TRAINERS

JUMPS STATISTICS 2014-2015

Edited by Mark Brown

Raceform

Published in 2015 by Raceform Ltd
27 Kingfisher Court, Hambridge Road, Newbury, Berkshire RG14 5SJ

A catalogue record of this book is available from the British Library.

ISBN 978-1-909471-90-0

Printed and bound by Printondemandworldwide.com, 9 Culley Court,
Orton Southgate, Peterborough, PE2 6XD

CONTENTS

WINNING BRITISH TRAINERS	5
LEADING TRAINERS BY COURSE	195
LEADING TRAINERS BY MONTH	216
LEADING PRIZEMONEY WINNERS	228

WINNING TRAINERS

Jumps statistics for the 2014-2015 season for winning British-based trainers. Trainers with less than ten winners are shown with abbreviated statistics.

Winning horses preceded by an asterisk joined the stable during the course of the season; an asterisk following the horse's name denotes a switch to another trainer during the season. Names may be abbreviated due to the pressure of space.

N W ALEXANDER

KINNESTON, PERTH & KINROSS

	No. of Hrs	Races Run	1st	2nd	3rd	Unpl	Per cent	£1 Level Stake
NH Flat	*14*	*23*	*1*	*0*	*1*	*21*	*4.3*	*-10.00*
Hurdles	*30*	*108*	*6*	*12*	*10*	*80*	*5.6*	*-68.75*
Chases	*20*	*62*	*2*	*8*	*9*	*43*	*3.2*	*-44.00*
Totals	**46**	**193**	**9**	**20**	**20**	**144**	**4.7**	**-122.75**
13-14	*47*	*188*	*25*	*22*	*25*	*116*	*13.3*	*+49.54*
12-13	*40*	*181*	*28*	*22*	*16*	*115*	*15.5*	*+3.90*

JOCKEYS

	W-R	Per cent	£1 Level Stake
Lucy Alexander	5-95	5.3	-53.75
Brian Harding	1-6	16.7	+4.00
Peter Buchanan	1-8	12.5	0.00
Mr Kit Alexander	1-30	3.3	-26.50
Stephen Mulqueen	1-41	2.4	-33.50

COURSE RECORD

	Total W-R	Non-Hndcps Hurdles	Non-Hndcps Chases	Hndcps Hurdles	Hndcps Chases	NH Flat	Per cent	£1 Level Stake
Musselbgh	2-19	0-5	0-0	2-7	0-6	0-1	10.5	-8.00
Kelso	2-34	1-10	0-1	0-8	1-11	0-4	5.9	-22.25
Ayr	2-39	0-8	0-0	1-13	0-11	1-7	5.1	-17.00
Hexham	1-14	0-4	0-0	1-4	0-2	0-4	7.1	-8.50
Perth	1-28	0-4	0-3	0-14	1-5	0-2	3.6	-18.00
Newcastle	1-30	0-9	0-0	1-9	0-9	0-3	3.3	-20.00

WINNING HORSES

Horse	Races Run	1st	2nd	3rd	£
Isla Pearl Fisher	6	1	0	0	7148
Little Glenshee	7	1	2	2	6498
Landecker	7	1	1	0	5198
The Flaming Matron	8	1	1	0	4106
Humphrey Bee	2	1	0	1	3798
Bracing	7	1	1	0	3249
Always Tipsy	9	1	2	3	3249
Northern Acres	9	1	1	4	2274
Benny's Secret	3	1	0	0	1625

Total winning prize-money **£37145**

Favourites **1-5** **20.0%** **-1.50**

S R ANDREWS

LUTON, BEDS

	No. of Hrs	Races Run	1st	2nd	3rd	Unpl	Per cent	£1 Level Stake
NH Flat	*0*	*0*	*0*	*0*	*0*	*0*	*0.0*	*0.00*
Hurdles	*0*	*0*	*0*	*0*	*0*	*0*	*0.0*	*0.00*
Chases	*1*	*3*	*1*	*1*	*0*	*1*	*33.3*	*-0.63*
Totals	**1**	**3**	**1**	**1**	**0**	**1**	**33.3**	**-0.63**
13-14	*1*	*1*	*0*	*0*	*0*	*1*	*0.0*	*-1.00*
12-13	*1*	*1*	*0*	*0*	*1*	*0*	*0.0*	*-1.00*

JOCKEYS

	W-R	Per cent	£1 Level Stake
Miss G Andrews	1-3	33.3	-0.63

COURSE RECORD

	Total W-R	Non-Hndcps Hurdles	Non-Hndcps Chases	Hndcps Hurdles	Hndcps Chases	NH Flat	Per cent	£1 Level Stake
Fakenham	1-2	0-0	1-2	0-0	0-0	0-0	50.0	+0.38

WINNING HORSES

Horse	Races Run	1st	2nd	3rd	£
*Can Mestret	3	1	1	0	1920

Total winning prize-money **£1920**

Favourites **0-1** **0.0%** **-1.00**

MICHAEL APPLEBY

DANETHORPE, NOTTS

	No. of Hrs	Races Run	1st	2nd	3rd	Unpl	Per cent	£1 Level Stake
NH Flat	*1*	*2*	*0*	*0*	*0*	*2*	*0.0*	*-2.00*
Hurdles	*13*	*38*	*6*	*5*	*6*	*21*	*15.8*	*-2.42*
Chases	*0*	*0*	*0*	*0*	*0*	*0*	*0.0*	*0.00*
Totals	**14**	**40**	**6**	**5**	**6**	**23**	**15.0**	**-4.42**
13-14	*19*	*56*	*4*	*5*	*9*	*38*	*7.1*	*-32.09*
12-13	*19*	*47*	*3*	*7*	*2*	*35*	*6.4*	*+9.25*

JOCKEYS

	W-R	Per cent	£1 Level Stake
Richard Johnson	2-6	33.3	+6.33
Jonathan England	2-15	13.3	-7.75
A P McCoy	1-1	100.0	+2.00
Killian Moore	1-2	50.0	+11.00

COURSE RECORD

	Total W-R	Non-Hndcps Hurdles	Non-Hndcps Chases	Hndcps Hurdles	Hndcps Chases	NH Flat	Per cent	£1 Level Stake
Doncaster	2-5	0-1	0-0	2-3	0-0	0-1	40.0	+6.25
Catterick	1-2	0-1	0-0	1-1	0-0	0-0	50.0	+1.00
Huntingdon	1-5	0-1	0-0	1-3	0-0	0-1	20.0	-0.67
Stratford	1-6	0-2	0-0	1-4	0-0	0-0	16.7	+7.00
Mrket Rsn	1-8	0-2	0-0	1-6	0-0	0-0	12.5	-4.00

WINNING HORSES

Horse	Races Run	1st	2nd	3rd	£
Favorite Girl	8	3	1	1	12996
*Mawaqeet	3	1	0	0	5064
Dewala	4	2	1	1	7148

Total winning prize-money			**£25208**
Favourites	**2-4**	**50.0%**	**2.25**

DAVID ARBUTHNOT

BEARE GREEN, SURREY

	No. of Hrs	Races Run	1st	2nd	3rd	Unpl	Per cent	£1 Level Stake
NH Flat	*1*	*2*	*0*	*0*	*1*	*1*	*0.0*	*-2.00*
Hurdles	*8*	*30*	*3*	*2*	*2*	*23*	*10.0*	*-4.50*
Chases	*4*	*13*	*1*	*2*	*1*	*9*	*7.7*	*+2.00*
Totals	**11**	**45**	**4**	**4**	**4**	**33**	**8.9**	**-4.50**
13-14	*10*	*40*	*3*	*4*	*4*	*29*	*7.5*	*-24.90*
12-13	*17*	*63*	*6*	*7*	*7*	*43*	*9.5*	*-20.00*

JOCKEYS

	W-R	Per cent	£1 Level Stake
Tom Cannon	2-23	8.7	+2.00
Joshua Moore	1-4	25.0	+4.50
Nico de Boinville	1-4	25.0	+3.00

COURSE RECORD

	Total W-R	Non-Hndcps Hurdles	Non-Hndcps Chases	Hndcps Hurdles	Hndcps Chases	NH Flat	Per cent	£1 Level Stake
Cheltenham	1-1	0-0	0-0	1-1	0-0	0-0	100.0	+6.00
Taunton	1-2	0-0	0-0	0-1	1-1	0-0	50.0	+13.00
Wincanton	1-2	0-0	0-0	1-2	0-0	0-0	50.0	+8.00
Fontwell	1-6	0-1	0-0	1-4	0-0	0-1	16.7	+2.50

WINNING HORSES

Horse	Races Run	1st	2nd	3rd	£
Starluck	5	1	0	1	7507
Strollawaynow	6	1	0	1	3861
Urcalin	8	2	0	0	7343
Total winning prize-money					**£18711**
Favourites	**0-1**		**0.0%**		**-1.00**

JOHN ARMSTRONG

TRIMDON STATION, CO. DURHAM

	No. of Hrs	Races Run	1st	2nd	3rd	Unpl	Per cent	£1 Level Stake
NH Flat	*0*	*0*	*0*	*0*	*0*	*0*	*0.0*	*0.00*
Hurdles	*0*	*0*	*0*	*0*	*0*	*0*	*0.0*	*0.00*
Chases	*1*	*2*	*1*	*0*	*0*	*1*	*50.0*	*+3.50*
Totals	**1**	**2**	**1**	**0**	**0**	**1**	**50.0**	**+3.50**

JOCKEYS

	W-R	Per cent	£1 Level Stake
Mr C Dawson	1-2	50.0	+3.50

COURSE RECORD

	Total W-R	Non-Hndcps Hurdles	Non-Hndcps Chases	Hndcps Hurdles	Hndcps Chases	NH Flat	Per cent	£1 Level Stake
Cartmel	1-1	0-0	1-1	0-0	0-0	0-0	100.0	+4.50

WINNING HORSES

Horse	Races Run	1st	2nd	3rd	£
*Sposalizio	2	1	0	0	1560
Total winning prize-money					**£1560**
Favourites	**0-0**		**0.0%**		**0.00**

PETER ATKINSON

YAFFORTH, N YORKS

	No. of Hrs	Races Run	1st	2nd	3rd	Unpl	Per cent	£1 Level Stake
NH Flat	*0*	*0*	*0*	*0*	*0*	*0*	*0.0*	*0.00*
Hurdles	*1*	*4*	*2*	*1*	*0*	*1*	*50.0*	*+7.00*
Chases	*1*	*1*	*0*	*0*	*0*	*1*	*0.0*	*-1.00*
Totals	**2**	**5**	**2**	**1**	**0**	**2**	**40.0**	**+6.00**
13-14	*2*	*14*	*4*	*2*	*0*	*8*	*28.6*	*+10.00*
12-13	*2*	*11*	*2*	*0*	*1*	*8*	*18.2*	*+7.50*

JOCKEYS

	W-R	Per cent	£1 Level Stake
Henry Brooke	2-5	40.0	+6.00

COURSE RECORD

	Total W-R	Non-Hndcps Hurdles	Non-Hndcps Chases	Hndcps Hurdles	Hndcps Chases	NH Flat	Per cent	£1 Level Stake
Sedgefield	2-2	0-0	0-0	2-2	0-0	0-0	100.0	+9.00

WINNING HORSES

Horse	Races Run	1st	2nd	3rd	£
Sparkling Hand	4	2	1	0	7278
Total winning prize-money					**£7278**
Favourites	**0-0**		**0.0%**		**0.00**

KIM BAILEY

ANDOVERSFORD, GLOUCS

	No. of Hrs	Races Run	1st	2nd	3rd	Unpl	Per cent	£1 Level Stake
NH Flat	*16*	*21*	*3*	*3*	*1*	*14*	*14.3*	*-8.50*
Hurdles	*40*	*153*	*34*	*17*	*19*	*83*	*22.2*	*-1.95*
Chases	*22*	*94*	*24*	*12*	*11*	*47*	*25.5*	*+34.53*
Totals	**66**	**268**	**61**	**32**	**31**	**144**	**22.8**	**+24.08**
13-14	*62*	*261*	*34*	*25*	*33*	*169*	*13.0*	*-43.73*
12-13	*68*	*240*	*27*	*32*	*37*	*144*	*11.3*	*-57.24*

BY MONTH

NH Flat	W-R	Per cent	£1 Level Stake
May	0-0	0.0	0.00
June	0-1	0.0	-1.00
July	0-0	0.0	0.00
August	0-0	0.0	0.00
September	0-0	0.0	0.00
October	1-3	33.3	-1.00
November	0-1	0.0	-1.00
December	0-1	0.0	-1.00
January	0-1	0.0	-1.00
February	0-0	0.0	0.00
March	0-6	0.0	-6.00
April	2-8	25.0	+2.50

Hurdles	W-R	Per cent	£1 Level Stake
May	2-20	10.0	-11.38
June	3-3	100.0	+4.28
July	1-4	25.0	+3.50
August	2-3	66.7	+1.71
September	3-6	50.0	+0.38
October	5-25	20.0	-3.83
November	2-18	11.1	-9.75
December	2-14	14.3	-8.15
January	2-11	18.2	+1.10
February	7-14	50.0	+24.85
March	2-24	8.3	-13.33
April	3-11	27.3	+8.68

Chases	W-R	Per cent	£1 Level Stake
May	3-11	27.3	+8.50
June	3-5	60.0	+2.71
July	0-1	0.0	-1.00
August	2-3	66.7	+6.00
September	3-4	75.0	+4.16
October	1-11	9.1	-4.00
November	4-15	26.7	+0.78
December	3-10	30.0	+1.50
January	0-5	0.0	-5.00
February	2-7	28.6	+1.38
March	2-12	16.7	+25.75
April	1-10	10.0	-6.25

Totals	W-R	Per cent	£1 Level Stake
May	5-31	16.1	-2.88
June	6-9	66.7	+5.99
July	1-5	20.0	+2.50
August	4-6	66.7	+7.71
September	6-10	60.0	+4.54
October	7-39	17.9	-8.83
November	6-34	17.6	-9.97
December	5-25	20.0	-7.65
January	2-17	11.8	-4.90
February	9-21	42.9	+26.23
March	4-42	9.5	+6.42
April	6-29	20.7	+4.93

DISTANCE

Hurdles	W-R	Per cent	£1 Level Stake
2m-2m3f	10-44	22.7	-6.89
2m4f-2m7f	13-49	26.5	+14.01
3m+	2-15	13.3	-2.00

Chases	W-R	Per cent	£1 Level Stake
2m-2m3f	9-15	60.0	+23.74
2m4f-2m7f	8-35	22.9	+30.88
3m+	4-31	12.9	-15.59

TYPE OF RACE

Non-Handicaps	W-R	Per cent	£1 Level Stake
Nov Hrdls	13-43	30.2	-10.45
Hrdls	6-28	21.4	-10.28
Nov Chs	6-20	30.0	-1.93
Chases	1-5	20.0	+6.00
Sell/Claim	0-1	0.0	-1.00

Handicaps	W-R	Per cent	£1 Level Stake
Nov Hrdls	1-10	10.0	-6.00
Hrdls	14-70	20.0	+26.78
Nov Chs	8-22	36.4	+12.25
Chases	9-47	19.1	+18.21
Sell/Claim	0-0	0.0	0.00

RACE CLASS

	W-R	Per cent	£1 Level Stake
Class 1	1-19	5.3	+15.00
Class 2	2-20	10.0	-9.75
Class 3	16-59	27.1	+6.17
Class 4	30-121	24.8	+7.59
Class 5	10-33	30.3	+14.06
Class 6	2-16	12.5	-9.00

FIRST TIME OUT

	W-R	Per cent	£1 Level Stake
Bumpers	2-16	12.5	-8.50
Hurdles	5-32	15.6	-16.73
Chases	6-18	33.3	+15.25
Totals	13-66	19.7	-9.98

JOCKEYS

	W-R	Per cent	£1 Level Stake
A P McCoy	17-35	48.6	+14.88
David Bass	16-61	26.2	+38.64
Jason Maguire	15-54	27.8	+22.71
Ed Cookson	6-46	13.0	-19.38
Tom Bellamy	4-18	22.2	+8.63
Richard Johnson	1-2	50.0	+0.10
Mr H A A Bannister	1-4	25.0	+2.00
Andrew Thornton	1-5	20.0	-0.50

COURSE RECORD

	Total W-R	Non-Hndcps Hurdles	Non-Hndcps Chases	Hndcps Hurdles	Hndcps Chases	NH Flat	Per cent	£1 Level Stake
Worcester	6-13	2-3	1-2	0-4	3-3	0-1	46.2	+14.00
Towcester	5-14	1-2	1-2	1-6	1-3	1-1	35.7	+10.13
Southwell	4-9	1-3	0-0	1-1	2-3	0-2	44.4	+2.22
Bangor	4-11	2-4	1-1	0-3	0-2	1-1	36.4	+0.31
Huntingdon	4-12	0-2	1-2	2-2	1-3	0-3	33.3	+8.00
Uttoxeter	4-22	0-6	1-2	3-10	0-3	0-1	18.2	+0.41
Nton Abbot	3-4	2-3	0-0	0-0	1-1	0-0	75.0	+2.96
Wincanton	3-11	1-3	0-0	2-6	0-1	0-1	27.3	+3.30
Ludlow	3-17	0-6	0-1	1-6	1-3	1-1	17.6	-2.63
Hexham	2-3	1-1	1-1	0-0	0-1	0-0	66.7	+4.50
Newcastle	2-3	2-2	0-0	0-0	0-1	0-0	66.7	+3.38
Sedgefield	2-5	1-2	0-0	0-1	1-2	0-0	40.0	+1.60
Doncaster	2-10	0-1	1-2	1-4	0-3	0-0	20.0	-4.72
Ffos Las	2-11	1-3	0-0	1-6	0-1	0-1	18.2	-5.58
Cheltenham	2-24	0-3	0-4	0-5	2-11	0-1	8.3	+16.00
Fakenham	1-1	0-0	0-0	0-0	1-1	0-0	100.0	+2.50
Plumpton	1-1	1-1	0-0	0-0	0-0	0-0	100.0	+1.88
Perth	1-2	1-1	0-1	0-0	0-0	0-0	50.0	+0.88
Cartmel	1-3	1-3	0-0	0-0	0-0	0-0	33.3	-0.13
Catterick	1-3	0-1	0-0	0-1	1-1	0-0	33.3	-0.50
Ascot	1-4	0-1	0-0	0-2	1-1	0-0	25.0	-0.25
Wetherby	1-4	0-2	0-1	1-1	0-0	0-0	25.0	+13.00
Chepstow	1-6	0-2	0-0	1-3	0-1	0-0	16.7	+9.00
Taunton	1-6	1-4	0-0	0-0	0-2	0-0	16.7	-4.33
Exeter	1-7	0-4	0-1	1-1	0-1	0-0	14.3	-0.50
Mrket Rsn	1-10	0-1	0-1	0-2	1-3	0-3	10.0	-6.25
Newbury	1-10	0-1	0-1	0-4	1-3	0-1	10.0	-5.00
Stratford	1-10	1-4	0-0	0-1	0-3	0-2	10.0	-8.09

WINNING HORSES

Horse	Races Run	1st	2nd	3rd	£
Darna	5	2	0	0	57598
Un Ace	7	3	2	0	35421
Able Deputy	6	4	2	0	32610
Charingworth	6	1	1	0	11992
Gallery Exhibition	8	2	1	2	13321
Jimmy The Jetplane	5	3	0	1	19819
Knockanrawley	6	2	1	2	11696

Supreme Present	6	4	0	1	14685
Molly's A Diva	8	2	2	2	11891
Up For An Oscar	7	2	0	0	10099
Derrintogher Bliss	7	2	1	1	8642
Mrs Peachey	8	1	0	3	5198
Crazy Jack	7	2	2	0	5198
Allez Encore	4	2	1	0	7473
Midnight Oscar	11	2	1	3	7400
Viking Ridge	3	1	0	0	3994
Thedrinkymeister	6	1	1	1	3994
Faerie Reel	6	2	0	1	7148
Premier Portrait	9	2	0	0	7538
Bonne Fee	9	3	3	2	9153
Amazing D'Azy	5	2	1	1	5562
Patsys Castle	3	3	0	0	9653
Magic Money	6	1	0	0	3249
Grand March	7	2	0	0	5328
Ballyknock Lad	6	1	0	0	3249
Mere Anarchy	1	1	0	0	3249
Azure Aware	5	1	0	1	3119
A Shade Of Bay	6	1	1	0	3119
West End	10	1	1	2	2599
Milord	3	1	2	0	2599
Knocklayde Express	4	1	0	0	2469
Monkhouse	2	1	1	0	2053
Agent Fedora	4	1	1	0	1949
Gold Man	4	1	0	0	1560
Total winning prize-money					**£334627**
Favourites	**25-54**		**46.3%**		**2.20**

CAROLINE BAILEY

HOLDENBY, NORTHANTS

	No. of Hrs	Races Run	1st	2nd	3rd	Unpl	Per cent	£1 Level Stake
NH Flat	*3*	*3*	*0*	*0*	*0*	*3*	*0.0*	*-3.00*
Hurdles	*19*	*59*	*4*	*3*	*3*	*49*	*6.8*	*-25.13*
Chases	*11*	*55*	*8*	*11*	*9*	*27*	*14.5*	*+18.63*
Totals	**27**	**117**	**12**	**14**	**12**	**79**	**10.3**	**-9.50**
13-14	*25*	*116*	*11*	*14*	*10*	*81*	*9.5*	*-44.15*
12-13	*22*	*86*	*13*	*6*	*15*	*52*	*15.1*	*-8.00*

BY MONTH

NH Flat	W-R	Per cent	£1 Level Stake
May	0-1	0.0	-1.00
June	0-0	0.0	0.00
July	0-0	0.0	0.00
August	0-0	0.0	0.00
September	0-0	0.0	0.00
October	0-0	0.0	0.00
November	0-0	0.0	0.00
December	0-0	0.0	0.00
January	0-0	0.0	0.00
February	0-0	0.0	0.00
March	0-0	0.0	0.00
April	0-2	0.0	-2.00

Hurdles	W-R	Per cent	£1 Level Stake
May	0-5	0.0	-5.00
June	2-10	20.0	-1.50
July	1-4	25.0	-1.63
August	0-2	0.0	-2.00
September	0-1	0.0	-1.00
October	1-4	25.0	+19.00
November	0-4	0.0	-4.00
December	0-6	0.0	-6.00
January	0-8	0.0	-8.00
February	0-4	0.0	-4.00
March	0-9	0.0	-9.00
April	0-2	0.0	-2.00

Chases	W-R	Per cent	£1 Level Stake
May	1-3	33.3	+4.00
June	1-3	33.3	+0.50
July	1-6	16.7	-1.50
August	0-3	0.0	-3.00
September	1-3	33.3	+5.50
October	1-6	16.7	+1.00
November	0-6	0.0	-6.00
December	2-8	25.0	+1.13
January	0-3	0.0	-3.00
February	0-4	0.0	-4.00
March	1-4	25.0	+30.00
April	0-6	0.0	-6.00

Totals	W-R	Per cent	£1 Level Stake
May	1-9	11.1	-2.00
June	3-13	23.1	-1.00
July	2-10	20.0	-3.13
August	0-5	0.0	-5.00
September	1-4	25.0	+4.50
October	2-10	20.0	+20.00
November	0-10	0.0	-10.00
December	2-14	14.3	-4.87
January	0-11	0.0	-11.00
February	0-8	0.0	-8.00
March	1-13	7.7	+21.00
April	0-10	0.0	-10.00

DISTANCE

Hurdles	W-R	Per cent	£1 Level Stake
2m-2m3f	1-22	4.5	-19.00
2m4f-2m7f	1-13	7.7	+10.00
3m+	0-0	0.0	0.00

Chases	W-R	Per cent	£1 Level Stake
2m-2m3f	1-9	11.1	-0.50
2m4f-2m7f	3-25	12.0	-10.88
3m+	4-16	25.0	+35.00

TYPE OF RACE

Non-Handicaps	W-R	Per cent	£1 Level Stake
Nov Hrdls	0-17	0.0	-17.00
Hrdls	0-11	0.0	-11.00
Nov Chs	0-2	0.0	-2.00
Chases	0-0	0.0	0.00
Sell/Claim	0-0	0.0	0.00

Handicaps	W-R	Per cent	£1 Level Stake
Nov Hrdls	0-4	0.0	-4.00
Hrdls	4-27	14.8	+6.88
Nov Chs	1-5	20.0	-2.38
Chases	7-48	14.6	+23.00
Sell/Claim	0-0	0.0	0.00

RACE CLASS

	W-R	Per cent	£1 Level Stake
Class 1	0-2	0.0	-2.00
Class 2	0-0	0.0	0.00
Class 3	1-30	3.3	+4.00
Class 4	10-67	14.9	+1.00
Class 5	1-15	6.7	-9.50
Class 6	0-3	0.0	-3.00

FIRST TIME OUT

	W-R	Per cent	£1 Level Stake
Bumpers	0-3	0.0	-3.00
Hurdles	0-15	0.0	-15.00
Chases	1-9	11.1	-2.00
Totals	1-27	3.7	-20.00

JOCKEYS

	W-R	Per cent	£1 Level Stake
Andrew Thornton	7-80	8.8	-24.38
Adam Pogson	2-6	33.3	+34.50
Jake Greenall	1-4	25.0	+1.50
Richard Johnson	1-4	25.0	-1.63
Tom Scudamore	1-7	14.3	-3.50

COURSE RECORD

	Total W-R	Non-Hndcps Hurdles	Non-Hndcps Chases	Hndcps Hurdles	Hndcps Chases	NH Flat	Per cent	£1 Level Stake
Worcester	3-10	0-1	0-0	1-3	2-6	0-0	30.0	+6.00

Southwell	3-21	0-9	0-1	3-8	0-3	0-0	14.3	+9.88
Uttoxeter	2-12	0-2	0-1	0-5	2-4	0-0	16.7	-1.50
Newcastle	1-3	0-0	0-0	0-0	1-3	0-0	33.3	-0.38
Stratford	1-4	0-0	0-0	0-2	1-2	0-0	25.0	+3.00
Warwick	1-4	0-1	0-0	0-0	1-2	0-1	25.0	+30.00
Mrket Rsn	1-11	0-1	0-0	0-5	1-5	0-0	9.1	-4.50

WINNING HORSES

Horse	Races Run	1st	2nd	3rd	£
Carli King	6	2	1	1	14296
Gold Ingot	5	1	2	1	4540
High Ron	9	2	0	0	7994
Prince Des Marais	9	1	2	0	3899
*Quinsman	7	1	1	2	3899
Dealing River	12	4	2	2	3769
Trapper Peak	8	1	0	3	3119
Total winning prize-money					**£41516**
Favourites	**3-9**		**33.3%**		**-1.00**

TRACEY L BAILEY

CROOKED SOLEY, WILTS

	No. of Hrs	Races Run	1st	2nd	3rd	Unpl	Per cent	£1 Level Stake
NH Flat	*0*	*0*	*0*	*0*	*0*	*0*	*0.0*	*0.00*
Hurdles	*1*	*1*	*0*	*0*	*1*	*0*	*0.0*	*-1.00*
Chases	*3*	*12*	*1*	*2*	*1*	*8*	*8.3*	*-4.50*
Totals	**3**	**13**	**1**	**2**	**2**	**8**	**7.7**	**-5.50**
13-14	*3*	*12*	*0*	*1*	*3*	*8*	*0.0*	*-12.00*
12-13	*1*	*3*	*1*	*0*	*0*	*2*	*33.3*	*+8.00*

JOCKEYS

	W-R	Per cent	£1 Level Stake
Mark Grant	1-2	50.0	+5.50

COURSE RECORD

	Total W-R	Non-Hndcps Hurdles	Non-Hndcps Chases	Hndcps Hurdles	Hndcps Chases	NH Flat	Per cent	£1 Level Stake
Uttoxeter	1-2	0-0	0-0	0-0	1-2	0-0	50.0	+5.50

WINNING HORSES

Horse	Races Run	1st	2nd	3rd	£
Broadway Symphony	7	1	2	1	3899
Total winning prize-money					**£3899**
Favourites	**0-2**		**0.0%**		**-2.00**

EMMA BAKER

NAUNTON, GLOUCS

	No. of Hrs	Races Run	1st	2nd	3rd	Unpl	Per cent	£1 Level Stake
NH Flat	*3*	*6*	*0*	*0*	*0*	*6*	*0.0*	*-6.00*
Hurdles	*10*	*36*	*1*	*3*	*5*	*27*	*2.8*	*-25.00*
Chases	*2*	*16*	*3*	*0*	*2*	*11*	*18.8*	*-4.75*
Totals	**13**	**58**	**4**	**3**	**7**	**44**	**6.9**	**-35.75**
13-14	*9*	*42*	*3*	*1*	*9*	*29*	*7.1*	*-27.50*
12-13	*8*	*40*	*2*	*3*	*5*	*30*	*5.0*	*-9.00*

JOCKEYS

	W-R	Per cent	£1 Level Stake
James Banks	4-48	8.3	-25.75

COURSE RECORD

	Total W-R	Non-Hndcps Hurdles	Non-Hndcps Chases	Hndcps Hurdles	Hndcps Chases	NH Flat	Per cent	£1 Level Stake
Fakenham	2-6	0-0	0-0	0-1	2-4	0-1	33.3	+0.75
Leicester	1-1	0-0	0-0	0-0	1-1	0-0	100.0	+3.50
Ffos Las	1-3	0-1	0-0	1-2	0-0	0-0	33.3	+8.00

WINNING HORSES

Horse	Races Run	1st	2nd	3rd	£
Midnight Charmer	10	2	0	1	7798
Snowell	10	1	1	1	3899
Church Hall	5	1	0	2	3119
Total winning prize-money					**£14816**
Favourites	**2-4**		**50.0%**		**2.75**

GEORGE BAKER

MANTON, WILTS

	No. of Hrs	Races Run	1st	2nd	3rd	Unpl	Per cent	£1 Level Stake
NH Flat	*3*	*4*	*1*	*0*	*0*	*3*	*25.0*	*-2.78*
Hurdles	*8*	*14*	*1*	*0*	*3*	*10*	*7.1*	*+3.00*
Chases	*2*	*5*	*1*	*1*	*1*	*2*	*20.0*	*+16.00*
Totals	**12**	**23**	**3**	**1**	**4**	**15**	**13.0**	**+16.22**
13-14	*16*	*38*	*8*	*1*	*3*	*26*	*21.1*	*+60.95*
12-13	*11*	*24*	*3*	*5*	*1*	*15*	*12.5*	*-6.00*

JOCKEYS

	W-R	Per cent	£1 Level Stake
Andrew Tinkler	2-16	12.5	+2.22
Ciaran Gethings	1-2	50.0	+19.00

COURSE RECORD

	Total W-R	Non-Hndcps Hurdles	Non-Hndcps Chases	Hndcps Hurdles	Hndcps Chases	NH Flat	Per cent	£1 Level Stake
Southwell	1-1	0-0	0-0	1-1	0-0	0-0	100.0	+16.00
Wincanton	1-2	0-0	0-1	0-0	0-0	1-1	50.0	-0.78
Taunton	1-3	0-2	1-1	0-0	0-0	0-0	33.3	+18.00

WINNING HORSES

Horse	Races Run	1st	2nd	3rd	£
Sinbad The Sailor	1	1	0	0	3119
Double Dash	2	1	1	0	1976

Horse	Races Run	1st	2nd	3rd	£
Preseli Star	1	1	0	0	1625
Total winning prize-money					**£6720**
Favourites	**337-338**		**99.7%**		**73.81**

ANDREW BALDING

KINGSCLERE, HANTS

	No. of Hrs	Races Run	1st	2nd	3rd	Unpl	Per cent	£1 Level Stake
NH Flat	*2*	*2*	*1*	*0*	*0*	*1*	*50.0*	*+15.00*
Hurdles	*3*	*10*	*0*	*1*	*2*	*7*	*0.0*	*-10.00*
Chases	*0*	*0*	*0*	*0*	*0*	*0*	*0.0*	*0.00*
Totals	**5**	**12**	**1**	**1**	**2**	**8**	**8.3**	**+5.00**
13-14	*3*	*4*	*0*	*2*	*0*	*2*	*0.0*	*-4.00*
12-13	*1*	*4*	*1*	*0*	*0*	*3*	*25.0*	*+5.00*

JOCKEYS

	W-R	Per cent	£1 Level Stake
Barry Geraghty	1-1	100.0	+16.00

COURSE RECORD

	Total W-R	Non-Hndcps Hurdles	Non-Hndcps Chases	Hndcps Hurdles	Hndcps Chases	NH Flat	Per cent	£1 Level Stake
Ascot	1-1	0-0	0-0	0-0	0-0	1-1	100.0	+16.00

WINNING HORSES

Horse	Races Run	1st	2nd	3rd	£
Supasundae	1	1	0	0	11390
Total winning prize-money					**£11390**
Favourites	**0-1**		**0.0%**		**-1.00**

MARC BARBER

AMROTH, PEMBROKES

	No. of Hrs	Races Run	1st	2nd	3rd	Unpl	Per cent	£1 Level Stake
NH Flat	*0*	*0*	*0*	*0*	*0*	*0*	*0.0*	*0.00*
Hurdles	*0*	*0*	*0*	*0*	*0*	*0*	*0.0*	*0.00*
Chases	*2*	*2*	*1*	*1*	*0*	*0*	*50.0*	*+0.25*
Totals	**2**	**2**	**1**	**1**	**0**	**0**	**50.0**	**+0.25**
13-14	*21*	*55*	*2*	*4*	*4*	*45*	*3.6*	*-46.50*
12-13	*10*	*21*	*0*	*0*	*0*	*21*	*0.0*	*-21.00*

JOCKEYS

	W-R	Per cent	£1 Level Stake
Mr J F Mathias	1-1	100.0	+1.25

COURSE RECORD

	Total W-R	Non-Hndcps Hurdles	Non-Hndcps Chases	Hndcps Hurdles	Hndcps Chases	NH Flat	Per cent	£1 Level Stake
Chepstow	1-2	0-0	1-2	0-0	0-0	0-0	50.0	+0.25

WINNING HORSES

Horse	Races Run	1st	2nd	3rd	£
*Desertmore View	1	1	0	0	2371
Total winning prize-money					**£2371**
Favourites	**1-1**		**100.0%**		**1.25**

MAURICE BARNES

FARLAM, CUMBRIA

	No. of Hrs	Races Run	1st	2nd	3rd	Unpl	Per cent	£1 Level Stake
NH Flat	*5*	*8*	*0*	*0*	*0*	*8*	*0.0*	*-8.00*
Hurdles	*24*	*86*	*5*	*9*	*11*	*61*	*5.8*	*-36.00*
Chases	*12*	*54*	*8*	*8*	*11*	*27*	*14.8*	*+29.50*
Totals	**33**	**148**	**13**	**17**	**22**	**96**	**8.8**	**-14.50**
13-14	*31*	*149*	*11*	*21*	*18*	*99*	*7.4*	*-75.65*
12-13	*24*	*116*	*10*	*11*	*18*	*77*	*8.6*	*+56.75*

BY MONTH

NH Flat	W-R	Per cent	£1 Level Stake	Hurdles	W-R	Per cent	£1 Level Stake
May	0-2	0.0	-2.00	May	0-13	0.0	-13.00
June	0-1	0.0	-1.00	June	0-6	0.0	-6.00
July	0-1	0.0	-1.00	July	0-8	0.0	-8.00
August	0-0	0.0	0.00	August	1-2	50.0	+5.00
September	0-0	0.0	0.00	September	0-6	0.0	-6.00
October	0-1	0.0	-1.00	October	0-11	0.0	-11.00
November	0-1	0.0	-1.00	November	0-11	0.0	-11.00
December	0-1	0.0	-1.00	December	2-9	22.2	+24.50
January	0-0	0.0	0.00	January	1-2	50.0	+3.50
February	0-0	0.0	0.00	February	1-6	16.7	-2.00
March	0-0	0.0	0.00	March	0-7	0.0	-7.00
April	0-1	0.0	-1.00	April	0-5	0.0	-5.00

Chases	W-R	Per cent	£1 Level Stake	Totals	W-R	Per cent	£1 Level Stake
May	0-5	0.0	-5.00	May	0-20	0.0	-20.00
June	0-7	0.0	-7.00	June	0-14	0.0	-14.00
July	3-8	37.5	+14.50	July	3-17	17.6	+5.50
August	1-3	33.3	+12.00	August	2-5	40.0	+17.00
September	0-3	0.0	-3.00	September	0-9	0.0	-9.00
October	1-6	16.7	0.00	October	1-18	5.6	-12.00
November	1-5	20.0	-1.00	November	1-17	5.9	-13.00
December	0-3	0.0	-3.00	December	2-13	15.4	+20.50
January	0-3	0.0	-3.00	January	1-5	20.0	+0.50
February	0-2	0.0	-2.00	February	1-8	12.5	-4.00
March	2-5	40.0	+31.00	March	2-12	16.7	+24.00
April	0-4	0.0	-4.00	April	0-10	0.0	-10.00

DISTANCE

Hurdles	W-R	Per cent	£1 Level Stake	Chases	W-R	Per cent	£1 Level Stake
2m-2m3f	4-62	6.5	-38.00	2m-2m3f	2-11	18.2	+13.00
2m4f-2m7f	1-14	7.1	+12.00	2m4f-2m7f	4-24	16.7	+25.50

3m+	0-4	0.0	-4.00	3m+	0-12	0.0	-12.00

TYPE OF RACE

Non-Handicaps	W-R	Per cent	£1 Level Stake	Handicaps	W-R	Per cent	£1 Level Stake
Nov Hrdls	1-25	4.0	-19.50	Nov Hrdls	0-5	0.0	-5.00
Hrdls	1-19	5.3	+7.00	Hrdls	3-35	8.6	-16.50
Nov Chs	0-3	0.0	-3.00	Nov Chs	0-8	0.0	-8.00
Chases	0-1	0.0	-1.00	Chases	8-42	19.0	+41.50
Sell/Claim	0-2	0.0	-2.00	Sell/Claim	0-0	0.0	0.00

RACE CLASS / FIRST TIME OUT

RACE CLASS	W-R	Per cent	£1 Level Stake	FIRST TIME OUT	W-R	Per cent	£1 Level Stake
Class 1	0-1	0.0	-1.00	Bumpers	0-5	0.0	-5.00
Class 2	0-4	0.0	-4.00	Hurdles	0-20	0.0	-20.00
Class 3	3-20	15.0	+14.00	Chases	2-8	25.0	+22.00
Class 4	7-75	9.3	-17.50				
Class 5	3-42	7.1	0.00	Totals	2-33	6.1	-3.00
Class 6	0-6	0.0	-6.00				

JOCKEYS

	W-R	Per cent	£1 Level Stake
Michael McAlister	7-71	9.9	+8.50
Stephen Mulqueen	4-40	10.0	-16.00
Daragh Bourke	2-25	8.0	+5.00

COURSE RECORD

	Total W-R	Non-Hndcps Hurdles	Non-Hndcps Chases	Hndcps Hurdles	Hndcps Chases	NH Flat	Per cent	£1 Level Stake
Sedgefield	3-21	1-9	0-0	1-4	1-6	0-2	14.3	+27.00
Newcastle	2-5	0-0	0-0	1-2	1-3	0-0	40.0	+12.50
Cartmel	2-9	0-1	0-1	0-2	2-5	0-0	22.2	+7.00
Haydock	1-3	0-1	0-0	0-0	1-2	0-0	33.3	+23.00
Ayr	1-7	0-3	0-0	1-1	0-3	0-0	14.3	-3.00
Carlisle	1-12	0-4	0-0	0-4	1-3	0-1	8.3	-8.00
Wetherby	1-15	1-6	0-0	0-4	0-5	0-0	6.7	-9.50
Perth	1-20	0-2	0-0	0-7	1-9	0-2	5.0	-13.50
Hexham	1-26	0-10	0-2	0-4	1-9	0-1	3.8	-20.00

WINNING HORSES

Horse	Races Run	1st	2nd	3rd	£
Carrigdhoun	3	1	1	0	8123
Bobs Lady Tamure	11	3	3	1	12902
Indian Voyage	6	1	0	0	6330
Harrys Whim	9	1	3	3	5198
Toledo Gold	8	3	0	3	11052
Attycran	6	1	0	2	3899
Apache Pilot	9	1	1	1	3769
Dynamic Drive	12	1	3	2	2469
Dibdabs	5	1	0	2	2464
Total winning prize-money					**£56206**
Favourites	**1-6**		**16.7%**		**-2.00**

BRIAN BARR

LONGBURTON, DORSET

	No. of Hrs	Races Run	1st	2nd	3rd	Unpl	Per cent	£1 Level Stake
NH Flat	*2*	*4*	*0*	*2*	*1*	*1*	*0.0*	*-4.00*
Hurdles	*8*	*40*	*5*	*4*	*8*	*23*	*12.5*	*-21.50*
Chases	*1*	*6*	*0*	*2*	*2*	*2*	*0.0*	*-6.00*
Totals	**9**	**50**	**5**	**8**	**11**	**26**	**10.0**	**-31.50**
13-14	*11*	*38*	*5*	*4*	*2*	*27*	*13.2*	*+22.50*
12-13	*11*	*22*	*1*	*2*	*3*	*16*	*4.5*	*-17.50*

JOCKEYS

	W-R	Per cent	£1 Level Stake
Dave Crosse	3-6	50.0	+5.50
William Featherstone	1-2	50.0	+1.50
Michael Heard	1-3	33.3	+0.50

COURSE RECORD

	Total W-R	Non-Hndcps Hurdles	Non-Hndcps Chases	Hndcps Hurdles	Hndcps Chases	NH Flat	Per cent	£1 Level Stake
Wincanton	2-6	1-2	0-0	1-3	0-0	0-1	33.3	-0.50
Taunton	2-13	0-2	0-0	2-6	0-5	0-0	15.4	-6.00
Fontwell	1-7	0-2	0-0	1-4	0-0	0-1	14.3	-1.00

WINNING HORSES

Horse	Races Run	1st	2nd	3rd	£
Castlemorris King	5	1	0	1	5254
Norfolk Sky	6	1	1	1	3249
Follow The Tracks	8	2	2	2	5848
Bostin	3	1	0	0	1949
Total winning prize-money					**£16300**
Favourites	**3-5**		**60.0%**		**4.00**

ALISON BATCHELOR

PETWORTH, W SUSSEX

	No. of Hrs	Races Run	1st	2nd	3rd	Unpl	Per cent	£1 Level Stake
NH Flat	*0*	*0*	*0*	*0*	*0*	*0*	*0.0*	*0.00*
Hurdles	*8*	*29*	*2*	*4*	*2*	*21*	*6.9*	*-14.25*
Chases	*3*	*6*	*2*	*0*	*2*	*2*	*33.3*	*+3.50*
Totals	**9**	**35**	**4**	**4**	**4**	**23**	**11.4**	**-10.75**
13-14	*10*	*26*	*3*	*2*	*3*	*18*	*11.5*	*-2.50*
12-13	*10*	*34*	*0*	*4*	*4*	*26*	*0.0*	*-34.00*

JOCKEYS

	W-R	Per cent	£1 Level Stake
Leighton Aspell	3-10	30.0	+3.25
Tom Cannon	1-5	20.0	+6.00

COURSE RECORD

	Total W-R	Non-Hndcps Hurdles	Non-Hndcps Chases	Hndcps Hurdles	Hndcps Chases	NH Flat	Per cent	£1 Level Stake
Fontwell	2-12	0-4	0-1	0-4	2-3	0-0	16.7	-2.50
Huntingdon	1-1	0-0	0-0	1-1	0-0	0-0	100.0	+2.75
Wincanton	1-1	1-1	0-0	0-0	0-0	0-0	100.0	+10.00

WINNING HORSES

Horse	Races Run	1st	2nd	3rd	£
*Tara Dove	4	1	0	0	4185
Try Catch Me	4	2	0	1	6108
*Mr Lando	4	1	3	0	3249
Total winning prize-money					**£13542**
Favourites	**0-1**		**0.0%**		**-1.00**

CHRIS BEALBY

BARROWBY, LINCS

	No. of Hrs	Races Run	1st	2nd	3rd	Unpl	Per cent	£1 Level Stake
NH Flat	*2*	*3*	*0*	*0*	*0*	*3*	*0.0*	*-3.00*
Hurdles	*12*	*33*	*2*	*2*	*6*	*23*	*6.1*	*-22.00*
Chases	*7*	*33*	*5*	*2*	*7*	*19*	*15.2*	*-6.50*
Totals	**18**	**69**	**7**	**4**	**13**	**45**	**10.1**	**-31.50**
13-14	*27*	*64*	*3*	*4*	*1*	*56*	*4.7*	*-42.00*
12-13	*29*	*83*	*5*	*8*	*11*	*59*	*6.0*	*-59.88*

JOCKEYS

	W-R	Per cent	£1 Level Stake
Tom Messenger	6-57	10.5	-24.00
Trevor Ryan	1-1	100.0	+3.50

COURSE RECORD

	Total W-R	Non-Hndcps Hurdles	Non-Hndcps Chases	Hndcps Hurdles	Hndcps Chases	NH Flat	Per cent	£1 Level Stake
Mrket Rsn	3-14	0-3	0-0	1-4	2-6	0-1	21.4	+4.00
Worcester	1-1	1-1	0-0	0-0	0-0	0-0	100.0	+5.50
Warwick	1-3	0-1	0-0	0-0	1-2	0-0	33.3	0.00
Fakenham	1-11	0-2	0-0	0-2	1-7	0-0	9.1	-5.50
Southwell	1-22	0-7	0-0	0-7	1-7	0-1	4.5	-17.50

WINNING HORSES

Horse	Races Run	1st	2nd	3rd	£
Benevolent	6	2	0	2	14621
Sir Lynx	10	2	1	2	5508
Ruaraidh Hugh	8	1	1	0	2738
Chac Du Cadran	4	1	0	1	2274
Intent	2	1	0	0	1949
Total winning prize-money					**£27090**
Favourites	**2-3**		**66.7%**		**4.50**

JIM BEST

LEWES, E SUSSEX

	No. of Hrs	Races Run	1st	2nd	3rd	Unpl	Per cent	£1 Level Stake
NH Flat	*6*	*11*	*2*	*3*	*2*	*4*	*18.2*	*+2.88*
Hurdles	*26*	*100*	*15*	*19*	*10*	*56*	*15.0*	*-25.28*
Chases	*1*	*4*	*1*	*2*	*0*	*1*	*25.0*	*-1.63*
Totals	**30**	**115**	**18**	**24**	**12**	**61**	**15.7**	**-24.03**
13-14	*35*	*115*	*20*	*12*	*12*	*71*	*17.4*	*-35.09*
12-13	*30*	*104*	*7*	*11*	*9*	*77*	*6.7*	*-68.63*

BY MONTH

NH Flat	W-R	Per cent	£1 Level Stake	Hurdles	W-R	Per cent	£1 Level Stake
May	0-0	0.0	0.00	May	1-6	16.7	-2.75
June	0-0	0.0	0.00	June	0-7	0.0	-7.00
July	1-2	50.0	+0.88	July	2-8	25.0	+11.00
August	0-2	0.0	-2.00	August	3-6	50.0	+5.25
September	0-1	0.0	-1.00	September	1-8	12.5	-5.90
October	0-1	0.0	-1.00	October	1-7	14.3	-3.00
November	0-2	0.0	-2.00	November	1-10	10.0	+1.00
December	0-1	0.0	-1.00	December	0-9	0.0	-9.00
January	1-1	100.0	+10.00	January	2-7	28.6	+4.00
February	0-1	0.0	-1.00	February	2-7	28.6	-1.88
March	0-0	0.0	0.00	March	1-17	5.9	-11.50
April	0-0	0.0	0.00	April	1-8	12.5	-5.50

Chases	W-R	Per cent	£1 Level Stake	Totals	W-R	Per cent	£1 Level Stake
May	0-0	0.0	0.00	May	1-6	16.7	-2.75
June	0-0	0.0	0.00	June	0-7	0.0	-7.00
July	0-1	0.0	-1.00	July	3-11	27.3	+10.88
August	1-2	50.0	+0.38	August	4-10	40.0	+3.63
September	0-1	0.0	-1.00	September	1-10	10.0	-7.90
October	0-0	0.0	0.00	October	1-8	12.5	-4.00
November	0-0	0.0	0.00	November	1-12	8.3	-1.00
December	0-0	0.0	0.00	December	0-10	0.0	-10.00
January	0-0	0.0	0.00	January	3-8	37.5	+14.00
February	0-0	0.0	0.00	February	2-8	25.0	-2.88
March	0-0	0.0	0.00	March	1-17	5.9	-11.50
April	0-0	0.0	0.00	April	1-8	12.5	-5.50

DISTANCE

Hurdles	W-R	Per cent	£1 Level Stake	Chases	W-R	Per cent	£1 Level Stake
2m-2m3f	9-56	16.1	-3.13	2m-2m3f	0-0	0.0	0.00
2m4f-2m7f	2-16	12.5	-6.75	2m4f-2m7f	0-1	0.0	-1.00
3m+	0-3	0.0	-3.00	3m+	1-3	33.3	-0.63

TYPE OF RACE

Non-Handicaps	W-R	Per cent	£1 Level Stake	Handicaps	W-R	Per cent	£1 Level Stake
Nov Hrdls	3-17	17.6	-8.88	Nov Hrdls	2-6	33.3	+2.75
Hrdls	5-32	15.6	-1.00	Hrdls	3-39	7.7	-28.40

Nov Chs	0-0	0.0	0.00	Nov Chs	0-0	0.0	0.00
Chases	0-0	0.0	0.00	Chases	1-4	25.0	-1.63
Sell/Claim	2-2	100.0	+14.25	Sell/Claim	0-4	0.0	-4.00

RACE CLASS / FIRST TIME OUT

	W-R	Per cent	£1 Level Stake		W-R	Per cent	£1 Level Stake
Class 1	0-5	0.0	-5.00	Bumpers	1-6	16.7	-3.13
Class 2	0-2	0.0	-2.00	Hurdles	5-24	20.8	+10.00
Class 3	1-4	25.0	+1.50	Chases	0-0	0.0	0.00
Class 4	6-52	11.5	-28.64				
Class 5	9-43	20.9	+5.23	Totals	6-30	20.0	+6.87
Class 6	2-9	22.2	+4.88				

JOCKEYS

	W-R	Per cent	£1 Level Stake
A P McCoy	10-25	40.0	+8.85
Tom Scudamore	3-17	17.6	+2.11
Barry Geraghty	1-2	50.0	+4.50
Daryl Jacob	1-4	25.0	+1.50
Dougie Costello	1-4	25.0	+7.00
Sam Twiston-Davies	1-6	16.7	+5.00
Jason Maguire	1-7	14.3	-3.00

COURSE RECORD

	Total W-R	Non-Hndcps Hurdles	Non-Hndcps Chases	Hndcps Hurdles	Hndcps Chases	NH Flat	Per cent	£1 Level Stake
Worcester	3-9	2-4	0-0	1-3	0-0	0-2	33.3	+13.25
Plumpton	3-17	2-6	0-0	0-8	0-0	1-3	17.6	+2.00
Uttoxeter	2-5	0-2	0-0	1-2	0-0	1-1	40.0	+3.88
Nton Abbot	2-6	0-2	0-0	1-2	1-1	0-1	33.3	-0.88
Wetherby	1-1	1-1	0-0	0-0	0-0	0-0	100.0	+10.00
Lingfield	1-2	1-1	0-0	0-1	0-0	0-0	50.0	-0.39
Mrket Rsn	1-2	0-0	0-0	1-2	0-0	0-0	50.0	+0.50
Southwell	1-2	0-1	0-0	1-1	0-0	0-0	50.0	+0.10
Kempton	1-6	1-5	0-0	0-1	0-0	0-0	16.7	+0.50
Ludlow	1-6	1-3	0-0	0-2	0-0	0-1	16.7	-3.50
Fakenham	1-8	1-5	0-0	0-3	0-0	0-0	12.5	-4.00
Stratford	1-10	1-5	0-0	0-3	0-1	0-1	10.0	-4.50

WINNING HORSES

Horse	Races Run	1st	2nd	3rd	£
*New Street	1	1	0	0	5381
Kiama Bay	9	2	3	1	8772
Slowfoot	2	2	0	0	6628
*Officer Drivel	9	2	1	1	5952
Boru's Brook	5	2	1	1	6498
Sugar Hiccup	1	1	0	0	3249
Crannaghmore Boy	5	1	2	0	2924
Dorry K	3	1	1	0	2599
Money Money Money	2	1	0	0	2209
Saint Helena	7	1	1	1	1949
Conducting	1	1	0	0	1949
Slaney Star	2	1	0	0	1949
Missile Man	3	1	0	0	1819
Generous Jack	3	1	2	0	1560
Total winning prize-money					**£53438**
Favourites	**6-26**		**23.1%**		**-11.41**

JAMES BETHELL

MIDDLEHAM MOOR, N YORKS

	No. of Hrs	Races Run	1st	2nd	3rd	Unpl	Per cent	£1 Level Stake
NH Flat	*0*	*0*	*0*	*0*	*0*	*0*	*0.0*	*0.00*
Hurdles	*3*	*11*	*3*	*0*	*2*	*6*	*27.3*	*+84.50*
Chases	*0*	*0*	*0*	*0*	*0*	*0*	*0.0*	*0.00*
Totals	**3**	**11**	**3**	**0**	**2**	**6**	**27.3**	**+84.50**
13-14	*3*	*3*	*0*	*0*	*0*	*3*	*0.0*	*-3.00*
12-13	*3*	*6*	*0*	*0*	*1*	*5*	*0.0*	*-6.00*

JOCKEYS

	W-R	Per cent	£1 Level Stake
Joe Colliver	2-7	28.6	+79.50
Jack Sherwood	1-1	100.0	+8.00

COURSE RECORD

	Total W-R	Non-Hndcps Hurdles	Non-Hndcps Chases	Hndcps Hurdles	Hndcps Chases	NH Flat	Per cent	£1 Level Stake
Perth	2-3	1-1	0-0	1-2	0-0	0-0	66.7	+87.00
Musselbgh	1-2	1-2	0-0	0-0	0-0	0-0	50.0	+3.50

WINNING HORSES

Horse	Races Run	1st	2nd	3rd	£
Last Supper	4	2	0	0	8816
Thankyou Very Much	6	1	0	2	2599
Total winning prize-money					**£11415**
Favourites	**0-1**		**0.0%**		**-1.00**

HARRIET BETHELL

ARNOLD, E YORKS

	No. of Hrs	Races Run	1st	2nd	3rd	Unpl	Per cent	£1 Level Stake
NH Flat	*0*	*0*	*0*	*0*	*0*	*0*	*0.0*	*0.00*
Hurdles	*5*	*16*	*0*	*1*	*1*	*14*	*0.0*	*-16.00*
Chases	*4*	*11*	*1*	*3*	*2*	*5*	*9.1*	*-6.50*
Totals	**6**	**27**	**1**	**4**	**3**	**19**	**3.7**	**-22.50**

JOCKEYS

	W-R	Per cent	£1 Level Stake
Jonathan England	1-8	12.5	-3.50

COURSE RECORD

	Total W-R	Non-Hndcps Hurdles	Non-Hndcps Chases	Hndcps Hurdles	Hndcps Chases	NH Flat	Per cent	£1 Level Stake
Towcester	1-2	0-0	0-0	0-0	1-2	0-0	50.0	+2.50

WINNING HORSES

Horse	Races Run	1st	2nd	3rd	£
Nalim	7	1	2	2	3249
Total winning prize-money					**£3249**
Favourites	**0-1**		**0.0%**		**-1.00**

GEORGE BEWLEY

BONCHESTER BRIDGE, BORDERS

	No. of Hrs	Races Run	1st	2nd	3rd	Unpl	Per cent	£1 Level Stake
NH Flat	*3*	*5*	*0*	*2*	*0*	*3*	*0.0*	*-5.00*
Hurdles	*10*	*38*	*2*	*2*	*6*	*28*	*5.3*	*-7.50*
Chases	*7*	*25*	*2*	*0*	*7*	*16*	*8.0*	*-7.00*
Totals	**17**	**68**	**4**	**4**	**13**	**47**	**5.9**	**-19.50**
13-14	*14*	*58*	*5*	*5*	*6*	*42*	*8.6*	*+33.00*
12-13	*14*	*55*	*8*	*4*	*9*	*34*	*14.5*	*-5.75*

JOCKEYS

	W-R	Per cent	£1 Level Stake
Miss J Walton	2-10	20.0	+8.50
Jonathon Bewley	2-51	3.9	-21.00

COURSE RECORD

	Total W-R	Non-Hndcps Hurdles	Non-Hndcps Chases	Hndcps Hurdles	Hndcps Chases	NH Flat	Per cent	£1 Level Stake
Hexham	1-6	0-0	0-0	1-5	0-1	0-0	16.7	+3.50
Sedgefield	1-7	0-1	0-0	0-3	1-2	0-1	14.3	+2.00
Kelso	1-12	0-0	0-0	1-6	0-6	0-0	8.3	+9.00
Carlisle	1-13	0-1	0-0	0-4	1-6	0-2	7.7	-4.00

WINNING HORSES

Horse	Races Run	1st	2nd	3rd	£
Carters Rest	7	1	0	1	4159
Romany Ryme	9	1	0	1	3899
Hunters Belt	11	1	0	4	3249
Rev Up Ruby	7	1	1	1	3120
Total winning prize-money					**£14427**
Favourites	**0-1**		**0.0%**		**-1.00**

ROBERT BEWLEY

JEDBURGH, BORDERS

	No. of Hrs	Races Run	1st	2nd	3rd	Unpl	Per cent	£1 Level Stake
NH Flat	*2*	*3*	*1*	*0*	*0*	*2*	*33.3*	*+16.00*
Hurdles	*2*	*8*	*0*	*1*	*1*	*6*	*0.0*	*-8.00*
Chases	*1*	*1*	*0*	*0*	*0*	*1*	*0.0*	*-1.00*
Totals	**4**	**12**	**1**	**1**	**1**	**9**	**8.3**	**+7.00**
13-14	*4*	*17*	*0*	*2*	*3*	*12*	*0.0*	*-17.00*
12-13	*3*	*9*	*1*	*1*	*1*	*6*	*11.1*	*-3.00*

JOCKEYS

	W-R	Per cent	£1 Level Stake
Graham Watters	1-1	100.0	+18.00

COURSE RECORD

	Total W-R	Non-Hndcps Hurdles	Non-Hndcps Chases	Hndcps Hurdles	Hndcps Chases	NH Flat	Per cent	£1 Level Stake
Sedgefield	1-2	0-1	0-0	0-0	0-0	1-1	50.0	+17.00

WINNING HORSES

Horse	Races Run	1st	2nd	3rd	£
Daring Exit	7	1	0	0	1560
Total winning prize-money					**£1560**
Favourites	**0-0**		**0.0%**		**0.00**

KEVIN BISHOP

SPAXTON, SOMERSET

	No. of Hrs	Races Run	1st	2nd	3rd	Unpl	Per cent	£1 Level Stake
NH Flat	*2*	*5*	*1*	*0*	*0*	*4*	*20.0*	*-1.50*
Hurdles	*8*	*26*	*2*	*4*	*6*	*14*	*7.7*	*-11.50*
Chases	*4*	*11*	*2*	*1*	*1*	*7*	*18.2*	*+4.50*
Totals	**9**	**42**	**5**	**5**	**7**	**25**	**11.9**	**-8.50**
13-14	*18*	*55*	*4*	*3*	*4*	*44*	*7.3*	*+21.50*
12-13	*23*	*86*	*15*	*8*	*8*	*55*	*17.4*	*+67.42*

JOCKEYS

	W-R	Per cent	£1 Level Stake
Conor Smith	2-8	25.0	+6.50
James Best	2-23	8.7	-15.00
Ciaran Gethings	1-2	50.0	+9.00

COURSE RECORD

	Total W-R	Non-Hndcps Hurdles	Non-Hndcps Chases	Hndcps Hurdles	Hndcps Chases	NH Flat	Per cent	£1 Level Stake
Towcester	3-5	0-0	0-0	2-2	1-3	0-0	60.0	+20.50
Fontwell	2-6	0-0	0-0	0-1	1-3	1-2	33.3	+2.00

WINNING HORSES

Horse	Races Run	1st	2nd	3rd	£
Tara Tavey	10	2	3	4	9747
Just Spot	6	1	1	0	4549
Withy Mills	8	1	0	1	2530
Somerset Jem	4	1	0	0	1560
Total winning prize-money					**£18386**
Favourites	**0-1**		**0.0%**		**-1.00**

LINDA BLACKFORD

RACKENFORD, DEVON

	No. of Hrs	Races Run	1st	2nd	3rd	Unpl	Per cent	£1 Level Stake
NH Flat	*0*	*0*	*0*	*0*	*0*	*0*	*0.0*	*0.00*
Hurdles	*5*	*17*	*0*	*2*	*1*	*14*	*0.0*	*-17.00*
Chases	*4*	*19*	*2*	*1*	*5*	*11*	*10.5*	*-4.00*
Totals	**8**	**36**	**2**	**3**	**6**	**25**	**5.6**	**-21.00**
13-14	*10*	*33*	*1*	*2*	*4*	*26*	*3.0*	*-29.00*
12-13	*9*	*13*	*0*	*0*	*0*	*13*	*0.0*	*-13.00*

JOCKEYS

	W-R	Per cent	£1 Level Stake
Nick Scholfield	2-2	100.0	+13.00

COURSE RECORD

	Total W-R	Non-Hndcps Hurdles	Non-Hndcps Chases	Hndcps Hurdles	Hndcps Chases	NH Flat	Per cent	£1 Level Stake
Taunton	1-6	0-1	0-0	0-1	1-4	0-0	16.7	-2.00
Wincanton	1-8	0-1	0-0	0-2	1-5	0-0	12.5	+3.00

WINNING HORSES

Horse	Races Run	1st	2nd	3rd	£
Chance Encounter	8	2	1	3	6043
Total winning prize-money					**£6043**
Favourites	**0-0**		**0.0%**		**0.00**

MICHAEL BLAKE

TROWBRIDGE, WILTS

	No. of Hrs	Races Run	1st	2nd	3rd	Unpl	Per cent	£1 Level Stake
NH Flat	*1*	*2*	*0*	*0*	*0*	*2*	*0.0*	*-2.00*
Hurdles	*7*	*21*	*4*	*4*	*2*	*11*	*19.0*	*-1.25*
Chases	*5*	*13*	*1*	*2*	*0*	*10*	*7.7*	*-9.75*
Totals	**11**	**36**	**5**	**6**	**2**	**23**	**13.9**	**-13.00**
13-14	*20*	*100*	*14*	*7*	*12*	*67*	*14.0*	*-36.38*
12-13	*21*	*94*	*12*	*8*	*13*	*61*	*12.8*	*-24.87*

JOCKEYS

	W-R	Per cent	£1 Level Stake
Tom Scudamore	3-7	42.9	+6.25
Nick Scholfield	2-13	15.4	-3.25

COURSE RECORD

	Total W-R	Non-Hndcps Hurdles	Non-Hndcps Chases	Hndcps Hurdles	Hndcps Chases	NH Flat	Per cent	£1 Level Stake
Southwell	3-4	1-1	0-0	1-1	1-2	0-0	75.0	+9.00
Exeter	1-1	1-1	0-0	0-0	0-0	0-0	100.0	+4.00
Taunton	1-2	1-1	0-0	0-0	0-1	0-0	50.0	+3.00

WINNING HORSES

Horse	Races Run	1st	2nd	3rd	£
Rocky Rebel	4	2	0	0	5523
Stow	7	1	2	0	2738
Typical Oscar	6	1	2	0	2274
Lamps	5	1	0	2	1949
Total winning prize-money					**£12484**
Favourites	**2-8**		**25.0%**		**-1.00**

MARTIN BOSLEY

CHALFONT ST GILES, BUCKS

	No. of Hrs	Races Run	1st	2nd	3rd	Unpl	Per cent	£1 Level Stake
NH Flat	*0*	*0*	*0*	*0*	*0*	*0*	*0.0*	*0.00*
Hurdles	*6*	*14*	*0*	*1*	*0*	*13*	*0.0*	*-14.00*
Chases	*3*	*15*	*3*	*1*	*4*	*7*	*20.0*	*+13.00*
Totals	**9**	**29**	**3**	**2**	**4**	**20**	**10.3**	**-1.00**
13-14	*13*	*46*	*2*	*1*	*3*	*40*	*4.3*	*+59.00*
12-13	*13*	*41*	*4*	*0*	*4*	*33*	*9.8*	*-7.67*

JOCKEYS

	W-R	Per cent	£1 Level Stake
Mr Z Baker	3-18	16.7	+10.00

COURSE RECORD

	Total W-R	Non-Hndcps Hurdles	Non-Hndcps Chases	Hndcps Hurdles	Hndcps Chases	NH Flat	Per cent	£1 Level Stake
Huntingdon	1-2	0-0	0-0	0-0	1-2	0-0	50.0	+3.50
Worcester	1-3	0-0	0-1	0-0	1-2	0-0	33.3	+14.00
Ludlow	1-4	0-1	0-0	0-1	1-2	0-0	25.0	+1.50

WINNING HORSES

Horse	Races Run	1st	2nd	3rd	£
Topthorn	9	2	1	1	6394
Carobello	5	1	0	3	3743
Total winning prize-money					**£10137**
Favourites	**0-1**		**0.0%**		**-1.00**

PETER BOWEN

LITTLE NEWCASTLE, PEMBROKES

	No. of Hrs	Races Run	1st	2nd	3rd	Unpl	Per cent	£1 Level Stake
NH Flat	*25*	*59*	*12*	*7*	*13*	*27*	*20.3*	*-8.13*
Hurdles	*46*	*191*	*30*	*30*	*30*	*101*	*15.7*	*-36.56*
Chases	*26*	*123*	*15*	*21*	*23*	*64*	*12.2*	*-45.38*
Totals	**76**	**373**	**57**	**58**	**66**	**192**	**15.3**	**-90.07**
13-14	*73*	*356*	*69*	*62*	*36*	*189*	*19.4*	*+57.06*
12-13	*83*	*364*	*49*	*53*	*42*	*220*	*13.5*	*-89.84*

BY MONTH

NH Flat	W-R	Per cent	£1 Level Stake	Hurdles	W-R	Per cent	£1 Level Stake
May	0-4	0.0	-4.00	May	7-22	31.8	+12.45
June	1-6	16.7	-3.00	June	3-16	18.8	-7.95
July	1-10	10.0	-7.75	July	2-13	15.4	-7.00
August	0-3	0.0	-3.00	August	0-6	0.0	-6.00
September	0-5	0.0	-5.00	September	1-17	5.9	-13.50
October	0-6	0.0	-6.00	October	2-23	8.7	-5.00
November	0-2	0.0	-2.00	November	0-11	0.0	-11.00
December	3-6	50.0	+5.50	December	4-22	18.2	+6.88
January	1-2	50.0	-0.33	January	3-15	20.0	+2.50
February	1-2	50.0	+0.20	February	1-18	5.6	-16.00
March	1-6	16.7	-1.00	March	2-12	16.7	+7.00
April	4-7	57.1	+18.25	April	5-16	31.3	+1.06

Chases	W-R	Per cent	£1 Level Stake	Totals	W-R	Per cent	£1 Level Stake
May	3-12	25.0	+9.50	May	10-38	26.3	+17.95
June	3-16	18.8	-0.75	June	7-38	18.4	-11.70
July	1-13	7.7	-10.13	July	4-36	11.1	-24.88
August	1-10	10.0	-5.00	August	1-19	5.3	-14.00
September	1-9	11.1	-3.50	September	2-31	6.5	-22.00
October	2-11	18.2	-1.00	October	4-40	10.0	-12.00
November	0-9	0.0	-9.00	November	0-22	0.0	-22.00
December	0-15	0.0	-15.00	December	7-43	16.3	-2.62
January	0-7	0.0	-7.00	January	4-24	16.7	-4.83
February	2-4	50.0	+6.50	February	4-24	16.7	-9.30
March	1-6	16.7	-2.00	March	4-24	16.7	+4.00
April	1-11	9.1	-8.00	April	10-34	29.4	+11.31

DISTANCE

Hurdles	W-R	Per cent	£1 Level Stake	Chases	W-R	Per cent	£1 Level Stake
2m-2m3f	5-46	10.9	-28.05	2m-2m3f	0-10	0.0	-10.00
2m4f-2m7f	14-68	20.6	-5.62	2m4f-2m7f	6-35	17.1	-4.25
3m+	3-26	11.5	0.00	3m+	5-50	10.0	-21.63

TYPE OF RACE

Non-Handicaps	W-R	Per cent	£1 Level Stake	Handicaps	W-R	Per cent	£1 Level Stake
Nov Hrdls	6-39	15.4	-10.70	Nov Hrdls	0-10	0.0	-10.00
Hrdls	5-29	17.2	-9.55	Hrdls	17-105	16.2	-6.04
Nov Chs	0-7	0.0	-7.00	Nov Chs	2-10	20.0	+0.50
Chases	0-0	0.0	0.00	Chases	13-106	12.3	-38.88
Sell/Claim	1-6	16.7	-4.27	Sell/Claim	1-2	50.0	+4.00

RACE CLASS

	W-R	Per cent	£1 Level Stake
Class 1	1-27	3.7	-18.00
Class 2	3-20	15.0	+6.00
Class 3	10-83	12.0	-24.04
Class 4	24-131	18.3	-14.25
Class 5	12-66	18.2	-16.70
Class 6	7-46	15.2	-23.08

FIRST TIME OUT

	W-R	Per cent	£1 Level Stake
Bumpers	4-25	16.0	-7.25
Hurdles	5-34	14.7	-5.80
Chases	3-17	17.6	+1.50
Totals	12-76	15.8	-11.55

JOCKEYS

	W-R	Per cent	£1 Level Stake
Sean Bowen	26-127	20.5	+3.23
Jamie Moore	16-91	17.6	-10.75
Donal Devereux	9-97	9.3	-48.50
Robert Dunne	1-2	50.0	+1.75
Paddy Brennan	1-2	50.0	+3.00
Miss Jodie Hughes	1-2	50.0	+1.75
A P McCoy	1-4	25.0	-1.80
Denis O'Regan	1-6	16.7	-0.50
Richard Johnson	1-13	7.7	-9.25

COURSE RECORD

	Total W-R	Non-Hndcps Hurdles	Non-Hndcps Chases	Hndcps Hurdles	Hndcps Chases	NH Flat	Per cent	£1 Level Stake
Ffos Las	12-85	5-28	0-1	2-22	4-21	1-13	14.1	-33.31
Chepstow	9-31	0-9	0-1	3-9	3-8	3-4	29.0	+17.50
Perth	4-14	1-1	0-0	2-4	0-6	1-3	28.6	0.00
Mrket Rsn	4-21	1-3	0-1	1-6	2-9	0-2	19.0	-6.00
Cartmel	3-7	1-1	0-1	1-3	1-2	0-0	42.9	+6.38
Nton Abbot	3-17	1-2	0-0	1-7	1-7	0-1	17.6	-4.50
Kempton	2-2	0-0	0-0	1-1	0-0	1-1	100.0	+6.20
Carlisle	2-3	1-1	0-0	0-1	1-1	0-0	66.7	+13.00
Bangor	2-8	1-1	0-0	0-3	0-2	1-2	25.0	-2.80
Warwick	2-9	0-0	0-0	1-4	0-3	1-2	22.2	+4.50
Plumpton	2-11	0-0	0-0	2-5	0-5	0-1	18.2	+2.88
Worcester	2-16	0-2	0-2	0-2	1-7	1-3	12.5	-6.75
Aintree	2-18	0-1	0-0	1-9	0-6	1-2	11.1	-3.00
Taunton	1-3	0-0	0-0	0-2	0-0	1-1	33.3	+0.75
Fakenham	1-4	0-0	0-0	1-2	0-1	0-1	25.0	-0.25
Newbury	1-6	1-1	0-0	0-3	0-2	0-0	16.7	-2.50
Haydock	1-7	0-2	0-0	0-2	0-2	1-1	14.3	+1.00
Cheltenham	1-8	0-0	0-0	1-4	0-3	0-1	12.5	+3.00
Fontwell	1-8	0-0	0-0	0-2	1-5	0-1	12.5	-3.00
Exeter	1-10	0-4	0-0	1-2	0-4	0-0	10.0	-8.17
Stratford	1-13	0-1	0-0	0-2	1-3	0-7	7.7	-3.00

WINNING HORSES

Horse	Races Run	1st	2nd	3rd	£
Hollies Pearl	5	3	1	1	20455
Land Of Vic	6	1	0	1	12686
Rolling Maul	12	5	1	3	29017
Awaywiththegreys	7	1	0	0	9747
Book'Em Danno	5	2	0	0	11696
*Tanerko Emery	3	2	0	0	9870
Grape Tree Flame	9	3	1	1	12996
*Velator	9	1	3	2	6963
Dark Glacier	10	3	1	1	12828
Ballybough Gorta	7	1	0	2	6498
Letbeso	9	2	2	2	11047
Sandynow	4	2	1	1	8123
Buachaill Alainn	6	1	1	2	4874

Cygnet	8	2	1	2	6498
Forever My Friend	7	1	0	2	3899
The Road Ahead	7	2	2	0	7473
Princess Tara	8	2	3	1	7148
Strumble Head	10	2	1	2	7538
Rons Dream	7	2	1	1	6693
Get Home Now	10	1	3	0	3249
Vinnie My Boy	8	1	0	1	3249
Handmaid	7	2	1	2	6498
Henllan Harri	4	2	0	1	6368
Squeeze Me	2	1	0	0	2634
Cruising Bye	11	1	6	3	2599
Ghost River	5	3	0	1	6602
Tough Talkin Man	6	1	1	3	2144
Princess Roania	2	1	1	0	2053
G'Dai Sydney	7	1	0	1	1949
Western Xpress	4	1	0	2	1949
Red Six	2	1	0	0	1949
Cresswell Prince	3	1	0	2	1598
Thunder And Rain	4	1	3	0	1560
Desertmore Hill	2	1	0	1	1560
Total winning prize-money					**£242010**
Favourites	**18-54**		**33.3%**		**-3.32**

MICKEY BOWEN

HAVERFORDWEST, PEMBROKES

	No. of Hrs	Races Run	1st	2nd	3rd	Unpl	Per cent	£1 Level Stake
NH Flat	*0*	*0*	*0*	*0*	*0*	*0*	*0.0*	*0.00*
Hurdles	*0*	*0*	*0*	*0*	*0*	*0*	*0.0*	*0.00*
Chases	*2*	*5*	*2*	*0*	*0*	*3*	*40.0*	*+5.00*
Totals	**2**	**5**	**2**	**0**	**0**	**3**	**40.0**	**+5.00**
13-14	*1*	*1*	*0*	*0*	*0*	*1*	*0.0*	*-1.00*

JOCKEYS

	W-R	Per cent	£1 Level Stake
Ciaran Gethings	2-3	66.7	+7.00

COURSE RECORD

	Total W-R	Non-Hndcps Hurdles	Non-Hndcps Chases	Hndcps Hurdles	Hndcps Chases	NH Flat	Per cent	£1 Level Stake
Chepstow	1-1	0-0	1-1	0-0	0-0	0-0	100.0	+5.50
Ffos Las	1-1	0-0	1-1	0-0	0-0	0-0	100.0	+2.50

WINNING HORSES

Horse	Races Run	1st	2nd	3rd	£
Bobs Law	4	2	0	0	6108
Total winning prize-money					**£6108**
Favourites	**0-1**		**0.0%**		**-1.00**

DAVID BRACE

PYLE, BRIDGEND

	No. of Hrs	Races Run	1st	2nd	3rd	Unpl	Per cent	£1 Level Stake
NH Flat	*0*	*0*	*0*	*0*	*0*	*0*	*0.0*	*0.00*
Hurdles	*7*	*18*	*1*	*4*	*1*	*12*	*5.6*	*-9.50*
Chases	*2*	*3*	*0*	*0*	*0*	*3*	*0.0*	*-3.00*
Totals	**9**	**21**	**1**	**4**	**1**	**15**	**4.8**	**-12.50**
13-14	*11*	*22*	*1*	*1*	*1*	*19*	*4.5*	*-19.75*
12-13	*9*	*14*	*0*	*0*	*0*	*14*	*0.0*	*-14.00*

JOCKEYS

	W-R	Per cent	£1 Level Stake
Sean Bowen	1-10	10.0	-1.50

COURSE RECORD

	Total W-R	Non-Hndcps Hurdles	Non-Hndcps Chases	Hndcps Hurdles	Hndcps Chases	NH Flat	Per cent	£1 Level Stake
Worcester	1-7	0-3	0-0	1-2	0-2	0-0	14.3	+1.50

WINNING HORSES

Horse	Races Run	1st	2nd	3rd	£
*Bajan Blu	7	1	3	1	3119
Total winning prize-money					**£3119**
Favourites	**0-4**		**0.0%**		**-4.00**

MARK BRADSTOCK

LETCOMBE BASSETT, OXON

	No. of Hrs	Races Run	1st	2nd	3rd	Unpl	Per cent	£1 Level Stake
NH Flat	*4*	*5*	*0*	*1*	*1*	*3*	*0.0*	*-5.00*
Hurdles	*4*	*9*	*3*	*0*	*1*	*5*	*33.3*	*+8.25*
Chases	*2*	*11*	*5*	*0*	*1*	*5*	*45.5*	*+16.21*
Totals	**9**	**25**	**8**	**1**	**3**	**13**	**32.0**	**+19.46**
13-14	*9*	*26*	*1*	*1*	*5*	*19*	*3.8*	*-22.00*
12-13	*10*	*28*	*7*	*1*	*1*	*19*	*25.0*	*+5.98*

JOCKEYS

	W-R	Per cent	£1 Level Stake
Nico de Boinville	6-22	27.3	+15.83
Sean Bowen	1-1	100.0	+2.75
Richard Johnson	1-1	100.0	+1.88

COURSE RECORD

	Total W-R	Non-Hndcps Hurdles	Non-Hndcps Chases	Hndcps Hurdles	Hndcps Chases	NH Flat	Per cent	£1 Level Stake
Newbury	3-4	0-0	2-2	0-1	1-1	0-0	75.0	+10.88
Ascot	1-1	0-0	0-0	1-1	0-0	0-0	100.0	+7.00
Kempton	1-1	0-0	1-1	0-0	0-0	0-0	100.0	+3.33

Ffos Las	1-2	0-0	0-0	1-1	0-0	0-1	50.0	+1.75
Cheltenham	1-3	0-0	1-2	0-0	0-1	0-0	33.3	+5.00
Chepstow	1-3	0-0	0-0	1-1	0-2	0-0	33.3	+2.50

WINNING HORSES

Horse	Races Run	1st	2nd	3rd	£
Coneygree	4	4	0	0	401931
Carruthers	7	1	0	1	12512
Flintham	6	3	0	1	14898
Total winning prize-money					**£429341**
Favourites	**1-1**		**100.0%**		**1.88**

GILES BRAVERY

NEWMARKET, SUFFOLK

	No. of Hrs	Races Run	1st	2nd	3rd	Unpl	Per cent	£1 Level Stake
NH Flat	*1*	*2*	*1*	*0*	*0*	*1*	*50.0*	*+19.00*
Hurdles	*0*	*0*	*0*	*0*	*0*	*0*	*0.0*	*0.00*
Chases	*0*	*0*	*0*	*0*	*0*	*0*	*0.0*	*0.00*
Totals	**1**	**2**	**1**	**0**	**0**	**1**	**50.0**	**+19.00**
13-14	*2*	*4*	*1*	*1*	*0*	*2*	*25.0*	*+1.50*

JOCKEYS

	W-R	Per cent	£1 Level Stake
Jack Quinlan	1-2	50.0	+19.00

COURSE RECORD

	Total W-R	Non-Hndcps Hurdles	Non-Hndcps Chases	Hndcps Hurdles	Hndcps Chases	NH Flat	Per cent	£1 Level Stake
Fontwell	1-1	0-0	0-0	0-0	0-0	1-1	100.0	+20.00

WINNING HORSES

Horse	Races Run	1st	2nd	3rd	£
Amber Spyglass	2	1	0	0	1560
Total winning prize-money					**£1560**
Favourites	**0-0**		**0.0%**		**0.00**

BARRY BRENNAN

UPPER LAMBOURN, BERKS

	No. of Hrs	Races Run	1st	2nd	3rd	Unpl	Per cent	£1 Level Stake
NH Flat	*1*	*1*	*0*	*0*	*0*	*1*	*0.0*	*-1.00*
Hurdles	*11*	*29*	*3*	*1*	*2*	*23*	*10.3*	*-14.75*
Chases	*5*	*11*	*0*	*1*	*1*	*9*	*0.0*	*-11.00*
Totals	**12**	**41**	**3**	**2**	**3**	**33**	**7.3**	**-26.75**
13-14	*25*	*71*	*2*	*4*	*7*	*58*	*2.8*	*-55.50*
12-13	*25*	*59*	*9*	*5*	*6*	*39*	*15.3*	*-3.88*

JOCKEYS

	W-R	Per cent	£1 Level Stake
James Banks	2-13	15.4	-2.50
Sam Twiston-Davies	1-4	25.0	-0.25

COURSE RECORD

	Total W-R	Non-Hndcps Hurdles	Non-Hndcps Chases	Hndcps Hurdles	Hndcps Chases	NH Flat	Per cent	£1 Level Stake
Fakenham	1-3	0-1	0-0	1-2	0-0	0-0	33.3	+0.50
Southwell	1-3	0-0	0-0	1-3	0-0	0-0	33.3	+4.00
Leicester	1-6	1-3	0-1	0-2	0-0	0-0	16.7	-2.25

WINNING HORSES

Horse	Races Run	1st	2nd	3rd	£
Bathcounty	5	2	0	0	6173
*Swampfire	7	1	1	1	2599
Total winning prize-money					**£8772**
Favourites	**0-1**		**0.0%**		**-1.00**

DAVID BRIDGWATER

ICOMB, GLOUCS

	No. of Hrs	Races Run	1st	2nd	3rd	Unpl	Per cent	£1 Level Stake
NH Flat	*4*	*6*	*0*	*0*	*1*	*5*	*0.0*	*-6.00*
Hurdles	*25*	*78*	*12*	*12*	*10*	*44*	*15.4*	*-14.99*
Chases	*27*	*100*	*21*	*14*	*15*	*50*	*21.0*	*+3.82*
Totals	**49**	**184**	**33**	**26**	**26**	**99**	**17.9**	**-17.17**
13-14	*52*	*211*	*21*	*28*	*29*	*133*	*10.0*	*-44.64*
12-13	*26*	*100*	*16*	*20*	*12*	*52*	*16.0*	*-21.27*

BY MONTH

NH Flat	W-R	Per cent	£1 Level Stake	Hurdles	W-R	Per cent	£1 Level Stake
May	0-0	0.0	0.00	May	1-11	9.1	-1.00
June	0-0	0.0	0.00	June	0-6	0.0	-6.00
July	0-0	0.0	0.00	July	3-12	25.0	+3.60
August	0-0	0.0	0.00	August	2-5	40.0	+2.50
September	0-0	0.0	0.00	September	1-5	20.0	-2.25
October	0-0	0.0	0.00	October	0-4	0.0	-4.00
November	0-4	0.0	-4.00	November	0-5	0.0	-5.00
December	0-1	0.0	-1.00	December	1-6	16.7	-3.50
January	0-0	0.0	0.00	January	3-9	33.3	+13.75
February	0-0	0.0	0.00	February	1-5	20.0	-3.09
March	0-1	0.0	-1.00	March	0-8	0.0	-8.00
April	0-0	0.0	0.00	April	0-2	0.0	-2.00

Chases	W-R	Per cent	£1 Level Stake	Totals	W-R	Per cent	£1 Level Stake
May	3-11	27.3	+7.50	May	4-22	18.2	+6.50
June	1-8	12.5	-4.25	June	1-14	7.1	-10.25
July	1-8	12.5	-4.25	July	4-20	20.0	-0.65
August	0-7	0.0	-7.00	August	2-12	16.7	-4.50
September	0-3	0.0	-3.00	September	1-8	12.5	-5.25
October	1-6	16.7	-2.75	October	1-10	10.0	-6.75
November	4-14	28.6	+12.75	November	4-23	17.4	+3.75
December	0-6	0.0	-6.00	December	1-13	7.7	-10.50
January	2-7	28.6	-2.84	January	5-16	31.3	+10.91

February	3-11	27.3	-1.00	February	4-16	25.0	-4.09
March	5-12	41.7	+18.91	March	5-21	23.8	+9.91
April	1-7	14.3	-4.25	April	1-9	11.1	-6.25

DISTANCE

Hurdles	W-R	Per cent	£1 Level Stake	Chases	W-R	Per cent	£1 Level Stake
2m-2m3f	7-44	15.9	-7.34	2m-2m3f	8-29	27.6	+5.91
2m4f-2m7f	3-20	15.0	-5.40	2m4f-2m7f	5-25	20.0	+7.25
3m+	0-0	0.0	0.00	3m+	3-28	10.7	-9.50

TYPE OF RACE

Non-Handicaps	W-R	Per cent	£1 Level Stake	Handicaps	W-R	Per cent	£1 Level Stake
Nov Hrdls	3-36	8.3	-14.50	Nov Hrdls	3-7	42.9	+18.50
Hrdls	3-16	18.8	-7.15	Hrdls	0-11	0.0	-11.00
Nov Chs	0-2	0.0	-2.00	Nov Chs	2-18	11.1	-11.09
Chases	0-4	0.0	-4.00	Chases	19-76	25.0	+20.91
Sell/Claim	3-7	42.9	+0.16	Sell/Claim	0-0	0.0	0.00

RACE CLASS

	W-R	Per cent	£1 Level Stake
Class 1	0-11	0.0	-11.00
Class 2	2-8	25.0	+10.00
Class 3	2-16	12.5	+6.50
Class 4	18-101	17.8	-10.24
Class 5	11-44	25.0	-8.43
Class 6	0-4	0.0	-4.00

FIRST TIME OUT

	W-R	Per cent	£1 Level Stake
Bumpers	0-4	0.0	-4.00
Hurdles	5-23	21.7	+13.25
Chases	7-22	31.8	+10.25
Totals	12-49	24.5	+19.50

JOCKEYS

	W-R	Per cent	£1 Level Stake
Tom Scudamore	18-68	26.5	+13.76
Jake Hodson	7-58	12.1	-13.34
Tom Cannon	3-14	21.4	+7.91
Miss A E Stirling	1-2	50.0	+1.75
Mr J Launchbury	1-3	33.3	+0.75
Sam Twiston-Davies	1-4	25.0	-0.75
Tom O'Brien	1-5	20.0	+0.50
Alain Cawley	1-14	7.1	-11.75

COURSE RECORD

	Total W-R	Non-Hndcps Hurdles	Non-Hndcps Chases	Hndcps Hurdles	Hndcps Chases	NH Flat	Per cent	£1 Level Stake
Plumpton	6-19	1-7	0-0	0-2	5-10	0-0	31.6	-1.59
Southwell	4-7	0-1	0-0	0-0	4-6	0-0	57.1	+6.91
Nton Abbot	4-13	1-3	0-0	1-3	2-7	0-0	30.8	+8.25
Towcester	3-11	1-3	0-0	0-0	2-7	0-1	27.3	+6.25
Fontwell	3-13	1-4	0-0	0-0	2-8	0-1	23.1	-0.75
Stratford	3-25	0-12	0-1	1-4	2-8	0-0	12.0	+10.50
Leicester	2-6	2-3	0-0	0-1	0-2	0-0	33.3	-0.75
Fakenham	1-1	0-0	0-0	0-0	1-1	0-0	100.0	+0.50
Newbury	1-1	0-0	0-0	0-0	1-1	0-0	100.0	+6.00
Haydock	1-2	0-0	0-1	0-0	1-1	0-0	50.0	+9.00
Chepstow	1-4	0-2	0-0	0-0	1-2	0-0	25.0	+1.50
Mrket Rsn	1-5	1-3	0-0	0-1	0-1	0-0	20.0	-1.00
Taunton	1-6	1-5	0-0	0-0	0-0	0-1	16.7	-4.09
Uttoxeter	1-9	0-2	0-0	1-2	0-5	0-0	11.1	+2.00
Worcester	1-18	1-8	0-0	0-1	0-9	0-0	5.6	-15.90

WINNING HORSES

Horse	Races Run	1st	2nd	3rd	£
No Buts	5	1	1	0	31280
According To Trev	6	1	1	0	21896
Oscar Hill	4	1	0	1	6498
Dont Do Mondays	5	2	1	0	10489
*De Kerry Man	2	2	0	0	10318
Plum Pudding	4	1	1	0	5198
Russian Bolero	4	1	0	2	4549
Nomadic Storm	8	5	1	2	17115
Bravo Riquet	5	2	1	0	6628
Engai	6	1	0	1	3833
Ringa Bay	7	2	1	2	6343
Collodi	4	2	0	1	3509
Garnock	6	2	2	1	6448
Gino Trail	1	1	0	0	3249
Vinnieslittle Lamb	6	1	1	1	3249
Bawden Rocks	2	1	0	0	3249
Saffron Prince	4	1	1	0	3249
*Faith Jicaro	1	1	0	0	3119
Lord Navits	7	2	1	1	5337
Tempuran	6	2	1	0	4934
Regal One	7	1	0	2	2144

Total winning prize-money **£162634**

Favourites **10-29** **34.5%** **-7.02**

CHARLIE BROOKS

SARSDEN, OXON

	No. of Hrs	Races Run	1st	2nd	3rd	Unpl	Per cent	£1 Level Stake
NH Flat	*1*	*1*	*0*	*0*	*0*	*1*	*0.0*	*-1.00*
Hurdles	*3*	*10*	*1*	*3*	*1*	*5*	*10.0*	*-2.00*
Chases	*0*	*0*	*0*	*0*	*0*	*0*	*0.0*	*0.00*
Totals	**4**	**11**	**1**	**3**	**1**	**6**	**9.1**	**-3.00**
13-14	*7*	*25*	*3*	*7*	*0*	*15*	*12.0*	*+0.50*
12-13	*7*	*10*	*1*	*2*	*0*	*7*	*10.0*	*-3.00*

JOCKEYS

	W-R	Per cent	£1 Level Stake
Liam Treadwell	1-10	10.0	-2.00

COURSE RECORD

	Total W-R	Non-Hndcps Hurdles	Non-Hndcps Chases	Hndcps Hurdles	Hndcps Chases	NH Flat	Per cent	£1 Level Stake
Aintree	1-3	0-0	0-0	1-3	0-0	0-0	33.3	+5.00

WINNING HORSES

Horse	Races Run	1st	2nd	3rd	£
Max Ward	4	1	3	0	5848
Total winning prize-money					**£5848**
Favourites	**0-0**		**0.0%**		**0.00**

ALAN BROWN

YEDINGHAM, N YORKS

	No. of Hrs	Races Run	1st	2nd	3rd	Unpl	Per cent	£1 Level Stake
NH Flat	*1*	*1*	*0*	*0*	*0*	*1*	*0.0*	*-1.00*
Hurdles	*6*	*20*	*1*	*2*	*2*	*15*	*5.0*	*+6.00*
Chases	*3*	*8*	*1*	*1*	*0*	*6*	*12.5*	*-3.50*
Totals	**7**	**29**	**2**	**3**	**2**	**22**	**6.9**	**+1.50**
13-14	*8*	*31*	*0*	*3*	*4*	*24*	*0.0*	*-31.00*
12-13	*6*	*26*	*1*	*0*	*1*	*24*	*3.8*	*-5.00*

JOCKEYS

	W-R	Per cent	£1 Level Stake
Jonathan England	1-4	25.0	+0.50
G Lavery	1-16	6.3	+10.00

COURSE RECORD

	Total W-R	Non-Hndcps Hurdles	Non-Hndcps Chases	Hndcps Hurdles	Hndcps Chases	NH Flat	Per cent	£1 Level Stake
Bangor	1-3	0-0	0-0	0-1	1-2	0-0	33.3	+1.50
Wetherby	1-7	1-2	0-0	0-4	0-1	0-0	14.3	+19.00

WINNING HORSES

Horse	Races Run	1st	2nd	3rd	£
*Harris	9	2	2	0	8551
Total winning prize-money					**£8551**
Favourites	**0-0**		**0.0%**		**0.00**

GARY BROWN

LAMBOURN, BERKS

	No. of Hrs	Races Run	1st	2nd	3rd	Unpl	Per cent	£1 Level Stake
NH Flat	*1*	*1*	*0*	*0*	*0*	*1*	*0.0*	*-1.00*
Hurdles	*1*	*1*	*0*	*0*	*0*	*1*	*0.0*	*-1.00*
Chases	*2*	*4*	*1*	*0*	*0*	*3*	*25.0*	*+4.00*
Totals	**3**	**6**	**1**	**0**	**0**	**5**	**16.7**	**+2.00**
13-14	*7*	*29*	*2*	*5*	*6*	*16*	*6.9*	*-19.50*
12-13	*11*	*37*	*2*	*2*	*2*	*31*	*5.4*	*-27.75*

JOCKEYS

	W-R	Per cent	£1 Level Stake
Jamie Moore	1-2	50.0	+6.00

COURSE RECORD

	Total W-R	Non-Hndcps Hurdles	Non-Hndcps Chases	Hndcps Hurdles	Hndcps Chases	NH Flat	Per cent	£1 Level Stake
Huntingdon	1-2	0-1	0-0	0-0	1-1	0-0	50.0	+6.00

WINNING HORSES

Horse	Races Run	1st	2nd	3rd	£
Chestnut Ben	2	1	0	0	3899
Total winning prize-money					**£3899**
Favourites	**0-0**		**0.0%**		**0.00**

KATE BUCKETT

UPHAM, HANTS

	No. of Hrs	Races Run	1st	2nd	3rd	Unpl	Per cent	£1 Level Stake
NH Flat	*0*	*0*	*0*	*0*	*0*	*0*	*0.0*	*0.00*
Hurdles	*4*	*15*	*3*	*0*	*3*	*9*	*20.0*	*+43.00*
Chases	*2*	*5*	*0*	*0*	*1*	*4*	*0.0*	*-5.00*
Totals	**4**	**20**	**3**	**0**	**4**	**13**	**15.0**	**+38.00**
13-14	*5*	*26*	*2*	*2*	*1*	*21*	*7.7*	*+46.00*
12-13	*5*	*27*	*3*	*4*	*3*	*17*	*11.1*	*-19.13*

JOCKEYS

	W-R	Per cent	£1 Level Stake
Kieron Edgar	3-12	25.0	+46.00

COURSE RECORD

	Total W-R	Non-Hndcps Hurdles	Non-Hndcps Chases	Hndcps Hurdles	Hndcps Chases	NH Flat	Per cent	£1 Level Stake
Lingfield	2-2	1-1	0-0	1-1	0-0	0-0	100.0	+39.00
Fontwell	1-6	0-1	0-0	1-4	0-1	0-0	16.7	+11.00

WINNING HORSES

Horse	Races Run	1st	2nd	3rd	£
Boardwalk Empire	5	1	0	1	3379
Join The Navy	6	1	0	2	2599
Upham Running	4	1	0	0	1949
Total winning prize-money					**£7927**
Favourites	**0-2**		**0.0%**		**-2.00**

BOB BUCKLER

HENLEY, SOMERSET

	No. of Hrs	Races Run	1st	2nd	3rd	Unpl	Per cent	£1 Level Stake
NH Flat	*3*	*5*	*0*	*1*	*0*	*4*	*0.0*	*-5.00*
Hurdles	*9*	*27*	*1*	*5*	*5*	*16*	*3.7*	*-25.33*
Chases	*3*	*23*	*7*	*3*	*2*	*11*	*30.4*	*+13.60*
Totals	**10**	**55**	**8**	**9**	**7**	**31**	**14.5**	**-16.73**
13-14	*14*	*60*	*4*	*4*	*9*	*43*	*6.7*	*-7.50*
12-13	*25*	*88*	*9*	*7*	*7*	*65*	*10.2*	*+0.58*

JOCKEYS

	W-R	Per cent	£1 Level Stake
Liam Heard	5-40	12.5	-10.33
Gary Derwin	3-13	23.1	-4.40

COURSE RECORD

	Total W-R	Non-Hndcps Hurdles	Non-Hndcps Chases	Hndcps Hurdles	Hndcps Chases	NH Flat	Per cent	£1 Level Stake
Taunton	4-13	0-3	0-0	0-2	4-8	0-0	30.8	+1.88
Kempton	1-1	0-0	0-0	0-0	1-1	0-0	100.0	+8.00
Ffos Las	1-1	0-0	0-0	0-0	1-1	0-0	100.0	+0.73
Newbury	1-2	0-0	1-1	0-1	0-0	0-0	50.0	+9.00
Chepstow	1-5	1-2	0-0	0-1	0-1	0-1	20.0	-3.33

WINNING HORSES

Horse	Races Run	1st	2nd	3rd	£
Tinker Time	9	2	1	1	21652
The Happy Warrior	11	1	2	0	3769
Ballyegan	11	4	3	3	12333
Ugolin De Beaumont	4	1	2	0	3249
Total winning prize-money					**£41003**
Favourites	**4-7**		**57.1%**		**1.27**

DAI BURCHELL

BRIERY HILL, BLAENAU GWENT

	No. of Hrs	Races Run	1st	2nd	3rd	Unpl	Per cent	£1 Level Stake
NH Flat	*1*	*1*	*0*	*0*	*0*	*1*	*0.0*	*-1.00*
Hurdles	*15*	*45*	*2*	*3*	*5*	*35*	*4.4*	*-11.00*
Chases	*7*	*27*	*5*	*5*	*5*	*12*	*18.5*	*+10.00*
Totals	**18**	**73**	**7**	**8**	**10**	**48**	**9.6**	**-2.00**
13-14	*24*	*88*	*10*	*11*	*10*	*57*	*11.4*	*-40.52*
12-13	*15*	*61*	*6*	*4*	*2*	*49*	*9.8*	*+0.50*

JOCKEYS

	W-R	Per cent	£1 Level Stake
Robert Dunne	5-43	11.6	+20.50
Paul John	2-5	40.0	+2.50

COURSE RECORD

	Total W-R	Non-Hndcps Hurdles	Non-Hndcps Chases	Hndcps Hurdles	Hndcps Chases	NH Flat	Per cent	£1 Level Stake
Leicester	2-3	0-0	0-0	0-0	2-3	0-0	66.7	+3.50
Warwick	1-3	0-1	0-0	1-2	0-0	0-0	33.3	+10.00
Worcester	1-4	0-0	0-1	0-1	1-2	0-0	25.0	+5.00
Chepstow	1-9	0-2	0-0	0-3	1-3	0-1	11.1	+8.00
Ludlow	1-10	1-7	0-0	0-2	0-1	0-0	10.0	+11.00
Ffos Las	1-10	0-1	0-0	0-5	1-4	0-0	10.0	-5.50

WINNING HORSES

Horse	Races Run	1st	2nd	3rd	£
Rebeccas Choice	7	1	1	1	12660
Cardigan Island	7	1	1	2	4061
One For The Boss	10	3	3	1	8772
King Alfonso	4	1	0	1	3899
*Guanciale	4	1	0	1	3249
Total winning prize-money					**£32641**
Favourites	**1-3**		**33.3%**		**0.00**

K R BURKE

MIDDLEHAM MOOR, N YORKS

	No. of Hrs	Races Run	1st	2nd	3rd	Unpl	Per cent	£1 Level Stake
NH Flat	*0*	*0*	*0*	*0*	*0*	*0*	*0.0*	*0.00*
Hurdles	*2*	*6*	*2*	*1*	*1*	*2*	*33.3*	*+2.50*
Chases	*1*	*1*	*0*	*0*	*0*	*1*	*0.0*	*-1.00*
Totals	**2**	**7**	**2**	**1**	**1**	**3**	**28.6**	**+1.50**
13-14	*3*	*11*	*1*	*2*	*1*	*7*	*9.1*	*-2.50*

JOCKEYS

	W-R	Per cent	£1 Level Stake
Brian Hughes	2-5	40.0	+3.50

COURSE RECORD

	Total W-R	Non-Hndcps Hurdles	Non-Hndcps Chases	Hndcps Hurdles	Hndcps Chases	NH Flat	Per cent	£1 Level Stake
Catterick	1-1	1-1	0-0	0-0	0-0	0-0	100.0	+0.50
Doncaster	1-1	1-1	0-0	0-0	0-0	0-0	100.0	+6.00

WINNING HORSES

Horse	Races Run	1st	2nd	3rd	£
*Intense Tango	5	2	1	1	24686
Total winning prize-money					**£24686**
Favourites	**1-1**		**100.0%**		**0.50**

HUGH BURNS

ALNWICK, NORTHUMBERLAND

	No. of Hrs	Races Run	1st	2nd	3rd	Unpl	Per cent	£1 Level Stake
NH Flat	*1*	*1*	*0*	*0*	*0*	*1*	*0.0*	*-1.00*
Hurdles	*2*	*5*	*1*	*1*	*0*	*3*	*20.0*	*+4.50*
Chases	*0*	*0*	*0*	*0*	*0*	*0*	*0.0*	*0.00*
Totals	**3**	**6**	**1**	**1**	**0**	**4**	**16.7**	**+3.50**
13-14	*4*	*9*	*0*	*0*	*0*	*9*	*0.0*	*-9.00*
12-13	*6*	*15*	*0*	*0*	*0*	*15*	*0.0*	*-15.00*

JOCKEYS

	W-R	Per cent	£1 Level Stake
Brian Hughes	1-5	20.0	+4.50

COURSE RECORD

	Total W-R	Non-Hndcps Hurdles	Non-Hndcps Chases	Hndcps Hurdles	Hndcps Chases	NH Flat	Per cent	£1 Level Stake
Perth	1-2	0-0	0-0	1-1	0-0	0-1	50.0	+7.50

WINNING HORSES

Horse	Races Run	1st	2nd	3rd	£
Oxalido	3	1	1	0	3249
Total winning prize-money					**£3249**
Favourites	**0-0**		**0.0%**		**0.00**

JOHN BUTLER

NEWMARKET, SUFFOLK

	No. of Hrs	Races Run	1st	2nd	3rd	Unpl	Per cent	£1 Level Stake
NH Flat	*2*	*3*	*0*	*0*	*0*	*3*	*0.0*	*-3.00*
Hurdles	*5*	*16*	*2*	*3*	*2*	*9*	*12.5*	*-9.17*
Chases	*2*	*3*	*1*	*0*	*0*	*2*	*33.3*	*+4.00*
Totals	**9**	**22**	**3**	**3**	**2**	**14**	**13.6**	**-8.17**
13-14	*8*	*12*	*1*	*0*	*2*	*9*	*8.3*	*-6.00*
12-13	*4*	*8*	*0*	*0*	*1*	*7*	*0.0*	*-8.00*

JOCKEYS

	W-R	Per cent	£1 Level Stake
Sam Twiston-Davies	1-1	100.0	+4.00
A P McCoy	1-2	50.0	-0.17
Gavin Sheehan	1-9	11.1	-2.00

COURSE RECORD

	Total W-R	Non-Hndcps Hurdles	Non-Hndcps Chases	Hndcps Hurdles	Hndcps Chases	NH Flat	Per cent	£1 Level Stake
Huntingdon	1-1	0-0	0-0	1-1	0-0	0-0	100.0	+4.00
Stratford	1-1	0-0	0-0	0-0	1-1	0-0	100.0	+6.00
Uttoxeter	1-4	1-2	0-0	0-1	0-1	0-0	25.0	-2.17

WINNING HORSES

Horse	Races Run	1st	2nd	3rd	£
Minella For Value	2	1	0	0	11574
Deadly Sting	7	2	3	0	5458
Total winning prize-money					**£17032**
Favourites	**1-110**		**0.9%**		**-108.17**

PADDY BUTLER

EAST CHILTINGTON, E SUSSEX

	No. of Hrs	Races Run	1st	2nd	3rd	Unpl	Per cent	£1 Level Stake
NH Flat	*0*	*0*	*0*	*0*	*0*	*0*	*0.0*	*0.00*
Hurdles	*2*	*7*	*0*	*0*	*1*	*6*	*0.0*	*-7.00*
Chases	*2*	*16*	*1*	*2*	*4*	*9*	*6.3*	*-13.50*
Totals	**3**	**23**	**1**	**2**	**5**	**15**	**4.3**	**-20.50**
13-14	*7*	*24*	*0*	*0*	*1*	*23*	*0.0*	*-24.00*
12-13	*4*	*9*	*0*	*1*	*1*	*7*	*0.0*	*-9.00*

JOCKEYS

	W-R	Per cent	£1 Level Stake
Marc Goldstein	1-11	9.1	-8.50

COURSE RECORD

	Total W-R	Non-Hndcps Hurdles	Non-Hndcps Chases	Hndcps Hurdles	Hndcps Chases	NH Flat	Per cent	£1 Level Stake
Fontwell	1-7	0-0	0-0	0-1	1-6	0-0	14.3	-4.50

WINNING HORSES

Horse	Races Run	1st	2nd	3rd	£
My Silver Cloud	9	1	2	2	2729
Total winning prize-money					**£2729**
Favourites	**1-2**		**50.0%**		**0.50**

BARBARA BUTTERWORTH

BOLTON, CUMBRIA

	No. of Hrs	Races Run	1st	2nd	3rd	Unpl	Per cent	£1 Level Stake
NH Flat	*0*	*0*	*0*	*0*	*0*	*0*	*0.0*	*0.00*
Hurdles	*4*	*21*	*3*	*3*	*3*	*12*	*14.3*	*+17.00*
Chases	*1*	*1*	*0*	*0*	*0*	*1*	*0.0*	*-1.00*
Totals	**5**	**22**	**3**	**3**	**3**	**13**	**13.6**	**+16.00**
13-14	*4*	*29*	*1*	*0*	*6*	*22*	*3.4*	*-26.38*
12-13	*4*	*33*	*2*	*1*	*4*	*26*	*6.1*	*+8.00*

JOCKEYS

	W-R	Per cent	£1 Level Stake
Harry Challoner	2-4	50.0	+28.00
Sean Quinlan	1-13	7.7	-7.00

COURSE RECORD

	Total W-R	Non-Hndcps Hurdles	Non-Hndcps Chases	Hndcps Hurdles	Hndcps Chases	NH Flat	Per cent	£1 Level Stake
Catterick	1-2	0-0	0-0	1-2	0-0	0-0	50.0	+4.00
Newcastle	1-2	0-0	0-0	1-2	0-0	0-0	50.0	+4.00
Carlisle	1-7	0-0	0-0	1-7	0-0	0-0	14.3	+19.00

WINNING HORSES

Horse	Races Run	1st	2nd	3rd	£
Snowed In	13	1	3	3	5198
Age Of Glory	1	1	0	0	4224
Knight Valliant	6	1	0	0	2274
Total winning prize-money					**£11696**
Favourites	**0-2**		**0.0%**		**-2.00**

A CAMPBELL

MORETON-IN-MARSH, GLOUCS

	No. of Hrs	Races Run	1st	2nd	3rd	Unpl	Per cent	£1 Level Stake
NH Flat	*0*	*0*	*0*	*0*	*0*	*0*	*0.0*	*0.00*
Hurdles	*0*	*0*	*0*	*0*	*0*	*0*	*0.0*	*0.00*
Chases	*6*	*11*	*1*	*1*	*0*	*9*	*9.1*	*+6.00*
Totals	**6**	**11**	**1**	**1**	**0**	**9**	**9.1**	**+6.00**
13-14	*2*	*6*	*1*	*0*	*0*	*5*	*16.7*	*+95.00*

JOCKEYS

	W-R	Per cent	£1 Level Stake
Mr H F Nugent	1-5	20.0	+12.00

COURSE RECORD

	Total W-R	Non-Hndcps Hurdles	Non-Hndcps Chases	Hndcps Hurdles	Hndcps Chases	NH Flat	Per cent	£1 Level Stake
Exeter	1-1	0-0	1-1	0-0	0-0	0-0	100.0	+16.00

WINNING HORSES

Horse	Races Run	1st	2nd	3rd	£
*Moscow Chancer	4	1	1	0	936
Total winning prize-money					**£936**
Favourites	**0-0**		**0.0%**		**0.00**

JENNIE CANDLISH

BASFORD GREEN, STAFFS

	No. of Hrs	Races Run	1st	2nd	3rd	Unpl	Per cent	£1 Level Stake
NH Flat	*3*	*5*	*0*	*1*	*0*	*4*	*0.0*	*-5.00*
Hurdles	*25*	*94*	*9*	*11*	*10*	*64*	*9.6*	*-53.52*
Chases	*9*	*34*	*4*	*6*	*6*	*18*	*11.8*	*+4.38*
Totals	**31**	**133**	**13**	**18**	**16**	**86**	**9.8**	**-54.14**
13-14	*44*	*213*	*18*	*26*	*31*	*138*	*8.5*	*-123.38*
12-13	*37*	*173*	*12*	*19*	*26*	*116*	*6.9*	*-104.17*

BY MONTH

NH Flat	W-R	Per cent	£1 Level Stake	**Hurdles**	W-R	Per cent	£1 Level Stake
May	0-1	0.0	-1.00	May	0-7	0.0	-7.00
June	0-1	0.0	-1.00	June	0-4	0.0	-4.00
July	0-1	0.0	-1.00	July	0-5	0.0	-5.00
August	0-0	0.0	0.00	August	0-1	0.0	-1.00
September	0-0	0.0	0.00	September	0-1	0.0	-1.00
October	0-0	0.0	0.00	October	0-8	0.0	-8.00
November	0-0	0.0	0.00	November	0-1	0.0	-1.00
December	0-0	0.0	0.00	December	2-16	12.5	-8.40
January	0-0	0.0	0.00	January	3-17	17.6	-5.25
February	0-1	0.0	-1.00	February	1-12	8.3	-8.25
March	0-1	0.0	-1.00	March	3-13	23.1	+4.38
April	0-0	0.0	0.00	April	0-9	0.0	-9.00

Chases	W-R	Per cent	£1 Level Stake	**Totals**	W-R	Per cent	£1 Level Stake
May	0-4	0.0	-4.00	May	0-12	0.0	-12.00
June	0-2	0.0	-2.00	June	0-7	0.0	-7.00
July	0-4	0.0	-4.00	July	0-10	0.0	-10.00
August	0-0	0.0	0.00	August	0-1	0.0	-1.00
September	0-0	0.0	0.00	September	0-1	0.0	-1.00
October	0-1	0.0	-1.00	October	0-9	0.0	-9.00
November	0-2	0.0	-2.00	November	0-3	0.0	-3.00
December	1-4	25.0	-1.13	December	3-20	15.0	-9.53
January	0-5	0.0	-5.00	January	3-22	13.6	-10.25
February	0-4	0.0	-4.00	February	1-17	5.9	-13.25
March	2-5	40.0	+21.50	March	5-19	26.3	+24.88
April	1-3	33.3	+6.00	April	1-12	8.3	-3.00

DISTANCE

Hurdles	W-R	Per cent	£1 Level Stake	**Chases**	W-R	Per cent	£1 Level Stake
2m-2m3f	7-43	16.3	-13.02	2m-2m3f	0-7	0.0	-7.00
2m4f-2m7f	0-14	0.0	-14.00	2m4f-2m7f	0-16	0.0	-16.00
3m+	2-11	18.2	-0.50	3m+	4-9	44.4	+29.38

TYPE OF RACE

Non-Handicaps	W-R	Per cent	£1 Level Stake	**Handicaps**	W-R	Per cent	£1 Level Stake
Nov Hrdls	3-27	11.1	-18.27	Nov Hrdls	0-5	0.0	-5.00
Hrdls	0-14	0.0	-14.00	Hrdls	6-47	12.8	-15.25
Nov Chs	0-5	0.0	-5.00	Nov Chs	1-4	25.0	+17.00
Chases	0-0	0.0	0.00	Chases	3-25	12.0	-7.63
Sell/Claim	0-0	0.0	0.00	Sell/Claim	0-0	0.0	0.00

RACE CLASS

	W-R	Per cent	£1 Level Stake
Class 1	0-6	0.0	-6.00
Class 2	0-9	0.0	-9.00
Class 3	4-24	16.7	+10.50
Class 4	8-64	12.5	-26.65
Class 5	1-26	3.8	-19.00
Class 6	0-4	0.0	-4.00

FIRST TIME OUT

	W-R	Per cent	£1 Level Stake
Bumpers	0-3	0.0	-3.00
Hurdles	0-22	0.0	-22.00
Chases	0-6	0.0	-6.00
Totals	0-31	0.0	-31.00

JOCKEYS

	W-R	Per cent	£1 Level Stake
Peter Carberry	6-44	13.6	-23.15

Jason Maguire	2-14	14.3	-5.50
Conor Walsh	1-2	50.0	+5.00
Richard Johnson	1-4	25.0	+17.00
Noel Fehily	1-5	20.0	0.00
Henry Brooke	1-5	20.0	+4.00
Aidan Coleman	1-7	14.3	+0.50

COURSE RECORD

	Total W-R	Non-Hndcps Hurdles	Non-Hndcps Chases	Hndcps Hurdles	Hndcps Chases	NH Flat	Per cent	£1 Level Stake
Carlisle	4-16	1-6	0-1	0-4	3-5	0-0	25.0	+4.25
Sedgefield	3-9	1-2	0-0	2-5	0-2	0-0	33.3	+5.50
Haydock	2-6	0-1	0-0	2-4	0-1	0-0	33.3	+2.50
Uttoxeter	2-19	0-9	0-1	1-6	1-3	0-0	10.5	+9.50
Kempton	1-2	0-0	0-0	1-2	0-0	0-0	50.0	+3.00
Bangor	1-12	1-5	0-0	0-5	0-1	0-1	8.3	-9.90

WINNING HORSES

Horse	Races Run	1st	2nd	3rd	£
Barafundle	5	2	2	0	19549
Sleepy Haven	7	2	1	0	13444
Basford Ben	7	3	1	0	12671
The Horsechesnut	3	1	0	1	3798
Astaroland	8	1	2	1	3379
Grove Silver	7	2	2	0	6628
*Restraint Of Trade	5	1	0	2	3119
Kilkenny Kim	11	1	1	1	2469
Total winning prize-money					**£65057**
Favourites	**4-17**		**23.5%**		**-5.28**

GRANT CANN

BATH, GLOUCESTERSHIRE

	No. of Hrs	Races Run	1st	2nd	3rd	Unpl	Per cent	£1 Level Stake
NH Flat	*0*	*0*	*0*	*0*	*0*	*0*	*0.0*	*0.00*
Hurdles	*4*	*10*	*0*	*0*	*0*	*10*	*0.0*	*-10.00*
Chases	*6*	*15*	*2*	*1*	*2*	*10*	*13.3*	*-4.20*
Totals	**8**	**25**	**2**	**1**	**2**	**20**	**8.0**	**-14.20**
13-14	*6*	*17*	*0*	*3*	*4*	*10*	*0.0*	*-17.00*
12-13	*8*	*32*	*1*	*6*	*5*	*20*	*3.1*	*-29.38*

JOCKEYS

	W-R	Per cent	£1 Level Stake
Tom O'Brien	1-4	25.0	-2.20
Nick Scholfield	1-13	7.7	-4.00

COURSE RECORD

	Total W-R	Non-Hndcps Hurdles	Non-Hndcps Chases	Hndcps Hurdles	Hndcps Chases	NH Flat	Per cent	£1 Level Stake
Wincanton	2-7	0-0	0-1	0-2	2-4	0-0	28.6	+3.80

WINNING HORSES

Horse	Races Run	1st	2nd	3rd	£
I'm In Charge	7	2	0	2	7798
Total winning prize-money					**£7798**
Favourites	**1-2**		**50.0%**		**-0.20**

DON CANTILLON

NEWMARKET, SUFFOLK

	No. of Hrs	Races Run	1st	2nd	3rd	Unpl	Per cent	£1 Level Stake
NH Flat	*2*	*3*	*0*	*1*	*0*	*2*	*0.0*	*-3.00*
Hurdles	*6*	*26*	*5*	*1*	*4*	*16*	*19.2*	*+26.30*
Chases	*3*	*5*	*0*	*0*	*0*	*5*	*0.0*	*-5.00*
Totals	**8**	**34**	**5**	**2**	**4**	**23**	**14.7**	**+18.30**
13-14	*9*	*38*	*11*	*9*	*6*	*12*	*28.9*	*+2.07*
12-13	*4*	*15*	*5*	*2*	*4*	*4*	*33.3*	*-2.55*

JOCKEYS

	W-R	Per cent	£1 Level Stake
Conor Shoemark	2-8	25.0	+29.00
Mikey Hamill	1-1	100.0	+0.80
Mr Charlie Deutsch	1-2	50.0	+3.50
Leighton Aspell	1-10	10.0	-2.00

COURSE RECORD

	Total W-R	Non-Hndcps Hurdles	Non-Hndcps Chases	Hndcps Hurdles	Hndcps Chases	NH Flat	Per cent	£1 Level Stake
Doncaster	1-1	0-0	0-0	1-1	0-0	0-0	100.0	+7.00
Nton Abbot	1-2	0-1	0-0	1-1	0-0	0-0	50.0	+1.00
Sedgefield	1-3	0-0	0-0	1-3	0-0	0-0	33.3	-1.20
Huntingdon	1-5	0-2	0-0	1-2	0-1	0-0	20.0	+0.50
Stratford	1-5	0-1	0-0	1-3	0-1	0-0	20.0	+29.00

WINNING HORSES

Horse	Races Run	1st	2nd	3rd	£
Truckers Darling	6	1	0	0	3119
Speed Check	10	3	1	2	7538
Oscars Way	8	1	0	1	2274
Total winning prize-money					**£12931**
Favourites	**2-6**		**33.3%**		**-1.20**

RUTH CARR

HUBY, N YORKS

	No. of Hrs	Races Run	1st	2nd	3rd	Unpl	Per cent	£1 Level Stake
NH Flat	*0*	*0*	*0*	*0*	*0*	*0*	*0.0*	*0.00*
Hurdles	*2*	*14*	*1*	*0*	*1*	*12*	*7.1*	*-7.50*
Chases	*1*	*2*	*1*	*0*	*1*	*0*	*50.0*	*+1.75*
Totals	**2**	**16**	**2**	**0**	**2**	**12**	**12.5**	**-5.75**

13-14	*1*	*7*	*2*	*1*	*1*	*3*	*28.6*	*+17.50*

JOCKEYS

	W-R	Per cent	£1 Level Stake
Andrew Thornton	1-3	33.3	+3.50
Jake Greenall	1-10	10.0	-6.25

COURSE RECORD

	Total W-R	Non-Hndcps Hurdles	Non-Hndcps Chases	Hndcps Hurdles	Hndcps Chases	NH Flat	Per cent	£1 Level Stake
Newcastle	1-3	0-0	0-0	1-3	0-0	0-0	33.3	+3.50
Sedgefield	1-6	0-1	0-0	0-4	1-1	0-0	16.7	-2.25

WINNING HORSES

Horse	Races Run	1st	2nd	3rd	£
Light The City	10	2	0	2	7148
Total winning prize-money					**£7148**
Favourites	**0-0**		**0.0%**		**0.00**

TONY CARROLL

CROPTHORNE, WORCS

	No. of Hrs	Races Run	1st	2nd	3rd	Unpl	Per cent	£1 Level Stake
NH Flat	*4*	*6*	*0*	*0*	*1*	*5*	*0.0*	*-6.00*
Hurdles	*30*	*84*	*7*	*7*	*13*	*57*	*8.3*	*-36.95*
Chases	*10*	*41*	*6*	*4*	*5*	*26*	*14.6*	*+8.50*
Totals	**35**	**131**	**13**	**11**	**19**	**88**	**9.9**	**-34.45**
13-14	*48*	*186*	*14*	*18*	*18*	*136*	*7.5*	*-105.54*
12-13	*59*	*186*	*17*	*15*	*14*	*140*	*9.1*	*-69.97*

BY MONTH

NH Flat	W-R	Per cent	£1 Level Stake	**Hurdles**	W-R	Per cent	£1 Level Stake
May	0-0	0.0	0.00	May	1-11	9.1	-8.75
June	0-0	0.0	0.00	June	0-5	0.0	-5.00
July	0-1	0.0	-1.00	July	0-6	0.0	-6.00
August	0-0	0.0	0.00	August	0-2	0.0	-2.00
September	0-1	0.0	-1.00	September	1-5	20.0	+1.50
October	0-1	0.0	-1.00	October	1-7	14.3	+2.00
November	0-1	0.0	-1.00	November	1-9	11.1	0.00
December	0-1	0.0	-1.00	December	1-7	14.3	-0.50
January	0-1	0.0	-1.00	January	0-7	0.0	-7.00
February	0-0	0.0	0.00	February	2-9	22.2	+4.80
March	0-0	0.0	0.00	March	0-14	0.0	-14.00
April	0-0	0.0	0.00	April	0-2	0.0	-2.00

Chases	W-R	Per cent	£1 Level Stake	**Totals**	W-R	Per cent	£1 Level Stake
May	1-4	25.0	+9.00	May	2-15	13.3	+0.25
June	2-4	50.0	+15.50	June	2-9	22.2	+10.50
July	1-2	50.0	+2.50	July	1-9	11.1	-4.50
August	0-0	0.0	0.00	August	0-2	0.0	-2.00
September	0-0	0.0	0.00	September	1-6	16.7	+0.50
October	0-2	0.0	-2.00	October	1-10	10.0	-1.00
November	0-4	0.0	-4.00	November	1-14	7.1	-5.00
December	0-9	0.0	-9.00	December	1-17	5.9	-10.50
January	0-8	0.0	-8.00	January	0-16	0.0	-16.00
February	2-4	50.0	+8.50	February	4-13	30.8	+13.30
March	0-2	0.0	-2.00	March	0-16	0.0	-16.00
April	0-2	0.0	-2.00	April	0-4	0.0	-4.00

DISTANCE

Hurdles	W-R	Per cent	£1 Level Stake	**Chases**	W-R	Per cent	£1 Level Stake
2m-2m3f	5-60	8.3	-24.20	2m-2m3f	3-16	18.8	+8.00
2m4f-2m7f	0-5	0.0	-5.00	2m4f-2m7f	2-14	14.3	+4.50
3m+	0-1	0.0	-1.00	3m+	0-2	0.0	-2.00

TYPE OF RACE

Non-Handicaps	W-R	Per cent	£1 Level Stake	**Handicaps**	W-R	Per cent	£1 Level Stake
Nov Hrdls	0-6	0.0	-6.00	Nov Hrdls	0-7	0.0	-7.00
Hrdls	1-11	9.1	-9.20	Hrdls	5-48	10.4	-9.25
Nov Chs	0-0	0.0	0.00	Nov Chs	3-13	23.1	+9.00
Chases	0-0	0.0	0.00	Chases	3-28	10.7	-0.50
Sell/Claim	1-9	11.1	-2.50	Sell/Claim	0-4	0.0	-4.00

RACE CLASS / FIRST TIME OUT

RACE CLASS	W-R	Per cent	£1 Level Stake	FIRST TIME OUT	W-R	Per cent	£1 Level Stake
Class 1	0-2	0.0	-2.00	Bumpers	0-4	0.0	-4.00
Class 2	0-2	0.0	-2.00	Hurdles	1-28	3.6	-19.00
Class 3	1-12	8.3	-3.00	Chases	1-3	33.3	+10.00
Class 4	6-61	9.8	-12.50				
Class 5	6-49	12.2	-9.95	Totals	2-35	5.7	-13.00
Class 6	0-5	0.0	-5.00				

JOCKEYS

	W-R	Per cent	£1 Level Stake
Lee Edwards	10-72	13.9	+3.80
Mr H A A Bannister	1-1	100.0	+1.25
Josh Hamer	1-10	10.0	-0.50
Trevor Whelan	1-21	4.8	-12.00

COURSE RECORD

	Total W-R	Non-Hndcps Hurdles	Non-Hndcps Chases	Hndcps Hurdles	Hndcps Chases	NH Flat	Per cent	£1 Level Stake
Leicester	3-16	1-5	0-0	1-4	1-7	0-0	18.8	+5.00
Worcester	2-8	0-0	0-0	0-4	2-3	0-1	25.0	+14.50
Towcester	2-9	0-2	0-0	2-5	0-2	0-0	22.2	+2.25
Doncaster	1-3	0-0	0-0	1-2	0-1	0-0	33.3	+9.00
Ffos Las	1-3	0-0	0-0	0-1	1-2	0-0	33.3	+4.00
Ayr	1-5	1-2	0-0	0-1	0-2	0-0	20.0	-3.20
Chepstow	1-8	0-1	0-0	1-5	0-1	0-1	12.5	-1.50
Stratford	1-10	0-1	0-0	0-7	1-2	0-0	10.0	0.00
Uttoxeter	1-14	0-1	0-0	0-9	1-3	0-1	7.1	-9.50

WINNING HORSES

Horse	Races Run	1st	2nd	3rd	£
Malanos	6	1	1	2	6498
Great Link	9	1	0	1	4224
Vivacissimo	6	1	0	0	3899
Got Attitude	5	3	1	0	9800
Expanding Universe	6	1	0	3	3769
Smart Catch	5	1	1	0	3119
Prairie Town	4	1	0	0	2274
Vertueux	9	1	1	0	1949
Taroum	8	1	1	3	1949
Boston Blue	3	1	0	2	1949
Vedani	3	1	0	2	1949
Total winning prize-money					**£41379**
Favourites	**2-10**		**20.0%**		**-5.95**

ANTHONY CARSON

NEWMARKET, SUFFOLK

	No. of Hrs	Races Run	1st	2nd	3rd	Unpl	Per cent	£1 Level Stake
NH Flat	*0*	*0*	*0*	*0*	*0*	*0*	*0.0*	*0.00*
Hurdles	*1*	*3*	*1*	*1*	*0*	*1*	*33.3*	*+0.75*
Chases	*0*	*0*	*0*	*0*	*0*	*0*	*0.0*	*0.00*
Totals	**1**	**3**	**1**	**1**	**0**	**1**	**33.3**	**+0.75**
13-14	*2*	*5*	*0*	*2*	*2*	*1*	*0.0*	*-5.00*
12-13	*2*	*2*	*0*	*0*	*0*	*2*	*0.0*	*-2.00*

JOCKEYS

	W-R	Per cent	£1 Level Stake
Paddy Brennan	1-1	100.0	+2.75

COURSE RECORD

	Total W-R	Non-Hndcps Hurdles	Non-Hndcps Chases	Hndcps Hurdles	Hndcps Chases	NH Flat	Per cent	£1 Level Stake
Southwell	1-1	1-1	0-0	0-0	0-0	0-0	100.0	+2.75

WINNING HORSES

Horse	Races Run	1st	2nd	3rd	£
May Hay	3	1	1	0	3899
Total winning prize-money					**£3899**
Favourites	**0-89**		**0.0%**		**-89.00**

BEN CASE

EDGCOTE, NORTHANTS

	No. of Hrs	Races Run	1st	2nd	3rd	Unpl	Per cent	£1 Level Stake
NH Flat	*9*	*14*	*1*	*1*	*4*	*8*	*7.1*	*-3.00*
Hurdles	*24*	*100*	*12*	*11*	*17*	*60*	*12.0*	*-33.13*
Chases	*11*	*35*	*5*	*3*	*7*	*20*	*14.3*	*-12.29*
Totals	**35**	**149**	**18**	**15**	**28**	**88**	**12.1**	**-48.42**
13-14	*23*	*91*	*13*	*17*	*10*	*51*	*14.3*	*+35.79*
12-13	*22*	*94*	*10*	*9*	*16*	*59*	*10.6*	*+9.00*

BY MONTH

NH Flat	W-R	Per cent	£1 Level Stake	Hurdles	W-R	Per cent	£1 Level Stake
May	1-2	50.0	+9.00	May	3-8	37.5	+11.00
June	0-0	0.0	0.00	June	1-4	25.0	+1.50
July	0-0	0.0	0.00	July	0-4	0.0	-4.00
August	0-0	0.0	0.00	August	1-1	100.0	+7.00
September	0-0	0.0	0.00	September	0-2	0.0	-2.00
October	0-1	0.0	-1.00	October	0-8	0.0	-8.00
November	0-1	0.0	-1.00	November	0-17	0.0	-17.00
December	0-1	0.0	-1.00	December	1-13	7.7	-10.38
January	0-1	0.0	-1.00	January	1-13	7.7	-4.00
February	0-2	0.0	-2.00	February	1-9	11.1	-3.00
March	0-2	0.0	-2.00	March	2-10	20.0	0.00
April	0-4	0.0	-4.00	April	2-11	18.2	-4.25

Chases	W-R	Per cent	£1 Level Stake	Totals	W-R	Per cent	£1 Level Stake
May	0-1	0.0	-1.00	May	4-11	36.4	+19.00
June	0-0	0.0	0.00	June	1-4	25.0	+1.50
July	0-3	0.0	-3.00	July	0-7	0.0	-7.00
August	0-2	0.0	-2.00	August	1-3	33.3	+5.00
September	0-0	0.0	0.00	September	0-2	0.0	-2.00
October	1-2	50.0	+2.33	October	1-11	9.1	-6.67
November	1-6	16.7	+3.00	November	1-24	4.2	-15.00
December	0-3	0.0	-3.00	December	1-17	5.9	-14.38
January	0-2	0.0	-2.00	January	1-16	6.3	-7.00
February	1-4	25.0	-0.50	February	2-15	13.3	-5.50
March	2-8	25.0	-2.13	March	4-20	20.0	-4.13
April	0-4	0.0	-4.00	April	2-19	10.5	-12.25

DISTANCE

Hurdles	W-R	Per cent	£1 Level Stake	Chases	W-R	Per cent	£1 Level Stake
2m-2m3f	5-30	16.7	+1.50	2m-2m3f	3-9	33.3	+7.83
2m4f-2m7f	4-44	9.1	-28.13	2m4f-2m7f	2-11	18.2	-5.13
3m+	1-7	14.3	-0.50	3m+	0-3	0.0	-3.00

TYPE OF RACE

Non-Handicaps	W-R	Per cent	£1 Level Stake	Handicaps	W-R	Per cent	£1 Level Stake
Nov Hrdls	4-30	13.3	-9.50	Nov Hrdls	1-8	12.5	+1.00
Hrdls	1-16	6.3	-13.38	Hrdls	6-46	13.0	-11.25
Nov Chs	0-3	0.0	-3.00	Nov Chs	2-13	15.4	-5.17
Chases	0-1	0.0	-1.00	Chases	3-18	16.7	-3.13
Sell/Claim	0-0	0.0	0.00	Sell/Claim	0-0	0.0	0.00

RACE CLASS / FIRST TIME OUT

RACE CLASS	W-R	Per cent	£1 Level Stake	FIRST TIME OUT	W-R	Per cent	£1 Level Stake
Class 1	0-13	0.0	-13.00	Bumpers	1-9	11.1	+2.00
Class 2	1-10	10.0	-1.00	Hurdles	3-19	15.8	0.00

Class 3	2-18	11.1	-7.50	Chases	1-7	14.3	-2.67
Class 4	10-69	14.5	-15.42				
Class 5	4-29	13.8	-12.50	Totals	5-35	14.3	-0.67
Class 6	1-10	10.0	+1.00				

JOCKEYS

	W-R	Per cent	£1 Level Stake
Kielan Woods	8-55	14.5	+0.33
Daryl Jacob	7-50	14.0	-20.00
Richard Johnson	1-1	100.0	+4.50
David Bass	1-2	50.0	+1.75
Mr M J P Kendrick	1-21	4.8	-15.00

COURSE RECORD

	Total W-R	Non-Hndcps Hurdles	Non-Hndcps Chases	Hndcps Hurdles	Hndcps Chases	NH Flat	Per cent	£1 Level Stake
Taunton	2-2	1-1	0-0	0-0	1-1	0-0	100.0	+7.50
Worcester	2-7	1-3	0-0	1-2	0-2	0-0	28.6	+6.50
Leicester	2-8	0-1	0-1	0-2	2-4	0-0	25.0	-2.13
Towcester	2-14	1-7	0-0	0-3	0-3	1-1	14.3	+3.00
Huntingdon	2-16	0-3	0-0	2-7	0-4	0-2	12.5	-6.00
Ascot	1-2	0-0	0-0	0-0	1-2	0-0	50.0	+7.00
Ffos Las	1-2	0-0	0-0	1-2	0-0	0-0	50.0	+5.00
Chepstow	1-4	1-2	0-0	0-1	0-1	0-0	25.0	-1.00
Uttoxeter	1-4	0-0	0-0	0-1	1-1	0-2	25.0	+0.33
Fakenham	1-7	1-3	0-0	0-3	0-1	0-0	14.3	-4.38
Warwick	1-7	0-2	0-0	1-4	0-0	0-1	14.3	+2.00
Mrket Rsn	1-8	0-2	0-0	1-3	0-0	0-3	12.5	-4.25
Southwell	1-12	0-6	0-0	1-3	0-2	0-1	8.3	-6.00

WINNING HORSES

Horse	Races Run	1st	2nd	3rd	£
Croco Bay	7	1	0	3	43330
Moss On The Mill	1	1	0	0	6498
Crookstown	6	2	1	0	10459
Phare Isle	6	2	0	2	7148
Thoresby	5	1	1	1	3899
Midnight Jazz	8	3	2	1	8790
Bebinn	10	1	1	3	3249
Gamain	7	1	0	2	3249
Vesuvhill	8	1	1	0	3249
Breaking The Bank	6	2	0	1	6238
Wither Yenot	5	1	0	1	3119
Mr Grey	4	1	1	0	2144
My Nosy Rosy	8	1	1	3	2112
Total winning prize-money					**£103484**
Favourites	**4-15**		**26.7%**		**-2.75**

MICK CHANNON

WEST ILSLEY, BERKS

	No. of Hrs	Races Run	1st	2nd	3rd	Unpl	Per cent	£1 Level Stake
NH Flat	*3*	*6*	*0*	*2*	*0*	*4*	*0.0*	*-6.00*
Hurdles	*8*	*17*	*1*	*1*	*0*	*15*	*5.9*	*-14.80*
Chases	*8*	*32*	*7*	*8*	*1*	*16*	*21.9*	*-12.87*
Totals	**16**	**55**	**8**	**11**	**1**	**35**	**14.5**	**-33.67**
13-14	*16*	*60*	*10*	*10*	*13*	*27*	*16.7*	*-13.22*
12-13	*21*	*77*	*10*	*13*	*10*	*44*	*13.0*	*-15.47*

JOCKEYS

	W-R	Per cent	£1 Level Stake
Brian Hughes	6-21	28.6	-9.87
Wayne Hutchinson	1-1	100.0	+7.00
Andrew Thornton	1-7	14.3	-4.80

COURSE RECORD

	Total W-R	Non-Hndcps Hurdles	Non-Hndcps Chases	Hndcps Hurdles	Hndcps Chases	NH Flat	Per cent	£1 Level Stake
Fakenham	2-4	0-2	2-2	0-0	0-0	0-0	50.0	+1.38
Plumpton	1-1	1-1	0-0	0-0	0-0	0-0	100.0	+1.20
Uttoxeter	1-1	0-0	1-1	0-0	0-0	0-0	100.0	+0.73
Wincanton	1-2	0-0	0-0	0-0	1-2	0-0	50.0	+6.00
Carlisle	1-3	0-0	1-1	0-0	0-2	0-0	33.3	-1.88
Mrket Rsn	1-4	0-1	1-1	0-0	0-2	0-0	25.0	-2.60
Huntingdon	1-5	0-1	1-2	0-1	0-1	0-0	20.0	-3.50

WINNING HORSES

Horse	Races Run	1st	2nd	3rd	£
Loch Ba	5	1	0	0	9514
Warden Hill	4	2	1	0	15470
Knock House	5	2	1	0	10592
Sgt Reckless	4	2	0	0	8022
Needless Shouting	4	1	1	0	3899
Total winning prize-money					**£47497**
Favourites	**6-12**		**50.0%**		**-1.17**

MICHAEL CHAPMAN

MARKET RASEN, LINCS

	No. of Hrs	Races Run	1st	2nd	3rd	Unpl	Per cent	£1 Level Stake
NH Flat	*0*	*0*	*0*	*0*	*0*	*0*	*0.0*	*0.00*
Hurdles	*12*	*48*	*3*	*2*	*1*	*42*	*6.3*	*-7.00*
Chases	*7*	*51*	*3*	*10*	*6*	*32*	*5.9*	*-11.50*
Totals	**17**	**99**	**6**	**12**	**7**	**74**	**6.1**	**-18.50**
13-14	*13*	*87*	*5*	*7*	*11*	*64*	*5.7*	*+9.00*
12-13	*11*	*98*	*4*	*3*	*18*	*73*	*4.1*	*-65.25*

JOCKEYS

	W-R	Per cent	£1 Level Stake
Joe Cornwall	4-75	5.3	-25.00
Mr John Dawson	1-5	20.0	+21.00
Alice Mills	1-6	16.7	-1.50

COURSE RECORD

	Total W-R	Non-Hndcps Hurdles	Non-Hndcps Chases	Hndcps Hurdles	Hndcps Chases	NH Flat	Per cent	£1 Level Stake
Stratford	2-8	0-2	0-0	2-2	0-4	0-0	25.0	+16.00
Fakenham	1-9	0-3	0-0	0-1	1-5	0-0	11.1	-4.50
Cartmel	1-12	1-3	0-0	0-2	0-7	0-0	8.3	+5.00
Southwell	1-23	0-3	0-0	0-9	1-11	0-0	4.3	+3.00
Mrket Rsn	1-34	0-5	0-2	0-10	1-17	0-0	2.9	-25.00

WINNING HORSES

Horse	Races Run	1st	2nd	3rd	£
Tayarat	6	2	0	1	6173
Epee Celeste	10	1	2	0	3249
Volcanic Jack	10	1	0	0	3249
Galley Slave	4	2	0	0	4874
Total winning prize-money					**£17545**
Favourites	**1-2**		**50.0%**		**2.50**

GEORGE CHARLTON

STOCKSFIELD, NORTHUMBERLAND

	No. of Hrs	Races Run	1st	2nd	3rd	Unpl	Per cent	£1 Level Stake
NH Flat	*3*	*6*	*0*	*0*	*0*	*6*	*0.0*	*-6.00*
Hurdles	*5*	*15*	*1*	*4*	*1*	*9*	*6.7*	*-9.50*
Chases	*1*	*1*	*0*	*0*	*0*	*1*	*0.0*	*-1.00*
Totals	**8**	**22**	**1**	**4**	**1**	**16**	**4.5**	**-16.50**
13-14	*10*	*24*	*3*	*3*	*4*	*14*	*12.5*	*+59.00*
12-13	*21*	*57*	*1*	*5*	*6*	*45*	*1.8*	*-53.50*

JOCKEYS

	W-R	Per cent	£1 Level Stake
Ryan Mania	1-5	20.0	+0.50

COURSE RECORD

	Total W-R	Non-Hndcps Hurdles	Non-Hndcps Chases	Hndcps Hurdles	Hndcps Chases	NH Flat	Per cent	£1 Level Stake
Kelso	1-11	0-2	0-0	1-7	0-1	0-1	9.1	-5.50

WINNING HORSES

Horse	Races Run	1st	2nd	3rd	£
Ballyvoque	6	1	2	1	2924
Total winning prize-money					**£2924**
Favourites	**0-1**		**0.0%**		**-1.00**

ANGELA CLARKE

LLANGADOG, CARMARTHENS

	No. of Hrs	Races Run	1st	2nd	3rd	Unpl	Per cent	£1 Level Stake
NH Flat	*1*	*2*	*0*	*0*	*0*	*2*	*0.0*	*-2.00*
Hurdles	*1*	*6*	*2*	*0*	*0*	*4*	*33.3*	*+107.00*
Chases	*0*	*0*	*0*	*0*	*0*	*0*	*0.0*	*0.00*
Totals	**2**	**8**	**2**	**0**	**0**	**6**	**25.0**	**+105.00**
13-14	*3*	*8*	*0*	*1*	*1*	*6*	*0.0*	*-8.00*
12-13	*2*	*5*	*0*	*0*	*0*	*5*	*0.0*	*-5.00*

JOCKEYS

	W-R	Per cent	£1 Level Stake
Miss Jodie Hughes	2-4	50.0	+109.00

COURSE RECORD

	Total W-R	Non-Hndcps Hurdles	Non-Hndcps Chases	Hndcps Hurdles	Hndcps Chases	NH Flat	Per cent	£1 Level Stake
Ffos Las	1-2	0-0	0-0	1-1	0-0	0-1	50.0	+10.00
Worcester	1-4	1-1	0-0	0-2	0-0	0-1	25.0	+97.00

WINNING HORSES

Horse	Races Run	1st	2nd	3rd	£
Panache	6	2	0	0	5068
Total winning prize-money					**£5068**
Favourites	**0-0**		**0.0%**		**0.00**

PAUL COLLINS

SALTBURN, CLEVELAND

	No. of Hrs	Races Run	1st	2nd	3rd	Unpl	Per cent	£1 Level Stake
NH Flat	*0*	*0*	*0*	*0*	*0*	*0*	*0.0*	*0.00*
Hurdles	*0*	*0*	*0*	*0*	*0*	*0*	*0.0*	*0.00*
Chases	*2*	*5*	*1*	*0*	*2*	*2*	*20.0*	*-1.75*
Totals	**2**	**5**	**1**	**0**	**2**	**2**	**20.0**	**-1.75**
12-13	*1*	*1*	*0*	*0*	*0*	*1*	*0.0*	*-1.00*

JOCKEYS

	W-R	Per cent	£1 Level Stake
Mr P Collins	1-4	25.0	-0.75

COURSE RECORD

	Total W-R	Non-Hndcps Hurdles	Non-Hndcps Chases	Hndcps Hurdles	Hndcps Chases	NH Flat	Per cent	£1 Level Stake
Cartmel	1-1	0-0	1-1	0-0	0-0	0-0	100.0	+2.25

WINNING HORSES

Horse	Races Run	1st	2nd	3rd	£
Dica	4	1	0	2	1560
Total winning prize-money					**£1560**
Favourites	**0-0**		**0.0%**		**0.00**

STUART COLTHERD

SELKIRK, BORDERS

	No. of Hrs	Races Run	1st	2nd	3rd	Unpl	Per cent	£1 Level Stake
NH Flat	*4*	*7*	*0*	*1*	*0*	*6*	*0.0*	*-7.00*

Hurdles	*14*	*43*	*0*	*2*	*4*	*36*	*0.0*	*-43.00*
Chases	*11*	*47*	*12*	*4*	*7*	*24*	*25.5*	*+43.25*
Totals	**22**	**97**	**12**	**7**	**11**	**66**	**12.4**	**-6.75**
13-14	*19*	*103*	*17*	*13*	*4*	*69*	*16.5*	*-0.38*
12-13	*18*	*73*	*5*	*13*	*5*	*50*	*6.8*	*+56.25*

BY MONTH

NH Flat	W-R	Per cent	£1 Level Stake
May	0-0	0.0	0.00
June	0-0	0.0	0.00
July	0-1	0.0	-1.00
August	0-0	0.0	0.00
September	0-0	0.0	0.00
October	0-1	0.0	-1.00
November	0-3	0.0	-3.00
December	0-2	0.0	-2.00
January	0-0	0.0	0.00
February	0-0	0.0	0.00
March	0-0	0.0	0.00
April	0-0	0.0	0.00

Hurdles	W-R	Per cent	£1 Level Stake
May	0-3	0.0	-3.00
June	0-2	0.0	-2.00
July	0-2	0.0	-2.00
August	0-0	0.0	0.00
September	0-0	0.0	0.00
October	0-0	0.0	0.00
November	0-9	0.0	-9.00
December	0-6	0.0	-6.00
January	0-6	0.0	-6.00
February	0-4	0.0	-4.00
March	0-8	0.0	-8.00
April	0-3	0.0	-3.00

Chases	W-R	Per cent	£1 Level Stake
May	0-0	0.0	0.00
June	0-0	0.0	0.00
July	0-2	0.0	-2.00
August	0-0	0.0	0.00
September	0-0	0.0	0.00
October	0-0	0.0	0.00
November	0-8	0.0	-8.00
December	3-9	33.3	+11.50
January	0-7	0.0	-7.00
February	3-8	37.5	+8.50
March	2-7	28.6	+24.00
April	4-6	66.7	+16.25

Totals	W-R	Per cent	£1 Level Stake
May	0-3	0.0	-3.00
June	0-2	0.0	-2.00
July	0-5	0.0	-5.00
August	0-0	0.0	0.00
September	0-0	0.0	0.00
October	0-1	0.0	-1.00
November	0-20	0.0	-20.00
December	3-17	17.6	+3.50
January	0-13	0.0	-13.00
February	3-12	25.0	+4.50
March	2-15	13.3	+16.00
April	4-9	44.4	+13.25

DISTANCE

Hurdles	W-R	Per cent	£1 Level Stake
2m-2m3f	0-28	0.0	-28.00
2m4f-2m7f	0-11	0.0	-11.00
3m+	0-3	0.0	-3.00

Chases	W-R	Per cent	£1 Level Stake
2m-2m3f	4-12	33.3	+6.00
2m4f-2m7f	5-20	25.0	+34.00
3m+	1-11	9.1	-7.75

TYPE OF RACE

Non-Handicaps

	W-R	Per cent	£1 Level Stake
Nov Hrdls	0-13	0.0	-13.00
Hrdls	0-6	0.0	-6.00
Nov Chs	0-2	0.0	-2.00
Chases	0-3	0.0	-3.00
Sell/Claim	0-2	0.0	-2.00

Handicaps

	W-R	Per cent	£1 Level Stake
Nov Hrdls	0-2	0.0	-2.00
Hrdls	0-20	0.0	-20.00
Nov Chs	2-13	15.4	+2.00
Chases	10-29	34.5	+46.25
Sell/Claim	0-0	0.0	0.00

RACE CLASS

	W-R	Per cent	£1 Level Stake
Class 1	0-1	0.0	-1.00
Class 2	0-2	0.0	-2.00
Class 3	1-11	9.1	-8.00
Class 4	6-49	12.2	-13.00
Class 5	5-26	19.2	+25.25
Class 6	0-8	0.0	-8.00

FIRST TIME OUT

	W-R	Per cent	£1 Level Stake
Bumpers	0-4	0.0	-4.00
Hurdles	0-10	0.0	-10.00
Chases	0-8	0.0	-8.00
Totals	0-22	0.0	-22.00

JOCKEYS

	W-R	Per cent	£1 Level Stake
James Reveley	8-30	26.7	+14.00
Derek Fox	2-17	11.8	-1.75
Dale Irving	1-4	25.0	+1.00
John Kington	1-17	5.9	+9.00

COURSE RECORD

	Total W-R	Non-Hndcps Hurdles	Non-Hndcps Chases	Hndcps Hurdles	Hndcps Chases	NH Flat	Per cent	£1 Level Stake
Hexham	4-13	0-3	0-0	0-3	4-7	0-0	30.8	+31.75
Ayr	2-8	0-1	0-0	0-0	2-6	0-1	25.0	-1.50
Sedgefield	2-9	0-2	0-0	0-3	2-3	0-1	22.2	+1.00
Wetherby	1-7	0-1	0-1	0-1	1-3	0-1	14.3	-2.50
Newcastle	1-14	0-2	0-0	0-7	1-5	0-0	7.1	-5.50
Carlisle	1-15	0-3	0-0	0-5	1-4	0-3	6.7	-3.00
Kelso	1-19	0-7	0-3	0-1	1-8	0-0	5.3	-15.00

WINNING HORSES

Horse	Races Run	1st	2nd	3rd	£
Aye Well	8	3	2	1	17740
Sharney Sike	8	2	0	2	8429
Amethyst Rose	9	3	1	1	4549
Resolute Reformer	7	2	0	0	6238
Hotgrove Boy	3	1	0	1	2599
*Oxalido	12	1	0	1	2209
Total winning prize-money					**£41764**
Favourites	**2-4**		**50.0%**		**2.25**

JOHN COOMBE

FLEET, DORSET

	No. of Hrs	Races Run	1st	2nd	3rd	Unpl	Per cent	£1 Level Stake
NH Flat	*0*	*0*	*0*	*0*	*0*	*0*	*0.0*	*0.00*
Hurdles	*3*	*12*	*1*	*3*	*2*	*6*	*8.3*	*+9.00*
Chases	*0*	*0*	*0*	*0*	*0*	*0*	*0.0*	*0.00*
Totals	**3**	**12**	**1**	**3**	**2**	**6**	**8.3**	**+9.00**
13-14	*2*	*8*	*0*	*1*	*0*	*7*	*0.0*	*-8.00*
12-13	*5*	*21*	*0*	*3*	*2*	*16*	*0.0*	*-21.00*

JOCKEYS

	W-R	Per cent	£1 Level Stake
Mr Louis Muspratt	1-9	11.1	+12.00

COURSE RECORD

	Total W-R	Non-Hndcps Hurdles	Non-Hndcps Chases	Hndcps Hurdles	Hndcps Chases	NH Flat	Per cent	£1 Level Stake
Uttoxeter	1-4	0-0	0-0	1-4	0-0	0-0	25.0	+17.00

WINNING HORSES

Horse	Races Run	1st	2nd	3rd	£
Dais Return	5	1	2	2	2339
Total winning prize-money					**£2339**
Favourites	**0-1**		**0.0%**		**-1.00**

SUSAN CORBETT

OTTERBURN, NORTHUMBERLAND

	No. of Hrs	Races Run	1st	2nd	3rd	Unpl	Per cent	£1 Level Stake
NH Flat	*6*	*12*	*2*	*0*	*0*	*10*	*16.7*	*+13.00*
Hurdles	*15*	*56*	*4*	*8*	*6*	*38*	*7.1*	*-33.75*
Chases	*2*	*4*	*0*	*0*	*0*	*4*	*0.0*	*-4.00*
Totals	**18**	**72**	**6**	**8**	**6**	**52**	**8.3**	**-24.75**
13-14	*17*	*44*	*0*	*2*	*1*	*40*	*0.0*	*-44.00*
12-13	*10*	*44*	*2*	*0*	*3*	*39*	*4.5*	*+8.00*

JOCKEYS

	W-R	Per cent	£1 Level Stake
James Corbett	5-66	7.6	-22.75
Gary Rutherford	1-2	50.0	+2.00

COURSE RECORD

	Total W-R	Non-Hndcps Hurdles	Non-Hndcps Chases	Hndcps Hurdles	Hndcps Chases	NH Flat	Per cent	£1 Level Stake
Hexham	3-22	0-8	0-0	3-9	0-2	0-3	13.6	-5.75
Carlisle	1-4	0-0	0-0	0-3	0-0	1-1	25.0	+17.00
Newcastle	1-6	0-1	0-0	0-2	0-1	1-2	16.7	-2.00
Perth	1-6	0-0	0-0	1-6	0-0	0-0	16.7	0.00

WINNING HORSES

Horse	Races Run	1st	2nd	3rd	£
Super Collider	9	1	1	2	3798
Dun To Perfection	7	2	2	1	5068
Ballyreesode	8	1	2	0	1949
Virnon	4	2	0	0	3184
Total winning prize-money					**£13999**
Favourites	**1-3**		**33.3%**		**0.25**

JOHN CORNWALL

LONG CLAWSON, LEICS

	No. of Hrs	Races Run	1st	2nd	3rd	Unpl	Per cent	£1 Level Stake
NH Flat	*0*	*0*	*0*	*0*	*0*	*0*	*0.0*	*0.00*
Hurdles	*2*	*2*	*0*	*0*	*0*	*2*	*0.0*	*-2.00*
Chases	*7*	*45*	*1*	*2*	*6*	*36*	*2.2*	*-39.50*
Totals	**7**	**47**	**1**	**2**	**6**	**38**	**2.1**	**-41.50**
13-14	*10*	*83*	*3*	*10*	*10*	*60*	*3.6*	*-48.00*
12-13	*10*	*59*	*4*	*5*	*9*	*41*	*6.8*	*-23.00*

JOCKEYS

	W-R	Per cent	£1 Level Stake
Joe Cornwall	1-45	2.2	-39.50

COURSE RECORD

	Total W-R	Non-Hndcps Hurdles	Non-Hndcps Chases	Hndcps Hurdles	Hndcps Chases	NH Flat	Per cent	£1 Level Stake
Uttoxeter	1-8	0-0	0-0	0-0	1-8	0-0	12.5	-2.50

WINNING HORSES

Horse	Races Run	1st	2nd	3rd	£
Flichity	14	1	1	3	2929
Total winning prize-money					**£2929**
Favourites	**0-0**		**0.0%**		**0.00**

PAUL COWLEY

CULWORTH, NORTHANTS

	No. of Hrs	Races Run	1st	2nd	3rd	Unpl	Per cent	£1 Level Stake
NH Flat	*3*	*5*	*0*	*0*	*0*	*5*	*0.0*	*-5.00*
Hurdles	*2*	*12*	*2*	*2*	*0*	*8*	*16.7*	*+1.00*
Chases	*3*	*8*	*1*	*0*	*2*	*5*	*12.5*	*-4.75*
Totals	**8**	**25**	**3**	**2**	**2**	**18**	**12.0**	**-8.75**
13-14	*7*	*25*	*2*	*1*	*6*	*16*	*8.0*	*+2.00*
12-13	*2*	*4*	*0*	*0*	*2*	*2*	*0.0*	*-4.00*

JOCKEYS

	W-R	Per cent	£1 Level Stake
Miss G Andrews	3-7	42.9	+9.25

COURSE RECORD

	Total W-R	Non-Hndcps Hurdles	Non-Hndcps Chases	Hndcps Hurdles	Hndcps Chases	NH Flat	Per cent	£1 Level Stake
Stratford	1-3	0-0	0-0	1-1	0-1	0-1	33.3	+1.00
Warwick	1-3	0-0	0-0	1-2	0-0	0-1	33.3	+6.00
Towcester	1-6	0-0	0-0	0-0	1-4	0-2	16.7	-2.75

WINNING HORSES

Horse	Races Run	1st	2nd	3rd	£
Seas Of Green	8	2	2	0	5302
Grand Article	4	1	0	0	2184
Total winning prize-money					**£7486**
Favourites	**1-1**		**100.0%**		**2.25**

TONY COYLE

NORTON, N YORKS

	No. of Hrs	Races Run	1st	2nd	3rd	Unpl	Per cent	£1 Level Stake
NH Flat	*6*	*11*	*1*	*1*	*0*	*9*	*9.1*	*-6.67*
Hurdles	*13*	*29*	*1*	*1*	*7*	*20*	*3.4*	*-23.50*
Chases	*7*	*41*	*3*	*9*	*7*	*22*	*7.3*	*-20.50*
Totals	**21**	**81**	**5**	**11**	**14**	**51**	**6.2**	**-50.67**
13-14	*20*	*75*	*14*	*7*	*15*	*39*	*18.7*	*+12.28*
12-13	*15*	*63*	*5*	*10*	*10*	*38*	*7.9*	*-40.88*

JOCKEYS

	W-R	Per cent	£1 Level Stake
Dougie Costello	4-52	7.7	-27.17
Leighton Aspell	1-4	25.0	+1.50

COURSE RECORD

	Total W-R	Non-Hndcps Hurdles	Non-Hndcps Chases	Hndcps Hurdles	Hndcps Chases	NH Flat	Per cent	£1 Level Stake
Fakenham	1-1	0-0	0-0	0-0	1-1	0-0	100.0	+5.00
Huntingdon	1-1	0-0	0-0	0-0	1-1	0-0	100.0	+4.50
Worcester	1-3	0-0	0-0	0-0	0-2	1-1	33.3	+1.33
Wetherby	1-7	0-1	0-0	1-3	0-3	0-0	14.3	-1.50
Mrket Rsn	1-17	0-1	0-2	0-5	1-6	0-3	5.9	-8.00

WINNING HORSES

Horse	Races Run	1st	2nd	3rd	£
*Frizzo	9	2	0	2	8892
Qoubilai	8	1	3	1	3899
Silver Dragon	7	1	2	2	3249
Probably Sorry	3	1	1	0	1560
Total winning prize-money					**£17600**
Favourites	**0-1**		**0.0%**		**-1.00**

ANDREW CROOK

MIDDLEHAM MOOR, N YORKS

	No. of Hrs	Races Run	1st	2nd	3rd	Unpl	Per cent	£1 Level Stake
NH Flat	*5*	*11*	*0*	*0*	*1*	*10*	*0.0*	*-11.00*
Hurdles	*14*	*33*	*2*	*1*	*1*	*29*	*6.1*	*+6.50*
Chases	*2*	*19*	*2*	*3*	*2*	*12*	*10.5*	*+1.50*
Totals	**20**	**63**	**4**	**4**	**4**	**51**	**6.3**	**-3.00**
13-14	*22*	*89*	*2*	*7*	*10*	*70*	*2.2*	*-71.90*
12-13	*21*	*78*	*4*	*1*	*6*	*67*	*5.1*	*+40.00*

JOCKEYS

	W-R	Per cent	£1 Level Stake
John Kington	4-58	6.9	+2.00

COURSE RECORD

	Total W-R	Non-Hndcps Hurdles	Non-Hndcps Chases	Hndcps Hurdles	Hndcps Chases	NH Flat	Per cent	£1 Level Stake
Sedgefield	2-17	0-3	0-0	0-6	2-7	0-1	11.8	+3.50
Catterick	1-7	0-1	0-0	1-2	0-2	0-2	14.3	-1.50
Hexham	1-7	0-2	0-0	1-2	0-2	0-1	14.3	+27.00

WINNING HORSES

Horse	Races Run	1st	2nd	3rd	£
Zazamix	14	2	2	2	5458
Air Chief	9	1	1	1	2599
Sohcahtoa	4	1	0	0	2053
Total winning prize-money					**£10110**
Favourites	**0-0**		**0.0%**		**0.00**

MRS SHEILA CROW

SHREWSBURY, SHROPSHIRE

	No. of Hrs	Races Run	1st	2nd	3rd	Unpl	Per cent	£1 Level Stake
NH Flat	*0*	*0*	*0*	*0*	*0*	*0*	*0.0*	*0.00*
Hurdles	*0*	*0*	*0*	*0*	*0*	*0*	*0.0*	*0.00*
Chases	*3*	*7*	*1*	*3*	*1*	*2*	*14.3*	*-4.80*
Totals	**3**	**7**	**1**	**3**	**1**	**2**	**14.3**	**-4.80**
13-14	*2*	*5*	*3*	*1*	*0*	*1*	*60.0*	*+2.24*
12-13	*4*	*7*	*1*	*2*	*0*	*4*	*14.3*	*-4.25*

JOCKEYS

	W-R	Per cent	£1 Level Stake
Mr P Gerety	1-7	14.3	-4.80

COURSE RECORD

	Total W-R	Non-Hndcps Hurdles	Non-Hndcps Chases	Hndcps Hurdles	Hndcps Chases	NH Flat	Per cent	£1 Level Stake
Southwell	1-1	0-0	1-1	0-0	0-0	0-0	100.0	+1.20

WINNING HORSES

Horse	Races Run	1st	2nd	3rd	£
*Mr Mercurial	4	1	2	1	1248
Total winning prize-money					**£1248**
Favourites	**1-3**		**33.3%**		**-0.80**

REBECCA CURTIS

NEWPORT, PEMBROKESHIRE

	No. of Hrs	Races Run	1st	2nd	3rd	Unpl	Per cent	£1 Level Stake
NH Flat	*24*	*34*	*6*	*9*	*7*	*12*	*17.6*	*-12.00*
Hurdles	*36*	*108*	*22*	*17*	*20*	*49*	*20.4*	*+1.17*
Chases	*22*	*79*	*17*	*8*	*12*	*42*	*21.5*	*+34.25*

Totals	**60**	**221**	**45**	**34**	**39**	**103**	**20.4**	**+23.42**
13-14	*67*	*236*	*38*	*39*	*37*	*122*	*16.1*	*-94.57*
12-13	*56*	*210*	*49*	*33*	*28*	*100*	*23.3*	*-18.22*

BY MONTH

NH Flat	W-R	Per cent	£1 Level Stake
May	0-0	0.0	0.00
June	0-0	0.0	0.00
July	0-0	0.0	0.00
August	0-0	0.0	0.00
September	0-0	0.0	0.00
October	3-10	30.0	+1.75
November	0-5	0.0	-5.00
December	2-5	40.0	+2.25
January	0-3	0.0	-3.00
February	0-3	0.0	-3.00
March	1-4	25.0	-1.00
April	0-4	0.0	-4.00

Hurdles	W-R	Per cent	£1 Level Stake
May	0-4	0.0	-4.00
June	1-1	100.0	+1.75
July	0-0	0.0	0.00
August	0-0	0.0	0.00
September	0-0	0.0	0.00
October	4-20	20.0	-2.00
November	2-14	14.3	-5.25
December	2-16	12.5	-10.75
January	5-14	35.7	+8.91
February	2-11	18.2	-2.13
March	3-16	18.8	+1.83
April	3-12	25.0	+12.80

Chases	W-R	Per cent	£1 Level Stake
May	0-0	0.0	0.00
June	2-3	66.7	+7.00
July	1-1	100.0	+2.00
August	0-0	0.0	0.00
September	0-0	0.0	0.00
October	4-12	33.3	+10.25
November	1-18	5.6	-15.00
December	0-14	0.0	-14.00
January	2-8	25.0	+30.00
February	1-6	16.7	-3.00
March	3-11	27.3	+7.25
April	3-6	50.0	+9.75

Totals	W-R	Per cent	£1 Level Stake
May	0-4	0.0	-4.00
June	3-4	75.0	+8.75
July	1-1	100.0	+2.00
August	0-0	0.0	0.00
September	0-0	0.0	0.00
October	11-42	26.2	+10.00
November	3-37	8.1	-25.25
December	4-35	11.4	-22.50
January	7-25	28.0	+35.91
February	3-20	15.0	-8.13
March	7-31	22.6	+8.08
April	6-22	27.3	+18.55

DISTANCE

Hurdles	W-R	Per cent	£1 Level Stake
2m-2m3f	6-25	24.0	+24.75
2m4f-2m7f	9-41	22.0	-11.58
3m+	1-15	6.7	-10.50

Chases	W-R	Per cent	£1 Level Stake
2m-2m3f	2-16	12.5	-4.50
2m4f-2m7f	6-19	31.6	+13.50
3m+	6-31	19.4	+26.75

TYPE OF RACE

Non-Handicaps	W-R	Per cent	£1 Level Stake
Nov Hrdls	8-41	19.5	-8.82
Hrdls	5-34	14.7	-13.09
Nov Chs	2-17	11.8	-10.75
Chases	1-2	50.0	+1.00
Sell/Claim	0-2	0.0	-2.00

Handicaps	W-R	Per cent	£1 Level Stake
Nov Hrdls	2-3	66.7	+20.50
Hrdls	7-28	25.0	+4.58
Nov Chs	5-32	15.6	+3.00
Chases	9-28	32.1	+41.00
Sell/Claim	0-0	0.0	0.00

RACE CLASS

	W-R	Per cent	£1 Level Stake
Class 1	2-24	8.3	-4.50
Class 2	3-18	16.7	+6.75
Class 3	11-54	20.4	-2.79
Class 4	19-78	24.4	+35.80
Class 5	8-25	32.0	+4.91
Class 6	2-22	9.1	-16.75

FIRST TIME OUT

	W-R	Per cent	£1 Level Stake
Bumpers	6-24	25.0	-2.00
Hurdles	3-19	15.8	-6.50
Chases	5-17	29.4	+7.50
Totals	14-60	23.3	-1.00

JOCKEYS

	W-R	Per cent	£1 Level Stake
Paul Townend	10-32	31.3	+40.46
Tom Scudamore	7-38	18.4	-5.00
A P McCoy	7-41	17.1	-24.34
Barry Geraghty	5-17	29.4	+10.75
Paul Carberry	2-4	50.0	+5.75
Leighton Aspell	2-6	33.3	+4.30
Davy Russell	2-7	28.6	-1.75
Paul Moloney	2-11	18.2	-4.25
Sean Bowen	1-2	50.0	+0.25
Mr J J Codd	1-2	50.0	+1.00
James Reveley	1-2	50.0	+19.00
Jamie Moore	1-4	25.0	-1.50
Richie McLernon	1-4	25.0	+2.00
Noel Fehily	1-6	16.7	-2.25
Jason Maguire	1-6	16.7	+1.00
Conor Brassil	1-9	11.1	+8.00

COURSE RECORD

	Total W-R	Non-Hndcps Hurdles	Non-Hndcps Chases	Hndcps Hurdles	Hndcps Chases	NH Flat	Per cent	£1 Level Stake
Ffos Las	14-43	4-18	0-0	3-10	6-8	1-7	32.6	+31.66
Bangor	6-19	3-7	1-3	1-3	0-3	1-3	31.6	+3.46
Stratford	4-7	1-1	1-1	1-1	1-2	0-2	57.1	+23.30
Worcester	4-14	1-3	0-1	1-3	2-4	0-3	28.6	+4.00
Chepstow	4-30	3-8	0-3	0-2	1-10	0-7	13.3	-12.50
Ludlow	3-11	1-4	0-0	1-1	0-4	1-2	27.3	-2.25
Aintree	2-8	0-2	0-1	1-1	0-3	1-1	25.0	+4.00
Uttoxeter	2-11	0-5	0-1	0-0	1-3	1-2	18.2	-0.50
Cheltenham	2-12	0-4	1-2	0-2	1-3	0-1	16.7	+3.25
Taunton	1-3	0-1	0-0	0-0	0-1	1-1	33.3	+0.50
Exeter	1-6	0-2	0-0	0-0	1-3	0-1	16.7	-2.00
Doncaster	1-7	0-2	0-1	0-1	1-2	0-1	14.3	+14.00
Ascot	1-11	0-2	0-1	1-2	0-4	0-2	9.1	-4.50

WINNING HORSES

Horse	Races Run	1st	2nd	3rd	£
The Romford Pele	3	3	0	0	41836
Irish Cavalier	5	1	1	2	34170
Bob Ford	7	2	1	0	25344
Peckhamecho	5	1	1	0	13763
Beast Of Burden	5	3	1	0	12931
One Term	5	1	0	0	7596
Red Devil Lads	7	4	0	1	20898
Bob Keown	2	2	0	0	12021
Tara Road	6	2	0	0	12128
Doing Fine	5	1	1	0	6498
Ballyhollow	6	1	2	1	6498
Binge Drinker	6	4	0	0	9617
Lookslikerainted	7	1	1	0	6330

Audacious Plan	7	2	2	3	8317
Guard of Honour	6	1	1	2	3899
Champagne Rian	6	1	0	1	3899
Carningli	5	2	0	0	6498
Scorpiancer	6	1	1	3	3899
Relentless Dreamer	5	1	2	0	3899
Glenwood Star	6	1	0	0	3899
Foryourinformation	6	2	1	1	5848
Vintage Vinnie	7	1	1	3	3249
Globalisation	4	1	1	1	3249
Golden Milan	4	1	0	1	3119
Imagine The Chat	3	1	0	0	3080
Wild Rover	4	1	0	1	2053
Going For Broke	2	1	0	0	2053
Definite Outcome	1	1	0	0	1689
Teaforthree	2	1	0	0	1317
Total winning prize-money					**£269597**
Favourites	**21-47**		**44.7%**		**12.29**

LUKE DACE

PULBOROUGH, W SUSSEX

	No. of Hrs	Races Run	1st	2nd	3rd	Unpl	Per cent	£1 Level Stake
NH Flat	*0*	*0*	*0*	*0*	*0*	*0*	*0.0*	*0.00*
Hurdles	*3*	*10*	*0*	*0*	*2*	*8*	*0.0*	*-10.00*
Chases	*2*	*8*	*1*	*0*	*0*	*7*	*12.5*	*+1.00*
Totals	**4**	**18**	**1**	**0**	**2**	**15**	**5.6**	**-9.00**
13-14	*5*	*19*	*3*	*1*	*1*	*14*	*15.8*	*+4.75*
12-13	*9*	*25*	*1*	*0*	*0*	*24*	*4.0*	*-14.00*

JOCKEYS

	W-R	Per cent	£1 Level Stake
Tom Cannon	1-3	33.3	+6.00

COURSE RECORD

	Total W-R	Non-Hndcps Hurdles	Non-Hndcps Chases	Hndcps Hurdles	Hndcps Chases	NH Flat	Per cent	£1 Level Stake
Kempton	1-4	0-0	0-0	0-1	1-3	0-0	25.0	+5.00

WINNING HORSES

Horse	Races Run	1st	2nd	3rd	£
American Spin	6	1	0	0	6498
Total winning prize-money					**£6498**
Favourites	**0-0**		**0.0%**		**0.00**

KEITH DALGLEISH

CARLUKE, S LANARKS

	No. of Hrs	Races Run	1st	2nd	3rd	Unpl	Per cent	£1 Level Stake
NH Flat	*4*	*6*	*0*	*0*	*0*	*6*	*0.0*	*-6.00*
Hurdles	*14*	*40*	*4*	*4*	*1*	*31*	*10.0*	*-22.31*
Chases	*1*	*6*	*5*	*0*	*0*	*1*	*83.3*	*+15.50*
Totals	**19**	**52**	**9**	**4**	**1**	**38**	**17.3**	**-12.81**
13-14	*13*	*41*	*9*	*4*	*6*	*22*	*22.0*	*+20.17*
12-13	*3*	*9*	*0*	*2*	*0*	*7*	*0.0*	*-9.00*

JOCKEYS

	W-R	Per cent	£1 Level Stake
Wilson Renwick	7-34	20.6	-1.81
Craig Nichol	2-7	28.6	0.00

COURSE RECORD

	Total W-R	Non-Hndcps Hurdles	Non-Hndcps Chases	Hndcps Hurdles	Hndcps Chases	NH Flat	Per cent	£1 Level Stake
Newcastle	3-7	0-2	0-0	0-2	3-3	0-0	42.9	+4.50
Carlisle	1-1	0-0	0-0	0-0	1-1	0-0	100.0	+2.50
Haydock	1-1	0-0	0-0	1-1	0-0	0-0	100.0	+8.00
Hexham	1-3	1-1	0-0	0-2	0-0	0-0	33.3	-1.56
Ayr	1-4	1-3	0-0	0-0	0-0	0-1	25.0	-0.25
Sedgefield	1-8	0-1	0-0	0-6	1-1	0-0	12.5	-1.50
Musselbgh	1-10	0-5	0-0	1-4	0-0	0-1	10.0	-6.50

WINNING HORSES

Horse	Races Run	1st	2nd	3rd	£
Nexius	5	2	0	0	12346
Montoya's Son	6	5	0	0	25277
Hurricane Hollow	2	2	0	0	5497
Total winning prize-money					**£43120**
Favourites	**2-4**		**50.0%**		**0.94**

HENRY DALY

STANTON LACY, SHROPSHIRE

	No. of Hrs	Races Run	1st	2nd	3rd	Unpl	Per cent	£1 Level Stake
NH Flat	*13*	*18*	*1*	*9*	*1*	*7*	*5.6*	*-5.00*
Hurdles	*27*	*105*	*13*	*22*	*9*	*61*	*12.4*	*+25.25*
Chases	*17*	*58*	*7*	*11*	*8*	*32*	*12.1*	*-23.83*
Totals	**49**	**181**	**21**	**42**	**18**	**100**	**11.6**	**-3.58**
13-14	*43*	*182*	*36*	*31*	*21*	*94*	*19.8*	*+5.20*
12-13	*50*	*172*	*19*	*17*	*22*	*114*	*11.0*	*-64.68*

BY MONTH

NH Flat	W-R	Per cent	£1 Level Stake	**Hurdles**	W-R	Per cent	£1 Level Stake
May	0-3	0.0	-3.00	May	1-5	20.0	-2.25
June	0-0	0.0	0.00	June	0-3	0.0	-3.00
July	0-0	0.0	0.00	July	0-2	0.0	-2.00
August	0-1	0.0	-1.00	August	0-3	0.0	-3.00
September	0-0	0.0	0.00	September	0-2	0.0	-2.00
October	0-2	0.0	-2.00	October	1-11	9.1	+23.00
November	0-3	0.0	-3.00	November	0-12	0.0	-12.00
December	0-1	0.0	-1.00	December	5-17	29.4	+16.11
January	0-1	0.0	-1.00	January	1-14	7.1	-9.50
February	1-3	33.3	+10.00	February	2-12	16.7	-5.33
March	0-2	0.0	-2.00	March	1-12	8.3	+29.00

April	0-2	0.0	-2.00	April	2-12	16.7	-3.78

Chases	W-R	Per cent	£1 Level Stake	Totals	W-R	Per cent	£1 Level Stake
May	1-4	25.0	-1.00	May	2-12	16.7	-6.25
June	0-1	0.0	-1.00	June	0-4	0.0	-4.00
July	0-0	0.0	0.00	July	0-2	0.0	-2.00
August	0-0	0.0	0.00	August	0-4	0.0	-4.00
September	0-1	0.0	-1.00	September	0-3	0.0	-3.00
October	0-8	0.0	-8.00	October	1-21	4.8	+13.00
November	1-8	12.5	-4.75	November	1-23	4.3	-19.75
December	1-9	11.1	+4.00	December	6-27	22.2	+19.11
January	1-9	11.1	-4.67	January	2-24	8.3	-15.17
February	1-5	20.0	0.00	February	4-20	20.0	+4.67
March	1-6	16.7	-2.25	March	2-20	10.0	+24.75
April	1-7	14.3	-5.17	April	3-21	14.3	-10.95

DISTANCE

Hurdles	W-R	Per cent	£1 Level Stake	Chases	W-R	Per cent	£1 Level Stake
2m-2m3f	2-29	6.9	+13.22	2m-2m3f	0-3	0.0	-3.00
2m4f-2m7f	5-31	16.1	-9.64	2m4f-2m7f	2-13	15.4	-6.83
3m+	2-17	11.8	-5.00	3m+	5-35	14.3	-7.00

TYPE OF RACE

Non-Handicaps	W-R	Per cent	£1 Level Stake	Handicaps	W-R	Per cent	£1 Level Stake
Nov Hrdls	3-21	14.3	+15.84	Nov Hrdls	2-7	28.6	-0.83
Hrdls	1-12	8.3	-6.50	Hrdls	7-65	10.8	+16.75
Nov Chs	1-7	14.3	+6.00	Nov Chs	1-10	10.0	-6.75
Chases	3-8	37.5	+1.83	Chases	2-33	6.1	-24.92
Sell/Claim	0-0	0.0	0.00	Sell/Claim	0-0	0.0	0.00

RACE CLASS

	W-R	Per cent	£1 Level Stake
Class 1	0-17	0.0	-17.00
Class 2	0-10	0.0	-10.00
Class 3	4-52	7.7	+12.75
Class 4	9-68	13.2	+4.17
Class 5	6-23	26.1	+1.50
Class 6	2-11	18.2	+5.00

FIRST TIME OUT

	W-R	Per cent	£1 Level Stake
Bumpers	1-13	7.7	0.00
Hurdles	3-21	14.3	+17.37
Chases	2-15	13.3	-8.75
Totals	6-49	12.2	+8.62

JOCKEYS

	W-R	Per cent	£1 Level Stake
Jake Greenall	6-79	7.6	+24.75
Richard Johnson	4-42	9.5	-21.41
Tom Bellamy	2-3	66.7	+3.17
Miss J C Williams	2-6	33.3	-1.17
Tom O'Brien	2-15	13.3	-3.00
Kieron Edgar	1-1	100.0	+12.00
Sam Twiston-Davies	1-1	100.0	+3.00
Mr O Greenall	1-2	50.0	+3.00
A P McCoy	1-3	33.3	+1.33
Andrew Tinkler	1-13	7.7	-9.25

COURSE RECORD

	Total W-R	Non-Hndcps Hurdles	Non-Hndcps Chases	Hndcps Hurdles	Hndcps Chases	NH Flat	Per cent	£1 Level Stake
Fakenham	2-4	0-0	1-2	1-1	0-1	0-0	50.0	+1.75
Bangor	2-13	0-1	0-0	2-5	0-4	0-3	15.4	+1.00
Ludlow	2-26	1-4	1-2	0-8	0-10	0-2	7.7	-22.55
Hexham	1-1	0-0	0-0	0-0	1-1	0-0	100.0	+2.25
Perth	1-2	1-1	0-0	0-0	0-1	0-0	50.0	-0.78
Haydock	1-3	0-0	1-1	0-1	0-1	0-0	33.3	+2.00
Sandown	1-4	0-2	0-0	1-1	0-1	0-0	25.0	+11.00
Taunton	1-5	0-1	0-0	0-2	1-2	0-0	20.0	-1.25
Doncaster	1-6	0-0	0-0	0-1	0-2	1-3	16.7	+7.00
Southwell	1-6	1-2	0-0	0-2	0-1	0-1	16.7	-0.50
Towcester	1-6	0-3	0-0	1-2	0-0	0-1	16.7	-2.00
Uttoxeter	1-6	0-2	1-1	0-2	0-1	0-0	16.7	+7.00
Wetherby	1-6	0-1	0-1	0-2	1-2	0-0	16.7	-1.67
Exeter	1-7	0-1	0-1	1-3	0-2	0-0	14.3	-2.50
Chepstow	1-8	0-2	0-0	1-5	0-1	0-0	12.5	-6.33
Stratford	1-10	0-2	0-1	1-5	0-2	0-0	10.0	+31.00
Aintree	1-11	1-2	0-0	0-6	0-1	0-2	9.1	+23.00
Warwick	1-12	0-4	0-1	1-4	0-3	0-0	8.3	-7.00

WINNING HORSES

Horse	Races Run	1st	2nd	3rd	£
Kayfleur	5	1	0	0	9384
Grove Pride	5	1	0	2	6657
Pearlysteps	3	1	1	0	6239
Mighty Minnie	5	1	1	3	5848
Oyster Shell	7	1	2	0	5523
Chicoria	4	1	1	0	5198
Tara Mist	5	2	1	0	8672
Brave Buck	2	1	0	0	4595
Heronshaw	5	1	0	0	4549
Top Totti	6	1	1	1	3833
Arctic Ben	5	1	1	0	3769
Queen Spud	4	1	1	0	3249
Nightline	5	1	1	0	3249
Nordic Nymph	6	3	1	0	7252
Rockiteer	6	2	2	0	3813
Toot Sweet	5	1	1	0	1949
Score Card	1	1	0	0	1560
Total winning prize-money					**£85339**
Favourites	**7-26**		**26.9%**		**-9.33**

VICTOR DARTNALL

BRAYFORD, DEVON

	No. of Hrs	Races Run	1st	2nd	3rd	Unpl	Per cent	£1 Level Stake
NH Flat	*6*	*8*	*0*	*0*	*0*	*8*	*0.0*	*-8.00*
Hurdles	*17*	*66*	*8*	*9*	*5*	*44*	*12.1*	*-16.42*
Chases	*14*	*38*	*6*	*7*	*3*	*22*	*15.8*	*+0.75*

Totals	**30**	**112**	**14**	**16**	**8**	**74**	**12.5**	**-23.67**
13-14	*33*	*131*	*12*	*17*	*19*	*83*	*9.2*	*-64.84*
12-13	*37*	*116*	*15*	*10*	*3*	*88*	*12.9*	*+7.41*

BY MONTH

NH Flat	W-R	Per cent	£1 Level Stake
May	0-3	0.0	-3.00
June	0-0	0.0	0.00
July	0-0	0.0	0.00
August	0-0	0.0	0.00
September	0-0	0.0	0.00
October	0-0	0.0	0.00
November	0-1	0.0	-1.00
December	0-1	0.0	-1.00
January	0-2	0.0	-2.00
February	0-1	0.0	-1.00
March	0-0	0.0	0.00
April	0-0	0.0	0.00

Hurdles	W-R	Per cent	£1 Level Stake
May	0-2	0.0	-2.00
June	0-1	0.0	-1.00
July	0-1	0.0	-1.00
August	1-4	25.0	-0.75
September	1-1	100.0	+2.75
October	0-2	0.0	-2.00
November	0-7	0.0	-7.00
December	4-17	23.5	-0.42
January	1-9	11.1	+8.00
February	1-7	14.3	+2.00
March	0-7	0.0	-7.00
April	0-8	0.0	-8.00

Chases	W-R	Per cent	£1 Level Stake
May	1-3	33.3	+3.00
June	1-3	33.3	+14.00
July	0-2	0.0	-2.00
August	0-0	0.0	0.00
September	0-4	0.0	-4.00
October	1-2	50.0	+1.75
November	2-8	25.0	-1.00
December	1-7	14.3	-2.00
January	0-1	0.0	-1.00
February	0-3	0.0	-3.00
March	0-2	0.0	-2.00
April	0-3	0.0	-3.00

Totals	W-R	Per cent	£1 Level Stake
May	1-8	12.5	-2.00
June	1-4	25.0	+13.00
July	0-3	0.0	-3.00
August	1-4	25.0	-0.75
September	1-5	20.0	-1.25
October	1-4	25.0	-0.25
November	2-16	12.5	-9.00
December	5-25	20.0	-3.42
January	1-12	8.3	+5.00
February	1-11	9.1	-2.00
March	0-9	0.0	-9.00
April	0-11	0.0	-11.00

DISTANCE

Hurdles	W-R	Per cent	£1 Level Stake
2m-2m3f	5-32	15.6	-12.17
2m4f-2m7f	3-21	14.3	+8.75
3m+	0-1	0.0	-1.00

Chases	W-R	Per cent	£1 Level Stake
2m-2m3f	4-13	30.8	+16.50
2m4f-2m7f	1-13	7.7	-9.75
3m+	1-6	16.7	0.00

TYPE OF RACE

Non-Handicaps	W-R	Per cent	£1 Level Stake
Nov Hrdls	0-12	0.0	-12.00
Hrdls	0-8	0.0	-8.00
Nov Chs	0-0	0.0	0.00
Chases	0-0	0.0	0.00
Sell/Claim	0-0	0.0	0.00

Handicaps	W-R	Per cent	£1 Level Stake
Nov Hrdls	1-4	25.0	-0.25
Hrdls	7-42	16.7	+3.83
Nov Chs	0-8	0.0	-8.00
Chases	6-30	20.0	+8.75
Sell/Claim	0-0	0.0	0.00

RACE CLASS

	W-R	Per cent	£1 Level Stake
Class 1	0-2	0.0	-2.00
Class 2	0-4	0.0	-4.00
Class 3	5-27	18.5	+14.50
Class 4	7-47	14.9	-7.17
Class 5	2-26	7.7	-19.00
Class 6	0-6	0.0	-6.00

FIRST TIME OUT

	W-R	Per cent	£1 Level Stake
Bumpers	0-6	0.0	-6.00
Hurdles	2-13	15.4	-5.75
Chases	3-11	27.3	+15.75
Totals	5-30	16.7	+4.00

JOCKEYS

	W-R	Per cent	£1 Level Stake
Jack Doyle	5-23	21.7	+15.75
Denis O'Regan	4-50	8.0	-20.92
Paul John	3-7	42.9	+3.75
Aidan Coleman	1-3	33.3	+3.00
Giles Hawkins	1-17	5.9	-13.25

COURSE RECORD

	Total W-R	Non-Hndcps Hurdles	Non-Hndcps Chases	Hndcps Hurdles	Hndcps Chases	NH Flat	Per cent	£1 Level Stake
Exeter	5-28	0-7	0-0	3-13	2-5	0-3	17.9	-8.25
Fontwell	4-9	0-0	0-0	2-4	2-4	0-1	44.4	+21.00
Kempton	1-2	0-0	0-0	1-1	0-1	0-0	50.0	+7.00
Southwell	1-2	0-0	0-0	0-0	1-2	0-0	50.0	+1.25
Wincanton	1-10	0-3	0-0	1-4	0-3	0-0	10.0	+7.00
Chepstow	1-12	0-2	0-0	0-6	1-3	0-1	8.3	-7.00
Taunton	1-12	0-2	0-0	1-7	0-1	0-2	8.3	-7.67

WINNING HORSES

Horse	Races Run	1st	2nd	3rd	£
Shammick Boy	8	3	1	1	24104
Seebright	1	1	0	0	7596
Tolkeins Tango	6	2	1	1	10397
Jewellery	9	4	3	1	12736
Overclear	4	1	0	0	3769
Un Bleu A L'Aam	4	1	0	0	3574
Exmoor Mist	2	1	0	0	3249
Unefille De Guye	11	1	1	1	2274
Total winning prize-money					**£67699**
Favourites	**3-13**		**23.1%**		**-2.00**

TRISTAN DAVIDSON

IRTHINGTON, CUMBRIA

	No. of Hrs	Races Run	1st	2nd	3rd	Unpl	Per cent	£1 Level Stake
NH Flat	*1*	*1*	*0*	*0*	*0*	*1*	*0.0*	*-1.00*
Hurdles	*3*	*15*	*1*	*0*	*1*	*13*	*6.7*	*-9.00*
Chases	*0*	*0*	*0*	*0*	*0*	*0*	*0.0*	*0.00*
Totals	**4**	**16**	**1**	**0**	**1**	**14**	**6.3**	**-10.00**
13-14	*4*	*10*	*0*	*0*	*0*	*10*	*0.0*	*-10.00*
12-13	*1*	*3*	*2*	*0*	*1*	*0*	*66.7*	*+9.50*

JOCKEYS

	W-R	Per cent	£1 Level Stake
Jonathan England	1-10	10.0	-4.00

COURSE RECORD

	Total W-R	Non-Hndcps Hurdles	Non-Hndcps Chases	Hndcps Hurdles	Hndcps Chases	NH Flat	Per cent	£1 Level Stake
Sedgefield	1-2	0-0	0-0	1-1	0-0	0-1	50.0	+4.00

WINNING HORSES

Horse	Races Run	1st	2nd	3rd	£
*Orchard Road	5	1	0	0	2339

Total winning prize-money **£2339**

Favourites **0-1** **0.0%** **-1.00**

PAUL DAVIES

BROMYARD, H'FORDS

	No. of Hrs	Races Run	1st	2nd	3rd	Unpl	Per cent	£1 Level Stake
NH Flat	*0*	*0*	*0*	*0*	*0*	*0*	*0.0*	*0.00*
Hurdles	*1*	*2*	*0*	*0*	*0*	*2*	*0.0*	*-2.00*
Chases	*1*	*3*	*1*	*0*	*1*	*1*	*33.3*	*+2.50*
Totals	**2**	**5**	**1**	**0**	**1**	**3**	**20.0**	**+0.50**
13-14	*3*	*5*	*1*	*1*	*0*	*3*	*20.0*	*+2.50*
12-13	*4*	*9*	*2*	*1*	*1*	*5*	*22.2*	*+43.00*

JOCKEYS

	W-R	Per cent	£1 Level Stake
Peter Carberry	1-4	25.0	+1.50

COURSE RECORD

	Total W-R	Non-Hndcps Hurdles	Non-Hndcps Chases	Hndcps Hurdles	Hndcps Chases	NH Flat	Per cent	£1 Level Stake
Warwick	1-1	0-0	0-0	0-0	1-1	0-0	100.0	+4.50

WINNING HORSES

Horse	Races Run	1st	2nd	3rd	£
Emma Soda	3	1	0	1	3899

Total winning prize-money **£3899**

Favourites **0-0** **0.0%** **0.00**

SARAH-JAYNE DAVIES

LEOMINSTER, H'FORDS

	No. of Hrs	Races Run	1st	2nd	3rd	Unpl	Per cent	£1 Level Stake
NH Flat	*2*	*2*	*0*	*0*	*0*	*2*	*0.0*	*-2.00*
Hurdles	*22*	*68*	*2*	*4*	*6*	*56*	*2.9*	*-53.50*
Chases	*16*	*41*	*4*	*5*	*6*	*26*	*9.8*	*-27.50*
Totals	**31**	**111**	**6**	**9**	**12**	**84**	**5.4**	**-83.00**
13-14	*26*	*95*	*10*	*5*	*4*	*76*	*10.5*	*+21.00*
12-13	*8*	*23*	*1*	*4*	*2*	*16*	*4.3*	*-16.50*

JOCKEYS

	W-R	Per cent	£1 Level Stake
A P McCoy	2-5	40.0	-0.75
Tom Scudamore	1-4	25.0	+3.50
Mr J Mahot	1-8	12.5	-4.75
Michael Heard	1-13	7.7	-6.00
Will Kennedy	1-31	3.2	-25.00

COURSE RECORD

	Total W-R	Non-Hndcps Hurdles	Non-Hndcps Chases	Hndcps Hurdles	Hndcps Chases	NH Flat	Per cent	£1 Level Stake
Nton Abbot	2-13	0-1	0-0	0-4	2-8	0-0	15.4	-3.75
Huntingdon	1-1	0-0	0-0	0-0	1-1	0-0	100.0	+1.25
Towcester	1-4	0-1	0-0	1-1	0-2	0-0	25.0	+3.00
Ffos Las	1-8	0-1	0-0	1-3	0-4	0-0	12.5	-0.50
Worcester	1-13	0-1	0-1	0-5	1-6	0-0	7.7	-11.00

WINNING HORSES

Horse	Races Run	1st	2nd	3rd	£
Respectueux	7	2	1	0	6823
Passing Fiesta	7	1	0	1	3899
Pembroke House	7	1	0	1	2599
Accessallareas	10	1	1	3	2274
Capisci	6	1	3	1	2274

Total winning prize-money **£17869**

Favourites **3-8** **37.5%** **-0.50**

JO DAVIS

EAST GARSTON, BERKS

	No. of Hrs	Races Run	1st	2nd	3rd	Unpl	Per cent	£1 Level Stake
NH Flat	*5*	*5*	*0*	*1*	*1*	*3*	*0.0*	*-5.00*
Hurdles	*8*	*22*	*2*	*1*	*2*	*17*	*9.1*	*+11.00*
Chases	*5*	*9*	*0*	*1*	*2*	*6*	*0.0*	*-9.00*
Totals	**13**	**36**	**2**	**3**	**5**	**26**	**5.6**	**-3.00**
13-14	*15*	*54*	*1*	*2*	*7*	*44*	*1.9*	*-44.00*
12-13	*16*	*55*	*4*	*8*	*1*	*42*	*7.3*	*-40.00*

JOCKEYS

	W-R	Per cent	£1 Level Stake
Sam Jones	2-20	10.0	+13.00

COURSE RECORD

	Total W-R	Non-Hndcps Hurdles	Non-Hndcps Chases	Hndcps Hurdles	Hndcps Chases	NH Flat	Per cent	£1 Level Stake
Lingfield	1-1	0-0	0-0	1-1	0-0	0-0	100.0	+25.00
Uttoxeter	1-3	1-1	0-0	0-0	0-1	0-1	33.3	+4.00

WINNING HORSES

Horse	Races Run	1st	2nd	3rd	£
Mr Fitzroy	4	1	0	2	6330

Rose Of The World	5	1	1	0	3249

Total winning prize-money			**£9579**
Favourites	**0-1**	**0.0%**	**-1.00**

DOMINIC FFRENCH DAVIS

LAMBOURN, BERKS

	No. of Hrs	Races Run	1st	2nd	3rd	Unpl	Per cent	£1 Level Stake
NH Flat	*2*	*5*	*1*	*0*	*1*	*3*	*20.0*	*+12.00*
Hurdles	*9*	*22*	*0*	*1*	*3*	*18*	*0.0*	*-22.00*
Chases	*1*	*6*	*0*	*0*	*1*	*5*	*0.0*	*-6.00*
Totals	**10**	**33**	**1**	**1**	**5**	**26**	**3.0**	**-16.00**
13-14	*9*	*18*	*1*	*0*	*4*	*13*	*5.6*	*+11.00*
12-13	*4*	*4*	*0*	*1*	*0*	*3*	*0.0*	*-4.00*

JOCKEYS

	W-R	Per cent	£1 Level Stake
Ben Ffrench Davis	1-15	6.7	+2.00

COURSE RECORD

	Total W-R	Non-Hndcps Hurdles	Non-Hndcps Chases	Hndcps Hurdles	Hndcps Chases	NH Flat	Per cent	£1 Level Stake
Stratford	1-3	0-0	0-0	0-0	0-1	1-2	33.3	+14.00

WINNING HORSES

Horse	Races Run	1st	2nd	3rd	£
Whatthebutlersaw	6	1	0	1	1625
Total winning prize-money					**£1625**
Favourites	**0-0**		**0.0%**		**0.00**

ZOE DAVISON

HAMMERWOOD, E SUSSEX

	No. of Hrs	Races Run	1st	2nd	3rd	Unpl	Per cent	£1 Level Stake
NH Flat	*3*	*6*	*0*	*2*	*0*	*4*	*0.0*	*-6.00*
Hurdles	*14*	*52*	*2*	*3*	*4*	*43*	*3.8*	*-30.00*
Chases	*5*	*14*	*0*	*1*	*2*	*11*	*0.0*	*-14.00*
Totals	**18**	**72**	**2**	**6**	**6**	**58**	**2.8**	**-50.00**
13-14	*23*	*92*	*1*	*3*	*5*	*83*	*1.1*	*-88.50*
12-13	*24*	*92*	*6*	*9*	*11*	*66*	*6.5*	*-31.75*

JOCKEYS

	W-R	Per cent	£1 Level Stake
Gemma Gracey-Davison	2-41	4.9	-19.00

COURSE RECORD

	Total W-R	Non-Hndcps Hurdles	Non-Hndcps Chases	Hndcps Hurdles	Hndcps Chases	NH Flat	Per cent	£1 Level Stake
Bangor	1-1	0-0	0-0	1-1	0-0	0-0	100.0	+12.00
Stratford	1-3	0-1	0-0	1-1	0-1	0-0	33.3	+6.00

WINNING HORSES

Horse	Races Run	1st	2nd	3rd	£
Jumeirah Liberty	6	1	0	0	2599
Frank N Fair	10	1	1	0	2274
Total winning prize-money					**£4873**
Favourites	**0-2**		**0.0%**		**-2.00**

M N DAWSON

GRAINTHORPE, LINCOLNSHIRE

	No. of Hrs	Races Run	1st	2nd	3rd	Unpl	Per cent	£1 Level Stake
NH Flat	*0*	*0*	*0*	*0*	*0*	*0*	*0.0*	*0.00*
Hurdles	*0*	*0*	*0*	*0*	*0*	*0*	*0.0*	*0.00*
Chases	*2*	*3*	*2*	*0*	*1*	*0*	*66.7*	*+1.04*
Totals	**2**	**3**	**2**	**0**	**1**	**0**	**66.7**	**+1.04**

JOCKEYS

	W-R	Per cent	£1 Level Stake
Miss C V Hart	2-3	66.7	+1.04

COURSE RECORD

	Total W-R	Non-Hndcps Hurdles	Non-Hndcps Chases	Hndcps Hurdles	Hndcps Chases	NH Flat	Per cent	£1 Level Stake
Carlisle	1-1	0-0	1-1	0-0	0-0	0-0	100.0	+0.67
Leicester	1-1	0-0	1-1	0-0	0-0	0-0	100.0	+1.38

WINNING HORSES

Horse	Races Run	1st	2nd	3rd	£
*Palypso De Creek	2	2	0	0	8931
Total winning prize-money					**£8931**
Favourites	**2-2**		**100.0%**		**2.04**

MRS J DAWSON

GRAINTHORPE, LINCS

	No. of Hrs	Races Run	1st	2nd	3rd	Unpl	Per cent	£1 Level Stake
NH Flat	*0*	*0*	*0*	*0*	*0*	*0*	*0.0*	*0.00*
Hurdles	*0*	*0*	*0*	*0*	*0*	*0*	*0.0*	*0.00*
Chases	*1*	*2*	*1*	*1*	*0*	*0*	*50.0*	*+1.25*
Totals	**1**	**2**	**1**	**1**	**0**	**0**	**50.0**	**+1.25**
13-14	*1*	*3*	*2*	*1*	*0*	*0*	*66.7*	*+2.00*
12-13	*1*	*1*	*1*	*0*	*0*	*0*	*100.0*	*+2.00*

JOCKEYS

	W-R	Per cent	£1 Level Stake
Miss C V Hart	1-2	50.0	+1.25

COURSE RECORD

	Total W-R	Non-Hndcps Hurdles	Non-Hndcps Chases	Hndcps Hurdles	Chases	NH Flat	Per cent	£1 Level Stake
Wetherby	1-1	0-0	1-1	0-0	0-0	0-0	100.0	+2.25

WINNING HORSES

Horse	Races Run	1st	2nd	3rd	£
*Palypso De Creek	2	1	1	0	988
Total winning prize-money					**£988**
Favourites	**0-0**		**0.0%**		**0.00**

ANTHONY DAY

WOLVEY, LEICS

	No. of Hrs	Races Run	1st	2nd	3rd	Unpl	Per cent	£1 Level Stake
NH Flat	*2*	*4*	*0*	*0*	*0*	*4*	*0.0*	*-4.00*
Hurdles	*2*	*3*	*0*	*0*	*0*	*3*	*0.0*	*-3.00*
Chases	*1*	*8*	*2*	*1*	*1*	*4*	*25.0*	*-1.88*
Totals	**4**	**15**	**2**	**1**	**1**	**11**	**13.3**	**-8.88**
13-14	*1*	*6*	*0*	*0*	*0*	*6*	*0.0*	*-6.00*
12-13	*3*	*10*	*1*	*0*	*0*	*9*	*10.0*	*+3.00*

JOCKEYS

	W-R	Per cent	£1 Level Stake
Danny Burton	2-7	28.6	-0.88

COURSE RECORD

	Total W-R	Non-Hndcps Hurdles	Non-Hndcps Chases	Hndcps Hurdles	Chases	NH Flat	Per cent	£1 Level Stake
Chepstow	1-1	0-0	0-0	0-0	1-1	0-0	100.0	+2.25
Plumpton	1-2	0-0	0-0	0-0	1-2	0-0	50.0	+0.88

WINNING HORSES

Horse	Races Run	1st	2nd	3rd	£
Charming Lad	8	2	1	1	5393
Total winning prize-money					**£5393**
Favourites	**1-2**		**50.0%**		**0.88**

GEOFFREY DEACON

COMPTON, BERKS

	No. of Hrs	Races Run	1st	2nd	3rd	Unpl	Per cent	£1 Level Stake
NH Flat	*0*	*0*	*0*	*0*	*0*	*0*	*0.0*	*0.00*
Hurdles	*5*	*13*	*2*	*0*	*2*	*9*	*15.4*	*+15.00*
Chases	*1*	*1*	*0*	*0*	*0*	*1*	*0.0*	*-1.00*
Totals	**6**	**14**	**2**	**0**	**2**	**10**	**14.3**	**+14.00**
13-14	*12*	*27*	*0*	*2*	*2*	*23*	*0.0*	*-27.00*
12-13	*9*	*18*	*0*	*0*	*2*	*16*	*0.0*	*-18.00*

JOCKEYS

	W-R	Per cent	£1 Level Stake
Mark Grant	2-11	18.2	+17.00

COURSE RECORD

	Total W-R	Non-Hndcps Hurdles	Non-Hndcps Chases	Hndcps Hurdles	Chases	NH Flat	Per cent	£1 Level Stake
Plumpton	2-3	0-1	0-0	2-2	0-0	0-0	66.7	+25.00

WINNING HORSES

Horse	Races Run	1st	2nd	3rd	£
Moon Trip	2	1	0	1	2274
Banks Road	4	1	0	0	1949
Total winning prize-money					**£4223**
Favourites	**0-0**		**0.0%**		**0.00**

TIM DENNIS

BUDE, CORNWALL

	No. of Hrs	Races Run	1st	2nd	3rd	Unpl	Per cent	£1 Level Stake
NH Flat	*0*	*0*	*0*	*0*	*0*	*0*	*0.0*	*0.00*
Hurdles	*3*	*13*	*2*	*0*	*0*	*11*	*15.4*	*-5.50*
Chases	*2*	*5*	*0*	*0*	*0*	*5*	*0.0*	*-5.00*
Totals	**4**	**18**	**2**	**0**	**0**	**16**	**11.1**	**-10.50**
13-14	*4*	*10*	*0*	*0*	*1*	*9*	*0.0*	*-10.00*
12-13	*2*	*7*	*0*	*0*	*1*	*6*	*0.0*	*-7.00*

JOCKEYS

	W-R	Per cent	£1 Level Stake
Nick Scholfield	2-12	16.7	-4.50

COURSE RECORD

	Total W-R	Non-Hndcps Hurdles	Non-Hndcps Chases	Hndcps Hurdles	Chases	NH Flat	Per cent	£1 Level Stake
Taunton	1-3	0-0	0-0	1-1	0-2	0-0	33.3	0.00
Exeter	1-7	0-6	0-0	1-1	0-0	0-0	14.3	-2.50

WINNING HORSES

Horse	Races Run	1st	2nd	3rd	£
Its A Long Road	6	2	0	0	4874
Total winning prize-money					**£4874**
Favourites	**1-1**		**100.0%**		**2.00**

DAVID DENNIS

HANLEY SWAN, WORCESTERSHIRE

	No. of Hrs	Races Run	1st	2nd	3rd	Unpl	Per cent	£1 Level Stake
NH Flat	*10*	*19*	*3*	*1*	*4*	*11*	*15.8*	*+12.00*
Hurdles	*30*	*146*	*22*	*8*	*24*	*92*	*15.1*	*-12.65*

Chases	*8*	*43*	*7*	*3*	*9*	*24*	*16.3*	*-1.25*
Totals	**34**	**208**	**32**	**12**	**37**	**127**	**15.4**	**-1.90**
13-14	*18*	*79*	*7*	*12*	*9*	*51*	*8.9*	*-45.91*

BY MONTH

NH Flat	W-R	Per cent	£1 Level Stake
May	0-2	0.0	-2.00
June	0-0	0.0	0.00
July	0-0	0.0	0.00
August	0-0	0.0	0.00
September	0-1	0.0	-1.00
October	0-1	0.0	-1.00
November	0-4	0.0	-4.00
December	0-3	0.0	-3.00
January	2-3	66.7	+24.50
February	0-3	0.0	-3.00
March	0-1	0.0	-1.00
April	1-1	100.0	+2.50

Hurdles	W-R	Per cent	£1 Level Stake
May	2-14	14.3	+6.00
June	1-10	10.0	-4.00
July	0-8	0.0	-8.00
August	1-7	14.3	-4.13
September	2-5	40.0	+4.25
October	2-12	16.7	+9.00
November	0-14	0.0	-14.00
December	1-7	14.3	0.00
January	3-18	16.7	-10.00
February	2-10	20.0	-1.47
March	3-21	14.3	-7.50
April	5-20	25.0	+17.20

Chases	W-R	Per cent	£1 Level Stake
May	0-2	0.0	-2.00
June	1-2	50.0	+9.00
July	0-3	0.0	-3.00
August	0-2	0.0	-2.00
September	0-2	0.0	-2.00
October	0-2	0.0	-2.00
November	2-7	28.6	+0.75
December	4-6	66.7	+17.00
January	0-3	0.0	-3.00
February	0-4	0.0	-4.00
March	0-5	0.0	-5.00
April	0-5	0.0	-5.00

Totals	W-R	Per cent	£1 Level Stake
May	2-18	11.1	+2.00
June	2-12	16.7	+5.00
July	0-11	0.0	-11.00
August	1-9	11.1	-6.13
September	2-8	25.0	+1.25
October	2-15	13.3	+6.00
November	2-25	8.0	-17.25
December	5-16	31.3	+14.00
January	5-24	20.8	+11.50
February	2-17	11.8	-8.47
March	3-27	11.1	-13.50
April	6-26	23.1	+14.70

DISTANCE

Hurdles	W-R	Per cent	£1 Level Stake
2m-2m3f	10-66	15.2	+12.66
2m4f-2m7f	5-41	12.2	-17.13
3m+	1-6	16.7	-3.75

Chases	W-R	Per cent	£1 Level Stake
2m-2m3f	2-13	15.4	-2.00
2m4f-2m7f	2-15	13.3	-1.25
3m+	0-4	0.0	-4.00

TYPE OF RACE

Non-Handicaps	W-R	Per cent	£1 Level Stake
Nov Hrdls	3-19	15.8	-7.93
Hrdls	2-27	7.4	-22.84
Nov Chs	0-0	0.0	0.00
Chases	0-0	0.0	0.00
Sell/Claim	0-1	0.0	-1.00

Handicaps	W-R	Per cent	£1 Level Stake
Nov Hrdls	2-22	9.1	+1.88
Hrdls	15-75	20.0	+19.25
Nov Chs	4-14	28.6	+14.50
Chases	3-29	10.3	-15.75
Sell/Claim	0-2	0.0	-2.00

RACE CLASS

	W-R	Per cent	£1 Level Stake
Class 1	0-9	0.0	-9.00
Class 2	1-5	20.0	+8.00
Class 3	4-44	9.1	-13.75
Class 4	19-87	21.8	+5.10
Class 5	5-49	10.2	-9.25
Class 6	3-14	21.4	+17.00

FIRST TIME OUT

	W-R	Per cent	£1 Level Stake
Bumpers	1-10	10.0	+16.00
Hurdles	0-22	0.0	-22.00
Chases	0-2	0.0	-2.00
Totals	1-34	2.9	-8.00

JOCKEYS

	W-R	Per cent	£1 Level Stake
Aidan Coleman	6-41	14.6	-13.25
Noel Fehily	5-31	16.1	+13.07
Shane Quinlan	4-18	22.2	+10.88
A P McCoy	3-4	75.0	+8.13
Sam Twiston-Davies	3-16	18.8	+7.00
Kieron Edgar	2-3	66.7	+9.50
Gavin Sheehan	2-25	8.0	-16.00
Jake Hodson	1-3	33.3	+3.00
Brian Harding	1-3	33.3	-0.25
Trevor Whelan	1-4	25.0	+3.00
Leighton Aspell	1-4	25.0	+1.50
Dougie Costello	1-4	25.0	+17.00
Jamie Bargary	1-6	16.7	-1.00
Brian Hughes	1-10	10.0	-8.47

COURSE RECORD

	Total W-R	Non-Hndcps Hurdles	Non-Hndcps Chases	Hndcps Hurdles	Hndcps Chases	NH Flat	Per cent	£1 Level Stake
Huntingdon	5-13	1-3	0-0	2-6	2-3	0-1	38.5	+15.63
Fontwell	3-8	0-0	0-0	3-5	0-2	0-1	37.5	+6.88
Ludlow	3-13	2-6	0-0	1-4	0-3	0-0	23.1	+1.57
Taunton	3-15	0-2	0-0	2-9	1-3	0-1	20.0	-2.00
Mrket Rsn	2-6	0-0	0-0	1-3	0-2	1-1	33.3	-0.25
Stratford	2-14	0-3	0-0	2-8	0-3	0-0	14.3	+6.00
Uttoxeter	2-14	1-4	0-0	0-6	1-1	0-3	14.3	-5.00
Newcastle	1-1	1-1	0-0	0-0	0-0	0-0	100.0	+0.53
Musselbgh	1-2	0-1	0-0	0-0	1-1	0-0	50.0	+3.00
Cheltenham	1-4	0-0	0-0	1-4	0-0	0-0	25.0	+13.00
Fakenham	1-4	0-1	0-0	1-3	0-0	0-0	25.0	0.00
Plumpton	1-5	0-0	0-0	1-3	0-1	0-1	20.0	+16.00
Ffos Las	1-5	0-0	0-0	0-2	1-3	0-0	20.0	+6.00
Bangor	1-6	0-0	0-0	0-4	0-1	1-1	16.7	-4.50
Wetherby	1-6	0-2	0-0	0-1	1-3	0-0	16.7	-3.25
Chepstow	1-9	0-1	0-0	0-3	0-2	1-3	11.1	+17.00
Doncaster	1-9	0-4	0-0	1-4	0-0	0-1	11.1	-6.75
Nton Abbot	1-9	0-2	0-0	1-7	0-0	0-0	11.1	-4.00
Worcester	1-20	0-6	0-0	1-10	0-3	0-1	5.0	-16.75

WINNING HORSES

Horse	Races Run	1st	2nd	3rd	£
Roman Flight	12	3	0	1	28363
Marju's Quest	13	4	2	4	15010
Un Anjou	12	2	2	3	9097
*Lucky Jim	5	1	1	1	4874
Ballybough Andy	4	1	0	0	4549
Steel Summit	18	6	0	4	11853
Set The Trend	4	2	0	1	7798
Maller Tree	13	2	0	3	7148
Key To The West	9	1	0	1	3899

Doctor Phoenix	6	2	1	2	3899
*Norse Light	7	1	0	1	3899
Cyclop	8	1	0	2	3249
*Anginola	7	1	0	0	2599
Nether Stream	11	2	0	3	3899
Final Nudge	5	1	1	0	1949
Wade Harper	2	1	1	0	1643
Silent Alliance	1	1	0	0	1560
Total winning prize-money					**£115288**
Favourites	**8-110**		**7.3%**		**-91.27**

ROBIN DICKIN

ALCESTER, WARWICKS

	No. of Hrs	Races Run	1st	2nd	3rd	Unpl	Per cent	£1 Level Stake
NH Flat	*12*	*22*	*0*	*1*	*4*	*17*	*0.0*	*-22.00*
Hurdles	*21*	*61*	*4*	*2*	*4*	*51*	*6.6*	*+46.00*
Chases	*13*	*51*	*3*	*11*	*7*	*30*	*5.9*	*-40.00*
Totals	**36**	**134**	**7**	**14**	**15**	**98**	**5.2**	**-16.00**
13-14	*35*	*139*	*10*	*14*	*12*	*103*	*7.2*	*-43.50*
12-13	*36*	*110*	*13*	*5*	*9*	*83*	*11.8*	*-9.30*

JOCKEYS

	W-R	Per cent	£1 Level Stake
Joseph Palmowski	3-41	7.3	+0.50
Charlie Poste	2-74	2.7	-67.50
Miss Francesca Nimmo	1-1	100.0	+18.00
Mr T W Wheeler	1-11	9.1	+40.00

COURSE RECORD

	Total W-R	Non-Hndcps Hurdles	Non-Hndcps Chases	Hndcps Hurdles	Hndcps Chases	NH Flat	Per cent	£1 Level Stake
Towcester	2-14	0-6	1-1	0-0	1-2	0-5	14.3	-7.50
Huntingdon	1-1	0-0	0-0	1-1	0-0	0-0	100.0	+18.00
Worcester	1-6	0-1	0-0	0-0	1-4	0-1	16.7	-1.50
Warwick	1-10	1-6	0-1	0-1	0-1	0-1	10.0	+41.00
Kempton	1-13	0-3	0-1	1-3	0-3	0-3	7.7	-2.00
Ludlow	1-19	1-6	0-0	0-6	0-1	0-6	5.3	+7.00

WINNING HORSES

Horse	Races Run	1st	2nd	3rd	£
Garrahalish	7	2	1	1	10426
Queen Of The Stage	4	1	0	0	3899
Under The Phone	9	1	1	1	3249
Be My Witness	7	1	0	1	3249
Bally Lagan	4	1	2	0	2599
Galactic Power	7	1	0	0	2395
Total winning prize-money					**£25817**
Favourites	**1-11**		**9.1%**		**-6.50**

JOHN DIXON

THURSBY, CUMBRIA

	No. of Hrs	Races Run	1st	2nd	3rd	Unpl	Per cent	£1 Level Stake
NH Flat	*1*	*1*	*0*	*0*	*0*	*1*	*0.0*	*-1.00*
Hurdles	*2*	*13*	*1*	*3*	*1*	*8*	*7.7*	*-9.75*
Chases	*0*	*0*	*0*	*0*	*0*	*0*	*0.0*	*0.00*
Totals	**3**	**14**	**1**	**3**	**1**	**9**	**7.1**	**-10.75**
13-14	*3*	*12*	*2*	*1*	*1*	*8*	*16.7*	*+12.00*
12-13	*3*	*12*	*0*	*0*	*0*	*12*	*0.0*	*-12.00*

JOCKEYS

	W-R	Per cent	£1 Level Stake
Mr J Dixon	1-14	7.1	-10.75

COURSE RECORD

	Total W-R	Non-Hndcps Hurdles	Non-Hndcps Chases	Hndcps Hurdles	Hndcps Chases	NH Flat	Per cent	£1 Level Stake
Ayr	1-3	0-0	0-0	1-3	0-0	0-0	33.3	+0.25

WINNING HORSES

Horse	Races Run	1st	2nd	3rd	£
Circus Star	5	1	1	1	5848
Total winning prize-money					**£5848**
Favourites	**1-1**		**100.0%**		**2.25**

ROSE DOBBIN

SOUTH HAZELRIGG, NORTHUMBRIA

	No. of Hrs	Races Run	1st	2nd	3rd	Unpl	Per cent	£1 Level Stake
NH Flat	*9*	*13*	*3*	*0*	*1*	*9*	*23.1*	*+15.75*
Hurdles	*24*	*94*	*3*	*7*	*10*	*74*	*3.2*	*-66.75*
Chases	*12*	*62*	*10*	*11*	*13*	*28*	*16.1*	*-10.88*
Totals	**36**	**169**	**16**	**18**	**24**	**111**	**9.5**	**-61.88**
13-14	*34*	*145*	*15*	*10*	*14*	*106*	*10.3*	*+34.75*
12-13	*26*	*102*	*8*	*9*	*10*	*75*	*7.8*	*-28.25*

BY MONTH

NH Flat	W-R	Per cent	£1 Level Stake	**Hurdles**	W-R	Per cent	£1 Level Stake
May	1-3	33.3	+0.75	May	0-7	0.0	-7.00
June	0-0	0.0	0.00	June	1-3	33.3	+3.50
July	0-0	0.0	0.00	July	1-3	33.3	+0.75
August	0-0	0.0	0.00	August	0-0	0.0	0.00
September	0-0	0.0	0.00	September	0-3	0.0	-3.00
October	1-4	25.0	+17.00	October	1-10	10.0	+7.00
November	0-1	0.0	-1.00	November	0-10	0.0	-10.00
December	1-1	100.0	+3.00	December	0-9	0.0	-9.00
January	0-0	0.0	0.00	January	0-10	0.0	-10.00
February	0-2	0.0	-2.00	February	0-11	0.0	-11.00

	W-R	Per cent	£1 Level Stake
March	0-1	0.0	-1.00
April	0-1	0.0	-1.00

Chases	W-R	Per cent	£1 Level Stake
May	3-8	37.5	+8.50
June	0-5	0.0	-5.00
July	2-6	33.3	+0.88
August	0-0	0.0	0.00
September	2-5	40.0	+1.75
October	1-9	11.1	-4.00
November	1-9	11.1	+1.00
December	0-3	0.0	-3.00
January	1-6	16.7	0.00
February	0-1	0.0	-1.00
March	0-5	0.0	-5.00
April	0-5	0.0	-5.00

	W-R	Per cent	£1 Level Stake
March	0-15	0.0	-15.00
April	0-13	0.0	-13.00

Totals	W-R	Per cent	£1 Level Stake
May	4-18	22.2	+2.25
June	1-8	12.5	-1.50
July	3-9	33.3	+1.63
August	0-0	0.0	0.00
September	2-8	25.0	-1.25
October	3-23	13.0	+20.00
November	1-20	5.0	-10.00
December	1-13	7.7	-9.00
January	1-16	6.3	-10.00
February	0-14	0.0	-14.00
March	0-21	0.0	-21.00
April	0-19	0.0	-19.00

DISTANCE

Hurdles	W-R	Per cent	£1 Level Stake
2m-2m3f	2-53	3.8	-42.75
2m4f-2m7f	1-18	5.6	-1.00
3m+	0-11	0.0	-11.00

Chases	W-R	Per cent	£1 Level Stake
2m-2m3f	4-17	23.5	-2.88
2m4f-2m7f	2-20	10.0	-10.00
3m+	1-13	7.7	-7.00

TYPE OF RACE

Non-Handicaps

	W-R	Per cent	£1 Level Stake
Nov Hrdls	0-23	0.0	-23.00
Hrdls	0-5	0.0	-5.00
Nov Chs	0-0	0.0	0.00
Chases	0-1	0.0	-1.00
Sell/Claim	0-0	0.0	0.00

Handicaps

	W-R	Per cent	£1 Level Stake
Nov Hrdls	2-9	22.2	+1.25
Hrdls	1-57	1.8	-40.00
Nov Chs	6-19	31.6	+7.25
Chases	4-42	9.5	-17.13
Sell/Claim	0-0	0.0	0.00

RACE CLASS

	W-R	Per cent	£1 Level Stake
Class 1	0-0	0.0	0.00
Class 2	0-1	0.0	-1.00
Class 3	2-12	16.7	-1.00
Class 4	8-93	8.6	-52.13
Class 5	4-52	7.7	-21.75
Class 6	2-11	18.2	+14.00

FIRST TIME OUT

	W-R	Per cent	£1 Level Stake
Bumpers	2-9	22.2	+15.75
Hurdles	0-17	0.0	-17.00
Chases	3-10	30.0	+6.50
Totals	5-36	13.9	+5.25

JOCKEYS

	W-R	Per cent	£1 Level Stake
Wilson Renwick	7-48	14.6	+3.00
Craig Nichol	6-66	9.1	-43.88
Phil Dennis	1-3	33.3	+14.00
Harry Challoner	1-5	20.0	+5.00
Graham Watters	1-13	7.7	-6.00

COURSE RECORD

	Total W-R	Non-Hndcps Hurdles	Non-Hndcps Chases	Hndcps Hurdles	Hndcps Chases	NH Flat	Per cent	£1 Level Stake
Perth	4-19	0-0	0-0	1-9	3-9	0-1	21.1	-4.63
Musselbgh	3-16	0-1	0-0	0-7	2-6	1-2	18.8	+4.00
Kelso	3-29	0-8	0-0	1-12	1-6	1-3	10.3	-4.75
Carlisle	2-15	0-3	0-0	0-5	2-5	0-2	13.3	-3.00
Sedgefield	2-20	0-3	0-1	0-7	1-8	1-1	10.0	+4.00
Cartmel	1-2	0-0	0-0	0-0	1-2	0-0	50.0	+4.00
Uttoxeter	1-4	0-0	0-0	1-2	0-2	0-0	25.0	+2.50

WINNING HORSES

Horse	Races Run	1st	2nd	3rd	£
Jurisdiction	2	1	0	0	9097
Robin's Command	10	5	2	0	23925
Purcell's Bridge	9	2	2	3	10267
Shady Sadie	7	1	2	1	3899
Another Dimension	8	1	0	2	3249
Politeness	6	2	1	1	5588
Everylasting	8	1	1	3	2729
Doktor Glaz	6	1	0	2	2599
Professor Plum	4	2	1	0	3509
Total winning prize-money					**£64862**
Favourites	**3-16**		**18.8%**		**-5.75**

DES DONOVAN

NEWMARKET, SUFFOLK

	No. of Hrs	Races Run	1st	2nd	3rd	Unpl	Per cent	£1 Level Stake
NH Flat	*1*	*2*	*0*	*0*	*0*	*2*	*0.0*	*-2.00*
Hurdles	*2*	*8*	*1*	*0*	*2*	*5*	*12.5*	*+3.00*
Chases	*0*	*0*	*0*	*0*	*0*	*0*	*0.0*	*0.00*
Totals	**3**	**10**	**1**	**0**	**2**	**7**	**10.0**	**+1.00**
13-14	*2*	*5*	*0*	*1*	*1*	*3*	*0.0*	*-5.00*

JOCKEYS

	W-R	Per cent	£1 Level Stake
Trevor Whelan	1-5	20.0	+6.00

COURSE RECORD

	Total W-R	Non-Hndcps Hurdles	Non-Hndcps Chases	Hndcps Hurdles	Hndcps Chases	NH Flat	Per cent	£1 Level Stake
Southwell	1-3	1-1	0-0	0-1	0-0	0-1	33.3	+8.00

WINNING HORSES

Horse	Races Run	1st	2nd	3rd	£
Recway Lass	6	1	0	2	1949
Total winning prize-money					**£1949**
Favourites	**0-0**		**0.0%**		**0.00**

CONOR DORE

HUBBERT'S BRIDGE, LINCS

	No. of Hrs	Races Run	1st	2nd	3rd	Unpl	Per cent	£1 Level Stake
NH Flat	0	0	0	0	0	0	0.0	0.00
Hurdles	6	26	2	5	3	16	7.7	-1.50
Chases	1	8	1	0	0	7	12.5	-4.25
Totals	**6**	**34**	**3**	**5**	**3**	**23**	**8.8**	**-5.75**
13-14	*4*	*30*	*1*	*4*	*9*	*16*	*3.3*	*-20.00*

JOCKEYS

	W-R	Per cent	£1 Level Stake
Peter Carberry	2-21	9.5	-0.25
Tom O'Brien	1-3	33.3	+4.50

COURSE RECORD

	Total W-R	Non-Hndcps Hurdles	Non-Hndcps Chases	Hndcps Hurdles	Hndcps Chases	NH Flat	Per cent	£1 Level Stake
Fontwell	1-1	0-0	0-0	0-0	1-1	0-0	100.0	+2.75
Towcester	1-2	1-1	0-0	0-1	0-0	0-0	50.0	+15.00
Mrket Rsn	1-3	0-1	0-0	1-2	0-0	0-0	33.3	+4.50

WINNING HORSES

Horse	Races Run	1st	2nd	3rd	£
A Little Bit Dusty	9	1	3	1	3249
Yasir	9	1	2	1	2599
Johnnys Legacy	9	1	0	0	2144
Total winning prize-money					**£7992**
Favourites	**0-2**		**0.0%**		**-2.00**

CHRIS DOWN

MUTTERTON, DEVON

	No. of Hrs	Races Run	1st	2nd	3rd	Unpl	Per cent	£1 Level Stake
NH Flat	6	9	0	0	1	8	0.0	-9.00
Hurdles	21	108	12	13	17	66	11.1	+36.00
Chases	5	13	0	1	1	11	0.0	-13.00
Totals	**28**	**130**	**12**	**14**	**19**	**85**	**9.2**	**+14.00**
13-14	*27*	*119*	*7*	*10*	*14*	*87*	*5.9*	*-61.50*
12-13	*25*	*91*	*9*	*5*	*13*	*64*	*9.9*	*+61.88*

BY MONTH

NH Flat	W-R	Per cent	£1 Level Stake
May	0-1	0.0	-1.00
June	0-2	0.0	-2.00
July	0-1	0.0	-1.00
August	0-0	0.0	0.00
September	0-0	0.0	0.00
October	0-1	0.0	-1.00
November	0-1	0.0	-1.00
December	0-0	0.0	0.00
January	0-0	0.0	0.00
February	0-1	0.0	-1.00
March	0-0	0.0	0.00
April	0-2	0.0	-2.00

Hurdles	W-R	Per cent	£1 Level Stake
May	3-11	27.3	+7.00
June	0-4	0.0	-4.00
July	0-4	0.0	-4.00
August	1-1	100.0	+2.50
September	0-3	0.0	-3.00
October	0-7	0.0	-7.00
November	1-13	7.7	+21.00
December	0-9	0.0	-9.00
January	1-11	9.1	-2.50
February	2-10	20.0	+32.50
March	1-13	7.7	-6.00
April	3-22	13.6	+8.50

Chases	W-R	Per cent	£1 Level Stake
May	0-0	0.0	0.00
June	0-1	0.0	-1.00
July	0-4	0.0	-4.00
August	0-0	0.0	0.00
September	0-1	0.0	-1.00
October	0-2	0.0	-2.00
November	0-1	0.0	-1.00
December	0-1	0.0	-1.00
January	0-1	0.0	-1.00
February	0-1	0.0	-1.00
March	0-1	0.0	-1.00
April	0-0	0.0	0.00

Totals	W-R	Per cent	£1 Level Stake
May	3-12	25.0	+6.00
June	0-7	0.0	-7.00
July	0-9	0.0	-9.00
August	1-1	100.0	+2.50
September	0-4	0.0	-4.00
October	0-10	0.0	-10.00
November	1-15	6.7	+19.00
December	0-10	0.0	-10.00
January	1-12	8.3	-3.50
February	2-12	16.7	+30.50
March	1-14	7.1	-7.00
April	3-24	12.5	+6.50

DISTANCE

Hurdles	W-R	Per cent	£1 Level Stake
2m-2m3f	7-60	11.7	+53.00
2m4f-2m7f	3-31	9.7	-11.50
3m+	0-3	0.0	-3.00

Chases	W-R	Per cent	£1 Level Stake
2m-2m3f	0-5	0.0	-5.00
2m4f-2m7f	0-7	0.0	-7.00
3m+	0-1	0.0	-1.00

TYPE OF RACE

Non-Handicaps	W-R	Per cent	£1 Level Stake
Nov Hrdls	0-8	0.0	-8.00
Hrdls	0-9	0.0	-9.00
Nov Chs	0-5	0.0	-5.00
Chases	0-0	0.0	0.00
Sell/Claim	0-1	0.0	-1.00

Handicaps	W-R	Per cent	£1 Level Stake
Nov Hrdls	1-13	7.7	-2.00
Hrdls	10-76	13.2	+52.00
Nov Chs	0-3	0.0	-3.00
Chases	0-5	0.0	-5.00
Sell/Claim	1-2	50.0	+3.00

RACE CLASS

	W-R	Per cent	£1 Level Stake
Class 1	0-4	0.0	-4.00
Class 2	0-2	0.0	-2.00
Class 3	2-16	12.5	-1.50
Class 4	3-55	5.5	-32.50
Class 5	7-45	15.6	+62.00
Class 6	0-8	0.0	-8.00

FIRST TIME OUT

	W-R	Per cent	£1 Level Stake
Bumpers	0-6	0.0	-6.00
Hurdles	4-20	20.0	+32.00
Chases	0-2	0.0	-2.00
Totals	4-28	14.3	+24.00

JOCKEYS

	W-R	Per cent	£1 Level Stake
James Davies	6-72	8.3	+36.00
Conor Shoemark	1-1	100.0	+3.50
Wayne Hutchinson	1-1	100.0	+7.50
Mr Charlie Deutsch	1-1	100.0	+4.00
Tom Scudamore	1-3	33.3	+3.00

Ciaran Gethings	1-11	9.1	-2.50
Giles Hawkins	1-18	5.6	-14.50

COURSE RECORD

	Total W-R	Non-Hndcps Hurdles	Non-Hndcps Chases	Hndcps Hurdles	Hndcps Chases	NH Flat	Per cent	£1 Level Stake
Taunton	4-21	0-1	0-0	4-19	0-0	0-1	19.0	+43.50
Nton Abbot	3-25	0-4	0-1	3-16	0-2	0-2	12.0	-5.50
Wincanton	2-11	0-2	0-1	2-8	0-0	0-0	18.2	+0.50
Exeter	2-28	0-7	0-2	2-17	0-1	0-1	7.1	-13.50
Chepstow	1-8	0-0	0-0	1-8	0-0	0-0	12.5	+26.00

WINNING HORSES

Horse	Races Run	1st	2nd	3rd	£
Dragon's Den	9	2	1	1	10917
*Ice Tres	8	1	1	0	3899
Frozen Over	7	2	0	1	6823
Lily Potts	3	1	0	0	2924
Thedeboftheyear	3	1	0	0	2738
Key To Milan	7	1	1	1	2738
Aroseforoscar	9	1	0	2	2599
Hot Pepper	4	1	0	0	2274
Nothing Is Forever	3	1	0	0	1949
Sunshine Buddy	7	1	0	3	1949
Total winning prize-money					**£38810**
Favourites	**0-2**		**0.0%**		**-2.00**

RICHARD DRAKE

ILKLEY, W YORKS

	No. of Hrs	Races Run	1st	2nd	3rd	Unpl	Per cent	£1 Level Stake
NH Flat	*1*	*1*	*0*	*1*	*0*	*0*	*0.0*	*-1.00*
Hurdles	*4*	*14*	*2*	*3*	*0*	*9*	*14.3*	*0.00*
Chases	*4*	*10*	*0*	*0*	*1*	*9*	*0.0*	*-10.00*
Totals	**7**	**25**	**2**	**4**	**1**	**18**	**8.0**	**-11.00**
13-14	*5*	*23*	*1*	*0*	*1*	*21*	*4.3*	*-15.00*

JOCKEYS

	W-R	Per cent	£1 Level Stake
Jonathan England	2-10	20.0	+4.00

COURSE RECORD

	Total W-R	Non-Hndcps Hurdles	Non-Hndcps Chases	Hndcps Hurdles	Hndcps Chases	NH Flat	Per cent	£1 Level Stake
Mrket Rsn	2-5	0-2	0-0	2-3	0-0	0-0	40.0	+9.00

WINNING HORSES

Horse	Races Run	1st	2nd	3rd	£
Raktiman	6	2	3	0	9292
Total winning prize-money					**£9292**
Favourites	**0-0**		**0.0%**		**0.00**

MRS C DRURY

SHERIFF HUTTON, N YORKS

	No. of Hrs	Races Run	1st	2nd	3rd	Unpl	Per cent	£1 Level Stake
NH Flat	*0*	*0*	*0*	*0*	*0*	*0*	*0.0*	*0.00*
Hurdles	*0*	*0*	*0*	*0*	*0*	*0*	*0.0*	*0.00*
Chases	*2*	*6*	*1*	*3*	*1*	*1*	*16.7*	*+11.00*
Totals	**2**	**6**	**1**	**3**	**1**	**1**	**16.7**	**+11.00**
13-14	*1*	*2*	*1*	*0*	*0*	*1*	*50.0*	*+3.50*
12-13	*1*	*1*	*0*	*1*	*0*	*0*	*0.0*	*-1.00*

JOCKEYS

	W-R	Per cent	£1 Level Stake
Miss E Todd	1-4	25.0	+13.00

COURSE RECORD

	Total W-R	Non-Hndcps Hurdles	Non-Hndcps Chases	Hndcps Hurdles	Hndcps Chases	NH Flat	Per cent	£1 Level Stake
Musselbgh	1-1	0-0	1-1	0-0	0-0	0-0	100.0	+16.00

WINNING HORSES

Horse	Races Run	1st	2nd	3rd	£
Drom	3	1	0	1	1872
Total winning prize-money					**£1872**
Favourites	**0-0**		**0.0%**		**0.00**

IAN DUNCAN

COYLTON, AYRSHIRE

	No. of Hrs	Races Run	1st	2nd	3rd	Unpl	Per cent	£1 Level Stake
NH Flat	*3*	*4*	*0*	*0*	*0*	*4*	*0.0*	*-4.00*
Hurdles	*2*	*5*	*1*	*0*	*1*	*3*	*20.0*	*+29.00*
Chases	*5*	*16*	*3*	*0*	*2*	*11*	*18.8*	*+11.00*
Totals	**9**	**25**	**4**	**0**	**3**	**18**	**16.0**	**+36.00**
13-14	*6*	*26*	*2*	*1*	*4*	*19*	*7.7*	*-14.17*
12-13	*6*	*19*	*2*	*4*	*1*	*12*	*10.5*	*-4.75*

JOCKEYS

	W-R	Per cent	£1 Level Stake
Graham Watters	4-19	21.1	+42.00

COURSE RECORD

	Total W-R	Non-Hndcps Hurdles	Non-Hndcps Chases	Hndcps Hurdles	Hndcps Chases	NH Flat	Per cent	£1 Level Stake
Newcastle	1-1	0-0	0-0	0-0	1-1	0-0	100.0	+18.00
Bangor	1-2	0-0	0-0	0-0	1-1	0-1	50.0	+1.50
Carlisle	1-3	0-0	0-1	0-0	1-2	0-0	33.3	+1.50
Ayr	1-11	1-3	0-1	0-2	0-3	0-2	9.1	+23.00

WINNING HORSES

Horse	Races Run	1st	2nd	3rd	£
Milborough	5	2	0	0	51590
Golden Sparkle	3	1	0	1	3994
Spring Over	4	1	0	1	2530
Total winning prize-money					**£58114**
Favourites	**0-2**		**0.0%**		**-2.00**

ALEXANDRA DUNN

WEST BUCKLAND, SOMERSET

	No. of Hrs	Races Run	1st	2nd	3rd	Unpl	Per cent	£1 Level Stake
NH Flat	*5*	*5*	*0*	*0*	*0*	*5*	*0.0*	*-5.00*
Hurdles	*30*	*95*	*5*	*7*	*9*	*74*	*5.3*	*-44.75*
Chases	*14*	*38*	*6*	*3*	*2*	*27*	*15.8*	*+35.00*
Totals	**39**	**138**	**11**	**10**	**11**	**106**	**8.0**	**-14.75**
13-14	*19*	*58*	*6*	*5*	*7*	*40*	*10.3*	*-24.36*
12-13	*7*	*17*	*4*	*2*	*2*	*9*	*23.5*	*+2.33*

BY MONTH

NH Flat	W-R	Per cent	£1 Level Stake	Hurdles	W-R	Per cent	£1 Level Stake
May	0-0	0.0	0.00	May	0-7	0.0	-7.00
June	0-0	0.0	0.00	June	0-5	0.0	-5.00
July	0-2	0.0	-2.00	July	0-3	0.0	-3.00
August	0-0	0.0	0.00	August	0-6	0.0	-6.00
September	0-0	0.0	0.00	September	0-6	0.0	-6.00
October	0-1	0.0	-1.00	October	0-5	0.0	-5.00
November	0-0	0.0	0.00	November	2-14	14.3	-5.75
December	0-0	0.0	0.00	December	1-12	8.3	-1.00
January	0-0	0.0	0.00	January	1-6	16.7	-1.00
February	0-0	0.0	0.00	February	0-7	0.0	-7.00
March	0-1	0.0	-1.00	March	1-19	5.3	+7.00
April	0-1	0.0	-1.00	April	0-5	0.0	-5.00

Chases	W-R	Per cent	£1 Level Stake	Totals	W-R	Per cent	£1 Level Stake
May	1-8	12.5	-4.00	May	1-15	6.7	-11.00
June	0-3	0.0	-3.00	June	0-8	0.0	-8.00
July	1-1	100.0	+33.00	July	1-6	16.7	+28.00
August	2-4	50.0	+8.00	August	2-10	20.0	+2.00
September	0-2	0.0	-2.00	September	0-8	0.0	-8.00
October	1-6	16.7	0.00	October	1-12	8.3	-6.00
November	0-2	0.0	-2.00	November	2-16	12.5	-7.75
December	0-3	0.0	-3.00	December	1-15	6.7	-4.00
January	1-1	100.0	+16.00	January	2-7	28.6	+15.00
February	0-3	0.0	-3.00	February	0-10	0.0	-10.00
March	0-4	0.0	-4.00	March	1-24	4.2	+2.00
April	0-1	0.0	-1.00	April	0-7	0.0	-7.00

DISTANCE

Hurdles	W-R	Per cent	£1 Level Stake	Chases	W-R	Per cent	£1 Level Stake
2m-2m3f	4-62	6.5	-37.75	2m-2m3f	4-14	28.6	+21.00
2m4f-2m7f	1-17	5.9	+9.00	2m4f-2m7f	0-10	0.0	-10.00
3m+	0-2	0.0	-2.00	3m+	2-9	22.2	+29.00

TYPE OF RACE

Non-Handicaps	W-R	Per cent	£1 Level Stake	Handicaps	W-R	Per cent	£1 Level Stake
Nov Hrdls	0-13	0.0	-13.00	Nov Hrdls	1-10	10.0	+16.00
Hrdls	0-16	0.0	-16.00	Hrdls	4-49	8.2	-24.75
Nov Chs	0-2	0.0	-2.00	Nov Chs	0-6	0.0	-6.00
Chases	1-2	50.0	+2.00	Chases	5-28	17.9	+41.00
Sell/Claim	0-4	0.0	-4.00	Sell/Claim	0-3	0.0	-3.00

RACE CLASS / FIRST TIME OUT

RACE CLASS	W-R	Per cent	£1 Level Stake	FIRST TIME OUT	W-R	Per cent	£1 Level Stake
Class 1	0-1	0.0	-1.00	Bumpers	0-5	0.0	-5.00
Class 2	0-3	0.0	-3.00	Hurdles	1-25	4.0	-21.75
Class 3	3-22	13.6	+23.50	Chases	2-9	22.2	+29.00
Class 4	4-62	6.5	-9.25				
Class 5	3-44	6.8	-23.00	Totals	3-39	7.7	+2.25
Class 6	1-6	16.7	-2.00				

JOCKEYS

	W-R	Per cent	£1 Level Stake
Mrs Alex Dunn	4-27	14.8	-9.75
Adam Wedge	4-30	13.3	-1.00
Conor O'Farrell	2-10	20.0	+33.00
Ian Popham	1-4	25.0	+30.00

COURSE RECORD

	Total W-R	Non-Hndcps Hurdles	Non-Hndcps Chases	Hndcps Hurdles	Hndcps Chases	NH Flat	Per cent	£1 Level Stake
Fontwell	2-4	0-0	1-1	1-3	0-0	0-0	50.0	+5.00
Taunton	2-24	0-7	0-0	2-14	0-2	0-1	8.3	-9.75
Wetherby	1-2	0-0	0-0	0-1	1-1	0-0	50.0	+4.00
Bangor	1-3	0-0	0-0	0-0	1-3	0-0	33.3	+3.50
Fakenham	1-3	0-0	0-0	1-3	0-0	0-0	33.3	+2.00
Chepstow	1-7	0-1	0-0	0-4	1-2	0-0	14.3	+10.00
Exeter	1-11	0-2	0-2	1-5	0-1	0-1	9.1	+15.00
Stratford	1-11	0-6	0-0	0-1	1-3	0-1	9.1	-5.50
Nton Abbot	1-14	0-4	0-0	0-8	1-2	0-0	7.1	+20.00

WINNING HORSES

Horse	Races Run	1st	2nd	3rd	£
Prince Tom	4	1	1	0	6963
Nikos Extra	8	3	1	0	17241
Come On Annie	4	2	0	0	7993
Black Narcissus	7	1	0	1	3249
Zero Visibility	11	2	1	2	4874
Worldor	13	1	0	0	2274
*Double Mead	1	1	0	0	936
Total winning prize-money					**£43530**
Favourites	**0-1**		**0.0%**		**-1.00**

DAVID DUNSDON

SHERE, SURREY

	No. of Hrs	Races Run	1st	2nd	3rd	Unpl	Per cent	£1 Level Stake
NH Flat	*0*	*0*	*0*	*0*	*0*	*0*	*0.0*	*0.00*
Hurdles	*0*	*0*	*0*	*0*	*0*	*0*	*0.0*	*0.00*
Chases	*1*	*2*	*2*	*0*	*0*	*0*	*100.0*	*+3.75*
Totals	**1**	**2**	**2**	**0**	**0**	**0**	**100.0**	**+3.75**
13-14	*1*	*1*	*1*	*0*	*0*	*0*	*100.0*	*+3.50*

JOCKEYS

	W-R	Per cent	£1 Level Stake
Mr D H Dunsdon	2-2	100.0	+3.75

COURSE RECORD

	Total W-R	Non-Hndcps Hurdles	Non-Hndcps Chases	Hndcps Hurdles	Hndcps Chases	NH Flat	Per cent	£1 Level Stake
Fontwell	1-1	0-0	1-1	0-0	0-0	0-0	100.0	+2.00
Stratford	1-1	0-0	1-1	0-0	0-0	0-0	100.0	+1.75

WINNING HORSES

Horse	Races Run	1st	2nd	3rd	£
Utopian	2	2	0	0	3120
Total winning prize-money					**£3120**
Favourites	**1-1**		**100.0%**		**1.75**

SEAMUS DURACK

UPPER LAMBOURN, BERKSHIRE

	No. of Hrs	Races Run	1st	2nd	3rd	Unpl	Per cent	£1 Level Stake
NH Flat	*2*	*5*	*1*	*1*	*1*	*2*	*20.0*	*+12.00*
Hurdles	*2*	*3*	*1*	*0*	*0*	*2*	*33.3*	*-0.75*
Chases	*1*	*1*	*0*	*0*	*0*	*1*	*0.0*	*-1.00*
Totals	**5**	**9**	**2**	**1**	**1**	**5**	**22.2**	**+10.25**
13-14	*12*	*35*	*0*	*4*	*9*	*22*	*0.0*	*-35.00*
12-13	*12*	*35*	*5*	*0*	*4*	*26*	*14.3*	*+2.25*

JOCKEYS

	W-R	Per cent	£1 Level Stake
Conor O'Farrell	2-7	28.6	+12.25

COURSE RECORD

	Total W-R	Non-Hndcps Hurdles	Non-Hndcps Chases	Hndcps Hurdles	Hndcps Chases	NH Flat	Per cent	£1 Level Stake
Nton Abbot	1-1	1-1	0-0	0-0	0-0	0-0	100.0	+1.25
Worcester	1-3	0-0	0-0	0-1	0-0	1-2	33.3	+14.00

WINNING HORSES

Horse	Races Run	1st	2nd	3rd	£
Bohemian Rhapsody	2	1	0	0	2738
Paolozzi	3	1	1	1	1560
Total winning prize-money					**£4298**
Favourites	**1-1**		**100.0%**		**1.25**

CLAIRE DYSON

CLEEVE PRIOR, WORCS

	No. of Hrs	Races Run	1st	2nd	3rd	Unpl	Per cent	£1 Level Stake
NH Flat	*4*	*5*	*0*	*0*	*1*	*4*	*0.0*	*-5.00*
Hurdles	*16*	*68*	*1*	*4*	*12*	*51*	*1.5*	*-62.00*
Chases	*10*	*41*	*1*	*8*	*4*	*28*	*2.4*	*-20.00*
Totals	**26**	**114**	**2**	**12**	**17**	**83**	**1.8**	**-87.00**
13-14	*27*	*144*	*9*	*5*	*10*	*120*	*6.3*	*-60.50*
12-13	*27*	*118*	*13*	*9*	*12*	*84*	*11.0*	*+4.63*

JOCKEYS

	W-R	Per cent	£1 Level Stake
Nick Scholfield	1-9	11.1	-3.00
Trevor Whelan	1-53	1.9	-32.00

COURSE RECORD

	Total W-R	Non-Hndcps Hurdles	Non-Hndcps Chases	Hndcps Hurdles	Hndcps Chases	NH Flat	Per cent	£1 Level Stake
Huntingdon	2-12	0-1	0-0	1-7	1-4	0-0	16.7	+15.00

WINNING HORSES

Horse	Races Run	1st	2nd	3rd	£
Giveitachance	6	1	0	3	3249
Forresters Folly	7	1	1	0	2599
Total winning prize-money					**£5848**
Favourites	**0-4**		**0.0%**		**-4.00**

SIMON EARLE

TYTHERINGTON, WILTS

	No. of Hrs	Races Run	1st	2nd	3rd	Unpl	Per cent	£1 Level Stake
NH Flat	*0*	*0*	*0*	*0*	*0*	*0*	*0.0*	*0.00*
Hurdles	*7*	*18*	*0*	*0*	*1*	*17*	*0.0*	*-18.00*
Chases	*1*	*3*	*1*	*0*	*0*	*2*	*33.3*	*+2.00*
Totals	**8**	**21**	**1**	**0**	**1**	**19**	**4.8**	**-16.00**
13-14	*9*	*39*	*4*	*3*	*6*	*26*	*10.3*	*-5.60*
12-13	*8*	*29*	*4*	*3*	*0*	*22*	*13.8*	*+17.75*

JOCKEYS

	W-R	Per cent	£1 Level Stake
Paddy Brennan	1-6	16.7	-1.00

COURSE RECORD

	Total W-R	Non-Hndcps Hurdles	Non-Hndcps Chases	Hndcps Hurdles	Hndcps Chases	NH Flat	Per cent	£1 Level Stake
Exeter	1-3	0-1	0-0	0-1	1-1	0-0	33.3	+2.00

WINNING HORSES

Horse	Races Run	1st	2nd	3rd	£
Headly's Bridge	3	1	0	0	9495
Total winning prize-money					**£9495**
Favourites	**0-0**		**0.0%**		**0.00**

TIM EASTERBY

GREAT HABTON, N YORKS

	No. of Hrs	Races Run	1st	2nd	3rd	Unpl	Per cent	£1 Level Stake
NH Flat	*9*	*16*	*1*	*3*	*3*	*9*	*6.3*	*+5.00*
Hurdles	*22*	*69*	*4*	*10*	*7*	*48*	*5.8*	*+5.88*
Chases	*4*	*13*	*2*	*0*	*2*	*9*	*15.4*	*-0.25*
Totals	**31**	**98**	**7**	**13**	**12**	**66**	**7.1**	**+10.63**
13-14	*24*	*101*	*13*	*17*	*12*	*59*	*12.9*	*-17.40*
12-13	*28*	*99*	*16*	*11*	*12*	*60*	*16.2*	*-4.22*

JOCKEYS

	W-R	Per cent	£1 Level Stake
Brian Harding	2-10	20.0	+2.75
James Reveley	2-21	9.5	+38.00
Tom Scudamore	1-2	50.0	+0.88
Jamie Moore	1-3	33.3	+18.00
Brian Hughes	1-4	25.0	+9.00

COURSE RECORD

	Total W-R	Non-Hndcps Hurdles	Non-Hndcps Chases	Hndcps Hurdles	Hndcps Chases	NH Flat	Per cent	£1 Level Stake
Doncaster	2-6	1-4	0-0	0-0	1-1	0-1	33.3	+48.75
Aintree	1-1	0-0	0-0	1-1	0-0	0-0	100.0	+12.00
Towcester	1-1	0-0	0-0	0-0	0-0	1-1	100.0	+20.00
Cartmel	1-2	0-1	0-0	1-1	0-0	0-0	50.0	+0.88
Kelso	1-3	0-2	0-0	0-0	1-1	0-0	33.3	+6.00
Newcastle	1-6	0-2	0-1	1-2	0-0	0-1	16.7	+2.00

WINNING HORSES

Horse	Races Run	1st	2nd	3rd	£
Hawk High	5	1	1	1	25024
Dark Dune	11	1	2	3	9495
Tiptoeaway	5	2	0	0	11696
Monita Bonita	5	1	0	0	3249
Two B'S	2	1	0	0	3249
Colour Of The Wind	3	1	1	0	1560
Total winning prize-money					**£54273**
Favourites	**1-5**		**20.0%**		**-2.13**

MICHAEL EASTERBY

SHERIFF HUTTON, N YORKS

	No. of Hrs	Races Run	1st	2nd	3rd	Unpl	Per cent	£1 Level Stake
NH Flat	*6*	*11*	*0*	*1*	*1*	*9*	*0.0*	*-11.00*
Hurdles	*17*	*46*	*3*	*4*	*6*	*33*	*6.5*	*-27.75*
Chases	*6*	*21*	*7*	*3*	*3*	*8*	*33.3*	*+23.95*
Totals	**23**	**78**	**10**	**8**	**10**	**50**	**12.8**	**-14.80**
13-14	*25*	*79*	*2*	*4*	*5*	*68*	*2.5*	*-65.00*
12-13	*29*	*92*	*9*	*10*	*8*	*65*	*9.8*	*-17.00*

BY MONTH

NH Flat	W-R	Per cent	£1 Level Stake	Hurdles	W-R	Per cent	£1 Level Stake
May	0-0	0.0	0.00	May	0-4	0.0	-4.00
June	0-0	0.0	0.00	June	0-0	0.0	0.00
July	0-0	0.0	0.00	July	0-0	0.0	0.00
August	0-0	0.0	0.00	August	0-2	0.0	-2.00
September	0-0	0.0	0.00	September	0-5	0.0	-5.00
October	0-0	0.0	0.00	October	1-8	12.5	+1.00
November	0-4	0.0	-4.00	November	0-8	0.0	-8.00
December	0-1	0.0	-1.00	December	1-4	25.0	-0.25
January	0-2	0.0	-2.00	January	1-4	25.0	+1.50
February	0-2	0.0	-2.00	February	0-2	0.0	-2.00
March	0-2	0.0	-2.00	March	0-4	0.0	-4.00
April	0-0	0.0	0.00	April	0-5	0.0	-5.00

Chases	W-R	Per cent	£1 Level Stake	Totals	W-R	Per cent	£1 Level Stake
May	0-1	0.0	-1.00	May	0-5	0.0	-5.00
June	0-0	0.0	0.00	June	0-0	0.0	0.00
July	0-0	0.0	0.00	July	0-0	0.0	0.00
August	0-0	0.0	0.00	August	0-2	0.0	-2.00
September	0-0	0.0	0.00	September	0-5	0.0	-5.00
October	1-1	100.0	+20.00	October	2-9	22.2	+21.00
November	1-2	50.0	+2.00	November	1-14	7.1	-10.00
December	2-3	66.7	+2.95	December	3-8	37.5	+1.70
January	0-2	0.0	-2.00	January	1-8	12.5	-2.50
February	0-3	0.0	-3.00	February	0-7	0.0	-7.00
March	2-5	40.0	+4.00	March	2-11	18.2	-2.00
April	1-4	25.0	+1.00	April	1-9	11.1	-4.00

DISTANCE

Hurdles	W-R	Per cent	£1 Level Stake	Chases	W-R	Per cent	£1 Level Stake
2m-2m3f	2-26	7.7	-13.25	2m-2m3f	2-6	33.3	+1.50
2m4f-2m7f	1-6	16.7	-0.50	2m4f-2m7f	4-11	36.4	+19.95
3m+	0-7	0.0	-7.00	3m+	0-1	0.0	-1.00

TYPE OF RACE

Non-Handicaps

	W-R	Per cent	£1 Level Stake
Nov Hrdls	0-12	0.0	-12.00
Hrdls	0-10	0.0	-10.00
Nov Chs	0-0	0.0	0.00
Chases	0-0	0.0	0.00
Sell/Claim	0-1	0.0	-1.00

Handicaps

	W-R	Per cent	£1 Level Stake
Nov Hrdls	0-3	0.0	-3.00
Hrdls	3-20	15.0	-1.75
Nov Chs	5-8	62.5	+13.45
Chases	2-13	15.4	+10.50
Sell/Claim	0-0	0.0	0.00

RACE CLASS

	W-R	Per cent	£1 Level Stake
Class 1	1-3	33.3	+18.00
Class 2	0-5	0.0	-5.00
Class 3	4-15	26.7	+3.70
Class 4	4-36	11.1	-18.00
Class 5	1-9	11.1	-3.50
Class 6	0-10	0.0	-10.00

FIRST TIME OUT

	W-R	Per cent	£1 Level Stake
Bumpers	0-6	0.0	-6.00
Hurdles	0-14	0.0	-14.00
Chases	1-3	33.3	+1.00
Totals	1-23	4.3	-19.00

JOCKEYS

	W-R	Per cent	£1 Level Stake
Mr H A A Bannister	4-29	13.8	-8.25
Jake Greenall	3-29	10.3	-14.75
Denis O'Regan	1-2	50.0	+3.00
Wilson Renwick	1-3	33.3	-0.80
Brian Harding	1-8	12.5	+13.00

COURSE RECORD

	Total W-R	Non-Hndcps Hurdles	Chases	Hndcps Hurdles	Chases	NH Flat	Per cent	£1 Level Stake
Wetherby	6-17	0-2	0-0	3-8	3-5	0-2	35.3	+28.20
Catterick	2-6	0-1	0-0	0-1	2-3	0-1	33.3	+3.00
Stratford	1-2	0-0	0-0	0-0	1-2	0-0	50.0	+3.00
Doncaster	1-8	0-3	0-0	0-0	1-3	0-2	12.5	-4.00

WINNING HORSES

Horse	Races Run	1st	2nd	3rd	£
Shadows Lengthen	7	1	0	1	15946
Saints And Sinners	5	3	0	0	16653
Lightening Rod	7	2	1	1	11372
Narcissist	8	2	1	2	5198
Classinaglass	3	1	0	2	5198
*Billy Two Tongues	8	1	0	2	2909
Total winning prize-money					£57276
Favourites	3-10		30.0%		-1.30

MRS SARAH EASTERBY

MALTON, NORTH YORKS

	No. of Hrs	Races Run	1st	2nd	3rd	Unpl	Per cent	£1 Level Stake
NH Flat	0	0	0	0	0	0	0.0	0.00
Hurdles	0	0	0	0	0	0	0.0	0.00
Chases	2	5	1	0	1	3	20.0	+21.00
Totals	2	5	1	0	1	3	20.0	+21.00
13-14	4	4	0	0	1	3	0.0	-4.00
12-13	2	2	0	1	1	0	0.0	-2.00

JOCKEYS

	W-R	Per cent	£1 Level Stake
Mr W Easterby	1-5	20.0	+21.00

COURSE RECORD

	Total W-R	Non-Hndcps Hurdles	Chases	Hndcps Hurdles	Chases	NH Flat	Per cent	£1 Level Stake
Catterick	1-1	0-0	1-1	0-0	0-0	0-0	100.0	+25.00

WINNING HORSES

Horse	Races Run	1st	2nd	3rd	£
*Soleil D'Avril	2	1	0	0	1872
Total winning prize-money					£1872
Favourites	0-0		0.0%		0.00

BRIAN ECKLEY

LLANSPYDDID, POWYS

	No. of Hrs	Races Run	1st	2nd	3rd	Unpl	Per cent	£1 Level Stake
NH Flat	3	5	0	0	2	3	0.0	-5.00
Hurdles	3	15	2	0	3	10	13.3	+3.73
Chases	0	0	0	0	0	0	0.0	0.00
Totals	5	20	2	0	5	13	10.0	-1.27
13-14	6	12	0	0	0	12	0.0	-12.00
12-13	7	32	1	2	4	25	3.1	-25.00

JOCKEYS

	W-R	Per cent	£1 Level Stake
Donal Devereux	2-18	11.1	+0.73

COURSE RECORD

	Total W-R	Non-Hndcps Hurdles	Chases	Hndcps Hurdles	Chases	NH Flat	Per cent	£1 Level Stake
Bangor	1-6	0-1	0-0	1-2	0-0	0-3	16.7	+11.00
Ffos Las	1-7	0-1	0-0	1-4	0-0	0-2	14.3	-5.27

WINNING HORSES

Horse	Races Run	1st	2nd	3rd	£
Jaunty Inflight	10	2	0	2	8447
Total winning prize-money					**£8447**
Favourites	**1-2**		**50.0%**		**-0.27**

ROBERT EDDERY

NEWMARKET, SUFFOLK

	No. of Hrs	Races Run	1st	2nd	3rd	Unpl	Per cent	£1 Level Stake
NH Flat	*0*	*0*	*0*	*0*	*0*	*0*	*0.0*	*0.00*
Hurdles	*3*	*6*	*1*	*0*	*2*	*3*	*16.7*	*-1.00*
Chases	*0*	*0*	*0*	*0*	*0*	*0*	*0.0*	*0.00*
Totals	**3**	**6**	**1**	**0**	**2**	**3**	**16.7**	**-1.00**
13-14	*1*	*1*	*0*	*0*	*0*	*1*	*0.0*	*-1.00*
12-13	*1*	*1*	*0*	*0*	*0*	*1*	*0.0*	*-1.00*

JOCKEYS

	W-R	Per cent	£1 Level Stake
Tom O'Brien	1-2	50.0	+3.00

COURSE RECORD

	Total W-R	Non-Hndcps Hurdles	Non-Hndcps Chases	Hndcps Hurdles	Hndcps Chases	NH Flat	Per cent	£1 Level Stake
Fakenham	1-3	1-3	0-0	0-0	0-0	0-0	33.3	+2.00

WINNING HORSES

Horse	Races Run	1st	2nd	3rd	£
Isabella Liberty	3	1	0	1	5848
Total winning prize-money					**£5848**
Favourites	**0-0**		**0.0%**		**0.00**

STUART EDMUNDS

NEWPORT PAGNELL, BUCKS

	No. of Hrs	Races Run	1st	2nd	3rd	Unpl	Per cent	£1 Level Stake
NH Flat	*4*	*5*	*0*	*0*	*0*	*5*	*0.0*	*-5.00*
Hurdles	*7*	*13*	*1*	*3*	*2*	*7*	*7.7*	*-8.00*
Chases	*1*	*3*	*0*	*0*	*1*	*2*	*0.0*	*-3.00*
Totals	**11**	**21**	**1**	**3**	**3**	**14**	**4.8**	**-16.00**

JOCKEYS

	W-R	Per cent	£1 Level Stake
Brendan Powell	1-2	50.0	+3.00

COURSE RECORD

	Total W-R	Non-Hndcps Hurdles	Non-Hndcps Chases	Hndcps Hurdles	Hndcps Chases	NH Flat	Per cent	£1 Level Stake
Warwick	1-2	0-0	0-0	1-1	0-1	0-0	50.0	+3.00

WINNING HORSES

Horse	Races Run	1st	2nd	3rd	£
*Dawn Commander	2	1	0	0	12512
Total winning prize-money					**£12512**
Favourites	**0-1**		**0.0%**		**-1.00**

LUCINDA EGERTON

MALTON, NORTH YORKS

	No. of Hrs	Races Run	1st	2nd	3rd	Unpl	Per cent	£1 Level Stake
NH Flat	*1*	*1*	*0*	*0*	*0*	*1*	*0.0*	*-1.00*
Hurdles	*8*	*23*	*0*	*2*	*3*	*18*	*0.0*	*-23.00*
Chases	*3*	*18*	*2*	*1*	*4*	*11*	*11.1*	*-8.00*
Totals	**9**	**42**	**2**	**3**	**7**	**30**	**4.8**	**-32.00**
13-14	*5*	*16*	*0*	*1*	*0*	*15*	*0.0*	*-16.00*

JOCKEYS

	W-R	Per cent	£1 Level Stake
Jake Greenall	1-3	33.3	+1.00
Danny Cook	1-15	6.7	-9.00

COURSE RECORD

	Total W-R	Non-Hndcps Hurdles	Non-Hndcps Chases	Hndcps Hurdles	Hndcps Chases	NH Flat	Per cent	£1 Level Stake
Newcastle	1-4	0-1	0-0	0-1	1-2	0-0	25.0	0.00
Mrket Rsn	1-5	0-0	0-2	0-2	1-1	0-0	20.0	+1.00

WINNING HORSES

Horse	Races Run	1st	2nd	3rd	£
Safari Journey	9	1	1	3	3769
Hi Bob	5	1	1	0	3249
Total winning prize-money					**£7018**
Favourites	**1-1**		**100.0%**		**3.00**

BRIAN ELLISON

NORTON, N YORKS

	No. of Hrs	Races Run	1st	2nd	3rd	Unpl	Per cent	£1 Level Stake
NH Flat	*6*	*11*	*2*	*3*	*2*	*4*	*18.2*	*-5.25*
Hurdles	*65*	*205*	*25*	*39*	*28*	*113*	*12.2*	*-126.08*
Chases	*25*	*74*	*8*	*13*	*11*	*42*	*10.8*	*-43.00*
Totals	**77**	**290**	**35**	**55**	**41**	**159**	**12.1**	**-174.33**
13-14	*73*	*274*	*37*	*42*	*40*	*155*	*13.5*	*-37.93*
12-13	*64*	*265*	*39*	*41*	*30*	*155*	*14.7*	*-15.99*

BY MONTH

Per £1 Level Per £1 Level

NH Flat	W-R	Per cent	£1 Level Stake
May	0-0	0.0	0.00
June	0-0	0.0	0.00
July	0-0	0.0	0.00
August	0-0	0.0	0.00
September	0-0	0.0	0.00
October	0-1	0.0	-1.00
November	1-4	25.0	-1.13
December	0-1	0.0	-1.00
January	0-0	0.0	0.00
February	0-3	0.0	-3.00
March	1-1	100.0	+1.88
April	0-1	0.0	-1.00

Hurdles	W-R	Per cent	£1 Level Stake
May	0-11	0.0	-11.00
June	2-9	22.2	-2.38
July	1-16	6.3	-11.00
August	4-16	25.0	-5.00
September	2-11	18.2	-5.96
October	1-9	11.1	-7.47
November	4-23	17.4	-5.00
December	3-18	16.7	-6.25
January	3-15	20.0	-9.30
February	2-37	5.4	-31.84
March	2-22	9.1	-15.25
April	1-18	5.6	-15.63

Chases	W-R	Per cent	£1 Level Stake
May	1-3	33.3	-0.50
June	0-3	0.0	-3.00
July	1-2	50.0	+2.50
August	0-0	0.0	0.00
September	1-4	25.0	-0.50
October	0-10	0.0	-10.00
November	3-12	25.0	0.00
December	0-5	0.0	-5.00
January	1-8	12.5	-5.50
February	1-11	9.1	-5.00
March	0-7	0.0	-7.00
April	0-9	0.0	-9.00

Totals	W-R	Per cent	£1 Level Stake
May	1-14	7.1	-11.50
June	2-12	16.7	-5.38
July	2-18	11.1	-8.50
August	4-16	25.0	-5.00
September	3-15	20.0	-6.46
October	1-20	5.0	-18.47
November	8-39	20.5	-6.13
December	3-24	12.5	-12.25
January	4-23	17.4	-14.80
February	3-51	5.9	-39.84
March	3-30	10.0	-20.37
April	1-28	3.6	-25.63

DISTANCE

Hurdles	W-R	Per cent	£1 Level Stake
2m-2m3f	18-110	16.4	-50.97
2m4f-2m7f	2-34	5.9	-27.38
3m+	2-15	13.3	-10.39

Chases	W-R	Per cent	£1 Level Stake
2m-2m3f	3-19	15.8	-9.50
2m4f-2m7f	0-19	0.0	-19.00
3m+	3-21	14.3	-6.25

TYPE OF RACE

Non-Handicaps	W-R	Per cent	£1 Level Stake
Nov Hrdls	11-50	22.0	-17.30
Hrdls	9-34	26.5	-3.06
Nov Chs	3-11	27.3	-1.75
Chases	0-0	0.0	0.00
Sell/Claim	2-13	15.4	-6.63

Handicaps	W-R	Per cent	£1 Level Stake
Nov Hrdls	0-8	0.0	-8.00
Hrdls	3-99	3.0	-90.09
Nov Chs	2-12	16.7	-1.00
Chases	3-51	5.9	-40.25
Sell/Claim	0-1	0.0	-1.00

RACE CLASS

	W-R	Per cent	£1 Level Stake
Class 1	2-26	7.7	-21.22
Class 2	0-30	0.0	-30.00
Class 3	5-73	6.8	-56.59
Class 4	23-114	20.2	-34.14
Class 5	3-37	8.1	-28.13
Class 6	2-10	20.0	-4.25

FIRST TIME OUT

	W-R	Per cent	£1 Level Stake
Bumpers	1-6	16.7	-3.13
Hurdles	8-60	13.3	-31.54
Chases	0-11	0.0	-11.00
Totals	9-77	11.7	-45.67

JOCKEYS

	W-R	Per cent	£1 Level Stake
Danny Cook	19-91	20.9	-28.52
Will Kennedy	5-22	22.7	-7.68
Richard Johnson	3-10	30.0	+2.75
G Lavery	3-16	18.8	-6.88
James Cowley	1-1	100.0	+1.63
Jason Maguire	1-1	100.0	+2.75
Wilson Renwick	1-8	12.5	-3.50
A P McCoy	1-10	10.0	-7.38
Nathan Moscrop	1-38	2.6	-34.50

COURSE RECORD

	Total W-R	Non-Hndcps Hurdles	Non-Hndcps Chases	Hndcps Hurdles	Hndcps Chases	NH Flat	Per cent	£1 Level Stake
Mrket Rsn	6-30	6-12	0-1	0-11	0-6	0-0	20.0	-7.00
Catterick	5-14	3-7	1-2	0-1	1-3	0-1	35.7	+0.95
Sedgefield	5-25	4-15	0-0	0-3	0-5	1-2	20.0	-12.46
Bangor	3-11	1-4	0-0	0-2	1-3	1-2	27.3	-0.38
Hexham	3-13	1-7	0-0	1-3	1-3	0-0	23.1	-1.38
Wetherby	3-27	3-12	0-1	0-9	0-5	0-0	11.1	-18.22
Cartmel	2-7	0-2	0-0	0-3	2-2	0-0	28.6	0.00
Musselbgh	2-31	0-6	0-1	2-18	0-4	0-2	6.5	-26.09
Leicester	1-1	1-1	0-0	0-0	0-0	0-0	100.0	+5.00
Nton Abbot	1-1	1-1	0-0	0-0	0-0	0-0	100.0	+2.25
Fakenham	1-5	1-2	0-0	0-1	0-2	0-0	20.0	-2.00
Haydock	1-6	1-1	0-0	0-4	0-1	0-0	16.7	-2.75
Southwell	1-13	0-3	1-1	0-9	0-0	0-0	7.7	-9.50
Carlisle	1-15	0-3	1-2	0-6	0-4	0-0	6.7	-11.75

WINNING HORSES

Horse	Races Run	1st	2nd	3rd	£
*Definitly Red	3	2	0	0	20608
Full Day	6	3	1	1	18798
Presented	6	1	0	0	7988
Streets Of Newyork	4	2	2	0	12996
Yorkist	8	2	4	1	12078
Teenage Dream	6	2	1	1	9747
*Jac The Legend	4	1	1	1	6498
Racing Europe	7	2	2	1	6585
Apterix	6	2	2	0	7928
Moyode Wood	6	1	0	2	4328
Come On Sunshine	5	2	0	2	3970
*Announcement	6	1	1	1	3899
Gone Forever	4	1	3	0	3899
*Seamour	2	2	0	0	7148
George Fernbeck	8	2	1	2	6888
Admiral Hawke	6	2	0	0	5458
*The Grey Taylor	4	1	2	1	3422
Five In A Row	5	1	1	1	3379
Manhattan Swing	2	1	0	1	3249
Lucky Cody	6	1	2	1	3249
Zaidiyn	5	1	0	1	3249
It's A Mans World	10	1	0	0	2599

Oscar Blue	3	1	0	1	1560
Total winning prize-money					**£159523**
Favourites	**17-52**		**32.7%**		**-10.45**

M E ELLWOOD

KINROSS, PERTH

	No. of Hrs	Races Run	1st	2nd	3rd	Unpl	Per cent	£1 Level Stake
NH Flat	*0*	*0*	*0*	*0*	*0*	*0*	*0.0*	*0.00*
Hurdles	*0*	*0*	*0*	*0*	*0*	*0*	*0.0*	*0.00*
Chases	*1*	*1*	*1*	*0*	*0*	*0*	*100.0*	*+6.00*
Totals	**1**	**1**	**1**	**0**	**0**	**0**	**100.0**	**+6.00**
13-14	*1*	*3*	*0*	*1*	*1*	*1*	*0.0*	*-3.00*
12-13	*1*	*2*	*0*	*0*	*1*	*1*	*0.0*	*-2.00*

JOCKEYS

	W-R	Per cent	£1 Level Stake
Mr J Lyttle	1-1	100.0	+6.00

COURSE RECORD

	Total W-R	Non-Hndcps Hurdles	Non-Hndcps Chases	Hndcps Hurdles	Hndcps Chases	NH Flat	Per cent	£1 Level Stake
Hexham	1-1	0-0	1-1	0-0	0-0	0-0	100.0	+6.00

WINNING HORSES

Horse	Races Run	1st	2nd	3rd	£
A New Rising	1	1	0	0	2496
Total winning prize-money					**£2496**
Favourites	**0-0**		**0.0%**		**0.00**

SARA ENDER

MALTON, N YORKS

	No. of Hrs	Races Run	1st	2nd	3rd	Unpl	Per cent	£1 Level Stake
NH Flat	*2*	*5*	*0*	*0*	*0*	*5*	*0.0*	*-5.00*
Hurdles	*5*	*8*	*1*	*0*	*1*	*6*	*12.5*	*-5.75*
Chases	*1*	*1*	*0*	*0*	*0*	*1*	*0.0*	*-1.00*
Totals	**7**	**14**	**1**	**0**	**1**	**12**	**7.1**	**-11.75**
13-14	*6*	*10*	*0*	*0*	*0*	*10*	*0.0*	*-10.00*

JOCKEYS

	W-R	Per cent	£1 Level Stake
Nathan Moscrop	1-10	10.0	-7.75

COURSE RECORD

	Total W-R	Non-Hndcps Hurdles	Non-Hndcps Chases	Hndcps Hurdles	Hndcps Chases	NH Flat	Per cent	£1 Level Stake
Hexham	1-2	1-2	0-0	0-0	0-0	0-0	50.0	+0.25

WINNING HORSES

Horse	Races Run	1st	2nd	3rd	£
Grey Monk	1	1	0	0	2053
Total winning prize-money					**£2053**
Favourites	**0-0**		**0.0%**		**0.00**

JAMES EUSTACE

NEWMARKET, SUFFOLK

	No. of Hrs	Races Run	1st	2nd	3rd	Unpl	Per cent	£1 Level Stake
NH Flat	*0*	*0*	*0*	*0*	*0*	*0*	*0.0*	*0.00*
Hurdles	*4*	*13*	*1*	*2*	*3*	*7*	*7.7*	*-8.00*
Chases	*0*	*0*	*0*	*0*	*0*	*0*	*0.0*	*0.00*
Totals	**4**	**13**	**1**	**2**	**3**	**7**	**7.7**	**-8.00**
13-14	*5*	*21*	*3*	*1*	*5*	*12*	*14.3*	*+7.00*
12-13	*6*	*19*	*3*	*0*	*2*	*14*	*15.8*	*-6.50*

JOCKEYS

	W-R	Per cent	£1 Level Stake
Jack Quinlan	1-9	11.1	-4.00

COURSE RECORD

	Total W-R	Non-Hndcps Hurdles	Non-Hndcps Chases	Hndcps Hurdles	Hndcps Chases	NH Flat	Per cent	£1 Level Stake
Fakenham	1-2	1-1	0-0	0-1	0-0	0-0	50.0	+3.00

WINNING HORSES

Horse	Races Run	1st	2nd	3rd	£
Aviator	2	1	1	0	4224
Total winning prize-money					**£4224**
Favourites	**0-0**		**0.0%**		**0.00**

DAVID EVANS

PANDY, MONMOUTHS

	No. of Hrs	Races Run	1st	2nd	3rd	Unpl	Per cent	£1 Level Stake
NH Flat	*3*	*4*	*0*	*0*	*1*	*3*	*0.0*	*-4.00*
Hurdles	*7*	*20*	*2*	*2*	*1*	*15*	*10.0*	*-6.75*
Chases	*2*	*5*	*1*	*1*	*1*	*2*	*20.0*	*-0.50*
Totals	**9**	**29**	**3**	**3**	**3**	**20**	**10.3**	**-11.25**
13-14	*17*	*36*	*0*	*3*	*2*	*31*	*0.0*	*-36.00*
12-13	*28*	*103*	*10*	*10*	*17*	*66*	*9.7*	*-30.26*

JOCKEYS

	W-R	Per cent	£1 Level Stake
Peter Carberry	2-8	25.0	+6.50
Mr H A A Bannister	1-3	33.3	+0.25

COURSE RECORD

	Total W-R	Non-Hndcps Hurdles	Non-Hndcps Chases	Hndcps Hurdles	Hndcps Chases	NH Flat	Per cent	£1 Level Stake
Mrket Rsn	1-3	0-0	0-0	1-1	0-2	0-0	33.3	+7.00
Stratford	1-3	0-0	0-0	0-1	1-1	0-1	33.3	+1.50
Ludlow	1-5	0-2	0-0	1-2	0-0	0-1	20.0	-1.75

WINNING HORSES

Horse	Races Run	1st	2nd	3rd	£
*Foundry Square	4	1	0	1	9495
Annaluna	6	1	2	0	3743
Scotsbrook Cloud	5	1	0	1	3249
Total winning prize-money					**£16487**
Favourites	**1-4**		**25.0%**		**-0.75**

JAMES EVANS

BROADWAS, WORCS

	No. of Hrs	Races Run	1st	2nd	3rd	Unpl	Per cent	£1 Level Stake
NH Flat	*2*	*3*	*1*	*1*	*0*	*1*	*33.3*	*-0.13*
Hurdles	*12*	*33*	*3*	*3*	*5*	*22*	*9.1*	*-23.50*
Chases	*4*	*14*	*1*	*3*	*1*	*9*	*7.1*	*-11.00*
Totals	**13**	**50**	**5**	**7**	**6**	**32**	**10.0**	**-34.63**
13-14	*13*	*44*	*8*	*3*	*6*	*27*	*18.2*	*+24.83*
12-13	*14*	*58*	*8*	*6*	*8*	*36*	*13.8*	*-0.92*

JOCKEYS

	W-R	Per cent	£1 Level Stake
Liam Treadwell	3-17	17.6	-8.63
Conor Ring	1-2	50.0	+2.00
Mark Quinlan	1-12	8.3	-9.00

COURSE RECORD

	Total W-R	Non-Hndcps Hurdles	Non-Hndcps Chases	Hndcps Hurdles	Hndcps Chases	NH Flat	Per cent	£1 Level Stake
Mrket Rsn	3-6	0-0	0-0	1-1	1-4	1-1	50.0	+3.88
Catterick	1-1	1-1	0-0	0-0	0-0	0-0	100.0	+0.50
Ascot	1-4	1-1	0-0	0-1	0-1	0-1	25.0	0.00

WINNING HORSES

Horse	Races Run	1st	2nd	3rd	£
Desilvano	6	3	1	1	12478
*Minella Bliss	9	1	4	1	4549
It's Oscar	8	1	1	2	2599
Total winning prize-money					**£19626**
Favourites	**3-7**		**42.9%**		**1.38**

JAMES EWART

LANGHOLM, DUMFRIES & G'WAY

	No. of Hrs	Races Run	1st	2nd	3rd	Unpl	Per cent	£1 Level Stake
NH Flat	*14*	*27*	*1*	*3*	*3*	*20*	*3.7*	*-25.20*
Hurdles	*29*	*74*	*12*	*12*	*8*	*42*	*16.2*	*-4.15*
Chases	*20*	*62*	*7*	*8*	*7*	*40*	*11.3*	*-19.25*
Totals	**45**	**163**	**20**	**23**	**18**	**102**	**12.3**	**-48.60**
13-14	*34*	*132*	*19*	*19*	*15*	*79*	*14.4*	*-9.42*
12-13	*34*	*129*	*15*	*14*	*20*	*80*	*11.6*	*-84.48*

BY MONTH

NH Flat	W-R	Per cent	£1 Level Stake	Hurdles	W-R	Per cent	£1 Level Stake
May	0-0	0.0	0.00	May	0-2	0.0	-2.00
June	0-0	0.0	0.00	June	0-3	0.0	-3.00
July	0-0	0.0	0.00	July	0-3	0.0	-3.00
August	0-0	0.0	0.00	August	1-1	100.0	+8.00
September	0-0	0.0	0.00	September	1-1	100.0	+2.00
October	0-3	0.0	-3.00	October	2-9	22.2	-2.25
November	0-6	0.0	-6.00	November	0-13	0.0	-13.00
December	0-4	0.0	-4.00	December	0-9	0.0	-9.00
January	1-7	14.3	-5.20	January	1-12	8.3	-7.50
February	0-2	0.0	-2.00	February	1-5	20.0	-2.60
March	0-2	0.0	-2.00	March	3-7	42.9	+17.20
April	0-3	0.0	-3.00	April	3-9	33.3	+11.00

Chases	W-R	Per cent	£1 Level Stake	Totals	W-R	Per cent	£1 Level Stake
May	0-4	0.0	-4.00	May	0-6	0.0	-6.00
June	0-2	0.0	-2.00	June	0-5	0.0	-5.00
July	0-5	0.0	-5.00	July	0-8	0.0	-8.00
August	0-2	0.0	-2.00	August	1-3	33.3	+6.00
September	0-0	0.0	0.00	September	1-1	100.0	+2.00
October	1-2	50.0	+1.75	October	3-14	21.4	-3.50
November	4-13	30.8	+7.00	November	4-32	12.5	-12.00
December	0-14	0.0	-14.00	December	0-27	0.0	-27.00
January	1-7	14.3	+6.00	January	3-26	11.5	-6.70
February	0-5	0.0	-5.00	February	1-12	8.3	-9.60
March	0-6	0.0	-6.00	March	3-15	20.0	+9.20
April	1-2	50.0	+4.00	April	4-14	28.6	+12.00

DISTANCE

Hurdles	W-R	Per cent	£1 Level Stake	Chases	W-R	Per cent	£1 Level Stake
2m-2m3f	7-48	14.6	-11.05	2m-2m3f	5-26	19.2	+7.00
2m4f-2m7f	3-11	27.3	+15.00	2m4f-2m7f	0-18	0.0	-18.00
3m+	1-6	16.7	-1.50	3m+	1-10	10.0	-6.25

TYPE OF RACE

Non-Handicaps	W-R	Per cent	£1 Level Stake	Handicaps	W-R	Per cent	£1 Level Stake
Nov Hrdls	2-22	9.1	-17.05	Nov Hrdls	1-7	14.3	-4.00
Hrdls	1-10	10.0	-7.60	Hrdls	8-35	22.9	+24.50
Nov Chs	0-5	0.0	-5.00	Nov Chs	0-11	0.0	-11.00

Chases	0-0	0.0	0.00	Chases	7-46	15.2	-3.25
Sell/Claim	0-0	0.0	0.00	Sell/Claim	0-0	0.0	0.00

RACE CLASS

	W-R	Per cent	£1 Level Stake
Class 1	0-0	0.0	0.00
Class 2	0-4	0.0	-4.00
Class 3	7-38	18.4	+20.75
Class 4	7-74	9.5	-48.05
Class 5	5-23	21.7	+4.90
Class 6	1-24	4.2	-22.20

FIRST TIME OUT

	W-R	Per cent	£1 Level Stake
Bumpers	1-14	7.1	-12.20
Hurdles	1-19	5.3	-16.25
Chases	0-12	0.0	-12.00
Totals	2-45	4.4	-40.45

JOCKEYS

	W-R	Per cent	£1 Level Stake
Dale Irving	12-51	23.5	+19.65
Lucy Alexander	5-59	8.5	-27.00
Daragh Bourke	2-18	11.1	-12.25
Ryan Mania	1-13	7.7	-7.00

COURSE RECORD

	Total W-R	Non-Hndcps Hurdles	Non-Hndcps Chases	Hndcps Hurdles	Hndcps Chases	NH Flat	Per cent	£1 Level Stake
Kelso	5-13	0-1	0-1	3-5	2-6	0-0	38.5	+14.50
Ayr	4-30	0-6	0-0	3-9	1-7	0-8	13.3	+2.25
Hexham	3-13	1-3	0-0	0-1	2-5	0-4	23.1	-0.50
Sedgefield	2-12	0-3	0-0	1-5	1-4	0-0	16.7	+4.00
Cartmel	1-3	0-1	0-0	1-1	0-1	0-0	33.3	+6.00
Catterick	1-8	1-4	0-0	0-0	0-2	0-2	12.5	-5.60
Doncaster	1-8	0-0	0-0	0-1	1-4	0-3	12.5	-4.25
Wetherby	1-12	1-2	0-1	0-2	0-7	0-0	8.3	-9.80
Newcastle	1-15	0-5	0-0	1-3	0-5	0-2	6.7	-8.00
Musselbgh	1-16	0-3	0-0	0-4	0-3	1-6	6.3	-14.20

WINNING HORSES

Horse	Races Run	1st	2nd	3rd	£
Rockawango	4	1	0	0	9747
Avidity	5	2	1	0	13191
Aristo Du Plessis	8	3	1	1	13646
Sa Suffit	4	2	0	1	6498
Premier Grand Cru	4	1	0	0	6498
Snuker	7	2	1	0	7669
Wilde Pastures	5	1	0	0	3899
Sleep In First	9	3	0	0	9877
Be My Present	4	1	0	0	3899
Lord Wishes	6	1	0	0	3899
Thorlak	3	1	0	0	3249
Civil Unrest	6	1	1	2	2339
Catching Shadows	1	1	0	0	1949

Total winning prize-money **£86360**

Favourites 5-15 33.3% -2.85

RICHARD FAHEY

MUSLEY BANK, N YORKS

	No. of Hrs	Races Run	1st	2nd	3rd	Unpl	Per cent	£1 Level Stake
NH Flat	*3*	*6*	*1*	*0*	*1*	*4*	*16.7*	*+3.00*
Hurdles	*1*	*1*	*0*	*0*	*0*	*1*	*0.0*	*-1.00*
Chases	*0*	*0*	*0*	*0*	*0*	*0*	*0.0*	*0.00*
Totals	**4**	**7**	**1**	**0**	**1**	**5**	**14.3**	**+2.00**
13-14	*1*	*1*	*0*	*0*	*0*	*1*	*0.0*	*-1.00*
12-13	*9*	*29*	*2*	*5*	*4*	*18*	*6.9*	*-23.00*

JOCKEYS

	W-R	Per cent	£1 Level Stake
Brian Hughes	1-3	33.3	+6.00

COURSE RECORD

	Total W-R	Non-Hndcps Hurdles	Non-Hndcps Chases	Hndcps Hurdles	Hndcps Chases	NH Flat	Per cent	£1 Level Stake
Sedgefield	1-1	0-0	0-0	0-0	0-0	1-1	100.0	+8.00

WINNING HORSES

Horse	Races Run	1st	2nd	3rd	£
Clonalig House	2	1	0	1	1560

Total winning prize-money **£1560**

Favourites **0-1** **0.0%** **-1.00**

JOHNNY FARRELLY

ENMORE, SOMERSET

	No. of Hrs	Races Run	1st	2nd	3rd	Unpl	Per cent	£1 Level Stake
NH Flat	*3*	*4*	*0*	*0*	*0*	*4*	*0.0*	*-4.00*
Hurdles	*24*	*78*	*10*	*8*	*6*	*54*	*12.8*	*+10.50*
Chases	*6*	*24*	*4*	*3*	*2*	*15*	*16.7*	*-4.00*
Totals	**28**	**106**	**14**	**11**	**8**	**73**	**13.2**	**+2.50**
13-14	*20*	*57*	*4*	*4*	*3*	*46*	*7.0*	*-23.50*

BY MONTH

NH Flat	W-R	Per cent	£1 Level Stake	**Hurdles**	W-R	Per cent	£1 Level Stake
May	0-1	0.0	-1.00	May	3-8	37.5	+7.50
June	0-0	0.0	0.00	June	0-5	0.0	-5.00
July	0-0	0.0	0.00	July	0-6	0.0	-6.00
August	0-0	0.0	0.00	August	1-4	25.0	+1.50
September	0-0	0.0	0.00	September	1-5	20.0	-1.00
October	0-0	0.0	0.00	October	0-4	0.0	-4.00
November	0-0	0.0	0.00	November	1-5	20.0	+8.00
December	0-1	0.0	-1.00	December	0-8	0.0	-8.00
January	0-0	0.0	0.00	January	1-8	12.5	+5.00
February	0-2	0.0	-2.00	February	1-3	33.3	+4.50
March	0-0	0.0	0.00	March	0-15	0.0	-15.00
April	0-0	0.0	0.00	April	2-7	28.6	+23.00

Chases	W-R	Per cent	£1 Level Stake
May	1-2	50.0	+4.00
June	0-1	0.0	-1.00
July	0-1	0.0	-1.00
August	0-2	0.0	-2.00
September	0-1	0.0	-1.00
October	0-0	0.0	0.00
November	0-1	0.0	-1.00
December	1-4	25.0	-0.50
January	0-1	0.0	-1.00
February	1-5	20.0	-1.00
March	1-5	20.0	+1.50
April	0-1	0.0	-1.00

Totals	W-R	Per cent	£1 Level Stake
May	4-11	36.4	+10.50
June	0-6	0.0	-6.00
July	0-7	0.0	-7.00
August	1-6	16.7	-0.50
September	1-6	16.7	-2.00
October	0-4	0.0	-4.00
November	1-6	16.7	+7.00
December	1-13	7.7	-9.50
January	1-9	11.1	+4.00
February	2-10	20.0	+1.50
March	1-20	5.0	-13.50
April	2-8	25.0	+22.00

DISTANCE

Hurdles	W-R	Per cent	£1 Level Stake
2m-2m3f	2-36	5.6	-6.00
2m4f-2m7f	4-26	15.4	+2.50
3m+	2-4	50.0	+5.50

Chases	W-R	Per cent	£1 Level Stake
2m-2m3f	0-1	0.0	-1.00
2m4f-2m7f	1-7	14.3	-1.00
3m+	3-14	21.4	0.00

TYPE OF RACE

Non-Handicaps	W-R	Per cent	£1 Level Stake
Nov Hrdls	0-8	0.0	-8.00
Hrdls	0-7	0.0	-7.00
Nov Chs	0-0	0.0	0.00
Chases	0-0	0.0	0.00
Sell/Claim	0-0	0.0	0.00

Handicaps	W-R	Per cent	£1 Level Stake
Nov Hrdls	0-4	0.0	-4.00
Hrdls	10-59	16.9	+29.50
Nov Chs	2-7	28.6	+3.00
Chases	2-17	11.8	-7.00
Sell/Claim	0-0	0.0	0.00

RACE CLASS

	W-R	Per cent	£1 Level Stake
Class 1	0-3	0.0	-3.00
Class 2	0-2	0.0	-2.00
Class 3	4-23	17.4	+20.00
Class 4	4-42	9.5	-13.50
Class 5	6-33	18.2	+4.00
Class 6	0-3	0.0	-3.00

FIRST TIME OUT

	W-R	Per cent	£1 Level Stake
Bumpers	0-3	0.0	-3.00
Hurdles	1-23	4.3	-17.50
Chases	0-2	0.0	-2.00
Totals	1-28	3.6	-22.50

JOCKEYS

	W-R	Per cent	£1 Level Stake
Mr Robert Hawker	5-22	22.7	+18.00
Brendan Powell	4-27	14.8	+5.00
Mr J F Mathias	1-1	100.0	+6.50
Dougie Costello	1-3	33.3	+1.00
Richie McLernon	1-4	25.0	+2.50
Leighton Aspell	1-7	14.3	+6.00
Richard Johnson	1-9	11.1	-3.50

COURSE RECORD

	Total W-R	Non-Hndcps Hurdles	Non-Hndcps Chases	Hndcps Hurdles	Hndcps Chases	NH Flat	Per cent	£1 Level Stake
Nton Abbot	3-12	0-3	0-0	2-7	1-2	0-0	25.0	+3.00
Ludlow	2-4	0-1	0-0	2-3	0-0	0-0	50.0	+16.50
Stratford	2-5	0-0	0-0	1-3	1-2	0-0	40.0	+7.00
Southwell	2-6	0-1	0-0	0-2	2-3	0-0	33.3	+1.50
Worcester	2-7	0-0	0-0	2-5	0-2	0-0	28.6	+3.50
Taunton	2-12	0-3	0-0	2-7	0-2	0-0	16.7	+18.00
Wincanton	1-6	0-0	0-0	1-5	0-0	0-1	16.7	+7.00

WINNING HORSES

Horse	Races Run	1st	2nd	3rd	£
*Ascendant	7	2	2	0	12867
Sporting Boy	8	2	0	0	14419
Qulinton	9	2	0	1	11853
Finish The Story	12	4	1	2	8511
Bedouin Bay	13	2	0	1	6506
Perfect Timing	6	1	1	0	3080
*Exemplary	3	1	1	0	2599
Total winning prize-money					**£59835**
Favourites	**0-5**		**0.0%**		**-5.00**

JOHN FERGUSON

COWLINGE, SUFFOLK

	No. of Hrs	Races Run	1st	2nd	3rd	Unpl	Per cent	£1 Level Stake
NH Flat	*16*	*28*	*7*	*7*	*0*	*14*	*25.0*	*-10.36*
Hurdles	*52*	*162*	*46*	*38*	*17*	*61*	*28.4*	*+19.32*
Chases	*12*	*24*	*3*	*4*	*1*	*16*	*12.5*	*-17.78*
Totals	**71**	**214**	**56**	**49**	**18**	**91**	**26.2**	**-8.82**
13-14	*71*	*218*	*50*	*35*	*22*	*111*	*22.9*	*-37.02*
12-13	*54*	*125*	*23*	*17*	*17*	*68*	*18.4*	*-47.26*

BY MONTH

NH Flat	W-R	Per cent	£1 Level Stake
May	0-0	0.0	0.00
June	0-0	0.0	0.00
July	0-2	0.0	-2.00
August	1-1	100.0	+2.00
September	2-2	100.0	+1.54
October	1-6	16.7	-3.90
November	2-5	40.0	+1.25
December	0-2	0.0	-2.00
January	0-1	0.0	-1.00
February	1-7	14.3	-4.25
March	0-1	0.0	-1.00
April	0-1	0.0	-1.00

Hurdles	W-R	Per cent	£1 Level Stake
May	4-12	33.3	+1.21
June	3-18	16.7	-6.67
July	8-19	42.1	+12.72
August	5-12	41.7	+1.74
September	3-8	37.5	-2.60
October	2-8	25.0	-5.37
November	5-19	26.3	+20.37
December	4-17	23.5	+1.70
January	6-21	28.6	+0.07
February	5-11	45.5	+8.82
March	0-8	0.0	-8.00
April	1-9	11.1	-4.67

Chases	W-R	Per cent	£1 Level Stake
May	0-4	0.0	-4.00
June	0-1	0.0	-1.00
July	0-0	0.0	0.00
August	0-0	0.0	0.00
September	0-0	0.0	0.00
October	0-1	0.0	-1.00

Totals	W-R	Per cent	£1 Level Stake
May	4-16	25.0	-2.79
June	3-19	15.8	-7.67
July	8-21	38.1	+10.72
August	6-13	46.2	+3.74
September	5-10	50.0	-1.06
October	3-15	20.0	-10.27

November	1-1	100.0	+1.75	November	8-25	32.0	+23.37
December	1-4	25.0	-2.20	December	5-23	21.7	-2.50
January	1-4	25.0	-2.33	January	7-26	26.9	-3.26
February	0-3	0.0	-3.00	February	6-21	28.6	+1.57
March	0-3	0.0	-3.00	March	0-12	0.0	-12.00
April	0-3	0.0	-3.00	April	1-13	7.7	-8.67

DISTANCE

Hurdles	W-R	Per cent	£1 Level Stake	Chases	W-R	Per cent	£1 Level Stake
2m-2m3f	23-94	24.5	-22.73	2m-2m3f	2-8	25.0	-4.53
2m4f-2m7f	5-24	20.8	+6.30	2m4f-2m7f	0-4	0.0	-4.00
3m+	0-4	0.0	-4.00	3m+	0-5	0.0	-5.00

TYPE OF RACE

Non-Handicaps	W-R	Per cent	£1 Level Stake	Handicaps	W-R	Per cent	£1 Level Stake
Nov Hrdls	20-55	36.4	+9.06	Nov Hrdls	1-2	50.0	+7.00
Hrdls	11-39	28.2	-12.78	Hrdls	14-66	21.2	+16.04
Nov Chs	3-9	33.3	-2.78	Nov Chs	0-5	0.0	-5.00
Chases	0-6	0.0	-6.00	Chases	0-4	0.0	-4.00
Sell/Claim	0-0	0.0	0.00	Sell/Claim	0-0	0.0	0.00

RACE CLASS

	W-R	Per cent	£1 Level Stake
Class 1	6-41	14.6	+11.17
Class 2	5-20	25.0	+2.21
Class 3	10-39	25.6	+5.19
Class 4	24-72	33.3	-11.18
Class 5	5-21	23.8	-9.85
Class 6	6-21	28.6	-6.36

FIRST TIME OUT

	W-R	Per cent	£1 Level Stake
Bumpers	5-16	31.3	-2.71
Hurdles	11-45	24.4	-12.97
Chases	1-10	10.0	-7.25
Totals	17-71	23.9	-22.93

JOCKEYS

	W-R	Per cent	£1 Level Stake
A P McCoy	26-86	30.2	-22.58
Barry Geraghty	6-16	37.5	+7.31
Jack Quinlan	5-29	17.2	-9.57
Brian Hughes	4-10	40.0	+2.05
Sam Twiston-Davies	4-19	21.1	-4.00
Mikey Ennis	3-7	42.9	+25.00
Noel Fehily	3-15	20.0	+4.00
Denis O'Regan	2-4	50.0	+7.50
Sean Bowen	1-1	100.0	+1.38
Aidan Coleman	1-2	50.0	+2.33
Jack Sherwood	1-4	25.0	-1.25

COURSE RECORD

	Total W-R	Non-Hndcps Hurdles	Non-Hndcps Chases	Hndcps Hurdles	Hndcps Chases	NH Flat	Per cent	£1 Level Stake
Huntingdon	9-14	6-8	0-1	0-1	0-0	3-4	64.3	+12.11
Stratford	5-10	4-5	0-0	1-4	0-0	0-1	50.0	+2.08
Worcester	4-12	2-7	0-0	1-3	0-0	1-2	33.3	-0.58
Nton Abbot	4-13	1-5	0-0	2-7	0-0	1-1	30.8	+0.74
Cheltenham	4-20	2-6	0-1	2-9	0-1	0-3	20.0	+5.78
Catterick	3-4	2-2	0-0	0-0	0-1	1-1	75.0	+6.00
Southwell	3-8	1-1	0-0	2-4	0-1	0-2	37.5	+3.88
Mrket Rsn	3-9	1-5	0-0	1-2	0-0	1-2	33.3	+3.16
Musselbgh	3-11	1-5	0-1	2-5	0-0	0-0	27.3	+4.70
Fontwell	2-5	2-3	0-0	0-1	0-0	0-1	40.0	+0.33
Doncaster	2-6	1-3	1-2	0-0	0-0	0-1	33.3	-2.89
Wetherby	2-6	1-2	0-1	1-2	0-0	0-1	33.3	-1.10
Newbury	2-7	2-3	0-0	0-3	0-0	0-1	28.6	+5.50
Leicester	1-1	0-0	1-1	0-0	0-0	0-0	100.0	+1.75
Bangor	1-3	0-1	0-0	1-2	0-0	0-0	33.3	0.00
Newcastle	1-3	0-2	1-1	0-0	0-0	0-0	33.3	-1.20
Wincanton	1-3	0-1	0-0	1-1	0-0	0-1	33.3	+14.00
Hexham	1-4	0-1	0-0	1-2	0-0	0-1	25.0	-0.50
Uttoxeter	1-4	1-2	0-0	0-2	0-0	0-0	25.0	-2.17
Fakenham	1-5	1-3	0-2	0-0	0-0	0-0	20.0	-1.25
Sedgefield	1-5	1-4	0-0	0-0	0-0	0-1	20.0	-3.33
Sandown	1-7	1-2	0-0	0-4	0-1	0-0	14.3	-3.00
Kempton	1-10	1-6	0-1	0-2	0-0	0-1	10.0	-8.83

WINNING HORSES

Horse	Races Run	1st	2nd	3rd	£
Purple Bay	4	2	2	0	54103
Ruacana	4	1	0	0	25992
Parlour Games	8	4	4	0	43386
Three Kingdoms	6	3	1	0	29050
Shubaat	3	3	0	0	22268
Retrieve	3	2	1	0	16837
*Arabian Revolution	4	2	1	0	17173
Aqalim	8	3	2	1	17327
Ittirad	7	3	4	0	18286
Bordoni	5	1	1	0	7535
Chesterfield	5	3	1	0	14655
Qewy	4	1	0	2	6498
Commissioned	4	2	0	0	10155
Aalim	8	2	2	1	11047
Dubai Prince	2	1	0	1	5393
Zip Top	5	2	1	0	7148
El Namoose	4	3	0	0	7018
*Mantou	2	1	0	0	3899
Honour System	3	1	1	0	3509
Manjakani	5	2	3	0	6758
Authorship	3	2	0	0	6498
My Direction	6	3	2	0	9487
*Devilment	5	2	2	0	6158
*Buckwheat	2	1	0	1	3249
Arabic History	5	3	2	0	6212
Southern Strife	2	1	0	0	1949
Joe Farrell	3	1	1	0	1625
Avenue Of Honour	2	1	0	0	1560

Total winning prize-money **£364775**

Favourites **32-78** **41.0%** **-11.99**

MARJORIE FIFE

STILLINGTON, N YORKS

	No. of Hrs	Races Run	1st	2nd	3rd	Unpl	Per cent	£1 Level Stake
NH Flat	0	0	0	0	0	0	0.0	0.00
Hurdles	5	17	1	2	1	13	5.9	-9.50
Chases	1	1	0	0	0	1	0.0	-1.00
Totals	**5**	**18**	**1**	**2**	**1**	**14**	**5.6**	**-10.50**
13-14	*5*	*13*	*0*	*0*	*0*	*13*	*0.0*	*-13.00*
12-13	*5*	*25*	*2*	*0*	*3*	*20*	*8.0*	*+31.00*

JOCKEYS

	W-R	Per cent	£1 Level Stake
Jeremiah McGrath	1-10	10.0	-2.50

COURSE RECORD

	Total W-R	Non-Hndcps Hurdles	Non-Hndcps Chases	Hndcps Hurdles	Hndcps Chases	NH Flat	Per cent	£1 Level Stake
Ayr	1-2	0-1	0-0	1-1	0-0	0-0	50.0	+5.50

WINNING HORSES

Horse	Races Run	1st	2nd	3rd	£
Simmply Sam	5	1	1	0	2599
Total winning prize-money					**£2599**
Favourites	**0-0**		**0.0%**		**0.00**

D M G FITCH-PEYTON

TETBURY, GLOUCS

	No. of Hrs	Races Run	1st	2nd	3rd	Unpl	Per cent	£1 Level Stake
NH Flat	0	0	0	0	0	0	0.0	0.00
Hurdles	0	0	0	0	0	0	0.0	0.00
Chases	1	2	1	0	0	1	50.0	+8.00
Totals	**1**	**2**	**1**	**0**	**0**	**1**	**50.0**	**+8.00**

JOCKEYS

	W-R	Per cent	£1 Level Stake
Miss H Lewis	1-2	50.0	+8.00

COURSE RECORD

	Total W-R	Non-Hndcps Hurdles	Non-Hndcps Chases	Hndcps Hurdles	Hndcps Chases	NH Flat	Per cent	£1 Level Stake
Stratford	1-1	0-0	1-1	0-0	0-0	0-0	100.0	+9.00

WINNING HORSES

Horse	Races Run	1st	2nd	3rd	£
*Bound For Glory	2	1	0	0	1872
Total winning prize-money					**£1872**
Favourites	**0-0**		**0.0%**		**0.00**

TIM FITZGERALD

NORTON, N YORKS

	No. of Hrs	Races Run	1st	2nd	3rd	Unpl	Per cent	£1 Level Stake
NH Flat	2	2	1	0	0	1	50.0	+3.00
Hurdles	0	0	0	0	0	0	0.0	0.00
Chases	2	6	0	2	0	4	0.0	-6.00
Totals	**4**	**8**	**1**	**2**	**0**	**5**	**12.5**	**-3.00**
13-14	*10*	*30*	*2*	*4*	*4*	*20*	*6.7*	*-14.50*
12-13	*7*	*23*	*2*	*3*	*2*	*16*	*8.7*	*-3.50*

JOCKEYS

	W-R	Per cent	£1 Level Stake
Andrew Tinkler	1-4	25.0	+1.00

COURSE RECORD

	Total W-R	Non-Hndcps Hurdles	Non-Hndcps Chases	Hndcps Hurdles	Hndcps Chases	NH Flat	Per cent	£1 Level Stake
Newcastle	1-1	0-0	0-0	0-0	0-0	1-1	100.0	+4.00

WINNING HORSES

Horse	Races Run	1st	2nd	3rd	£
Captain Chaos	1	1	0	0	1560
Total winning prize-money					**£1560**
Favourites	**0-0**		**0.0%**		**0.00**

JOHN FLINT

KENFIG HILL, BRIDGEND

	No. of Hrs	Races Run	1st	2nd	3rd	Unpl	Per cent	£1 Level Stake
NH Flat	2	3	0	0	0	3	0.0	-3.00
Hurdles	9	26	3	3	3	17	11.5	-13.00
Chases	3	17	0	4	6	7	0.0	-17.00
Totals	**12**	**46**	**3**	**7**	**9**	**27**	**6.5**	**-33.00**
13-14	*22*	*57*	*5*	*5*	*8*	*39*	*8.8*	*-17.50*
12-13	*40*	*127*	*11*	*14*	*16*	*86*	*8.7*	*-63.75*

JOCKEYS

	W-R	Per cent	£1 Level Stake
Tom O'Brien	2-8	25.0	+1.25
A P McCoy	1-2	50.0	+1.75

COURSE RECORD

	Total W-R	Non-Hndcps Hurdles	Non-Hndcps Chases	Hndcps Hurdles	Hndcps Chases	NH Flat	Per cent	£1 Level Stake
Nton Abbot	1-1	0-0	0-0	1-1	0-0	0-0	100.0	+4.50
Southwell	1-2	1-1	0-0	0-0	0-0	0-1	50.0	+1.75
Ffos Las	1-12	0-2	0-0	1-6	0-3	0-1	8.3	-8.25

WINNING HORSES

Horse	Races Run	1st	2nd	3rd	£
Lac Sacre	9	1	2	3	5393
*Stonemadforspeed	4	1	0	2	3249
Bernisdale	5	1	1	0	2738
Total winning prize-money					**£11380**
Favourites	**0-1**		**0.0%**		**-1.00**

DAVID FLOOD

CHISELDON, WILTSHIRE

	No. of Hrs	Races Run	1st	2nd	3rd	Unpl	Per cent	£1 Level Stake
NH Flat	*1*	*1*	*0*	*0*	*0*	*1*	*0.0*	*-1.00*
Hurdles	*2*	*3*	*0*	*0*	*0*	*3*	*0.0*	*-3.00*
Chases	*2*	*10*	*2*	*1*	*1*	*6*	*20.0*	*+35.00*
Totals	**5**	**14**	**2**	**1**	**1**	**10**	**14.3**	**+31.00**
12-13	*2*	*2*	*0*	*0*	*0*	*2*	*0.0*	*-2.00*

JOCKEYS

	W-R	Per cent	£1 Level Stake
Dave Crosse	1-4	25.0	+30.00
Patrick Corbett	1-4	25.0	+7.00

COURSE RECORD

	Total W-R	Non-Hndcps Hurdles	Non-Hndcps Chases	Hndcps Hurdles	Hndcps Chases	NH Flat	Per cent	£1 Level Stake
Ffos Las	1-1	0-0	0-0	0-0	1-1	0-0	100.0	+10.00
Plumpton	1-2	0-0	0-0	0-0	1-2	0-0	50.0	+32.00

WINNING HORSES

Horse	Races Run	1st	2nd	3rd	£
Petit Ecuyer	9	2	1	1	5449
Total winning prize-money					**£5449**
Favourites	**0-0**		**0.0%**		**0.00**

STEVE FLOOK

LEOMINSTER, HEREFORDSHIRE

	No. of Hrs	Races Run	1st	2nd	3rd	Unpl	Per cent	£1 Level Stake
NH Flat	*3*	*5*	*0*	*0*	*0*	*5*	*0.0*	*-5.00*
Hurdles	*3*	*4*	*0*	*0*	*0*	*4*	*0.0*	*-4.00*
Chases	*6*	*28*	*3*	*4*	*6*	*15*	*10.7*	*+7.80*
Totals	**12**	**37**	**3**	**4**	**6**	**24**	**8.1**	**-1.20**
13-14	*7*	*21*	*4*	*6*	*1*	*10*	*19.0*	*+0.25*
12-13	*8*	*32*	*5*	*6*	*3*	*18*	*15.6*	*-10.09*

JOCKEYS

	W-R	Per cent	£1 Level Stake
Miss G Andrews	1-5	20.0	-3.20
Ben Poste	1-8	12.5	-3.00
Ciaran Gethings	1-10	10.0	+19.00

COURSE RECORD

	Total W-R	Non-Hndcps Hurdles	Non-Hndcps Chases	Hndcps Hurdles	Hndcps Chases	NH Flat	Per cent	£1 Level Stake
Fontwell	1-1	0-0	1-1	0-0	0-0	0-0	100.0	+0.80
Leicester	1-4	0-0	0-3	0-0	1-1	0-0	25.0	+1.00
Ludlow	1-7	0-2	1-4	0-0	0-0	0-1	14.3	+22.00

WINNING HORSES

Horse	Races Run	1st	2nd	3rd	£
*Gentle George	3	1	0	2	5198
Bermuda Boy	9	1	1	1	2560
Foundry Square	8	1	3	2	1280
Total winning prize-money					**£9038**
Favourites	**1-2**		**50.0%**		**-0.20**

TONY FORBES

STRAMSHALL, STAFFS

	No. of Hrs	Races Run	1st	2nd	3rd	Unpl	Per cent	£1 Level Stake
NH Flat	*0*	*0*	*0*	*0*	*0*	*0*	*0.0*	*0.00*
Hurdles	*2*	*7*	*1*	*1*	*0*	*5*	*14.3*	*0.00*
Chases	*1*	*2*	*0*	*0*	*0*	*2*	*0.0*	*-2.00*
Totals	**2**	**9**	**1**	**1**	**0**	**7**	**11.1**	**-2.00**
13-14	*1*	*11*	*1*	*2*	*2*	*6*	*9.1*	*-4.00*
12-13	*2*	*5*	*0*	*0*	*1*	*4*	*0.0*	*-5.00*

JOCKEYS

	W-R	Per cent	£1 Level Stake
Josh Wall	1-6	16.7	+1.00

COURSE RECORD

	Total W-R	Non-Hndcps Hurdles	Non-Hndcps Chases	Hndcps Hurdles	Hndcps Chases	NH Flat	Per cent	£1 Level Stake
Uttoxeter	1-8	0-0	0-0	1-6	0-2	0-0	12.5	-1.00

WINNING HORSES

Horse	Races Run	1st	2nd	3rd	£
Nolecce	3	1	0	0	2339
Total winning prize-money					**£2339**
Favourites	**0-0**		**0.0%**		**0.00**

RICHARD FORD

GARSTANG, LANCS

	No. of Hrs	Races Run	1st	2nd	3rd	Unpl	Per cent	£1 Level Stake
NH Flat	*2*	*3*	*0*	*1*	*0*	*2*	*0.0*	*-3.00*
Hurdles	*10*	*25*	*5*	*4*	*1*	*15*	*20.0*	*+3.75*
Chases	*6*	*26*	*3*	*4*	*4*	*15*	*11.5*	*-15.93*

Totals	**14**	**54**	**8**	**9**	**5**	**32**	**14.8**	**-15.18**
13-14	*17*	*53*	*2*	*7*	*7*	*37*	*3.8*	*-33.50*
12-13	*17*	*41*	*5*	*6*	*1*	*29*	*12.2*	*-14.75*

JOCKEYS

	W-R	Per cent	£1 Level Stake
Harry Challoner	6-47	12.8	-21.68
Craig Nichol	1-1	100.0	+7.00
Miss J Walton	1-1	100.0	+4.50

COURSE RECORD

	Total W-R	Non-Hndcps Hurdles	Non-Hndcps Chases	Hndcps Hurdles	Hndcps Chases	NH Flat	Per cent	£1 Level Stake
Cartmel	2-9	0-0	1-1	1-3	0-5	0-0	22.2	+3.20
Carlisle	1-1	0-0	0-0	0-0	1-1	0-0	100.0	+3.00
Perth	1-1	0-0	0-0	1-1	0-0	0-0	100.0	+4.50
Worcester	1-2	1-2	0-0	0-0	0-0	0-0	50.0	+1.25
Stratford	1-4	1-4	0-0	0-0	0-0	0-0	25.0	-1.00
Uttoxeter	1-4	1-2	0-1	0-0	0-0	0-1	25.0	+4.00
Sedgefield	1-7	0-0	0-0	0-1	1-6	0-0	14.3	-4.13

WINNING HORSES

Horse	Races Run	1st	2nd	3rd	£
Swaledale Lad	9	2	2	2	10683
Debt To Society	16	4	6	1	10072
Reckless Romeo	1	1	0	0	2599
Makellys Blackpool	3	1	0	0	2599

Total winning prize-money **£25953**

Favourites **1-8** **12.5%** **-5.13**

RICHENDA FORD

BROCKHAMPTON GREEN, DORSET

	No. of Hrs	Races Run	1st	2nd	3rd	Unpl	Per cent	£1 Level Stake
NH Flat	*0*	*0*	*0*	*0*	*0*	*0*	*0.0*	*0.00*
Hurdles	*1*	*2*	*0*	*0*	*0*	*2*	*0.0*	*-2.00*
Chases	*4*	*28*	*1*	*6*	*4*	*17*	*3.6*	*-23.00*
Totals	**4**	**30**	**1**	**6**	**4**	**19**	**3.3**	**-25.00**
13-14	*6*	*16*	*1*	*1*	*2*	*12*	*6.3*	*-12.25*
12-13	*4*	*15*	*1*	*1*	*1*	*12*	*6.7*	*-9.50*

JOCKEYS

	W-R	Per cent	£1 Level Stake
Adam Wedge	1-18	5.6	-13.00

COURSE RECORD

	Total W-R	Non-Hndcps Hurdles	Non-Hndcps Chases	Hndcps Hurdles	Hndcps Chases	NH Flat	Per cent	£1 Level Stake
Nton Abbot	1-1	0-0	0-0	0-0	1-1	0-0	100.0	+4.00

WINNING HORSES

Horse	Races Run	1st	2nd	3rd	£
Ball Hopper	9	1	1	3	3899

Total winning prize-money **£3899**

Favourites **0-1** **0.0%** **-1.00**

SANDY FORSTER

KIRK YETHOLM, ROXBURGHSHIRE

	No. of Hrs	Races Run	1st	2nd	3rd	Unpl	Per cent	£1 Level Stake
NH Flat	*2*	*2*	*0*	*0*	*0*	*2*	*0.0*	*-2.00*
Hurdles	*4*	*18*	*2*	*2*	*1*	*13*	*11.1*	*+30.00*
Chases	*1*	*1*	*0*	*0*	*0*	*1*	*0.0*	*-1.00*
Totals	**7**	**21**	**2**	**2**	**1**	**16**	**9.5**	**+27.00**
13-14	*12*	*36*	*1*	*4*	*3*	*28*	*2.8*	*-29.50*
12-13	*11*	*32*	*0*	*4*	*4*	*24*	*0.0*	*-32.00*

JOCKEYS

	W-R	Per cent	£1 Level Stake
Miss J Walton	1-1	100.0	+18.00
Mr T Hamilton	1-15	6.7	+14.00

COURSE RECORD

	Total W-R	Non-Hndcps Hurdles	Non-Hndcps Chases	Hndcps Hurdles	Hndcps Chases	NH Flat	Per cent	£1 Level Stake
Perth	2-2	0-0	0-0	2-2	0-0	0-0	100.0	+46.00

WINNING HORSES

Horse	Races Run	1st	2nd	3rd	£
High Fair	7	1	1	1	4431
See The Legend	6	1	1	0	3120

Total winning prize-money **£7551**

Favourites **0-0** **0.0%** **0.00**

JOANNE FOSTER

MENSTON, W YORKS

	No. of Hrs	Races Run	1st	2nd	3rd	Unpl	Per cent	£1 Level Stake
NH Flat	*1*	*1*	*0*	*0*	*0*	*1*	*0.0*	*-1.00*
Hurdles	*9*	*19*	*0*	*0*	*1*	*18*	*0.0*	*-19.00*
Chases	*11*	*49*	*6*	*4*	*10*	*29*	*12.2*	*+10.00*
Totals	**15**	**69**	**6**	**4**	**11**	**48**	**8.7**	**-10.00**
13-14	*12*	*52*	*3*	*4*	*5*	*40*	*5.8*	*-27.00*
12-13	*13*	*66*	*10*	*9*	*15*	*32*	*15.2*	*+58.00*

JOCKEYS

	W-R	Per cent	£1 Level Stake
Samantha Drake	3-16	18.8	+8.50
Mr John Dawson	2-17	11.8	-3.50
Dougie Costello	1-15	6.7	+6.00

COURSE RECORD

	Total W-R	Non-Hndcps Hurdles	Non-Hndcps Chases	Hndcps Hurdles	Hndcps Chases	NH Flat	Per cent	£1 Level Stake
Sedgefield	4-30	0-5	0-0	0-3	4-22	0-0	13.3	+15.50

Cartmel	1-4	0-0	0-0	0-1	1-3	0-0	25.0	+2.50
Hexham	1-7	0-0	0-1	0-0	1-6	0-0	14.3	0.00

WINNING HORSES

Horse	Races Run	1st	2nd	3rd	£
Cross To Boston	3	1	1	0	5198
*Houndscourt	8	2	0	3	7950
Urban Gale	9	1	0	5	3925
Cara Court	13	1	2	1	3249
Pindar	11	1	1	1	2794
Total winning prize-money					**£23116**
Favourites	**0-2**		**0.0%**		**-2.00**

JIMMY FROST

BUCKFAST, DEVON

	No. of Hrs	Races Run	1st	2nd	3rd	Unpl	Per cent	£1 Level Stake
NH Flat	*1*	*3*	*0*	*0*	*0*	*3*	*0.0*	*-3.00*
Hurdles	*26*	*77*	*3*	*4*	*4*	*66*	*3.9*	*-61.25*
Chases	*4*	*15*	*2*	*3*	*2*	*8*	*13.3*	*-8.13*
Totals	**28**	**95**	**5**	**7**	**6**	**77**	**5.3**	**-72.38**
13-14	*16*	*54*	*5*	*3*	*3*	*43*	*9.3*	*+23.50*
12-13	*21*	*64*	*2*	*3*	*3*	*56*	*3.1*	*-22.00*

JOCKEYS

	W-R	Per cent	£1 Level Stake
Hadden Frost	4-33	12.1	-14.38
Nico de Boinville	1-2	50.0	+2.00

COURSE RECORD

	Total W-R	Non-Hndcps Hurdles	Non-Hndcps Chases	Hndcps Hurdles	Hndcps Chases	NH Flat	Per cent	£1 Level Stake
Nton Abbot	5-31	0-8	0-1	3-13	2-9	0-0	16.1	-8.38

WINNING HORSES

Horse	Races Run	1st	2nd	3rd	£
Union Saint	4	1	1	0	6173
*Decoy	1	1	0	0	3899
Rusty Nail	7	2	2	1	5848
Strong Wind	11	1	1	1	2738
Total winning prize-money					**£18658**
Favourites	**3-5**		**60.0%**		**5.63**

KEVIN FROST

RED HILL, WARWICKSHIRE

	No. of Hrs	Races Run	1st	2nd	3rd	Unpl	Per cent	£1 Level Stake
NH Flat	*2*	*3*	*0*	*0*	*0*	*3*	*0.0*	*-3.00*
Hurdles	*9*	*29*	*1*	*4*	*4*	*20*	*3.4*	*-26.25*
Chases	*2*	*10*	*2*	*3*	*1*	*4*	*20.0*	*+35.00*
Totals	**10**	**42**	**3**	**7**	**5**	**27**	**7.1**	**+5.75**
13-14	*4*	*15*	*2*	*3*	*2*	*8*	*13.3*	*+13.50*

JOCKEYS

	W-R	Per cent	£1 Level Stake
Brian Hughes	3-11	27.3	+36.75

COURSE RECORD

	Total W-R	Non-Hndcps Hurdles	Non-Hndcps Chases	Hndcps Hurdles	Hndcps Chases	NH Flat	Per cent	£1 Level Stake
Aintree	2-3	0-0	0-0	0-0	2-3	0-0	66.7	+42.00
Wetherby	1-1	1-1	0-0	0-0	0-0	0-0	100.0	+1.75

WINNING HORSES

Horse	Races Run	1st	2nd	3rd	£
Surf And Turf	10	2	5	2	51898
Walkabout Creek	7	1	1	0	2599
Total winning prize-money					**£54497**
Favourites	**1-3**		**33.3%**		**-0.25**

HUGO FROUD

BRUTON, SOMERSET

	No. of Hrs	Races Run	1st	2nd	3rd	Unpl	Per cent	£1 Level Stake
NH Flat	*4*	*4*	*0*	*0*	*0*	*4*	*0.0*	*-4.00*
Hurdles	*4*	*9*	*0*	*0*	*0*	*9*	*0.0*	*-9.00*
Chases	*3*	*19*	*1*	*4*	*2*	*12*	*5.3*	*-13.00*
Totals	**9**	**32**	**1**	**4**	**2**	**25**	**3.1**	**-26.00**
13-14	*7*	*23*	*0*	*5*	*1*	*17*	*0.0*	*-23.00*
12-13	*2*	*4*	*0*	*2*	*0*	*2*	*0.0*	*-4.00*

JOCKEYS

	W-R	Per cent	£1 Level Stake
Dave Crosse	1-16	6.3	-10.00

COURSE RECORD

	Total W-R	Non-Hndcps Hurdles	Non-Hndcps Chases	Hndcps Hurdles	Hndcps Chases	NH Flat	Per cent	£1 Level Stake
Nton Abbot	1-4	0-1	0-0	0-1	1-2	0-0	25.0	+2.00

WINNING HORSES

Horse	Races Run	1st	2nd	3rd	£
Marky Bob	5	1	0	0	3249
Total winning prize-money					**£3249**
Favourites	**0-0**		**0.0%**		**0.00**

HARRY FRY

SEABOROUGH, DORSET

	No. of Hrs	Races Run	1st	2nd	3rd	Unpl	Per cent	£1 Level Stake
NH Flat	*15*	*23*	*2*	*1*	*6*	*14*	*8.7*	*-12.50*

Hurdles	*33*	*106*	*26*	*16*	*18*	*46*	*24.5*	*-14.84*
Chases	*11*	*29*	*8*	*4*	*3*	*14*	*27.6*	*-3.17*
Totals	**50**	**158**	**36**	**21**	**27**	**74**	**22.8**	**-30.51**
13-14	*37*	*111*	*32*	*17*	*9*	*53*	*28.8*	*+17.44*
12-13	*27*	*70*	*19*	*11*	*9*	*31*	*27.1*	*+41.02*

BY MONTH

NH Flat	W-R	Per cent	£1 Level Stake
May	0-2	0.0	-2.00
June	0-0	0.0	0.00
July	0-0	0.0	0.00
August	0-0	0.0	0.00
September	0-0	0.0	0.00
October	1-4	25.0	+1.50
November	1-5	20.0	0.00
December	0-5	0.0	-5.00
January	0-1	0.0	-1.00
February	0-4	0.0	-4.00
March	0-2	0.0	-2.00
April	0-0	0.0	0.00

Hurdles	W-R	Per cent	£1 Level Stake
May	0-3	0.0	-3.00
June	0-2	0.0	-2.00
July	0-1	0.0	-1.00
August	1-3	33.3	+1.50
September	0-0	0.0	0.00
October	2-7	28.6	-0.50
November	9-22	40.9	-2.32
December	5-14	35.7	+2.65
January	6-16	37.5	+8.60
February	1-10	10.0	-1.00
March	2-15	13.3	-4.78
April	0-13	0.0	-13.00

Chases	W-R	Per cent	£1 Level Stake
May	2-3	66.7	+2.25
June	0-1	0.0	-1.00
July	0-0	0.0	0.00
August	0-0	0.0	0.00
September	0-1	0.0	-1.00
October	0-1	0.0	-1.00
November	0-4	0.0	-4.00
December	1-6	16.7	-4.33
January	1-2	50.0	-0.17
February	2-5	40.0	+2.25
March	1-2	50.0	+3.50
April	1-4	25.0	+0.33

Totals	W-R	Per cent	£1 Level Stake
May	2-8	25.0	-2.75
June	0-3	0.0	-3.00
July	0-1	0.0	-1.00
August	1-3	33.3	+1.50
September	0-1	0.0	-1.00
October	3-12	25.0	0.00
November	10-31	32.3	-6.32
December	6-25	24.0	-6.68
January	7-19	36.8	+7.43
February	3-19	15.8	-2.75
March	3-19	15.8	-3.28
April	1-17	5.9	-12.67

DISTANCE

Hurdles	W-R	Per cent	£1 Level Stake
2m-2m3f	8-41	19.5	-15.95
2m4f-2m7f	13-33	39.4	+12.16
3m+	1-4	25.0	-1.80

Chases	W-R	Per cent	£1 Level Stake
2m-2m3f	1-7	14.3	-4.50
2m4f-2m7f	4-6	66.7	+9.67
3m+	2-12	16.7	-6.00

TYPE OF RACE

Non-Handicaps	W-R	Per cent	£1 Level Stake
Nov Hrdls	13-45	28.9	-0.25
Hrdls	5-23	21.7	-10.35
Nov Chs	1-6	16.7	-4.33
Chases	1-3	33.3	-1.17
Sell/Claim	0-0	0.0	0.00

Handicaps	W-R	Per cent	£1 Level Stake
Nov Hrdls	1-5	20.0	-1.50
Hrdls	7-33	21.2	-2.75
Nov Chs	0-1	0.0	-1.00
Chases	6-19	31.6	+3.33
Sell/Claim	0-0	0.0	0.00

RACE CLASS

	W-R	Per cent	£1 Level Stake
Class 1	4-33	12.1	-20.42
Class 2	6-17	35.3	+5.60
Class 3	12-30	40.0	+11.47
Class 4	13-48	27.1	-2.66
Class 5	0-13	0.0	-13.00
Class 6	1-17	5.9	-11.50

FIRST TIME OUT

	W-R	Per cent	£1 Level Stake
Bumpers	2-15	13.3	-4.50
Hurdles	6-26	23.1	-2.59
Chases	3-9	33.3	-0.50
Totals	11-50	22.0	-7.59

JOCKEYS

	W-R	Per cent	£1 Level Stake
Noel Fehily	15-76	19.7	-12.65
A P McCoy	5-10	50.0	+0.58
Nick Scholfield	5-12	41.7	+0.82
Ryan Mahon	5-28	17.9	-9.62
Gary Derwin	4-13	30.8	+1.75
R Walsh	1-1	100.0	+1.10
Conor Brassil	1-6	16.7	-0.50

COURSE RECORD

	Total W-R	Non-Hndcps Hurdles	Non-Hndcps Chases	Hndcps Hurdles	Hndcps Chases	NH Flat	Per cent	£1 Level Stake
Wincanton	7-22	2-7	0-0	3-7	2-4	0-4	31.8	+1.25
Exeter	5-12	3-7	0-2	1-1	1-1	0-1	41.7	+7.71
Ascot	4-6	4-4	0-0	0-1	0-0	0-1	66.7	+5.60
Cheltenham	4-17	3-6	0-1	0-6	0-3	1-1	23.5	-0.25
Fontwell	3-8	1-3	0-0	1-2	1-1	0-2	37.5	+0.30
Newbury	3-12	1-4	0-1	1-3	1-2	0-2	25.0	+2.13
Kempton	2-4	1-2	0-0	1-1	0-0	0-1	50.0	+0.50
Nton Abbot	2-8	0-2	0-0	1-5	0-0	1-1	25.0	+2.00
Doncaster	1-3	0-1	1-2	0-0	0-0	0-0	33.3	-1.17
Warwick	1-3	1-1	0-0	0-0	0-0	0-2	33.3	-0.80
Huntingdon	1-4	0-0	1-1	0-1	0-1	0-1	25.0	-2.33
Ludlow	1-7	0-2	0-1	0-1	1-2	0-1	14.3	-3.75
Sandown	1-8	1-3	0-1	0-3	0-1	0-0	12.5	+1.00
Taunton	1-16	1-10	0-0	0-3	0-0	0-3	6.3	-14.70

WINNING HORSES

Horse	Races Run	1st	2nd	3rd	£
Bitofapuzzle	5	3	1	1	43114
Rock On Ruby	4	2	1	1	38420
Henryville	8	2	2	0	32189
Highland Retreat	4	2	1	0	22283
Fletchers Flyer	4	2	1	1	15807
Polamco	6	2	0	2	15472
Jolly's Cracked It	6	2	1	0	17517
Blue Buttons	5	1	1	1	9495
Jollyallan	5	3	1	0	21198
Opening Batsman	6	2	1	0	13996
Shuil Royale	2	2	0	0	13803
Karinga Dancer	5	1	0	2	6330
Thomas Brown	5	2	1	0	11779
Zulu Oscar	2	1	0	0	5393
Presenting Arms	3	2	0	0	8123
Oscarslad	2	1	0	0	3899
*Desert Queen	2	2	0	0	7798
Mendip Express	4	1	2	0	3249

Assam Black	4	1	0	2	3249
Sir Ivan	5	1	0	2	3249
Dashing Oscar	2	1	0	0	2053
Total winning prize-money					**£298416**
Favourites	**21-43**		**48.8%**		**6.53**

SUE GARDNER

LONGDOWN, DEVON

	No. of Hrs	Races Run	1st	2nd	3rd	Unpl	Per cent	£1 Level Stake
NH Flat	*8*	*12*	*0*	*2*	*0*	*10*	*0.0*	*-12.00*
Hurdles	*20*	*82*	*6*	*5*	*4*	*67*	*7.3*	*-57.25*
Chases	*6*	*17*	*0*	*0*	*1*	*16*	*0.0*	*-17.00*
Totals	**29**	**111**	**6**	**7**	**5**	**93**	**5.4**	**-86.25**
13-14	*30*	*98*	*10*	*4*	*10*	*74*	*10.2*	*-17.17*
12-13	*34*	*163*	*20*	*19*	*15*	*109*	*12.3*	*+32.45*

JOCKEYS

	W-R	Per cent	£1 Level Stake
Lucy Gardner	6-77	7.8	-52.25

COURSE RECORD

	Total W-R	Non-Hndcps Hurdles	Non-Hndcps Chases	Hndcps Hurdles	Hndcps Chases	NH Flat	Per cent	£1 Level Stake
Exeter	2-31	0-10	0-1	2-14	0-5	0-1	6.5	-22.25
Chepstow	1-4	0-1	0-0	1-2	0-0	0-1	25.0	-0.25
Fontwell	1-4	0-0	0-0	1-3	0-0	0-1	25.0	-2.00
Plumpton	1-6	0-0	0-0	1-4	0-1	0-1	16.7	+1.00
Ffos Las	1-8	0-0	0-0	1-3	0-2	0-3	12.5	-4.75

WINNING HORSES

Horse	Races Run	1st	2nd	3rd	£
*Tea Time Fred	7	1	1	0	3249
Bredon Hill Lad	5	3	0	0	6407
*Sirop De Menthe	4	1	2	0	2274
Rafafie	3	1	0	1	1949
Total winning prize-money					**£13879**
Favourites	**3-6**		**50.0%**		**2.50**

ROSEMARY GASSON

BALSCOTE, OXON

	No. of Hrs	Races Run	1st	2nd	3rd	Unpl	Per cent	£1 Level Stake
NH Flat	*3*	*5*	*0*	*0*	*0*	*5*	*0.0*	*-5.00*
Hurdles	*3*	*11*	*0*	*0*	*2*	*9*	*0.0*	*-11.00*
Chases	*4*	*22*	*3*	*5*	*2*	*12*	*13.6*	*+2.88*
Totals	**8**	**38**	**3**	**5**	**4**	**26**	**7.9**	**-13.12**
13-14	*9*	*41*	*3*	*3*	*4*	*31*	*7.3*	*-25.50*
12-13	*8*	*43*	*2*	*10*	*4*	*27*	*4.7*	*-32.00*

JOCKEYS

	W-R	Per cent	£1 Level Stake
Ben Poste	3-35	8.6	-10.13

COURSE RECORD

	Total W-R	Non-Hndcps Hurdles	Non-Hndcps Chases	Hndcps Hurdles	Hndcps Chases	NH Flat	Per cent	£1 Level Stake
Stratford	1-4	0-0	0-0	0-1	1-2	0-1	25.0	-1.13
Bangor	1-5	0-2	0-0	0-1	1-2	0-0	20.0	+8.00
Towcester	1-10	0-1	0-0	0-0	1-8	0-1	10.0	-1.00

WINNING HORSES

Horse	Races Run	1st	2nd	3rd	£
Kilcascan	6	2	2	0	5743
Jolly Boys Outing	8	1	1	1	2144
Total winning prize-money					**£7887**
Favourites	**0-1**		**0.0%**		**-1.00**

MICHAEL GATES

CLIFFORD CHAMBERS, WARWICKS

	No. of Hrs	Races Run	1st	2nd	3rd	Unpl	Per cent	£1 Level Stake
NH Flat	*1*	*2*	*0*	*0*	*0*	*2*	*0.0*	*-2.00*
Hurdles	*6*	*17*	*2*	*1*	*0*	*14*	*11.8*	*-5.50*
Chases	*3*	*10*	*3*	*1*	*0*	*6*	*30.0*	*+8.50*
Totals	**7**	**29**	**5**	**2**	**0**	**22**	**17.2**	**+1.00**
13-14	*9*	*77*	*9*	*9*	*5*	*54*	*11.7*	*-0.75*
12-13	*6*	*42*	*2*	*1*	*2*	*37*	*4.8*	*-31.75*

JOCKEYS

	W-R	Per cent	£1 Level Stake
Mikey Hamill	3-11	27.3	+7.50
Miss A E Stirling	1-3	33.3	+4.00
Peter Carberry	1-12	8.3	-7.50

COURSE RECORD

	Total W-R	Non-Hndcps Hurdles	Non-Hndcps Chases	Hndcps Hurdles	Hndcps Chases	NH Flat	Per cent	£1 Level Stake
Stratford	2-7	0-3	0-0	2-3	0-0	0-1	28.6	+4.50
Fakenham	2-10	0-1	0-0	0-3	2-6	0-0	20.0	+3.00
Worcester	1-7	0-1	0-0	0-3	1-2	0-1	14.3	-1.50

WINNING HORSES

Horse	Races Run	1st	2nd	3rd	£
Full Ov Beans	7	3	1	0	13293
Carn Rock	4	1	1	0	3249
Handsome Buddy	5	1	0	0	2274
Total winning prize-money					**£18816**
Favourites	**0-0**		**0.0%**		**0.00**

JONATHAN GEAKE

EAST KENNETT, WILTS

	No. of Hrs	Races Run	1st	2nd	3rd	Unpl	Per cent	£1 Level Stake
NH Flat	*3*	*4*	*0*	*0*	*0*	*4*	*0.0*	*-4.00*
Hurdles	*4*	*17*	*1*	*0*	*4*	*12*	*5.9*	*-7.00*
Chases	*1*	*1*	*0*	*0*	*0*	*1*	*0.0*	*-1.00*
Totals	**7**	**22**	**1**	**0**	**4**	**17**	**4.5**	**-12.00**
13-14	*8*	*23*	*1*	*1*	*2*	*19*	*4.3*	*-8.00*
12-13	*9*	*28*	*2*	*7*	*2*	*17*	*7.1*	*-21.67*

JOCKEYS

	W-R	Per cent	£1 Level Stake
Gerard Tumelty	1-2	50.0	+8.00

COURSE RECORD

	Total W-R	Non-Hndcps Hurdles	Non-Hndcps Chases	Hndcps Hurdles	Hndcps Chases	NH Flat	Per cent	£1 Level Stake
Taunton	1-8	0-2	0-0	1-5	0-0	0-1	12.5	+2.00

WINNING HORSES

Horse	Races Run	1st	2nd	3rd	£
Shot In The Dark	9	1	0	1	2395
Total winning prize-money					**£2395**
Favourites	**0-0**		**0.0%**		**0.00**

TOM GEORGE

SLAD, GLOUCS

	No. of Hrs	Races Run	1st	2nd	3rd	Unpl	Per cent	£1 Level Stake
NH Flat	*15*	*21*	*2*	*5*	*1*	*13*	*9.5*	*-5.50*
Hurdles	*29*	*70*	*7*	*13*	*4*	*46*	*10.0*	*+6.66*
Chases	*41*	*171*	*27*	*22*	*33*	*89*	*15.8*	*-49.21*
Totals	**66**	**262**	**36**	**40**	**38**	**148**	**13.7**	**-48.05**
13-14	*83*	*289*	*40*	*48*	*25*	*176*	*13.8*	*-92.26*
12-13	*69*	*243*	*39*	*38*	*30*	*136*	*16.0*	*-49.75*

BY MONTH

NH Flat	W-R	Per cent	£1 Level Stake
May	0-0	0.0	0.00
June	0-0	0.0	0.00
July	0-0	0.0	0.00
August	0-0	0.0	0.00
September	0-0	0.0	0.00
October	2-4	50.0	+11.50
November	0-6	0.0	-6.00
December	0-2	0.0	-2.00
January	0-1	0.0	-1.00
February	0-2	0.0	-2.00
March	0-4	0.0	-4.00
April	0-2	0.0	-2.00

Hurdles	W-R	Per cent	£1 Level Stake
May	0-8	0.0	-8.00
June	0-3	0.0	-3.00
July	0-0	0.0	0.00
August	0-0	0.0	0.00
September	0-0	0.0	0.00
October	0-3	0.0	-3.00
November	3-10	30.0	+5.91
December	1-7	14.3	-4.75
January	0-11	0.0	-11.00
February	2-9	22.2	+45.00
March	1-14	7.1	-9.50
April	0-5	0.0	-5.00

Chases	W-R	Per cent	£1 Level Stake
May	1-9	11.1	-6.00
June	1-5	20.0	-2.00
July	0-4	0.0	-4.00
August	0-0	0.0	0.00
September	0-1	0.0	-1.00
October	2-13	15.4	+0.33
November	6-28	21.4	-1.00
December	3-30	10.0	-15.50
January	2-18	11.1	-12.13
February	5-22	22.7	+4.58
March	2-20	10.0	-14.38
April	5-21	23.8	+1.88

Totals	W-R	Per cent	£1 Level Stake
May	1-17	5.9	-14.00
June	1-8	12.5	-5.00
July	0-4	0.0	-4.00
August	0-0	0.0	0.00
September	0-1	0.0	-1.00
October	4-20	20.0	+8.83
November	9-44	20.5	-1.09
December	4-39	10.3	-22.25
January	2-30	6.7	-24.13
February	7-33	21.2	+47.58
March	3-38	7.9	-27.88
April	5-28	17.9	-5.12

DISTANCE

Hurdles	W-R	Per cent	£1 Level Stake
2m-2m3f	3-42	7.1	+21.50
2m4f-2m7f	1-10	10.0	-8.09
3m+	0-1	0.0	-1.00

Chases	W-R	Per cent	£1 Level Stake
2m-2m3f	4-34	11.8	-11.25
2m4f-2m7f	8-52	15.4	-20.29
3m+	9-50	18.0	-5.63

TYPE OF RACE

Non-Handicaps	W-R	Per cent	£1 Level Stake
Nov Hrdls	4-26	15.4	+38.50
Hrdls	1-20	5.0	-17.75
Nov Chs	1-6	16.7	-3.00
Chases	1-11	9.1	-9.17
Sell/Claim	0-0	0.0	0.00

Handicaps	W-R	Per cent	£1 Level Stake
Nov Hrdls	0-4	0.0	-4.00
Hrdls	2-20	10.0	-10.09
Nov Chs	8-45	17.8	-9.38
Chases	17-109	15.6	-27.67
Sell/Claim	0-0	0.0	0.00

RACE CLASS

	W-R	Per cent	£1 Level Stake
Class 1	1-32	3.1	-23.00
Class 2	3-35	8.6	-23.67
Class 3	11-77	14.3	-20.75
Class 4	13-71	18.3	+30.63
Class 5	5-34	14.7	-15.59
Class 6	3-13	23.1	+4.33

FIRST TIME OUT

	W-R	Per cent	£1 Level Stake
Bumpers	2-15	13.3	+0.50
Hurdles	2-17	11.8	-8.75
Chases	6-34	17.6	-3.17
Totals	10-66	15.2	-11.42

JOCKEYS

	W-R	Per cent	£1 Level Stake
Paddy Brennan	34-200	17.0	+3.12
Tom O'Brien	1-1	100.0	+8.00
Mr W Biddick	1-2	50.0	-0.17

COURSE RECORD

	Total W-R	Non-Hndcps Hurdles	Non-Hndcps Chases	Hndcps Hurdles	Hndcps Chases	NH Flat	Per cent	£1 Level Stake
Ludlow	6-22	0-5	0-0	0-0	6-15	0-2	27.3	+3.50
Southwell	5-10	2-3	0-0	1-1	1-4	1-2	50.0	+9.91
Leicester	3-11	0-0	0-0	0-0	3-11	0-0	27.3	+1.75
Wincanton	3-11	0-2	1-1	0-0	2-8	0-0	27.3	-3.29

Exeter	2-11	0-3	0-0	1-2	1-6	0-0	18.2	+6.00
Kempton	2-13	0-2	0-2	0-1	2-7	0-1	15.4	-4.00
Newbury	2-15	1-3	0-0	0-4	1-7	0-1	13.3	-2.50
Cheltenham	2-23	0-6	0-2	0-1	2-12	0-2	8.7	-11.50
Musselbgh	1-2	1-1	0-0	0-0	0-1	0-0	50.0	+1.00
Fontwell	1-3	0-0	0-0	0-0	0-2	1-1	33.3	+6.00
Catterick	1-4	0-0	0-0	0-0	1-3	0-1	25.0	-0.75
Warwick	1-6	0-2	0-0	0-0	1-3	0-1	16.7	-2.25
Mrket Rsn	1-7	0-1	1-1	0-2	0-2	0-1	14.3	-4.00
Doncaster	1-8	1-4	0-0	0-1	0-3	0-0	12.5	+43.00
Aintree	1-11	0-0	0-2	0-2	1-7	0-0	9.1	-6.67
Stratford	1-12	0-2	0-1	0-0	1-8	0-1	8.3	-3.00
Chepstow	1-13	0-4	0-0	0-1	1-7	0-1	7.7	-10.25
Perth	1-15	0-1	0-1	0-4	1-8	0-1	6.7	-12.00
Sandown	1-17	0-1	0-5	0-2	1-9	0-0	5.9	-11.00

WINNING HORSES

Horse	Races Run	1st	2nd	3rd	£
God's Own	6	1	2	1	35594
Ballinvarrig	6	1	1	0	25024
Parsnip Pete	6	1	0	0	12558
Stellar Notion	4	2	0	0	18768
Gorsky Island	6	2	1	0	22007
Some Plan	4	2	1	0	15631
Kilbree Kid	8	2	3	3	15595
A Good Skin	8	2	3	0	14703
Saint Are	5	1	1	3	7798
No Duffer	6	2	0	2	11696
Ballyallia Man	5	1	0	2	7347
O Maonlai	5	1	0	0	7148
Sir Valentino	5	1	1	1	6498
The Ould Lad	7	2	2	1	10229
Whats Happening	5	1	0	2	6256
Until Winning	8	3	0	3	13757
Henri De Boistron	5	1	0	1	4549
On The Case	4	1	0	0	3899
Double Shuffle	4	2	0	0	6996
Moonlight Maggie	6	1	2	0	3249
Definitely Better	8	2	1	2	4549
Some Buckle	5	1	1	0	1949
Storming Strumpet	4	1	2	0	1643
Just Before Dawn	1	1	0	0	1560
Big Fella Thanks	4	1	1	0	960
Total winning prize-money					**£259963**
Favourites	**15-46**		**32.6%**		**-2.30**

NICK GIFFORD

FINDON, W SUSSEX

	No. of Hrs	Races Run	1st	2nd	3rd	Unpl	Per cent	£1 Level Stake
NH Flat	*5*	*8*	*1*	*0*	*2*	*5*	*12.5*	*-1.00*
Hurdles	*9*	*33*	*1*	*9*	*6*	*17*	*3.0*	*-27.00*
Chases	*9*	*30*	*4*	*3*	*6*	*17*	*13.3*	*-5.25*
Totals	**18**	**71**	**6**	**12**	**14**	**39**	**8.5**	**-33.25**
13-14	*28*	*108*	*12*	*10*	*13*	*73*	*11.1*	*-10.38*
12-13	*24*	*98*	*10*	*10*	*14*	*64*	*10.2*	*-7.26*

JOCKEYS

	W-R	Per cent	£1 Level Stake
Tom Cannon	3-37	8.1	-20.75
Daryl Jacob	2-5	40.0	+10.50
Liam Treadwell	1-7	14.3	-1.00

COURSE RECORD

	Total W-R	Non-Hndcps Hurdles	Non-Hndcps Chases	Hndcps Hurdles	Hndcps Chases	NH Flat	Per cent	£1 Level Stake
Huntingdon	2-3	0-0	0-0	0-1	1-1	1-1	66.7	+7.25
Sandown	2-9	0-0	0-0	0-2	2-7	0-0	22.2	+5.50
Cheltenham	1-4	0-0	0-0	0-1	1-2	0-1	25.0	+3.00
Fontwell	1-8	0-1	0-0	1-5	0-1	0-1	12.5	-2.00

WINNING HORSES

Horse	Races Run	1st	2nd	3rd	£
Generous Ransom	7	2	0	2	23147
Fairy Rath	5	1	1	0	9384
*Doctor Ric	1	1	0	0	6498
Prouts Pub	7	1	2	1	3249
Theo's Charm	3	1	0	1	1625
Total winning prize-money					**£43903**
Favourites	**1-17**		**5.9%**		**-13.75**

MARK GILLARD

HOLWELL, DORSET

	No. of Hrs	Races Run	1st	2nd	3rd	Unpl	Per cent	£1 Level Stake
NH Flat	*2*	*4*	*0*	*1*	*0*	*3*	*0.0*	*-4.00*
Hurdles	*20*	*87*	*10*	*9*	*7*	*61*	*11.5*	*+4.25*
Chases	*13*	*59*	*8*	*6*	*9*	*36*	*13.6*	*-7.67*
Totals	**27**	**150**	**18**	**16**	**16**	**100**	**12.0**	**-7.42**
13-14	*29*	*148*	*5*	*14*	*16*	*113*	*3.4*	*-108.75*
12-13	*19*	*88*	*9*	*10*	*10*	*59*	*10.2*	*-32.00*

BY MONTH

NH Flat	W-R	Per cent	£1 Level Stake	**Hurdles**	W-R	Per cent	£1 Level Stake
May	0-1	0.0	-1.00	May	1-10	10.0	-6.25
June	0-1	0.0	-1.00	June	1-6	16.7	+1.00
July	0-0	0.0	0.00	July	1-7	14.3	-4.00
August	0-0	0.0	0.00	August	1-7	14.3	-4.00
September	0-0	0.0	0.00	September	0-2	0.0	-2.00
October	0-0	0.0	0.00	October	0-5	0.0	-5.00
November	0-0	0.0	0.00	November	0-8	0.0	-8.00
December	0-0	0.0	0.00	December	1-8	12.5	+26.00
January	0-0	0.0	0.00	January	0-6	0.0	-6.00
February	0-0	0.0	0.00	February	3-13	23.1	+7.50
March	0-1	0.0	-1.00	March	2-9	22.2	+11.00
April	0-1	0.0	-1.00	April	0-6	0.0	-6.00

Chases	W-R	Per cent	£1 Level Stake	Totals	W-R	Per cent	£1 Level Stake
May	2-8	25.0	+6.50	May	3-19	15.8	-0.75
June	0-5	0.0	-5.00	June	1-12	8.3	-5.00
July	1-4	25.0	-0.50	July	2-11	18.2	-4.50
August	1-2	50.0	+1.00	August	2-9	22.2	-3.00
September	1-8	12.5	-3.67	September	1-10	10.0	-5.67
October	0-5	0.0	-5.00	October	0-10	0.0	-10.00
November	0-7	0.0	-7.00	November	0-15	0.0	-15.00
December	1-3	33.3	+6.00	December	2-11	18.2	+32.00
January	0-6	0.0	-6.00	January	0-12	0.0	-12.00
February	0-2	0.0	-2.00	February	3-15	20.0	+5.50
March	1-6	16.7	+7.00	March	3-16	18.8	+17.00
April	1-3	33.3	+1.00	April	1-10	10.0	-6.00

DISTANCE

Hurdles	W-R	Per cent	£1 Level Stake	Chases	W-R	Per cent	£1 Level Stake
2m-2m3f	3-50	6.0	-26.00	2m-2m3f	1-29	3.4	-21.50
2m4f-2m7f	3-18	16.7	-9.00	2m4f-2m7f	4-18	22.2	-3.17
3m+	1-3	33.3	+14.00	3m+	0-4	0.0	-4.00

TYPE OF RACE

Non-Handicaps	W-R	Per cent	£1 Level Stake	Handicaps	W-R	Per cent	£1 Level Stake
Nov Hrdls	2-16	12.5	-6.00	Nov Hrdls	1-9	11.1	+25.00
Hrdls	0-12	0.0	-12.00	Hrdls	5-40	12.5	-4.75
Nov Chs	0-4	0.0	-4.00	Nov Chs	1-9	11.1	-2.00
Chases	0-0	0.0	0.00	Chases	7-46	15.2	-1.67
Sell/Claim	1-6	16.7	-3.00	Sell/Claim	1-4	25.0	+5.00

RACE CLASS / FIRST TIME OUT

RACE CLASS	W-R	Per cent	£1 Level Stake	FIRST TIME OUT	W-R	Per cent	£1 Level Stake
Class 1	0-4	0.0	-4.00	Bumpers	0-2	0.0	-2.00
Class 2	0-1	0.0	-1.00	Hurdles	0-17	0.0	-17.00
Class 3	0-2	0.0	-2.00	Chases	1-8	12.5	-0.50
Class 4	5-64	7.8	-25.25				
Class 5	13-77	16.9	+26.83	Totals	1-27	3.7	-19.50
Class 6	0-2	0.0	-2.00				

JOCKEYS

	W-R	Per cent	£1 Level Stake
Paul John	4-13	30.8	+51.00
Tom O'Brien	4-15	26.7	+2.83
Tom Cannon	4-45	8.9	-17.00
Gary Derwin	2-13	15.4	+1.50
Tom Bellamy	1-1	100.0	+2.50
A P McCoy	1-2	50.0	+1.75
Sean Bowen	1-4	25.0	-1.00
Mr T Gillard	1-5	20.0	+3.00

COURSE RECORD

	Total W-R	Non-Hndcps Hurdles	Non-Hndcps Chases	Hndcps Hurdles	Hndcps Chases	NH Flat	Per cent	£1 Level Stake
Towcester	5-13	0-0	0-0	1-3	4-10	0-0	38.5	+27.25
Nton Abbot	5-27	1-4	0-1	1-12	3-10	0-0	18.5	+8.33
Wincanton	3-14	0-3	0-0	3-10	0-1	0-0	21.4	+26.50
Worcester	3-21	2-7	0-0	0-3	1-11	0-0	14.3	-11.50
Fakenham	1-4	0-0	0-0	1-3	0-0	0-1	25.0	+5.00
Taunton	1-17	0-6	0-1	1-9	0-1	0-0	5.9	-9.00

WINNING HORSES

Horse	Races Run	1st	2nd	3rd	£
Enchanting Smile	6	1	0	2	6173
Comical Red	8	1	0	1	4106
*Dont Call Me Oscar	7	3	1	0	8980
Revaader	4	1	1	1	3574
Wicklewood	12	4	1	2	5393
Lamb's Cross	12	1	3	1	3249
Byron Blue	9	2	2	1	5198
Tenby Jewel	12	1	1	1	3119
*Gorteenwood	7	3	2	0	7993
Karl Marx	10	1	2	0	2274

Total winning prize-money **£50059**

Favourites **4-6** **66.7%** **7.25**

J L GLEDSON

BELLINGHAM, NORTHUMBERLAND

	No. of Hrs	Races Run	1st	2nd	3rd	Unpl	Per cent	£1 Level Stake
NH Flat	*1*	*3*	*0*	*0*	*0*	*3*	*0.0*	*-3.00*
Hurdles	*1*	*5*	*1*	*0*	*0*	*4*	*20.0*	*+10.00*
Chases	*1*	*1*	*0*	*0*	*0*	*1*	*0.0*	*-1.00*
Totals	**2**	**9**	**1**	**0**	**0**	**8**	**11.1**	**+6.00**
13-14	*1*	*4*	*0*	*0*	*0*	*4*	*0.0*	*-4.00*

JOCKEYS

	W-R	Per cent	£1 Level Stake
Mr John Dawson	1-5	20.0	+10.00

COURSE RECORD

	Total W-R	Non-Hndcps Hurdles	Non-Hndcps Chases	Hndcps Hurdles	Hndcps Chases	NH Flat	Per cent	£1 Level Stake
Kelso	1-3	0-0	0-0	1-3	0-0	0-0	33.3	+12.00

WINNING HORSES

Horse	Races Run	1st	2nd	3rd	£
Neville Woods	6	1	0	0	3249

Total winning prize-money **£3249**

Favourites **0-0** **0.0%** **0.00**

JIM GOLDIE

UPLAWMOOR, E RENFREWS

	No. of Hrs	Races Run	1st	2nd	3rd	Unpl	Per cent	£1 Level Stake
NH Flat	2	3	0	1	0	2	0.0	-3.00
Hurdles	17	56	3	4	6	43	5.4	-39.50
Chases	3	16	2	1	3	10	12.5	-6.50
Totals	**21**	**75**	**5**	**6**	**9**	**55**	**6.7**	**-49.00**
13-14	*26*	*107*	*15*	*9*	*12*	*71*	*14.0*	*-1.58*
12-13	*34*	*134*	*9*	*11*	*18*	*96*	*6.7*	*-66.63*

JOCKEYS

	W-R	Per cent	£1 Level Stake
Mr H Stock	1-2	50.0	+2.50
Brian Hughes	1-5	20.0	+0.50
Brian Harding	1-5	20.0	+2.00
Dale Irving	1-6	16.7	-2.00
Ryan Day	1-20	5.0	-15.00

COURSE RECORD

	Total W-R	Non-Hndcps Hurdles	Non-Hndcps Chases	Hndcps Hurdles	Hndcps Chases	NH Flat	Per cent	£1 Level Stake
Ayr	3-33	1-3	0-0	0-17	2-11	0-2	9.1	-18.50
Perth	1-10	0-2	0-0	1-7	0-1	0-0	10.0	-5.50
Musselbgh	1-15	0-4	0-0	1-11	0-0	0-0	6.7	-8.00

WINNING HORSES

Horse	Races Run	1st	2nd	3rd	£
Too Cool To Fool	9	1	1	0	6886
*Silver Duke	6	1	0	3	6256
Plus Jamais	8	1	1	3	4549
Los Nadis	6	1	0	0	3035
Lochnell	6	1	0	0	1949
Total winning prize-money					**£22675**
Favourites	**0-3**		**0.0%**		**-3.00**

STEVE GOLLINGS

SCAMBLESBY, LINCS

	No. of Hrs	Races Run	1st	2nd	3rd	Unpl	Per cent	£1 Level Stake
NH Flat	3	3	1	0	0	2	33.3	0.00
Hurdles	13	26	5	5	4	12	19.2	+7.88
Chases	2	4	0	1	0	3	0.0	-4.00
Totals	**16**	**33**	**6**	**6**	**4**	**17**	**18.2**	**+3.88**
13-14	*23*	*103*	*14*	*16*	*17*	*56*	*13.6*	*-36.13*
12-13	*19*	*71*	*16*	*10*	*5*	*40*	*22.5*	*+4.88*

JOCKEYS

	W-R	Per cent	£1 Level Stake
Trevor Ryan	3-13	23.1	+6.88
Richard Johnson	2-7	28.6	+5.50
A P McCoy	1-5	20.0	-0.50

COURSE RECORD

	Total W-R	Non-Hndcps Hurdles	Non-Hndcps Chases	Hndcps Hurdles	Hndcps Chases	NH Flat	Per cent	£1 Level Stake
Mrket Rsn	2-9	0-2	0-0	2-5	0-1	0-1	22.2	-4.13
Catterick	1-1	0-0	0-0	1-1	0-0	0-0	100.0	+3.50
Cheltenham	1-1	0-0	0-0	0-0	0-0	1-1	100.0	+2.00
Sedgefield	1-1	0-0	0-0	1-1	0-0	0-0	100.0	+14.00
Wetherby	1-1	1-1	0-0	0-0	0-0	0-0	100.0	+8.50

WINNING HORSES

Horse	Races Run	1st	2nd	3rd	£
Make Me A Fortune	9	3	1	4	18880
Definity Red	2	1	1	0	11390
Local Hero	2	1	0	0	6498
The Grey Taylor	1	1	0	0	5523
Total winning prize-money					**£42291**
Favourites	**2-5**		**40.0%**		**-0.13**

CHRIS GORDON

MORESTEAD, HAMPSHIRE

	No. of Hrs	Races Run	1st	2nd	3rd	Unpl	Per cent	£1 Level Stake
NH Flat	10	17	0	1	1	15	0.0	-17.00
Hurdles	32	125	18	19	14	74	14.4	+18.00
Chases	16	56	12	11	9	24	21.4	+6.02
Totals	**42**	**198**	**30**	**31**	**24**	**113**	**15.2**	**+7.02**
13-14	*38*	*211*	*19*	*27*	*30*	*135*	*9.0*	*-51.29*
12-13	*33*	*165*	*14*	*20*	*19*	*112*	*8.5*	*-22.63*

BY MONTH

NH Flat	W-R	Per cent	£1 Level Stake	Hurdles	W-R	Per cent	£1 Level Stake
May	0-2	0.0	-2.00	May	5-13	38.5	+44.50
June	0-0	0.0	0.00	June	0-5	0.0	-5.00
July	0-0	0.0	0.00	July	0-5	0.0	-5.00
August	0-0	0.0	0.00	August	0-6	0.0	-6.00
September	0-1	0.0	-1.00	September	0-2	0.0	-2.00
October	0-4	0.0	-4.00	October	2-12	16.7	+14.00
November	0-3	0.0	-3.00	November	3-19	15.8	+12.50
December	0-2	0.0	-2.00	December	4-16	25.0	-2.75
January	0-2	0.0	-2.00	January	1-13	7.7	-8.50
February	0-2	0.0	-2.00	February	2-13	15.4	-5.75
March	0-0	0.0	0.00	March	0-13	0.0	-13.00
April	0-1	0.0	-1.00	April	1-8	12.5	-5.00

Chases	W-R	Per cent	£1 Level Stake
May	0-7	0.0	-7.00
June	0-3	0.0	-3.00
July	1-2	50.0	+15.00
August	0-1	0.0	-1.00
September	0-0	0.0	0.00
October	2-4	50.0	+3.25
November	2-9	22.2	-1.40
December	1-5	20.0	0.00
January	0-3	0.0	-3.00
February	2-5	40.0	+9.33
March	3-8	37.5	-1.17
April	1-9	11.1	-5.00

Totals	W-R	Per cent	£1 Level Stake
May	5-22	22.7	+35.50
June	0-8	0.0	-8.00
July	1-7	14.3	+10.00
August	0-7	0.0	-7.00
September	0-3	0.0	-3.00
October	4-20	20.0	+13.25
November	5-31	16.1	+8.10
December	5-23	21.7	-4.75
January	1-18	5.6	-13.50
February	4-20	20.0	+1.58
March	3-21	14.3	-14.17
April	2-18	11.1	-11.00

DISTANCE

Hurdles	W-R	Per cent	£1 Level Stake
2m-2m3f	11-55	20.0	-1.00
2m4f-2m7f	4-34	11.8	+13.25
3m+	1-14	7.1	-11.25

Chases	W-R	Per cent	£1 Level Stake
2m-2m3f	5-24	20.8	+4.83
2m4f-2m7f	4-15	26.7	-0.07
3m+	2-10	20.0	+2.75

TYPE OF RACE

Non-Handicaps

	W-R	Per cent	£1 Level Stake
Nov Hrdls	3-25	12.0	-17.00
Hrdls	3-14	21.4	+31.50
Nov Chs	0-1	0.0	-1.00
Chases	0-1	0.0	-1.00
Sell/Claim	0-0	0.0	0.00

Handicaps

	W-R	Per cent	£1 Level Stake
Nov Hrdls	0-12	0.0	-12.00
Hrdls	12-72	16.7	+17.50
Nov Chs	3-13	23.1	-0.25
Chases	9-41	22.0	+8.27
Sell/Claim	0-2	0.0	-2.00

RACE CLASS

	W-R	Per cent	£1 Level Stake
Class 1	0-4	0.0	-4.00
Class 2	1-8	12.5	-3.50
Class 3	5-31	16.1	+3.58
Class 4	16-82	19.5	+12.10
Class 5	8-59	13.6	+12.83
Class 6	0-14	0.0	-14.00

FIRST TIME OUT

	W-R	Per cent	£1 Level Stake
Bumpers	0-10	0.0	-10.00
Hurdles	6-20	30.0	+70.50
Chases	2-12	16.7	-2.75
Totals	8-42	19.0	+57.75

JOCKEYS

	W-R	Per cent	£1 Level Stake
Tom Cannon	25-143	17.5	+7.68
Marc Goldstein	2-19	10.5	+12.50
Richard Johnson	1-1	100.0	+3.33
Mr Louis Muspratt	1-5	20.0	+10.00
Sean Bowen	1-8	12.5	-4.50

COURSE RECORD

	Total W-R	Non-Hndcps Hurdles	Non-Hndcps Chases	Hndcps Hurdles	Hndcps Chases	NH Flat	Per cent	£1 Level Stake
Fontwell	13-60	2-17	0-1	7-20	4-17	0-5	21.7	+4.33
Plumpton	6-38	3-6	0-0	0-18	3-10	0-4	15.8	+15.00
Kempton	4-9	0-1	0-0	1-3	3-4	0-1	44.4	+28.43
Lingfield	3-8	1-2	0-0	2-3	0-3	0-0	37.5	+3.00
Warwick	1-1	0-0	0-0	0-0	1-1	0-0	100.0	+1.75
Cheltenham	1-3	0-0	0-0	1-2	0-1	0-0	33.3	+1.50
Wincanton	1-8	0-1	0-0	1-6	0-1	0-0	12.5	+7.00
Stratford	1-10	0-2	0-0	0-6	1-2	0-0	10.0	+7.00

WINNING HORSES

Horse	Races Run	1st	2nd	3rd	£
Lightentertainment	10	5	2	0	38931
Sea Wall	6	1	0	2	6844
Comeonginger	5	3	0	1	14815
Ballyheigue Bay	8	3	1	3	14966
Tigre D'Aron	3	1	1	0	4549
Chilworth Screamer	2	1	0	0	4549
Noble Friend	12	2	2	3	8123
*Coolking	3	1	1	0	3994
Very Noble	10	2	1	1	7148
Remiluc	5	1	2	0	3899
King Edmund	10	2	4	1	6671
*Owner Occupier	6	1	1	2	3249
Sweet Boy Vic	8	1	3	1	3119
*Norse Legend	4	1	2	0	3119
*Star Presenter	4	1	2	1	2729
*Jebril	6	1	1	0	2274
Osmosia	12	2	0	1	4094
The Kings Assassin	8	1	2	2	2079
Total winning prize-money					**£135152**
Favourites	**8-27**		**29.6%**		**-5.98**

HARRIET GRAHAM

PHILIP LAW, BORDERS

	No. of Hrs	Races Run	1st	2nd	3rd	Unpl	Per cent	£1 Level Stake
NH Flat	*0*	*0*	*0*	*0*	*0*	*0*	*0.0*	*0.00*
Hurdles	*4*	*21*	*2*	*1*	*1*	*17*	*9.5*	*-7.75*
Chases	*4*	*17*	*1*	*2*	*2*	*12*	*5.9*	*-11.00*
Totals	**6**	**38**	**3**	**3**	**3**	**29**	**7.9**	**-18.75**
13-14	*8*	*42*	*5*	*5*	*6*	*26*	*11.9*	*-5.50*
12-13	*7*	*37*	*3*	*3*	*4*	*27*	*8.1*	*-18.25*

JOCKEYS

	W-R	Per cent	£1 Level Stake
Callum Bewley	2-15	13.3	-1.75
James Reveley	1-7	14.3	-1.00

COURSE RECORD

	Total W-R	Non-Hndcps Hurdles	Non-Hndcps Chases	Hndcps Hurdles	Hndcps Chases	NH Flat	Per cent	£1 Level Stake
Catterick	2-3	0-0	0-0	1-2	1-1	0-0	66.7	+13.00
Ayr	1-4	0-1	0-0	1-3	0-0	0-0	25.0	-0.75

WINNING HORSES

Horse	Races Run	1st	2nd	3rd	£
Scotswell	9	1	2	0	12512
*Macgillycuddy	11	1	0	1	3899
Maggie Blue	10	1	1	0	3329
Total winning prize-money					**£19740**
Favourites	**1-4**		**25.0%**		**2.00**

CHRIS GRANT

NEWTON BEWLEY, CO DURHAM

	No. of Hrs	Races Run	1st	2nd	3rd	Unpl	Per cent	£1 Level Stake
NH Flat	*15*	*29*	*2*	*0*	*3*	*24*	*6.9*	*-3.00*
Hurdles	*31*	*74*	*8*	*7*	*7*	*52*	*10.8*	*-10.53*
Chases	*14*	*60*	*8*	*6*	*9*	*37*	*13.3*	*+20.25*
Totals	**46**	**163**	**18**	**13**	**19**	**113**	**11.0**	**+6.72**
13-14	*49*	*183*	*8*	*18*	*30*	*127*	*4.4*	*-59.55*
12-13	*54*	*213*	*20*	*30*	*30*	*133*	*9.4*	*-59.38*

BY MONTH

NH Flat	W-R	Per cent	£1 Level Stake
May	0-2	0.0	-2.00
June	1-2	50.0	+19.00
July	0-0	0.0	0.00
August	0-0	0.0	0.00
September	0-1	0.0	-1.00
October	1-2	50.0	+3.00
November	0-6	0.0	-6.00
December	0-4	0.0	-4.00
January	0-4	0.0	-4.00
February	0-1	0.0	-1.00
March	0-5	0.0	-5.00
April	0-2	0.0	-2.00

Hurdles	W-R	Per cent	£1 Level Stake
May	1-13	7.7	+13.00
June	0-1	0.0	-1.00
July	0-1	0.0	-1.00
August	0-1	0.0	-1.00
September	0-1	0.0	-1.00
October	1-6	16.7	-3.38
November	2-10	20.0	-3.28
December	1-10	10.0	-7.25
January	1-5	20.0	-2.63
February	1-12	8.3	+5.00
March	1-10	10.0	-4.00
April	0-4	0.0	-4.00

Chases	W-R	Per cent	£1 Level Stake
May	0-4	0.0	-4.00
June	0-3	0.0	-3.00
July	0-5	0.0	-5.00
August	0-3	0.0	-3.00
September	0-2	0.0	-2.00
October	2-4	50.0	+5.25
November	1-8	12.5	-5.25
December	1-6	16.7	-1.50
January	1-6	16.7	-2.25
February	2-5	40.0	+21.00
March	0-8	0.0	-8.00
April	1-6	16.7	+28.00

Totals	W-R	Per cent	£1 Level Stake
May	1-19	5.3	+7.00
June	1-6	16.7	+15.00
July	0-6	0.0	-6.00
August	0-4	0.0	-4.00
September	0-4	0.0	-4.00
October	4-12	33.3	+4.87
November	3-24	12.5	-14.53
December	2-20	10.0	-12.75
January	2-15	13.3	-8.88
February	3-18	16.7	+25.00
March	1-23	4.3	-17.00
April	1-12	8.3	+22.00

DISTANCE

Hurdles	W-R	Per cent	£1 Level Stake
2m-2m3f	1-24	4.2	-22.78
2m4f-2m7f	3-39	7.7	-17.00
3m+	4-9	44.4	+31.25

Chases	W-R	Per cent	£1 Level Stake
2m-2m3f	1-14	7.1	-10.25
2m4f-2m7f	3-18	16.7	+13.25
3m+	3-19	15.8	+22.50

TYPE OF RACE

Non-Handicaps	W-R	Per cent	£1 Level Stake
Nov Hrdls	2-32	6.3	-28.40
Hrdls	1-10	10.0	-7.38
Nov Chs	0-10	0.0	-10.00
Chases	0-0	0.0	0.00
Sell/Claim	0-3	0.0	-3.00

Handicaps	W-R	Per cent	£1 Level Stake
Nov Hrdls	0-2	0.0	-2.00
Hrdls	5-26	19.2	+31.25
Nov Chs	1-9	11.1	-4.50
Chases	7-41	17.1	+34.75
Sell/Claim	0-1	0.0	-1.00

RACE CLASS

	W-R	Per cent	£1 Level Stake
Class 1	0-0	0.0	0.00
Class 2	0-3	0.0	-3.00
Class 3	3-18	16.7	+45.00
Class 4	5 78	6.4	-49.15
Class 5	8-36	22.2	+15.88
Class 6	2-28	7.1	-2.00

FIRST TIME OUT

	W-R	Per cent	£1 Level Stake
Bumpers	1-15	6.7	+6.00
Hurdles	3-23	13.0	+2.13
Chases	0-8	0.0	-8.00
Totals	4-46	8.7	+0.13

JOCKEYS

	W-R	Per cent	£1 Level Stake
Diarmuid O'Regan	11-84	13.1	+6.10
Brian Hughes	4-26	15.4	+19.13
Miss G Andrews	1-1	100.0	+25.00
Mr John Dawson	1-3	33.3	0.00
Dougie Costello	1-9	11.1	-3.50

COURSE RECORD

	Total W-R	Non-Hndcps Hurdles	Non-Hndcps Chases	Hndcps Hurdles	Hndcps Chases	NH Flat	Per cent	£1 Level Stake
Kelso	4-11	1-6	0-0	1-3	2-2	0-0	36.4	+36.88
Newcastle	3-26	0-8	0-0	2-4	1-8	0-6	11.5	-11.75
Sedgefield	3-26	1-8	0-1	0-1	2-7	0-9	11.5	-16.53
Musselbgh	2-10	0-3	0-0	0-2	2-4	0-1	20.0	-3.25
Wetherby	2-20	0-8	0-2	2-4	0-4	0-2	10.0	+8.75
Bangor	1-1	0-0	0-0	0-0	0-0	1-1	100.0	+4.00
Haydock	1-2	0-1	0-0	0-0	1-1	0-0	50.0	+32.00
Uttoxeter	1-2	0-0	0-0	0-0	0-1	1-1	50.0	+19.00
Hexham	1-11	1-2	0-0	0-2	0-5	0-2	9.1	-8.38

WINNING HORSES

Horse	Races Run	1st	2nd	3rd	£
William Money	5	2	0	0	14621
Donna's Diamond	7	2	2	0	8707
Generous Chief	6	1	0	1	4793
Muwalla	7	1	2	1	4527
Local Present	8	1	2	2	3899
Jacks Last Hope	5	3	1	0	6909
Beau Dandy	8	2	0	3	6369
Lucematic	2	1	0	0	3249
Notonebuttwo	6	3	0	0	6693

Ride The Range	2	1	1	0	2274
Papillon Parc	2	1	0	0	2053
Total winning prize-money					**£64094**
Favourites	**6-10**		**60.0%**		**5.47**

CARROLL GRAY

MOORLAND, SOMERSET

	No. of Hrs	Races Run	1st	2nd	3rd	Unpl	Per cent	£1 Level Stake
NH Flat	*1*	*1*	*0*	*0*	*0*	*1*	*0.0*	*-1.00*
Hurdles	*10*	*18*	*0*	*1*	*0*	*17*	*0.0*	*-18.00*
Chases	*5*	*15*	*1*	*3*	*2*	*9*	*6.7*	*-8.50*
Totals	**13**	**34**	**1**	**4**	**2**	**27**	**2.9**	**-27.50**
13-14	*11*	*45*	*5*	*3*	*4*	*33*	*11.1*	*+64.25*
12-13	*10*	*32*	*1*	*3*	*4*	*24*	*3.1*	*-28.25*

JOCKEYS

	W-R	Per cent	£1 Level Stake
James Best	1-6	16.7	+0.50

COURSE RECORD

	Total W-R	Non-Hndcps Hurdles	Non-Hndcps Chases	Hndcps Hurdles	Hndcps Chases	NH Flat	Per cent	£1 Level Stake
Fontwell	1-2	0-0	0-0	0-0	1-2	0-0	50.0	+4.50

WINNING HORSES

Horse	Races Run	1st	2nd	3rd	£
Volio Vincente	3	1	0	0	2144
Total winning prize-money					**£2144**
Favourites	**0-2**		**0.0%**		**-2.00**

WARREN GREATREX

UPPER LAMBOURN, BERKS

	No. of Hrs	Races Run	1st	2nd	3rd	Unpl	Per cent	£1 Level Stake
NH Flat	*27*	*31*	*11*	*2*	*2*	*16*	*35.5*	*+7.45*
Hurdles	*59*	*198*	*35*	*25*	*24*	*114*	*17.7*	*-69.61*
Chases	*19*	*43*	*5*	*4*	*8*	*26*	*11.6*	*-17.75*
Totals	**81**	**272**	**51**	**31**	**34**	**156**	**18.8**	**-79.91**
13-14	*48*	*178*	*41*	*25*	*25*	*87*	*23.0*	*+37.26*
12-13	*28*	*109*	*12*	*16*	*11*	*70*	*11.0*	*-37.55*

BY MONTH

NH Flat	W-R	Per cent	£1 Level Stake	Hurdles	W-R	Per cent	£1 Level Stake
May	4-7	57.1	+7.53	May	4-9	44.4	+1.72
June	0-0	0.0	0.00	June	3-6	50.0	+1.58
July	1-1	100.0	+0.50	July	2-5	40.0	+1.30
August	0-0	0.0	0.00	August	1-7	14.3	-5.09
September	0-0	0.0	0.00	September	0-5	0.0	-5.00
October	3-5	60.0	+8.00	October	3-12	25.0	-1.38
November	0-4	0.0	-4.00	November	10-27	37.0	+0.04
December	0-4	0.0	-4.00	December	4-27	14.8	-11.27
January	0-0	0.0	0.00	January	0-26	0.0	-26.00
February	1-2	50.0	+2.33	February	3-15	20.0	-5.90
March	0-2	0.0	-2.00	March	4-33	12.1	+1.38
April	2-6	33.3	-0.92	April	1-26	3.8	-21.00

Chases	W-R	Per cent	£1 Level Stake	Totals	W-R	Per cent	£1 Level Stake
May	1-2	50.0	+0.50	May	9-18	50.0	+9.75
June	1-2	50.0	+2.00	June	4-8	50.0	+3.58
July	0-0	0.0	0.00	July	3-6	50.0	+1.80
August	0-1	0.0	-1.00	August	1-8	12.5	-6.09
September	0-1	0.0	-1.00	September	0-6	0.0	-6.00
October	0-2	0.0	-2.00	October	6-19	31.6	+4.62
November	1-7	14.3	-4.75	November	11-38	28.9	-8.71
December	1-9	11.1	+6.00	December	5-40	12.5	-9.27
January	0-2	0.0	-2.00	January	0-28	0.0	-28.00
February	1-4	25.0	-2.50	February	5-21	23.8	-6.07
March	0-6	0.0	-6.00	March	4-41	9.8	-6.62
April	0-7	0.0	-7.00	April	3-39	7.7	-28.92

DISTANCE

Hurdles	W-R	Per cent	£1 Level Stake	Chases	W-R	Per cent	£1 Level Stake
2m-2m3f	16-77	20.8	-15.99	2m-2m3f	0-1	0.0	-1.00
2m4f-2m7f	11-57	19.3	-22.83	2m4f-2m7f	0-12	0.0	-12.00
3m+	3-20	15.0	-10.25	3m+	4-19	21.1	+2.25

TYPE OF RACE

Non-Handicaps	W-R	Per cent	£1 Level Stake	Handicaps	W-R	Per cent	£1 Level Stake
Nov Hrdls	13-63	20.6	-22.47	Nov Hrdls	1-5	20.0	-3.20
Hrdls	9-54	16.7	-11.13	Hrdls	12-74	16.2	-30.81
Nov Chs	1-5	20.0	-2.75	Nov Chs	0-11	0.0	-11.00
Chases	2-4	50.0	0.00	Chases	2-23	8.7	-4.00
Sell/Claim	0-2	0.0	-2.00	Sell/Claim	0-0	0.0	0.00

RACE CLASS

	W-R	Per cent	£1 Level Stake
Class 1	3-33	9.1	+0.25
Class 2	2-15	13.3	-3.00
Class 3	4-39	10.3	-26.99
Class 4	23-137	16.8	-58.87
Class 5	7-29	24.1	-12.25
Class 6	12-19	63.2	+20.95

FIRST TIME OUT

	W-R	Per cent	£1 Level Stake
Bumpers	11-27	40.7	+11.45
Hurdles	13-40	32.5	-3.30
Chases	1-14	7.1	-11.50
Totals	25-81	30.9	-3.35

JOCKEYS

	W-R	Per cent	£1 Level Stake
Gavin Sheehan	40-175	22.9	-20.57
Dougie Costello	5-45	11.1	-22.86
Mr S Waley-Cohen	2-4	50.0	0.00
A P McCoy	2-5	40.0	-0.99
Andrew Tinkler	1-3	33.3	-0.50
Conor Walsh	1-14	7.1	-9.00

COURSE RECORD

	Total W-R	Non-Hndcps Hurdles	Non-Hndcps Chases	Hndcps Hurdles	Hndcps Chases	NH Flat	Per cent	£1 Level Stake
Wetherby	7-16	4-9	1-1	1-4	1-1	0-1	43.8	+15.68
Mrket Rsn	5-10	3-6	0-0	1-3	0-0	1-1	50.0	+6.61
Nton Abbot	4-8	0-0	0-0	3-6	0-1	1-1	50.0	+3.92
Uttoxeter	4-10	1-4	0-0	1-3	0-0	2-3	40.0	+2.25
Ffos Las	4-13	2-5	0-0	0-3	1-4	1-1	30.8	-2.84
Doncaster	4-14	1-8	1-2	1-2	0-1	1-1	28.6	-4.64
Wincanton	3-10	1-3	0-0	1-6	0-0	1-1	30.0	+2.75
Stratford	3-11	2-8	1-1	0-2	0-0	0-0	27.3	-3.75
Worcester	3-11	0-1	0-1	1-5	0-2	2-2	27.3	-2.67
Plumpton	3-14	2-11	0-0	0-2	0-0	1-1	21.4	-2.55
Fontwell	2-6	1-3	0-0	1-3	0-0	0-0	33.3	0.00
Cheltenham	2-15	2-8	0-2	0-1	0-0	0-4	13.3	+6.00
Lingfield	1-2	1-1	0-0	0-0	0-1	0-0	50.0	-0.27
Southwell	1-5	1-1	0-0	0-1	0-1	0-2	20.0	+2.50
Bangor	1-7	0-3	0-0	1-2	0-1	0-1	14.3	-4.90
Warwick	1-7	0-6	0-0	0-0	0-0	1-1	14.3	-4.50
Exeter	1-10	0-4	0-0	1-3	0-2	0-1	10.0	-5.00
Chepstow	1-12	1-5	0-0	0-3	0-3	0-1	8.3	-7.00
Newbury	1-14	0-7	0-0	1-3	0-4	0-0	7.1	-4.50

WINNING HORSES

Horse	Races Run	1st	2nd	3rd	£
Cole Harden	6	2	2	1	191922
*Alzammaar	6	1	1	3	25992
Dolatulo	7	1	1	0	22780
Paint The Clouds	4	2	0	1	16238
Seedling	5	3	0	0	12706
Kaysersberg	5	2	0	0	10002
Centasia	4	1	0	0	5523
Chalk It Down	3	2	1	0	9422
Good Of Luck	3	1	0	2	4224
Andi'Amu	4	1	1	1	3899
*Blue Atlantic	3	1	0	1	3899
Warrantor	6	2	0	0	7018
Bells 'N' Banjos	6	1	2	0	3899
Horsted Valley	5	1	0	0	3899
High Kite	7	1	0	3	3769
Hannah's Princess	5	1	3	1	3574
Silent Knight	5	2	1	0	5458
Shantou Bob	6	3	1	1	7104
One Track Mind	4	2	0	0	6541
*Boite	3	1	2	0	3249
Easy Beesy	4	1	0	1	3249
Chestertern	4	1	0	0	3249
Chase The Wind	6	2	0	1	6498
Miss Sophierose	4	2	0	0	4892
Tsar Alexandre	2	1	1	0	3249
Detour Ahead	2	2	0	0	4687
Relentless Pursuit	4	1	0	0	2053
Missed Approach	3	2	0	1	3509
Con Forza	1	1	0	0	1711
La Bague Au Roi	1	1	0	0	1711
Bon Enfant	1	1	0	0	1625
Davy Doubt	3	1	0	0	1560
Always Managing	4	1	0	0	1560
Knight Bachelor	5	1	1	0	1560
Alphabet Bay	6	1	0	0	1560
Going For Gold	5	1	0	0	1560
Total winning prize-money					**£395351**
Favourites	**27-68**		**39.7%**		**-11.37**

MISS R A GREEN

BRIDGWATER, SOMERSET

	No. of Hrs	Races Run	1st	2nd	3rd	Unpl	Per cent	£1 Level Stake
NH Flat	*0*	*0*	*0*	*0*	*0*	*0*	*0.0*	*0.00*
Hurdles	*0*	*0*	*0*	*0*	*0*	*0*	*0.0*	*0.00*
Chases	*1*	*1*	*1*	*0*	*0*	*0*	*100.0*	*+33.00*
Totals	**1**	**1**	**1**	**0**	**0**	**0**	**100.0**	**+33.00**

JOCKEYS

	W-R	Per cent	£1 Level Stake
Mr H Cobden	1-1	100.0	+33.00

COURSE RECORD

	Total W-R	Non-Hndcps Hurdles	Non-Hndcps Chases	Hndcps Hurdles	Hndcps Chases	NH Flat	Per cent	£1 Level Stake
Leicester	1-1	0-0	1-1	0-0	0-0	0-0	100.0	+33.00

WINNING HORSES

Horse	Races Run	1st	2nd	3rd	£
*El Mondo	1	1	0	0	1560
Total winning prize-money					**£1560**
Favourites	**0-0**		**0.0%**		**0.00**

TOM GRETTON

HOLBERROW GREEN, WORCS

	No. of Hrs	Races Run	1st	2nd	3rd	Unpl	Per cent	£1 Level Stake
NH Flat	*2*	*4*	*0*	*0*	*0*	*4*	*0.0*	*-4.00*
Hurdles	*9*	*20*	*0*	*1*	*1*	*18*	*0.0*	*-20.00*
Chases	*7*	*26*	*3*	*4*	*6*	*13*	*11.5*	*+7.00*
Totals	**14**	**50**	**3**	**5**	**7**	**35**	**6.0**	**-17.00**
13-14	*16*	*52*	*1*	*11*	*1*	*39*	*1.9*	*-49.75*
12-13	*17*	*41*	*5*	*4*	*4*	*28*	*12.2*	*-24.58*

JOCKEYS

	W-R	Per cent	£1 Level Stake
Felix De Giles	2-15	13.3	+1.00
James Davies	1-2	50.0	+15.00

COURSE RECORD

	Total W-R	Non-Hndcps Hurdles	Non-Hndcps Chases	Hndcps Hurdles	Hndcps Chases	NH Flat	Per cent	£1 Level Stake
Plumpton	1-1	0-0	0-0	0-0	1-1	0-0	100.0	+16.00
Chepstow	1-2	0-0	0-0	0-0	1-1	0-1	50.0	+5.00
Stratford	1-5	0-0	0-0	0-1	1-3	0-1	20.0	+4.00

WINNING HORSES

Horse	Races Run	1st	2nd	3rd	£
Little Jimmy	8	2	2	1	6173
Thats Ben	3	1	0	0	3249
Total winning prize-money					**£9422**
Favourites	**0-4**		**0.0%**		**-4.00**

DIANA GRISSELL

BRIGHTLING, E SUSSEX

	No. of Hrs	Races Run	1st	2nd	3rd	Unpl	Per cent	£1 Level Stake
NH Flat	*1*	*1*	*0*	*0*	*0*	*1*	*0.0*	*-1.00*
Hurdles	*7*	*17*	*2*	*0*	*1*	*14*	*11.8*	*+2.00*
Chases	*5*	*19*	*2*	*4*	*6*	*7*	*10.5*	*+1.00*
Totals	**11**	**37**	**4**	**4**	**7**	**22**	**10.8**	**+2.00**
13-14	*10*	*32*	*0*	*0*	*2*	*30*	*0.0*	*-32.00*
12-13	*12*	*37*	*5*	*1*	*5*	*26*	*13.5*	*-6.50*

JOCKEYS

	W-R	Per cent	£1 Level Stake
Marc Goldstein	2-14	14.3	-5.00
Andrew Thornton	1-2	50.0	+11.00
Liam Treadwell	1-4	25.0	+13.00

COURSE RECORD

	Total W-R	Non-Hndcps Hurdles	Non-Hndcps Chases	Hndcps Hurdles	Hndcps Chases	NH Flat	Per cent	£1 Level Stake
Fontwell	2-10	0-1	0-0	1-4	1-5	0-0	20.0	+20.00
Huntingdon	1-4	0-0	0-0	0-0	1-4	0-0	25.0	-1.00
Plumpton	1-15	1-5	0-0	0-4	0-5	0-1	6.7	-9.00

WINNING HORSES

Horse	Races Run	1st	2nd	3rd	£
Arbeo	6	1	0	2	4224
Blue Bear	3	1	0	1	3249
*Sitting Back	5	1	2	1	2339
*Wor Rom	1	1	0	0	1949
Total winning prize-money					**£11761**
Favourites	**1-1**		**100.0%**		**2.00**

MISS ROSE GRISSELL

ROBERTSBRIDGE, EAST SUSSEX

	No. of Hrs	Races Run	1st	2nd	3rd	Unpl	Per cent	£1 Level Stake
NH Flat	*0*	*0*	*0*	*0*	*0*	*0*	*0.0*	*0.00*
Hurdles	*0*	*0*	*0*	*0*	*0*	*0*	*0.0*	*0.00*
Chases	*6*	*8*	*1*	*0*	*0*	*7*	*12.5*	*0.00*
Totals	**6**	**8**	**1**	**0**	**0**	**7**	**12.5**	**0.00**
13-14	*4*	*7*	*1*	*2*	*0*	*4*	*14.3*	*-5.47*
12-13	*6*	*8*	*0*	*1*	*1*	*6*	*0.0*	*-8.00*

JOCKEYS

	W-R	Per cent	£1 Level Stake
Miss H Grissell	1-3	33.3	+5.00

COURSE RECORD

	Total W-R	Non-Hndcps Hurdles	Non-Hndcps Chases	Hndcps Hurdles	Hndcps Chases	NH Flat	Per cent	£1 Level Stake
Fontwell	1-3	0-0	1-3	0-0	0-0	0-0	33.3	+5.00

WINNING HORSES

Horse	Races Run	1st	2nd	3rd	£
Ashanti Moon	1	1	0	0	936
Total winning prize-money					**£936**
Favourites	**0-0**		**0.0%**		**0.00**

RICHARD GUEST

INGMANTHORPE, W YORKS

	No. of Hrs	Races Run	1st	2nd	3rd	Unpl	Per cent	£1 Level Stake
NH Flat	*2*	*2*	*0*	*1*	*0*	*1*	*0.0*	*-2.00*
Hurdles	*8*	*19*	*0*	*1*	*0*	*18*	*0.0*	*-19.00*
Chases	*1*	*4*	*1*	*0*	*0*	*3*	*25.0*	*+2.50*
Totals	**10**	**25**	**1**	**2**	**0**	**22**	**4.0**	**-18.50**
13-14	*18*	*56*	*3*	*5*	*6*	*42*	*5.4*	*-35.25*
12-13	*12*	*49*	*4*	*5*	*3*	*37*	*8.2*	*-31.00*

JOCKEYS

	W-R	Per cent	£1 Level Stake
Jack Quinlan	1-5	20.0	+1.50

COURSE RECORD

	Total W-R	Non-Hndcps Hurdles	Non-Hndcps Chases	Hndcps Hurdles	Hndcps Chases	NH Flat	Per cent	£1 Level Stake
Mrket Rsn	1-6	0-1	0-0	0-1	1-3	0-1	16.7	+0.50

WINNING HORSES

Horse	Races Run	1st	2nd	3rd	£
Balinroab	4	1	0	0	3899
Total winning prize-money					**£3899**
Favourites	**0-2**		**0.0%**		**-2.00**

POLLY GUNDRY

OTTERY ST MARY, DEVON

	No. of Hrs	Races Run	1st	2nd	3rd	Unpl	Per cent	£1 Level Stake
NH Flat	*5*	*7*	*1*	*0*	*0*	*6*	*14.3*	*+10.00*
Hurdles	*9*	*31*	*2*	*4*	*0*	*25*	*6.5*	*-10.50*
Chases	*7*	*28*	*3*	*5*	*3*	*17*	*10.7*	*+11.25*
Totals	**17**	**66**	**6**	**9**	**3**	**48**	**9.1**	**+10.75**
13-14	*18*	*38*	*2*	*3*	*3*	*30*	*5.3*	*-24.00*
12-13	*19*	*43*	*1*	*1*	*5*	*36*	*2.3*	*-34.50*

JOCKEYS

	W-R	Per cent	£1 Level Stake
James Davies	2-6	33.3	+30.00
Andrew Thornton	2-7	28.6	+13.50
Nick Scholfield	2-21	9.5	-0.75

COURSE RECORD

	Total W-R	Non-Hndcps Hurdles	Non-Hndcps Chases	Hndcps Hurdles	Hndcps Chases	NH Flat	Per cent	£1 Level Stake
Taunton	2-10	0-3	0-0	1-3	1-4	0-0	20.0	+28.00
Plumpton	1-2	0-0	0-0	1-2	0-0	0-0	50.0	+1.50
Uttoxeter	1-5	0-0	0-0	0-1	0-3	1-1	20.0	+12.00
Wincanton	1-6	0-0	0-0	0-1	1-5	0-0	16.7	-2.75
Worcester	1-12	0-3	0-1	0-0	1-4	0-4	8.3	+3.00

WINNING HORSES

Horse	Races Run	1st	2nd	3rd	£
Harry's Farewell	6	1	3	1	3899
Dawson City	7	2	2	0	6823
*Captain Knock	7	2	0	0	5361
Fivefortyfive	1	1	0	0	1560
Total winning prize-money					**£17643**
Favourites	**2-25**		**8.0%**		**-18.25**

BEN DE HAAN

LAMBOURN, BERKS

	No. of Hrs	Races Run	1st	2nd	3rd	Unpl	Per cent	£1 Level Stake
NH Flat	*0*	*0*	*0*	*0*	*0*	*0*	*0.0*	*0.00*
Hurdles	*2*	*4*	*0*	*1*	*1*	*2*	*0.0*	*-4.00*
Chases	*3*	*9*	*1*	*3*	*1*	*4*	*11.1*	*-2.00*
Totals	**5**	**13**	**1**	**4**	**2**	**6**	**7.7**	**-6.00**
13-14	*7*	*24*	*1*	*5*	*4*	*14*	*4.2*	*+2.00*
12-13	*9*	*21*	*1*	*6*	*1*	*13*	*4.8*	*-10.00*

JOCKEYS

	W-R	Per cent	£1 Level Stake
Jack Doyle	1-11	9.1	-4.00

COURSE RECORD

	Total W-R	Non-Hndcps Hurdles	Non-Hndcps Chases	Hndcps Hurdles	Hndcps Chases	NH Flat	Per cent	£1 Level Stake
Stratford	1-2	0-0	0-0	0-0	1-2	0-0	50.0	+5.00

WINNING HORSES

Horse	Races Run	1st	2nd	3rd	£
Deciding Moment	6	1	2	1	6498
Total winning prize-money					**£6498**
Favourites	**0-0**		**0.0%**		**0.00**

ALEX HALES

EDGCOTE, NORTHAMPTONSHIRE

	No. of Hrs	Races Run	1st	2nd	3rd	Unpl	Per cent	£1 Level Stake
NH Flat	*3*	*3*	*0*	*0*	*0*	*3*	*0.0*	*-3.00*
Hurdles	*18*	*67*	*7*	*10*	*6*	*44*	*10.4*	*-13.50*
Chases	*6*	*32*	*6*	*9*	*6*	*11*	*18.8*	*-4.02*
Totals	**23**	**102**	**13**	**19**	**12**	**58**	**12.7**	**-20.52**
13-14	*25*	*88*	*7*	*6*	*13*	*62*	*8.0*	*-21.40*
12-13	*17*	*68*	*6*	*6*	*9*	*47*	*8.8*	*-24.25*

BY MONTH

NH Flat	W-R	Per cent	£1 Level Stake
May	0-0	0.0	0.00
June	0-0	0.0	0.00
July	0-0	0.0	0.00
August	0-0	0.0	0.00
September	0-0	0.0	0.00
October	0-0	0.0	0.00
November	0-1	0.0	-1.00
December	0-0	0.0	0.00
January	0-0	0.0	0.00
February	0-0	0.0	0.00
March	0-1	0.0	-1.00
April	0-1	0.0	-1.00

Hurdles	W-R	Per cent	£1 Level Stake
May	1-2	50.0	+6.50
June	0-3	0.0	-3.00
July	0-0	0.0	0.00
August	0-0	0.0	0.00
September	0-3	0.0	-3.00
October	0-4	0.0	-4.00
November	0-11	0.0	-11.00
December	1-10	10.0	+2.00
January	1-9	11.1	-5.00
February	1-9	11.1	-5.00
March	2-10	20.0	+6.00
April	1-6	16.7	+3.00

Chases	W-R	Per cent	£1 Level Stake
May	0-0	0.0	0.00
June	0-0	0.0	0.00
July	0-0	0.0	0.00
August	0-0	0.0	0.00
September	0-0	0.0	0.00
October	0-1	0.0	-1.00
November	0-3	0.0	-3.00
December	1-5	20.0	+6.00
January	2-8	25.0	-2.27
February	1-7	14.3	-3.50
March	2-8	25.0	-0.25
April	0-0	0.0	0.00

Totals	W-R	Per cent	£1 Level Stake
May	1-2	50.0	+6.50
June	0-3	0.0	-3.00
July	0-0	0.0	0.00
August	0-0	0.0	0.00
September	0-3	0.0	-3.00
October	0-5	0.0	-5.00
November	0-15	0.0	-15.00
December	2-15	13.3	+8.00
January	3-17	17.6	-7.27
February	2-16	12.5	-8.50
March	4-19	21.1	+4.75
April	1-7	14.3	+2.00

DISTANCE

Hurdles	W-R	Per cent	£1 Level Stake	Chases	W-R	Per cent	£1 Level Stake
2m-2m3f	2-30	6.7	-10.00	2m-2m3f	2-6	33.3	+9.00
2m4f-2m7f	3-21	14.3	-1.00	2m4f-2m7f	1-7	14.3	-5.27
3m+	1-2	50.0	+3.00	3m+	1-8	12.5	-4.00

TYPE OF RACE

Non-Handicaps	W-R	Per cent	£1 Level Stake	Handicaps	W-R	Per cent	£1 Level Stake
Nov Hrdls	1-16	6.3	-5.00	Nov Hrdls	2-3	66.7	+14.50
Hrdls	0-13	0.0	-13.00	Hrdls	4-33	12.1	-8.00
Nov Chs	0-0	0.0	0.00	Nov Chs	3-8	37.5	+8.73
Chases	0-0	0.0	0.00	Chases	3-24	12.5	-12.75
Sell/Claim	0-1	0.0	-1.00	Sell/Claim	0-0	0.0	0.00

RACE CLASS / FIRST TIME OUT

	W-R	Per cent	£1 Level Stake		W-R	Per cent	£1 Level Stake
Class 1	0-3	0.0	-3.00	Bumpers	0-3	0.0	-3.00
Class 2	0-1	0.0	-1.00	Hurdles	3-17	17.6	+14.50
Class 3	0-8	0.0	-8.00	Chases	0-3	0.0	-3.00
Class 4	8-62	12.9	-10.75				
Class 5	5-26	19.2	+4.23	Totals	3-23	13.0	+8.50
Class 6	0-2	0.0	-2.00				

JOCKEYS

	W-R	Per cent	£1 Level Stake
Kielan Woods	4-39	10.3	-18.27
Noel Fehily	3-8	37.5	+4.25
Daryl Jacob	2-6	33.3	+10.00
James Banks	2-7	28.6	+13.00
Paddy Brennan	1-4	25.0	+4.50
Conor Shoemark	1-10	10.0	-6.00

COURSE RECORD

	Total W-R	Non-Hndcps Hurdles	Non-Hndcps Chases	Hndcps Hurdles	Hndcps Chases	NH Flat	Per cent	£1 Level Stake
Fakenham	5-15	0-2	0-0	2-9	3-4	0-0	33.3	+14.73
Mrket Rsn	2-17	0-5	0-0	1-7	1-4	0-1	11.8	-1.25
Lingfield	1-3	0-1	0-0	1-1	0-1	0-0	33.3	+1.00
Uttoxeter	1-3	0-1	0-0	1-1	0-1	0-0	33.3	+5.50
Warwick	1-5	1-4	0-0	0-1	0-0	0-0	20.0	+6.00
Plumpton	1-7	0-3	0-0	1-2	0-2	0-0	14.3	-2.00
Stratford	1-7	0-3	0-0	0-3	1-1	0-0	14.3	-3.00
Huntingdon	1-10	0-1	0-0	0-3	1-6	0-0	10.0	-6.50

WINNING HORSES

Horse	Races Run	1st	2nd	3rd	£
*Ogaritmo	7	1	1	0	6498
Shinooki	9	3	3	2	10588
Ultimatum Du Roy	7	2	2	1	7798
Midnight Chorister	9	2	0	3	7760
*Running Wolf	8	1	2	0	3249
Gilzean	7	3	1	1	8967
Take Two	1	1	0	0	3249
Total winning prize-money					**£48109**
Favourites	**2-9**		**22.2%**		**-3.77**

SALLY HALL

MIDDLEHAM MOOR, N YORKS

	No. of Hrs	Races Run	1st	2nd	3rd	Unpl	Per cent	£1 Level Stake
NH Flat	*1*	*1*	*0*	*1*	*0*	*0*	*0.0*	*-1.00*
Hurdles	*1*	*4*	*1*	*0*	*2*	*1*	*25.0*	*+5.00*
Chases	*0*	*0*	*0*	*0*	*0*	*0*	*0.0*	*0.00*
Totals	**2**	**5**	**1**	**1**	**2**	**1**	**20.0**	**+4.00**
13-14	*3*	*10*	*1*	*2*	*2*	*5*	*10.0*	*-2.00*
12-13	*3*	*9*	*0*	*1*	*0*	*8*	*0.0*	*-9.00*

JOCKEYS

	W-R	Per cent	£1 Level Stake
Adam Nicol	1-3	33.3	+6.00

COURSE RECORD

	Total W-R	Non-Hndcps Hurdles	Non-Hndcps Chases	Hndcps Hurdles	Hndcps Chases	NH Flat	Per cent	£1 Level Stake
Wetherby	1-3	0-2	0-0	1-1	0-0	0-0	33.3	+6.00

WINNING HORSES

Horse	Races Run	1st	2nd	3rd	£
Rock A Doodle Doo	4	1	0	2	4549
Total winning prize-money					**£4549**
Favourites	**0-0**		**0.0%**		**0.00**

DEBRA HAMER

NANTYCAWS, CARMARTHENS

	No. of Hrs	Races Run	1st	2nd	3rd	Unpl	Per cent	£1 Level Stake
NH Flat	*4*	*9*	*0*	*0*	*0*	*9*	*0.0*	*-9.00*
Hurdles	*9*	*32*	*2*	*6*	*2*	*22*	*6.3*	*-24.00*
Chases	*6*	*20*	*1*	*4*	*3*	*12*	*5.0*	*-3.00*
Totals	**15**	**61**	**3**	**10**	**5**	**43**	**4.9**	**-36.00**
13-14	*12*	*54*	*3*	*3*	*4*	*44*	*5.6*	*-16.25*
12-13	*15*	*37*	*4*	*1*	*4*	*28*	*10.8*	*-19.17*

JOCKEYS

	W-R	Per cent	£1 Level Stake
James Davies	1-7	14.3	+10.00
Tom O'Brien	1-10	10.0	-7.50
Paul Moloney	1-14	7.1	-8.50

COURSE RECORD

	Total W-R	Non-Hndcps Hurdles	Non-Hndcps Chases	Hndcps Hurdles	Hndcps Chases	NH Flat	Per cent	£1 Level Stake
Ffos Las	2-17	0-2	0-0	1-5	1-8	0-2	11.8	+2.50
Worcester	1-9	0-3	0-0	1-5	0-1	0-0	11.1	-3.50

WINNING HORSES

Horse	Races Run	1st	2nd	3rd	£
Magical Man	6	1	1	2	3861
Pennant Dancer	7	1	2	0	2599
Who Am I	7	1	3	0	1949
Total winning prize-money					**£8409**
Favourites	**2-2**		**100.0%**		**6.00**

ANN HAMILTON

GREAT BAVINGTON, NORTHUMBLAND

	No. of Hrs	Races Run	1st	2nd	3rd	Unpl	Per cent	£1 Level Stake
NH Flat	*2*	*2*	*0*	*0*	*1*	*1*	*0.0*	*-2.00*
Hurdles	*2*	*5*	*1*	*0*	*0*	*4*	*20.0*	*-1.00*
Chases	*3*	*22*	*5*	*10*	*0*	*7*	*22.7*	*+3.00*
Totals	**6**	**29**	**6**	**10**	**1**	**12**	**20.7**	**0.00**
13-14	*7*	*43*	*3*	*8*	*8*	*24*	*7.0*	*-29.13*
12-13	*9*	*38*	*6*	*5*	*5*	*22*	*15.8*	*-3.25*

JOCKEYS

	W-R	Per cent	£1 Level Stake
Wilson Renwick	3-10	30.0	+2.25
Brian Hughes	2-12	16.7	-5.25
Tony Kelly	1-6	16.7	+4.00

COURSE RECORD

	Total W-R	Non-Hndcps Hurdles	Non-Hndcps Chases	Hndcps Hurdles	Hndcps Chases	NH Flat	Per cent	£1 Level Stake
Newcastle	2-7	0-0	1-1	0-0	1-6	0-0	28.6	+6.50
Sedgefield	1-2	0-0	0-0	0-0	1-2	0-0	50.0	+1.25
Cartmel	1-3	0-1	0-1	0-0	1-1	0-0	33.3	+2.00
Hexham	1-4	0-0	0-0	1-2	0-1	0-1	25.0	0.00
Kelso	1-4	0-0	1-2	0-1	0-1	0-0	25.0	-0.75

WINNING HORSES

Horse	Races Run	1st	2nd	3rd	£
Runswick Royal	7	2	3	0	21064
Edmund	7	2	2	0	10423
Trust Thomas	11	2	5	0	10397
Total winning prize-money					**£41884**
Favourites	**2-9**		**22.2%**		**-0.75**

J P G HAMILTON

HAWICK, SCOTTISH BORDERS

	No. of Hrs	Races Run	1st	2nd	3rd	Unpl	Per cent	£1 Level Stake
NH Flat	*0*	*0*	*0*	*0*	*0*	*0*	*0.0*	*0.00*
Hurdles	*0*	*0*	*0*	*0*	*0*	*0*	*0.0*	*0.00*
Chases	*1*	*3*	*2*	*0*	*0*	*1*	*66.7*	*+4.50*
Totals	**1**	**3**	**2**	**0**	**0**	**1**	**66.7**	**+4.50**

JOCKEYS

	W-R	Per cent	£1 Level Stake
Mr H A A Bannister	2-2	100.0	+5.50

COURSE RECORD

	Total W-R	Non-Hndcps Hurdles	Non-Hndcps Chases	Hndcps Hurdles	Hndcps Chases	NH Flat	Per cent	£1 Level Stake
Kelso	1-1	0-0	1-1	0-0	0-0	0-0	100.0	+3.50
Perth	1-1	0-0	1-1	0-0	0-0	0-0	100.0	+2.00

WINNING HORSES

Horse	Races Run	1st	2nd	3rd	£
*Wayupinthesky	3	2	0	0	6863
Total winning prize-money					**£6863**
Favourites	**0-0**		**0.0%**		**0.00**

ALISON HAMILTON

DENHOLM, BORDERS

	No. of Hrs	Races Run	1st	2nd	3rd	Unpl	Per cent	£1 Level Stake
NH Flat	*1*	*4*	*0*	*1*	*0*	*3*	*0.0*	*-4.00*
Hurdles	*10*	*33*	*0*	*4*	*1*	*28*	*0.0*	*-33.00*
Chases	*7*	*14*	*1*	*3*	*1*	*9*	*7.1*	*-5.00*
Totals	**11**	**51**	**1**	**8**	**2**	**40**	**2.0**	**-42.00**
13-14	*7*	*35*	*6*	*5*	*2*	*22*	*17.1*	*+18.08*
12-13	*5*	*18*	*0*	*3*	*2*	*13*	*0.0*	*-18.00*

JOCKEYS

	W-R	Per cent	£1 Level Stake
Mr T Hamilton	1-20	5.0	-11.00

COURSE RECORD

	Total W-R	Non-Hndcps Hurdles	Non-Hndcps Chases	Hndcps Hurdles	Hndcps Chases	NH Flat	Per cent	£1 Level Stake
Kelso	1-6	0-0	0-0	0-1	1-5	0-0	16.7	+3.00

WINNING HORSES

Horse	Races Run	1st	2nd	3rd	£
Some Lad	8	1	2	0	4874
Total winning prize-money					**£4874**
Favourites	**0-2**		**0.0%**		**-2.00**

MIKE HAMMOND

ABBERLEY, WORCS

	No. of Hrs	Races Run	1st	2nd	3rd	Unpl	Per cent	£1 Level Stake
NH Flat	*1*	*1*	*0*	*0*	*0*	*1*	*0.0*	*-1.00*
Hurdles	*2*	*9*	*1*	*3*	*0*	*5*	*11.1*	*-5.00*
Chases	*1*	*1*	*0*	*0*	*0*	*1*	*0.0*	*-1.00*
Totals	**4**	**11**	**1**	**3**	**0**	**7**	**9.1**	**-7.00**
13-14	*2*	*2*	*0*	*0*	*0*	*2*	*0.0*	*-2.00*
12-13	*6*	*12*	*0*	*0*	*0*	*12*	*0.0*	*-12.00*

JOCKEYS

	W-R	Per cent	£1 Level Stake
Denis O'Regan	1-4	25.0	0.00

COURSE RECORD

	Total W-R	Non-Hndcps Hurdles	Non-Hndcps Chases	Hndcps Hurdles	Hndcps Chases	NH Flat	Per cent	£1 Level Stake
Worcester	1-2	0-0	0-0	1-1	0-0	0-1	50.0	+2.00

WINNING HORSES

Horse	Races Run	1st	2nd	3rd	£
Provincial Pride	6	1	3	0	3119
Total winning prize-money					**£3119**
Favourites	**0-2**		**0.0%**		**-2.00**

MICKY HAMMOND

MIDDLEHAM, N YORKS

	No. of Hrs	Races Run	1st	2nd	3rd	Unpl	Per cent	£1 Level Stake
NH Flat	*8*	*19*	*3*	*4*	*1*	*11*	*15.8*	*+12.25*
Hurdles	*30*	*130*	*14*	*11*	*14*	*91*	*10.8*	*-33.54*
Chases	*12*	*45*	*4*	*7*	*0*	*34*	*8.9*	*-22.25*
Totals	**40**	**194**	**21**	**22**	**15**	**136**	**10.8**	**-43.54**
13-14	*21*	*94*	*12*	*10*	*8*	*64*	*12.8*	*-18.42*
12-13	*32*	*108*	*7*	*8*	*7*	*86*	*6.5*	*-49.50*

BY MONTH

NH Flat	W-R	Per cent	£1 Level Stake
May	0-1	0.0	-1.00
June	0-0	0.0	0.00
July	0-0	0.0	0.00
August	0-0	0.0	0.00
September	0-0	0.0	0.00
October	0-0	0.0	0.00
November	0-0	0.0	0.00
December	0-2	0.0	-2.00
January	2-3	66.7	+25.00
February	0-1	0.0	-1.00
March	1-8	12.5	-4.75
April	0-4	0.0	-4.00

Hurdles	W-R	Per cent	£1 Level Stake
May	1-5	20.0	-2.75
June	2-7	28.6	+0.38
July	1-6	16.7	-1.50
August	1-6	16.7	+3.00
September	0-6	0.0	-6.00
October	1-6	16.7	-1.67
November	1-13	7.7	+13.00
December	0-28	0.0	-28.00
January	3-24	12.5	-1.75
February	2-9	22.2	+0.50
March	2-14	14.3	-2.75
April	0-6	0.0	-6.00

Chases	W-R	Per cent	£1 Level Stake
May	0-1	0.0	-1.00
June	0-0	0.0	0.00
July	0-2	0.0	-2.00
August	0-2	0.0	-2.00
September	0-1	0.0	-1.00
October	0-2	0.0	-2.00
November	0-5	0.0	-5.00
December	0-6	0.0	-6.00
January	0-6	0.0	-6.00
February	2-7	28.6	+5.50
March	1-6	16.7	-2.25
April	1-7	14.3	-0.50

Totals	W-R	Per cent	£1 Level Stake
May	1-7	14.3	-4.75
June	2-7	28.6	+0.38
July	1-8	12.5	-3.50
August	1-8	12.5	+1.00
September	0-7	0.0	-7.00
October	1-8	12.5	-3.67
November	1-18	5.6	+8.00
December	0-36	0.0	-36.00
January	5-33	15.2	+17.25
February	4-17	23.5	+5.00
March	4-28	14.3	-9.75
April	1-17	5.9	-10.50

DISTANCE

Hurdles	W-R	Per cent	£1 Level Stake
2m-2m3f	7-70	10.0	-38.63
2m4f-2m7f	6-41	14.6	+13.08
3m+	1-8	12.5	+3.00

Chases	W-R	Per cent	£1 Level Stake
2m-2m3f	3-16	18.8	+3.00
2m4f-2m7f	0-11	0.0	-11.00
3m+	0-11	0.0	-11.00

TYPE OF RACE

Non-Handicaps	W-R	Per cent	£1 Level Stake
Nov Hrdls	6-33	18.2	-13.29
Hrdls	0-7	0.0	-7.00
Nov Chs	2-3	66.7	+5.75
Chases	0-0	0.0	0.00
Sell/Claim	0-2	0.0	-2.00

Handicaps	W-R	Per cent	£1 Level Stake
Nov Hrdls	0-9	0.0	-9.00
Hrdls	8-78	10.3	-1.25
Nov Chs	1-10	10.0	-3.50
Chases	1-32	3.1	-24.50
Sell/Claim	0-1	0.0	-1.00

RACE CLASS

	W-R	Per cent	£1 Level Stake
Class 1	0-4	0.0	-4.00
Class 2	1-5	20.0	+21.00
Class 3	3-24	12.5	-10.50
Class 4	10-100	10.0	-51.79
Class 5	4-45	8.9	-13.50
Class 6	3-16	18.8	+15.25

FIRST TIME OUT

	W-R	Per cent	£1 Level Stake
Bumpers	2-8	25.0	+20.00
Hurdles	2-28	7.1	-21.42
Chases	0-4	0.0	-4.00
Totals	4-40	10.0	-5.42

JOCKEYS

	W-R	Per cent	£1 Level Stake
Joe Colliver	16-97	16.5	+8.71
Jamie Bargary	2-8	25.0	+2.75
Wilson Renwick	2-33	6.1	-14.00
Henry Brooke	1-25	4.0	-10.00

COURSE RECORD

	Total W-R	Non-Hndcps Hurdles	Non-Hndcps Chases	Hndcps Hurdles	Hndcps Chases	NH Flat	Per cent	£1 Level Stake
Sedgefield	5-34	0-4	0-0	2-18	1-9	2-3	14.7	+5.00
Wetherby	5-42	2-11	0-0	2-22	0-5	1-4	11.9	-3.42

Mrket Rsn	4-22	1-3	0-0	3-13	0-4	0-2	18.2	+22.00
Hexham	2-13	2-5	0-0	0-3	0-3	0-2	15.4	-8.88
Ayr	1-2	0-0	1-1	0-0	0-1	0-0	50.0	+3.00
Haydock	1-3	0-0	0-0	0-1	1-2	0-0	33.3	+3.50
Kelso	1-6	1-5	0-0	0-1	0-0	0-0	16.7	-1.50
Newcastle	1-7	0-0	0-0	1-4	0-1	0-2	14.3	-2.00
Carlisle	1-13	0-1	1-1	0-4	0-5	0-2	7.7	-9.25

WINNING HORSES

Horse	Races Run	1st	2nd	3rd	£
Master Of The Hall	12	3	2	1	20144
*Just Cameron	6	4	0	0	23328
*Endless Credit	4	2	0	1	6671
Pay The King	6	1	0	1	3422
Typhon	4	1	0	0	3379
Alderbrook Lad	11	3	3	1	9888
Rayadour	5	1	1	0	2909
Stickleback	4	1	0	0	2762
Auldthunder	11	1	0	0	2729
*Politbureau	8	1	0	2	2469
Sherry	4	1	1	0	1643
Libby Mae	3	2	0	1	3202
Total winning prize-money					**£82546**
Favourites	**2-12**		**16.7%**		**-8.50**

GEOFFREY HARKER

THIRKLEBY, N YORKS

	No. of Hrs	Races Run	1st	2nd	3rd	Unpl	Per cent	£1 Level Stake
NH Flat	*2*	*4*	*0*	*0*	*1*	*3*	*0.0*	*-4.00*
Hurdles	*3*	*8*	*1*	*2*	*0*	*5*	*12.5*	*+18.00*
Chases	*0*	*0*	*0*	*0*	*0*	*0*	*0.0*	*0.00*
Totals	**5**	**12**	**1**	**2**	**1**	**8**	**8.3**	**+14.00**
13-14	*4*	*12*	*0*	*1*	*1*	*10*	*0.0*	*-12.00*
12-13	*5*	*7*	*0*	*0*	*0*	*7*	*0.0*	*-7.00*

JOCKEYS

	W-R	Per cent	£1 Level Stake
Peter Buchanan	1-2	50.0	+24.00

COURSE RECORD

	Total W-R	Non-Hndcps Hurdles	Non-Hndcps Chases	Hndcps Hurdles	Hndcps Chases	NH Flat	Per cent	£1 Level Stake
Wetherby	1-2	1-1	0-0	0-0	0-0	0-1	50.0	+24.00

WINNING HORSES

Horse	Races Run	1st	2nd	3rd	£
Conjola	6	1	2	0	3195
Total winning prize-money					**£3195**
Favourites	**0-0**		**0.0%**		**0.00**

MRS PAULINE HARKIN

CHIPPING WARDEN, NORTHANTS

	No. of Hrs	Races Run	1st	2nd	3rd	Unpl	Per cent	£1 Level Stake
NH Flat	*0*	*0*	*0*	*0*	*0*	*0*	*0.0*	*0.00*
Hurdles	*0*	*0*	*0*	*0*	*0*	*0*	*0.0*	*0.00*
Chases	*2*	*4*	*3*	*0*	*0*	*1*	*75.0*	*+2.70*
Totals	**2**	**4**	**3**	**0**	**0**	**1**	**75.0**	**+2.70**
13-14	*2*	*4*	*1*	*1*	*1*	*1*	*25.0*	*+0.50*
12-13	*1*	*2*	*1*	*0*	*0*	*1*	*50.0*	*+3.00*

JOCKEYS

	W-R	Per cent	£1 Level Stake
Mr J Docker	2-3	66.7	+1.20
Mr P Mann	1-1	100.0	+1.50

COURSE RECORD

	Total W-R	Non-Hndcps Hurdles	Non-Hndcps Chases	Hndcps Hurdles	Hndcps Chases	NH Flat	Per cent	£1 Level Stake
Cheltenham	2-2	0-0	2-2	0-0	0-0	0-0	100.0	+2.70
Southwell	1-1	0-0	1-1	0-0	0-0	0-0	100.0	+1.00

WINNING HORSES

Horse	Races Run	1st	2nd	3rd	£
Doctor Kingsley	1	1	0	0	4679
Popaway	3	2	0	0	4055
Total winning prize-money					**£8734**
Favourites	**3-3**		**100.0%**		**3.70**

SHAUN HARRIS

CARBURTON, NOTTS

	No. of Hrs	Races Run	1st	2nd	3rd	Unpl	Per cent	£1 Level Stake
NH Flat	*2*	*5*	*0*	*1*	*1*	*3*	*0.0*	*-5.00*
Hurdles	*10*	*32*	*2*	*1*	*0*	*29*	*6.3*	*-13.00*
Chases	*1*	*5*	*1*	*0*	*0*	*4*	*20.0*	*-1.00*
Totals	**12**	**42**	**3**	**2**	**1**	**36**	**7.1**	**-19.00**
13-14	*11*	*60*	*5*	*7*	*4*	*44*	*8.3*	*+4.00*
12-13	*7*	*32*	*1*	*2*	*6*	*23*	*3.1*	*-27.00*

JOCKEYS

	W-R	Per cent	£1 Level Stake
Jonathan England	2-5	40.0	+12.00
Sam Twiston-Davies	1-3	33.3	+3.00

COURSE RECORD

	Total W-R	Non-Hndcps Hurdles	Non-Hndcps Chases	Hndcps Hurdles	Hndcps Chases	NH Flat	Per cent	£1 Level Stake
Huntingdon	1-3	0-1	0-0	1-1	0-1	0-0	33.3	+3.00
Mrket Rsn	1-4	0-2	0-0	1-2	0-0	0-0	25.0	+9.00

Fakenham	1-5	0-1	0-0	0-3	1-1	0-0	20.0	-1.00

WINNING HORSES

Horse	Races Run	1st	2nd	3rd	£
Lord Fox	5	1	0	0	3607
Whatsupjack	5	1	0	0	3249
Hear The Chimes	10	1	1	1	3249
Total winning prize-money					**£10105**
Favourites	**0-1**		**0.0%**		**-1.00**

GRACE HARRIS

SHIRENEWTON, MONMOUTHSHIRE

	No. of Hrs	Races Run	1st	2nd	3rd	Unpl	Per cent	£1 Level Stake
NH Flat	*1*	*2*	*0*	*1*	*0*	*1*	*0.0*	*-2.00*
Hurdles	*3*	*4*	*0*	*0*	*0*	*4*	*0.0*	*-4.00*
Chases	*2*	*6*	*2*	*1*	*0*	*3*	*33.3*	*+34.00*
Totals	**5**	**12**	**2**	**2**	**0**	**8**	**16.7**	**+28.00**
13-14	*4*	*10*	*0*	*0*	*0*	*10*	*0.0*	*-10.00*

JOCKEYS

	W-R	Per cent	£1 Level Stake
Rhys Flint	1-4	25.0	+30.00
Conor Ring	1-4	25.0	+2.00

COURSE RECORD

	Total W-R	Non-Hndcps Hurdles	Non-Hndcps Chases	Hndcps Hurdles	Hndcps Chases	NH Flat	Per cent	£1 Level Stake
Lingfield	1-1	0-0	0-0	0-0	1-1	0-0	100.0	+33.00
Chepstow	1-2	0-0	0-0	0-0	1-1	0-1	50.0	+4.00

WINNING HORSES

Horse	Races Run	1st	2nd	3rd	£
Paddy The Oscar	6	2	1	0	7018
Total winning prize-money					**£7018**
Favourites	**0-1**		**0.0%**		**-1.00**

LISA HARRISON

ALDOTH, CUMBRIA

	No. of Hrs	Races Run	1st	2nd	3rd	Unpl	Per cent	£1 Level Stake
NH Flat	*6*	*14*	*0*	*1*	*1*	*12*	*0.0*	*-14.00*
Hurdles	*13*	*48*	*4*	*11*	*5*	*28*	*8.3*	*+3.50*
Chases	*6*	*18*	*4*	*5*	*2*	*7*	*22.2*	*+5.33*
Totals	**15**	**80**	**8**	**17**	**8**	**47**	**10.0**	**-5.17**
13-14	*8*	*50*	*4*	*8*	*11*	*27*	*8.0*	*-14.00*
12-13	*8*	*44*	*1*	*3*	*2*	*38*	*2.3*	*-32.00*

JOCKEYS

	W-R	Per cent	£1 Level Stake
Ryan Day	6-55	10.9	+6.83
Stephen Mulqueen	1-4	25.0	+1.50
Grant Cockburn	1-5	20.0	+2.50

COURSE RECORD

	Total W-R	Non-Hndcps Hurdles	Non-Hndcps Chases	Hndcps Hurdles	Hndcps Chases	NH Flat	Per cent	£1 Level Stake
Perth	7-33	0-6	0-0	3-15	4-7	0-5	21.2	+15.83
Hexham	1-5	0-0	0-0	1-2	0-2	0-1	20.0	+21.00

WINNING HORSES

Horse	Races Run	1st	2nd	3rd	£
Solway Dandy	7	1	3	1	5064
Solway Bay	4	1	0	0	4549
Solway Dornal	14	3	5	2	7148
Solway Sam	16	2	6	2	7047
*Willie Hall	5	1	1	0	2601
Total winning prize-money					**£26409**
Favourites	**0-5**		**0.0%**		**-5.00**

MISS C V HART

CHIPPING CAMPDEN, GLOS

	No. of Hrs	Races Run	1st	2nd	3rd	Unpl	Per cent	£1 Level Stake
NH Flat	*0*	*0*	*0*	*0*	*0*	*0*	*0.0*	*0.00*
Hurdles	*0*	*0*	*0*	*0*	*0*	*0*	*0.0*	*0.00*
Chases	*1*	*4*	*1*	*0*	*1*	*2*	*25.0*	*+2.00*
Totals	**1**	**4**	**1**	**0**	**1**	**2**	**25.0**	**+2.00**
13-14	*1*	*1*	*1*	*0*	*0*	*0*	*100.0*	*+5.50*
12-13	*2*	*2*	*0*	*0*	*1*	*1*	*0.0*	*-2.00*

JOCKEYS

	W-R	Per cent	£1 Level Stake
Miss C V Hart	1-4	25.0	+2.00

COURSE RECORD

	Total W-R	Non-Hndcps Hurdles	Non-Hndcps Chases	Hndcps Hurdles	Hndcps Chases	NH Flat	Per cent	£1 Level Stake
Warwick	1-1	0-0	1-1	0-0	0-0	0-0	100.0	+5.00

WINNING HORSES

Horse	Races Run	1st	2nd	3rd	£
Vincitore	4	1	0	1	1248
Total winning prize-money					**£1248**
Favourites	**0-0**		**0.0%**		**0.00**

BEN HASLAM

MIDDLEHAM MOOR, N YORKS

	No. of Hrs	Races Run	1st	2nd	3rd	Unpl	Per cent	£1 Level Stake
NH Flat	*1*	*1*	*0*	*1*	*0*	*0*	*0.0*	*-1.00*

Hurdles	*9*	*28*	*4*	*2*	*6*	*16*	*14.3*	*-10.43*
Chases	*4*	*7*	*3*	*0*	*0*	*4*	*42.9*	*-1.33*
Totals	**11**	**36**	**7**	**3**	**6**	**20**	**19.4**	**-12.76**
13-14	*8*	*37*	*3*	*2*	*6*	*26*	*8.1*	*-23.88*
12-13	*8*	*14*	*1*	*1*	*1*	*11*	*7.1*	*-1.00*

JOCKEYS

	W-R	Per cent	£1 Level Stake
A P McCoy	5-7	71.4	+3.84
Ryan D Clark	1-5	20.0	+4.00
Andrew Tinkler	1-14	7.1	-10.60

COURSE RECORD

	Total W-R	Non-Hndcps Hurdles	Non-Hndcps Chases	Hndcps Hurdles	Hndcps Chases	NH Flat	Per cent	£1 Level Stake
Sedgefield	4-9	0-1	0-0	2-6	2-2	0-0	44.4	+7.63
Uttoxeter	2-3	0-0	0-0	2-3	0-0	0-0	66.7	+2.17
Southwell	1-3	0-0	0-0	0-1	1-1	0-1	33.3	-1.56

WINNING HORSES

Horse	Races Run	1st	2nd	3rd	£
Ever So Much	6	4	0	1	12606
Hi Dancer	3	1	0	0	2469
Mad For Road	7	1	1	3	2339
Operateur	4	1	1	1	2209
Total winning prize-money					**£19623**
Favourites	**6-10**		**60.0%**		**4.24**

NIGEL HAWKE

STOODLEIGH, DEVON

	No. of Hrs	Races Run	1st	2nd	3rd	Unpl	Per cent	£1 Level Stake
NH Flat	*9*	*13*	*2*	*2*	*1*	*8*	*15.4*	*+9.00*
Hurdles	*22*	*63*	*5*	*7*	*4*	*47*	*7.9*	*-31.22*
Chases	*12*	*52*	*12*	*4*	*3*	*33*	*23.1*	*+28.86*
Totals	**32**	**128**	**19**	**13**	**8**	**88**	**14.8**	**+6.64**
13-14	*20*	*131*	*20*	*14*	*6*	*91*	*15.3*	*-6.59*
12-13	*14*	*62*	*5*	*9*	*7*	*41*	*8.1*	*-26.63*

BY MONTH

NH Flat	W-R	Per cent	£1 Level Stake
May	0-0	0.0	0.00
June	0-0	0.0	0.00
July	0-0	0.0	0.00
August	0-0	0.0	0.00
September	0-1	0.0	-1.00
October	0-3	0.0	-3.00
November	0-3	0.0	-3.00
December	0-0	0.0	0.00
January	0-0	0.0	0.00
February	1-3	33.3	+16.00
March	1-2	50.0	+1.00
April	0-1	0.0	-1.00

Hurdles	W-R	Per cent	£1 Level Stake
May	0-4	0.0	-4.00
June	1-3	33.3	-1.09
July	0-3	0.0	-3.00
August	0-1	0.0	-1.00
September	0-0	0.0	0.00
October	0-4	0.0	-4.00
November	0-8	0.0	-8.00
December	0-10	0.0	-10.00
January	0-6	0.0	-6.00
February	0-8	0.0	-8.00
March	4-7	57.1	+22.88
April	0-9	0.0	-9.00

Chases	W-R	Per cent	£1 Level Stake
May	0-4	0.0	-4.00
June	1-2	50.0	+5.50
July	3-4	75.0	+10.63
August	0-4	0.0	-4.00
September	0-1	0.0	-1.00
October	0-4	0.0	-4.00
November	1-4	25.0	+0.50
December	0-6	0.0	-6.00
January	0-2	0.0	-2.00
February	1-5	20.0	+12.00
March	4-8	50.0	+8.73
April	2-8	25.0	+12.50

Totals	W-R	Per cent	£1 Level Stake
May	0-8	0.0	-8.00
June	2-5	40.0	+4.41
July	3-7	42.9	+7.63
August	0-5	0.0	-5.00
September	0-2	0.0	-2.00
October	0-11	0.0	-11.00
November	1-15	6.7	-10.50
December	0-16	0.0	-16.00
January	0-8	0.0	-8.00
February	2-16	12.5	+20.00
March	9-17	52.9	+32.61
April	2-18	11.1	+2.50

DISTANCE

Hurdles	W-R	Per cent	£1 Level Stake
2m-2m3f	2-42	4.8	-34.13
2m4f-2m7f	3-14	21.4	+9.91
3m+	0-1	0.0	-1.00

Chases	W-R	Per cent	£1 Level Stake
2m-2m3f	5-21	23.8	+14.96
2m4f-2m7f	3-14	21.4	+14.50
3m+	1-11	9.1	-8.00

TYPE OF RACE

Non-Handicaps

	W-R	Per cent	£1 Level Stake
Nov Hrdls	0-19	0.0	-19.00
Hrdls	0-15	0.0	-15.00
Nov Chs	1-2	50.0	+15.00
Chases	0-0	0.0	0.00
Sell/Claim	0-0	0.0	0.00

Handicaps

	W-R	Per cent	£1 Level Stake
Nov Hrdls	2-9	22.2	+0.88
Hrdls	3-20	15.0	+1.91
Nov Chs	2-8	25.0	+2.50
Chases	9-42	21.4	+11.36
Sell/Claim	0-0	0.0	0.00

RACE CLASS

	W-R	Per cent	£1 Level Stake
Class 1	1-7	14.3	+6.00
Class 2	0-8	0.0	-8.00
Class 3	3-17	17.6	+1.25
Class 4	12-62	19.4	+4.39
Class 5	1-26	3.8	-11.00
Class 6	2-8	25.0	+14.00

FIRST TIME OUT

	W-R	Per cent	£1 Level Stake
Bumpers	1-9	11.1	+10.00
Hurdles	0-17	0.0	-17.00
Chases	1-6	16.7	-1.50
Totals	2-32	6.3	-8.50

JOCKEYS

	W-R	Per cent	£1 Level Stake
Tom Scudamore	11-42	26.2	+14.89
Dave Crosse	3-19	15.8	+24.00
James Best	2-28	7.1	-16.00
A P McCoy	1-2	50.0	+0.75
Tom Bellamy	1-2	50.0	+3.00
Gavin Sheehan	1-3	33.3	+12.00

COURSE RECORD

	Total W-R	Non-Hndcps Hurdles	Non-Hndcps Chases	Hndcps Hurdles	Hndcps Chases	NH Flat	Per cent	£1 Level Stake

Mrket Rsn	4-10	0-3	0-0	0-0	4-7	0-0	40.0	+10.71
Carlisle	2-4	0-0	0-0	1-1	0-2	1-1	50.0	+1.88
Southwell	2-5	0-2	0-0	1-1	1-1	0-1	40.0	+11.40
Exeter	2-20	0-11	0-1	1-5	1-2	0-1	10.0	-12.00
Sandown	1-2	0-0	0-0	0-1	1-1	0-0	50.0	+6.00
Wetherby	1-2	0-1	0-0	0-0	0-0	1-1	50.0	+17.00
Wincanton	1-2	0-0	0-0	1-1	0-1	0-0	50.0	+5.00
Doncaster	1-4	0-0	1-1	0-1	0-2	0-0	25.0	+13.00
Worcester	1-4	0-1	0-0	0-0	1-3	0-0	25.0	-1.25
Ffos Las	1-5	0-1	0-0	1-2	0-2	0-0	20.0	-3.09
Uttoxeter	1-7	0-2	0-0	0-1	1-4	0-0	14.3	+0.50
Cheltenham	1-8	0-0	0-0	0-3	1-4	0-1	12.5	+5.00
Chepstow	1-17	0-3	0-0	0-6	1-7	0-1	5.9	-9.50

WINNING HORSES

Horse	Races Run	1st	2nd	3rd	£
Anay Turge	6	2	1	0	37859
Samingarry	5	1	0	0	7798
Sedgemoor Express	10	3	0	3	13247
Master Neo	7	1	0	0	4549
Mister Wiseman	11	3	3	0	4289
Kadalkin	3	1	0	0	3899
Pagham Belle	8	2	0	0	6498
*Midnight Request	6	2	0	2	7798
Greybougg	8	2	1	0	6498
Pomme	2	1	0	0	1643
Speredek	2	1	0	1	1560
Total winning prize-money					**£95638**
Favourites	**5-10**		**50.0%**		**2.18**

JONATHAN HAYNES

LOW ROW, CUMBRIA

	No. of Hrs	Races Run	1st	2nd	3rd	Unpl	Per cent	£1 Level Stake
NH Flat	*0*	*0*	*0*	*0*	*0*	*0*	*0.0*	*0.00*
Hurdles	*3*	*36*	*3*	*5*	*2*	*26*	*8.3*	*-7.00*
Chases	*2*	*4*	*0*	*0*	*0*	*4*	*0.0*	*-4.00*
Totals	**5**	**40**	**3**	**5**	**2**	**30**	**7.5**	**-11.00**
13-14	*4*	*42*	*0*	*0*	*6*	*36*	*0.0*	*-42.00*
12-13	*7*	*24*	*1*	*1*	*2*	*20*	*4.2*	*-19.00*

JOCKEYS

	W-R	Per cent	£1 Level Stake
Diarmuid O'Regan	3-22	13.6	+7.00

COURSE RECORD

	Total W-R	Non-Hndcps Hurdles	Non-Hndcps Chases	Hndcps Hurdles	Hndcps Chases	NH Flat	Per cent	£1 Level Stake
Hexham	2-9	0-0	0-0	2-7	0-2	0-0	22.2	+14.00
Newcastle	1-4	0-0	0-0	1-4	0-0	0-0	25.0	+2.00

WINNING HORSES

Horse	Races Run	1st	2nd	3rd	£
Beyondtemptation	13	2	5	1	5371
Mrs Grass	12	1	0	1	2738
Total winning prize-money					**£8109**
Favourites	**0-1**		**0.0%**		**-1.00**

GAIL HAYWOOD

MORETONHAMPSTEAD, DEVON

	No. of Hrs	Races Run	1st	2nd	3rd	Unpl	Per cent	£1 Level Stake
NH Flat	*0*	*0*	*0*	*0*	*0*	*0*	*0.0*	*0.00*
Hurdles	*3*	*4*	*1*	*0*	*0*	*3*	*25.0*	*+77.00*
Chases	*0*	*0*	*0*	*0*	*0*	*0*	*0.0*	*0.00*
Totals	**3**	**4**	**1**	**0**	**0**	**3**	**25.0**	**+77.00**
13-14	*1*	*1*	*0*	*0*	*0*	*1*	*0.0*	*-1.00*

JOCKEYS

	W-R	Per cent	£1 Level Stake
Alice Mills	1-2	50.0	+79.00

COURSE RECORD

	Total W-R	Non-Hndcps Hurdles	Non-Hndcps Chases	Hndcps Hurdles	Hndcps Chases	NH Flat	Per cent	£1 Level Stake
Nton Abbot	1-1	1-1	0-0	0-0	0-0	0-0	100.0	+80.00

WINNING HORSES

Horse	Races Run	1st	2nd	3rd	£
*Hija	1	1	0	0	3422
Total winning prize-money					**£3422**
Favourites	**0-0**		**0.0%**		**0.00**

PAUL HENDERSON

WHITSBURY, HANTS

	No. of Hrs	Races Run	1st	2nd	3rd	Unpl	Per cent	£1 Level Stake
NH Flat	*7*	*11*	*1*	*0*	*1*	*9*	*9.1*	*-7.25*
Hurdles	*25*	*68*	*1*	*5*	*3*	*59*	*1.5*	*-61.00*
Chases	*22*	*81*	*8*	*12*	*13*	*48*	*9.9*	*-27.00*
Totals	**43**	**160**	**10**	**17**	**17**	**116**	**6.3**	**-95.25**
13-14	*38*	*183*	*15*	*16*	*18*	*134*	*8.2*	*-48.00*
12-13	*29*	*131*	*16*	*10*	*9*	*96*	*12.2*	*+10.63*

BY MONTH

NH Flat	W-R	Per cent	£1 Level Stake	**Hurdles**	W-R	Per cent	£1 Level Stake
May	0-1	0.0	-1.00	May	0-9	0.0	-9.00
June	0-1	0.0	-1.00	June	0-1	0.0	-1.00
July	0-1	0.0	-1.00	July	1-3	33.3	+4.00
August	0-2	0.0	-2.00	August	0-4	0.0	-4.00
September	1-1	100.0	+2.75	September	0-3	0.0	-3.00
October	0-0	0.0	0.00	October	0-7	0.0	-7.00
November	0-2	0.0	-2.00	November	0-9	0.0	-9.00

December	0-1	0.0	-1.00	December	0-7	0.0	-7.00
January	0-1	0.0	-1.00	January	0-6	0.0	-6.00
February	0-1	0.0	-1.00	February	0-6	0.0	-6.00
March	0-0	0.0	0.00	March	0-8	0.0	-8.00
April	0-0	0.0	0.00	April	0-5	0.0	-5.00

Chases	W-R	Per cent	£1 Level Stake	Totals	W-R	Per cent	£1 Level Stake
May	1-7	14.3	-1.50	May	1-17	5.9	-11.50
June	3-8	37.5	+18.00	June	3-10	30.0	+16.00
July	1-4	25.0	+6.00	July	2-8	25.0	+9.00
August	0-2	0.0	-2.00	August	0-8	0.0	-8.00
September	0-3	0.0	-3.00	September	1-7	14.3	-3.25
October	1-6	16.7	-0.50	October	1-13	7.7	-7.50
November	1-6	16.7	-2.50	November	1-17	5.9	-13.50
December	0-11	0.0	-11.00	December	0-19	0.0	-19.00
January	1-11	9.1	-7.50	January	1-18	5.6	-14.50
February	0-7	0.0	-7.00	February	0-14	0.0	-14.00
March	0-6	0.0	-6.00	March	0-14	0.0	-14.00
April	0-10	0.0	-10.00	April	0-15	0.0	-15.00

DISTANCE

Hurdles	W-R	Per cent	£1 Level Stake	Chases	W-R	Per cent	£1 Level Stake
2m-2m3f	0-19	0.0	-19.00	2m-2m3f	1-16	6.3	-6.00
2m4f-2m7f	1-32	3.1	-25.00	2m4f-2m7f	2-25	8.0	-6.50
3m+	0-5	0.0	-5.00	3m+	1-25	4.0	-19.50

TYPE OF RACE

Non-Handicaps	W-R	Per cent	£1 Level Stake	Handicaps	W-R	Per cent	£1 Level Stake
Nov Hrdls	0-17	0.0	-17.00	Nov Hrdls	0-6	0.0	-6.00
Hrdls	1-6	16.7	+1.00	Hrdls	0-38	0.0	-38.00
Nov Chs	0-5	0.0	-5.00	Nov Chs	1-12	8.3	-8.00
Chases	0-0	0.0	0.00	Chases	7-64	10.9	-14.00
Sell/Claim	0-0	0.0	0.00	Sell/Claim	0-0	0.0	0.00

RACE CLASS / FIRST TIME OUT

	W-R	Per cent	£1 Level Stake		W-R	Per cent	£1 Level Stake
Class 1	0-1	0.0	-1.00	Bumpers	0-7	0.0	-7.00
Class 2	1-8	12.5	+2.00	Hurdles	1-19	5.3	-12.00
Class 3	2-27	7.4	-5.00	Chases	1-17	5.9	-11.50
Class 4	3-81	3.7	-64.50				
Class 5	3-32	9.4	-19.50	Totals	2-43	4.7	-30.50
Class 6	1-11	9.1	-7.25				

JOCKEYS

	W-R	Per cent	£1 Level Stake
Tom O'Brien	6-68	8.8	-24.25
Jamie Moore	1-4	25.0	-0.50
Mr G Treacy	1-9	11.1	-5.50
Richard Johnson	1-15	6.7	-8.00
Nick Scholfield	1-18	5.6	-11.00

COURSE RECORD

	Total W-R	Non-Hndcps Hurdles	Non-Hndcps Chases	Hndcps Hurdles	Hndcps Chases	NH Flat	Per cent	£1 Level Stake
Plumpton	3-19	0-2	0-0	0-4	3-13	0-0	15.8	-4.50
Ffos Las	2-6	0-0	0-0	0-1	2-5	0-0	33.3	+5.00
Fakenham	2-9	0-0	0-0	0-1	2-8	0-0	22.2	+9.50
Huntingdon	1-4	0-0	0-0	0-1	0-1	1-2	25.0	-0.25
Stratford	1-10	0-1	0-0	0-5	1-2	0-2	10.0	0.00
Nton Abbot	1-17	1-4	0-2	0-3	0-8	0-0	5.9	-10.00

WINNING HORSES

Horse	Races Run	1st	2nd	3rd	£
Fair Dilemma	6	2	1	0	20310
Carloswayback	4	1	0	0	6498
West Cork Flash	3	2	0	1	9707
Alright Benny	11	3	4	0	4527
One More Tune	5	1	0	0	4224
Katcha Kopek	7	1	0	1	1560
Total winning prize-money					**£46826**
Favourites	**0-2**		**0.0%**		**-2.00**

NICKY HENDERSON

UPPER LAMBOURN, BERKS

	No. of Hrs	Races Run	1st	2nd	3rd	Unpl	Per cent	£1 Level Stake
NH Flat	*46*	*78*	*23*	*13*	*11*	*31*	*29.5*	*-6.02*
Hurdles	*102*	*318*	*90*	*60*	*33*	*135*	*28.3*	*-12.30*
Chases	*36*	*109*	*16*	*19*	*18*	*56*	*14.7*	*-35.68*
Totals	**157**	**505**	**129**	**92**	**62**	**222**	**25.5**	**-54.00**
13-14	*158*	*499*	*116*	*72*	*55*	*256*	*23.2*	*-43.56*
12-13	*159*	*487*	*122*	*72*	*52*	*240*	*25.1*	*-27.85*

BY MONTH

NH Flat	W-R	Per cent	£1 Level Stake	Hurdles	W-R	Per cent	£1 Level Stake
May	5-19	26.3	-6.56	May	2-16	12.5	-7.13
June	1-6	16.7	-0.50	June	5-12	41.7	+4.55
July	0-0	0.0	0.00	July	0-2	0.0	-2.00
August	0-0	0.0	0.00	August	0-1	0.0	-1.00
September	1-2	50.0	+0.25	September	1-4	25.0	-2.80
October	1-2	50.0	+2.00	October	3-18	16.7	-7.25
November	3-10	30.0	+3.83	November	13-52	25.0	-4.00
December	2-4	50.0	-0.77	December	14-44	31.8	+13.34
January	0-5	0.0	-5.00	January	14-35	40.0	+10.09
February	4-9	44.4	+3.00	February	12-35	34.3	-7.78
March	2-8	25.0	-2.25	March	14-50	28.0	+2.41
April	4-13	30.8	-0.02	April	12-49	24.5	-10.73

Chases	W-R	Per cent	£1 Level Stake	Totals	W-R	Per cent	£1 Level Stake
May	5-13	38.5	+9.83	May	12-48	25.0	-3.86
June	2-3	66.7	+2.41	June	8-21	38.1	+6.46
July	0-3	0.0	-3.00	July	0-5	0.0	-5.00

August	0-0	0.0	0.00	August	0-1	0.0	-1.00
September	1-2	50.0	-0.43	September	3-8	37.5	-2.98
October	1-4	25.0	+1.00	October	5-24	20.8	-4.25
November	1-13	7.7	-10.13	November	17-75	22.7	-10.30
December	1-20	5.0	-17.63	December	17-68	25.0	-5.06
January	1-16	6.3	-14.64	January	15-56	26.8	-9.55
February	1-8	12.5	-6.60	February	17-52	32.7	-11.38
March	0-14	0.0	-14.00	March	16-72	22.2	-13.84
April	3-13	23.1	+17.50	April	19-75	25.3	+6.75

DISTANCE

Hurdles	W-R	Per cent	£1 Level Stake	Chases	W-R	Per cent	£1 Level Stake
2m-2m3f	43-138	31.2	-15.73	2m-2m3f	6-23	26.1	-2.00
2m4f-2m7f	20-80	25.0	-11.55	2m4f-2m7f	5-47	10.6	-19.96
3m+	4-18	22.2	+1.25	3m+	3-25	12.0	-7.60

TYPE OF RACE

Non-Handicaps	W-R	Per cent	£1 Level Stake	Handicaps	W-R	Per cent	£1 Level Stake
Nov Hrdls	32-101	31.7	-15.83	Nov Hrdls	3-11	27.3	+6.00
Hrdls	34-85	40.0	+17.90	Hrdls	21-121	17.4	-20.38
Nov Chs	10-29	34.5	-5.05	Nov Chs	2-16	12.5	-4.63
Chases	0-19	0.0	-19.00	Chases	4-45	8.9	-7.00
Sell/Claim	0-0	0.0	0.00	Sell/Claim	0-0	0.0	0.00

RACE CLASS

	W-R	Per cent	£1 Level Stake
Class 1	20-137	14.6	-49.11
Class 2	13-71	18.3	-8.34
Class 3	24-100	24.0	-6.92
Class 4	38-110	34.5	-7.93
Class 5	21-43	48.8	+24.47
Class 6	13-44	29.5	-5.17

FIRST TIME OUT

	W-R	Per cent	£1 Level Stake
Bumpers	13-46	28.3	-5.36
Hurdles	22-79	27.8	+5.73
Chases	8-32	25.0	+7.70
Totals	43-157	27.4	+8.07

JOCKEYS

	W-R	Per cent	£1 Level Stake
Barry Geraghty	38-168	22.6	-36.19
Nico de Boinville	23-74	31.1	+12.35
David Bass	17-61	27.9	-6.86
Andrew Tinkler	12-70	17.1	-28.83
A P McCoy	10-16	62.5	+8.04
Peter Carberry	9-32	28.1	-7.60
Jeremiah McGrath	9-34	26.5	+7.13
Daryl Jacob	6-21	28.6	-0.24
Freddie Mitchell	2-10	20.0	-6.20
Mr S Waley-Cohen	2-12	16.7	+10.00
Noel Fehily	1-4	25.0	-2.60

COURSE RECORD

	Total W-R	Non-Hndcps Hurdles	Non-Hndcps Chases	Hndcps Hurdles	Hndcps Chases	NH Flat	Per cent	£1 Level Stake
Sandown	11-37	5-11	0-4	4-14	2-7	0-1	29.7	+26.69
Kempton	11-45	3-18	0-6	4-12	0-5	4-4	24.4	-2.03
Doncaster	9-14	7-10	1-1	1-3	0-0	0-0	64.3	+14.01
Mrket Rsn	8-14	3-4	0-1	1-3	1-1	3-5	57.1	+20.17
Aintree	8-37	3-12	1-5	2-11	2-6	0-3	21.6	+14.50
Ludlow	7-24	4-13	0-1	0-1	0-3	3-6	29.2	-9.06
Ascot	7-32	4-12	0-4	1-10	1-2	1-4	21.9	-10.76
Newbury	7-35	6-17	0-0	1-8	0-6	0-4	20.0	-12.26
Uttoxeter	6-15	4-5	1-2	0-4	0-1	1-3	40.0	-2.42
Cheltenham	6-71	5-25	0-4	1-22	0-17	0-3	8.5	-48.92
Fakenham	5-6	3-3	1-1	0-0	0-0	1-2	83.3	+3.96
Towcester	5-12	3-4	0-1	1-2	0-0	1-5	41.7	+3.36
Huntingdon	5-13	3-6	0-2	1-1	0-1	1-3	38.5	+6.35
Worcester	5-16	1-4	2-3	0-1	0-1	2-7	31.3	+0.62
Nton Abbot	4-5	1-1	1-1	1-2	0-0	1-1	80.0	+5.36
Ffos Las	3-6	2-3	0-0	0-1	0-0	1-2	50.0	-0.56
Stratford	3-14	1-3	1-2	1-4	0-3	0-2	21.4	-7.53
Musselbgh	2-4	1-2	0-0	1-2	0-0	0-0	50.0	+1.11
Ayr	2-7	1-2	0-0	0-4	0-0	1-1	28.6	-3.26
Haydock	2-8	1-1	0-2	1-5	0-0	0-0	25.0	-3.85
Southwell	2-10	0-4	0-2	0-0	0-0	2-4	20.0	-3.25
Exeter	2-12	1-5	0-2	1-1	0-0	0-4	16.7	-8.57
Wincanton	2-13	0-2	1-2	1-5	0-1	0-3	15.4	-3.63
Hexham	1-2	1-1	0-0	0-1	0-0	0-0	50.0	-0.17
Kelso	1-2	0-0	1-1	0-0	0-0	0-1	50.0	+1.25
Lingfield	1-2	1-2	0-0	0-0	0-0	0-0	50.0	-0.43
Plumpton	1-2	1-1	0-0	0-1	0-0	0-0	50.0	+1.50
Taunton	1-7	0-3	0-0	1-4	0-0	0-0	14.3	-2.00
Chepstow	1-8	1-3	0-0	0-3	0-1	0-1	12.5	-4.00
Fontwell	1-11	0-2	0-0	0-2	0-1	1-6	9.1	-9.20

WINNING HORSES

Horse	Races Run	1st	2nd	3rd	£
Hadrian's Approach	3	1	0	0	85425
Peace And Co	3	3	0	0	101301
Whisper	3	1	1	0	67582
Rajdhani Express	6	1	0	0	67356
Call The Cops	4	2	1	0	55307
Snake Eyes	1	1	0	0	34170
Polly Peachum	5	2	2	0	44115
Theinval	6	3	1	0	50878
Sign Of A Victory	4	1	1	0	28135
L'Ami Serge	4	3	0	0	64961
Cocktails At Dawn	5	1	1	0	18768
Vyta Du Roc	7	4	2	0	42327
Days Of Heaven	6	3	0	2	24233
Caracci Apache	7	3	1	0	27877
Anquetta	6	1	1	0	15640
Dawalan	7	2	2	0	28636
Volnay De Thaix	5	1	1	1	15640
Different Gravey	4	3	0	0	27262
Hargam	5	2	1	1	26750
Bear's Affair	7	1	2	1	14076
Vasco Du Ronceray	6	1	0	1	12996
Cup Final	2	1	0	1	12512
Might Bite	3	2	0	1	13524
Top Notch	4	3	1	0	22743

Lessons In Milan	3	2	0	1	12503
Golden Hoof	6	1	2	2	8791
Makari	2	2	0	0	11458
Big Hands Harry	5	1	0	0	6882
Clean Sheet	3	2	1	0	9626
Out Sam	3	2	0	0	12996
Aigle De La See	4	2	0	0	10267
Bivouac	4	2	0	1	12996
William Henry	3	2	0	0	9097
Close Touch	4	1	0	1	6389
Laudatory	5	1	1	0	6238
One Lucky Lady	7	2	1	1	9842
Springinherstep	6	1	1	2	5523
Medieval Chapel	4	1	1	1	5198
Hunters Hoof	2	2	0	0	8317
Special Agent	5	2	1	0	6823
Quiet Candid	8	2	3	0	8447
Broxbourne	5	2	1	1	8347
Sweet Deal	6	2	1	0	8347
Master Of The Game	1	1	0	0	3899
Heronry	3	1	1	1	3899
Josses Hill	5	1	2	1	3899
Maestro Royal	1	1	0	0	3899
One For The Guv'Nr	4	2	1	0	6498
Jack Frost	6	4	1	0	12108
Leaderofthedance	6	2	0	1	5458
Gold Present	4	2	2	0	7148
Mister Dillon	2	1	1	0	3769
Laurium	4	2	1	0	6823
Sugar Baron	3	2	0	0	5764
Son Du Berlais	2	1	0	0	3509
Cardinal Walter	4	2	1	0	5198
Vodka 'n Tonic	6	1	1	1	3249
Hel Tara	3	1	0	1	3249
Nicolas Chauvin	7	2	2	2	3249
Kilcrea Vale	1	1	0	0	3249
New Horizons	6	1	1	1	3249
Chocca Wocca	2	1	1	0	3249
Robins Reef	4	2	0	0	4297
Saint Charles	3	1	1	0	2599
Area Fifty One	4	1	1	0	2599
Champagne Express	2	1	0	1	2599
Forever Field	4	2	0	0	4159
Peggy Do	1	1	0	0	2397
Taylor	4	1	2	0	2274
Newsworthy	1	1	0	0	2274
Ok Corral	1	1	0	0	2274
Spartan Angel	6	1	1	1	1949
Coole Charmer	1	1	0	0	1949
Playhara	1	1	0	0	1949
Premier Bond	3	1	0	2	1643
Summer Storm	3	1	1	0	1643
Magna Cartor	1	1	0	0	1560
Chapel Hall	2	1	0	1	1560
Lolli	3	1	0	1	1560
Altior	2	1	0	1	1560
O O Seven	3	1	1	0	1560
Princess Ombu	5	1	0	1	0

Total winning prize-money			**£1204071**
Favourites	**99-202**	**49.0%**	**34.80**

CHRISTOPHER HENN

BRACKLEY, NORTHANTS

	No. of Hrs	Races Run	1st	2nd	3rd	Unpl	Per cent	£1 Level Stake
NH Flat	*0*	*0*	*0*	*0*	*0*	*0*	*0.0*	*0.00*
Hurdles	*0*	*0*	*0*	*0*	*0*	*0*	*0.0*	*0.00*
Chases	*1*	*1*	*1*	*0*	*0*	*0*	*100.0*	*+2.25*
Totals	**1**	**1**	**1**	**0**	**0**	**0**	**100.0**	**+2.25**

JOCKEYS

	W-R	Per cent	£1 Level Stake
Mr T A Mcclorey	1-1	100.0	+2.25

COURSE RECORD

	Total W-R	Non-Hndcps Hurdles	Non-Hndcps Chases	Hndcps Hurdles	Hndcps Chases	NH Flat	Per cent	£1 Level Stake
Towcester	1-1	0-0	1-1	0-0	0-0	0-0	100.0	+2.25

WINNING HORSES

Horse	Races Run	1st	2nd	3rd	£
*Legal Legend	1	1	0	0	988

Total winning prize-money			**£988**
Favourites	**0-0**	**0.0%**	**0.00**

PHILIP HIDE

FINDON, W SUSSEX

	No. of Hrs	Races Run	1st	2nd	3rd	Unpl	Per cent	£1 Level Stake
NH Flat	*1*	*1*	*1*	*0*	*0*	*0*	*100.0*	*+3.50*
Hurdles	*2*	*2*	*0*	*0*	*0*	*2*	*0.0*	*-2.00*
Chases	*0*	*0*	*0*	*0*	*0*	*0*	*0.0*	*0.00*
Totals	**3**	**3**	**1**	**0**	**0**	**2**	**33.3**	**+1.50**
13-14	*6*	*11*	*0*	*0*	*1*	*10*	*0.0*	*-11.00*
12-13	*4*	*7*	*0*	*0*	*0*	*7*	*0.0*	*-7.00*

JOCKEYS

	W-R	Per cent	£1 Level Stake
Sam Twiston-Davies	1-1	100.0	+3.50

COURSE RECORD

	Total W-R	Non-Hndcps Hurdles	Non-Hndcps Chases	Hndcps Hurdles	Hndcps Chases	NH Flat	Per cent	£1 Level Stake
Fontwell	1-1	0-0	0-0	0-0	0-0	1-1	100.0	+3.50

WINNING HORSES

Horse	Races Run	1st	2nd	3rd	£
Cougar Kid	1	1	0	0	1560
Total winning prize-money					**£1560**
Favourites	**0-0**		**0.0%**		**0.00**

ALAN HILL

ASTON ROWANT, OXFORDSHIRE

	No. of Hrs	Races Run	1st	2nd	3rd	Unpl	Per cent	£1 Level Stake
NH Flat	*0*	*0*	*0*	*0*	*0*	*0*	*0.0*	*0.00*
Hurdles	*0*	*0*	*0*	*0*	*0*	*0*	*0.0*	*0.00*
Chases	*8*	*11*	*2*	*3*	*0*	*6*	*18.2*	*-3.50*
Totals	**8**	**11**	**2**	**3**	**0**	**6**	**18.2**	**-3.50**
13-14	*10*	*16*	*3*	*1*	*3*	*9*	*18.8*	*-5.13*
12-13	*4*	*9*	*2*	*2*	*2*	*3*	*22.2*	*-3.65*

JOCKEYS

	W-R	Per cent	£1 Level Stake
Mr J E Tudor	2-6	33.3	+1.50

COURSE RECORD

	Total W-R	Non-Hndcps Hurdles	Non-Hndcps Chases	Hndcps Hurdles	Hndcps Chases	NH Flat	Per cent	£1 Level Stake
Cheltenham	1-3	0-0	1-3	0-0	0-0	0-0	33.3	-0.50
Fontwell	1-3	0-0	1-3	0-0	0-0	0-0	33.3	+2.00

WINNING HORSES

Horse	Races Run	1st	2nd	3rd	£
Sharp Suit	2	1	0	0	4367
Start Royal	1	1	0	0	1872
Total winning prize-money					**£6239**
Favourites	**1-2**		**50.0%**		**0.50**

LAWNEY HILL

ASTON ROWANT, OXON

	No. of Hrs	Races Run	1st	2nd	3rd	Unpl	Per cent	£1 Level Stake
NH Flat	*2*	*3*	*1*	*1*	*0*	*1*	*33.3*	*+1.50*
Hurdles	*16*	*54*	*4*	*9*	*5*	*36*	*7.4*	*-30.27*
Chases	*14*	*43*	*2*	*6*	*7*	*28*	*4.7*	*-34.67*
Totals	**28**	**100**	**7**	**16**	**12**	**65**	**7.0**	**-63.44**
13-14	*34*	*126*	*15*	*16*	*14*	*81*	*11.9*	*-25.25*
12-13	*41*	*129*	*15*	*15*	*12*	*87*	*11.6*	*-43.20*

JOCKEYS

	W-R	Per cent	£1 Level Stake
David Bass	3-24	12.5	-8.77
Aidan Coleman	2-12	16.7	-3.67
Miss A E Stirling	1-1	100.0	+8.00
Trevor Whelan	1-5	20.0	-1.00

COURSE RECORD

	Total W-R	Non-Hndcps Hurdles	Non-Hndcps Chases	Hndcps Hurdles	Hndcps Chases	NH Flat	Per cent	£1 Level Stake
Uttoxeter	2-3	1-1	0-0	0-0	1-2	0-0	66.7	+2.73
Plumpton	1-5	0-1	0-0	0-1	0-1	1-2	20.0	-0.50
Sedgefield	1-5	0-1	0-0	1-2	0-2	0-0	20.0	-1.00
Nton Abbot	1-6	0-0	0-0	1-2	0-4	0-0	16.7	+3.00
Towcester	1-7	0-1	0-0	1-3	0-3	0-0	14.3	+2.00
Fontwell	1-12	0-0	0-0	0-6	1-6	0-0	8.3	-7.67

WINNING HORSES

Horse	Races Run	1st	2nd	3rd	£
Giant O Murchu	7	1	1	0	3769
El Toreros	9	1	2	2	3369
Mighty Mambo	5	1	0	0	2924
*Rogue Dancer	5	1	3	1	2599
*Champion Versions	4	1	1	0	2469
*Take A Bow	3	1	0	0	2209
Rude And Crude	4	1	2	0	1625
Total winning prize-money					**£18964**
Favourites	**3-12**		**25.0%**		**-2.27**

MARTIN HILL

LITTLEHEMPSTON, DEVON

	No. of Hrs	Races Run	1st	2nd	3rd	Unpl	Per cent	£1 Level Stake
NH Flat	*4*	*8*	*1*	*0*	*1*	*6*	*12.5*	*+1.00*
Hurdles	*16*	*33*	*5*	*1*	*5*	*22*	*15.2*	*+28.00*
Chases	*5*	*10*	*1*	*4*	*0*	*5*	*10.0*	*-7.63*
Totals	**21**	**51**	**7**	**5**	**6**	**33**	**13.7**	**+21.37**
13-14	*21*	*73*	*11*	*9*	*12*	*41*	*15.1*	*+14.25*
12-13	*14*	*36*	*3*	*1*	*2*	*30*	*8.3*	*+27.00*

JOCKEYS

	W-R	Per cent	£1 Level Stake
Hadden Frost	6-29	20.7	+35.38
Alice Mills	1-7	14.3	+1.00

COURSE RECORD

	Total W-R	Non-Hndcps Hurdles	Non-Hndcps Chases	Hndcps Hurdles	Hndcps Chases	NH Flat	Per cent	£1 Level Stake
Nton Abbot	5-27	0-4	1-1	3-14	0-5	1-3	18.5	+9.38
Exeter	1-2	1-1	0-0	0-0	0-0	0-1	50.0	+24.00
Worcester	1-6	0-0	0-0	1-3	0-0	0-3	16.7	+4.00

WINNING HORSES

Horse	Races Run	1st	2nd	3rd	£
Tzora	3	2	0	1	16772
Detroit Red	4	2	0	0	13959
Sheriff Hutton	4	1	1	1	5523
*Ocean Venture	1	1	0	0	3249

Watcombe Heights	2	1	0	0	2395
Total winning prize-money					**£41898**
Favourites	**0-6**		**0.0%**		**-6.00**

PHILIP HOBBS

WITHYCOMBE, SOMERSET

	No. of Hrs	Races Run	1st	2nd	3rd	Unpl	Per cent	£1 Level Stake
NH Flat	*32*	*43*	*11*	*11*	*4*	*17*	*25.6*	*+5.88*
Hurdles	*67*	*220*	*34*	*40*	*27*	*119*	*15.5*	*-65.72*
Chases	*67*	*291*	*58*	*42*	*46*	*145*	*19.9*	*-19.47*
Totals	**136**	**554**	**103**	**93**	**77**	**281**	**18.6**	**-79.31**
13-14	*131*	*545*	*105*	*74*	*54*	*312*	*19.3*	*+14.62*
12-13	*138*	*502*	*68*	*76*	*57*	*300*	*13.5*	*-82.28*

BY MONTH

NH Flat	W-R	Per cent	£1 Level Stake	**Hurdles**	W-R	Per cent	£1 Level Stake
May	0-4	0.0	-4.00	May	4-22	18.2	+0.38
June	0-0	0.0	0.00	June	1-7	14.3	-3.00
July	0-0	0.0	0.00	July	1-7	14.3	-4.00
August	0-0	0.0	0.00	August	0-2	0.0	-2.00
September	0-2	0.0	-2.00	September	0-4	0.0	-4.00
October	3-7	42.9	+1.38	October	5-32	15.6	-14.88
November	0-0	0.0	0.00	November	7-30	23.3	-8.06
December	1-3	33.3	+8.00	December	3-30	10.0	-19.75
January	2-2	100.0	+6.00	January	4-27	14.8	-2.50
February	2-7	28.6	+3.50	February	1-15	6.7	-12.13
March	1-9	11.1	-4.00	March	4-25	16.0	-2.76
April	2-9	22.2	-3.00	April	4-19	21.1	+6.98

Chases	W-R	Per cent	£1 Level Stake	**Totals**	W-R	Per cent	£1 Level Stake
May	4-23	17.4	-10.02	May	8-49	16.3	-13.64
June	1-6	16.7	-2.75	June	2-13	15.4	-5.75
July	1-7	14.3	-4.38	July	2-14	14.3	-8.38
August	1-8	12.5	-6.70	August	1-10	10.0	-8.70
September	2-6	33.3	+6.75	September	2-12	16.7	+0.75
October	6-30	20.0	+12.67	October	14-69	20.3	-0.83
November	12-46	26.1	+25.07	November	19-76	25.0	+17.01
December	8-39	20.5	-0.35	December	12-72	16.7	-12.10
January	9-35	25.7	-1.26	January	15-64	23.4	+2.24
February	2-19	10.5	-13.50	February	5-41	12.2	-22.13
March	2-38	5.3	-31.00	March	7-72	9.7	-37.76
April	10-34	29.4	+6.00	April	16-62	25.8	+9.98

DISTANCE

Hurdles	W-R	Per cent	£1 Level Stake	**Chases**	W-R	Per cent	£1 Level Stake
2m-2m3f	15-93	16.1	-13.53	2m-2m3f	11-50	22.0	-5.63
2m4f-2m7f	12-64	18.8	-17.79	2m4f-2m7f	19-80	23.8	-5.68
3m+	0-9	0.0	-9.00	3m+	20-122	16.4	-23.40

TYPE OF RACE

Non-Handicaps	W-R	Per cent	£1 Level Stake	**Handicaps**	W-R	Per cent	£1 Level Stake
Nov Hrdls	11-66	16.7	-24.54	Nov Hrdls	0-12	0.0	-12.00
Hrdls	7-39	17.9	-14.25	Hrdls	14-101	13.9	-18.50
Nov Chs	13-40	32.5	-4.28	Nov Chs	6-46	13.0	-18.50
Chases	6-21	28.6	+6.82	Chases	33-184	17.9	-3.51
Sell/Claim	0-0	0.0	0.00	Sell/Claim	0-0	0.0	0.00

RACE CLASS

	W-R	Per cent	£1 Level Stake
Class 1	13-89	14.6	-1.63
Class 2	12-76	15.8	-13.43
Class 3	31-138	22.5	+4.27
Class 4	33-175	18.9	-48.53
Class 5	5-47	10.6	-26.88
Class 6	9-29	31.0	+6.88

FIRST TIME OUT

	W-R	Per cent	£1 Level Stake
Bumpers	7-32	21.9	+2.00
Hurdles	7-56	12.5	-19.63
Chases	12-48	25.0	+19.63
Totals	26-136	19.1	+2.00

JOCKEYS

	W-R	Per cent	£1 Level Stake
Richard Johnson	64-300	21.3	-0.35
Tom O'Brien	16-126	12.7	-57.25
Micheal Nolan	5-30	16.7	-4.58
James Best	5-34	14.7	-11.93
A P McCoy	4-13	30.8	-1.13
Ciaran Gethings	4-19	21.1	+0.68
Thomas Cheesman	3-12	25.0	+9.50
Mr D Maxwell	1-4	25.0	-1.75
Conor Smith	1-10	10.0	-6.50

COURSE RECORD

	Total W-R	Non-Hndcps Hurdles	Non-Hndcps Chases	Hndcps Hurdles	Hndcps Chases	NH Flat	Per cent	£1 Level Stake
Exeter	12-50	4-10	2-8	1-12	3-15	2-5	24.0	+12.73
Cheltenham	12-56	1-3	5-16	1-10	4-23	1-4	21.4	+13.85
Worcester	6-24	2-6	0-0	1-4	3-13	0-1	25.0	-1.13
Chepstow	6-27	2-8	1-1	0-2	2-13	1-3	22.2	-9.12
Newbury	6-28	1-4	0-0	0-4	5-19	0-1	21.4	+2.50
Ludlow	6-29	1-10	0-1	3-3	2-13	0-2	20.7	-1.50
Wincanton	6-52	0-11	1-2	1-14	3-22	1-3	11.5	-31.50
Warwick	5-22	1-6	1-2	0-2	1-8	2-4	22.7	-7.00
Nton Abbot	5-28	1-8	1-4	2-6	1-9	0-1	17.9	-3.70
Sandown	4-21	1-2	2-4	1-4	0-10	0-1	19.0	+0.25
Leicester	3-6	0-1	0-0	0-0	3-5	0-0	50.0	+2.25
Fontwell	3-14	2-8	0-0	1-3	0-2	0-1	21.4	-6.80
Stratford	3-17	0-4	1-1	0-1	2-10	0-1	17.6	-1.54
Uttoxeter	3-20	0-1	0-0	1-7	1-11	1-1	15.0	+3.25
Aintree	3-23	0-1	0-4	0-6	3-12	0-0	13.0	+2.50
Perth	2-4	1-1	0-0	0-0	1-3	0-0	50.0	+1.35
Wetherby	2-6	0-0	2-4	0-0	0-2	0-0	33.3	+4.83
Doncaster	2-9	0-2	0-1	0-3	2-3	0-0	22.2	-0.25
Kempton	2-18	2-3	0-3	0-5	0-5	0-2	11.1	-14.23
Ascot	2-19	0-2	0-3	0-6	1-7	1-1	10.5	-6.50
Taunton	2-21	0-7	0-0	1-7	0-4	1-3	9.5	-12.38
Catterick	1-1	0-0	1-1	0-0	0-0	0-0	100.0	+0.25
Musselbgh	1-1	0-0	0-0	0-0	1-1	0-0	100.0	+0.91

Fakenham	1-1	0-0	1-1	0-0	0-0	0-0	100.0	+0.73
Hexham	1-1	1-1	0-0	0-0	0-0	0-0	100.0	+0.44
Ayr	1-4	0-0	0-0	1-2	0-2	0-0	25.0	+7.00
Huntingdon	1-10	0-3	1-2	0-1	0-3	0-1	10.0	-2.50
Ffos Las	1-11	0-0	0-0	0-3	0-5	1-3	9.1	-8.50
Haydock	1-12	0-0	0-2	0-5	1-4	0-1	8.3	-6.50

WINNING HORSES

Horse	Races Run	1st	2nd	3rd	£
Menorah	6	3	1	0	113900
Cheltenian	4	1	1	1	56950
Garde La Victoire	5	2	0	1	71188
If In Doubt	5	2	1	0	50701
Wishfull Thinking	6	2	0	1	73559
Duke Of Lucca	6	1	0	0	33791
Roalco De Farges	7	1	1	0	31280
Bold Henry	5	1	0	0	28152
Dunraven Storm	8	2	1	1	23991
Brother Tedd	7	3	1	0	25786
Royal Player	5	2	0	0	25667
Golden Doyen	7	2	2	0	20334
Gas Line Boy	6	2	0	0	24555
Balthazar King	2	1	0	0	15640
Uncle Jimmy	4	1	1	1	15640
Cloud Creeper	7	3	2	0	26726
Champagne West	4	2	1	0	25948
Ballygarvey	4	1	0	0	12686
Filbert	7	1	0	4	12512
Lamb Or Cod	8	3	2	0	28902
Wishfull Dreaming	2	1	1	0	11888
Royal Regatta	7	2	1	2	22834
Bertie Boru	5	2	1	0	16508
Return Spring	8	1	0	2	9495
Onenightinvienna	3	2	1	0	12917
Bincombe	7	2	0	1	13933
Silver Commander	3	1	1	0	7988
Toowoomba	5	2	0	1	11162
Irish Buccaneer	5	1	2	0	7596
Al Alfa	6	1	1	0	7507
The Skyfarmer	4	1	0	0	7148
Mountain King	7	1	1	1	6963
Thomas Wild	7	1	2	1	6498
Tony Star	5	1	0	1	6498
Allthekingshorses	7	2	1	1	6498
Village Vic	5	1	1	1	6498
August Hill	6	2	2	2	10267
Pull The Chord	4	2	0	1	9747
Carrigmorna King	6	1	1	1	6330
Powerful Action	4	2	0	2	12178
No Likey	8	2	1	1	10054
Woodford County	6	1	0	2	6055
Rock The Kasbah	6	3	1	1	10610
Princely Player	3	1	0	0	5393
Trickaway	9	2	1	4	9097
Sausalito Sunrise	4	1	2	0	4549
Wait For Me	2	1	0	1	4549
Danandy	6	1	1	1	4419
According To Sarah	10	2	2	1	6961
Meetmeatthemoon	3	1	2	0	3899
Scoop The Pot	3	1	1	0	3899
Ballytober	2	1	0	0	3769
Horizontal Speed	7	1	2	2	3769
River Deep	7	2	0	0	3509
Hello George	7	1	1	2	3249
Free Of Charge	6	1	2	0	3249
Risk A Fine	7	1	1	1	3249
Kublai	8	1	1	0	3249
War Sound	4	2	0	0	6498
Stilletto	2	1	0	0	3119
Lord Lescribaa	5	1	0	0	2924
Dry Ol'Party	3	1	2	0	2053
Sykes	2	1	0	0	1949
Duke Des Champs	2	1	0	0	1949
Copper Kay	2	1	0	0	1949
Drumlee Sunset	1	1	0	0	1625
Kayf Adventure	2	1	0	0	1625
Kayf Willow	2	1	1	0	1625
Star Trouper	1	1	0	0	1625
Onefitzall	1	1	0	0	1560
Out Now	3	1	0	1	1248

Total winning prize-money **£1041638**

Favourites **42-117** **35.9%** **-9.24**

JOHN HODGE

CUMNOCK, AYRSHIRE

	No. of Hrs	Races Run	1st	2nd	3rd	Unpl	Per cent	£1 Level Stake
NH Flat	*0*	*0*	*0*	*0*	*0*	*0*	*0.0*	*0.00*
Hurdles	*2*	*5*	*0*	*0*	*1*	*4*	*0.0*	*-5.00*
Chases	*1*	*4*	*1*	*1*	*0*	*2*	*25.0*	*+7.00*
Totals	**3**	**9**	**1**	**1**	**1**	**6**	**11.1**	**+2.00**
12-13	*1*	*2*	*0*	*0*	*0*	*2*	*0.0*	*-2.00*

JOCKEYS

	W-R	Per cent	£1 Level Stake
Grant Cockburn	1-4	25.0	+7.00

COURSE RECORD

	Total W-R	Non-Hndcps Hurdles	Non-Hndcps Chases	Hndcps Hurdles	Hndcps Chases	NH Flat	Per cent	£1 Level Stake
Hexham	1-5	0-2	0-0	0-0	1-3	0-0	20.0	+6.00

WINNING HORSES

Horse	Races Run	1st	2nd	3rd	£
*Flaming Thistle	4	1	1	0	2924

Total winning prize-money **£2924**

Favourites **0-0** **0.0%** **0.00**

RON HODGES

CHARLTON MACKRELL, SOMERSET

	No. of Hrs	Races Run	1st	2nd	3rd	Unpl	Per cent	£1 Level Stake
NH Flat	*1*	*1*	*0*	*0*	*0*	*1*	*0.0*	*-1.00*
Hurdles	*3*	*8*	*0*	*0*	*0*	*8*	*0.0*	*-8.00*
Chases	*1*	*5*	*1*	*2*	*0*	*2*	*20.0*	*+1.00*
Totals	**5**	**14**	**1**	**2**	**0**	**11**	**7.1**	**-8.00**
13-14	*10*	*28*	*2*	*1*	*2*	*23*	*7.1*	*-17.50*
12-13	*12*	*35*	*1*	*0*	*1*	*33*	*2.9*	*-26.50*

JOCKEYS

	W-R	Per cent	£1 Level Stake
Ian Popham	1-2	50.0	+4.00

COURSE RECORD

	Total W-R	Non-Hndcps Hurdles	Non-Hndcps Chases	Hndcps Hurdles	Hndcps Chases	NH Flat	Per cent	£1 Level Stake
Nton Abbot	1-4	0-0	0-0	0-1	1-3	0-0	25.0	+2.00

WINNING HORSES

Horse	Races Run	1st	2nd	3rd	£
Miss Tenacious	5	1	2	0	3899

Total winning prize-money **£3899**

Favourites **0-0** **0.0%** **0.00**

HENRY HOGARTH

STILLINGTON, N YORKS

	No. of Hrs	Races Run	1st	2nd	3rd	Unpl	Per cent	£1 Level Stake
NH Flat	*1*	*1*	*0*	*0*	*0*	*1*	*0.0*	*-1.00*
Hurdles	*11*	*23*	*1*	*3*	*4*	*15*	*4.3*	*-18.50*
Chases	*5*	*16*	*2*	*1*	*1*	*12*	*12.5*	*+3.50*
Totals	**14**	**40**	**3**	**4**	**5**	**28**	**7.5**	**-16.00**
13-14	*14*	*61*	*7*	*4*	*7*	*43*	*11.5*	*+29.50*
12-13	*13*	*51*	*2*	*2*	*11*	*36*	*3.9*	*-33.00*

JOCKEYS

	W-R	Per cent	£1 Level Stake
Adam Nicol	1-2	50.0	+2.50
Henry Brooke	1-4	25.0	+11.00
Graham Watters	1-12	8.3	-7.50

COURSE RECORD

	Total W-R	Non-Hndcps Hurdles	Non-Hndcps Chases	Hndcps Hurdles	Hndcps Chases	NH Flat	Per cent	£1 Level Stake
Catterick	2-5	0-0	0-0	1-3	1-2	0-0	40.0	+14.50
Newcastle	1-8	0-1	0-0	0-4	1-2	0-1	12.5	-3.50

WINNING HORSES

Horse	Races Run	1st	2nd	3rd	£
Pamak D'Airy	4	1	0	1	3769
Over And Above	7	1	0	0	3249
Deny	7	1	2	1	2738

Total winning prize-money **£9756**

Favourites **1-5** **20.0%** **-0.50**

MRS J M HOLLANDS

WESTRUTHER, BORDERS

	No. of Hrs	Races Run	1st	2nd	3rd	Unpl	Per cent	£1 Level Stake
NH Flat	*0*	*0*	*0*	*0*	*0*	*0*	*0.0*	*0.00*
Hurdles	*0*	*0*	*0*	*0*	*0*	*0*	*0.0*	*0.00*
Chases	*1*	*4*	*1*	*2*	*0*	*1*	*25.0*	*0.00*
Totals	**1**	**4**	**1**	**2**	**0**	**1**	**25.0**	**0.00**
13-14	*1*	*4*	*0*	*0*	*3*	*1*	*0.0*	*-4.00*
12-13	*1*	*1*	*0*	*1*	*0*	*0*	*0.0*	*-1.00*

JOCKEYS

	W-R	Per cent	£1 Level Stake
Mr G Crow	1-3	33.3	+1.00

COURSE RECORD

	Total W-R	Non-Hndcps Hurdles	Non-Hndcps Chases	Hndcps Hurdles	Hndcps Chases	NH Flat	Per cent	£1 Level Stake
Perth	1-1	0-0	1-1	0-0	0-0	0-0	100.0	+3.00

WINNING HORSES

Horse	Races Run	1st	2nd	3rd	£
Barachois Silver	4	1	2	0	1872

Total winning prize-money **£1872**

Favourites **0-0** **0.0%** **0.00**

D HOLMES

MORPETH, NORTHUMBERLAND

	No. of Hrs	Races Run	1st	2nd	3rd	Unpl	Per cent	£1 Level Stake
NH Flat	*0*	*0*	*0*	*0*	*0*	*0*	*0.0*	*0.00*
Hurdles	*0*	*0*	*0*	*0*	*0*	*0*	*0.0*	*0.00*
Chases	*3*	*6*	*2*	*0*	*0*	*4*	*33.3*	*+7.00*
Totals	**3**	**6**	**2**	**0**	**0**	**4**	**33.3**	**+7.00**
13-14	*3*	*7*	*1*	*0*	*0*	*6*	*14.3*	*0.00*
12-13	*2*	*2*	*0*	*1*	*0*	*1*	*0.0*	*-2.00*

JOCKEYS

	W-R	Per cent	£1 Level Stake
Mr R Smith	1-1	100.0	+9.00
Miss R McDonald	1-1	100.0	+2.00

COURSE RECORD

	Total W-R	Non-Hndcps Hurdles	Non-Hndcps Chases	Hndcps Hurdles	Hndcps Chases	NH Flat	Per cent	£1 Level Stake
Hexham	1-1	0-0	1-1	0-0	0-0	0-0	100.0	+2.00
Kelso	1-2	0-0	1-2	0-0	0-0	0-0	50.0	+8.00

WINNING HORSES

Horse	Races Run	1st	2nd	3rd	£
*Beggar's Velvet	3	2	0	0	5241
Total winning prize-money					**£5241**
Favourites	**0-0**		**0.0%**		**0.00**

PATRICK HOLMES

MIDDLEHAM, N YORKS

	No. of Hrs	Races Run	1st	2nd	3rd	Unpl	Per cent	£1 Level Stake
NH Flat	*1*	*1*	*0*	*0*	*0*	*1*	*0.0*	*-1.00*
Hurdles	*13*	*28*	*2*	*1*	*5*	*20*	*7.1*	*-10.00*
Chases	*4*	*18*	*1*	*4*	*1*	*12*	*5.6*	*-13.50*
Totals	**14**	**47**	**3**	**5**	**6**	**33**	**6.4**	**-24.50**
13-14	*9*	*33*	*2*	*2*	*2*	*27*	*6.1*	*0.00*
12-13	*7*	*17*	*0*	*4*	*1*	*12*	*0.0*	*-17.00*

JOCKEYS

	W-R	Per cent	£1 Level Stake
John Kington	2-24	8.3	-12.50
Barry Keniry	1-9	11.1	+2.00

COURSE RECORD

	Total W-R	Non-Hndcps Hurdles	Non-Hndcps Chases	Hndcps Hurdles	Hndcps Chases	NH Flat	Per cent	£1 Level Stake
Carlisle	1-3	0-0	0-0	1-3	0-0	0-0	33.3	+8.00
Kelso	1-5	0-0	0-0	1-4	0-1	0-0	20.0	+2.00
Catterick	1-8	0-1	0-1	0-1	1-4	0-1	12.5	-3.50

WINNING HORSES

Horse	Races Run	1st	2nd	3rd	£
Foot The Bill	14	2	4	3	12483
Yourholidayisover	9	1	0	0	3119
Total winning prize-money					**£15602**
Favourites	**0-1**		**0.0%**		**-1.00**

ANTHONY HONEYBALL

MOSTERTON, DORSET

	No. of Hrs	Races Run	1st	2nd	3rd	Unpl	Per cent	£1 Level Stake
NH Flat	*15*	*28*	*6*	*6*	*4*	*12*	*21.4*	*+9.16*
Hurdles	*31*	*110*	*17*	*8*	*11*	*74*	*15.5*	*-8.77*
Chases	*13*	*39*	*4*	*8*	*5*	*22*	*10.3*	*-12.50*
Totals	**41**	**177**	**27**	**22**	**20**	**108**	**15.3**	**-12.11**
13-14	*41*	*139*	*21*	*18*	*13*	*87*	*15.1*	*-29.95*
12-13	*35*	*105*	*19*	*12*	*11*	*62*	*18.1*	*-16.75*

BY MONTH

NH Flat	W-R	Per cent	£1 Level Stake	Hurdles	W-R	Per cent	£1 Level Stake
May	2-4	50.0	+20.00	May	1-13	7.7	-7.00
June	1-1	100.0	+0.91	June	0-2	0.0	-2.00
July	0-1	0.0	-1.00	July	1-4	25.0	+3.00
August	0-0	0.0	0.00	August	1-4	25.0	+1.50
September	1-1	100.0	+4.00	September	1-1	100.0	+1.38
October	1-3	33.3	0.00	October	3-11	27.3	-0.13
November	0-6	0.0	-6.00	November	2-15	13.3	-2.20
December	0-6	0.0	-6.00	December	0-8	0.0	-8.00
January	0-2	0.0	-2.00	January	1-14	7.1	+7.00
February	1-3	33.3	+0.25	February	6-17	35.3	+16.06
March	0-1	0.0	-1.00	March	1-17	5.9	-14.38
April	0-0	0.0	0.00	April	0-4	0.0	-4.00

Chases	W-R	Per cent	£1 Level Stake	Totals	W-R	Per cent	£1 Level Stake
May	0-0	0.0	0.00	May	3-17	17.6	+13.00
June	0-2	0.0	-2.00	June	1-5	20.0	-3.09
July	0-1	0.0	-1.00	July	1-6	16.7	+1.00
August	0-0	0.0	0.00	August	1-4	25.0	+1.50
September	0-0	0.0	0.00	September	2-2	100.0	+5.38
October	1-4	25.0	+13.00	October	5-18	27.8	+12.87
November	0-7	0.0	-7.00	November	2-28	7.1	-15.20
December	0-5	0.0	-5.00	December	0-19	0.0	-19.00
January	1-9	11.1	-5.50	January	2-25	8.0	-0.50
February	0-4	0.0	-4.00	February	7-24	29.2	+12.31
March	2-5	40.0	+1.00	March	3-23	13.0	-14.38
April	0-2	0.0	-2.00	April	0-6	0.0	-6.00

DISTANCE

Hurdles	W-R	Per cent	£1 Level Stake	Chases	W-R	Per cent	£1 Level Stake
2m-2m3f	5-51	9.8	-5.20	2m-2m3f	1-10	10.0	-6.50
2m4f-2m7f	3-24	12.5	-7.77	2m4f-2m7f	1-13	7.7	-10.00
3m+	3-8	37.5	-0.25	3m+	1-10	10.0	-7.00

TYPE OF RACE

Non-Handicaps	W-R	Per cent	£1 Level Stake	Handicaps	W-R	Per cent	£1 Level Stake
Nov Hrdls	1-35	2.9	-33.20	Nov Hrdls	2-4	50.0	+3.33
Hrdls	1-17	5.9	-11.00	Hrdls	13-54	24.1	+32.10
Nov Chs	0-1	0.0	-1.00	Nov Chs	1-11	9.1	-8.00
Chases	0-1	0.0	-1.00	Chases	3-26	11.5	-2.50
Sell/Claim	0-0	0.0	0.00	Sell/Claim	0-0	0.0	0.00

RACE CLASS

	W-R	Per cent	£1 Level Stake
Class 1	0-12	0.0	-12.00
Class 2	2-8	25.0	+18.00
Class 3	3-32	9.4	-23.63
Class 4	10-78	12.8	-26.27

FIRST TIME OUT

	W-R	Per cent	£1 Level Stake
Bumpers	3-15	20.0	+14.00
Hurdles	2-20	10.0	-15.82
Chases	1-6	16.7	+11.00

Class 5	6-25	24.0	+16.63	Totals	6-41	14.6	+9.18
Class 6	6-22	27.3	+15.16				

JOCKEYS

	W-R	Per cent	£1 Level Stake
Rachael Green	11-68	16.2	+0.13
Aidan Coleman	7-28	25.0	-1.15
Denis O'Regan	3-18	16.7	+21.80
Ryan Mahon	3-28	10.7	-11.09
Will Kennedy	1-3	33.3	+6.00
Mr D G Noonan	1-4	25.0	-2.17
Daryl Jacob	1-5	20.0	-2.63

COURSE RECORD

	Total W-R	Non-Hndcps Hurdles	Non-Hndcps Chases	Hndcps Hurdles	Hndcps Chases	NH Flat	Per cent	£1 Level Stake
Uttoxeter	5-12	1-3	0-0	4-7	0-2	0-0	41.7	+11.38
Exeter	5-20	0-6	0-1	2-7	2-4	1-2	25.0	+29.50
Taunton	4-19	0-8	0-0	4-6	0-3	0-2	21.1	+0.96
Ffos Las	4-24	1-6	0-0	1-8	0-5	2-5	16.7	-3.79
Fontwell	3-6	0-1	0-0	1-1	0-1	2-3	50.0	+4.38
Plumpton	2-5	0-1	0-0	1-2	0-1	1-1	40.0	-0.02
Chepstow	2-18	0-7	0-0	1-5	1-6	0-0	11.1	+10.00
Warwick	1-2	0-0	0-0	0-0	1-1	0-1	50.0	+1.00
Wincanton	1-22	0-10	0-0	1-6	0-3	0-3	4.5	-16.50

WINNING HORSES

Horse	Races Run	1st	2nd	3rd	£
Victors Serenade	5	1	0	0	16245
Regal Encore	5	1	0	0	12512
Lily Waugh	8	1	4	0	7528
Chill Factor	7	3	0	0	11528
Royal Native	5	2	1	0	10443
Rouquine Sauvage	9	2	1	0	6173
Marie Des Anges	5	1	1	2	3899
Jaja De Jau	9	2	2	2	6108
Midnight Minx	3	1	0	1	3798
Cresswell Breeze	9	3	0	0	8935
Jackies Solitaire	6	1	1	2	3249
Oscarteea	2	1	1	0	3119
*River Dancing	3	1	0	1	2924
The Geegeez Geegee	10	2	0	3	4159
Miss Mobot	2	1	1	0	1949
Act Now	6	1	1	1	1819
Horace Hazel	6	1	0	1	1625
Fountains Blossom	7	2	0	0	3119
Total winning prize-money					**£109132**
Favourites	**10-32**		**31.3%**		**-7.86**

CHRIS HONOUR

ASHBURTON, DEVON

	No. of Hrs	Races Run	1st	2nd	3rd	Unpl	Per cent	£1 Level Stake
NH Flat	*0*	*0*	*0*	*0*	*0*	*0*	*0.0*	*0.00*
Hurdles	*0*	*0*	*0*	*0*	*0*	*0*	*0.0*	*0.00*
Chases	*1*	*3*	*2*	*0*	*0*	*1*	*66.7*	*+6.00*
Totals	**1**	**3**	**2**	**0**	**0**	**1**	**66.7**	**+6.00**

JOCKEYS

	W-R	Per cent	£1 Level Stake
Mr D Edwards	2-3	66.7	+6.00

COURSE RECORD

	Total W-R	Non-Hndcps Hurdles	Non-Hndcps Chases	Hndcps Hurdles	Hndcps Chases	NH Flat	Per cent	£1 Level Stake
Wincanton	2-2	0-0	2-2	0-0	0-0	0-0	100.0	+7.00

WINNING HORSES

Horse	Races Run	1st	2nd	3rd	£
*Coombe Hill	3	2	0	0	1924
Total winning prize-money					**£1924**
Favourites	**0-0**		**0.0%**		**0.00**

STUART HOWE

OAKFORD, DEVON

	No. of Hrs	Races Run	1st	2nd	3rd	Unpl	Per cent	£1 Level Stake
NH Flat	*0*	*0*	*0*	*0*	*0*	*0*	*0.0*	*0.00*
Hurdles	*3*	*18*	*1*	*4*	*0*	*13*	*5.6*	*-8.00*
Chases	*0*	*0*	*0*	*0*	*0*	*0*	*0.0*	*0.00*
Totals	**3**	**18**	**1**	**4**	**0**	**13**	**5.6**	**-8.00**
13-14	*4*	*17*	*4*	*1*	*2*	*10*	*23.5*	*+10.75*
12-13	*4*	*19*	*2*	*0*	*2*	*15*	*10.5*	*-6.17*

JOCKEYS

	W-R	Per cent	£1 Level Stake
Gavin Sheehan	1-4	25.0	+6.00

COURSE RECORD

	Total W-R	Non-Hndcps Hurdles	Non-Hndcps Chases	Hndcps Hurdles	Hndcps Chases	NH Flat	Per cent	£1 Level Stake
Exeter	1-4	0-1	0-0	1-3	0-0	0-0	25.0	+6.00

WINNING HORSES

Horse	Races Run	1st	2nd	3rd	£
Party Palace	7	1	1	0	6498
Total winning prize-money					**£6498**
Favourites	**0-0**		**0.0%**		**0.00**

MARK HUGHES

WIGTON, CUMBRIA

	No. of Hrs	Races Run	1st	2nd	3rd	Unpl	Per cent	£1 Level Stake
NH Flat	0	0	0	0	0	0	0.0	0.00
Hurdles	0	0	0	0	0	0	0.0	0.00
Chases	1	3	1	1	0	1	33.3	0.00
Totals	**1**	**3**	**1**	**1**	**0**	**1**	**33.3**	**0.00**
13-14	1	7	1	2	0	4	14.3	-4.80
12-13	1	9	3	1	1	4	33.3	-0.56

JOCKEYS

	W-R	Per cent	£1 Level Stake
Mr R Hogg	1-3	33.3	0.00

COURSE RECORD

	Total W-R	Non-Hndcps Hurdles	Non-Hndcps Chases	Hndcps Hurdles	Hndcps Chases	NH Flat	Per cent	£1 Level Stake
Sedgefield	1-1	0-0	1-1	0-0	0-0	0-0	100.0	+2.00

WINNING HORSES

Horse	Races Run	1st	2nd	3rd	£
*Special Portrait	3	1	1	0	1920
Total winning prize-money					**£1920**
Favourites	**1-1**		**100.0%**		**2.00**

MS N M HUGO

EDGE GREEN, CHESHIRE

	No. of Hrs	Races Run	1st	2nd	3rd	Unpl	Per cent	£1 Level Stake
NH Flat	0	0	0	0	0	0	0.0	0.00
Hurdles	1	2	0	0	0	2	0.0	-2.00
Chases	1	5	1	0	1	3	20.0	+4.00
Totals	**2**	**7**	**1**	**0**	**1**	**5**	**14.3**	**+2.00**
13-14	3	3	0	0	1	2	0.0	-3.00
12-13	4	8	0	0	0	8	0.0	-8.00

JOCKEYS

	W-R	Per cent	£1 Level Stake
Robert Dunne	1-4	25.0	+5.00

COURSE RECORD

	Total W-R	Non-Hndcps Hurdles	Non-Hndcps Chases	Hndcps Hurdles	Hndcps Chases	NH Flat	Per cent	£1 Level Stake
Huntingdon	1-2	0-0	0-0	0-0	1-2	0-0	50.0	+7.00

WINNING HORSES

Horse	Races Run	1st	2nd	3rd	£
Silent Cliche	5	1	0	1	2339
Total winning prize-money					**£2339**
Favourites	**0-0**		**0.0%**		**0.00**

SARAH HUMPHREY

WEST WRATTING, CAMBS

	No. of Hrs	Races Run	1st	2nd	3rd	Unpl	Per cent	£1 Level Stake
NH Flat	4	6	0	2	0	4	0.0	-6.00
Hurdles	14	42	4	1	9	28	9.5	-20.25
Chases	4	21	1	3	6	11	4.8	-13.00
Totals	**15**	**69**	**5**	**6**	**15**	**43**	**7.2**	**-39.25**
13-14	24	71	3	8	6	54	4.2	-48.63
12-13	26	71	5	4	11	51	7.0	-43.09

JOCKEYS

	W-R	Per cent	£1 Level Stake
Jack Quinlan	3-40	7.5	-23.25
James Banks	2-18	11.1	-5.00

COURSE RECORD

	Total W-R	Non-Hndcps Hurdles	Non-Hndcps Chases	Hndcps Hurdles	Hndcps Chases	NH Flat	Per cent	£1 Level Stake
Southwell	1-3	1-1	0-0	0-2	0-0	0-0	33.3	+6.00
Worcester	1-3	1-2	0-0	0-0	0-1	0-0	33.3	+0.25
Stratford	1-6	1-2	0-0	0-1	0-2	0-1	16.7	-1.50
Plumpton	1-7	0-1	0-0	1-2	0-2	0-2	14.3	-2.00
Fakenham	1-13	0-3	0-0	0-5	1-5	0-0	7.7	-5.00

WINNING HORSES

Horse	Races Run	1st	2nd	3rd	£
*Unknown Legend	5	1	0	2	9747
Larteta	14	1	3	5	3899
Minella Hero	2	1	0	0	3195
Flemi Two Toes	13	1	0	4	2274
Tales Of Milan	5	1	0	1	2274
Total winning prize-money					**£21389**
Favourites	**0-3**		**0.0%**		**-3.00**

KEVIN HUNTER

NATLAND, CUMBRIA

	No. of Hrs	Races Run	1st	2nd	3rd	Unpl	Per cent	£1 Level Stake
NH Flat	0	0	0	0	0	0	0.0	0.00
Hurdles	2	6	0	0	0	6	0.0	-6.00
Chases	3	15	1	1	2	11	6.7	-10.67
Totals	**3**	**21**	**1**	**1**	**2**	**17**	**4.8**	**-16.67**
13-14	3	7	1	0	1	5	14.3	-1.00
12-13	1	3	0	0	0	3	0.0	-3.00

JOCKEYS

	W-R	Per cent	£1 Level Stake
Callum Bewley	1-14	7.1	-9.67

COURSE RECORD

	Total W-R	Non-Hndcps Hurdles	Non-Hndcps Chases	Hndcps Hurdles	Hndcps Chases	NH Flat	Per cent	£1 Level Stake
Hexham	1-9	0-1	0-0	0-0	1-8	0-0	11.1	-4.67

WINNING HORSES

Horse	Races Run	1st	2nd	3rd	£
Milan Royale	9	1	1	0	2794
Total winning prize-money					**£2794**
Favourites	**0-0**		**0.0%**		**0.00**

LAURA HURLEY

KINETON, WARWICKS

	No. of Hrs	Races Run	1st	2nd	3rd	Unpl	Per cent	£1 Level Stake
NH Flat	*0*	*0*	*0*	*0*	*0*	*0*	*0.0*	*0.00*
Hurdles	*3*	*12*	*3*	*1*	*1*	*7*	*25.0*	*-0.77*
Chases	*4*	*10*	*0*	*0*	*0*	*10*	*0.0*	*-10.00*
Totals	**6**	**22**	**3**	**1**	**1**	**17**	**13.6**	**-10.77**
13-14	*7*	*21*	*2*	*1*	*2*	*16*	*9.5*	*+19.00*
12-13	*5*	*19*	*1*	*1*	*2*	*15*	*5.3*	*-7.00*

JOCKEYS

	W-R	Per cent	£1 Level Stake
Kieron Edgar	1-2	50.0	+2.00
David Bass	1-3	33.3	+2.50
Tom Bellamy	1-3	33.3	-1.27

COURSE RECORD

	Total W-R	Non-Hndcps Hurdles	Non-Hndcps Chases	Hndcps Hurdles	Hndcps Chases	NH Flat	Per cent	£1 Level Stake
Lingfield	1-1	0-0	0-0	1-1	0-0	0-0	100.0	+0.73
Plumpton	1-1	0-0	0-0	1-1	0-0	0-0	100.0	+3.00
Leicester	1-4	0-2	0-0	1-1	0-1	0-0	25.0	+1.50

WINNING HORSES

Horse	Races Run	1st	2nd	3rd	£
Catchin Time	6	3	0	0	7668
Total winning prize-money					**£7668**
Favourites	**2-3**		**66.7%**		**2.73**

F A HUTSBY

STRATFORD-UPON-AVON, WARWICKS

	No. of Hrs	Races Run	1st	2nd	3rd	Unpl	Per cent	£1 Level Stake
NH Flat	*0*	*0*	*0*	*0*	*0*	*0*	*0.0*	*0.00*
Hurdles	*0*	*0*	*0*	*0*	*0*	*0*	*0.0*	*0.00*
Chases	*5*	*9*	*1*	*2*	*2*	*4*	*11.1*	*-6.25*
Totals	**5**	**9**	**1**	**2**	**2**	**4**	**11.1**	**-6.25**
13-14	*3*	*9*	*2*	*1*	*3*	*3*	*22.2*	*-5.77*
12-13	*4*	*16*	*4*	*3*	*3*	*6*	*25.0*	*-3.89*

JOCKEYS

	W-R	Per cent	£1 Level Stake
Mr T Ellis	1-7	14.3	-4.25

COURSE RECORD

	Total W-R	Non-Hndcps Hurdles	Non-Hndcps Chases	Hndcps Hurdles	Hndcps Chases	NH Flat	Per cent	£1 Level Stake
Towcester	1-1	0-0	1-1	0-0	0-0	0-0	100.0	+1.75

WINNING HORSES

Horse	Races Run	1st	2nd	3rd	£
Penmore Mill	2	1	0	1	936
Total winning prize-money					**£936**
Favourites	**1-1**		**100.0%**		**1.75**

TINA JACKSON

LIVERTON, CLEVELAND

	No. of Hrs	Races Run	1st	2nd	3rd	Unpl	Per cent	£1 Level Stake
NH Flat	*1*	*2*	*0*	*0*	*0*	*2*	*0.0*	*-2.00*
Hurdles	*9*	*26*	*2*	*1*	*3*	*20*	*7.7*	*+3.00*
Chases	*3*	*4*	*0*	*1*	*0*	*3*	*0.0*	*-4.00*
Totals	**11**	**32**	**2**	**2**	**3**	**25**	**6.3**	**-3.00**
13-14	*9*	*36*	*2*	*2*	*1*	*31*	*5.6*	*-7.80*
12-13	*2*	*8*	*1*	*1*	*0*	*6*	*12.5*	*+5.00*

JOCKEYS

	W-R	Per cent	£1 Level Stake
Nico de Boinville	1-1	100.0	+2.00
Samantha Drake	1-19	5.3	+7.00

COURSE RECORD

	Total W-R	Non-Hndcps Hurdles	Non-Hndcps Chases	Hndcps Hurdles	Hndcps Chases	NH Flat	Per cent	£1 Level Stake
Newcastle	1-3	0-0	0-0	1-2	0-0	0-1	33.3	0.00
Hexham	1-9	1-5	0-0	0-1	0-3	0-0	11.1	+17.00

WINNING HORSES

Horse	Races Run	1st	2nd	3rd	£
Purple Harry	7	1	1	2	2274
Ardesia	5	1	0	0	2053
Total winning prize-money					**£4327**
Favourites	**1-1**		**100.0%**		**2.00**

LEE JAMES

NORTON, N YORKS

	No. of Hrs	Races Run	1st	2nd	3rd	Unpl	Per cent	£1 Level Stake
NH Flat	*0*	*0*	*0*	*0*	*0*	*0*	*0.0*	*0.00*
Hurdles	*2*	*3*	*1*	*0*	*0*	*2*	*33.3*	*+98.00*
Chases	*0*	*0*	*0*	*0*	*0*	*0*	*0.0*	*0.00*
Totals	**2**	**3**	**1**	**0**	**0**	**2**	**33.3**	**+98.00**
13-14	*2*	*3*	*0*	*0*	*0*	*3*	*0.0*	*-3.00*

JOCKEYS

	W-R	Per cent	£1 Level Stake
Kyle James	1-3	33.3	+98.00

COURSE RECORD

	Total W-R	Non-Hndcps Hurdles	Non-Hndcps Chases	Hndcps Hurdles	Hndcps Chases	NH Flat	Per cent	£1 Level Stake
Catterick	1-1	0-0	0-0	1-1	0-0	0-0	100.0	+100.00

WINNING HORSES

Horse	Races Run	1st	2nd	3rd	£
Freedom Flying	2	1	0	0	3249
Total winning prize-money					**£3249**
Favourites	**0-0**		**0.0%**		**0.00**

IAIN JARDINE

BONCHESTER BRIDGE, ROXBURGH

	No. of Hrs	Races Run	1st	2nd	3rd	Unpl	Per cent	£1 Level Stake
NH Flat	*4*	*5*	*0*	*0*	*0*	*5*	*0.0*	*-5.00*
Hurdles	*9*	*21*	*1*	*1*	*3*	*16*	*4.8*	*-17.75*
Chases	*1*	*4*	*2*	*0*	*0*	*2*	*50.0*	*+16.00*
Totals	**11**	**30**	**3**	**1**	**3**	**23**	**10.0**	**-6.75**
13-14	*15*	*35*	*1*	*2*	*1*	*31*	*2.9*	*-14.00*
12-13	*15*	*42*	*4*	*4*	*3*	*31*	*9.5*	*-16.13*

JOCKEYS

	W-R	Per cent	£1 Level Stake
Craig Nichol	3-7	42.9	+16.25

COURSE RECORD

	Total W-R	Non-Hndcps Hurdles	Non-Hndcps Chases	Hndcps Hurdles	Hndcps Chases	NH Flat	Per cent	£1 Level Stake
Aintree	1-1	0-0	0-0	0-0	1-1	0-0	100.0	+10.00
Perth	1-3	0-1	0-0	1-2	0-0	0-0	33.3	+0.25
Kelso	1-8	0-3	0-0	0-2	1-2	0-1	12.5	+1.00

WINNING HORSES

Horse	Races Run	1st	2nd	3rd	£
Double Whammy	4	2	0	0	9505
Push Me	4	1	1	0	2532
Total winning prize-money					**£12037**
Favourites	**0-2**		**0.0%**		**-2.00**

MALCOLM JEFFERSON

NORTON, N YORKS

	No. of Hrs	Races Run	1st	2nd	3rd	Unpl	Per cent	£1 Level Stake
NH Flat	*19*	*34*	*4*	*6*	*9*	*15*	*11.8*	*-13.75*
Hurdles	*23*	*56*	*9*	*6*	*0*	*41*	*16.1*	*-19.21*
Chases	*20*	*71*	*12*	*8*	*8*	*43*	*16.9*	*-16.13*
Totals	**49**	**161**	**25**	**20**	**17**	**99**	**15.5**	**-49.09**
13-14	*48*	*189*	*31*	*26*	*29*	*103*	*16.4*	*-17.81*
12-13	*38*	*152*	*23*	*21*	*18*	*90*	*15.1*	*+11.60*

BY MONTH

NH Flat	W-R	Per cent	£1 Level Stake
May	0-4	0.0	-4.00
June	1-2	50.0	+3.50
July	0-1	0.0	-1.00
August	0-1	0.0	-1.00
September	0-3	0.0	-3.00
October	1-4	25.0	+3.50
November	0-2	0.0	-2.00
December	0-3	0.0	-3.00
January	0-1	0.0	-1.00
February	0-2	0.0	-2.00
March	1-5	20.0	-1.75
April	1-6	16.7	-2.00

Hurdles	W-R	Per cent	£1 Level Stake
May	1-7	14.3	-3.00
June	0-3	0.0	-3.00
July	1-1	100.0	+2.75
August	0-2	0.0	-2.00
September	1-6	16.7	-4.00
October	0-7	0.0	-7.00
November	1-7	14.3	-2.50
December	1-8	12.5	-2.50
January	0-0	0.0	0.00
February	0-4	0.0	-4.00
March	2-5	40.0	+0.79
April	2-6	33.3	+5.25

Chases	W-R	Per cent	£1 Level Stake
May	1-4	25.0	-1.63
June	2-4	50.0	+8.00
July	1-3	33.3	-0.63
August	0-1	0.0	-1.00
September	0-1	0.0	-1.00
October	0-6	0.0	-6.00
November	0-8	0.0	-8.00
December	0-10	0.0	-10.00
January	1-8	12.5	-0.50
February	1-3	33.3	-0.38

Totals	W-R	Per cent	£1 Level Stake
May	2-15	13.3	-8.63
June	3-9	33.3	+8.50
July	2-5	40.0	+1.12
August	0-4	0.0	-4.00
September	1-10	10.0	-8.00
October	1-17	5.9	-9.50
November	1-17	5.9	-12.50
December	1-21	4.8	-15.50
January	1-9	11.1	-1.50
February	1-9	11.1	-6.38

March	5-14	35.7	+5.00	March	8-24	33.3	+4.04
April	1-9	11.1	0.00	April	4-21	19.0	+3.25

DISTANCE

Hurdles	W-R	Per cent	£1 Level Stake	Chases	W-R	Per cent	£1 Level Stake
2m-2m3f	6-36	16.7	-11.46	2m-2m3f	2-17	11.8	-7.13
2m4f-2m7f	3-11	27.3	+1.25	2m4f-2m7f	4-26	15.4	-10.13
3m+	0-3	0.0	-3.00	3m+	2-19	10.5	-6.75

TYPE OF RACE

Non-Handicaps	W-R	Per cent	£1 Level Stake	Handicaps	W-R	Per cent	£1 Level Stake
Nov Hrdls	5-20	25.0	-0.96	Nov Hrdls	0-2	0.0	-2.00
Hrdls	0-5	0.0	-5.00	Hrdls	4-27	14.8	-9.25
Nov Chs	0-7	0.0	-7.00	Nov Chs	2-11	18.2	-6.38
Chases	0-0	0.0	0.00	Chases	10-53	18.9	-2.75
Sell/Claim	0-1	0.0	-1.00	Sell/Claim	0-0	0.0	0.00

RACE CLASS / FIRST TIME OUT

Race Class	W-R	Per cent	£1 Level Stake	First Time Out	W-R	Per cent	£1 Level Stake
Class 1	1-17	5.9	-8.00	Bumpers	2-19	10.5	-10.25
Class 2	3-14	21.4	-0.50	Hurdles	1-15	6.7	-11.00
Class 3	6-31	19.4	-4.13	Chases	1-15	6.7	-12.63
Class 4	9-56	16.1	-18.46				
Class 5	2-14	14.3	-9.25	Totals	4-49	8.2	-33.88
Class 6	4-29	13.8	-8.75				

JOCKEYS

	W-R	Per cent	£1 Level Stake
Brian Hughes	25-146	17.1	-34.09

COURSE RECORD

	Total W-R	Non-Hndcps Hurdles	Non-Hndcps Chases	Hndcps Hurdles	Hndcps Chases	NH Flat	Per cent	£1 Level Stake
Sedgefield	5-26	2-5	0-0	1-7	2-7	0-7	19.2	-10.38
Newcastle	3-8	1-1	0-1	0-1	1-3	1-2	37.5	+2.38
Hexham	3-9	1-3	0-0	0-1	1-2	1-3	33.3	-0.71
Wetherby	3-16	0-2	0-0	1-5	2-8	0-1	18.8	+3.50
Mrket Rsn	3-20	0-5	0-0	2-5	0-3	1-7	15.0	-6.75
Ayr	2-13	0-2	0-1	0-0	1-6	1-4	15.4	-2.25
Perth	1-2	0-0	0-0	0-1	1-1	0-0	50.0	+7.00
Southwell	1-4	0-0	0-0	0-1	1-2	0-1	25.0	-1.63
Uttoxeter	1-8	0-3	0-0	0-2	1-3	0-0	12.5	+1.00
Carlisle	1-9	0-1	0-1	0-0	1-5	0-2	11.1	-6.50
Aintree	1-9	1-2	0-0	0-2	0-3	0-2	11.1	0.00
Kelso	1-14	0-2	0-1	0-0	1-9	0-2	7.1	-11.75

WINNING HORSES

Horse	Races Run	1st	2nd	3rd	£
Cyrus Darius	4	3	0	1	40296
Oscar Rock	5	2	1	0	21119
Firth Of The Clyde	6	1	2	1	11819
Enchanted Garden	3	2	0	0	17759
King Of The Wolds	6	1	1	0	7798
Sun Cloud	5	2	0	1	13926
Cape York	7	1	0	1	6498
Secrete Stream	3	1	0	0	5523
Grey Life	8	3	0	0	11826
The Panama Kid	5	1	0	0	3961
Nautical Twilight	8	1	2	0	3509
Pair Of Jacks	5	1	1	1	3379
Major Ivan	4	1	0	1	3379
Danby's Legend	6	1	0	0	2274
Cloudy Dream	2	1	0	1	1711
Double W's	5	1	2	1	1643
Chilly Miss	2	1	0	1	1560
Jurby	2	1	0	0	1560

Total winning prize-money **£159540**

Favourites **10-25** **40.0%** **-0.84**

J R JENKINS

ROYSTON, HERTS

	No. of Hrs	Races Run	1st	2nd	3rd	Unpl	Per cent	£1 Level Stake
NH Flat	*3*	*3*	*1*	*0*	*0*	*2*	*33.3*	*+23.00*
Hurdles	*10*	*33*	*3*	*4*	*2*	*24*	*9.1*	*-1.00*
Chases	*1*	*2*	*1*	*0*	*0*	*1*	*50.0*	*+2.50*
Totals	**13**	**38**	**5**	**4**	**2**	**27**	**13.2**	**+24.50**
13-14	*13*	*49*	*6*	*8*	*8*	*27*	*12.2*	*-18.30*
12-13	*8*	*33*	*3*	*0*	*4*	*26*	*9.1*	*-0.50*

JOCKEYS

	W-R	Per cent	£1 Level Stake
Aidan Coleman	2-9	22.2	+16.00
Paul Moloney	1-1	100.0	+25.00
Dougie Costello	1-2	50.0	+2.50
A P McCoy	1-4	25.0	+3.00

COURSE RECORD

	Total W-R	Non-Hndcps Hurdles	Non-Hndcps Chases	Hndcps Hurdles	Hndcps Chases	NH Flat	Per cent	£1 Level Stake
Huntingdon	2-8	0-2	0-0	1-4	0-0	1-2	25.0	+35.00
Fakenham	1-4	0-3	0-0	0-0	1-1	0-0	25.0	+0.50
Southwell	1-5	0-1	0-0	1-4	0-0	0-0	20.0	+3.00
Worcester	1-9	0-0	0-0	1-8	0-1	0-0	11.1	-2.00

WINNING HORSES

Horse	Races Run	1st	2nd	3rd	£
Hi Tide	6	3	0	0	11047
Tiradia	9	1	2	1	3249
Brave Richard	1	1	0	0	1625

Total winning prize-money **£15921**

Favourites **0-2** **0.0%** **-2.00**

LINDA JEWELL

SUTTON VALENCE, KENT

	No. of Hrs	Races Run	1st	2nd	3rd	Unpl	Per cent	£1 Level Stake
NH Flat	*1*	*1*	*0*	*0*	*0*	*1*	*0.0*	*-1.00*
Hurdles	*11*	*39*	*0*	*1*	*3*	*35*	*0.0*	*-39.00*
Chases	*3*	*14*	*3*	*3*	*1*	*7*	*21.4*	*+12.50*
Totals	**13**	**54**	**3**	**4**	**4**	**43**	**5.6**	**-27.50**
13-14	*11*	*38*	*5*	*1*	*2*	*30*	*13.2*	*-3.50*
12-13	*14*	*40*	*2*	*2*	*2*	*34*	*5.0*	*-2.00*

JOCKEYS

	W-R	Per cent	£1 Level Stake
Tom Cannon	2-12	16.7	+6.00
Thomas Garner	1-7	14.3	+1.50

COURSE RECORD

	Total W-R	Non-Hndcps Hurdles	Non-Hndcps Chases	Hndcps Hurdles	Hndcps Chases	NH Flat	Per cent	£1 Level Stake
Plumpton	2-22	0-5	0-0	0-11	2-5	0-1	9.1	-1.50
Fontwell	1-12	0-4	0-0	0-5	1-3	0-0	8.3	-6.00

WINNING HORSES

Horse	Races Run	1st	2nd	3rd	£
Itoldyou	6	2	2	0	19727
Red Anchor	7	1	1	1	2599
Total winning prize-money					**£22326**
Favourites	**0-1**		**0.0%**		**-1.00**

ROBERT JOHNSON

NEWBURN, TYNE & WEAR

	No. of Hrs	Races Run	1st	2nd	3rd	Unpl	Per cent	£1 Level Stake
NH Flat	*3*	*6*	*0*	*0*	*0*	*6*	*0.0*	*-6.00*
Hurdles	*6*	*22*	*1*	*3*	*3*	*15*	*4.5*	*-5.00*
Chases	*5*	*16*	*1*	*5*	*4*	*6*	*6.3*	*-10.50*
Totals	**10**	**44**	**2**	**8**	**7**	**27**	**4.5**	**-21.50**
13-14	*17*	*83*	*5*	*5*	*6*	*67*	*6.0*	*-56.00*
12-13	*19*	*58*	*0*	*7*	*9*	*42*	*0.0*	*-58.00*

JOCKEYS

	W-R	Per cent	£1 Level Stake
Peter Buchanan	1-10	10.0	-4.50
Mr T Dowson	1-13	7.7	+4.00

COURSE RECORD

	Total W-R	Non-Hndcps Hurdles	Non-Hndcps Chases	Hndcps Hurdles	Hndcps Chases	NH Flat	Per cent	£1 Level Stake
Kelso	1-4	0-2	0-0	0-0	1-2	0-0	25.0	+1.50
Newcastle	1-15	0-6	0-0	1-4	0-2	0-3	6.7	+2.00

WINNING HORSES

Horse	Races Run	1st	2nd	3rd	£
Lord Brendy	9	1	4	3	7798
*Captain Sharpe	7	1	0	2	2014
Total winning prize-money					**£9812**
Favourites	**0-1**		**0.0%**		**-1.00**

ALAN JONES

BICKHAM, SOMERSET

	No. of Hrs	Races Run	1st	2nd	3rd	Unpl	Per cent	£1 Level Stake
NH Flat	*2*	*3*	*0*	*0*	*0*	*3*	*0.0*	*-3.00*
Hurdles	*8*	*19*	*0*	*1*	*1*	*17*	*0.0*	*-19.00*
Chases	*5*	*16*	*5*	*2*	*1*	*8*	*31.3*	*+34.50*
Totals	**13**	**38**	**5**	**3**	**2**	**28**	**13.2**	**+12.50**
13-14	*17*	*57*	*1*	*3*	*4*	*49*	*1.8*	*-50.50*
12-13	*21*	*53*	*3*	*6*	*2*	*42*	*5.7*	*-35.75*

JOCKEYS

	W-R	Per cent	£1 Level Stake
Tom Scudamore	2-3	66.7	+6.00
Brendan Powell	1-1	100.0	+4.50
Sean Bowen	1-2	50.0	+19.00
Nick Scholfield	1-2	50.0	+13.00

COURSE RECORD

	Total W-R	Non-Hndcps Hurdles	Non-Hndcps Chases	Hndcps Hurdles	Hndcps Chases	NH Flat	Per cent	£1 Level Stake
Chepstow	1-2	0-0	0-0	0-0	1-2	0-0	50.0	+19.00
Ffos Las	1-2	0-0	0-0	0-0	1-2	0-0	50.0	+13.00
Bangor	1-3	0-0	0-0	0-1	1-2	0-0	33.3	+2.00
Uttoxeter	1-3	0-0	0-0	0-2	1-1	0-0	33.3	+2.50
Plumpton	1-4	0-0	0-0	0-0	1-4	0-0	25.0	0.00

WINNING HORSES

Horse	Races Run	1st	2nd	3rd	£
Quincy Des Pictons	4	1	0	0	14621
Bobbits Way	5	2	2	1	10267
Tiquer	3	1	0	0	5023
Humbel Ben	4	1	0	0	3769
Total winning prize-money					**£33680**
Favourites	**0-0**		**0.0%**		**0.00**

LUCY JONES

LAWRENNY, PEMBROKESHIRE

	No. of Hrs	Races Run	1st	2nd	3rd	Unpl	Per cent	£1 Level Stake

NH Flat	3	6	0	1	0	5	0.0	-6.00
Hurdles	5	24	1	3	0	20	4.2	-15.50
Chases	1	5	0	1	2	2	0.0	-5.00
Totals	**8**	**35**	**1**	**5**	**2**	**27**	**2.9**	**-26.50**
13-14	*9*	*33*	*1*	*3*	*6*	*23*	*3.0*	*-23.50*
12-13	*13*	*41*	*3*	*4*	*6*	*28*	*7.3*	*-18.50*

JOCKEYS

	W-R	Per cent	£1 Level Stake
Sam Twiston-Davies	1-2	50.0	+6.50

COURSE RECORD

	Total W-R	Non-Hndcps Hurdles	Non-Hndcps Chases	Hndcps Hurdles	Hndcps Chases	NH Flat	Per cent	£1 Level Stake
Worcester	1-8	0-0	0-0	1-6	0-1	0-1	12.5	+0.50

WINNING HORSES

Horse	Races Run	1st	2nd	3rd	£
Toe To Toe	5	1	0	0	1949

Total winning prize-money **£1949**

Favourites	**0-4**	**0.0%**	**-4.00**

MRS GILLIAN JONES

FORTHAMPTON, GLOUCS

	No. of Hrs	Races Run	1st	2nd	3rd	Unpl	Per cent	£1 Level Stake
NH Flat	*0*	*0*	*0*	*0*	*0*	*0*	*0.0*	*0.00*
Hurdles	*0*	*0*	*0*	*0*	*0*	*0*	*0.0*	*0.00*
Chases	*1*	*5*	*1*	*2*	*0*	*2*	*20.0*	*-3.00*
Totals	**1**	**5**	**1**	**2**	**0**	**2**	**20.0**	**-3.00**

JOCKEYS

	W-R	Per cent	£1 Level Stake
Miss H Lewis	1-4	25.0	-2.00

COURSE RECORD

	Total W-R	Non-Hndcps Hurdles	Non-Hndcps Chases	Hndcps Hurdles	Hndcps Chases	NH Flat	Per cent	£1 Level Stake
Huntingdon	1-1	0-0	1-1	0-0	0-0	0-0	100.0	+1.00

WINNING HORSES

Horse	Races Run	1st	2nd	3rd	£
Shoreacres	5	1	2	0	1317

Total winning prize-money **£1317**

Favourites	**1-2**	**50.0%**	**0.00**

CAROLINE KEEVIL

MOTCOMBE, DORSET

	No. of Hrs	Races Run	1st	2nd	3rd	Unpl	Per cent	£1 Level Stake
NH Flat	*7*	*8*	*0*	*0*	*0*	*8*	*0.0*	*-8.00*
Hurdles	*17*	*49*	*2*	*1*	*4*	*42*	*4.1*	*-23.00*
Chases	*9*	*38*	*5*	*6*	*3*	*24*	*13.2*	*+15.00*
Totals	**27**	**95**	**7**	**7**	**7**	**74**	**7.4**	**-16.00**
13-14	*27*	*126*	*15*	*6*	*14*	*91*	*11.9*	*+22.55*
12-13	*28*	*110*	*6*	*4*	*13*	*87*	*5.5*	*-81.75*

JOCKEYS

	W-R	Per cent	£1 Level Stake
James Best	5-50	10.0	+3.00
Mr L Drowne	2-8	25.0	+18.00

COURSE RECORD

	Total W-R	Non-Hndcps Hurdles	Non-Hndcps Chases	Hndcps Hurdles	Hndcps Chases	NH Flat	Per cent	£1 Level Stake
Plumpton	2-4	0-0	0-0	0-1	2-3	0-0	50.0	+24.00
Fontwell	2-14	0-1	0-0	1-7	1-5	0-1	14.3	+11.50
Taunton	2-18	0-2	0-0	1-7	1-7	0-2	11.1	-5.50
Stratford	1-6	0-0	0-0	0-3	1-3	0-0	16.7	+7.00

WINNING HORSES

Horse	Races Run	1st	2nd	3rd	£
Midnight Lira	8	2	3	0	10397
Regal Flow	8	2	2	2	6636
Pod	6	1	0	0	3899
Strawberry Hill	3	1	1	0	3769
Cinevator	3	1	0	0	3119

Total winning prize-money **£27820**

Favourites	**1-6**	**16.7%**	**-1.50**

FIONA KEHOE

STEWKLEY, BEDS

	No. of Hrs	Races Run	1st	2nd	3rd	Unpl	Per cent	£1 Level Stake
NH Flat	*0*	*0*	*0*	*0*	*0*	*0*	*0.0*	*0.00*
Hurdles	*3*	*5*	*2*	*0*	*1*	*2*	*40.0*	*+9.50*
Chases	*1*	*1*	*1*	*0*	*0*	*0*	*100.0*	*+7.00*
Totals	**3**	**6**	**3**	**0**	**1**	**2**	**50.0**	**+16.50**
13-14	*1*	*2*	*0*	*0*	*0*	*2*	*0.0*	*-2.00*
12-13	*1*	*1*	*0*	*0*	*0*	*1*	*0.0*	*-1.00*

JOCKEYS

	W-R	Per cent	£1 Level Stake
Sam Jones	3-6	50.0	+16.50

COURSE RECORD

	Total W-R	Non-Hndcps Hurdles	Non-Hndcps Chases	Hndcps Hurdles	Hndcps Chases	NH Flat	Per cent	£1 Level Stake
Fakenham	2-2	0-0	0-0	2-2	0-0	0-0	100.0	+12.50
Warwick	1-2	0-0	0-0	0-1	1-1	0-0	50.0	+6.00

WINNING HORSES

Horse	Races Run	1st	2nd	3rd	£
De Kerry Man	2	1	0	0	3994
Vision Du Coeur	3	2	0	1	7798
Total winning prize-money					**£11792**
Favourites	**0-1**		**0.0%**		**-1.00**

MARTIN KEIGHLEY

CONDICOTE, GLOUCS

	No. of Hrs	Races Run	1st	2nd	3rd	Unpl	Per cent	£1 Level Stake
NH Flat	*11*	*23*	*1*	*3*	*3*	*16*	*4.3*	*-8.00*
Hurdles	*33*	*103*	*6*	*14*	*15*	*68*	*5.8*	*-45.50*
Chases	*23*	*84*	*10*	*12*	*9*	*53*	*11.9*	*-3.25*
Totals	**50**	**210**	**17**	**29**	**27**	**137**	**8.1**	**-56.75**
13-14	*42*	*208*	*21*	*32*	*17*	*137*	*10.1*	*-90.40*
12-13	*45*	*195*	*29*	*24*	*24*	*118*	*14.9*	*-37.19*

BY MONTH

NH Flat	W-R	Per cent	£1 Level Stake
May	0-2	0.0	-2.00
June	0-2	0.0	-2.00
July	0-0	0.0	0.00
August	0-1	0.0	-1.00
September	0-1	0.0	-1.00
October	1-3	33.3	+12.00
November	0-0	0.0	0.00
December	0-3	0.0	-3.00
January	0-4	0.0	-4.00
February	0-2	0.0	-2.00
March	0-3	0.0	-3.00
April	0-2	0.0	-2.00

Hurdles	W-R	Per cent	£1 Level Stake
May	1-10	10.0	-7.00
June	0-7	0.0	-7.00
July	2-11	18.2	+10.00
August	1-6	16.7	+7.00
September	0-4	0.0	-4.00
October	0-9	0.0	-9.00
November	0-13	0.0	-13.00
December	0-7	0.0	-7.00
January	0-12	0.0	-12.00
February	1-7	14.3	+0.50
March	1-11	9.1	+2.00
April	0-6	0.0	-6.00

Chases	W-R	Per cent	£1 Level Stake
May	1-8	12.5	+0.50
June	0-6	0.0	-6.00
July	0-2	0.0	-2.00
August	0-4	0.0	-4.00
September	1-4	25.0	-1.50
October	1-8	12.5	-2.00
November	2-14	14.3	+1.25
December	2-8	25.0	+18.00
January	2-11	18.2	+8.00
February	0-1	0.0	-1.00
March	0-11	0.0	-11.00
April	1-7	14.3	-3.50

Totals	W-R	Per cent	£1 Level Stake
May	2-20	10.0	-8.50
June	0-15	0.0	-15.00
July	2-13	15.4	+8.00
August	1-11	9.1	+2.00
September	1-9	11.1	-6.50
October	2-20	10.0	+1.00
November	2-27	7.4	-11.75
December	2-18	11.1	+8.00
January	2-27	7.4	-8.00
February	1-10	10.0	-2.50
March	1-25	4.0	-12.00
April	1-15	6.7	-11.50

DISTANCE

Hurdles	W-R	Per cent	£1 Level Stake
2m-2m3f	2-38	5.3	-22.00
2m4f-2m7f	2-31	6.5	-10.00
3m+	0-9	0.0	-9.00

Chases	W-R	Per cent	£1 Level Stake
2m-2m3f	0-12	0.0	-12.00
2m4f-2m7f	2-25	8.0	-10.50
3m+	7-43	16.3	+20.7

TYPE OF RACE

Non-Handicaps	W-R	Per cent	£1 Level Stake
Nov Hrdls	0-14	0.0	-14.00
Hrdls	2-22	9.1	+4.00
Nov Chs	0-7	0.0	-7.00
Chases	0-2	0.0	-2.00
Sell/Claim	1-7	14.3	+6.00

Handicaps	W-R	Per cent	£1 Level Stake
Nov Hrdls	1-8	12.5	-5.00
Hrdls	2-52	3.8	-36.50
Nov Chs	2-13	15.4	-2.00
Chases	8-62	12.9	+7.75
Sell/Claim	0-0	0.0	0.00

RACE CLASS

	W-R	Per cent	£1 Level Stake
Class 1	2-12	16.7	+11.00
Class 2	1-13	7.7	-4.00
Class 3	1-21	4.8	-18.50
Class 4	3-82	3.7	-48.50
Class 5	9-65	13.8	+5.25
Class 6	1-17	5.9	-2.00

FIRST TIME OUT

	W-R	Per cent	£1 Level Stake
Bumpers	1-11	9.1	+4.00
Hurdles	1-26	3.8	-23.00
Chases	1-13	7.7	-10.50
Totals	3-50	6.0	-29.50

JOCKEYS

	W-R	Per cent	£1 Level Stake
Ian Popham	5-47	10.6	-1.50
Conor Smith	2-10	20.0	+10.50
Richard Johnson	2-13	15.4	-7.00
Mr H Stock	1-1	100.0	+7.00
Gavin Sheehan	1-4	25.0	+2.00
Aidan Coleman	1-10	10.0	-1.00
Tom Bellamy	1-11	9.1	+2.00
Christopher Ward	1-11	9.1	-8.75
Killian Moore	1-17	5.9	-4.00
Andrew Tinkler	1-20	5.0	-7.00
Conor Shoemark	1-26	3.8	-9.00

COURSE RECORD

	Total W-R	Non-Hndcps Hurdles	Non-Hndcps Chases	Hndcps Hurdles	Hndcps Chases	NH Flat	Per cent	£1 Level Stake
Worcester	4-38	0-10	0-0	2-10	1-14	1-4	10.5	-3.50
Cheltenham	3-18	0-1	0-3	0-1	3-12	0-1	16.7	+14.00
Towcester	2-16	0-3	0-0	0-4	2-8	0-1	12.5	-7.75
Ffos Las	1-3	0-0	0-0	1-2	0-0	0-1	33.3	+4.50
Huntingdon	1-4	1-2	0-0	0-1	0-0	0-1	25.0	+9.00
Nton Abbot	1-4	1-1	0-0	0-2	0-1	0-0	25.0	+9.00
Ludlow	1-9	0-1	0-0	0-2	1-4	0-2	11.1	+4.00
Warwick	1-10	0-0	0-0	0-2	1-6	0-2	10.0	+3.00
Exeter	1-13	0-1	0-2	0-3	1-6	0-1	7.7	-9.50

Uttoxeter	1-19	1-6	0-0	0-6	0-6	0-1	5.3	-6.00
Chepstow	1-20	0-5	0-0	0-6	1-4	0-5	5.0	-17.50

WINNING HORSES

Horse	Races Run	1st	2nd	3rd	£
Annacotty	5	1	0	1	28475
Benbane Head	7	1	0	1	25628
Any Currency	4	1	1	0	21896
Creepy	5	1	0	1	6498
Georgian King	7	2	3	0	6043
Monty's Revenge	8	1	1	1	3744
Always Bold	9	2	3	1	6823
*Classic Colori	5	1	1	0	3509
Kyles Faith	19	3	5	1	2924
Midnight Thomas	7	1	0	0	2274
Altesse De Guye	8	1	0	2	2274
Bold Tara	7	1	0	1	1872
Dueling Banjos	4	1	2	0	1560
Total winning prize-money					**£113520**
Favourites	**3-9**		**33.3%**		**-1.25**

CHRISTOPHER KELLETT

APPLEBY MAGNA, DERBYS

	No. of Hrs	Races Run	1st	2nd	3rd	Unpl	Per cent	£1 Level Stake
NH Flat	*4*	*6*	*0*	*0*	*0*	*6*	*0.0*	*-6.00*
Hurdles	*6*	*16*	*1*	*0*	*0*	*15*	*6.3*	*-9.50*
Chases	*0*	*0*	*0*	*0*	*0*	*0*	*0.0*	*0.00*
Totals	**9**	**22**	**1**	**0**	**0**	**21**	**4.5**	**-15.50**
13-14	*13*	*33*	*0*	*0*	*1*	*32*	*0.0*	*-33.00*
12-13	*14*	*42*	*0*	*1*	*1*	*40*	*0.0*	*-42.00*

JOCKEYS

	W-R	Per cent	£1 Level Stake
Alan Johns	1-3	33.3	+3.50

COURSE RECORD

	Total W-R	Non-Hndcps Hurdles	Non-Hndcps Chases	Hndcps Hurdles	Hndcps Chases	NH Flat	Per cent	£1 Level Stake
Southwell	1-4	0-0	0-0	1-2	0-0	0-2	25.0	+2.50

WINNING HORSES

Horse	Races Run	1st	2nd	3rd	£
Mr Squirrel	4	1	0	0	3249
Total winning prize-money					**£3249**
Favourites	**0-0**		**0.0%**		**0.00**

DAVID KEMP

THETFORD, NORFOLK

	No. of Hrs	Races Run	1st	2nd	3rd	Unpl	Per cent	£1 Level Stake
NH Flat	*0*	*0*	*0*	*0*	*0*	*0*	*0.0*	*0.00*
Hurdles	*0*	*0*	*0*	*0*	*0*	*0*	*0.0*	*0.00*
Chases	*4*	*6*	*3*	*1*	*1*	*1*	*50.0*	*+4.04*
Totals	**4**	**6**	**3**	**1**	**1**	**1**	**50.0**	**+4.04**
13-14	*4*	*4*	*0*	*1*	*1*	*2*	*0.0*	*-4.00*
12-13	*2*	*2*	*0*	*1*	*0*	*1*	*0.0*	*-2.00*

JOCKEYS

	W-R	Per cent	£1 Level Stake
Mr D Kemp	3-6	50.0	+4.04

COURSE RECORD

	Total W-R	Non-Hndcps Hurdles	Non-Hndcps Chases	Hndcps Hurdles	Hndcps Chases	NH Flat	Per cent	£1 Level Stake
Fakenham	2-3	0-0	2-3	0-0	0-0	0-0	66.7	+4.17
Huntingdon	1-1	0-0	1-1	0-0	0-0	0-0	100.0	+1.88

WINNING HORSES

Horse	Races Run	1st	2nd	3rd	£
*Moroman	2	2	0	0	3241
Master Workman	2	1	0	1	2184
Total winning prize-money					**£5425**
Favourites	**1-1**		**100.0%**		**0.67**

NICK KENT

BRIGG, LINCS

	No. of Hrs	Races Run	1st	2nd	3rd	Unpl	Per cent	£1 Level Stake
NH Flat	*2*	*3*	*0*	*0*	*0*	*3*	*0.0*	*-3.00*
Hurdles	*12*	*44*	*4*	*5*	*4*	*31*	*9.1*	*-12.50*
Chases	*5*	*8*	*0*	*3*	*1*	*4*	*0.0*	*-8.00*
Totals	**14**	**55**	**4**	**8**	**5**	**38**	**7.3**	**-23.50**
13-14	*11*	*56*	*2*	*9*	*4*	*41*	*3.6*	*-42.00*
12-13	*17*	*67*	*2*	*7*	*7*	*51*	*3.0*	*-56.75*

JOCKEYS

	W-R	Per cent	£1 Level Stake
Adam Wedge	3-27	11.1	+1.50
Mr Charlie Deutsch	1-8	12.5	-5.00

COURSE RECORD

	Total W-R	Non-Hndcps Hurdles	Non-Hndcps Chases	Hndcps Hurdles	Hndcps Chases	NH Flat	Per cent	£1 Level Stake
Mrket Rsn	3-17	0-4	0-0	3-9	0-3	0-1	17.6	+11.50
Towcester	1-4	0-0	0-0	1-4	0-0	0-0	25.0	-1.00

WINNING HORSES

Horse	Races Run	1st	2nd	3rd	£
Bowie	4	1	1	0	6498
Ivans Back	8	2	2	1	4549

Combustible Kate	7	1	1	1	1949
Total winning prize-money					**£12996**
Favourites	**0-4**		**0.0%**		**-4.00**

NEIL KING

BARBURY CASTLE, WILTSHIRE

	No. of Hrs	Races Run	1st	2nd	3rd	Unpl	Per cent	£1 Level Stake
NH Flat	*13*	*32*	*4*	*0*	*4*	*24*	*12.5*	*+18.83*
Hurdles	*28*	*122*	*17*	*19*	*28*	*58*	*13.9*	*+7.63*
Chases	*8*	*47*	*8*	*9*	*13*	*17*	*17.0*	*-14.88*
Totals	**40**	**201**	**29**	**28**	**45**	**99**	**14.4**	**+11.58**
13-14	*38*	*182*	*26*	*29*	*28*	*99*	*14.3*	*-8.44*
12-13	*40*	*165*	*21*	*24*	*16*	*104*	*12.7*	*+25.00*

BY MONTH

NH Flat	W-R	Per cent	£1 Level Stake	**Hurdles**	W-R	Per cent	£1 Level Stake
May	0-0	0.0	0.00	May	0-5	0.0	-5.00
June	0-1	0.0	-1.00	June	1-10	10.0	+41.00
July	1-1	100.0	+9.00	July	2-6	33.3	+2.75
August	0-0	0.0	0.00	August	0-7	0.0	-7.00
September	0-1	0.0	-1.00	September	0-5	0.0	-5.00
October	0-1	0.0	-1.00	October	1-7	14.3	-0.50
November	2-5	40.0	+1.83	November	3-13	23.1	-6.23
December	0-3	0.0	-3.00	December	4-16	25.0	+2.88
January	0-3	0.0	-3.00	January	0-22	0.0	-22.00
February	1-7	14.3	+27.00	February	0-7	0.0	-7.00
March	0-3	0.0	-3.00	March	2-13	15.4	+8.00
April	0-7	0.0	-7.00	April	4-11	36.4	+5.73

Chases	W-R	Per cent	£1 Level Stake	**Totals**	W-R	Per cent	£1 Level Stake
May	0-6	0.0	-6.00	May	0-11	0.0	-11.00
June	0-0	0.0	0.00	June	1-11	9.1	+40.00
July	0-0	0.0	0.00	July	3-7	42.9	+11.75
August	0-0	0.0	0.00	August	0-7	0.0	-7.00
September	0-1	0.0	-1.00	September	0-7	0.0	-7.00
October	0-6	0.0	-6.00	October	1-14	7.1	-7.50
November	4-8	50.0	+0.62	November	9-26	34.6	-3.78
December	1-4	25.0	+2.00	December	5-23	21.7	+1.88
January	1-6	16.7	-0.50	January	1-31	3.2	-25.50
February	0-3	0.0	-3.00	February	1-17	5.9	+17.00
March	1-5	20.0	-1.00	March	3-21	14.3	+4.00
April	1-8	12.5	0.00	April	5-26	19.2	-1.27

DISTANCE

Hurdles	W-R	Per cent	£1 Level Stake	**Chases**	W-R	Per cent	£1 Level Stake
2m-2m3f	4-44	9.1	+22.25	2m-2m3f	1-3	33.3	+5.00
2m4f-2m7f	4-32	12.5	-18.02	2m4f-2m7f	2-12	16.7	-7.39
3m+	4-22	18.2	-5.88	3m+	4-22	18.2	-6.49

TYPE OF RACE

Non-Handicaps	W-R	Per cent	£1 Level Stake	**Handicaps**	W-R	Per cent	£1 Level Stake
Nov Hrdls	5-31	16.1	+28.74	Nov Hrdls	0-1	0.0	-1.00
Hrdls	3-28	10.7	-18.86	Hrdls	7-58	12.1	-6.00
Nov Chs	0-2	0.0	-2.00	Nov Chs	1-8	12.5	-4.75
Chases	0-0	0.0	0.00	Chases	7-37	18.9	-8.13
Sell/Claim	2-3	66.7	+5.75	Sell/Claim	0-1	0.0	-1.00

RACE CLASS / FIRST TIME OUT

RACE CLASS	W-R	Per cent	£1 Level Stake	**FIRST TIME OUT**	W-R	Per cent	£1 Level Stake
Class 1	0-7	0.0	-7.00	Bumpers	1-13	7.7	-3.00
Class 2	3-10	30.0	+17.00	Hurdles	4-22	18.2	+47.16
Class 3	0-31	0.0	-31.00	Chases	1-5	20.0	-1.75
Class 4	16-99	16.2	+12.23				
Class 5	8-29	27.6	+38.52	Totals	6-40	15.0	+42.41
Class 6	2-25	8.0	-18.17				

JOCKEYS

	W-R	Per cent	£1 Level Stake
Trevor Whelan	22-152	14.5	+26.23
Harry Skelton	2-5	40.0	+6.25
Mark Grant	2-15	13.3	-3.50
Sean Bowen	1-1	100.0	+5.00
Bridget Andrews	1-6	16.7	-3.90
Lizzie Kelly	1-12	8.3	-8.50

COURSE RECORD

	Total W-R	Non-Hndcps Hurdles	Non-Hndcps Chases	Hndcps Hurdles	Hndcps Chases	NH Flat	Per cent	£1 Level Stake
Uttoxeter	8-15	4-9	0-0	2-2	0-0	2-4	53.3	+19.36
Fontwell	4-22	1-6	0-0	0-6	3-7	0-3	18.2	+41.61
Fakenham	3-15	0-3	0-2	1-6	1-3	1-1	20.0	+24.35
Stratford	2-8	0-2	0-0	1-5	0-0	1-1	25.0	+8.50
Plumpton	2-16	1-4	0-0	0-4	1-7	0-1	12.5	-6.50
Kelso	1-2	0-0	0-0	1-1	0-1	0-0	50.0	+9.00
Lingfield	1-2	0-1	0-0	0-0	1-1	0-0	50.0	-0.09
Ascot	1-3	0-1	0-0	1-1	0-0	0-1	33.3	+7.00
Sandown	1-3	0-1	0-0	1-2	0-0	0-0	33.3	+3.00
Sedgefield	1-3	0-0	0-0	0-0	1-3	0-0	33.3	+2.50
Southwell	1-3	1-1	0-0	0-1	0-1	0-0	33.3	-0.63
Warwick	1-10	1-1	0-0	0-3	0-2	0-4	10.0	-8.27
Doncaster	1-12	1-5	0-0	0-4	0-0	0-3	8.3	-10.75
Mrket Rsn	1-16	1-6	0-0	0-6	0-2	0-2	6.3	-10.50
Huntingdon	1-20	0-7	0-0	0-6	1-4	0-3	5.0	-16.00

WINNING HORSES

Horse	Races Run	1st	2nd	3rd	£
*Lil Rockerfeller	6	2	1	2	57272
Milansbar	5	3	1	1	23263
*Southway Star	9	4	0	1	15363
Delgany Demon	5	1	2	2	4549
Ballyvoneen	18	2	4	6	6628
Brass Monkey	7	1	0	1	4106

Town Mouse	9	1	0	3	4029
*Master Rajeem	7	1	3	1	3899
Tender Surprise	8	3	1	1	7278
Zeroeshadesofgrey	6	3	0	2	9097
Mercers Court	5	1	2	1	3249
*Dire Straits	3	1	1	0	3249
*Hazzaat	9	1	2	2	3119
Unbuckled	3	1	0	0	2738
Oh Land Abloom	5	1	0	1	2395
*Minnie Milan	7	1	0	1	1949
The Boss's Dream	8	2	3	0	3119
Total winning prize-money					**£155302**
Favourites	**41-53**		**77.4%**		**148.08**

ALAN KING

BARBURY CASTLE, WILTS

	No. of Hrs	Races Run	1st	2nd	3rd	Unpl	Per cent	£1 Level Stake
NH Flat	*32*	*61*	*12*	*9*	*6*	*34*	*19.7*	*-7.62*
Hurdles	*71*	*253*	*40*	*47*	*26*	*139*	*15.8*	*-96.43*
Chases	*37*	*138*	*24*	*22*	*12*	*80*	*17.4*	*-27.13*
Totals	**121**	**452**	**76**	**78**	**44**	**253**	**16.8**	**-131.18**
13-14	*130*	*437*	*76*	*63*	*48*	*250*	*17.4*	*-24.80*
12-13	*125*	*399*	*56*	*66*	*61*	*216*	*14.0*	*-49.19*

BY MONTH

NH Flat	W-R	Per cent	£1 Level Stake	Hurdles	W-R	Per cent	£1 Level Stake
May	1-9	11.1	+2.00	May	2-16	12.5	-9.06
June	0-0	0.0	0.00	June	3-8	37.5	+0.63
July	0-0	0.0	0.00	July	3-8	37.5	+3.57
August	0-0	0.0	0.00	August	0-4	0.0	-4.00
September	0-0	0.0	0.00	September	1-5	20.0	-1.00
October	1-3	33.3	-0.63	October	8-28	28.6	-0.69
November	2-8	25.0	-4.10	November	6-39	15.4	-14.71
December	3-8	37.5	+5.91	December	7-38	18.4	-17.59
January	0-4	0.0	-4.00	January	5-23	21.7	+6.33
February	3-12	25.0	+5.50	February	0-24	0.0	-24.00
March	2-11	18.2	-6.31	March	4-40	10.0	-24.92
April	0-6	0.0	-6.00	April	1-20	5.0	-11.00

Chases	W-R	Per cent	£1 Level Stake	Totals	W-R	Per cent	£1 Level Stake
May	2-15	13.3	-12.38	May	5-40	12.5	-19.44
June	0-3	0.0	-3.00	June	3-11	27.3	-2.37
July	0-2	0.0	-2.00	July	3-10	30.0	+1.57
August	2-3	66.7	+1.88	August	2-7	28.6	-2.12
September	0-1	0.0	-1.00	September	1-6	16.7	-2.00
October	3-10	30.0	+9.75	October	12-41	29.3	+8.43
November	5-31	16.1	-14.13	November	13-78	16.7	-32.94
December	2-16	12.5	-7.50	December	12-62	19.4	-19.18
January	4-17	23.5	-1.50	January	9-44	20.5	+0.83
February	4-11	36.4	+12.75	February	7-47	14.9	-5.75
March	2-16	12.5	+3.00	March	8-67	11.9	-28.23
April	0-13	0.0	-13.00	April	1-39	2.6	-30.00

DISTANCE

Hurdles	W-R	Per cent	£1 Level Stake	Chases	W-R	Per cent	£1 Level Stake
2m-2m3f	18-116	15.5	-58.44	2m-2m3f	6-36	16.7	-22.75
2m4f-2m7f	7-63	11.1	-24.60	2m4f-2m7f	7-38	18.4	+6.25
3m+	3-26	11.5	-6.00	3m+	7-47	14.9	-7.25

TYPE OF RACE

Non-Handicaps	W-R	Per cent	£1 Level Stake	Handicaps	W-R	Per cent	£1 Level Stake
Nov Hrdls	12-69	17.4	-28.88	Nov Hrdls	1-16	6.3	-12.00
Hrdls	15-52	28.8	-0.05	Hrdls	12-115	10.4	-54.50
Nov Chs	8-27	29.6	-1.38	Nov Chs	6-26	23.1	+3.00
Chases	4-18	22.2	+8.88	Chases	6-67	9.0	-37.63
Sell/Claim	0-0	0.0	0.00	Sell/Claim	0-0	0.0	0.00

RACE CLASS

	W-R	Per cent	£1 Level Stake
Class 1	11-93	11.8	-22.63
Class 2	4-40	10.0	-17.75
Class 3	18-108	16.7	-28.58
Class 4	29-145	20.0	-63.85
Class 5	4-30	13.3	-11.06
Class 6	10-36	27.8	+12.68

FIRST TIME OUT

	W-R	Per cent	£1 Level Stake
Bumpers	8-32	25.0	+12.78
Hurdles	14-58	24.1	-3.00
Chases	3-31	9.7	-22.10
Totals	25-121	20.7	-12.32

JOCKEYS

	W-R	Per cent	£1 Level Stake
Wayne Hutchinson	36-217	16.6	-70.92
Richard Johnson	12-33	36.4	+9.20
Tom Bellamy	8-66	12.1	-25.75
Denis O'Regan	6-33	18.2	-8.78
A P McCoy	3-8	37.5	+12.32
Aidan Coleman	3-22	13.6	-8.25
Noel Fehily	2-6	33.3	-1.00
James Banks	1-3	33.3	-0.13
Barry Geraghty	1-3	33.3	-0.13
Tom Cannon	1-4	25.0	+2.00
Paddy Brennan	1-6	16.7	-3.00
Jamie Moore	1-7	14.3	-3.75
Gerard Tumelty	1-7	14.3	+4.00

COURSE RECORD

	Total W-R	Non-Hndcps Hurdles	Non-Hndcps Chases	Hndcps Hurdles	Hndcps Chases	NH Flat	Per cent	£1 Level Stake
Huntingdon	8-21	5-9	1-2	0-2	1-4	1-4	38.1	-3.04
Exeter	7-28	2-7	1-3	2-9	1-5	1-4	25.0	+9.54
Newbury	7-40	1-10	1-3	0-8	1-10	4-9	17.5	-6.65
Warwick	5-21	1-6	1-3	2-7	0-2	1-3	23.8	-3.78
Wincanton	5-21	0-4	0-1	0-9	3-4	2-3	23.8	+15.00
Cheltenham	5-33	1-9	2-7	2-8	0-6	0-3	15.2	+16.38
Bangor	4-13	1-2	1-1	2-5	0-1	0-4	30.8	-4.03
Plumpton	3-10	1-1	1-1	0-6	1-1	0-1	30.0	-0.42

Fontwell	3-11	1-3	0-0	0-3	1-3	1-2	27.3	-4.56
Stratford	3-14	1-4	0-0	2-6	0-2	0-2	21.4	-2.43
Uttoxeter	3-21	2-7	0-1	1-8	0-3	0-2	14.3	-10.13
Kempton	3-33	2-8	1-5	0-10	0-5	0-5	9.1	-24.06
Nton Abbot	2-5	0-1	0-1	1-1	1-1	0-1	40.0	+1.25
Wetherby	2-10	0-4	2-3	0-1	0-2	0-0	20.0	-1.75
Chepstow	2-11	2-5	0-1	0-2	0-1	0-2	18.2	-4.25
Towcester	2-11	1-7	0-1	0-1	0-0	1-2	18.2	-0.09
Sandown	2-15	1-4	0-3	1-4	0-3	0-1	13.3	-3.75
Haydock	2-17	1-1	0-2	0-6	0-6	1-2	11.8	-13.18
Lingfield	1-2	0-1	0-0	0-0	1-1	0-0	50.0	+2.50
Southwell	1-6	1-2	0-0	0-2	0-2	0-0	16.7	-4.09
Worcester	1-6	1-2	0-1	0-2	0-1	0-0	16.7	-2.75
Leicester	1-7	0-2	0-1	0-1	1-3	0-0	14.3	-3.25
Ludlow	1-9	0-2	0-0	0-3	1-4	0-0	11.1	-5.25
Doncaster	1-13	1-4	0-0	0-3	0-5	0-1	7.7	-11.78
Ascot	1-14	0-3	1-1	0-5	0-3	0-2	7.1	-9.00
Aintree	1-21	1-5	0-4	0-5	0-4	0-3	4.8	-18.63

WINNING HORSES

Horse	Races Run	1st	2nd	3rd	£
Uxizandre	4	2	0	0	218403
Balder Succes	7	2	2	0	103515
The Unit	2	1	0	1	36911
Medinas	4	1	1	0	22780
L'Unique	6	1	0	1	18768
Ned Stark	5	3	0	0	31375
Carraig Mor	6	2	2	0	24027
Ordo Ab Chao	6	3	0	0	26182
Ulzana's Raid	4	2	0	0	21270
Sego Success	5	2	0	0	17059
West End Rocker	3	1	0	0	12972
Nyanza	4	2	1	0	16428
The Pirate's Queen	4	2	0	1	14639
Salmanazar	6	1	0	2	9583
Pantxoa	8	1	1	0	9495
Ziga Boy	6	1	0	0	9384
Uriah Heep	12	3	1	2	19469
Hollow Penny	10	3	3	0	18328
Grumeti	5	2	0	1	11696
The Tourard Man	8	2	2	3	11047
Handazan	8	1	0	2	6657
Laser Blazer	7	3	0	1	16917
Roberto Pegasus	6	2	0	1	10072
Pain Au Chocolat	4	2	1	0	9877
Desert Joe	5	1	2	1	6330
Chatez	4	2	0	0	7473
No Substitute	3	1	1	0	3899
*Shadarpour	4	1	1	0	3899
Simply A Legend	2	1	0	0	3899
Chosen Well	4	2	0	0	3899
Karezak	7	1	4	1	3899
Miles To Memphis	3	1	0	1	3899
Dundee	3	1	1	0	3798
Turn Over Sivola	8	1	2	3	3769
*Spellbound	3	1	1	1	3574
Gimme Five	6	2	2	1	6628
Inner Drive	2	1	1	0	3249
Prettyasapicture	10	1	2	3	2924
Winner Massagot	4	1	0	0	2599
Smart Motive	5	1	0	0	2395
Gabriella Rose	5	1	2	0	1949
Board Of Trade	2	2	0	0	3574
Angel Face	2	1	0	0	1949
Lady Persephone	4	1	1	0	1819
Miss Crick	2	1	0	0	1711
Yanworth	4	2	1	0	1689
Dusky Legend	5	1	3	0	1643
Katie Too	2	1	0	0	1625
Wishing And Hoping	3	1	0	0	1625
Presenting Lisa	3	1	0	0	1560
Total winning prize-money					**£782131**
Favourites	**37-88**		**42.0%**		**-6.35**

WILLIAM KINSEY

ASHTON, CHESHIRE

	No. of Hrs	Races Run	1st	2nd	3rd	Unpl	Per cent	£1 Level Stake
NH Flat	*3*	*5*	*0*	*1*	*0*	*4*	*0.0*	*-5.00*
Hurdles	*12*	*26*	*0*	*3*	*5*	*18*	*0.0*	*-26.00*
Chases	*7*	*16*	*1*	*3*	*2*	*10*	*6.3*	*-12.25*
Totals	**19**	**47**	**1**	**7**	**7**	**32**	**2.1**	**-43.25**
13-14	*19*	*67*	*5*	*12*	*6*	*44*	*7.5*	*-23.00*
12-13	*22*	*78*	*8*	*10*	*8*	*52*	*10.3*	*+10.38*

JOCKEYS

	W-R	Per cent	£1 Level Stake
James Reveley	1-6	16.7	-2.25

COURSE RECORD

	Total W-R	Non-Hndcps Hurdles	Non-Hndcps Chases	Hndcps Hurdles	Hndcps Chases	NH Flat	Per cent	£1 Level Stake
Carlisle	1-6	0-1	0-1	0-0	1-4	0-0	16.7	-2.25

WINNING HORSES

Horse	Races Run	1st	2nd	3rd	£
Shouldavboughtgold	3	1	1	0	4327
Total winning prize-money					**£4327**
Favourites	**0-1**		**0.0%**		**-1.00**

PHILIP KIRBY

MIDDLEHAM, N YORKS

	No. of Hrs	Races Run	1st	2nd	3rd	Unpl	Per cent	£1 Level Stake
NH Flat	*18*	*37*	*1*	*2*	*6*	*28*	*2.7*	*-31.00*
Hurdles	*42*	*145*	*12*	*12*	*12*	*109*	*8.3*	*-21.63*
Chases	*6*	*11*	*3*	*1*	*0*	*7*	*27.3*	*+5.33*
Totals	**60**	**193**	**16**	**15**	**18**	**144**	**8.3**	**-47.30**

13-14	*71*	*202*	*28*	*28*	*16*	*130*	*13.9*	*-9.20*
12-13	*52*	*165*	*24*	*19*	*10*	*112*	*14.5*	*+17.21*

BY MONTH

NH Flat	W-R	Per cent	£1 Level Stake
May	0-5	0.0	-5.00
June	0-2	0.0	-2.00
July	0-0	0.0	0.00
August	0-1	0.0	-1.00
September	0-0	0.0	0.00
October	0-4	0.0	-4.00
November	0-5	0.0	-5.00
December	1-4	25.0	+2.00
January	0-6	0.0	-6.00
February	0-5	0.0	-5.00
March	0-4	0.0	-4.00
April	0-1	0.0	-1.00

Hurdles	W-R	Per cent	£1 Level Stake
May	1-11	9.1	+2.00
June	1-15	6.7	-6.50
July	2-13	15.4	+23.00
August	2-5	40.0	+8.63
September	0-5	0.0	-5.00
October	1-12	8.3	-9.63
November	1-25	4.0	-14.00
December	3-11	27.3	+12.88
January	0-18	0.0	-18.00
February	0-10	0.0	-10.00
March	0-14	0.0	-14.00
April	1-6	16.7	+9.00

Chases	W-R	Per cent	£1 Level Stake
May	1-2	50.0	+3.00
June	0-0	0.0	0.00
July	0-1	0.0	-1.00
August	0-0	0.0	0.00
September	0-0	0.0	0.00
October	0-3	0.0	-3.00
November	1-2	50.0	+2.33
December	0-1	0.0	-1.00
January	0-0	0.0	0.00
February	1-1	100.0	+6.00
March	0-1	0.0	-1.00
April	0-0	0.0	0.00

Totals	W-R	Per cent	£1 Level Stake
May	2-18	11.1	0.00
June	1-17	5.9	-8.50
July	2-14	14.3	+22.00
August	2-6	33.3	+7.63
September	0-5	0.0	-5.00
October	1-19	5.3	-16.63
November	2-32	6.3	-16.67
December	4-16	25.0	+13.88
January	0-24	0.0	-24.00
February	1-16	6.3	-9.00
March	0-19	0.0	-19.00
April	1-7	14.3	+8.00

DISTANCE

Hurdles	W-R	Per cent	£1 Level Stake
2m-2m3f	3-82	3.7	-66.75
2m4f-2m7f	6-39	15.4	+24.13
3m+	1-9	11.1	+6.00

Chases	W-R	Per cent	£1 Level Stake
2m-2m3f	0-2	0.0	-2.00
2m4f-2m7f	2-6	33.3	+5.33
3m+	1-3	33.3	+2.00

TYPE OF RACE

Non-Handicaps	W-R	Per cent	£1 Level Stake
Nov Hrdls	3-48	6.3	-40.13
Hrdls	0-18	0.0	-18.00
Nov Chs	2-4	50.0	+7.33
Chases	0-0	0.0	0.00
Sell/Claim	1-2	50.0	+6.50

Handicaps	W-R	Per cent	£1 Level Stake
Nov Hrdls	2-14	14.3	+8.00
Hrdls	6-62	9.7	+23.00
Nov Chs	0-4	0.0	-4.00
Chases	1-3	33.3	+2.00
Sell/Claim	0-1	0.0	-1.00

RACE CLASS

	W-R	Per cent	£1 Level Stake
Class 1	0-1	0.0	-1.00
Class 2	1-7	14.3	+6.00
Class 3	4-22	18.2	+13.33
Class 4	7-98	7.1	-41.13
Class 5	3-35	8.6	-0.50
Class 6	1-30	3.3	-24.00

FIRST TIME OUT

	W-R	Per cent	£1 Level Stake
Bumpers	0-18	0.0	-18.00
Hurdles	6-37	16.2	+19.75
Chases	2-5	40.0	+4.33
Totals	8-60	13.3	+6.08

JOCKEYS

	W-R	Per cent	£1 Level Stake
Adam Nicol	7-91	7.7	-26.50
James Reveley	5-22	22.7	+18.21
Ryan Mania	1-1	100.0	+4.00
Phil Dennis	1-15	6.7	-9.00
Henry Brooke	1-20	5.0	-9.00
Kyle James	1-24	4.2	-5.00

COURSE RECORD

	Total W-R	Non-Hndcps Hurdles	Non-Hndcps Chases	Hndcps Hurdles	Hndcps Chases	NH Flat	Per cent	£1 Level Stake
Carlisle	2-12	0-1	1-1	1-7	0-2	0-1	16.7	+7.33
Mrket Rsn	2-14	1-4	1-1	0-6	0-0	0-3	14.3	-4.38
Sedgefield	2-17	0-4	0-1	1-6	0-0	1-6	11.8	-1.00
Hexham	2-18	2-14	0-0	0-2	0-0	0-2	11.1	-6.63
Worcester	1-2	1-1	0-0	0-0	0-0	0-1	50.0	+0.38
Fakenham	1-3	0-0	0-0	1-3	0-0	0-0	33.3	+8.00
Huntingdon	1-3	0-0	0-0	1-1	0-0	0-2	33.3	+8.00
Kelso	1-4	0-1	0-0	0-0	1-2	0-1	25.0	+1.00
Aintree	1-8	0-3	0-0	1-2	0-0	0-3	12.5	+5.00
Cartmel	1-10	0-4	0-0	1-6	0-0	0-0	10.0	+9.00
Southwell	1-10	0-3	0-0	1-6	0-0	0-1	10.0	+7.00
Wetherby	1-26	0-12	0-0	1-10	0-0	0-4	3.8	-15.00

WINNING HORSES

Horse	Races Run	1st	2nd	3rd	£
Goldan Jess	2	1	1	0	16245
Rumble Of Thunder	2	1	0	1	11574
Everaard	2	1	0	0	9747
Stopped Out	6	2	1	1	12996
Factor Fifty	6	1	3	0	3899
Istimraar	11	1	3	1	3418
Lady Buttons	5	1	0	0	3249
Jawaab	5	2	0	0	5302
Stags Leap	1	1	0	0	3249
Hail The Brave	7	1	0	0	3249
Aniknam	4	1	1	1	3249
Courtown Oscar	5	1	0	0	2274
Noir Girl	8	1	0	1	2130
Bedale Lane	2	1	0	0	1560
Total winning prize-money					**£82141**

Favourites **1-7** **14.3%** **-4.63**

STUART KITTOW

BLACKBOROUGH, DEVON

	No. of Hrs	Races Run	1st	2nd	3rd	Unpl	Per cent	£1 Level Stake
NH Flat	*3*	*6*	*3*	*0*	*0*	*3*	*50.0*	*+58.00*

Hurdles	*7*	*19*	*1*	*0*	*1*	*17*	*5.3*	*-15.25*
Chases	*0*	*0*	*0*	*0*	*0*	*0*	*0.0*	*0.00*
Totals	**9**	**25**	**4**	**0**	**1**	**20**	**16.0**	**+42.75**
13-14	*4*	*8*	*0*	*1*	*1*	*6*	*0.0*	*-8.00*
12-13	*1*	*1*	*0*	*0*	*0*	*1*	*0.0*	*-1.00*

JOCKEYS

	W-R	Per cent	£1 Level Stake
Tom O'Brien	2-6	33.3	+18.75
Paddy Brennan	2-7	28.6	+36.00

COURSE RECORD

	Total W-R	Non-Hndcps Hurdles	Non-Hndcps Chases	Hndcps Hurdles	Hndcps Chases	NH Flat	Per cent	£1 Level Stake
Taunton	2-5	0-2	0-0	1-2	0-0	1-1	40.0	+19.75
Cheltenham	1-2	0-0	0-0	0-0	0-0	1-2	50.0	+15.00
Exeter	1-2	0-0	0-0	0-0	0-0	1-2	50.0	+24.00

WINNING HORSES

Horse	Races Run	1st	2nd	3rd	£
Tobouggaloo	2	2	0	0	6498
May Be Some Time	5	1	0	0	3764
Pengo's Boy	3	1	0	1	2053
Total winning prize-money					**£12315**
Favourites	**0-1**		**0.0%**		**-1.00**

HENRIETTA KNIGHT

WEST LOCKINGE, OXON

	No. of Hrs	Races Run	1st	2nd	3rd	Unpl	Per cent	£1 Level Stake
NH Flat	*0*	*0*	*0*	*0*	*0*	*0*	*0.0*	*0.00*
Hurdles	*0*	*0*	*0*	*0*	*0*	*0*	*0.0*	*0.00*
Chases	*2*	*5*	*1*	*0*	*1*	*3*	*20.0*	*+4.00*
Totals	**2**	**5**	**1**	**0**	**1**	**3**	**20.0**	**+4.00**
12-13	*5*	*6*	*0*	*1*	*0*	*5*	*0.0*	*-6.00*

JOCKEYS

	W-R	Per cent	£1 Level Stake
Mr H A A Bannister	1-5	20.0	+4.00

COURSE RECORD

	Total W-R	Non-Hndcps Hurdles	Non-Hndcps Chases	Hndcps Hurdles	Hndcps Chases	NH Flat	Per cent	£1 Level Stake
Ascot	1-1	0-0	1-1	0-0	0-0	0-0	100.0	+8.00

WINNING HORSES

Horse	Races Run	1st	2nd	3rd	£
Calgary Bay	4	1	0	1	2808
Total winning prize-money					**£2808**
Favourites	**0-1**		**0.0%**		**-1.00**

TOM LACEY

CHIPPING NORTON, OXON

	No. of Hrs	Races Run	1st	2nd	3rd	Unpl	Per cent	£1 Level Stake
NH Flat	*7*	*9*	*2*	*1*	*1*	*5*	*22.2*	*+16.00*
Hurdles	*10*	*24*	*3*	*3*	*3*	*15*	*12.5*	*-4.50*
Chases	*3*	*5*	*0*	*0*	*0*	*5*	*0.0*	*-5.00*
Totals	**16**	**38**	**5**	**4**	**4**	**25**	**13.2**	**+6.50**
13-14	*3*	*4*	*0*	*0*	*0*	*4*	*0.0*	*-4.00*
12-13	*1*	*2*	*1*	*0*	*0*	*1*	*50.0*	*+5.00*

JOCKEYS

	W-R	Per cent	£1 Level Stake
Robert Dunne	4-24	16.7	+16.50
Mr Charlie Deutsch	1-1	100.0	+3.00

COURSE RECORD

	Total W-R	Non-Hndcps Hurdles	Non-Hndcps Chases	Hndcps Hurdles	Hndcps Chases	NH Flat	Per cent	£1 Level Stake
Southwell	2-9	0-4	0-0	0-1	0-0	2-4	22.2	+16.00
Exeter	1-2	1-2	0-0	0-0	0-0	0-0	50.0	+6.50
Taunton	1-2	0-0	0-0	1-2	0-0	0-0	50.0	+3.50
Ludlow	1-4	0-1	0-1	1-2	0-0	0-0	25.0	+1.50

WINNING HORSES

Horse	Races Run	1st	2nd	3rd	£
Brandon Hill	2	2	0	0	5848
*Cloudy Spirit	6	1	0	1	3764
Holly Bush Henry	1	1	0	0	1949
Younevercall	2	1	0	1	1949
Total winning prize-money					**£13510**
Favourites	**0-2**		**0.0%**		**-2.00**

EMMA LAVELLE

HATHERDEN, HANTS

	No. of Hrs	Races Run	1st	2nd	3rd	Unpl	Per cent	£1 Level Stake
NH Flat	*13*	*27*	*5*	*0*	*4*	*18*	*18.5*	*+8.33*
Hurdles	*31*	*93*	*11*	*9*	*13*	*60*	*11.8*	*-26.35*
Chases	*25*	*71*	*5*	*11*	*5*	*50*	*7.0*	*-38.50*
Totals	**64**	**191**	**21**	**20**	**22**	**128**	**11.0**	**-56.52**
13-14	*64*	*227*	*40*	*35*	*38*	*113*	*17.6*	*-35.35*
12-13	*57*	*172*	*12*	*25*	*26*	*109*	*7.0*	*-95.50*

BY MONTH

NH Flat	W-R	Per cent	£1 Level Stake
May	0-0	0.0	0.00
June	0-0	0.0	0.00
July	0-0	0.0	0.00
August	0-0	0.0	0.00

Hurdles	W-R	Per cent	£1 Level Stake
May	0-6	0.0	-6.00
June	0-1	0.0	-1.00
July	0-0	0.0	0.00
August	0-3	0.0	-3.00

September	0-0	0.0	0.00	September	1-1	100.0	+2.75
October	0-2	0.0	-2.00	October	3-18	16.7	+6.50
November	1-2	50.0	+3.00	November	3-17	17.6	-4.35
December	1-2	50.0	+11.00	December	1-10	10.0	-7.00
January	2-5	40.0	+7.33	January	1-13	7.7	-7.00
February	0-4	0.0	-4.00	February	2-11	18.2	+5.75
March	1-11	9.1	-6.00	March	0-8	0.0	-8.00
April	0-1	0.0	-1.00	April	0-5	0.0	-5.00

Chases	W-R	Per cent	£1 Level Stake	Totals	W-R	Per cent	£1 Level Stake
May	0-8	0.0	-8.00	May	0-14	0.0	-14.00
June	0-1	0.0	-1.00	June	0-2	0.0	-2.00
July	0-0	0.0	0.00	July	0-0	0.0	0.00
August	0-3	0.0	-3.00	August	0-6	0.0	-6.00
September	0-2	0.0	-2.00	September	1-3	33.3	+0.75
October	2-13	15.4	-2.75	October	5-33	15.2	+1.75
November	2-9	22.2	+10.25	November	6-28	21.4	+8.90
December	0-8	0.0	-8.00	December	2-20	10.0	-4.00
January	0-6	0.0	-6.00	January	3-24	12.5	-5.67
February	0-4	0.0	-4.00	February	2-19	10.5	-2.25
March	0-6	0.0	-6.00	March	1-25	4.0	-20.00
April	1-11	9.1	-8.00	April	1-17	5.9	-14.00

DISTANCE

Hurdles	W-R	Per cent	£1 Level Stake	Chases	W-R	Per cent	£1 Level Stake
2m-2m3f	4-22	18.2	-1.75	2m-2m3f	0-12	0.0	-12.00
2m4f-2m7f	3-43	7.0	-29.60	2m4f-2m7f	1-24	4.2	-21.75
3m+	4-18	22.2	+15.00	3m+	4-25	16.0	+5.25

TYPE OF RACE

Non-Handicaps	W-R	Per cent	£1 Level Stake	Handicaps	W-R	Per cent	£1 Level Stake
Nov Hrdls	1-24	4.2	-22.60	Nov Hrdls	1-5	20.0	+4.00
Hrdls	4-15	26.7	+13.75	Hrdls	5-49	10.2	-21.50
Nov Chs	0-5	0.0	-5.00	Nov Chs	0-3	0.0	-3.00
Chases	1-5	20.0	-2.75	Chases	4-58	6.9	-27.75
Sell/Claim	0-0	0.0	0.00	Sell/Claim	0-0	0.0	0.00

RACE CLASS / FIRST TIME OUT

RACE CLASS	W-R	Per cent	£1 Level Stake	FIRST TIME OUT	W-R	Per cent	£1 Level Stake
Class 1	2-36	5.6	-6.00	Bumpers	4-13	30.8	+18.00
Class 2	1-19	5.3	-15.75	Hurdles	1-29	3.4	-23.00
Class 3	6-43	14.0	-6.75	Chases	1-22	4.5	-15.50
Class 4	4-53	7.5	-41.10				
Class 5	3-25	12.0	-6.25	Totals	6-64	9.4	-20.50
Class 6	5-15	33.3	+20.33				

JOCKEYS

	W-R	Per cent	£1 Level Stake
Aidan Coleman	10-99	10.1	-40.60
Richie McLernon	4-32	12.5	-9.42
Richie O'Dea	3-20	15.0	+2.25
Daryl Jacob	2-7	28.6	+17.50
Gavin Sheehan	2-10	20.0	-3.25

COURSE RECORD

	Total W-R	Non-Hndcps Hurdles	Non-Hndcps Chases	Hndcps Hurdles	Hndcps Chases	NH Flat	Per cent	£1 Level Stake
Wincanton	4-14	1-2	0-1	0-5	1-4	2-2	28.6	+30.00
Haydock	3-3	1-1	0-0	2-2	0-0	0-0	100.0	+20.50
Doncaster	2-6	0-0	0-0	0-2	0-2	2-2	33.3	+3.33
Chepstow	2-11	1-3	0-1	1-2	0-2	0-3	18.2	-3.50
Exeter	2-16	0-5	0-0	0-5	2-4	0-2	12.5	-5.75
Leicester	1-3	1-1	0-0	0-0	0-2	0-0	33.3	-1.60
Plumpton	1-3	0-0	0-0	0-2	1-1	0-0	33.3	0.00
Uttoxeter	1-5	0-0	0-1	0-1	0-1	1-2	20.0	0.00
Worcester	1-6	1-3	0-0	0-1	0-2	0-0	16.7	0.00
Fontwell	1-7	0-0	0-0	1-5	0-1	0-1	14.3	+2.00
Taunton	1-8	0-3	0-0	1-2	0-1	0-2	12.5	-4.25
Aintree	1-10	0-3	0-1	1-1	0-5	0-0	10.0	-0.50
Kempton	1-20	0-6	1-2	0-4	0-6	0-2	5.0	-17.75

WINNING HORSES

Horse	Races Run	1st	2nd	3rd	£
Court By Surprise	3	2	0	0	41766
Closing Ceremony	5	3	1	0	40029
Parish Business	7	2	2	0	8831
*Albert Bridge	5	1	1	0	6498
Caulfields Venture	5	1	1	0	6330
Private Malone	3	3	0	0	12541
Fix It Right	3	1	0	1	4224
Casino Markets	2	1	0	0	3764
Demographic	2	1	0	0	1949
Out Of The Mist	4	2	0	0	3574
Fortunate George	3	1	0	1	1625
See The World	1	1	0	0	1625
Lets Hope So	1	1	0	0	1560
Fox Appeal	7	1	2	0	0
Total winning prize-money					**£134316**
Favourites	**5-23**		**21.7%**		**-8.10**

S J LEADBETTER

HAWICK, BORDERS

	No. of Hrs	Races Run	1st	2nd	3rd	Unpl	Per cent	£1 Level Stake
NH Flat	*0*	*0*	*0*	*0*	*0*	*0*	*0.0*	*0.00*
Hurdles	*0*	*0*	*0*	*0*	*0*	*0*	*0.0*	*0.00*
Chases	*2*	*3*	*1*	*0*	*0*	*2*	*33.3*	*+20.00*
Totals	**2**	**3**	**1**	**0**	**0**	**2**	**33.3**	**+20.00**
13-14	*1*	*1*	*0*	*0*	*0*	*1*	*0.0*	*-1.00*

JOCKEYS

	W-R	Per cent	£1 Level Stake
Mr N Orpwood	1-2	50.0	+21.00

COURSE RECORD

	Total W-R	Non-Hndcps Hurdles	Non-Hndcps Chases	Hndcps Hurdles	Hndcps Chases	NH Flat	Per cent	£1 Level Stake
Sedgefield	1-1	0-0	1-1	0-0	0-0	0-0	100.0	+22.00

WINNING HORSES

Horse	Races Run	1st	2nd	3rd	£
*Another Dark Rum	2	1	0	0	1248
Total winning prize-money					**£1248**
Favourites	**0-0**		**0.0%**		**0.00**

BARRY LEAVY

FORSBROOK, STAFFS

	No. of Hrs	Races Run	1st	2nd	3rd	Unpl	Per cent	£1 Level Stake
NH Flat	*0*	*0*	*0*	*0*	*0*	*0*	*0.0*	*0.00*
Hurdles	*11*	*23*	*2*	*3*	*4*	*14*	*8.7*	*-8.50*
Chases	*3*	*8*	*0*	*0*	*2*	*6*	*0.0*	*-8.00*
Totals	**12**	**31**	**2**	**3**	**6**	**20**	**6.5**	**-16.50**
13-14	*12*	*52*	*4*	*5*	*2*	*41*	*7.7*	*-28.17*
12-13	*13*	*45*	*5*	*4*	*5*	*31*	*11.1*	*+0.55*

JOCKEYS

	W-R	Per cent	£1 Level Stake
Richard Johnson	1-4	25.0	+0.50
Harry Challoner	1-18	5.6	-8.00

COURSE RECORD

	Total W-R	Non-Hndcps Hurdles	Non-Hndcps Chases	Hndcps Hurdles	Hndcps Chases	NH Flat	Per cent	£1 Level Stake
Stratford	1-1	1-1	0-0	0-0	0-0	0-0	100.0	+3.50
Uttoxeter	1-13	1-3	0-0	0-6	0-4	0-0	7.7	-3.00

WINNING HORSES

Horse	Races Run	1st	2nd	3rd	£
Ministerofinterior	3	1	1	0	2599
Ghaabesh	3	1	0	0	2079
Total winning prize-money					**£4678**
Favourites	**0-2**		**0.0%**		**-2.00**

RICHARD LEE

BYTON, H'FORDS

	No. of Hrs	Races Run	1st	2nd	3rd	Unpl	Per cent	£1 Level Stake
NH Flat	*2*	*4*	*0*	*1*	*0*	*3*	*0.0*	*-4.00*
Hurdles	*12*	*37*	*6*	*4*	*6*	*21*	*16.2*	*+17.25*
Chases	*18*	*67*	*13*	*11*	*8*	*35*	*19.4*	*+4.88*
Totals	**27**	**108**	**19**	**16**	**14**	**59**	**17.6**	**+18.13**
13-14	*33*	*156*	*17*	*28*	*29*	*82*	*10.9*	*-38.15*
12-13	*31*	*161*	*21*	*17*	*20*	*103*	*13.0*	*-31.69*

BY MONTH

NH Flat	W-R	Per cent	£1 Level Stake	Hurdles	W-R	Per cent	£1 Level Stake
May	0-1	0.0	-1.00	May	0-5	0.0	-5.00
June	0-0	0.0	0.00	June	0-0	0.0	0.00
July	0-0	0.0	0.00	July	0-0	0.0	0.00
August	0-0	0.0	0.00	August	0-2	0.0	-2.00
September	0-0	0.0	0.00	September	0-0	0.0	0.00
October	0-0	0.0	0.00	October	0-1	0.0	-1.00
November	0-1	0.0	-1.00	November	0-3	0.0	-3.00
December	0-0	0.0	0.00	December	1-6	16.7	+28.00
January	0-0	0.0	0.00	January	2-3	66.7	+2.75
February	0-0	0.0	0.00	February	1-4	25.0	+3.00
March	0-1	0.0	-1.00	March	1-7	14.3	-2.00
April	0-1	0.0	-1.00	April	1-6	16.7	-3.50

Chases	W-R	Per cent	£1 Level Stake	Totals	W-R	Per cent	£1 Level Stake
May	0-5	0.0	-5.00	May	0-11	0.0	-11.00
June	0-3	0.0	-3.00	June	0-3	0.0	-3.00
July	0-2	0.0	-2.00	July	0-2	0.0	-2.00
August	0-1	0.0	-1.00	August	0-3	0.0	-3.00
September	0-0	0.0	0.00	September	0-0	0.0	0.00
October	2-5	40.0	+15.00	October	2-6	33.3	+14.00
November	3-8	37.5	+5.13	November	3-12	25.0	+1.13
December	3-10	30.0	+5.75	December	4-16	25.0	+33.75
January	1-8	12.5	-5.50	January	3-11	27.3	-2.75
February	1-11	9.1	-6.00	February	2-15	13.3	-3.00
March	1-7	14.3	-1.00	March	2-15	13.3	-4.00
April	2-7	28.6	+2.50	April	3-14	21.4	-2.00

DISTANCE

Hurdles	W-R	Per cent	£1 Level Stake	Chases	W-R	Per cent	£1 Level Stake
2m-2m3f	2-16	12.5	-4.00	2m-2m3f	5-17	29.4	+4.38
2m4f-2m7f	3-11	27.3	+28.75	2m4f-2m7f	3-16	18.8	+0.50
3m+	0-1	0.0	-1.00	3m+	5-23	21.7	+11.00

TYPE OF RACE

Non-Handicaps	W-R	Per cent	£1 Level Stake	Handicaps	W-R	Per cent	£1 Level Stake
Nov Hrdls	2-11	18.2	-5.25	Nov Hrdls	0-0	0.0	0.00
Hrdls	2-3	66.7	+33.50	Hrdls	2-23	8.7	-11.00
Nov Chs	2-3	66.7	+4.13	Nov Chs	2-6	33.3	+0.25
Chases	0-1	0.0	-1.00	Chases	9-57	15.8	+1.50
Sell/Claim	0-0	0.0	0.00	Sell/Claim	0-0	0.0	0.00

RACE CLASS / FIRST TIME OUT

Race Class	W-R	Per cent	£1 Level Stake	First Time Out	W-R	Per cent	£1 Level Stake
Class 1	1-14	7.1	-10.00	Bumpers	0-2	0.0	-2.00
Class 2	2-12	16.7	+2.00	Hurdles	1-9	11.1	+25.00
Class 3	7-28	25.0	+14.25	Chases	4-16	25.0	+10.13
Class 4	7-34	20.6	+23.88				

Class 5	2-18	11.1	-10.00	Totals	5-27	18.5	+33.13
Class 6	0-2	0.0	-2.00				

JOCKEYS

	W-R	Per cent	£1 Level Stake
Jamie Moore	6-17	35.3	+40.38
Charlie Poste	5-21	23.8	+0.25
Tom Scudamore	2-9	22.2	+3.50
Richard Johnson	2-11	18.2	-2.00
Micheal Nolan	2-16	12.5	-2.00
Sam Twiston-Davies	1-1	100.0	+4.00
Jake Greenall	1-19	5.3	-12.00

COURSE RECORD

	Total W-R	Non-Hndcps Hurdles	Non-Hndcps Chases	Hndcps Hurdles	Hndcps Chases	NH Flat	Per cent	£1 Level Stake
Carlisle	3-4	0-0	0-0	0-0	3-4	0-0	75.0	+18.00
Wetherby	3-7	2-3	1-1	0-1	0-2	0-0	42.9	+1.88
Warwick	3-8	1-1	0-1	0-2	2-4	0-0	37.5	+34.75
Lingfield	2-3	0-0	0-0	0-0	2-3	0-0	66.7	+7.00
Newbury	2-6	0-1	0-0	1-1	1-4	0-0	33.3	+1.50
Ayr	1-2	0-0	1-1	0-1	0-0	0-0	50.0	+2.00
Fontwell	1-2	0-0	0-0	1-1	0-1	0-0	50.0	+5.00
Exeter	1-3	0-1	0-0	0-1	1-1	0-0	33.3	+4.00
Towcester	1-5	1-1	0-0	0-0	0-3	0-1	20.0	-2.50
Ffos Las	1-8	0-0	0-0	0-1	1-7	0-0	12.5	-2.50
Chepstow	1-10	0-3	0-0	0-1	1-5	0-1	10.0	-1.00

WINNING HORSES

Horse	Races Run	1st	2nd	3rd	£
Top Gamble	6	4	1	0	44299
Grey Gold	5	1	1	0	25320
Knock A Hand	5	1	0	1	10397
Gassin Golf	6	1	2	1	9747
Russe Blanc	5	2	2	1	17705
Simply Wings	4	1	0	2	9495
Incentivise	7	2	1	1	12021
Tresor De Bontee	4	1	1	0	3769
*Kylemore Lough	6	3	0	1	10267
*Definite Future	5	1	0	0	3249
Aces Over Eights	5	1	1	0	2599
Ravens Brook	4	1	1	1	2469
Total winning prize-money					**£151337**
Favourites	**6-12**		**50.0%**		**6.13**

SOPHIE LEECH

ELTON, GLOUCS

	No. of Hrs	Races Run	1st	2nd	3rd	Unpl	Per cent	£1 Level Stake
NH Flat	*2*	*3*	*0*	*0*	*1*	*2*	*0.0*	*-3.00*
Hurdles	*30*	*117*	*16*	*6*	*8*	*87*	*13.7*	*-15.53*
Chases	*14*	*44*	*4*	*5*	*3*	*32*	*9.1*	*-16.00*
Totals	**40**	**164**	**20**	**11**	**12**	**121**	**12.2**	**-34.53**
13-14	*38*	*166*	*13*	*12*	*18*	*122*	*7.8*	*-51.13*
12-13	*33*	*145*	*18*	*19*	*16*	*92*	*12.4*	*-11.38*

BY MONTH

NH Flat	W-R	Per cent	£1 Level Stake	Hurdles	W-R	Per cent	£1 Level Stake
May	0-1	0.0	-1.00	May	3-11	27.3	+2.00
June	0-0	0.0	0.00	June	0-6	0.0	-6.00
July	0-0	0.0	0.00	July	2-12	16.7	-1.00
August	0-0	0.0	0.00	August	0-6	0.0	-6.00
September	0-0	0.0	0.00	September	3-6	50.0	+13.10
October	0-0	0.0	0.00	October	3-16	18.8	+2.25
November	0-0	0.0	0.00	November	1-9	11.1	-4.00
December	0-1	0.0	-1.00	December	2-16	12.5	-2.50
January	0-0	0.0	0.00	January	1-12	8.3	+7.00
February	0-0	0.0	0.00	February	0-8	0.0	-8.00
March	0-1	0.0	-1.00	March	0-10	0.0	-10.00
April	0-0	0.0	0.00	April	1-5	20.0	-2.38

Chases	W-R	Per cent	£1 Level Stake	Totals	W-R	Per cent	£1 Level Stake
May	1-8	12.5	-2.00	May	4-20	20.0	-1.00
June	0-3	0.0	-3.00	June	0-9	0.0	-9.00
July	0-1	0.0	-1.00	July	2-13	15.4	-2.00
August	0-0	0.0	0.00	August	0-6	0.0	-6.00
September	0-2	0.0	-2.00	September	3-8	37.5	+11.10
October	0-3	0.0	-3.00	October	3-19	15.8	-0.75
November	2-6	33.3	+12.00	November	3-15	20.0	+8.00
December	0-6	0.0	-6.00	December	2-23	8.7	-9.50
January	1-3	33.3	+1.00	January	2-15	13.3	+8.00
February	0-3	0.0	-3.00	February	0-11	0.0	-11.00
March	0-3	0.0	-3.00	March	0-14	0.0	-14.00
April	0-6	0.0	-6.00	April	1-11	9.1	-8.38

DISTANCE

Hurdles	W-R	Per cent	£1 Level Stake	Chases	W-R	Per cent	£1 Level Stake
2m-2m3f	9-58	15.5	-2.38	2m-2m3f	1-14	7.1	-11.00
2m4f-2m7f	4-27	14.8	-14.15	2m4f-2m7f	2-13	15.4	+6.00
3m+	0-3	0.0	-3.00	3m+	1-9	11.1	-3.00

TYPE OF RACE

Non-Handicaps	W-R	Per cent	£1 Level Stake	Handicaps	W-R	Per cent	£1 Level Stake
Nov Hrdls	4-15	26.7	+3.72	Nov Hrdls	0-7	0.0	-7.00
Hrdls	1-7	14.3	-3.00	Hrdls	10-79	12.7	-5.75
Nov Chs	1-1	100.0	+5.00	Nov Chs	0-3	0.0	-3.00
Chases	0-2	0.0	-2.00	Chases	3-38	7.9	-16.00
Sell/Claim	0-4	0.0	-4.00	Sell/Claim	1-5	20.0	+0.50

RACE CLASS

FIRST TIME OUT

Race Class	W-R	Per cent	£1 Level Stake	First Time Out	W-R	Per cent	£1 Level Stake
Class 1	0-9	0.0	-9.00	Bumpers	0-2	0.0	-2.00
Class 2	0-3	0.0	-3.00	Hurdles	1-27	3.7	-23.00
Class 3	3-14	21.4	+6.50	Chases	2-11	18.2	-2.00

Class 4	8-67	11.9	-28.27
Class 5	9-66	13.6	+4.25
Class 6	0-5	0.0	-5.00
Totals	3-40	7.5	-27.00

JOCKEYS

	W-R	Per cent	£1 Level Stake
Killian Moore	11-58	19.0	+29.35
Paul Moloney	7-60	11.7	-28.88
Richard Johnson	1-1	100.0	+4.50
James Best	1-9	11.1	-3.50

COURSE RECORD

	Total W-R	Non-Hndcps Hurdles	Non-Hndcps Chases	Hndcps Hurdles	Hndcps Chases	NH Flat	Per cent	£1 Level Stake
Ffos Las	6-17	2-3	0-0	3-6	1-6	0-2	35.3	+14.75
Sedgefield	3-3	2-2	0-0	1-1	0-0	0-0	100.0	+16.10
Chepstow	2-19	1-6	0-0	1-9	0-4	0-0	10.5	-11.38
Lingfield	1-1	0-0	0-0	1-1	0-0	0-0	100.0	+3.50
Wetherby	1-2	0-0	1-1	0-1	0-0	0-0	50.0	+4.00
Fakenham	1-4	0-0	0-0	1-4	0-0	0-0	25.0	+1.50
Uttoxeter	1-5	0-0	0-0	0-3	1-2	0-0	20.0	-1.00
Nton Abbot	1-8	0-1	0-0	1-6	0-1	0-0	12.5	-2.50
Cartmel	1-10	0-1	0-0	1-6	0-3	0-0	10.0	-4.00
Towcester	1-11	0-0	0-0	0-5	1-5	0-1	9.1	+4.00
Stratford	1-12	0-3	0-0	1-6	0-3	0-0	8.3	-6.50
Taunton	1-12	0-1	0-0	1-11	0-0	0-0	8.3	+7.00

WINNING HORSES

Horse	Races Run	1st	2nd	3rd	£
Tamarillo Grove	6	3	1	0	14491
Radmores Revenge	5	1	0	0	5393
*Rocky Elsom	7	1	1	0	5198
Winston Churchill	5	2	1	0	7148
Lovcen	1	1	0	0	3769
*Man Of Plenty	4	2	0	1	6888
Anteros	9	3	1	0	9693
Olympian Boy	11	1	2	2	2599
Rolling Dough	9	1	1	2	2599
Le Grand Chene	8	1	0	1	2144
Seaside Shuffle	12	1	0	1	2053
Kapricorne	9	3	1	1	5848
Total winning prize-money					**£67823**
Favourites	**3-6**		**50.0%**		**5.35**

MISS H LEWIS

	No. of Hrs	Races Run	1st	2nd	3rd	Unpl	Per cent	£1 Level Stake
NH Flat	*0*	*0*	*0*	*0*	*0*	*0*	*0.0*	*0.00*
Hurdles	*0*	*0*	*0*	*0*	*0*	*0*	*0.0*	*0.00*
Chases	*1*	*1*	*1*	*0*	*0*	*0*	*100.0*	*+2.25*
Totals	**1**	**1**	**1**	**0**	**0**	**0**	**100.0**	**+2.25**
13-14	*1*	*2*	*0*	*1*	*0*	*1*	*0.0*	*-2.00*

JOCKEYS

	W-R	Per cent	£1 Level Stake
Miss H Lewis	1-1	100.0	+2.25

COURSE RECORD

	Total W-R	Non-Hndcps Hurdles	Non-Hndcps Chases	Hndcps Hurdles	Hndcps Chases	NH Flat	Per cent	£1 Level Stake
Ffos Las	1-1	0-0	1-1	0-0	0-0	0-0	100.0	+2.25

WINNING HORSES

Horse	Races Run	1st	2nd	3rd	£
*Catspan	1	1	0	0	1581
Total winning prize-money					**£1581**
Favourites	**1-1**		**100.0%**		**2.25**

SHEILA LEWIS

BRECON, POWYS

	No. of Hrs	Races Run	1st	2nd	3rd	Unpl	Per cent	£1 Level Stake
NH Flat	*0*	*0*	*0*	*0*	*0*	*0*	*0.0*	*0.00*
Hurdles	*2*	*9*	*1*	*1*	*0*	*7*	*11.1*	*-3.50*
Chases	*2*	*2*	*0*	*0*	*0*	*2*	*0.0*	*-2.00*
Totals	**3**	**11**	**1**	**1**	**0**	**9**	**9.1**	**-5.50**
13-14	*1*	*2*	*0*	*0*	*0*	*2*	*0.0*	*-2.00*

JOCKEYS

	W-R	Per cent	£1 Level Stake
Robert Williams	1-5	20.0	+0.50

COURSE RECORD

	Total W-R	Non-Hndcps Hurdles	Non-Hndcps Chases	Hndcps Hurdles	Hndcps Chases	NH Flat	Per cent	£1 Level Stake
Ffos Las	1-5	0-2	0-0	1-3	0-0	0-0	20.0	+0.50

WINNING HORSES

Horse	Races Run	1st	2nd	3rd	£
Try It Sometime	6	1	1	0	2274
Total winning prize-money					**£2274**
Favourites	**0-1**		**0.0%**		**-1.00**

ALASTAIR LIDDERDALE

LAMBOURN, BERKS

	No. of Hrs	Races Run	1st	2nd	3rd	Unpl	Per cent	£1 Level Stake
NH Flat	*2*	*5*	*2*	*0*	*1*	*2*	*40.0*	*+9.50*
Hurdles	*3*	*5*	*0*	*0*	*0*	*5*	*0.0*	*-5.00*
Chases	*0*	*0*	*0*	*0*	*0*	*0*	*0.0*	*0.00*
Totals	**5**	**10**	**2**	**0**	**1**	**7**	**20.0**	**+4.50**
13-14	*10*	*28*	*1*	*1*	*3*	*23*	*3.6*	*-21.00*
12-13	*11*	*23*	*0*	*1*	*0*	*22*	*0.0*	*-23.00*

JOCKEYS

	W-R	Per cent	£1 Level Stake
James Banks	2-6	33.3	+8.50

COURSE RECORD

	Total W-R	Non-Hndcps Hurdles	Non-Hndcps Chases	Hndcps Hurdles	Hndcps Chases	NH Flat	Per cent	£1 Level Stake
Stratford	1-2	0-0	0-0	0-0	0-0	1-2	50.0	+8.00
Worcester	1-3	0-1	0-0	0-0	0-0	1-2	33.3	+1.50

WINNING HORSES

Horse	Races Run	1st	2nd	3rd	£
Hannah Just Hannah	3	2	0	1	3509
Total winning prize-money					**£3509**
Favourites	**0-0**		**0.0%**		**0.00**

BERNARD LLEWELLYN

FOCHRIW, CAERPHILLY

	No. of Hrs	Races Run	1st	2nd	3rd	Unpl	Per cent	£1 Level Stake
NH Flat	*1*	*2*	*0*	*0*	*0*	*2*	*0.0*	*-2.00*
Hurdles	*25*	*115*	*9*	*18*	*22*	*66*	*7.8*	*-36.75*
Chases	*2*	*2*	*1*	*0*	*0*	*1*	*50.0*	*+1.75*
Totals	**27**	**119**	**10**	**18**	**22**	**69**	**8.4**	**-37.00**
13-14	*31*	*115*	*10*	*13*	*5*	*87*	*8.7*	*-15.25*
12-13	*33*	*127*	*9*	*10*	*14*	*94*	*7.1*	*+35.63*

BY MONTH

NH Flat	W-R	Per cent	£1 Level Stake	**Hurdles**	W-R	Per cent	£1 Level Stake
May	0-0	0.0	0.00	May	2-7	28.6	+17.00
June	0-0	0.0	0.00	June	0-2	0.0	-2.00
July	0-0	0.0	0.00	July	0-3	0.0	-3.00
August	0-0	0.0	0.00	August	1-2	50.0	+11.00
September	0-0	0.0	0.00	September	0-9	0.0	-9.00
October	0-0	0.0	0.00	October	0-14	0.0	-14.00
November	0-0	0.0	0.00	November	1-17	5.9	-11.00
December	0-2	0.0	-2.00	December	1-13	7.7	-4.50
January	0-0	0.0	0.00	January	1-11	9.1	-4.50
February	0-0	0.0	0.00	February	2-14	14.3	-0.25
March	0-0	0.0	0.00	March	1-13	7.7	-6.50
April	0-0	0.0	0.00	April	0-10	0.0	-10.00

Chases	W-R	Per cent	£1 Level Stake	**Totals**	W-R	Per cent	£1 Level Stake
May	1-1	100.0	+2.75	May	3-8	37.5	+19.75
June	0-0	0.0	0.00	June	0-2	0.0	-2.00
July	0-0	0.0	0.00	July	0-3	0.0	-3.00
August	0-0	0.0	0.00	August	1-2	50.0	+11.00
September	0-0	0.0	0.00	September	0-9	0.0	-9.00
October	0-0	0.0	0.00	October	0-14	0.0	-14.00
November	0-0	0.0	0.00	November	1-17	5.9	-11.00
December	0-0	0.0	0.00	December	1-15	6.7	-6.50
January	0-0	0.0	0.00	January	1-11	9.1	-4.50
February	0-1	0.0	-1.00	February	2-15	13.3	-1.25
March	0-0	0.0	0.00	March	1-13	7.7	-6.50
April	0-0	0.0	0.00	April	0-10	0.0	-10.00

DISTANCE

Hurdles	W-R	Per cent	£1 Level Stake	**Chases**	W-R	Per cent	£1 Level Stake
2m-2m3f	6-83	7.2	-35.25	2m-2m3f	1-2	50.0	+1.75
2m4f-2m7f	3-16	18.8	+14.50	2m4f-2m7f	0-0	0.0	0.00
3m+	0-0	0.0	0.00	3m+	0-0	0.0	0.00

TYPE OF RACE

Non-Handicaps	W-R	Per cent	£1 Level Stake	**Handicaps**	W-R	Per cent	£1 Level Stake
Nov Hrdls	0-14	0.0	-14.00	Nov Hrdls	0-7	0.0	-7.00
Hrdls	2-12	16.7	-2.75	Hrdls	7-70	10.0	-1.00
Nov Chs	0-0	0.0	0.00	Nov Chs	0-0	0.0	0.00
Chases	0-0	0.0	0.00	Chases	1-2	50.0	+1.75
Sell/Claim	0-10	0.0	-10.00	Sell/Claim	0-3	0.0	-3.00

RACE CLASS / FIRST TIME OUT

Race Class	W-R	Per cent	£1 Level Stake	**First Time Out**	W-R	Per cent	£1 Level Stake
Class 1	0-1	0.0	-1.00	Bumpers	0-1	0.0	-1.00
Class 2	0-2	0.0	-2.00	Hurdles	2-25	8.0	+5.00
Class 3	0-14	0.0	-14.00	Chases	1-1	100.0	+2.75
Class 4	4-49	8.2	-10.75				
Class 5	6-52	11.5	-8.25	Totals	3-27	11.1	+6.75
Class 6	0-1	0.0	-1.00				

JOCKEYS

	W-R	Per cent	£1 Level Stake
Robert Williams	5-70	7.1	-22.50
Jordan Williams	2-15	13.3	+6.50
Michael Byrne	1-4	25.0	-1.25
Sean Bowen	1-5	20.0	+1.50
Mark Quinlan	1-7	14.3	-3.25

COURSE RECORD

	Total W-R	Non-Hndcps Hurdles	Non-Hndcps Chases	Hndcps Hurdles	Hndcps Chases	NH Flat	Per cent	£1 Level Stake
Ffos Las	5-25	1-9	0-0	3-14	1-1	0-1	20.0	+12.00
Catterick	1-1	0-0	0-0	1-1	0-0	0-0	100.0	+7.50
Plumpton	1-3	0-0	0-0	1-3	0-0	0-0	33.3	+3.00
Stratford	1-5	0-0	0-0	1-5	0-0	0-0	20.0	+8.00
Nton Abbot	1-8	1-1	0-0	0-7	0-0	0-0	12.5	-1.50
Chepstow	1-26	0-8	0-0	1-17	0-0	0-1	3.8	-15.00

WINNING HORSES

Horse	Races Run	1st	2nd	3rd	£
Rime Avec Gentil	1	1	0	0	4224
Global Thrill	6	1	2	1	3899
Lights Of Broadway	4	2	0	1	6264

Fuzzy Logic	6	1	0	1	3249
Filatore	9	1	1	2	2599
L Frank Baum	6	1	1	1	2079
Kozmina Bay	11	2	1	0	3899
Going Nowhere Fast	4	1	0	0	1872
Total winning prize-money					**£28085**
Favourites	**1-4**		**25.0%**		**-1.25**

CHARLIE LONGSDON

OVER NORTON, OXON

	No. of Hrs	Races Run	1st	2nd	3rd	Unpl	Per cent	£1 Level Stake
NH Flat	*18*	*27*	*4*	*4*	*4*	*15*	*14.8*	*+3.38*
Hurdles	*58*	*199*	*30*	*30*	*25*	*114*	*15.1*	*-79.15*
Chases	*28*	*112*	*16*	*16*	*14*	*66*	*14.3*	*-50.58*
Totals	**85**	**338**	**50**	**50**	**43**	**195**	**14.8**	**-126.35**
13-14	*97*	*385*	*77*	*48*	*52*	*208*	*20.0*	*-88.51*
12-13	*115*	*384*	*51*	*46*	*44*	*243*	*13.3*	*-100.46*

BY MONTH

NH Flat	W-R	Per cent	£1 Level Stake
May	1-3	33.3	+5.50
June	0-1	0.0	-1.00
July	0-0	0.0	0.00
August	0-0	0.0	0.00
September	0-2	0.0	-2.00
October	1-8	12.5	-5.13
November	2-5	40.0	+14.00
December	0-1	0.0	-1.00
January	0-0	0.0	0.00
February	0-1	0.0	-1.00
March	0-2	0.0	-2.00
April	0-4	0.0	-4.00

Hurdles	W-R	Per cent	£1 Level Stake
May	1-8	12.5	-6.47
June	1-3	33.3	+7.00
July	1-3	33.3	+3.00
August	2-4	50.0	+0.98
September	4-4	100.0	+10.17
October	9-36	25.0	-6.73
November	1-34	2.9	-31.63
December	4-26	15.4	-10.72
January	2-21	9.5	-10.00
February	2-12	16.7	-6.00
March	3-24	12.5	-4.75
April	0-24	0.0	-24.00

Chases	W-R	Per cent	£1 Level Stake
May	1-9	11.1	-6.63
June	1-6	16.7	-2.75
July	0-8	0.0	-8.00
August	0-2	0.0	-2.00
September	3-5	60.0	+5.58
October	2-11	18.2	-7.85
November	2-17	11.8	-0.50
December	3-15	20.0	-2.00
January	0-8	0.0	-8.00
February	0-6	0.0	-6.00
March	3-10	30.0	+1.28
April	1-15	6.7	-13.71

Totals	W-R	Per cent	£1 Level Stake
May	3-20	15.0	-7.60
June	2-10	20.0	+3.25
July	1-11	9.1	-5.00
August	2-6	33.3	-1.02
September	7-11	63.6	+13.75
October	12-55	21.8	-19.71
November	5-56	8.9	-18.13
December	7-42	16.7	-13.72
January	2-29	6.9	-18.00
February	2-19	10.5	-13.00
March	6-36	16.7	-5.47
April	1-43	2.3	-41.71

DISTANCE

Hurdles	W-R	Per cent	£1 Level Stake
2m-2m3f	8-68	11.8	-39.02
2m4f-2m7f	12-71	16.9	-16.43
3m+	2-14	14.3	-8.77

Chases	W-R	Per cent	£1 Level Stake
2m-2m3f	1-16	6.3	-13.63
2m4f-2m7f	8-37	21.6	-9.19
3m+	5-40	12.5	-21.06

TYPE OF RACE

Non-Handicaps	W-R	Per cent	£1 Level Stake
Nov Hrdls	10-66	15.2	-30.72
Hrdls	8-26	30.8	-1.61
Nov Chs	5-15	33.3	-7.29
Chases	1-4	25.0	+1.50
Sell/Claim	0-0	0.0	0.00

Handicaps	W-R	Per cent	£1 Level Stake
Nov Hrdls	2-9	22.2	+5.50
Hrdls	10-97	10.3	-51.32
Nov Chs	3-20	15.0	-4.75
Chases	7-73	9.6	-40.04
Sell/Claim	0-0	0.0	0.00

RACE CLASS

	W-R	Per cent	£1 Level Stake
Class 1	2-35	5.7	-20.00
Class 2	3-28	10.7	-8.25
Class 3	10-77	13.0	-28.01
Class 4	27-146	18.5	-50.61
Class 5	6-33	18.2	-11.86
Class 6	2-19	10.5	-7.63

FIRST TIME OUT

	W-R	Per cent	£1 Level Stake
Bumpers	3-18	16.7	+10.38
Hurdles	10-48	20.8	-11.11
Chases	4-19	21.1	-10.23
Totals	17-85	20.0	-10.96

JOCKEYS

	W-R	Per cent	£1 Level Stake
Noel Fehily	25-154	16.2	-50.97
Mr Charlie Deutsch	7-42	16.7	-1.80
Aidan Coleman	6-32	18.8	-14.15
Richard Johnson	2-7	28.6	+4.75
Will Kennedy	2-9	22.2	-6.27
L-Bdr Sally Randell	1-1	100.0	+4.50
Ger Fox	1-2	50.0	+8.00
Leighton Aspell	1-2	50.0	+3.00
A P McCoy	1-3	33.3	-0.63
Jason Maguire	1-4	25.0	+0.33
Tom O'Brien	1-8	12.5	-5.63
Kielan Woods	1-9	11.1	-5.75
Daryl Jacob	1-17	5.9	-13.75

COURSE RECORD

	Total W-R	Non-Hndcps Hurdles	Chases	Hndcps Hurdles	Chases	NH Flat	Per cent	£1 Level Stake
Uttoxeter	6-21	3-9	1-1	2-5	0-4	0-2	28.6	-3.85
Mrket Rsn	6-31	2-7	0-0	1-8	3-12	0-4	19.4	-9.63
Southwell	5-16	2-6	1-1	2-5	0-2	0-2	31.3	+1.99
Fontwell	4-14	2-5	0-0	0-5	1-3	1-1	28.6	+4.25
Bangor	4-15	3-7	1-1	0-5	0-2	0-0	26.7	-6.73
Worcester	4-15	1-4	0-0	2-5	0-3	1-3	26.7	+5.54
Haydock	2-6	0-0	0-0	1-2	0-3	1-1	33.3	+2.50
Newbury	2-12	0-1	0-0	1-5	1-6	0-0	16.7	+5.00
Ascot	2-13	0-3	0-2	0-2	1-3	1-3	15.4	+15.00
Doncaster	2-13	1-5	0-2	0-2	1-4	0-0	15.4	-3.75
Nton Abbot	1-1	0-0	1-1	0-0	0-0	0-0	100.0	+0.83
Lingfield	1-4	0-0	0-0	0-1	1-3	0-0	25.0	-0.25
Taunton	1-6	0-1	0-0	1-4	0-1	0-0	16.7	-1.00
Carlisle	1-7	0-1	1-2	0-0	0-3	0-1	14.3	-5.47

Wetherby	1-9	0-2	0-0	0-4	1-3	0-0	11.1	-4.67
Ludlow	1-10	1-5	0-0	0-2	0-3	0-0	10.0	-7.63
Plumpton	1-10	0-5	0-0	0-1	1-4	0-0	10.0	-5.00
Towcester	1-10	1-3	0-1	0-5	0-0	0-1	10.0	-5.67
Sandown	1-11	0-1	1-2	0-3	0-4	0-1	9.1	-5.50
Huntingdon	1-14	0-3	0-1	1-5	0-3	0-2	7.1	-12.27
Aintree	1-15	0-1	0-1	1-6	0-6	0-1	6.7	-12.00
Kempton	1-16	1-5	0-0	0-7	0-4	0-0	6.3	-10.50
Warwick	1-16	1-6	0-0	0-6	0-2	0-2	6.3	-14.56

WINNING HORSES

Horse	Races Run	1st	2nd	3rd	£
Kilcooley	6	2	1	0	41322
Kalane	3	2	0	1	25899
Grandads Horse	12	3	1	0	34016
Vulcanite	4	2	0	0	22107
Sergeant Mattie	2	1	0	0	9384
Spirit Of Shankly	5	1	0	0	7507
Pure Style	6	2	2	0	10137
Azure Fly	9	2	2	2	10397
Shantou Magic	6	3	0	0	14296
Loose Chips	7	1	2	1	6239
No No Mac	5	1	3	0	5393
Java Rose	3	2	0	0	8447
Greenlaw	4	1	1	0	4874
Green Bank	7	1	1	0	4549
Long Wave	4	2	1	1	8317
Leith Hill Legasi	8	1	1	2	4328
Drop Out Joe	5	1	1	1	4224
Our Kaempfer	5	2	0	2	7148
Battle Born	1	1	0	0	3705
*Wilberdragon	5	3	0	0	9951
Germany Calling	5	2	0	2	6628
*Kilfinichen Bay	5	4	0	0	10236
Simply The West	6	1	3	0	3249
Midnight Shot	4	1	1	1	3249
Glowinginthedark	1	1	0	0	3119
St Johns Point	6	1	0	2	3119
Coologue	5	1	2	0	3119
A Vos Gardes	5	1	2	2	2738
Orby's Man	5	1	1	1	2599
Frampton	5	1	1	0	2209
Masterplan	7	1	0	0	1625
No No Manolito	3	1	0	0	1560

Total winning prize-money **£285690**

Favourites 27-64 42.2% -2.19

MRS ROSE LOXTON

BRUTON, SOMERSET

	No. of Hrs	Races Run	1st	2nd	3rd	Unpl	Per cent	£1 Level Stake
NH Flat	*0*	*0*	*0*	*0*	*0*	*0*	*0.0*	*0.00*
Hurdles	*0*	*0*	*0*	*0*	*0*	*0*	*0.0*	*0.00*
Chases	*2*	*4*	*2*	*0*	*0*	*2*	*50.0*	*+1.00*
Totals	**2**	**4**	**2**	**0**	**0**	**2**	**50.0**	**+1.00**
12-13	*1*	*1*	*1*	*0*	*0*	*0*	*100.0*	*+25.00*

JOCKEYS

	W-R	Per cent	£1 Level Stake
Megan Nicholls	1-1	100.0	+0.50
Miss B Frost	1-3	33.3	+0.50

COURSE RECORD

	Total W-R	Non-Hndcps Hurdles	Non-Hndcps Chases	Hndcps Hurdles	Hndcps Chases	NH Flat	Per cent	£1 Level Stake
Musselbgh	1-1	0-0	1-1	0-0	0-0	0-0	100.0	+2.50
Wincanton	1-1	0-0	1-1	0-0	0-0	0-0	100.0	+0.50

WINNING HORSES

Horse	Races Run	1st	2nd	3rd	£
*Current Event	3	1	0	0	5996
*Gwanako	1	1	0	0	2184

Total winning prize-money **£8180**

Favourites **2-2** **100.0%** **3.00**

R E LUKE

HAVERFORDWEST, PEMBROKESHIRE

	No. of Hrs	Races Run	1st	2nd	3rd	Unpl	Per cent	£1 Level Stake
NH Flat	*0*	*0*	*0*	*0*	*0*	*0*	*0.0*	*0.00*
Hurdles	*0*	*0*	*0*	*0*	*0*	*0*	*0.0*	*0.00*
Chases	*2*	*8*	*2*	*1*	*0*	*5*	*25.0*	*+3.50*
Totals	**2**	**8**	**2**	**1**	**0**	**5**	**25.0**	**+3.50**
13-14	*3*	*11*	*2*	*2*	*2*	*5*	*18.2*	*-4.00*
12-13	*1*	*3*	*0*	*1*	*1*	*1*	*0.0*	*-3.00*

JOCKEYS

	W-R	Per cent	£1 Level Stake
Mr E David	2-8	25.0	+3.50

COURSE RECORD

	Total W-R	Non-Hndcps Hurdles	Non-Hndcps Chases	Hndcps Hurdles	Hndcps Chases	NH Flat	Per cent	£1 Level Stake
Taunton	1-2	0-0	1-2	0-0	0-0	0-0	50.0	-0.50
Cheltenham	1-3	0-0	1-3	0-0	0-0	0-0	33.3	+7.00

WINNING HORSES

Horse	Races Run	1st	2nd	3rd	£
Chosen Milan	6	2	1	0	5719

Total winning prize-money **£5719**

Favourites **1-1** **100.0%** **0.50**

SHAUN LYCETT

CLAPTON-ON-THE-HILL, GLOUCS

	No. of Hrs	Races Run	1st	2nd	3rd	Unpl	Per cent	£1 Level Stake
NH Flat	*5*	*10*	*2*	*3*	*1*	*4*	*20.0*	*+7.25*
Hurdles	*12*	*31*	*0*	*1*	*4*	*26*	*0.0*	*-31.00*
Chases	*2*	*5*	*2*	*1*	*2*	*0*	*40.0*	*+3.25*
Totals	**17**	**46**	**4**	**5**	**7**	**30**	**8.7**	**-20.50**
13-14	*15*	*39*	*3*	*0*	*2*	*34*	*7.7*	*+11.25*
12-13	*13*	*36*	*1*	*5*	*4*	*26*	*2.8*	*-29.00*

JOCKEYS

	W-R	Per cent	£1 Level Stake
Peter Carberry	3-32	9.4	-21.50
Tom Scudamore	1-1	100.0	+14.00

COURSE RECORD

	Total W-R	Non-Hndcps Hurdles	Non-Hndcps Chases	Hndcps Hurdles	Hndcps Chases	NH Flat	Per cent	£1 Level Stake
Stratford	3-6	0-2	0-0	0-1	2-2	1-1	50.0	+17.25
Bangor	1-1	0-0	0-0	0-0	0-0	1-1	100.0	+1.25

WINNING HORSES

Horse	Races Run	1st	2nd	3rd	£
Kalamill	7	2	1	3	10229
Nutcracker Prince	3	1	1	1	2053
Kingussie	1	1	0	0	1949
Total winning prize-money					**£14231**
Favourites	**2-3**		**66.7%**		**2.50**

JOHN MACKIE

CHURCH BROUGHTON , DERBYS

	No. of Hrs	Races Run	1st	2nd	3rd	Unpl	Per cent	£1 Level Stake
NH Flat	*1*	*1*	*0*	*0*	*0*	*1*	*0.0*	*-1.00*
Hurdles	*6*	*19*	*1*	*1*	*3*	*14*	*5.3*	*-11.50*
Chases	*2*	*13*	*2*	*2*	*3*	*6*	*15.4*	*-3.50*
Totals	**8**	**33**	**3**	**3**	**6**	**21**	**9.1**	**-16.00**
13-14	*16*	*63*	*8*	*4*	*3*	*48*	*12.7*	*-10.75*
12-13	*13*	*44*	*2*	*3*	*4*	*35*	*4.5*	*-5.50*

JOCKEYS

	W-R	Per cent	£1 Level Stake
Paul Moloney	2-6	33.3	+3.50
Peter Carberry	1-11	9.1	-3.50

COURSE RECORD

	Total W-R	Non-Hndcps Hurdles	Non-Hndcps Chases	Hndcps Hurdles	Hndcps Chases	NH Flat	Per cent	£1 Level Stake
Uttoxeter	2-10	0-0	0-0	0-4	2-6	0-0	20.0	-0.50
Doncaster	1-1	0-0	0-0	1-1	0-0	0-0	100.0	+6.50

WINNING HORSES

Horse	Races Run	1st	2nd	3rd	£
River Purple	8	2	1	1	6657
Knight In Purple	12	1	1	3	3249
Total winning prize-money					**£9906**
Favourites	**1-4**		**25.0%**		**-1.50**

MICHAEL MADGWICK

DENMEAD, HANTS

	No. of Hrs	Races Run	1st	2nd	3rd	Unpl	Per cent	£1 Level Stake
NH Flat	*0*	*0*	*0*	*0*	*0*	*0*	*0.0*	*0.00*
Hurdles	*5*	*8*	*2*	*0*	*0*	*6*	*25.0*	*+13.00*
Chases	*1*	*4*	*0*	*0*	*0*	*4*	*0.0*	*-4.00*
Totals	**5**	**12**	**2**	**0**	**0**	**10**	**16.7**	**+9.00**
13-14	*8*	*30*	*2*	*2*	*2*	*24*	*6.7*	*-7.00*
12-13	*9*	*33*	*4*	*0*	*4*	*25*	*12.1*	*+1.50*

JOCKEYS

	W-R	Per cent	£1 Level Stake
Marc Goldstein	2-12	16.7	+9.00

COURSE RECORD

	Total W-R	Non-Hndcps Hurdles	Non-Hndcps Chases	Hndcps Hurdles	Hndcps Chases	NH Flat	Per cent	£1 Level Stake
Fontwell	1-3	1-1	0-0	0-2	0-0	0-0	33.3	+12.00
Plumpton	1-6	1-1	0-0	0-2	0-3	0-0	16.7	0.00

WINNING HORSES

Horse	Races Run	1st	2nd	3rd	£
Money Talks	3	2	0	0	5928
Total winning prize-money					**£5928**
Favourites	**0-0**		**0.0%**		**0.00**

GABE MAHON

STRATFORD UPON AVON

	No. of Hrs	Races Run	1st	2nd	3rd	Unpl	Per cent	£1 Level Stake
NH Flat	*0*	*0*	*0*	*0*	*0*	*0*	*0.0*	*0.00*
Hurdles	*0*	*0*	*0*	*0*	*0*	*0*	*0.0*	*0.00*
Chases	*1*	*2*	*1*	*0*	*0*	*1*	*50.0*	*+1.25*
Totals	**1**	**2**	**1**	**0**	**0**	**1**	**50.0**	**+1.25**

JOCKEYS

	W-R	Per cent	£1 Level Stake
Mr Leo Mahon	1-2	50.0	+1.25

COURSE RECORD

	Total W-R	Non-Hndcps Hurdles	Non-Hndcps Chases	Hndcps Hurdles	Hndcps Chases	NH Flat	Per cent	£1 Level Stake
Worcester	1-1	0-0	1-1	0-0	0-0	0-0	100.0	+2.25

WINNING HORSES

Horse	Races Run	1st	2nd	3rd	£
Lake Legend	2	1	0	0	936
Total winning prize-money					**£936**
Favourites	**0-0**		**0.0%**		**0.00**

CHARLIE MANN

UPPER LAMBOURN, BERKS

	No. of Hrs	Races Run	1st	2nd	3rd	Unpl	Per cent	£1 Level Stake
NH Flat	*6*	*9*	*1*	*0*	*0*	*8*	*11.1*	*-4.67*
Hurdles	*20*	*78*	*11*	*7*	*6*	*54*	*14.1*	*+2.50*
Chases	*14*	*64*	*11*	*12*	*6*	*35*	*17.2*	*+0.93*
Totals	**36**	**151**	**23**	**19**	**12**	**97**	**15.2**	**-1.24**
13-14	*29*	*118*	*14*	*11*	*19*	*74*	*11.9*	*-9.50*
12-13	*36*	*148*	*16*	*20*	*16*	*96*	*10.8*	*-38.38*

BY MONTH

NH Flat	W-R	Per cent	£1 Level Stake
May	1-2	50.0	+2.33
June	0-0	0.0	0.00
July	0-1	0.0	-1.00
August	0-0	0.0	0.00
September	0-0	0.0	0.00
October	0-0	0.0	0.00
November	0-1	0.0	-1.00
December	0-0	0.0	0.00
January	0-0	0.0	0.00
February	0-4	0.0	-4.00
March	0-1	0.0	-1.00
April	0-0	0.0	0.00

Hurdles	W-R	Per cent	£1 Level Stake
May	3-12	25.0	-1.75
June	1-5	20.0	+4.00
July	1-4	25.0	-1.00
August	1-3	33.3	-0.25
September	1-3	33.3	+10.00
October	0-2	0.0	-2.00
November	0-7	0.0	-7.00
December	0-8	0.0	-8.00
January	1-8	12.5	+5.00
February	0-7	0.0	-7.00
March	2-9	22.2	+1.50
April	1-10	10.0	+9.00

Chases	W-R	Per cent	£1 Level Stake
May	0-4	0.0	-4.00
June	1-3	33.3	-1.27
July	0-2	0.0	-2.00
August	1-3	33.3	+9.00
September	0-3	0.0	-3.00
October	2-6	33.3	+4.75
November	1-11	9.1	-8.80
December	1-10	10.0	+5.00
January	2-6	33.3	+1.00
February	2-7	28.6	+2.25
March	1-7	14.3	0.00
April	0-2	0.0	-2.00

Totals	W-R	Per cent	£1 Level Stake
May	4-18	22.2	-3.42
June	2-8	25.0	+2.73
July	1-7	14.3	-4.00
August	2-6	33.3	+8.75
September	1-6	16.7	+7.00
October	2-8	25.0	+2.75
November	1-19	5.3	-16.80
December	1-18	5.6	-3.00
January	3-14	21.4	+6.00
February	2-18	11.1	-8.75
March	3-17	17.6	+0.50
April	1-12	8.3	+7.00

DISTANCE

Hurdles	W-R	Per cent	£1 Level Stake
2m-2m3f	5-33	15.2	+0.75
2m4f-2m7f	1-23	4.3	-4.00
3m+	2-6	33.3	+2.75

Chases	W-R	Per cent	£1 Level Stake
2m-2m3f	3-22	13.6	-14.82
2m4f-2m7f	2-18	11.1	+4.00
3m+	1-10	10.0	+2.00

TYPE OF RACE

Non-Handicaps	W-R	Per cent	£1 Level Stake
Nov Hrdls	4-22	18.2	0.00
Hrdls	1-18	5.6	-5.00
Nov Chs	2-7	28.6	-1.52
Chases	0-2	0.0	-2.00
Sell/Claim	0-0	0.0	0.00

Handicaps	W-R	Per cent	£1 Level Stake
Nov Hrdls	1-7	14.3	-1.50
Hrdls	5-31	16.1	+9.00
Nov Chs	6-17	35.3	+17.95
Chases	3-38	7.9	-13.50
Sell/Claim	0-0	0.0	0.00

RACE CLASS

	W-R	Per cent	£1 Level Stake
Class 1	0-10	0.0	-10.00
Class 2	1-6	16.7	+1.00
Class 3	4-45	8.9	-16.75
Class 4	15-64	23.4	+32.18
Class 5	2-21	9.5	-7.00
Class 6	1-5	20.0	-0.67

FIRST TIME OUT

	W-R	Per cent	£1 Level Stake
Bumpers	1-6	16.7	-1.67
Hurdles	2-19	10.5	-2.75
Chases	2-11	18.2	+7.25
Totals	5-36	13.9	+2.83

JOCKEYS

	W-R	Per cent	£1 Level Stake
Gavin Sheehan	12-48	25.0	+21.23
Jason Maguire	2-4	50.0	+13.20
Mr H A A Bannister	2-12	16.7	-3.92
Tommy Dowling	2-22	9.1	-11.50
Noel Fehily	2-29	6.9	-23.25
Daryl Jacob	1-3	33.3	+4.00
Richie McLernon	1-3	33.3	+10.00
James Davies	1-4	25.0	+15.00

COURSE RECORD

	Total W-R	Non-Hndcps Hurdles	Non-Hndcps Chases	Hndcps Hurdles	Hndcps Chases	NH Flat	Per cent	£1 Level Stake
Uttoxeter	4-9	1-3	0-1	3-5	0-0	0-0	44.4	+11.75
Musselbgh	2-3	1-2	1-1	0-0	0-0	0-0	66.7	+13.75
Stratford	2-5	0-0	0-0	1-2	1-3	0-0	40.0	+2.00
Plumpton	2-6	1-1	0-0	0-1	1-4	0-0	33.3	+14.50
Southwell	2-8	1-5	0-0	0-1	1-2	0-0	25.0	+0.25
Fontwell	2-13	0-3	1-1	1-5	0-3	0-1	15.4	-6.27
Catterick	1-2	0-0	0-0	0-0	1-2	0-0	50.0	+1.00
Leicester	1-2	0-0	0-0	0-0	1-2	0-0	50.0	+13.00
Huntingdon	1-3	0-0	0-0	0-1	1-2	0-0	33.3	+1.00
Mrket Rsn	1-4	0-0	0-0	1-1	0-3	0-0	25.0	+15.00
Taunton	1-4	0-2	0-0	0-0	1-2	0-0	25.0	-1.80
Bangor	1-5	0-1	0-1	0-1	1-2	0-0	20.0	+7.00
Nton Abbot	1-5	0-0	0-0	0-2	0-1	1-2	20.0	-0.67

Ffos Las	1-6	1-1	0-0	0-5	0-0	0-0	16.7	-2.75
Warwick	1-7	0-2	0-1	0-1	1-3	0-0	14.3	0.00

WINNING HORSES

Horse	Races Run	1st	2nd	3rd	£
Seventh Sky	16	5	6	1	42623
Superb Story	4	1	0	0	9747
Cody Wyoming	7	3	3	0	20626
Verano	7	2	0	1	9375
Elmore Back	2	1	0	0	4549
Sureness	10	4	0	0	13646
Sands Cove	8	1	1	1	3899
Big Jer	1	1	0	0	3798
Western King	7	1	0	1	3422
Area Access	3	1	1	0	3249
*Libeccio	7	1	1	1	3249
*Bridal Suite	8	1	1	0	2599
Latelo	1	1	0	0	2053
Total winning prize-money					**£122835**
Favourites	**6-9**		**66.7%**		**8.18**

MRS JULIE MANSELL

DURSLEY, GLOUCS

	No. of Hrs	Races Run	1st	2nd	3rd	Unpl	Per cent	£1 Level Stake
NH Flat	*0*	*0*	*0*	*0*	*0*	*0*	*0.0*	*0.00*
Hurdles	*0*	*0*	*0*	*0*	*0*	*0*	*0.0*	*0.00*
Chases	*3*	*7*	*1*	*1*	*0*	*5*	*14.3*	*0.00*
Totals	**3**	**7**	**1**	**1**	**0**	**5**	**14.3**	**0.00**
13-14	*4*	*8*	*0*	*0*	*2*	*6*	*0.0*	*-8.00*
12-13	*6*	*13*	*0*	*2*	*3*	*8*	*0.0*	*-13.00*

JOCKEYS

	W-R	Per cent	£1 Level Stake
Mr D Mansell	1-6	16.7	+1.00

COURSE RECORD

	Total W-R	Non-Hndcps Hurdles	Non-Hndcps Chases	Hndcps Hurdles	Hndcps Chases	NH Flat	Per cent	£1 Level Stake
Nton Abbot	1-1	0-0	0-0	0-0	1-1	0-0	100.0	+6.00

WINNING HORSES

Horse	Races Run	1st	2nd	3rd	£
Swallows Delight	4	1	0	0	3743
Total winning prize-money					**£3743**
Favourites	**0-0**		**0.0%**		**0.00**

MISS NICKY MARTIN

MINEHEAD, SOMERSET

	No. of Hrs	Races Run	1st	2nd	3rd	Unpl	Per cent	£1 Level Stake
NH Flat	*0*	*0*	*0*	*0*	*0*	*0*	*0.0*	*0.00*
Hurdles	*0*	*0*	*0*	*0*	*0*	*0*	*0.0*	*0.00*
Chases	*2*	*7*	*1*	*0*	*1*	*5*	*14.3*	*-3.00*
Totals	**2**	**7**	**1**	**0**	**1**	**5**	**14.3**	**-3.00**

JOCKEYS

	W-R	Per cent	£1 Level Stake
Mr D Edwards	1-5	20.0	-1.00

COURSE RECORD

	Total W-R	Non-Hndcps Hurdles	Non-Hndcps Chases	Hndcps Hurdles	Hndcps Chases	NH Flat	Per cent	£1 Level Stake
Exeter	1-2	0-0	1-2	0-0	0-0	0-0	50.0	+2.00

WINNING HORSES

Horse	Races Run	1st	2nd	3rd	£
Bradley Brook	3	1	0	1	1996
Total winning prize-money					**£1996**
Favourites	**0-0**		**0.0%**		**0.00**

JENNIFER MASON

ABLINGTON, GLOUCS

	No. of Hrs	Races Run	1st	2nd	3rd	Unpl	Per cent	£1 Level Stake
NH Flat	*2*	*2*	*0*	*0*	*1*	*1*	*0.0*	*-2.00*
Hurdles	*1*	*3*	*0*	*0*	*0*	*3*	*0.0*	*-3.00*
Chases	*1*	*6*	*1*	*1*	*1*	*3*	*16.7*	*-3.00*
Totals	**3**	**11**	**1**	**1**	**2**	**7**	**9.1**	**-8.00**
13-14	*5*	*15*	*0*	*2*	*1*	*12*	*0.0*	*-15.00*
12-13	*7*	*26*	*0*	*3*	*5*	*18*	*0.0*	*-26.00*

JOCKEYS

	W-R	Per cent	£1 Level Stake
James Davies	1-1	100.0	+2.00

COURSE RECORD

	Total W-R	Non-Hndcps Hurdles	Non-Hndcps Chases	Hndcps Hurdles	Hndcps Chases	NH Flat	Per cent	£1 Level Stake
Taunton	1-4	0-1	0-0	0-0	1-2	0-1	25.0	-1.00

WINNING HORSES

Horse	Races Run	1st	2nd	3rd	£
*Shy John	6	1	1	1	4327
Total winning prize-money					**£4327**
Favourites	**0-1**		**0.0%**		**-1.00**

G C MAUNDRELL

OGBOURNE ST ANDREW, WILTS

	No. of Hrs	Races Run	1st	2nd	3rd	Unpl	Per cent	£1 Level Stake
NH Flat	*1*	*3*	*2*	*0*	*0*	*1*	*66.7*	*+81.00*
Hurdles	*1*	*6*	*1*	*1*	*1*	*3*	*16.7*	*-1.50*
Chases	*0*	*0*	*0*	*0*	*0*	*0*	*0.0*	*0.00*
Totals	**1**	**9**	**3**	**1**	**1**	**4**	**33.3**	**+79.50**
13-14	*2*	*7*	*0*	*0*	*0*	*7*	*0.0*	*-7.00*
12-13	*2*	*4*	*0*	*0*	*0*	*4*	*0.0*	*-4.00*

JOCKEYS

	W-R	Per cent	£1 Level Stake
Mr Z Baker	3-5	60.0	+83.50

COURSE RECORD

	Total W-R	Non-Hndcps Hurdles	Non-Hndcps Chases	Hndcps Hurdles	Hndcps Chases	NH Flat	Per cent	£1 Level Stake
Uttoxeter	1-1	0-0	0-0	1-1	0-0	0-0	100.0	+3.50
Ffos Las	1-2	0-0	0-0	0-1	0-0	1-1	50.0	+65.00
Plumpton	1-3	0-1	0-0	0-1	0-0	1-1	33.3	+14.00

WINNING HORSES

Horse	Races Run	1st	2nd	3rd	£
Tambura	9	3	1	1	5866
Total winning prize-money					**£5866**
Favourites	**0-1**		**0.0%**		**-1.00**

ALAN McCABE

BISHOP'S CASTLE, SHROPSHIRE

	No. of Hrs	Races Run	1st	2nd	3rd	Unpl	Per cent	£1 Level Stake
NH Flat	*4*	*5*	*1*	*0*	*2*	*2*	*20.0*	*-0.50*
Hurdles	*6*	*14*	*1*	*1*	*2*	*10*	*7.1*	*-3.00*
Chases	*3*	*5*	*1*	*1*	*0*	*3*	*20.0*	*+0.50*
Totals	**12**	**24**	**3**	**2**	**4**	**15**	**12.5**	**-3.00**
13-14	*2*	*2*	*1*	*0*	*1*	*0*	*50.0*	*+3.00*
12-13	*2*	*4*	*0*	*0*	*0*	*4*	*0.0*	*-4.00*

JOCKEYS

	W-R	Per cent	£1 Level Stake
Nico de Boinville	2-7	28.6	+8.50
Noel Fehily	1-1	100.0	+4.50

COURSE RECORD

	Total W-R	Non-Hndcps Hurdles	Non-Hndcps Chases	Hndcps Hurdles	Hndcps Chases	NH Flat	Per cent	£1 Level Stake
Catterick	1-1	0-0	0-0	0-0	0-0	1-1	100.0	+3.50
Doncaster	1-1	0-0	0-0	1-1	0-0	0-0	100.0	+10.00
Southwell	1-3	0-1	0-0	0-0	1-1	0-1	33.3	+2.50

WINNING HORSES

Horse	Races Run	1st	2nd	3rd	£
*Hi Vic	2	1	1	0	3899
*Old Pride	3	1	0	2	3249
Midnight Tour	1	1	0	0	1949
Total winning prize-money					**£9097**
Favourites	**0-1**		**0.0%**		**-1.00**

DONALD McCAIN

CHOLMONDELEY, CHESHIRE

	No. of Hrs	Races Run	1st	2nd	3rd	Unpl	Per cent	£1 Level Stake
NH Flat	*43*	*64*	*8*	*9*	*12*	*35*	*12.5*	*-32.55*
Hurdles	*137*	*417*	*64*	*66*	*60*	*227*	*15.3*	*-159.47*
Chases	*67*	*208*	*27*	*21*	*32*	*128*	*13.0*	*-80.28*
Totals	**192**	**689**	**99**	**96**	**104**	**390**	**14.4**	**-272.30**
13-14	*196*	*773*	*140*	*117*	*110*	*406*	*18.1*	*-150.72*
12-13	*195*	*727*	*147*	*115*	*95*	*370*	*20.2*	*-187.07*

BY MONTH

NH Flat	W-R	Per cent	£1 Level Stake	Hurdles	W-R	Per cent	£1 Level Stake
May	1-4	25.0	0.00	May	14-50	28.0	-8.18
June	0-3	0.0	-3.00	June	2-25	8.0	-22.46
July	1-6	16.7	-3.63	July	7-26	26.9	-6.72
August	0-2	0.0	-2.00	August	3-21	14.3	-8.50
September	0-1	0.0	-1.00	September	2-23	8.7	-17.71
October	0-8	0.0	-8.00	October	5-38	13.2	-18.84
November	1-7	14.3	-2.50	November	5-32	15.6	-13.48
December	1-7	14.3	-5.43	December	7-34	20.6	-6.93
January	0-6	0.0	-6.00	January	5-35	14.3	+11.80
February	3-6	50.0	+6.50	February	8-53	15.1	-21.07
March	1-12	8.3	-5.50	March	4-45	8.9	-29.88
April	0-2	0.0	-2.00	April	2-35	5.7	-17.50

Chases	W-R	Per cent	£1 Level Stake	Totals	W-R	Per cent	£1 Level Stake
May	2-21	9.5	-14.50	May	17-75	22.7	-22.68
June	2-6	33.3	+6.50	June	4-34	11.8	-18.96
July	4-13	30.8	+11.88	July	12-45	26.7	+1.53
August	1-6	16.7	-1.00	August	4-29	13.8	-11.50
September	1-8	12.5	-6.27	September	3-32	9.4	-24.98
October	2-34	5.9	-28.67	October	7-80	8.8	-55.51
November	1-11	9.1	-9.67	November	7-50	14.0	-25.65
December	1-25	4.0	-15.00	December	9-66	13.6	-27.36
January	7-22	31.8	+2.57	January	12-63	19.0	+8.37
February	0-22	0.0	-22.00	February	11-81	13.6	-36.57
March	3-18	16.7	+0.38	March	8-75	10.7	-35.00
April	3-22	13.6	-4.50	April	5-59	8.5	-24.00

DISTANCE

Hurdles	W-R	Per cent	£1 Level Stake	Chases	W-R	Per cent	£1 Level Stake
2m-2m3f	32-219	14.6	-110.63	2m-2m3f	4-56	7.1	-43.40
2m4f-2m7f	18-97	18.6	-40.14	2m4f-2m7f	15-59	25.4	+26.33
3m+	5-30	16.7	-9.70	3m+	7-50	14.0	-23.72

TYPE OF RACE

Non-Handicaps	W-R	Per cent	£1 Level Stake	Handicaps	W-R	Per cent	£1 Level Stake
Nov Hrdls	35-134	26.1	-34.06	Nov Hrdls	2-21	9.5	-6.00
Hrdls	15-88	17.0	-16.41	Hrdls	10-167	6.0	-107.00
Nov Chs	7-43	16.3	-26.28	Nov Chs	8-60	13.3	-14.63
Chases	0-2	0.0	-2.00	Chases	12-103	11.7	-37.38
Sell/Claim	1-6	16.7	+1.00	Sell/Claim	0-1	0.0	-1.00

RACE CLASS

	W-R	Per cent	£1 Level Stake
Class 1	0-30	0.0	-30.00
Class 2	4-44	9.1	-3.50
Class 3	10-134	7.5	-87.17
Class 4	63-344	18.3	-111.02
Class 5	16-88	18.2	-16.69
Class 6	6-49	12.2	-23.93

FIRST TIME OUT

	W-R	Per cent	£1 Level Stake
Bumpers	6-43	14.0	-19.55
Hurdles	14-103	13.6	-42.13
Chases	4-46	8.7	-32.17
Totals	24-192	12.5	-93.85

JOCKEYS

	W-R	Per cent	£1 Level Stake
Jason Maguire	31-208	14.9	-69.90
Wilson Renwick	23-159	14.5	-58.82
A P McCoy	16-52	30.8	+1.39
James Cowley	9-61	14.8	-26.25
Noel Fehily	5-23	21.7	-9.97
Sam Twiston-Davies	4-19	21.1	-1.25
Henry Brooke	4-27	14.8	-7.00
Nick Slatter	3-20	15.0	-5.75
Adrian Lane	2-61	3.3	-48.00
Bridget Andrews	1-1	100.0	+1.25
Wayne Hutchinson	1-13	7.7	-3.00

COURSE RECORD

	Total W-R	Non-Hndcps Hurdles	Non-Hndcps Chases	Hndcps Hurdles	Hndcps Chases	NH Flat	Per cent	£1 Level Stake
Sedgefield	12-59	7-24	0-1	2-14	2-13	1-7	20.3	-15.06
Bangor	12-65	7-21	2-5	0-18	2-12	1-9	18.5	-6.88
Cartmel	8-24	4-9	1-2	3-8	0-5	0-0	33.3	+0.86
Kelso	8-36	3-14	1-3	1-8	3-10	0-1	22.2	+0.58
Carlisle	8-40	4-15	0-3	0-8	3-9	1-5	20.0	-8.19
Perth	7-38	3-14	0-1	1-10	2-10	1-3	18.4	-10.30
Worcester	6-29	3-10	1-2	1-10	1-4	0-3	20.7	-5.07
Musselbgh	6-36	3-10	0-1	0-12	1-10	2-3	16.7	-15.70
Ayr	5-23	2-6	1-1	0-4	1-8	1-4	21.7	-2.93
Newcastle	5-26	3-12	0-1	0-3	2-6	0-4	19.2	-4.70
Catterick	5-33	3-13	0-2	1-8	0-5	1-5	15.2	-12.35
Hexham	3-25	3-13	0-1	0-7	0-2	0-2	12.0	-21.15
Uttoxeter	3-41	2-15	1-5	0-10	0-5	0-6	7.3	-25.25
Mrket Rsn	2-20	1-3	0-3	0-8	1-4	0-2	10.0	-5.75
Aintree	2-33	2-7	0-2	0-9	0-14	0-1	6.1	-26.67
Fontwell	1-2	0-0	0-0	0-1	1-1	0-0	50.0	+3.50
Huntingdon	1-5	1-3	0-0	0-1	0-1	0-0	20.0	+2.00
Sandown	1-9	0-1	0-1	1-4	0-3	0-0	11.1	+6.00
Doncaster	1-12	0-4	0-1	1-5	0-1	0-1	8.3	-3.00
Southwell	1-12	0-4	0-2	0-3	1-3	0-0	8.3	-8.50
Haydock	1-17	1-3	0-0	0-6	0-6	0-2	5.9	-14.75
Wetherby	1-31	0-10	0-2	1-11	0-6	0-2	3.2	-26.00

WINNING HORSES

Horse	Races Run	1st	2nd	3rd	£
Dispour	4	1	0	0	18768
The Last Samuri	6	3	2	0	28680
Witness In Court	5	1	0	0	15698
Diocles	4	1	0	1	14876
Oscatara	6	1	1	1	6963
Abbey Storm	2	1	0	1	6657
Sir Mangan	8	1	2	0	6657
Lively Baron	6	1	0	1	6498
Welsh Bard	8	2	3	1	9747
Ubaltique	7	1	1	2	6498
Tonvadosa	3	1	0	0	6498
Billfromthebar	2	1	1	0	6410
Kie	7	1	0	0	6330
Any Given Day	2	1	0	0	5523
Valleyofmilan	7	2	0	0	9097
Starchitect	6	2	2	0	8447
I Need Gold	4	1	0	0	4549
Degooch	10	4	1	2	14815
Silver Gent	4	1	0	0	4549
Whiskey Chaser	6	1	0	1	4224
Sealous Scout	6	1	1	1	4106
Blackwater King	6	1	0	1	3899
Mr Satco	5	1	0	3	3899
Kitchapoly	8	1	1	4	3899
Hester Flemen	2	2	0	0	5458
Three Faces West	4	3	0	0	10397
Subtle Grey	4	2	1	1	7148
Abricot De L'Oasis	6	1	1	0	3899
*Frederic	3	1	0	0	3899
Nodform Richard	3	1	0	0	3861
Up And Go	3	1	1	0	3861
Shantou Tiger	6	3	0	1	10166
Beeves	4	1	1	0	3769
Gabrial The Great	5	3	0	0	10072
Lough Derg Walk	3	2	0	0	6173
*Roserrow	5	2	0	0	6758
Right To Rule	10	1	2	2	3509
Master Dee	5	2	1	2	6172
Hellorboston	6	1	1	1	3379
Venue	3	1	2	0	3379
Mr Burgees	7	2	2	0	5491

Court Dismissed	6	1	2	2	3379
Book Of Excuses	7	2	1	2	6494
Lyric Street	4	3	1	0	8873
Trend Is My Friend	6	1	0	1	3249
Plan Again	3	1	1	0	3249
Never Never	9	1	5	0	3249
Volcanic	7	2	0	2	6498
Wilcos Mo Chara	4	1	1	0	3249
*Debdebdeb	3	1	1	1	3249
Go Conquer	4	1	1	1	3249
Jonny Eager	4	1	0	1	3249
Whatdoesthefoxsay	8	3	5	0	6498
Ardnahoe	5	2	1	0	5848
Lovely Job	4	1	0	2	3249
Gingili	3	3	0	0	7148
Red Spinner	4	2	1	0	6498
Zip Wire	4	1	0	1	2599
Nefyn Bay	6	3	0	1	7369
Mawaqeet	6	1	1	1	2555
Final Pass	1	1	0	0	2339
Ballyboker Breeze	6	1	2	3	2330
Short Takes	7	1	1	1	2274
Theatrical Style	1	1	0	0	2053
Black Jack Rover	4	1	2	0	1949
Duke Arcadio	1	1	0	0	1625
*Huehuecoytle	1	1	0	0	1560
Total winning prize-money					**£408559**
Favourites	**37-105**		**35.2%**		**-31.01**

PHIL MCENTEE

NEWMARKET, SUFFOLK

	No. of Hrs	Races Run	1st	2nd	3rd	Unpl	Per cent	£1 Level Stake
NH Flat	*0*	*0*	*0*	*0*	*0*	*0*	*0.0*	*0.00*
Hurdles	*2*	*3*	*1*	*0*	*0*	*2*	*33.3*	*-0.13*
Chases	*1*	*2*	*0*	*0*	*1*	*1*	*0.0*	*-2.00*
Totals	**3**	**5**	**1**	**0**	**1**	**3**	**20.0**	**-2.13**
13-14	6	*16*	*1*	*0*	*1*	*14*	6.3	*-3.00*
12-13	*2*	*2*	*0*	*0*	*0*	*2*	*0.0*	*-2.00*

JOCKEYS

	W-R	Per cent	£1 Level Stake
Jack Quinlan	1-3	33.3	-0.13

COURSE RECORD

	Total W-R	Non-Hndcps Hurdles	Non-Hndcps Chases	Hndcps Hurdles	Hndcps Chases	NH Flat	Per cent	£1 Level Stake
Fakenham	1-1	1-1	0-0	0-0	0-0	0-0	100.0	+1.88

WINNING HORSES

Horse	Races Run	1st	2nd	3rd	£
*Jonnie Skull	1	1	0	0	2053
Total winning prize-money					**£2053**
Favourites	**0-0**		**0.0%**		**0.00**

KAREN McLINTOCK

INGOE, NORTHUMBERLAND

	No. of Hrs	Races Run	1st	2nd	3rd	Unpl	Per cent	£1 Level Stake
NH Flat	*7*	*17*	*1*	*2*	*1*	*13*	*5.9*	*-8.00*
Hurdles	*7*	*32*	*3*	*5*	*1*	*23*	*9.4*	*-7.50*
Chases	*6*	*15*	*1*	*3*	*2*	*9*	*6.7*	*-7.50*
Totals	**15**	**64**	**5**	**10**	**4**	**45**	**7.8**	**-23.00**
13-14	*15*	*57*	*7*	*9*	*10*	*31*	*12.3*	*-26.00*
12-13	*20*	*57*	*9*	*10*	*6*	*32*	*15.8*	*-14.22*

JOCKEYS

	W-R	Per cent	£1 Level Stake
James Reveley	2-13	15.4	+3.50
Dale Irving	1-1	100.0	+7.00
Richard Johnson	1-6	16.7	+2.50
Brian Harding	1-12	8.3	-4.00

COURSE RECORD

	Total W-R	Non-Hndcps Hurdles	Non-Hndcps Chases	Hndcps Hurdles	Hndcps Chases	NH Flat	Per cent	£1 Level Stake
Kelso	3-11	0-2	0-1	2-5	1-1	0-2	27.3	+12.50
Worcester	1-2	1-1	0-0	0-0	0-1	0-0	50.0	+6.50
Hexham	1-6	0-2	0-0	0-0	0-0	1-4	16.7	+3.00

WINNING HORSES

Horse	Races Run	1st	2nd	3rd	£
Carlito Brigante	5	1	2	2	11047
Mason Hindmarsh	5	1	2	0	3899
Gurkha Brave	8	2	1	0	5198
Emperor Sakhee	3	1	0	0	1711
Total winning prize-money					**£21855**
Favourites	**0-2**		**0.0%**		**-2.00**

GRAEME McPHERSON

UPPER ODDINGTON, GLOUCS

	No. of Hrs	Races Run	1st	2nd	3rd	Unpl	Per cent	£1 Level Stake
NH Flat	*8*	*11*	*0*	*0*	*2*	*9*	*0.0*	*-11.00*
Hurdles	*28*	*112*	*8*	*10*	*20*	*74*	*7.1*	*-37.50*
Chases	*12*	*44*	*7*	*2*	*6*	*29*	*15.9*	*+27.75*
Totals	**34**	**167**	**15**	**12**	**28**	**112**	**9.0**	**-20.75**
13-14	*35*	*120*	*13*	*11*	*11*	*85*	*10.8*	*+3.13*
12-13	*39*	*108*	*7*	*12*	*14*	*75*	*6.5*	*-40.04*

BY MONTH

NH Flat	W-R	Per cent	£1 Level Stake	**Hurdles**	W-R	Per cent	£1 Level Stake
May	0-2	0.0	-2.00	May	1-14	7.1	-8.50
June	0-0	0.0	0.00	June	0-5	0.0	-5.00
July	0-0	0.0	0.00	July	1-7	14.3	+8.00

August	0-0	0.0	0.00	August	0-2	0.0	-2.00
September	0-0	0.0	0.00	September	0-1	0.0	-1.00
October	0-4	0.0	-4.00	October	2-11	18.2	+14.00
November	0-0	0.0	0.00	November	0-11	0.0	-11.00
December	0-1	0.0	-1.00	December	2-11	18.2	+0.50
January	0-0	0.0	0.00	January	0-14	0.0	-14.00
February	0-0	0.0	0.00	February	1-10	10.0	-3.50
March	0-2	0.0	-2.00	March	1-10	10.0	+1.00
April	0-2	0.0	-2.00	April	0-16	0.0	-16.00

Chases	W-R	Per cent	£1 Level Stake	Totals	W-R	Per cent	£1 Level Stake
May	0-1	0.0	-1.00	May	1-17	5.9	-11.50
June	0-3	0.0	-3.00	June	0-8	0.0	-8.00
July	1-1	100.0	+2.75	July	2-8	25.0	+10.75
August	0-1	0.0	-1.00	August	0-3	0.0	-3.00
September	0-0	0.0	0.00	September	0-1	0.0	-1.00
October	1-5	20.0	+3.00	October	3-20	15.0	+13.00
November	1-5	20.0	+29.00	November	1-16	6.3	+18.00
December	0-6	0.0	-6.00	December	2-18	11.1	-6.50
January	1-7	14.3	-1.50	January	1-21	4.8	-15.50
February	2-7	28.6	+6.50	February	3-17	17.6	+3.00
March	1-5	20.0	+2.00	March	2-17	11.8	+1.00
April	0-3	0.0	-3.00	April	0-21	0.0	-21.00

DISTANCE

Hurdles	W-R	Per cent	£1 Level Stake	Chases	W-R	Per cent	£1 Level Stake
2m-2m3f	3-35	8.6	-10.50	2m-2m3f	0-2	0.0	-2.00
2m4f-2m7f	2-37	5.4	-12.00	2m4f-2m7f	2-15	13.3	-3.25
3m+	1-15	6.7	-9.50	3m+	4-21	19.0	+30.50

TYPE OF RACE

Non-Handicaps	W-R	Per cent	£1 Level Stake	Handicaps	W-R	Per cent	£1 Level Stake
Nov Hrdls	0-21	0.0	-21.00	Nov Hrdls	3-14	21.4	+15.50
Hrdls	0-9	0.0	-9.00	Hrdls	5-64	7.8	-19.00
Nov Chs	0-0	0.0	0.00	Nov Chs	2-16	12.5	+26.00
Chases	0-0	0.0	0.00	Chases	5-28	17.9	+1.75
Sell/Claim	0-0	0.0	0.00	Sell/Claim	0-4	0.0	-4.00

RACE CLASS

	W-R	Per cent	£1 Level Stake
Class 1	0-0	0.0	0.00
Class 2	0-5	0.0	-5.00
Class 3	0-19	0.0	-19.00
Class 4	12-89	13.5	+36.25
Class 5	3-46	6.5	-25.00
Class 6	0-8	0.0	-8.00

FIRST TIME OUT

	W-R	Per cent	£1 Level Stake
Bumpers	0-8	0.0	-8.00
Hurdles	1-20	5.0	-14.50
Chases	0-6	0.0	-6.00
Totals	1-34	2.9	-28.50

JOCKEYS

	W-R	Per cent	£1 Level Stake
Ryan Hatch	4-21	19.0	+17.50
Charlie Poste	3-24	12.5	+22.50
Wayne Hutchinson	2-16	12.5	+3.00
Paul Moloney	2-30	6.7	-11.25
Aidan Coleman	1-2	50.0	+6.50
Mr M Ennis	1-3	33.3	+1.50
Gavin Sheehan	1-9	11.1	-4.00
Killian Moore	1-15	6.7	-9.50

COURSE RECORD

	Total W-R	Non-Hndcps Hurdles	Non-Hndcps Chases	Hndcps Hurdles	Hndcps Chases	NH Flat	Per cent	£1 Level Stake
Uttoxeter	3-18	0-1	0-0	3-13	0-4	0-0	16.7	+9.50
Bangor	2-15	0-3	0-0	0-5	2-3	0-4	13.3	+24.00
Exeter	1-3	0-1	0-0	1-1	0-1	0-0	33.3	+8.00
Nton Abbot	1-3	0-0	0-0	1-2	0-1	0-0	33.3	+5.00
Southwell	1-3	0-0	0-0	1-2	0-1	0-0	33.3	+1.50
Wetherby	1-3	0-0	0-0	1-3	0-0	0-0	33.3	+14.00
Haydock	1-4	0-0	0-0	0-1	1-2	0-1	25.0	+3.00
Kempton	1-4	0-1	0-0	1-3	0-0	0-0	25.0	+2.50
Ffos Las	1-6	0-0	0-0	0-2	1-4	0-0	16.7	+2.00
Mrket Rsn	1-8	0-4	0-0	0-2	1-2	0-0	12.5	+0.50
Doncaster	1-9	0-1	0-0	0-3	1-5	0-0	11.1	-3.50
Stratford	1-9	0-1	0-0	0-3	1-5	0-0	11.1	-5.25

WINNING HORSES

Horse	Races Run	1st	2nd	3rd	£
Red Admirable	9	2	0	1	11372
Achimota	7	2	1	0	10397
Our Maimie	9	2	0	2	8313
Bracken House	5	1	0	0	4549
Trillerin Minella	8	1	1	1	4549
Extreme Impact	10	1	1	1	3743
Trafficker	7	2	1	1	6021
Flying Light	8	1	0	1	3249
Kayf Blanco	7	1	3	2	3249
Phar Away Island	2	1	0	0	2339
Hollywood All Star	10	1	1	3	2209
Total winning prize-money					**£59990**
Favourites	**1-7**		**14.3%**		**-3.25**

N MECHIE

THIRSK, NORTH YORKS

	No. of Hrs	Races Run	1st	2nd	3rd	Unpl	Per cent	£1 Level Stake
NH Flat	*0*	*0*	*0*	*0*	*0*	*0*	*0.0*	*0.00*
Hurdles	*0*	*0*	*0*	*0*	*0*	*0*	*0.0*	*0.00*
Chases	*1*	*2*	*1*	*0*	*0*	*1*	*50.0*	*+8.00*
Totals	**1**	**2**	**1**	**0**	**0**	**1**	**50.0**	**+8.00**
13-14	*1*	*2*	*1*	*0*	*0*	*1*	*50.0*	*+7.00*
12-13	*1*	*2*	*1*	*0*	*0*	*1*	*50.0*	*+19.00*

JOCKEYS

	W-R	Per cent	£1 Level Stake
Miss C Walton	1-2	50.0	+8.00

COURSE RECORD

	Total W-R	Non-Hndcps Hurdles	Non-Hndcps Chases	Hndcps Hurdles	Hndcps Chases	NH Flat	Per cent	£1 Level Stake
Cheltenham	1-1	0-0	1-1	0-0	0-0	0-0	100.0	+9.00

WINNING HORSES

Horse	Races Run	1st	2nd	3rd	£
Ockey De Neulliac	2	1	0	0	2184
Total winning prize-money					**£2184**
Favourites	**0-0**		**0.0%**		**0.00**

REBECCA MENZIES

STEARSBY, N YORKS

	No. of Hrs	Races Run	1st	2nd	3rd	Unpl	Per cent	£1 Level Stake
NH Flat	*2*	*2*	*0*	*0*	*0*	*2*	*0.0*	*-2.00*
Hurdles	*14*	*39*	*0*	*3*	*2*	*34*	*0.0*	*-39.00*
Chases	*12*	*51*	*7*	*7*	*9*	*28*	*13.7*	*+14.50*
Totals	**21**	**92**	**7**	**10**	**11**	**64**	**7.6**	**-26.50**
13-14	*12*	*47*	*6*	*8*	*7*	*26*	*12.8*	*-3.93*

JOCKEYS

	W-R	Per cent	£1 Level Stake
Tony Kelly	5-73	6.8	-23.50
Henry Brooke	2-6	33.3	+10.00

COURSE RECORD

	Total W-R	Non-Hndcps Hurdles	Non-Hndcps Chases	Hndcps Hurdles	Hndcps Chases	NH Flat	Per cent	£1 Level Stake
Musselbgh	2-5	0-1	0-0	0-1	2-3	0-0	40.0	+29.00
Perth	1-2	0-0	0-0	0-1	1-1	0-0	50.0	+1.50
Newcastle	1-4	0-0	0-0	0-0	1-4	0-0	25.0	+4.00
Wetherby	1-6	0-1	0-0	0-3	1-2	0-0	16.7	+2.00
Ayr	1-8	0-1	0-0	0-0	1-7	0-0	12.5	-4.00
Hexham	1-17	0-4	0-1	0-2	1-9	0-1	5.9	-9.00

WINNING HORSES

Horse	Races Run	1st	2nd	3rd	£
Royal Macnab	9	3	1	1	17069
Chavoy	8	2	2	2	10554
Revolutionary Road	2	1	0	0	5198
Mister Wall Street	5	1	0	2	2599
Total winning prize-money					**£35420**
Favourites	**1-4**		**25.0%**		**0.00**

PHIL MIDDLETON

DORTON, BUCKS

	No. of Hrs	Races Run	1st	2nd	3rd	Unpl	Per cent	£1 Level Stake
NH Flat	*1*	*1*	*0*	*0*	*0*	*1*	*0.0*	*-1.00*
Hurdles	*7*	*29*	*5*	*2*	*2*	*20*	*17.2*	*-2.92*
Chases	*3*	*14*	*4*	*1*	*1*	*8*	*28.6*	*+20.00*
Totals	**9**	**44**	**9**	**3**	**3**	**29**	**20.5**	**+16.08**
13-14	*8*	*49*	*7*	*5*	*6*	*31*	*14.3*	*-14.08*
12-13	*8*	*54*	*6*	*11*	*6*	*31*	*11.1*	*-5.00*

JOCKEYS

	W-R	Per cent	£1 Level Stake
Conor Shoemark	2-5	40.0	+7.00
Harry Haynes	2-7	28.6	+11.00
Kielan Woods	2-9	22.2	+7.00
Richard Johnson	1-2	50.0	+4.50
Mr Charlie Deutsch	1-2	50.0	+2.33
Ryan Hatch	1-6	16.7	-2.75

COURSE RECORD

	Total W-R	Non-Hndcps Hurdles	Non-Hndcps Chases	Hndcps Hurdles	Hndcps Chases	NH Flat	Per cent	£1 Level Stake
Uttoxeter	3-8	0-1	0-0	2-3	1-4	0-0	37.5	+10.50
Sandown	2-3	0-0	0-1	1-1	1-1	0-0	66.7	+9.33
Doncaster	1-2	0-0	0-0	0-1	1-1	0-0	50.0	+8.00
Mrket Rsn	1-2	0-0	0-0	1-2	0-0	0-0	50.0	+5.00
Southwell	1-3	0-0	0-0	0-2	1-1	0-0	33.3	+6.00
Towcester	1-4	0-0	0-0	1-2	0-1	0-1	25.0	-0.75

WINNING HORSES

Horse	Races Run	1st	2nd	3rd	£
*Tales Of Milan	8	2	1	0	28923
Exitas	8	3	1	1	35823
Refer	4	1	0	0	6256
Alwaystheoptimist	2	1	0	0	3798
Sail And Return	6	1	0	1	3769
*Con Forza	9	1	1	1	1949
Total winning prize-money					**£80518**
Favourites	**2-4**		**50.0%**		**3.58**

ANTHONY MIDDLETON

CULWORTH, OXON

	No. of Hrs	Races Run	1st	2nd	3rd	Unpl	Per cent	£1 Level Stake
NH Flat	*2*	*4*	*1*	*0*	*0*	*3*	*25.0*	*+47.00*
Hurdles	*18*	*88*	*7*	*6*	*10*	*65*	*8.0*	*-48.75*
Chases	*8*	*25*	*1*	*5*	*5*	*14*	*4.0*	*-16.00*
Totals	**22**	**117**	**9**	**11**	**15**	**82**	**7.7**	**-17.75**
13-14	*30*	*139*	*6*	*24*	*12*	*97*	*4.3*	*-90.75*
12-13	*26*	*119*	*7*	*7*	*16*	*89*	*5.9*	*-62.50*

JOCKEYS

	W-R	Per cent	£1 Level Stake
James Banks	4-33	12.1	-14.25
Paddy Brennan	1-2	50.0	+2.00
Jake Greenall	1-2	50.0	+49.00
Kielan Woods	1-6	16.7	-2.50

Mr Charlie Deutsch	1-8	12.5	+1.00
Sean Quinlan	1-31	3.2	-18.00

COURSE RECORD

	Total W-R	Non-Hndcps Hurdles	Non-Hndcps Chases	Hndcps Hurdles	Hndcps Chases	NH Flat	Per cent	£1 Level Stake
Towcester	3-8	0-1	0-0	2-4	1-3	0-0	37.5	+19.00
Exeter	1-1	0-0	0-0	1-1	0-0	0-0	100.0	+1.75
Ludlow	1-6	0-1	0-0	1-5	0-0	0-0	16.7	-2.00
Fontwell	1-7	0-0	0-0	1-5	0-2	0-0	14.3	-2.00
Fakenham	1-9	0-2	0-0	1-5	0-1	0-1	11.1	-3.00
Uttoxeter	1-12	1-3	0-0	0-7	0-2	0-0	8.3	-8.50
Stratford	1-13	0-2	0-0	0-8	0-2	1-1	7.7	+38.00

WINNING HORSES

Horse	Races Run	1st	2nd	3rd	£
American Life	12	3	1	2	10229
Cafe Au Lait	12	1	1	2	6330
Future Security	6	1	0	1	3899
Unknown Legend	12	1	2	3	3899
Lough Coi	3	1	0	1	2144
*An Capall Mor	5	1	0	1	1949
Carnaross	7	1	0	1	1560
Total winning prize-money					**£30010**
Favourites	**2-7**		**28.6%**		**-0.25**

NICK MITCHELL

PIDDLETRENTHIDE, DORSET

	No. of Hrs	Races Run	1st	2nd	3rd	Unpl	Per cent	£1 Level Stake
NH Flat	*2*	*3*	*0*	*0*	*0*	*3*	*0.0*	*-3.00*
Hurdles	*7*	*18*	*1*	*1*	*3*	*13*	*5.6*	*-12.50*
Chases	*6*	*22*	*5*	*4*	*2*	*11*	*22.7*	*+28.58*
Totals	**13**	**43**	**6**	**5**	**5**	**27**	**14.0**	**+13.08**
13-14	*11*	*49*	*1*	*3*	*4*	*41*	*2.0*	*-41.50*
12-13	*18*	*60*	*2*	*6*	*7*	*45*	*3.3*	*-24.00*

JOCKEYS

	W-R	Per cent	£1 Level Stake
Daryl Jacob	2-4	50.0	+17.33
Tom Scudamore	2-9	22.2	+17.00
Gavin Sheehan	1-3	33.3	+2.50
Nick Scholfield	1-9	11.1	-5.75

COURSE RECORD

	Total W-R	Non-Hndcps Hurdles	Non-Hndcps Chases	Hndcps Hurdles	Hndcps Chases	NH Flat	Per cent	£1 Level Stake
Stratford	1-1	0-0	0-0	1-1	0-0	0-0	100.0	+4.50
Towcester	1-1	0-0	0-0	0-0	1-1	0-0	100.0	+16.00
Ascot	1-2	0-0	0-1	0-0	1-1	0-0	50.0	+2.33
Ffos Las	1-3	0-0	0-0	0-0	1-3	0-0	33.3	+2.00
Newbury	1-4	0-0	0-0	0-0	1-4	0-0	25.0	+17.00
Wincanton	1-6	0-3	0-0	0-1	1-2	0-0	16.7	-2.75

WINNING HORSES

Horse	Races Run	1st	2nd	3rd	£
Dance Floor King	4	3	0	1	18351
Phone Home	11	2	3	0	10722
Solitairy Girl	8	1	0	3	1949
Total winning prize-money					**£31022**
Favourites	**0-2**		**0.0%**		**-2.00**

RICHARD MITCHELL

PIDDLETRENTHIDE, DORSET

	No. of Hrs	Races Run	1st	2nd	3rd	Unpl	Per cent	£1 Level Stake
NH Flat	*0*	*0*	*0*	*0*	*0*	*0*	*0.0*	*0.00*
Hurdles	*3*	*20*	*3*	*4*	*1*	*12*	*15.0*	*+19.00*
Chases	*0*	*0*	*0*	*0*	*0*	*0*	*0.0*	*0.00*
Totals	**3**	**20**	**3**	**4**	**1**	**12**	**15.0**	**+19.00**
13-14	*6*	*22*	*1*	*0*	*2*	*19*	*4.5*	*-17.67*
12-13	*9*	*34*	*2*	*4*	*5*	*23*	*5.9*	*+3.00*

JOCKEYS

	W-R	Per cent	£1 Level Stake
Tom Bellamy	3-6	50.0	+33.00

COURSE RECORD

	Total W-R	Non-Hndcps Hurdles	Non-Hndcps Chases	Hndcps Hurdles	Hndcps Chases	NH Flat	Per cent	£1 Level Stake
Exeter	2-4	0-0	0-0	2-4	0-0	0-0	50.0	+30.00
Wincanton	1-5	0-2	0-0	1-3	0-0	0-0	20.0	0.00

WINNING HORSES

Horse	Races Run	1st	2nd	3rd	£
Thundering Home	10	3	2	0	12996
Total winning prize-money					**£12996**
Favourites	**0-2**		**0.0%**		**-2.00**

JAMES MOFFATT

CARTMEL, CUMBRIA

	No. of Hrs	Races Run	1st	2nd	3rd	Unpl	Per cent	£1 Level Stake
NH Flat	*0*	*0*	*0*	*0*	*0*	*0*	*0.0*	*0.00*
Hurdles	*15*	*74*	*5*	*8*	*6*	*55*	*6.8*	*-28.00*
Chases	*5*	*20*	*2*	*2*	*2*	*14*	*10.0*	*-13.50*
Totals	**17**	**94**	**7**	**10**	**8**	**69**	**7.4**	**-41.50**
13-14	*23*	*101*	*7*	*16*	*13*	*65*	*6.9*	*-64.50*
12-13	*20*	*68*	*7*	*9*	*5*	*47*	*10.3*	*+20.41*

JOCKEYS

	W-R	Per cent	£1 Level Stake
Brian Hughes	4-41	9.8	-5.00
Tony Kelly	3-24	12.5	-7.50

COURSE RECORD

	Total W-R	Non-Hndcps Hurdles	Non-Hndcps Chases	Hndcps Hurdles	Hndcps Chases	NH Flat	Per cent	£1 Level Stake
Ayr	2-7	0-0	0-0	0-4	2-3	0-0	28.6	-0.50
Cartmel	2-20	1-4	0-4	1-8	0-4	0-0	10.0	-4.50
Musselbgh	1-3	0-0	0-0	1-3	0-0	0-0	33.3	+12.00
Wetherby	1-3	0-0	0-0	1-2	0-1	0-0	33.3	+7.00
Kelso	1-11	0-2	0-0	1-9	0-0	0-0	9.1	-5.50

WINNING HORSES

Horse	Races Run	1st	2nd	3rd	£
Smart Ruler	5	2	0	2	19494
Redpender	9	2	0	0	8543
Quel Elite	8	1	2	0	3422
Captain Brown	9	1	1	0	3249
May's Boy	5	1	1	0	2599
Total winning prize-money					**£37307**
Favourites	**1-3**		**33.3%**		**0.00**

LAURA MONGAN

EPSOM, SURREY

	No. of Hrs	Races Run	1st	2nd	3rd	Unpl	Per cent	£1 Level Stake
NH Flat	*2*	*2*	*0*	*0*	*0*	*2*	*0.0*	*-2.00*
Hurdles	*15*	*58*	*4*	*7*	*4*	*43*	*6.9*	*+19.00*
Chases	*3*	*10*	*3*	*2*	*4*	*1*	*30.0*	*+9.50*
Totals	**18**	**70**	**7**	**9**	**8**	**46**	**10.0**	**+26.50**
13-14	*18*	*63*	*2*	*6*	*10*	*45*	*3.2*	*-44.00*
12-13	*17*	*56*	*1*	*7*	*9*	*39*	*1.8*	*-35.00*

JOCKEYS

	W-R	Per cent	£1 Level Stake
Tom Cannon	7-41	17.1	+55.50

COURSE RECORD

	Total W-R	Non-Hndcps Hurdles	Non-Hndcps Chases	Hndcps Hurdles	Hndcps Chases	NH Flat	Per cent	£1 Level Stake
Worcester	3-12	0-1	0-0	2-9	1-2	0-0	25.0	+39.50
Southwell	1-1	0-0	0-0	1-1	0-0	0-0	100.0	+12.00
Kempton	1-7	0-2	0-0	0-3	1-2	0-0	14.3	+2.00
Plumpton	1-11	0-3	0-0	1-7	0-1	0-0	9.1	+6.00
Fontwell	1-16	0-1	0-0	0-13	1-1	0-1	6.3	-10.00

WINNING HORSES

Horse	Races Run	1st	2nd	3rd	£
First Avenue	9	2	0	0	11723
*Madame De Guise	5	1	1	1	4549
Cinematique	7	1	0	1	3899
*Morgan's Bay	5	2	1	2	7538
Orsm	4	1	2	0	2599
Total winning prize-money					**£30308**
Favourites	**0-0**		**0.0%**		**0.00**

GARY MOORE

LOWER BEEDING, W SUSSEX

	No. of Hrs	Races Run	1st	2nd	3rd	Unpl	Per cent	£1 Level Stake
NH Flat	*7*	*14*	*2*	*4*	*1*	*7*	*14.3*	*-7.38*
Hurdles	*70*	*188*	*20*	*16*	*22*	*130*	*10.6*	*-52.23*
Chases	*30*	*113*	*18*	*17*	*10*	*68*	*15.9*	*-40.00*
Totals	**91**	**315**	**40**	**37**	**33**	**205**	**12.7**	**-99.61**
13-14	*87*	*311*	*45*	*35*	*47*	*184*	*14.5*	*-5.20*
12-13	*78*	*272*	*33*	*35*	*21*	*183*	*12.1*	*+7.35*

BY MONTH

NH Flat	W-R	Per cent	£1 Level Stake	**Hurdles**	W-R	Per cent	£1 Level Stake
May	0-1	0.0	-1.00	May	7-25	28.0	+24.63
June	0-0	0.0	0.00	June	1-7	14.3	+1.00
July	0-1	0.0	-1.00	July	0-1	0.0	-1.00
August	1-1	100.0	+2.75	August	2-4	50.0	+9.10
September	0-0	0.0	0.00	September	0-4	0.0	-4.00
October	0-0	0.0	0.00	October	1-16	6.3	-12.75
November	1-3	33.3	-0.13	November	2-32	6.3	-26.50
December	0-2	0.0	-2.00	December	2-21	9.5	-14.59
January	0-0	0.0	0.00	January	0-15	0.0	-15.00
February	0-3	0.0	-3.00	February	1-19	5.3	+2.00
March	0-2	0.0	-2.00	March	2-27	7.4	-5.00
April	0-1	0.0	-1.00	April	2-17	11.8	-10.13

Chases	W-R	Per cent	£1 Level Stake	**Totals**	W-R	Per cent	£1 Level Stake
May	0-5	0.0	-5.00	May	7-31	22.6	+18.63
June	0-2	0.0	-2.00	June	1-9	11.1	-1.00
July	0-1	0.0	-1.00	July	0-3	0.0	-3.00
August	0-2	0.0	-2.00	August	3-7	42.9	+9.85
September	0-0	0.0	0.00	September	0-4	0.0	-4.00
October	1-10	10.0	-1.00	October	2-26	7.7	-13.75
November	2-19	10.5	-13.50	November	5-54	9.3	-40.13
December	2-14	14.3	-9.83	December	4-37	10.8	-26.42
January	3-20	15.0	+3.00	January	3-35	8.6	-12.00
February	3-10	30.0	-3.13	February	4-32	12.5	-4.13
March	4-14	28.6	+3.38	March	6-43	14.0	-3.62
April	3-16	18.8	-8.91	April	5-34	14.7	-20.04

DISTANCE

Hurdles	W-R	Per cent	£1 Level Stake	**Chases**	W-R	Per cent	£1 Level Stake
2m-2m3f	7-95	7.4	-33.10	2m-2m3f	8-36	22.2	-17.55
2m4f-2m7f	3-27	11.1	-16.13	2m4f-2m7f	1-24	4.2	-21.75
3m+	1-6	16.7	+11.00	3m+	4-30	13.3	-6.70

TYPE OF RACE

Non-Handicaps	W-R	Per cent	£1 Level Stake	**Handicaps**	W-R	Per cent	£1 Level Stake
Nov Hrdls	4-43	9.3	-25.22	Nov Hrdls	2-13	15.4	+1.25
Hrdls	1-34	2.9	-30.50	Hrdls	8-89	9.0	-9.90

Nov Chs	5-23	21.7	-4.28	Nov Chs	9-38	23.7	+4.25
Chases	1-4	25.0	-2.71	Chases	3-48	6.3	-37.25
Sell/Claim	4-7	57.1	+9.80	Sell/Claim	1-1	100.0	+3.33

RACE CLASS

	W-R	Per cent	£1 Level Stake
Class 1	2-26	7.7	-3.71
Class 2	2-26	7.7	-21.50
Class 3	8-79	10.1	-48.58
Class 4	18-130	13.8	-12.92
Class 5	9-44	20.5	-6.64
Class 6	1-10	10.0	-6.25

FIRST TIME OUT

	W-R	Per cent	£1 Level Stake
Bumpers	1-7	14.3	-4.13
Hurdles	7-65	10.8	-21.15
Chases	3-19	15.8	-6.71
Totals	11-91	12.1	-31.99

JOCKEYS

	W-R	Per cent	£1 Level Stake
Jamie Moore	18-126	14.3	-26.94
Joshua Moore	16-122	13.1	-35.97
George Gorman	3-21	14.3	-2.00
Tom Cannon	1-3	33.3	-1.70
Leighton Aspell	1-6	16.7	-2.00
Mr Joseph Akehurst	1-7	14.3	-1.00

COURSE RECORD

	Total W-R	Non-Hndcps Hurdles	Non-Hndcps Chases	Hndcps Hurdles	Hndcps Chases	NH Flat	Per cent	£1 Level Stake
Plumpton	10-52	2-14	2-3	2-19	4-15	0-1	19.2	-20.92
Fontwell	5-60	0-12	2-3	2-26	0-15	1-4	8.3	-39.60
Exeter	4-7	1-1	0-1	2-2	1-3	0-0	57.1	+12.00
Huntingdon	4-19	0-6	0-3	2-5	2-4	0-1	21.1	+14.83
Sandown	4-21	1-6	1-2	0-5	1-7	1-1	19.0	-10.96
Towcester	3-5	2-2	0-1	1-2	0-0	0-0	60.0	+15.50
Newbury	3-27	1-8	0-1	1-7	1-8	0-3	11.1	+14.00
Lingfield	2-16	0-5	1-1	0-4	1-6	0-0	12.5	-1.00
Uttoxeter	1-2	0-0	0-0	1-2	0-0	0-0	50.0	+6.00
Worcester	1-2	1-1	0-0	0-1	0-0	0-0	50.0	-0.20
Ludlow	1-3	1-3	0-0	0-0	0-0	0-0	33.3	+1.50
Chepstow	1-7	0-3	0-2	0-0	1-2	0-0	14.3	-4.75
Wincanton	1-9	0-0	0-0	0-6	1-3	0-0	11.1	-1.00

WINNING HORSES

Horse	Races Run	1st	2nd	3rd	£
Violet Dancer	7	1	1	1	88273
Sire De Grugy	5	2	0	0	87013
Leo Luna	8	3	1	0	21289
Gores Island	8	3	0	2	23791
Chris Pea Green	8	2	4	0	14486
Traffic Fluide	5	2	1	1	14486
Cabimas	3	1	0	0	6498
Baron Alco	6	1	0	1	6498
*Remind Me Later	4	2	0	0	8967
Via Sundown	5	1	0	0	4549
Ar Mad	4	1	1	0	4224
Tothemoonandback	6	3	0	0	3994
Stentorian	3	1	0	0	3899
Puisque Tu Pars	4	1	1	0	3899
Jay Are	6	2	0	1	7668
Osgood	4	2	0	0	5198
The Green Ogre	8	1	1	3	3249
Stonegate	4	1	0	0	3249
Shadarpour	1	1	0	0	3119
Ilewin For Hannah	2	1	0	0	3119
Golanova	7	1	2	0	2924
Nebula Storm	4	1	0	0	2599
Ilewindelilah	5	1	0	1	2339
While You Wait	4	2	0	0	4224
Galiotto	2	1	0	0	1949
Couloir Extreme	1	1	0	0	1949
Uptendownone	7	1	2	2	1560

Total winning prize-money **£335012**

Favourites **19-47** **40.4%** **0.94**

GEORGE MOORE

MIDDLEHAM MOOR, N YORKS

	No. of Hrs	Races Run	1st	2nd	3rd	Unpl	Per cent	£1 Level Stake
NH Flat	*4*	*5*	*0*	*0*	*0*	*5*	*0.0*	*-5.00*
Hurdles	*15*	*50*	*4*	*7*	*5*	*34*	*8.0*	*+4.50*
Chases	*3*	*12*	*2*	*1*	*1*	*8*	*16.7*	*-4.50*
Totals	**19**	**67**	**6**	**8**	**6**	**47**	**9.0**	**-5.00**
13-14	*17*	*78*	*7*	*4*	*9*	*58*	*9.0*	*-49.38*
12-13	*13*	*45*	*3*	*5*	*3*	*34*	*6.7*	*-28.25*

JOCKEYS

	W-R	Per cent	£1 Level Stake
Joseph Palmowski	2-3	66.7	+27.50
Barry Keniry	2-30	6.7	-22.50
Joe Colliver	1-15	6.7	0.00
Henry Brooke	1-19	5.3	-10.00

COURSE RECORD

	Total W-R	Non-Hndcps Hurdles	Non-Hndcps Chases	Hndcps Hurdles	Hndcps Chases	NH Flat	Per cent	£1 Level Stake
Wetherby	2-18	0-11	0-1	2-4	0-1	0-1	11.1	-4.50
Carlisle	1-4	0-2	0-0	1-2	0-0	0-0	25.0	+22.00
Hexham	1-4	0-1	0-1	0-0	1-2	0-0	25.0	-1.00
Kelso	1-4	1-2	0-0	0-0	0-1	0-1	25.0	+11.00
Southwell	1-4	0-1	1-1	0-1	0-0	0-1	25.0	+0.50

WINNING HORSES

Horse	Races Run	1st	2nd	3rd	£
Wolf Shield	8	2	1	1	10397
Cowslip	6	3	0	0	9422
Medicine Hat	4	1	2	0	3249

Total winning prize-money **£23068**

Favourites **1-2** **50.0%** **2.50**

GARETH MOORE

BRIDGEND, BRIDGEND

	No. of Hrs	Races Run	1st	2nd	3rd	Unpl	Per cent	£1 Level Stake
NH Flat	*0*	*0*	*0*	*0*	*0*	*0*	*0.0*	*0.00*
Hurdles	*0*	*0*	*0*	*0*	*0*	*0*	*0.0*	*0.00*
Chases	*3*	*6*	*2*	*1*	*0*	*3*	*33.3*	*+0.50*
Totals	**3**	**6**	**2**	**1**	**0**	**3**	**33.3**	**+0.50**

JOCKEYS

	W-R	Per cent	£1 Level Stake
Miss H Lewis	1-1	100.0	+1.75
Mr Nick Williams	1-3	33.3	+0.75

COURSE RECORD

	Total W-R	Non-Hndcps Hurdles	Non-Hndcps Chases	Hndcps Hurdles	Hndcps Chases	NH Flat	Per cent	£1 Level Stake
Cheltenham	1-2	0-0	1-2	0-0	0-0	0-0	50.0	+1.75
Stratford	1-2	0-0	1-2	0-0	0-0	0-0	50.0	+0.75

WINNING HORSES

Horse	Races Run	1st	2nd	3rd	£
Universal Soldier	4	2	1	0	9982
Total winning prize-money					**£9982**
Favourites	**1-2**		**50.0%**		**0.75**

PAUL MORGAN

YSTRAD, RHONDDA C TAFF

	No. of Hrs	Races Run	1st	2nd	3rd	Unpl	Per cent	£1 Level Stake
NH Flat	*1*	*2*	*1*	*0*	*1*	*0*	*50.0*	*+5.00*
Hurdles	*7*	*14*	*1*	*0*	*0*	*13*	*7.1*	*-3.00*
Chases	*3*	*3*	*0*	*0*	*0*	*3*	*0.0*	*-3.00*
Totals	**10**	**19**	**2**	**0**	**1**	**16**	**10.5**	**-1.00**
13-14	*2*	*2*	*0*	*0*	*0*	*2*	*0.0*	*-2.00*

JOCKEYS

	W-R	Per cent	£1 Level Stake
Conor Shoemark	1-3	33.3	+4.00
Jack Doyle	1-8	12.5	+3.00

COURSE RECORD

	Total W-R	Non-Hndcps Hurdles	Non-Hndcps Chases	Hndcps Hurdles	Hndcps Chases	NH Flat	Per cent	£1 Level Stake
Exeter	1-1	0-0	0-0	1-1	0-0	0-0	100.0	+10.00
Chepstow	1-4	0-2	0-0	0-1	0-0	1-1	25.0	+3.00

WINNING HORSES

Horse	Races Run	1st	2nd	3rd	£
Thomas Junior	6	1	0	0	3899
Potters Corner	2	1	0	1	1560
Total winning prize-money					**£5459**
Favourites	**0-19**		**0.0%**		**-19.00**

KEVIN MORGAN

GAZELEY, SUFFOLK

	No. of Hrs	Races Run	1st	2nd	3rd	Unpl	Per cent	£1 Level Stake
NH Flat	*1*	*2*	*0*	*0*	*0*	*2*	*0.0*	*-2.00*
Hurdles	*4*	*15*	*2*	*0*	*2*	*11*	*13.3*	*-3.50*
Chases	*1*	*6*	*0*	*1*	*0*	*5*	*0.0*	*-6.00*
Totals	**5**	**23**	**2**	**1**	**2**	**18**	**8.7**	**-11.50**
13-14	*4*	*17*	*1*	*0*	*2*	*14*	*5.9*	*-8.00*
12-13	*4*	*8*	*1*	*0*	*1*	*6*	*12.5*	*+26.00*

JOCKEYS

	W-R	Per cent	£1 Level Stake
Adam Wedge	2-20	10.0	-8.50

COURSE RECORD

	Total W-R	Non-Hndcps Hurdles	Non-Hndcps Chases	Hndcps Hurdles	Hndcps Chases	NH Flat	Per cent	£1 Level Stake
Wincanton	1-1	0-0	0-0	1-1	0-0	0-0	100.0	+2.50
Worcester	1-8	0-0	0-0	1-5	0-3	0-0	12.5	0.00

WINNING HORSES

Horse	Races Run	1st	2nd	3rd	£
Taaresh	6	2	0	0	8642
Total winning prize-money					**£8642**
Favourites	**1-1**		**100.0%**		**2.50**

HUGHIE MORRISON

EAST ILSLEY, BERKS

	No. of Hrs	Races Run	1st	2nd	3rd	Unpl	Per cent	£1 Level Stake
NH Flat	*3*	*4*	*0*	*0*	*0*	*4*	*0.0*	*-4.00*
Hurdles	*2*	*5*	*1*	*0*	*1*	*3*	*20.0*	*-1.00*
Chases	*0*	*0*	*0*	*0*	*0*	*0*	*0.0*	*0.00*
Totals	**5**	**9**	**1**	**0**	**1**	**7**	**11.1**	**-5.00**
13-14	*4*	*11*	*2*	*1*	*1*	*7*	*18.2*	*+3.50*
12-13	*10*	*21*	*2*	*5*	*3*	*11*	*9.5*	*-9.00*

JOCKEYS

	W-R	Per cent	£1 Level Stake
Tom O'Brien	1-8	12.5	-4.00

COURSE RECORD

	Total W-R	Non-Hndcps Hurdles	Non-Hndcps Chases	Hndcps Hurdles	Hndcps Chases	NH Flat	Per cent	£1 Level Stake
Kempton	1-1	0-0	0-0	1-1	0-0	0-0	100.0	+3.00

WINNING HORSES

Horse	Races Run	1st	2nd	3rd	£
Brother Brian	4	1	0	1	11574
Total winning prize-money					**£11574**
Favourites	**0-0**		**0.0%**		**0.00**

NEIL MULHOLLAND

LIMPLEY STOKE, WILTS

	No. of Hrs	Races Run	1st	2nd	3rd	Unpl	Per cent	£1 Level Stake
NH Flat	*11*	*13*	*4*	*1*	*1*	*7*	*30.8*	*+34.78*
Hurdles	*49*	*161*	*31*	*22*	*17*	*91*	*19.3*	*-19.07*
Chases	*25*	*88*	*16*	*15*	*8*	*49*	*18.2*	*-7.02*
Totals	**65**	**262**	**51**	**38**	**26**	**147**	**19.5**	**+8.69**
13-14	*64*	*248*	*32*	*26*	*27*	*163*	*12.9*	*-44.24*
12-13	*54*	*183*	*17*	*15*	*22*	*129*	*9.3*	*-32.33*

BY MONTH

NH Flat	W-R	Per cent	£1 Level Stake
May	0-2	0.0	-2.00
June	2-2	100.0	+40.91
July	0-0	0.0	0.00
August	0-0	0.0	0.00
September	0-0	0.0	0.00
October	0-2	0.0	-2.00
November	0-1	0.0	-1.00
December	0-3	0.0	-3.00
January	0-0	0.0	0.00
February	0-0	0.0	0.00
March	2-3	66.7	+1.88
April	0-0	0.0	0.00

Hurdles	W-R	Per cent	£1 Level Stake
May	4-23	17.4	+2.33
June	3-14	21.4	-1.25
July	1-5	20.0	-3.43
August	2-5	40.0	+3.25
September	3-10	30.0	+5.25
October	6-25	24.0	-4.21
November	3-17	17.6	-6.25
December	1-10	10.0	-7.38
January	2-14	14.3	-5.25
February	1-11	9.1	-2.00
March	4-16	25.0	+7.61
April	1-11	9.1	-7.75

Chases	W-R	Per cent	£1 Level Stake
May	0-7	0.0	-7.00
June	0-6	0.0	-6.00
July	1-6	16.7	-3.75
August	0-2	0.0	-2.00
September	2-6	33.3	+16.80
October	3-15	20.0	-0.33
November	2-8	25.0	-3.33
December	3-8	37.5	+5.73
January	1-7	14.3	-1.00
February	1-3	33.3	-0.75
March	2-12	16.7	-1.38
April	1-8	12.5	-4.00

Totals	W-R	Per cent	£1 Level Stake
May	4-32	12.5	-6.67
June	5-22	22.7	+33.66
July	2-11	18.2	-7.18
August	2-7	28.6	+1.25
September	5-16	31.3	+22.05
October	9-42	21.4	-6.54
November	5-26	19.2	-10.58
December	4-21	19.0	-4.65
January	3-21	14.3	-6.25
February	2-14	14.3	-2.75
March	8-31	25.8	+8.11
April	2-19	10.5	-11.75

DISTANCE

Hurdles	W-R	Per cent	£1 Level Stake
2m-2m3f	13-76	17.1	-15.88
2m4f-2m7f	11-48	22.9	+12.07
3m+	0-2	0.0	-2.00

Chases	W-R	Per cent	£1 Level Stake
2m-2m3f	4-19	21.1	-9.36
2m4f-2m7f	3-35	8.6	-6.20
3m+	4-18	22.2	+5.61

TYPE OF RACE

Non-Handicaps	W-R	Per cent	£1 Level Stake
Nov Hrdls	5-29	17.2	-14.74
Hrdls	1-26	3.8	-23.90
Nov Chs	3-11	27.3	-4.59
Chases	0-1	0.0	-1.00
Sell/Claim	0-2	0.0	-2.00

Handicaps	W-R	Per cent	£1 Level Stake
Nov Hrdls	5-19	26.3	+5.08
Hrdls	20-85	23.5	+16.49
Nov Chs	2-25	8.0	-15.00
Chases	11-51	21.6	+13.56
Sell/Claim	0-0	0.0	0.00

RACE CLASS

	W-R	Per cent	£1 Level Stake
Class 1	3-13	23.1	+2.25
Class 2	1-11	9.1	-8.00
Class 3	6-28	21.4	+9.29
Class 4	20-109	18.3	-29.08
Class 5	17-89	19.1	-1.56
Class 6	4-12	33.3	+35.78

FIRST TIME OUT

	W-R	Per cent	£1 Level Stake
Bumpers	4-11	36.4	+36.78
Hurdles	8-38	21.1	+8.93
Chases	2-16	12.5	-12.53
Totals	14-65	21.5	+33.18

JOCKEYS

	W-R	Per cent	£1 Level Stake
A P McCoy	11-24	45.8	+1.68
Mark Quinlan	10-72	13.9	+37.75
Michael Byrne	6-44	13.6	-23.88
Dougie Costello	5-14	35.7	+12.73
Barry Geraghty	4-9	44.4	+15.25
Conor Shoemark	4-12	33.3	+10.33
Martin McIntyre	3-17	17.6	-8.23
Daryl Jacob	2-9	22.2	+0.50
Richard Johnson	2-14	14.3	-10.18
Mr J T Carroll	1-1	100.0	+9.00
Tom Scudamore	1-3	33.3	-1.00
Noel Fehily	1-7	14.3	-3.00
Mikey Hamill	1-10	10.0	-6.25

COURSE RECORD

	Total W-R	Non-Hndcps Hurdles	Non-Hndcps Chases	Hndcps Hurdles	Hndcps Chases	NH Flat	Per cent	£1 Level Stake
Worcester	7-21	0-3	1-2	5-10	1-6	0-0	33.3	+28.05
Uttoxeter	4-19	2-7	0-0	1-7	1-5	0-0	21.1	-7.71
Fontwell	4-20	1-6	0-2	2-7	1-4	0-1	20.0	-7.08
Wetherby	3-4	0-0	1-1	1-2	0-0	1-1	75.0	+8.62
Ludlow	2-2	0-0	0-0	2-2	0-0	0-0	100.0	+4.38
Mrket Rsn	2-4	0-0	0-0	1-1	0-2	1-1	50.0	+2.41
Ascot	2-5	0-1	0-0	0-2	2-2	0-0	40.0	+1.25
Towcester	2-5	0-0	0-0	1-2	0-1	1-2	40.0	+2.88
Huntingdon	2-6	1-2	0-0	0-1	1-3	0-0	33.3	-2.72
Southwell	2-6	0-0	0-0	0-2	1-3	1-1	33.3	+38.00
Bangor	2-7	0-2	0-2	2-3	0-0	0-0	28.6	+2.33
Newbury	2-7	0-0	0-0	2-4	0-3	0-0	28.6	+8.50
Cheltenham	2-10	0-3	0-1	0-2	2-4	0-0	20.0	+9.00
Exeter	2-11	0-4	1-1	1-4	0-2	0-0	18.2	-3.50
Chepstow	2-14	1-6	0-0	1-4	0-3	0-1	14.3	-4.25

Nton Abbot	2-16	1-4	0-0	1-8	0-3	0-1	12.5	-11.18
Ffos Las	2-16	0-1	0-0	2-6	0-7	0-2	12.5	0.00
Taunton	2-24	0-2	0-1	1-14	1-7	0-0	8.3	-15.50
Sedgefield	1-1	0-0	0-0	0-0	1-1	0-0	100.0	+0.73
Lingfield	1-4	0-0	0-0	1-4	0-0	0-0	25.0	+1.00
Fakenham	1-8	0-1	0-0	1-6	0-1	0-0	12.5	-4.75
Stratford	1-13	0-5	0-1	0-1	1-5	0-1	7.7	-10.75
Wincanton	1-15	0-3	0-0	0-7	1-3	0-2	6.7	-7.00

WINNING HORSES

Horse	Races Run	1st	2nd	3rd	£
The Young Master	5	3	0	0	67792
The Druids Nephew	6	2	1	0	57912
Carole's Destrier	7	3	1	0	43574
Leave It Be	4	1	0	1	12996
Minella Definitely	6	3	0	1	17214
Barton Heather	10	3	3	0	11614
Pass The Time	5	1	1	1	6498
Isthereadifference	7	2	4	0	8123
Southfield Royale	6	3	2	0	9357
Mr Burbidge	5	2	0	1	6823
Ebony Empress	7	3	1	1	10180
Ashcott Boy	3	2	0	0	5198
Indian Stream	2	1	1	0	3249
Ni Sin E Mo Ainm	2	1	1	0	3249
Barton Rose	7	1	1	1	3249
Minella Present	6	2	1	0	5848
Commitment	5	3	1	0	9162
Another Brandy	3	1	2	0	3119
Agapanthus	4	2	0	0	5597
Ballydague Lady	10	2	1	4	4874
Jim Job Jones	6	2	0	1	4796
Langarve Lady	4	1	0	1	2599
Johns Luck	9	1	2	2	2395
Special Report	6	1	1	2	2112
Realta Mo Croi	5	1	2	0	1949
Pure Poteen	4	1	1	0	1949
Fingerontheswitch	1	1	0	0	1949
Shantou Village	1	1	0	0	1711
General Montgomery	4	1	0	0	1560
Total winning prize-money					**£316648**
Favourites	**67-97**		**69.1%**		**105.69**

LAWRENCE MULLANEY

GREAT HABTON, N YORKS

	No. of Hrs	Races Run	1st	2nd	3rd	Unpl	Per cent	£1 Level Stake
NH Flat	*2*	*4*	*1*	*0*	*1*	*2*	*25.0*	*-0.25*
Hurdles	*0*	*0*	*0*	*0*	*0*	*0*	*0.0*	*0.00*
Chases	*0*	*0*	*0*	*0*	*0*	*0*	*0.0*	*0.00*
Totals	**2**	**4**	**1**	**0**	**1**	**2**	**25.0**	**-0.25**
12-13	*2*	*2*	*0*	*0*	*0*	*2*	*0.0*	*-2.00*

JOCKEYS

	W-R	Per cent	£1 Level Stake
Brian Hughes	1-2	50.0	+1.75

COURSE RECORD

	Total W-R	Non-Hndcps Hurdles	Non-Hndcps Chases	Hndcps Hurdles	Hndcps Chases	NH Flat	Per cent	£1 Level Stake
Hexham	1-1	0-0	0-0	0-0	0-0	1-1	100.0	+2.75

WINNING HORSES

Horse	Races Run	1st	2nd	3rd	£
Kara Tara	3	1	0	1	1711
Total winning prize-money					**£1711**
Favourites	**0-0**		**0.0%**		**0.00**

MICHAEL MULLINEAUX

ALPRAHAM, CHESHIRE

	No. of Hrs	Races Run	1st	2nd	3rd	Unpl	Per cent	£1 Level Stake
NH Flat	*7*	*17*	*0*	*1*	*1*	*15*	*0.0*	*-17.00*
Hurdles	*7*	*18*	*0*	*2*	*1*	*15*	*0.0*	*-18.00*
Chases	*1*	*11*	*1*	*2*	*4*	*4*	*9.1*	*-5.00*
Totals	**14**	**46**	**1**	**5**	**6**	**34**	**2.2**	**-40.00**
13-14	*14*	*42*	*5*	*1*	*3*	*33*	*11.9*	*+59.00*
12-13	*13*	*63*	*2*	*3*	*7*	*51*	*3.2*	*-42.50*

JOCKEYS

	W-R	Per cent	£1 Level Stake
Ryan Mania	1-3	33.3	+3.00

COURSE RECORD

	Total W-R	Non-Hndcps Hurdles	Non-Hndcps Chases	Hndcps Hurdles	Hndcps Chases	NH Flat	Per cent	£1 Level Stake
Hexham	1-6	0-0	0-0	0-0	1-3	0-3	16.7	0.00

WINNING HORSES

Horse	Races Run	1st	2nd	3rd	£
Molko Jack	11	1	2	4	2395
Total winning prize-money					**£2395**
Favourites	**0-0**		**0.0%**		**0.00**

SEAMUS MULLINS

WILSFORD-CUM-LAKE, WILTS

	No. of Hrs	Races Run	1st	2nd	3rd	Unpl	Per cent	£1 Level Stake
NH Flat	*14*	*23*	*1*	*1*	*3*	*18*	*4.3*	*-15.00*
Hurdles	*36*	*118*	*9*	*19*	*11*	*79*	*7.6*	*-58.75*
Chases	*24*	*97*	*14*	*21*	*13*	*49*	*14.4*	*-11.04*

Totals	**55**	**238**	**24**	**41**	**27**	**146**	**10.1**	**-84.79**
13-14	*55*	*217*	*24*	*25*	*24*	*144*	*11.1*	*-29.82*
12-13	*56*	*179*	*20*	*23*	*19*	*117*	*11.2*	*+12.08*

BY MONTH

NH Flat	W-R	Per cent	£1 Level Stake
May	0-7	0.0	-7.00
June	0-3	0.0	-3.00
July	1-1	100.0	+7.00
August	0-1	0.0	-1.00
September	0-1	0.0	-1.00
October	0-2	0.0	-2.00
November	0-1	0.0	-1.00
December	0-1	0.0	-1.00
January	0-0	0.0	0.00
February	0-3	0.0	-3.00
March	0-1	0.0	-1.00
April	0-2	0.0	-2.00

Hurdles	W-R	Per cent	£1 Level Stake
May	0-17	0.0	-17.00
June	0-8	0.0	-8.00
July	0-8	0.0	-8.00
August	0-2	0.0	-2.00
September	0-3	0.0	-3.00
October	0-6	0.0	-6.00
November	0-12	0.0	-12.00
December	2-13	15.4	-4.00
January	3-19	15.8	+2.50
February	0-9	0.0	-9.00
March	2-11	18.2	+10.50
April	2-10	20.0	-2.75

Chases	W-R	Per cent	£1 Level Stake
May	1-13	7.7	-10.00
June	1-8	12.5	+7.00
July	0-4	0.0	-4.00
August	0-0	0.0	0.00
September	0-0	0.0	0.00
October	2-9	22.2	+8.00
November	2-12	16.7	0.00
December	3-15	20.0	-3.00
January	3-10	30.0	+9.33
February	0-6	0.0	-6.00
March	1-11	9.1	-8.38
April	1-9	11.1	-4.00

Totals	W-R	Per cent	£1 Level Stake
May	1-37	2.7	-34.00
June	1-19	5.3	-4.00
July	1-13	7.7	-5.00
August	0-3	0.0	-3.00
September	0-4	0.0	-4.00
October	2-17	11.8	0.00
November	2-25	8.0	-13.00
December	5-29	17.2	-8.00
January	6-29	20.7	+11.83
February	0-18	0.0	-18.00
March	3-23	13.0	+1.12
April	3-21	14.3	-8.75

DISTANCE

Hurdles	W-R	Per cent	£1 Level Stake
2m-2m3f	2-44	4.5	-32.00
2m4f-2m7f	0-31	0.0	-31.00
3m+	2-8	25.0	-0.75

Chases	W-R	Per cent	£1 Level Stake
2m-2m3f	6-37	16.2	-2.50
2m4f-2m7f	2-17	11.8	+9.00
3m+	3-24	12.5	-8.17

TYPE OF RACE

Non-Handicaps	W-R	Per cent	£1 Level Stake
Nov Hrdls	1-25	4.0	-21.00
Hrdls	1-23	4.3	-15.00
Nov Chs	0-6	0.0	-6.00
Chases	0-0	0.0	0.00
Sell/Claim	0-1	0.0	-1.00

Handicaps	W-R	Per cent	£1 Level Stake
Nov Hrdls	1-14	7.1	-5.00
Hrdls	6-54	11.1	-15.75
Nov Chs	3-18	16.7	+5.00
Chases	11-73	15.1	-10.04
Sell/Claim	0-1	0.0	-1.00

RACE CLASS

	W-R	Per cent	£1 Level Stake
Class 1	0-4	0.0	-4.00
Class 2	0-5	0.0	-5.00
Class 3	4-28	14.3	-1.00
Class 4	8-97	8.2	-41.38
Class 5	11-84	13.1	-21.42
Class 6	1-20	5.0	-12.00

FIRST TIME OUT

	W-R	Per cent	£1 Level Stake
Bumpers	0-14	0.0	-14.00
Hurdles	1-22	4.5	-14.00
Chases	4-19	21.1	+19.00
Totals	5-55	9.1	-9.00

JOCKEYS

	W-R	Per cent	£1 Level Stake
Andrew Thornton	16-121	13.2	-29.54
Kevin Jones	6-49	12.2	-13.25
Lt Col Erica Bridge	1-1	100.0	+16.00
Ryan Mahon	1-22	4.5	-13.00

COURSE RECORD

	Total W-R	Non-Hndcps Hurdles	Non-Hndcps Chases	Hndcps Hurdles	Hndcps Chases	NH Flat	Per cent	£1 Level Stake
Plumpton	5-34	0-3	0-2	3-12	2-15	0-2	14.7	-14.92
Southwell	3-19	0-4	0-0	0-2	2-10	1-3	15.8	-3.38
Fontwell	3-28	0-2	0-0	0-5	3-18	0-3	10.7	0.00
Sandown	2-5	0-0	0-0	2-5	0-0	0-0	40.0	+16.50
Lingfield	2-7	0-2	0-1	0-0	2-4	0-0	28.6	-0.50
Wincanton	2-23	0-5	0-0	1-11	1-6	0-1	8.7	-3.00
Stratford	1-4	0-1	0-0	0-0	1-3	0-0	25.0	+8.00
Huntingdon	1-5	0-2	0-1	1-1	0-0	0-1	20.0	0.00
Leicester	1-5	0-1	0-0	0-0	1-4	0-0	20.0	-1.00
Warwick	1-7	1-3	0-0	0-2	0-2	0-0	14.3	+1.00
Chepstow	1-9	1-2	0-0	0-2	0-4	0-1	11.1	-5.00
Exeter	1-18	0-3	0-1	0-5	1-8	0-1	5.6	-11.50
Nton Abbot	1-21	0-5	0-0	0-9	1-5	0-2	4.8	-18.00

WINNING HORSES

Horse	Races Run	1st	2nd	3rd	£
Adrenalin Flight	9	1	1	0	12558
Song Light	9	1	4	1	10010
Somchine	6	3	1	1	14815
Ultimate Act	3	2	0	1	10722
Boss In Boots	8	2	3	0	9097
Kastani Beach	8	2	1	0	6018
Miss Sassypants	7	1	0	0	3249
Sidbury Hill	5	1	2	1	3119
Sportsreport	9	2	2	1	5133
The Informant	8	1	2	2	2729
Brunette'Sonly	8	1	1	1	2663
Flugzeug	6	2	2	0	5198
Head Spin	9	2	2	3	4549
*Gizzit	6	1	2	0	2274
*Righteous Glory	2	1	0	0	2144
Bahri Sugar	3	1	0	0	1949
Total winning prize-money					**£96227**
Favourites	**4-14**		**28.6%**		**-1.75**

PAT MURPHY

EAST GARSTON, BERKS

	No. of Hrs	Races Run	1st	2nd	3rd	Unpl	Per cent	£1 Level Stake
NH Flat	*1*	*1*	*0*	*0*	*0*	*1*	*0.0*	*-1.00*
Hurdles	*1*	*4*	*0*	*1*	*0*	*3*	*0.0*	*-4.00*
Chases	*2*	*14*	*1*	*1*	*2*	*10*	*7.1*	*-9.50*
Totals	**3**	**19**	**1**	**2**	**2**	**14**	**5.3**	**-14.50**
13-14	*5*	*22*	*2*	*4*	*8*	*8*	*9.1*	*+2.50*
12-13	*4*	*14*	*1*	*2*	*1*	*10*	*7.1*	*-6.00*

JOCKEYS

	W-R	Per cent	£1 Level Stake
Leighton Aspell	1-5	20.0	-0.50

COURSE RECORD

	Total W-R	Non-Hndcps Hurdles	Non-Hndcps Chases	Hndcps Hurdles	Hndcps Chases	NH Flat	Per cent	£1 Level Stake
Mrket Rsn	1-1	0-0	0-0	0-0	1-1	0-0	100.0	+3.50

WINNING HORSES

Horse	Races Run	1st	2nd	3rd	£
Cloudy Bob	12	1	1	2	9747
Total winning prize-money					**£9747**
Favourites	**0-0**		**0.0%**		**0.00**

ANABEL K MURPHY

WILMCOTE, WARWICKS

	No. of Hrs	Races Run	1st	2nd	3rd	Unpl	Per cent	£1 Level Stake
NH Flat	*0*	*0*	*0*	*0*	*0*	*0*	*0.0*	*0.00*
Hurdles	*6*	*37*	*6*	*4*	*4*	*23*	*16.2*	*+15.25*
Chases	*1*	*1*	*0*	*0*	*0*	*1*	*0.0*	*-1.00*
Totals	**6**	**38**	**6**	**4**	**4**	**24**	**15.8**	**+14.25**
13-14	*9*	*39*	*1*	*4*	*6*	*28*	*2.6*	*-24.00*
12-13	*15*	*51*	*5*	*5*	*4*	*37*	*9.8*	*-28.75*

JOCKEYS

	W-R	Per cent	£1 Level Stake
Miss Joanna Mason	2-4	50.0	+19.50
Sam Twiston-Davies	1-3	33.3	+6.00
A P McCoy	1-4	25.0	-0.25
Noel Fehily	1-4	25.0	+5.00
Tom Scudamore	1-5	20.0	+2.00

COURSE RECORD

	Total W-R	Non-Hndcps Hurdles	Non-Hndcps Chases	Hndcps Hurdles	Hndcps Chases	NH Flat	Per cent	£1 Level Stake
Bangor	2-3	0-0	0-0	2-3	0-0	0-0	66.7	+9.75
Mrket Rsn	2-6	0-0	0-0	2-6	0-0	0-0	33.3	+17.50
Fakenham	1-1	0-0	0-0	1-1	0-0	0-0	100.0	+6.00
Lingfield	1-1	0-0	0-0	1-1	0-0	0-0	100.0	+8.00

WINNING HORSES

Horse	Races Run	1st	2nd	3rd	£
Todd	7	1	1	0	3994
Dormouse	13	2	2	4	6368
King's Road	6	2	0	0	4471
Walter De La Mare	3	1	0	0	2274
Total winning prize-money					**£17107**
Favourites	**0-0**		**0.0%**		**0.00**

BARRY MURTAGH

LOW BRAITHWAITE, CUMBRIA

	No. of Hrs	Races Run	1st	2nd	3rd	Unpl	Per cent	£1 Level Stake
NH Flat	*4*	*6*	*0*	*0*	*1*	*5*	*0.0*	*-6.00*
Hurdles	*18*	*68*	*4*	*1*	*9*	*54*	*5.9*	*-32.00*
Chases	*6*	*29*	*0*	*3*	*4*	*22*	*0.0*	*-29.00*
Totals	**22**	**103**	**4**	**4**	**14**	**81**	**3.9**	**-67.00**
13-14	*21*	*119*	*7*	*10*	*12*	*90*	*5.9*	*-13.50*
12-13	*21*	*80*	*4*	*7*	*8*	*61*	*5.0*	*-37.00*

JOCKEYS

	W-R	Per cent	£1 Level Stake
Brian Harding	3-22	13.6	+7.00
Mr L A Murtagh	1-5	20.0	+2.00

COURSE RECORD

	Total W-R	Non-Hndcps Hurdles	Non-Hndcps Chases	Hndcps Hurdles	Hndcps Chases	NH Flat	Per cent	£1 Level Stake
Sedgefield	2-16	0-0	0-0	2-10	0-4	0-2	12.5	+5.50
Newcastle	1-8	0-0	0-0	1-7	0-0	0-1	12.5	-1.00
Ayr	1-9	0-0	0-0	1-5	0-4	0-0	11.1	-1.50

WINNING HORSES

Horse	Races Run	1st	2nd	3rd	£
*Cape Arrow	7	1	0	3	2469
Jebulani	5	1	0	0	2339
Baraboy	9	1	1	1	2339
King's Chorister	10	1	0	0	2274
Total winning prize-money					**£9421**
Favourites	**0-5**		**0.0%**		**-5.00**

WILLIE MUSSON

NEWMARKET, SUFFOLK

	No. of Hrs	Races Run	1st	2nd	3rd	Unpl	Per cent	£1 Level Stake
NH Flat	*1*	*3*	*0*	*1*	*0*	*2*	*0.0*	*-3.00*
Hurdles	*4*	*17*	*3*	*2*	*2*	*10*	*17.6*	*+14.00*
Chases	*0*	*0*	*0*	*0*	*0*	*0*	*0.0*	*0.00*

Totals	**5**	**20**	**3**	**3**	**2**	**12**	**15.0**	**+11.00**
13-14	*7*	*16*	*1*	*3*	*2*	*10*	*6.3*	*+1.00*
12-13	*6*	*15*	*1*	*0*	*1*	*13*	*6.7*	*-10.00*

JOCKEYS

	W-R	Per cent	£1 Level Stake
Adam Wedge	1-1	100.0	+8.00
Aidan Coleman	1-1	100.0	+2.00
Paul Moloney	1-4	25.0	+15.00

COURSE RECORD

	Total W-R	Non-Hndcps Hurdles	Non-Hndcps Chases	Hndcps Hurdles	Hndcps Chases	NH Flat	Per cent	£1 Level Stake
Fakenham	2-3	0-0	0-0	2-3	0-0	0-0	66.7	+25.00
Southwell	1-1	1-1	0-0	0-0	0-0	0-0	100.0	+2.00

WINNING HORSES

Horse	Races Run	1st	2nd	3rd	£
Bold Adventure	6	2	0	1	10397
Broughtons Warrior	3	1	1	0	1949
Total winning prize-money					**£12346**
Favourites	**0-1**		**0.0%**		**-1.00**

HELEN NELMES

WARMWELL, DORSET

	No. of Hrs	Races Run	1st	2nd	3rd	Unpl	Per cent	£1 Level Stake
NH Flat	*3*	*5*	*0*	*0*	*0*	*5*	*0.0*	*-5.00*
Hurdles	*9*	*20*	*1*	*1*	*5*	*13*	*5.0*	*-18.39*
Chases	*1*	*2*	*0*	*0*	*0*	*2*	*0.0*	*-2.00*
Totals	**12**	**27**	**1**	**1**	**5**	**20**	**3.7**	**-25.39**
13-14	*14*	*37*	*1*	*2*	*6*	*28*	*2.7*	*-20.00*
12-13	*13*	*42*	*5*	*7*	*4*	*26*	*11.9*	*+20.00*

JOCKEYS

	W-R	Per cent	£1 Level Stake
Paul Moloney	1-7	14.3	-5.38

COURSE RECORD

	Total W-R	Non-Hndcps Hurdles	Non-Hndcps Chases	Hndcps Hurdles	Hndcps Chases	NH Flat	Per cent	£1 Level Stake
Nton Abbot	1-2	1-2	0-0	0-0	0-0	0-0	50.0	-0.39

WINNING HORSES

Horse	Races Run	1st	2nd	3rd	£
Kalmbeforethestorm	2	1	0	0	2738
Total winning prize-money					**£2738**
Favourites	**1-1**		**100.0%**		**0.61**

DR RICHARD NEWLAND

CLAINES, WORCS

	No. of Hrs	Races Run	1st	2nd	3rd	Unpl	Per cent	£1 Level Stake
NH Flat	*0*	*0*	*0*	*0*	*0*	*0*	*0.0*	*0.00*
Hurdles	*32*	*106*	*27*	*16*	*14*	*49*	*25.5*	*-1.53*
Chases	*12*	*44*	*8*	*7*	*3*	*26*	*18.2*	*-14.39*
Totals	**35**	**150**	**35**	**23**	**17**	**75**	**23.3**	**-15.92**
13-14	*25*	*168*	*40*	*22*	*24*	*82*	*23.8*	*+14.98*
12-13	*26*	*145*	*33*	*26*	*19*	*67*	*22.8*	*-12.22*

BY MONTH

NH Flat	W-R	Per cent	£1 Level Stake	Hurdles	W-R	Per cent	£1 Level Stake
May	0-0	0.0	0.00	May	2-9	22.2	-0.50
June	0-0	0.0	0.00	June	6-16	37.5	+1.15
July	0-0	0.0	0.00	July	2-13	15.4	-9.40
August	0-0	0.0	0.00	August	2-9	22.2	-4.34
September	0-0	0.0	0.00	September	3-8	37.5	-0.24
October	0-0	0.0	0.00	October	3-8	37.5	-0.50
November	0-0	0.0	0.00	November	2-9	22.2	-3.63
December	0-0	0.0	0.00	December	3-10	30.0	-4.07
January	0-0	0.0	0.00	January	1-4	25.0	-1.00
February	0-0	0.0	0.00	February	0-3	0.0	-3.00
March	0-0	0.0	0.00	March	1-10	10.0	+24.00
April	0-0	0.0	0.00	April	2-7	28.6	0.00

Chases	W-R	Per cent	£1 Level Stake	Totals	W-R	Per cent	£1 Level Stake
May	2-3	66.7	+0.28	May	4-12	33.3	-0.22
June	1-2	50.0	-0.27	June	7-18	38.9	+0.88
July	0-0	0.0	0.00	July	2-13	15.4	-9.40
August	0-0	0.0	0.00	August	2-9	22.2	-4.34
September	1-3	33.3	+6.00	September	4-11	36.4	+5.76
October	2-6	33.3	+0.50	October	5-14	35.7	0.00
November	0-4	0.0	-4.00	November	2-13	15.4	-7.63
December	1-3	33.3	-0.90	December	4-13	30.8	-4.97
January	1-3	33.3	+4.00	January	2-7	28.6	+3.00
February	0-4	0.0	-4.00	February	0-7	0.0	-7.00
March	0-5	0.0	-5.00	March	1-15	6.7	+19.00
April	0-11	0.0	-11.00	April	2-18	11.1	-11.00

DISTANCE

Hurdles	W-R	Per cent	£1 Level Stake	Chases	W-R	Per cent	£1 Level Stake
2m-2m3f	12-49	24.5	-21.66	2m-2m3f	2-9	22.2	-4.15
2m4f-2m7f	7-24	29.2	-3.28	2m4f-2m7f	3-14	21.4	-1.61
3m+	1-7	14.3	-3.75	3m+	2-10	20.0	+0.75

TYPE OF RACE

Non-Handicaps	W-R	Per cent	£1 Level Stake	Handicaps	W-R	Per cent	£1 Level Stake
Nov Hrdls	6-20	30.0	-5.86	Nov Hrdls	0-5	0.0	-5.00
Hrdls	6-17	35.3	-1.83	Hrdls	12-58	20.7	+10.25

Nov Chs	1-3	33.3	-0.90	Nov Chs	0-4	0.0	-4.00
Chases	0-5	0.0	-5.00	Chases	7-32	21.9	-4.49
Sell/Claim	3-7	42.9	-0.09	Sell/Claim	0-0	0.0	0.00

RACE CLASS

	W-R	Per cent	£1 Level Stake
Class 1	2-19	10.5	+24.00
Class 2	2-19	10.5	-9.90
Class 3	3-22	13.6	-12.25
Class 4	18-61	29.5	-14.13
Class 5	10-26	38.5	-0.64
Class 6	0-3	0.0	-3.00

FIRST TIME OUT

	W-R	Per cent	£1 Level Stake
Bumpers	0-0	0.0	0.00
Hurdles	11-31	35.5	+4.50
Chases	1-4	25.0	+5.00
Totals	12-35	34.3	+9.50

JOCKEYS

	W-R	Per cent	£1 Level Stake
Sam Twiston-Davies	13-46	28.3	-11.58
Christopher Ward	6-38	15.8	-20.00
Will Kennedy	5-29	17.2	+18.24
Tom O'Brien	4-7	57.1	+2.01
Daryl Jacob	3-9	33.3	+5.75
Sean Bowen	2-2	100.0	+1.91
Noel Fehily	1-2	50.0	+0.75
Tom Scudamore	1-3	33.3	+1.00

COURSE RECORD

	Total W-R	Non-Hndcps Hurdles	Non-Hndcps Chases	Hndcps Hurdles	Hndcps Chases	NH Flat	Per cent	£1 Level Stake
Worcester	5-16	3-6	0-0	1-7	1-3	0-0	31.3	-3.00
Fontwell	4-6	2-3	0-0	1-2	1-1	0-0	66.7	+4.77
Uttoxeter	4-10	2-5	0-0	2-5	0-0	0-0	40.0	-1.34
Carlisle	2-3	2-2	0-0	0-1	0-0	0-0	66.7	+1.14
Ffos Las	2-5	0-1	0-0	2-3	0-1	0-0	40.0	+3.50
Chepstow	2-6	1-1	0-0	1-4	0-1	0-0	33.3	-1.09
Huntingdon	2-7	1-1	0-0	0-0	1-6	0-0	28.6	-0.88
Mrket Rsn	2-12	0-7	0-0	1-4	1-1	0-0	16.7	-0.63
Cartmel	1-1	1-1	0-0	0-0	0-0	0-0	100.0	+0.91
Sedgefield	1-2	0-1	0-0	0-0	1-1	0-0	50.0	+1.75
Haydock	1-3	0-0	1-1	0-2	0-0	0-0	33.3	-0.90
Wincanton	1-3	0-0	0-1	1-2	0-0	0-0	33.3	-0.50
Fakenham	1-4	1-2	0-0	0-1	0-1	0-0	25.0	-1.00
Kempton	1-4	0-0	0-0	0-1	1-3	0-0	25.0	+3.00
Southwell	1-4	1-1	0-0	0-3	0-0	0-0	25.0	-1.63
Nton Abbot	1-5	0-1	0-0	0-2	1-2	0-0	20.0	-3.27
Aintree	1-6	0-1	0-1	1-1	0-3	0-0	16.7	-2.75
Ludlow	1-6	0-0	0-1	1-5	0-0	0-0	16.7	-3.00
Stratford	1-6	1-2	0-0	0-1	0-3	0-0	16.7	-4.00
Sandown	1-8	0-0	0-0	1-5	0-3	0-0	12.5	+26.00

WINNING HORSES

Horse	Races Run	1st	2nd	3rd	£
*Ebony Express	6	3	0	0	46363
Mart Lane	2	1	0	0	28475
Royale Knight	6	1	1	1	12686
Ardkilly Witness	8	1	0	0	12021
Boondooma	5	2	1	0	21748
Bombadero	2	1	1	0	7798
Masterofdeception	5	2	1	0	7668
Hawdyerwheesht	9	3	0	2	7798
Neverownup	10	4	3	1	12179
*Lysino	9	2	3	2	6108
Express Du Berlais	1	1	0	0	3899
*Gran Maestro	6	1	2	2	3509
Discay	7	3	1	1	8447
*Aficionado	2	1	1	0	3249
*Vosne Romanee	7	2	2	1	6498
Jayo Time	6	2	0	1	6498
Slim Pickens	4	2	1	1	5068
Murtys Delight	10	1	2	1	2738
*Jazz Man	7	1	0	0	2599
Rock Gone	2	1	0	1	2209
Total winning prize-money					**£207558**
Favourites	**25-50**		**50.0%**		**9.33**

MISS CHLOE NEWMAN

CREWKERNE, SOMERSET

	No. of Hrs	Races Run	1st	2nd	3rd	Unpl	Per cent	£1 Level Stake
NH Flat	*0*	*0*	*0*	*0*	*0*	*0*	*0.0*	*0.00*
Hurdles	*0*	*0*	*0*	*0*	*0*	*0*	*0.0*	*0.00*
Chases	*2*	*4*	*1*	*2*	*1*	*0*	*25.0*	*-0.75*
Totals	**2**	**4**	**1**	**2**	**1**	**0**	**25.0**	**-0.75**

JOCKEYS

	W-R	Per cent	£1 Level Stake
Mr Joshua Newman	1-4	25.0	-0.75

COURSE RECORD

	Total W-R	Non-Hndcps Hurdles	Non-Hndcps Chases	Hndcps Hurdles	Hndcps Chases	NH Flat	Per cent	£1 Level Stake
Fontwell	1-2	0-0	1-2	0-0	0-0	0-0	50.0	+1.25

WINNING HORSES

Horse	Races Run	1st	2nd	3rd	£
Sobre Tresor	3	1	1	1	1248
Total winning prize-money					**£1248**
Favourites	**0-1**		**0.0%**		**-1.00**

ANNA NEWTON-SMITH

JEVINGTON, E SUSSEX

	No. of Hrs	Races Run	1st	2nd	3rd	Unpl	Per cent	£1 Level Stake
NH Flat	*1*	*1*	*0*	*0*	*0*	*1*	*0.0*	*-1.00*
Hurdles	*7*	*26*	*3*	*0*	*1*	*22*	*11.5*	*+25.00*
Chases	*3*	*10*	*0*	*2*	*0*	*8*	*0.0*	*-10.00*
Totals	**9**	**37**	**3**	**2**	**1**	**31**	**8.1**	**+14.00**
13-14	*14*	*54*	*1*	*6*	*3*	*44*	*1.9*	*-34.00*
12-13	*11*	*57*	*2*	*6*	*6*	*43*	*3.5*	*-36.75*

JOCKEYS

	W-R	Per cent	£1 Level Stake
Adam Wedge	2-11	18.2	+27.00
Trevor Whelan	1-2	50.0	+11.00

COURSE RECORD

	Total W-R	Non-Hndcps Hurdles	Non-Hndcps Chases	Hndcps Hurdles	Hndcps Chases	NH Flat	Per cent	£1 Level Stake
Plumpton	3-17	0-1	0-1	3-11	0-3	0-1	17.6	+34.00

WINNING HORSES

Horse	Races Run	1st	2nd	3rd	£
Little Roxy	6	2	0	0	4874
Hermosa Vaquera	6	1	0	0	2274
Total winning prize-money					**£7148**
Favourites	**0-0**		**0.0%**		**0.00**

PAUL NICHOLLS

DITCHEAT, SOMERSET

	No. of Hrs	Races Run	1st	2nd	3rd	Unpl	Per cent	£1 Level Stake
NH Flat	*19*	*29*	*6*	*5*	*4*	*14*	*20.7*	*-5.83*
Hurdles	*82*	*237*	*51*	*42*	*43*	*101*	*21.5*	*+23.66*
Chases	*69*	*261*	*68*	*42*	*35*	*116*	*26.1*	*+34.44*
Totals	**141**	**527**	**125**	**89**	**82**	**231**	**23.7**	**+52.27**
13-14	*163*	*565*	*115*	*101*	*65*	*284*	*20.4*	*-124.35*
12-13	*170*	*549*	*130*	*100*	*72*	*247*	*23.7*	*-94.66*

BY MONTH

NH Flat	W-R	Per cent	£1 Level Stake
May	0-1	0.0	-1.00
June	0-0	0.0	0.00
July	0-0	0.0	0.00
August	0-0	0.0	0.00
September	0-1	0.0	-1.00
October	0-2	0.0	-2.00
November	3-6	50.0	+2.67
December	1-5	20.0	+0.50
January	1-2	50.0	+4.00
February	1-5	20.0	-2.00
March	0-2	0.0	-2.00
April	0-5	0.0	-5.00

Hurdles	W-R	Per cent	£1 Level Stake
May	4-15	26.7	-3.29
June	1-5	20.0	0.00
July	0-4	0.0	-4.00
August	0-2	0.0	-2.00
September	0-0	0.0	0.00
October	4-23	17.4	+2.75
November	10-39	25.6	+29.55
December	3-24	12.5	-8.98
January	4-25	16.0	-6.13
February	5-28	17.9	-14.24
March	12-37	32.4	+27.03
April	8-35	22.9	+2.98

Chases	W-R	Per cent	£1 Level Stake
May	0-10	0.0	-10.00
June	1-1	100.0	+1.00
July	0-3	0.0	-3.00
August	0-0	0.0	0.00
September	0-1	0.0	-1.00
October	6-19	31.6	-5.83
November	15-45	33.3	+17.21
December	15-51	29.4	+4.04
January	8-24	33.3	+42.00
February	8-27	29.6	+0.40
March	5-29	17.2	+4.48
April	10-51	19.6	-14.86

Totals	W-R	Per cent	£1 Level Stake
May	4-26	15.4	-14.29
June	2-6	33.3	+1.00
July	0-7	0.0	-7.00
August	0-2	0.0	-2.00
September	0-2	0.0	-2.00
October	10-44	22.7	-5.08
November	28-90	31.1	+49.43
December	19-80	23.8	-4.44
January	13-51	25.5	+39.87
February	14-60	23.3	-15.84
March	17-68	25.0	+29.51
April	18-91	19.8	-16.88

DISTANCE

Hurdles	W-R	Per cent	£1 Level Stake
2m-2m3f	23-105	21.9	+22.05
2m4f-2m7f	19-77	24.7	+11.20
3m+	0-10	0.0	-10.00

Chases	W-R	Per cent	£1 Level Stake
2m-2m3f	27-60	45.0	+33.15
2m4f-2m7f	19-77	24.7	+1.98
3m+	16-90	17.8	+8.28

TYPE OF RACE

Non-Handicaps	W-R	Per cent	£1 Level Stake
Nov Hrdls	28-91	30.8	-1.78
Hrdls	10-56	17.9	-1.17
Nov Chs	23-55	41.8	-1.17
Chases	16-57	28.1	+0.42
Sell/Claim	0-0	0.0	0.00

Handicaps	W-R	Per cent	£1 Level Stake
Nov Hrdls	2-9	22.2	+12.00
Hrdls	11-81	13.6	+14.63
Nov Chs	8-36	22.2	-9.96
Chases	21-113	18.6	+45.15
Sell/Claim	0-0	0.0	0.00

RACE CLASS

	W-R	Per cent	£1 Level Stake
Class 1	35-168	20.8	+41.36
Class 2	21-92	22.8	+48.07
Class 3	27-125	21.6	-23.26
Class 4	32-105	30.5	-3.97
Class 5	5-21	23.8	-9.92
Class 6	5-16	31.3	0.00

FIRST TIME OUT

	W-R	Per cent	£1 Level Stake
Bumpers	4-19	21.1	-3.00
Hurdles	12-68	17.6	-2.23
Chases	13-54	24.1	+7.60
Totals	29-141	20.6	+2.37

JOCKEYS

	W-R	Per cent	£1 Level Stake
Sam Twiston-Davies	69-309	22.3	-38.18
Nick Scholfield	19-86	22.1	+18.88
Noel Fehily	10-27	37.0	+17.28
Sean Bowen	10-38	26.3	+30.04
Jack Sherwood	6-24	25.0	+28.00
A P McCoy	3-5	60.0	+5.00
Mr W Biddick	2-6	33.3	+10.73
Mr H Cobden	1-1	100.0	+1.20
R Walsh	1-2	50.0	+1.50
Mr J Sole	1-2	50.0	+0.20
Mr James King	1-4	25.0	-2.67
Harry Derham	1-5	20.0	-3.38
Megan Nicholls	1-7	14.3	-5.33

COURSE RECORD

	Total W-R	Non-Hndcps Hurdles	Non-Hndcps Chases	Hndcps Hurdles	Hndcps Chases	NH Flat	Per cent	£1 Level Stake
Taunton	14-38	8-18	1-2	0-8	4-7	1-3	36.8	+0.68
Wincanton	14-57	7-17	1-4	1-13	4-17	1-6	24.6	-19.82
Sandown	13-53	2-6	5-17	2-11	4-18	0-1	24.5	+24.95
Exeter	10-34	3-14	5-8	1-3	0-6	1-3	29.4	+7.90

Cheltenham	10-71	2-16	2-17	3-17	3-21	0-0	14.1	+35.50
Ascot	9-29	2-8	4-9	1-2	2-9	0-1	31.0	+21.33
Newbury	8-34	1-5	1-6	2-9	4-13	0-1	23.5	+15.25
Nton Abbot	7-25	4-10	3-7	0-4	0-3	0-1	28.0	-9.50
Kempton	6-32	0-8	3-11	0-3	3-7	0-3	18.8	+3.88
Warwick	5-8	0-2	3-3	0-0	1-2	1-1	62.5	+11.13
Aintree	5-36	2-7	3-9	0-5	0-12	0-3	13.9	-4.63
Haydock	4-12	0-2	2-3	1-4	1-2	0-1	33.3	+3.93
Worcester	3-8	3-5	0-0	0-2	0-1	0-0	37.5	+3.25
Fontwell	3-12	0-4	3-4	0-2	0-2	0-0	25.0	-6.97
Chepstow	3-21	1-6	1-1	0-1	1-12	0-1	14.3	-14.37
Doncaster	2-9	0-3	1-3	0-0	0-2	1-1	22.2	-4.83
Plumpton	2-9	0-5	0-1	1-2	1-1	0-0	22.2	-2.17
Leicester	1-1	1-1	0-0	0-0	0-0	0-0	100.0	+1.88
Newcastle	1-1	1-1	0-0	0-0	0-0	0-0	100.0	+1.50
Ffos Las	1-1	0-0	0-0	1-1	0-0	0-0	100.0	+8.00
Bangor	1-2	1-1	0-1	0-0	0-0	0-0	50.0	+0.25
Huntingdon	1-2	0-0	0-1	0-0	0-0	1-1	50.0	+3.50
Wetherby	1-2	0-0	0-1	0-0	1-1	0-0	50.0	-0.09
Ludlow	1-14	0-4	1-1	0-1	0-6	0-2	7.1	-12.27

WINNING HORSES

Horse	Races Run	1st	2nd	3rd	£
Dodging Bullets	4	3	0	1	355088
Silviniaco Conti	5	3	0	0	311343
Caid Du Berlais	5	1	0	1	91120
Just A Par	7	1	1	1	85425
Rocky Creek	4	1	0	0	56950
Irving	5	1	1	0	56270
All Yours	5	2	1	0	59844
Saphir Du Rheu	6	3	1	0	97475
Aux Ptits Soins	1	1	0	0	45560
Rebel Rebellion	9	2	1	0	56452
Qualando	3	2	1	0	45962
Hawkes Point	4	1	0	1	34170
As De Mee	7	3	1	1	47166
Unioniste	5	1	0	1	31280
Silsol	4	2	1	0	50774
Southfield Vic	7	4	1	1	45889
Mr Mole	5	3	0	1	61090
Al Ferof	4	1	1	1	28609
Sam Winner	4	2	0	0	54902
Southfield Theatre	6	4	2	0	65624
Sound Investment	6	2	2	1	53499
Ulck Du Lin	6	2	1	1	34657
Ruben Cotter	2	1	0	0	25992
Virak	6	4	0	2	64818
Vibrato Valtat	10	4	2	2	73323
Wonderful Charm	6	1	0	2	18941
Dormello Mo	6	2	0	0	25157
Ptit Zig	6	4	0	0	49516
Irish Saint	7	3	1	2	46912
Black Thunder	5	1	1	0	17085
Arpege D'Alene	3	2	0	0	15640
Mon Parrain	5	1	0	0	12512
Morito Du Berlais	7	3	1	1	21480
Tara Point	3	2	0	1	14639
Lifeboat Mona	4	2	0	1	12950
Vicente	4	1	1	0	10635
Art Mauresque	3	2	0	0	14296
Far West	6	2	3	0	16485
McIlhatton	3	1	2	0	7863
Howlongisafoot	7	2	2	0	14296
Wilton Milan	8	1	3	2	6498
Urubu D'Irlande	2	1	1	0	6498
Minellahalfcentury	4	1	0	0	6498
Black River	4	1	0	1	6498
Vesperal Dream	10	5	0	2	21261
Solar Impulse	8	1	4	1	6498
*Old Guard	5	1	1	1	6498
Pressies Girl	4	2	0	0	6389
Polisky	5	1	1	1	6330
Cowards Close	3	1	1	1	6239
Katgary	6	1	0	0	5848
Great Try	5	1	2	1	5475
Vide Cave	5	1	0	0	4874
Salubrious	1	1	0	0	4549
*It's A Close Call	3	2	0	0	7798
Ceasar Milan	4	1	0	2	3899
Vago Collonges	6	1	4	1	3899
Earthmoves	6	2	1	2	7663
Sirabad	2	1	0	0	3899
Monsieur Gibraltar	1	1	0	0	3899
She's Da One	6	2	1	0	6823
Port Melon	5	1	1	3	3422
Abidjan	4	1	1	2	3422
San Benedeto	3	1	1	0	3249
*The Eaglehaslanded	3	2	0	0	4874
Merrion Square	6	1	3	0	3119
Sergeant Thunder	4	1	0	2	3119
Ballycoe	2	1	0	0	2599
Pacha Du Polder	3	1	2	0	2496
Persian Delight	2	1	0	0	2395
No Loose Change	4	1	1	1	2017
Rainy City	3	1	1	0	1625
Present Man	2	1	0	0	1625

Total winning prize-money **£2403484**

Favourites **70-163** **42.9%** **-3.64**

PETER NIVEN

BARTON-LE-STREET, N YORKS

	No. of Hrs	Races Run	1st	2nd	3rd	Unpl	Per cent	£1 Level Stake
NH Flat	*11*	*16*	*1*	*3*	*3*	*9*	*6.3*	*-5.00*
Hurdles	*8*	*33*	*3*	*4*	*4*	*22*	*9.1*	*-18.88*
Chases	*0*	*0*	*0*	*0*	*0*	*0*	*0.0*	*0.00*
Totals	**17**	**49**	**4**	**7**	**7**	**31**	**8.2**	**-23.88**
13-14	*16*	*45*	*5*	*8*	*5*	*27*	*11.1*	*-13.38*
12-13	*16*	*47*	*2*	*5*	*10*	*30*	*4.3*	*-36.75*

JOCKEYS

	W-R	Per cent	£1 Level Stake
Brian Hughes	2-16	12.5	-10.38
Daryl Jacob	1-2	50.0	+9.00
Graham Watters	1-2	50.0	+6.50

COURSE RECORD

	Total W-R	Non-Hndcps Hurdles	Non-Hndcps Chases	Hndcps Hurdles	Hndcps Chases	NH Flat	Per cent	£1 Level Stake
Mrket Rsn	2-13	0-4	0-0	1-4	0-0	1-5	15.4	+6.50
Ayr	1-1	1-1	0-0	0-0	0-0	0-0	100.0	+1.38
Catterick	1-6	1-4	0-0	0-1	0-0	0-1	16.7	-2.75

WINNING HORSES

Horse	Races Run	1st	2nd	3rd	£
*Engrossing	6	1	1	1	2599
Sir Safir	6	1	1	0	2599
*Renegotiate	4	1	0	1	1949
Pixiepot	2	1	0	0	1643
Total winning prize-money					**£8790**
Favourites	**2-3**		**66.7%**		**2.63**

LUCY NORMILE

DUNCRIEVIE, PERTH & KINROSS

	No. of Hrs	Races Run	1st	2nd	3rd	Unpl	Per cent	£1 Level Stake
NH Flat	*1*	*3*	*0*	*0*	*0*	*3*	*0.0*	*-3.00*
Hurdles	*17*	*56*	*1*	*5*	*4*	*46*	*1.8*	*-41.00*
Chases	*4*	*12*	*1*	*3*	*3*	*5*	*8.3*	*-7.50*
Totals	**20**	**71**	**2**	**8**	**7**	**54**	**2.8**	**-51.50**
13-14	*24*	*98*	*9*	*8*	*8*	*73*	*9.2*	*-5.50*
12-13	*24*	*82*	*4*	*2*	*9*	*67*	*4.9*	*-7.00*

JOCKEYS

	W-R	Per cent	£1 Level Stake
Adam Nicol	1-5	20.0	+10.00
Adrian Lane	1-23	4.3	-18.50

COURSE RECORD

	Total W-R	Non-Hndcps Hurdles	Non-Hndcps Chases	Hndcps Hurdles	Hndcps Chases	NH Flat	Per cent	£1 Level Stake
Ayr	2-7	0-3	0-0	1-2	1-2	0-0	28.6	+12.50

WINNING HORSES

Horse	Races Run	1st	2nd	3rd	£
Silverton	7	1	3	2	4549
Cadore	5	1	0	0	3899
Total winning prize-money					**£8448**
Favourites	**0-1**		**0.0%**		**-1.00**

DANIEL O'BRIEN

CAPEL, KENT

	No. of Hrs	Races Run	1st	2nd	3rd	Unpl	Per cent	£1 Level Stake
NH Flat	*0*	*0*	*0*	*0*	*0*	*0*	*0.0*	*0.00*
Hurdles	*6*	*29*	*1*	*7*	*3*	*18*	*3.4*	*-21.50*
Chases	*3*	*5*	*0*	*0*	*1*	*4*	*0.0*	*-5.00*
Totals	**8**	**34**	**1**	**7**	**4**	**22**	**2.9**	**-26.50**
13-14	*4*	*12*	*1*	*1*	*0*	*10*	*8.3*	*+14.00*
12-13	*9*	*28*	*3*	*1*	*4*	*20*	*10.7*	*+2.91*

JOCKEYS

	W-R	Per cent	£1 Level Stake
Thomas Garner	1-3	33.3	+4.50

COURSE RECORD

	Total W-R	Non-Hndcps Hurdles	Non-Hndcps Chases	Hndcps Hurdles	Hndcps Chases	NH Flat	Per cent	£1 Level Stake
Plumpton	1-24	0-0	0-0	1-20	0-4	0-0	4.2	-16.50

WINNING HORSES

Horse	Races Run	1st	2nd	3rd	£
*Bostin	5	1	1	0	4549
Total winning prize-money					**£4549**
Favourites	**0-1**		**0.0%**		**-1.00**

FERGAL O'BRIEN

COLN ST. DENNIS, GLOUCS

	No. of Hrs	Races Run	1st	2nd	3rd	Unpl	Per cent	£1 Level Stake
NH Flat	*14*	*26*	*2*	*1*	*5*	*18*	*7.7*	*+2.00*
Hurdles	*39*	*120*	*10*	*19*	*12*	*79*	*8.3*	*-39.50*
Chases	*25*	*101*	*15*	*12*	*12*	*62*	*14.9*	*+8.38*
Totals	**61**	**247**	**27**	**32**	**29**	**159**	**10.9**	**-29.12**
13-14	*75*	*312*	*47*	*34*	*37*	*194*	*15.1*	*+24.15*
12-13	*60*	*226*	*28*	*36*	*25*	*137*	*12.4*	*-28.22*

BY MONTH

NH Flat	W-R	Per cent	£1 Level Stake	**Hurdles**	W-R	Per cent	£1 Level Stake
May	0-1	0.0	-1.00	May	2-18	11.1	-2.38
June	0-2	0.0	-2.00	June	0-8	0.0	-8.00
July	0-3	0.0	-3.00	July	0-13	0.0	-13.00
August	0-0	0.0	0.00	August	0-3	0.0	-3.00
September	0-0	0.0	0.00	September	0-7	0.0	-7.00
October	0-5	0.0	-5.00	October	2-10	20.0	+35.00
November	1-3	33.3	+18.00	November	3-15	20.0	-8.50
December	0-2	0.0	-2.00	December	0-9	0.0	-9.00
January	0-3	0.0	-3.00	January	1-10	10.0	-7.63
February	0-2	0.0	-2.00	February	0-5	0.0	-5.00

March	1-1	100.0	+6.00	March	1-11	9.1	-4.00
April	0-4	0.0	-4.00	April	1-11	9.1	-7.00

Chases	W-R	Per cent	£1 Level Stake	Totals	W-R	Per cent	£1 Level Stake
May	0-11	0.0	-11.00	May	2-30	6.7	-14.38
June	2-13	15.4	+2.00	June	2-23	8.7	-8.00
July	1-10	10.0	-4.00	July	1-26	3.8	-20.00
August	0-2	0.0	-2.00	August	0-5	0.0	-5.00
September	2-7	28.6	+3.00	September	2-14	14.3	-4.00
October	1-13	7.7	-6.00	October	3-28	10.7	+24.00
November	2-12	16.7	+3.38	November	6-30	20.0	+12.88
December	2-8	25.0	+8.00	December	2-19	10.5	-3.00
January	1-8	12.5	+7.00	January	2-21	9.5	-3.63
February	0-4	0.0	-4.00	February	0-11	0.0	-11.00
March	2-7	28.6	+7.50	March	4-19	21.1	+9.50
April	2-6	33.3	+4.50	April	3-21	14.3	-6.50

DISTANCE

Hurdles	W-R	Per cent	£1 Level Stake	Chases	W-R	Per cent	£1 Level Stake
2m-2m3f	3-47	6.4	-30.13	2m-2m3f	2-16	12.5	+1.00
2m4f-2m7f	5-35	14.3	-8.00	2m4f-2m7f	11-52	21.2	+21.88
3m+	1-13	7.7	-10.38	3m+	1-26	3.8	-13.00

TYPE OF RACE

Non-Handicaps	W-R	Per cent	£1 Level Stake	Handicaps	W-R	Per cent	£1 Level Stake
Nov Hrdls	5-39	12.8	-22.88	Nov Hrdls	0-14	0.0	-14.00
Hrdls	2-13	15.4	+23.38	Hrdls	3-41	7.3	-13.00
Nov Chs	0-5	0.0	-5.00	Nov Chs	4-20	20.0	+24.00
Chases	0-3	0.0	-3.00	Chases	11-73	15.1	-7.63
Sell/Claim	0-12	0.0	-12.00	Sell/Claim	0-1	0.0	-1.00

RACE CLASS

	W-R	Per cent	£1 Level Stake
Class 1	1-16	6.3	-12.00
Class 2	1-9	11.1	-3.50
Class 3	8-45	17.8	+26.00
Class 4	12-109	11.0	-43.00
Class 5	4-54	7.4	-3.63
Class 6	1-14	7.1	+7.00

FIRST TIME OUT

	W-R	Per cent	£1 Level Stake
Bumpers	0-14	0.0	-14.00
Hurdles	5-28	17.9	+3.88
Chases	2-19	10.5	+4.00
Totals	7-61	11.5	-6.12

JOCKEYS

	W-R	Per cent	£1 Level Stake
Paddy Brennan	19-92	20.7	+54.50
Conor Shoemark	6-85	7.1	-50.00
Alain Cawley	2-30	6.7	+6.38

COURSE RECORD

	Total W-R	Non-Hndcps Hurdles	Non-Hndcps Chases	Hndcps Hurdles	Hndcps Chases	NH Flat	Per cent	£1 Level Stake
Ludlow	3-14	1-7	0-0	0-0	2-6	0-1	21.4	+7.00
Perth	3-14	0-0	0-0	0-6	3-7	0-1	21.4	+7.50
Towcester	3-17	2-6	0-0	1-4	0-5	0-2	17.6	-0.38
Uttoxeter	3-27	1-9	0-0	0-7	2-9	0-2	11.1	-14.00
Wetherby	2-6	1-2	0-0	0-0	0-1	1-3	33.3	+17.63
Exeter	2-8	0-3	0-1	0-1	2-3	0-0	25.0	+13.00
Plumpton	1-2	1-1	0-0	0-1	0-0	0-0	50.0	+1.75
Ascot	1-4	0-2	0-0	0-0	1-2	0-0	25.0	+1.50
Bangor	1-7	0-1	0-0	0-0	1-5	0-1	14.3	-4.63
Leicester	1-7	0-1	0-0	0-1	1-5	0-0	14.3	+8.00
Newbury	1-7	0-1	0-0	0-3	1-3	0-0	14.3	+2.00
Chepstow	1-9	1-4	0-0	0-4	0-1	0-0	11.1	+25.00
Mrket Rsn	1-9	0-0	0-2	0-2	1-5	0-0	11.1	-4.50
Nton Abbot	1-16	0-4	0-1	0-3	1-7	0-1	6.3	-11.00
Cheltenham	1-17	0-1	0-1	1-3	0-6	0-6	5.9	-13.00
Stratford	1-17	0-3	0-1	0-5	0-6	1-2	5.9	-10.00
Worcester	1-20	0-7	0-1	1-4	0-6	0-2	5.0	-9.00

WINNING HORSES

Horse	Races Run	1st	2nd	3rd	£
Creevytennant	7	3	0	0	35732
The Govaness	5	2	1	0	15128
Rio Milan	8	2	1	0	17545
Owen Na View	10	1	2	0	6498
Me And Ben	4	1	0	0	6389
Our Cat	4	1	0	0	6330
Perfect Candidate	7	3	0	0	13443
Chase The Spud	3	1	0	0	6330
Rockchasebullett	4	2	1	0	10155
Lord Landen	8	1	1	3	4517
Double Silver	2	1	0	0	3899
Gunner Fifteen	1	1	0	0	3798
Jennys Surprise	3	2	0	0	6693
Ballygrooby Bertie	4	1	0	0	3119
Boherna Lady	3	1	1	0	3119
Allerton	8	1	2	1	2924
War On The Rocks	2	1	0	0	2599
Isla Fernandos	5	1	0	1	2053
An Poc Ar Buile	9	1	1	2	1949
Total winning prize-money					**£152220**
Favourites	**6-17**		**35.3%**		**1.38**

JEDD O'KEEFFE

MIDDLEHAM MOOR, N YORKS

	No. of Hrs	Races Run	1st	2nd	3rd	Unpl	Per cent	£1 Level Stake
NH Flat	*0*	*0*	*0*	*0*	*0*	*0*	*0.0*	*0.00*
Hurdles	*3*	*13*	*2*	*4*	*1*	*6*	*15.4*	*-7.63*
Chases	*1*	*8*	*0*	*2*	*3*	*3*	*0.0*	*-8.00*
Totals	**4**	**21**	**2**	**6**	**4**	**9**	**9.5**	**-15.63**
13-14	*6*	*13*	*1*	*1*	*4*	*7*	*7.7*	*-3.00*
12-13	*3*	*16*	*1*	*2*	*0*	*13*	*6.3*	*-3.00*

JOCKEYS

	W-R	Per cent	£1 Level Stake
Brian Harding	2-14	14.3	-8.63

COURSE RECORD

	Total W-R	Non-Hndcps Hurdles	Non-Hndcps Chases	Hndcps Hurdles	Hndcps Chases	NH Flat	Per cent	£1 Level Stake
Kelso	1-1	0-0	0-0	1-1	0-0	0-0	100.0	+2.00
Mrket Rsn	1-3	1-3	0-0	0-0	0-0	0-0	33.3	-0.63

WINNING HORSES

Horse	Races Run	1st	2nd	3rd	£
Satanic Beat	6	2	1	0	8642
Total winning prize-money					**£8642**
Favourites	**0-2**		**0.0%**		**-2.00**

DAVID O'MEARA

NAWTON, N YORKS

	No. of Hrs	Races Run	1st	2nd	3rd	Unpl	Per cent	£1 Level Stake
NH Flat	*2*	*4*	*1*	*0*	*0*	*3*	*25.0*	*+3.00*
Hurdles	*1*	*2*	*0*	*0*	*1*	*1*	*0.0*	*-2.00*
Chases	*2*	*13*	*1*	*5*	*0*	*7*	*7.7*	*-10.25*
Totals	**4**	**19**	**2**	**5**	**1**	**11**	**10.5**	**-9.25**
13-14	*9*	*26*	*4*	*4*	*4*	*14*	*15.4*	*-3.67*
12-13	*22*	*55*	*7*	*6*	*5*	*37*	*12.7*	*-14.34*

JOCKEYS

	W-R	Per cent	£1 Level Stake
A P McCoy	1-3	33.3	-0.25
Denis O'Regan	1-3	33.3	+4.00

COURSE RECORD

	Total W-R	Non-Hndcps Hurdles	Non-Hndcps Chases	Hndcps Hurdles	Hndcps Chases	NH Flat	Per cent	£1 Level Stake
Catterick	1-1	0-0	0-0	0-0	0-0	1-1	100.0	+6.00
Musselbgh	1-1	0-0	0-0	0-0	1-1	0-0	100.0	+1.75

WINNING HORSES

Horse	Races Run	1st	2nd	3rd	£
Ifandbutwhynot	9	1	5	1	12996
After Toniight	2	1	0	0	2053
Total winning prize-money					**£15049**
Favourites	**1-3**		**33.3%**		**-0.25**

JONJO O'NEILL

CHELTENHAM, GLOUCS

	No. of Hrs	Races Run	1st	2nd	3rd	Unpl	Per cent	£1 Level Stake
NH Flat	*19*	*24*	*6*	*4*	*1*	*13*	*25.0*	*+5.13*
Hurdles	*114*	*373*	*59*	*50*	*43*	*221*	*15.8*	*-124.21*
Chases	*56*	*238*	*39*	*33*	*26*	*139*	*16.4*	*-67.12*
Totals	**165**	**635**	**104**	**87**	**70**	**373**	**16.4**	**-186.20**
13-14	*188*	*805*	*134*	*105*	*90*	*475*	*16.6*	*-176.49*
12-13	*180*	*683*	*88*	*56*	*64*	*475*	*12.9*	*-200.36*

BY MONTH

NH Flat	W-R	Per cent	£1 Level Stake
May	0-4	0.0	-4.00
June	0-0	0.0	0.00
July	1-3	33.3	-0.13
August	0-0	0.0	0.00
September	0-0	0.0	0.00
October	0-4	0.0	-4.00
November	1-1	100.0	+2.50
December	0-1	0.0	-1.00
January	1-1	100.0	+8.00
February	1-1	100.0	+1.50
March	1-2	50.0	+7.00
April	1-7	14.3	-4.75

Hurdles	W-R	Per cent	£1 Level Stake
May	6-44	13.6	-21.70
June	6-31	19.4	-15.09
July	4-31	12.9	-18.49
August	5-16	31.3	+4.42
September	3-9	33.3	+14.75
October	4-43	9.3	-23.63
November	2-31	6.5	-3.00
December	0-19	0.0	-19.00
January	5-34	14.7	-12.65
February	14-55	25.5	-8.93
March	6-35	17.1	-17.69
April	4-25	16.0	-3.20

Chases	W-R	Per cent	£1 Level Stake
May	9-20	45.0	+8.92
June	3-25	12.0	-13.10
July	2-17	11.8	-9.50
August	6-17	35.3	+4.56
September	0-7	0.0	-7.00
October	5-29	17.2	-5.25
November	1-29	3.4	-26.00
December	0-15	0.0	-15.00
January	1-21	4.8	-8.00
February	6-13	46.2	+18.75
March	3-23	13.0	-10.50
April	3-22	13.6	-5.00

Totals	W-R	Per cent	£1 Level Stake
May	15-68	22.1	-16.78
June	9-56	16.1	-28.19
July	7-51	13.7	-28.12
August	11-33	33.3	+8.98
September	3-16	18.8	+7.75
October	9-76	11.8	-32.88
November	4-61	6.6	-26.50
December	0-35	0.0	-35.00
January	7-56	12.5	-12.65
February	21-69	30.4	+11.32
March	10-60	16.7	-21.19
April	8-54	14.8	-12.95

DISTANCE

Hurdles	W-R	Per cent	£1 Level Stake
2m-2m3f	16-132	12.1	-50.34
2m4f-2m7f	20-114	17.5	-34.54
3m+	8-43	18.6	-8.50

Chases	W-R	Per cent	£1 Level Stake
2m-2m3f	5-38	13.2	-18.58
2m4f-2m7f	20-93	21.5	+4.88
3m+	7-79	8.9	-58.50

TYPE OF RACE

Non-Handicaps

	W-R	Per cent	£1 Level Stake
Nov Hrdls	10-88	11.4	-62.02
Hrdls	10-61	16.4	-30.00

Handicaps

	W-R	Per cent	£1 Level Stake
Nov Hrdls	7-26	26.9	+3.49
Hrdls	31-194	16.0	-33.78

Nov Chs	4-11	36.4	-1.43	Nov Chs	8-39	20.5	+5.25
Chases	4-20	20.0	-10.75	Chases	23-168	13.7	-60.19
Sell/Claim	1-2	50.0	+0.10	Sell/Claim	0-0	0.0	0.00

RACE CLASS

	W-R	Per cent	£1 Level Stake
Class 1	1-59	1.7	-56.00
Class 2	6-54	11.1	-27.25
Class 3	22-116	19.0	-15.12
Class 4	53-331	16.0	-96.21
Class 5	16-54	29.6	+7.24
Class 6	6-21	28.6	+1.13

FIRST TIME OUT

	W-R	Per cent	£1 Level Stake
Bumpers	4-19	21.1	-2.38
Hurdles	10-104	9.6	-59.05
Chases	10-42	23.8	+0.50
Totals	24-165	14.5	-60.93

JOCKEYS

	W-R	Per cent	£1 Level Stake
A P McCoy	61-290	21.0	-75.81
Richie McLernon	12-154	7.8	-84.13
Will Kennedy	5-38	13.2	-5.38
Barry Geraghty	4-10	40.0	+8.25
Patrick Cowley	4-18	22.2	+2.25
Maurice Linehan	4-51	7.8	-29.90
Wayne Hutchinson	2-3	66.7	+9.00
Mr Tommie M O'Brien	2-8	25.0	-3.00
Jack Savage	2-12	16.7	+7.00
Dougie Costello	2-17	11.8	-4.00
Sean Bowen	1-1	100.0	+3.50
Noel Fehily	1-2	50.0	+0.25
Mr H A A Bannister	1-2	50.0	-1.00
Jason Maguire	1-3	33.3	+1.00
Richard Johnson	1-3	33.3	-0.25
Raymond O'Brien	1-9	11.1	0.00

COURSE RECORD

	Total W-R	Non-Hndcps Hurdles	Non-Hndcps Chases	Hndcps Hurdles	Hndcps Chases	NH Flat	Per cent	£1 Level Stake
Worcester	12-65	2-11	1-4	3-24	5-22	1-4	18.5	-17.59
Mrket Rsn	11-51	0-11	1-2	3-13	7-25	0-0	21.6	-1.17
Wetherby	8-18	3-6	0-2	3-4	2-6	0-0	44.4	+14.35
Huntingdon	7-20	1-6	0-0	2-7	3-5	1-2	35.0	+11.38
Southwell	7-30	2-8	0-0	3-14	2-7	0-1	23.3	-0.64
Warwick	6-24	1-7	0-0	4-10	0-5	1-2	25.0	+16.74
Ffos Las	5-26	1-5	0-0	3-9	1-10	0-2	19.2	-8.29
Uttoxeter	5-42	1-9	0-2	3-15	1-15	0-1	11.9	-22.00
Kempton	4-19	2-5	1-2	0-7	1-5	0-0	21.1	+4.80
Chepstow	4-20	3-10	0-0	1-5	0-5	0-0	20.0	-4.95
Newbury	4-23	1-9	1-2	1-7	1-4	0-1	17.4	-5.60
Bangor	4-25	0-6	0-0	2-6	1-11	1-2	16.0	-6.50
Carlisle	3-9	0-2	1-2	1-2	0-2	1-1	33.3	+1.25
Exeter	3-23	1-8	0-1	1-7	1-6	0-1	13.0	-7.38
Ludlow	3-23	1-9	1-1	0-5	0-7	1-1	13.0	-8.38
Stratford	3-25	1-6	1-1	1-10	0-6	0-2	12.0	-15.23
Fontwell	2-9	0-1	0-0	1-3	1-5	0-0	22.2	-2.00
Towcester	2-10	0-6	0-0	0-2	2-2	0-0	20.0	-4.25
Doncaster	2-14	0-1	0-0	2-9	0-4	0-0	14.3	-8.00
Cheltenham	2-34	1-3	0-3	0-14	1-13	0-1	5.9	-24.75
Cartmel	1-2	0-0	0-0	1-2	0-0	0-0	50.0	-0.20
Ayr	1-3	0-0	0-0	1-1	0-2	0-0	33.3	+3.50
Fakenham	1-3	0-1	0-0	1-1	0-1	0-0	33.3	-1.56
Kelso	1-3	0-0	1-1	0-1	0-1	0-0	33.3	-1.75
Haydock	1-12	0-0	0-1	0-9	1-2	0-0	8.3	-3.50
Sandown	1-17	0-4	0-0	1-6	0-6	0-1	5.9	-13.00
Aintree	1-23	0-3	0-4	0-8	1-7	0-1	4.3	-19.50

WINNING HORSES

Horse	Races Run	1st	2nd	3rd	£
Johns Spirit	5	1	1	1	31280
It's A Gimme	3	2	1	0	32244
Dursey Sound	9	1	1	0	14621
Holywell	5	1	0	2	12512
Shutthefrontdoor	2	1	0	0	12512
Forthefunofit	3	1	0	1	12021
Join The Clan	11	2	1	0	16967
Catching On	8	3	0	0	20825
Beg To Differ	6	3	0	1	10260
Oscar Fortune	6	1	1	0	8123
Capard King	7	3	0	2	15595
Spookydooky	5	2	1	2	10915
Lost Legend	7	2	2	0	13296
The Nephew	9	2	2	0	12996
Rum And Butter	6	3	0	0	16895
Master Malt	9	4	0	2	16440
Bandit Country	6	1	2	1	6498
Titchwood	3	1	0	1	6343
In The Rough	4	4	0	0	18669
Foundation Man	6	1	0	0	6256
Gray Hession	1	1	0	0	5523
Goodwood Mirage	4	1	0	0	5523
Milan Bound	5	1	1	0	5523
Whisky Yankee	2	1	0	0	5393
On The Record	4	3	0	0	11891
Ballylifen	3	1	0	0	5111
American Legend	10	1	3	3	4224
Favoured Nation	6	2	2	1	7733
O'Callaghan Strand	8	1	0	2	3899
Mission Complete	13	1	4	0	3899
Presence Felt	5	1	1	0	3899
Old Pals Act	6	2	1	0	7668
Rayak	7	1	1	1	3899
Mr Shantu	10	2	1	3	3899
Ivy Gate	3	1	0	0	3899
Mad Jack Mytton	5	2	2	1	7148
Less Time	8	1	1	3	3899
Champagne Present	5	1	2	0	3899
Optimistic Bias	3	1	1	0	3899
Last Shadow	4	1	1	0	3833
Vujiyama	10	1	2	0	3769
Cyclone	6	1	0	2	3422
Tarvini	7	2	0	0	6368
Finding Your Feet	8	2	0	1	6368
Clues And Arrows	4	2	2	0	5848
Fort Worth	2	1	0	0	3249

She's Late	5	1	2	1	3249
Full Throttle	3	2	0	0	5198
Mont Royale	7	1	1	1	3249
Hedley Lamarr	2	1	1	0	3249
Mackerye End	3	1	1	1	3249
Minella Rocco	2	2	0	0	6498
Listen And Learn	7	1	1	0	3119
Don Padeja	4	1	1	0	3119
Ustica	4	1	1	0	2859
It Is What It Is	2	2	0	0	4807
*Sebastian Beach	6	1	1	1	2599
Clubs Are Trumps	6	2	1	0	5198
Rock N Rhythm	2	1	0	1	2599
Rose Revived	4	1	1	0	2599
Twirling Magnet	6	2	0	1	3484
Playing The Field	2	2	0	0	4289
There Is No Point	3	1	0	0	2053
Suit Yourself	1	1	0	0	2053
Calaf	3	1	0	0	1949
Petrovic	7	1	0	0	1949
Bronco Billy	2	1	1	0	1625
Beggars Cross	1	1	0	0	1625
For Instance	1	1	0	0	1560
Ozzy Thomas	4	1	1	0	1560

Total winning prize-money **£502691**

Favourites **52-138** **37.7%** **-3.67**

J J O'SHEA

FARNWORTH, GT MANCHESTER

	No. of Hrs	Races Run	1st	2nd	3rd	Unpl	Per cent	£1 Level Stake
NH Flat	*0*	*0*	*0*	*0*	*0*	*0*	*0.0*	*0.00*
Hurdles	*0*	*0*	*0*	*0*	*0*	*0*	*0.0*	*0.00*
Chases	*5*	*18*	*2*	*2*	*3*	*11*	*11.1*	*-14.67*
Totals	**5**	**18**	**2**	**2**	**3**	**11**	**11.1**	**-14.67**
13-14	*4*	*7*	*1*	*0*	*0*	*6*	*14.3*	*-4.00*
12-13	*3*	*7*	*2*	*1*	*1*	*3*	*28.6*	*0.00*

JOCKEYS

	W-R	Per cent	£1 Level Stake
Mr Tom David	1-3	33.3	-0.75
Mr G Crow	1-11	9.1	-9.92

COURSE RECORD

	Total W-R	Non-Hndcps Hurdles	Non-Hndcps Chases	Hndcps Hurdles	Hndcps Chases	NH Flat	Per cent	£1 Level Stake
Wetherby	1-1	0-0	1-1	0-0	0-0	0-0	100.0	+0.08
Leicester	1-4	0-0	1-4	0-0	0-0	0-0	25.0	-1.75

WINNING HORSES

Horse	Races Run	1st	2nd	3rd	£
*Woodview Prince	2	1	0	1	1560
*Executive Benefit	2	1	0	0	1292

Total winning prize-money **£2852**

Favourites **2-3** **66.7%** **0.33**

JOHN O'SHEA

ELTON, GLOUCS

	No. of Hrs	Races Run	1st	2nd	3rd	Unpl	Per cent	£1 Level Stake
NH Flat	*5*	*7*	*0*	*0*	*0*	*7*	*0.0*	*-7.00*
Hurdles	*13*	*36*	*0*	*2*	*5*	*29*	*0.0*	*-36.00*
Chases	*4*	*19*	*2*	*0*	*1*	*16*	*10.5*	*-1.13*
Totals	**19**	**62**	**2**	**2**	**6**	**52**	**3.2**	**-44.13**
13-14	*27*	*117*	*7*	*18*	*15*	*77*	*6.0*	*-78.50*
12-13	*13*	*75*	*7*	*8*	*10*	*50*	*9.3*	*-27.90*

JOCKEYS

	W-R	Per cent	£1 Level Stake
Dave Crosse	2-13	15.4	+4.88

COURSE RECORD

	Total W-R	Non-Hndcps Hurdles	Non-Hndcps Chases	Hndcps Hurdles	Hndcps Chases	NH Flat	Per cent	£1 Level Stake
Warwick	1-1	0-0	0-0	0-0	1-1	0-0	100.0	+14.00
Plumpton	1-4	0-0	0-0	0-1	1-3	0-0	25.0	-1.13

WINNING HORSES

Horse	Races Run	1st	2nd	3rd	£
Tribal Dance	6	2	0	2	7763

Total winning prize-money **£7763**

Favourites **1-2** **50.0%** **0.88**

HENRY OLIVER

BROOMHALL, WORCS

	No. of Hrs	Races Run	1st	2nd	3rd	Unpl	Per cent	£1 Level Stake
NH Flat	*5*	*5*	*1*	*0*	*0*	*4*	*20.0*	*+10.00*
Hurdles	*16*	*59*	*12*	*12*	*8*	*27*	*20.3*	*+32.00*
Chases	*9*	*43*	*8*	*8*	*5*	*22*	*18.6*	*-1.29*
Totals	**27**	**107**	**21**	**20**	**13**	**53**	**19.6**	**+40.71**
13-14	*18*	*101*	*13*	*8*	*17*	*63*	*12.9*	*-6.45*
12-13	*5*	*14*	*2*	*0*	*0*	*12*	*14.3*	*-0.50*

BY MONTH

NH Flat	W-R	Per cent	£1 Level Stake	**Hurdles**	W-R	Per cent	£1 Level Stake
May	0-1	0.0	-1.00	May	0-6	0.0	-6.00
June	0-0	0.0	0.00	June	0-1	0.0	-1.00
July	0-0	0.0	0.00	July	0-5	0.0	-5.00
August	0-0	0.0	0.00	August	1-2	50.0	+2.50
September	0-0	0.0	0.00	September	0-1	0.0	-1.00
October	0-0	0.0	0.00	October	1-9	11.1	+25.00
November	0-0	0.0	0.00	November	1-5	20.0	-0.50
December	0-0	0.0	0.00	December	1-7	14.3	-2.50

January	0-1	0.0	-1.00	January	3-8	37.5	+7.25
February	0-0	0.0	0.00	February	1-4	25.0	-1.75
March	0-0	0.0	0.00	March	2-7	28.6	+9.00
April	1-3	33.3	+12.00	April	2-4	50.0	+6.00

Chases	W-R	Per cent	£1 Level Stake	Totals	W-R	Per cent	£1 Level Stake
May	0-5	0.0	-5.00	May	0-12	0.0	-12.00
June	0-0	0.0	0.00	June	0-1	0.0	-1.00
July	0-0	0.0	0.00	July	0-5	0.0	-5.00
August	0-0	0.0	0.00	August	1-2	50.0	+2.50
September	0-0	0.0	0.00	September	0-1	0.0	-1.00
October	0-3	0.0	-3.00	October	1-12	8.3	+22.00
November	2-9	22.2	+9.00	November	3-14	21.4	+8.50
December	2-6	33.3	+3.50	December	3-13	23.1	+1.00
January	1-6	16.7	-2.25	January	4-15	26.7	+4.00
February	2-6	33.3	+1.83	February	3-10	30.0	+0.08
March	1-5	20.0	-2.38	March	3-12	25.0	+6.62
April	0-3	0.0	-3.00	April	3-10	30.0	+15.00

DISTANCE

Hurdles	W-R	Per cent	£1 Level Stake	Chases	W-R	Per cent	£1 Level Stake
2m-2m3f	9-37	24.3	+38.00	2m-2m3f	5-18	27.8	+13.75
2m4f-2m7f	2-9	22.2	-1.00	2m4f-2m7f	1-13	7.7	-10.38
3m+	0-0	0.0	0.00	3m+	0-4	0.0	-4.00

TYPE OF RACE

Non-Handicaps	W-R	Per cent	£1 Level Stake	Handicaps	W-R	Per cent	£1 Level Stake
Nov Hrdls	0-10	0.0	-10.00	Nov Hrdls	1-4	25.0	+0.50
Hrdls	1-6	16.7	+28.00	Hrdls	10-38	26.3	+14.50
Nov Chs	0-0	0.0	0.00	Nov Chs	2-17	11.8	+1.75
Chases	0-0	0.0	0.00	Chases	6-26	23.1	-3.04
Sell/Claim	0-2	0.0	-2.00	Sell/Claim	0-0	0.0	0.00

RACE CLASS / FIRST TIME OUT

RACE CLASS	W-R	Per cent	£1 Level Stake	FIRST TIME OUT	W-R	Per cent	£1 Level Stake
Class 1	0-5	0.0	-5.00	Bumpers	1-5	20.0	+10.00
Class 2	2-10	20.0	-2.17	Hurdles	2-16	12.5	+22.50
Class 3	4-18	22.2	+10.75	Chases	0-6	0.0	-6.00
Class 4	11-51	21.6	+0.13				
Class 5	3-19	15.8	+26.00	Totals	3-27	11.1	+26.50
Class 6	1-4	25.0	+11.00				

JOCKEYS

	W-R	Per cent	£1 Level Stake
James Davies	10-42	23.8	+55.58
Jeremiah McGrath	3-4	75.0	+14.00
Adam Wedge	2-3	66.7	+8.75
Jack Sherwood	2-4	50.0	+2.75
Paddy Brennan	1-3	33.3	-0.38
Richard Johnson	1-3	33.3	+0.50
Killian Moore	1-4	25.0	+0.50
Liam Treadwell	1-5	20.0	-2.00

COURSE RECORD

	Total W-R	Non-Hndcps Hurdles	Non-Hndcps Chases	Hndcps Hurdles	Hndcps Chases	NH Flat	Per cent	£1 Level Stake
Chepstow	3-8	0-0	0-0	1-3	1-4	1-1	37.5	+27.50
Towcester	3-10	0-3	0-0	2-3	1-2	0-2	30.0	+9.00
Leicester	2-7	0-0	0-0	2-4	0-3	0-0	28.6	+1.00
Carlisle	1-1	0-0	0-0	1-1	0-0	0-0	100.0	+3.50
Doncaster	1-1	0-0	0-0	0-0	1-1	0-0	100.0	+2.50
Nton Abbot	1-1	0-0	0-0	1-1	0-0	0-0	100.0	+3.50
Sedgefield	1-1	0-0	0-0	1-1	0-0	0-0	100.0	+1.75
Wincanton	1-1	0-0	0-0	0-0	1-1	0-0	100.0	+3.33
Haydock	1-2	0-0	0-0	0-1	1-1	0-0	50.0	+4.50
Fakenham	1-3	0-0	0-0	1-2	0-1	0-0	33.3	+1.50
Southwell	1-3	0-2	0-0	0-0	1-1	0-0	33.3	-0.38
Taunton	1-3	0-0	0-0	0-1	1-2	0-0	33.3	+0.75
Wetherby	1-3	0-1	0-0	1-1	0-1	0-0	33.3	+6.00
Mrket Rsn	1-5	0-0	0-0	1-3	0-2	0-0	20.0	-2.75
Bangor	1-6	0-1	0-0	0-0	1-4	0-1	16.7	-3.00
Stratford	1-7	1-2	0-0	0-5	0-0	0-0	14.3	+27.00

WINNING HORSES

Horse	Races Run	1st	2nd	3rd	£
*Dresden	7	1	2	0	16245
Keel Haul	8	1	2	0	12512
Whispering Harry	7	3	1	1	24440
Theregoesthetruth	7	2	1	1	7596
Take The Crown	11	2	2	2	8447
*Ozzy Thomas	5	1	1	2	3899
Signed Request	3	2	0	0	6173
*Dazinski	3	1	0	1	3509
Beatabout The Bush	4	2	0	0	6628
*Tiger O'Toole	1	1	0	0	3249
Grimley Girl	7	2	4	1	6498
*Desert Recluse	8	1	2	1	2599
Crescent Beach	6	1	0	1	2144
After Hours	1	1	0	0	1949
Total winning prize-money					**£105888**
Favourites	**8-20**		**40.0%**		**5.88**

MS EMMA OLIVER

LOWER ASHTON, DEVON

	No. of Hrs	Races Run	1st	2nd	3rd	Unpl	Per cent	£1 Level Stake
NH Flat	*0*	*0*	*0*	*0*	*0*	*0*	*0.0*	*0.00*
Hurdles	*0*	*0*	*0*	*0*	*0*	*0*	*0.0*	*0.00*
Chases	*3*	*6*	*1*	*3*	*0*	*2*	*16.7*	*-3.25*
Totals	**3**	**6**	**1**	**3**	**0**	**2**	**16.7**	**-3.25**
13-14	*2*	*6*	*1*	*1*	*0*	*4*	*16.7*	*-3.50*
12-13	*3*	*5*	*0*	*1*	*1*	*3*	*0.0*	*-5.00*

JOCKEYS

	W-R	Per cent	£1 Level Stake
Mr M Woodward	1-5	20.0	-2.25

COURSE RECORD

	Total W-R	Non-Hndcps Hurdles	Non-Hndcps Chases	Hndcps Hurdles	Hndcps Chases	NH Flat	Per cent	£1 Level Stake
Taunton	1-2	0-0	1-2	0-0	0-0	0-0	50.0	+0.75

WINNING HORSES

Horse	Races Run	1st	2nd	3rd	£
Double Bank	4	1	3	0	2305
Total winning prize-money					**£2305**
Favourites	**0-0**		**0.0%**		**0.00**

KEVIN PARKER

MINEHEAD, SOMERSET

	No. of Hrs	Races Run	1st	2nd	3rd	Unpl	Per cent	£1 Level Stake
NH Flat	*0*	*0*	*0*	*0*	*0*	*0*	*0.0*	*0.00*
Hurdles	*0*	*0*	*0*	*0*	*0*	*0*	*0.0*	*0.00*
Chases	*1*	*2*	*1*	*0*	*0*	*1*	*50.0*	*+0.10*
Totals	**1**	**2**	**1**	**0**	**0**	**1**	**50.0**	**+0.10**

JOCKEYS

	W-R	Per cent	£1 Level Stake
Miss Natalie Parker	1-2	50.0	+0.10

COURSE RECORD

	Total W-R	Non-Hndcps Hurdles	Non-Hndcps Chases	Hndcps Hurdles	Hndcps Chases	NH Flat	Per cent	£1 Level Stake
Lingfield	1-1	0-0	1-1	0-0	0-0	0-0	100.0	+1.10

WINNING HORSES

Horse	Races Run	1st	2nd	3rd	£
*Aiteen Thirtythree	2	1	0	0	936
Total winning prize-money					**£936**
Favourites	**1-1**		**100.0%**		**1.10**

HILARY PARROTT

REDMARLEY, GLOUCS

	No. of Hrs	Races Run	1st	2nd	3rd	Unpl	Per cent	£1 Level Stake
NH Flat	*1*	*1*	*0*	*0*	*0*	*1*	*0.0*	*-1.00*
Hurdles	*3*	*6*	*0*	*1*	*0*	*5*	*0.0*	*-6.00*
Chases	*2*	*10*	*2*	*2*	*3*	*3*	*20.0*	*+42.00*
Totals	**6**	**17**	**2**	**3**	**3**	**9**	**11.8**	**+35.00**
13-14	*8*	*24*	*0*	*1*	*1*	*22*	*0.0*	*-24.00*
12-13	*5*	*10*	*2*	*1*	*0*	*7*	*20.0*	*-1.75*

JOCKEYS

	W-R	Per cent	£1 Level Stake
Robert Dunne	2-3	66.7	+49.00

COURSE RECORD

	Total W-R	Non-Hndcps Hurdles	Non-Hndcps Chases	Hndcps Hurdles	Hndcps Chases	NH Flat	Per cent	£1 Level Stake
Ayr	1-1	0-0	0-0	0-0	1-1	0-0	100.0	+25.00
Doncaster	1-3	0-2	0-0	0-0	1-1	0-0	33.3	+23.00

WINNING HORSES

Horse	Races Run	1st	2nd	3rd	£
Wayward Prince	6	2	0	1	152085
Total winning prize-money					**£152085**
Favourites	**0-2**		**0.0%**		**-2.00**

BEN PAULING

BOURTON-ON-THE-WATER, GLOUCS

	No. of Hrs	Races Run	1st	2nd	3rd	Unpl	Per cent	£1 Level Stake
NH Flat	*14*	*26*	*6*	*2*	*6*	*12*	*23.1*	*+37.90*
Hurdles	*31*	*92*	*5*	*8*	*9*	*70*	*5.4*	*-57.38*
Chases	*11*	*37*	*9*	*5*	*1*	*22*	*24.3*	*+14.63*
Totals	**43**	**155**	**20**	**15**	**16**	**104**	**12.9**	**-4.85**
13-14	*13*	*54*	*9*	*6*	*2*	*37*	*16.7*	*-11.50*

BY MONTH

NH Flat	W-R	Per cent	£1 Level Stake	Hurdles	W-R	Per cent	£1 Level Stake
May	0-0	0.0	0.00	May	0-3	0.0	-3.00
June	0-0	0.0	0.00	June	0-1	0.0	-1.00
July	0-0	0.0	0.00	July	0-0	0.0	0.00
August	0-0	0.0	0.00	August	0-0	0.0	0.00
September	0-0	0.0	0.00	September	0-0	0.0	0.00
October	0-1	0.0	-1.00	October	0-1	0.0	-1.00
November	1-8	12.5	+18.00	November	3-17	17.6	+11.00
December	1-6	16.7	0.00	December	0-9	0.0	-9.00
January	1-2	50.0	+11.00	January	2-14	14.3	-7.38
February	1-3	33.3	+8.00	February	0-14	0.0	-14.00
March	1-4	25.0	-2.60	March	0-19	0.0	-19.00
April	1-2	50.0	+4.50	April	0-14	0.0	-14.00

Chases	W-R	Per cent	£1 Level Stake	Totals	W-R	Per cent	£1 Level Stake
May	1-2	50.0	+0.88	May	1-5	20.0	-2.12
June	0-0	0.0	0.00	June	0-1	0.0	-1.00
July	0-1	0.0	-1.00	July	0-1	0.0	-1.00
August	0-1	0.0	-1.00	August	0-1	0.0	-1.00
September	0-0	0.0	0.00	September	0-0	0.0	0.00
October	0-0	0.0	0.00	October	0-2	0.0	-2.00
November	0-1	0.0	-1.00	November	4-26	15.4	+28.00
December	4-8	50.0	+24.13	December	5-23	21.7	+15.13
January	3-7	42.9	+6.75	January	6-23	26.1	+10.37

February	0-8	0.0	-8.00	February	1-25	4.0	-14.00
March	1-6	16.7	-3.13	March	2-29	6.9	-24.73
April	0-3	0.0	-3.00	April	1-19	5.3	-12.50

DISTANCE

Hurdles	W-R	Per cent	£1 Level Stake	Chases	W-R	Per cent	£1 Level Stake
2m-2m3f	1-42	2.4	-39.00	2m-2m3f	3-6	50.0	+14.38
2m4f-2m7f	2-25	8.0	0.00	2m4f-2m7f	0-7	0.0	-7.00
3m+	0-5	0.0	-5.00	3m+	5-21	23.8	+4.75

TYPE OF RACE

Non-Handicaps	W-R	Per cent	£1 Level Stake	Handicaps	W-R	Per cent	£1 Level Stake
Nov Hrdls	2-35	5.7	-14.00	Nov Hrdls	1-4	25.0	-1.00
Hrdls	0-14	0.0	-14.00	Hrdls	2-38	5.3	-27.38
Nov Chs	2-5	40.0	+13.50	Nov Chs	1-4	25.0	+0.50
Chases	0-0	0.0	0.00	Chases	6-28	21.4	+0.63
Sell/Claim	0-0	0.0	0.00	Sell/Claim	0-1	0.0	-1.00

RACE CLASS / FIRST TIME OUT

	W-R	Per cent	£1 Level Stake		W-R	Per cent	£1 Level Stake
Class 1	2-12	16.7	+5.50	Bumpers	2-14	14.3	+25.00
Class 2	0-2	0.0	-2.00	Hurdles	2-21	9.5	-15.38
Class 3	1-23	4.3	-12.00	Chases	3-8	37.5	+10.50
Class 4	10-74	13.5	-7.25				
Class 5	3-27	11.1	-18.50	Totals	7-43	16.3	+20.12
Class 6	4-17	23.5	+29.40				

JOCKEYS

	W-R	Per cent	£1 Level Stake
David Bass	8-66	12.1	+0.75
Nico de Boinville	6-26	23.1	+6.38
Jason Maguire	3-18	16.7	+5.63
James Davies	2-13	15.4	+1.40
Andrew Tinkler	1-1	100.0	+12.00

COURSE RECORD

	Total W-R	Non-Hndcps Hurdles	Non-Hndcps Chases	Hndcps Hurdles	Hndcps Chases	NH Flat	Per cent	£1 Level Stake
Towcester	5-16	0-4	0-0	2-5	3-6	0-1	31.3	+3.88
Doncaster	4-11	0-4	2-2	1-2	1-2	0-1	36.4	+15.00
Huntingdon	2-6	0-2	0-0	0-0	0-1	2-3	33.3	+21.40
Warwick	2-9	0-3	0-0	0-1	0-2	2-3	22.2	+10.00
Ludlow	2-10	2-7	0-0	0-2	0-0	0-1	20.0	+11.00
Aintree	1-1	0-0	0-0	0-0	0-0	1-1	100.0	+5.50
Leicester	1-4	0-0	0-0	0-0	1-4	0-0	25.0	+1.50
Fontwell	1-5	0-1	0-0	0-1	1-2	0-1	20.0	-2.13
Ffos Las	1-5	0-1	0-0	0-1	1-2	0-1	20.0	+6.00
Newbury	1-7	0-4	0-0	0-2	0-0	1-1	14.3	+4.00

WINNING HORSES

Horse	Races Run	1st	2nd	3rd	£
Barters Hill	4	4	0	0	31390
Cadeau George	6	1	1	0	6657
Newton Thistle	5	2	2	0	7343
Malibu Sun	8	3	0	0	11566
*Assirem	4	1	0	0	4549
Smart Freddy	5	2	0	1	8164
Ergo Sum	5	2	0	0	6173
Ewings	4	1	0	0	3899
Baths Well	6	1	0	1	3899
Cosway Spirit	6	1	2	0	3249
Ballyhenry	2	2	0	0	3249
Total winning prize-money					**£90138**
Favourites	**7-14**		**50.0%**		**5.40**

PAT PHELAN

EPSOM, SURREY

	No. of Hrs	Races Run	1st	2nd	3rd	Unpl	Per cent	£1 Level Stake
NH Flat	*2*	*4*	*0*	*0*	*0*	*4*	*0.0*	*-4.00*
Hurdles	*11*	*37*	*2*	*5*	*5*	*25*	*5.4*	*-15.00*
Chases	*2*	*6*	*1*	*1*	*0*	*4*	*16.7*	*+0.50*
Totals	**14**	**47**	**3**	**6**	**5**	**33**	**6.4**	**-18.50**
13-14	*11*	*34*	*0*	*4*	*4*	*26*	*0.0*	*-34.00*
12-13	*10*	*35*	*0*	*3*	*4*	*28*	*0.0*	*-35.00*

JOCKEYS

	W-R	Per cent	£1 Level Stake
Paddy Bradley	2-15	13.3	+7.00
Joshua Moore	1-13	7.7	-6.50

COURSE RECORD

	Total W-R	Non-Hndcps Hurdles	Non-Hndcps Chases	Hndcps Hurdles	Hndcps Chases	NH Flat	Per cent	£1 Level Stake
Sandown	1-3	0-1	0-0	1-2	0-0	0-0	33.3	+12.00
Fontwell	1-6	0-0	0-0	1-4	0-0	0-2	16.7	+1.00
Kempton	1-7	0-3	0-0	0-1	1-2	0-1	14.3	-0.50

WINNING HORSES

Horse	Races Run	1st	2nd	3rd	£
Representingceltic	5	1	1	0	6498
Right Step	4	1	0	0	3899
Epsom Flyer	6	1	1	1	2339
Total winning prize-money					**£12736**
Favourites	**0-1**		**0.0%**		**-1.00**

ALAN PHILLIPS

CALLOW END, WORCS

	No. of Hrs	Races Run	1st	2nd	3rd	Unpl	Per cent	£1 Level Stake
NH Flat	0	0	0	0	0	0	0.0	0.00
Hurdles	6	23	1	3	2	17	4.3	-10.00
Chases	2	6	0	2	0	4	0.0	-6.00
Totals	**7**	**29**	**1**	**5**	**2**	**21**	**3.4**	**-16.00**
13-14	*4*	*7*	*0*	*0*	*0*	*7*	*0.0*	*-7.00*

JOCKEYS

	W-R	Per cent	£1 Level Stake
Sean Bowen	1-3	33.3	+10.00

COURSE RECORD

	Total W-R	Non-Hndcps Hurdles	Non-Hndcps Chases	Hndcps Hurdles	Hndcps Chases	NH Flat	Per cent	£1 Level Stake
Cheltenham	1-1	0-0	0-0	1-1	0-0	0-0	100.0	+12.00

WINNING HORSES

Horse	Races Run	1st	2nd	3rd	£
Roll On Ruby	7	1	2	2	6256
Total winning prize-money					**£6256**
Favourites	**0-0**		**0.0%**		**0.00**

RICHARD PHILLIPS

ADLESTROP, GLOUCS

	No. of Hrs	Races Run	1st	2nd	3rd	Unpl	Per cent	£1 Level Stake
NH Flat	14	23	3	1	2	17	13.0	+20.00
Hurdles	23	111	11	12	13	75	9.9	+23.00
Chases	5	10	0	2	2	6	0.0	-10.00
Totals	**34**	**144**	**14**	**15**	**17**	**98**	**9.7**	**+33.00**
13-14	*28*	*94*	*4*	*6*	*12*	*72*	*4.3*	*-28.50*
12-13	*33*	*125*	*12*	*13*	*13*	*87*	*9.6*	*-37.88*

BY MONTH

NH Flat	W-R	Per cent	£1 Level Stake	Hurdles	W-R	Per cent	£1 Level Stake
May	1-7	14.3	+10.00	May	0-10	0.0	-10.00
June	0-2	0.0	-2.00	June	2-11	18.2	+2.00
July	0-4	0.0	-4.00	July	2-12	16.7	+1.00
August	0-1	0.0	-1.00	August	0-5	0.0	-5.00
September	1-1	100.0	+4.00	September	1-6	16.7	+1.00
October	0-1	0.0	-1.00	October	0-7	0.0	-7.00
November	0-1	0.0	-1.00	November	0-14	0.0	-14.00
December	0-0	0.0	0.00	December	1-11	9.1	-2.00
January	0-1	0.0	-1.00	January	1-9	11.1	+8.00
February	0-1	0.0	-1.00	February	2-10	20.0	+22.00
March	1-4	25.0	+17.00	March	0-9	0.0	-9.00
April	0-0	0.0	0.00	April	2-7	28.6	+36.00

Chases	W-R	Per cent	£1 Level Stake	Totals	W-R	Per cent	£1 Level Stake
May	0-2	0.0	-2.00	May	1-19	5.3	-2.00
June	0-1	0.0	-1.00	June	2-14	14.3	-1.00
July	0-1	0.0	-1.00	July	2-17	11.8	-4.00
August	0-0	0.0	0.00	August	0-6	0.0	-6.00
September	0-0	0.0	0.00	September	2-7	28.6	+5.00
October	0-1	0.0	-1.00	October	0-9	0.0	-9.00
November	0-0	0.0	0.00	November	0-15	0.0	-15.00
December	0-3	0.0	-3.00	December	1-14	7.1	-5.00
January	0-0	0.0	0.00	January	1-10	10.0	+7.00
February	0-1	0.0	-1.00	February	2-12	16.7	+20.00
March	0-1	0.0	-1.00	March	1-14	7.1	+7.00
April	0-0	0.0	0.00	April	2-7	28.6	+36.00

DISTANCE

Hurdles	W-R	Per cent	£1 Level Stake	Chases	W-R	Per cent	£1 Level Stake
2m-2m3f	5-43	11.6	+45.50	2m-2m3f	0-0	0.0	0.00
2m4f-2m7f	4-37	10.8	-3.50	2m4f-2m7f	0-7	0.0	-7.00
3m+	1-11	9.1	-6.00	3m+	0-2	0.0	-2.00

TYPE OF RACE

Non-Handicaps	W-R	Per cent	£1 Level Stake	Handicaps	W-R	Per cent	£1 Level Stake
Nov Hrdls	0-20	0.0	-20.00	Nov Hrdls	4-16	25.0	+44.00
Hrdls	2-16	12.5	-3.50	Hrdls	4-53	7.5	+1.00
Nov Chs	0-1	0.0	-1.00	Nov Chs	0-2	0.0	-2.00
Chases	0-0	0.0	0.00	Chases	0-7	0.0	-7.00
Sell/Claim	0-4	0.0	-4.00	Sell/Claim	1-3	33.3	+4.50

RACE CLASS

	W-R	Per cent	£1 Level Stake
Class 1	0-0	0.0	0.00
Class 2	0-0	0.0	0.00
Class 3	1-7	14.3	+2.00
Class 4	5-66	7.6	-2.50
Class 5	5-49	10.2	+12.50
Class 6	3-22	13.6	+21.00

FIRST TIME OUT

	W-R	Per cent	£1 Level Stake
Bumpers	2-14	14.3	+24.00
Hurdles	1-16	6.3	+7.00
Chases	0-4	0.0	-4.00
Totals	3-34	8.8	+27.00

JOCKEYS

	W-R	Per cent	£1 Level Stake
Daniel Hiskett	9-84	10.7	-7.00
Richard Johnson	2-19	10.5	+7.00
Aidan Coleman	1-1	100.0	+16.00
Gavin Sheehan	1-2	50.0	+21.00
Sean Quinlan	1-7	14.3	+27.00

COURSE RECORD

	Total W-R	Non-Hndcps Hurdles	Non-Hndcps Chases	Hndcps Hurdles	Hndcps Chases	NH Flat	Per cent	£1 Level Stake
Chepstow	2-5	0-0	0-0	2-4	0-0	0-1	40.0	+38.00
Ludlow	2-7	0-2	0-0	2-4	0-1	0-0	28.6	+11.00

Southwell	2-10	1-4	0-0	0-4	0-0	1-2	20.0	+18.00
Uttoxeter	2-19	0-4	0-0	1-8	0-4	1-3	10.5	+3.00
Worcester	2-19	1-7	0-0	1-5	0-2	0-5	10.5	-5.50
Nton Abbot	1-4	0-1	0-0	1-3	0-0	0-0	25.0	+3.50
Warwick	1-4	0-1	0-0	1-3	0-0	0-0	25.0	+19.00
Stratford	1-9	0-5	0-0	0-3	0-0	1-1	11.1	-4.00
Doncaster	1-10	0-3	0-0	1-6	0-0	0-1	10.0	+7.00

WINNING HORSES

Horse	Races Run	1st	2nd	3rd	£
Seaviper	11	4	0	3	15595
Temlett	2	1	0	0	4549
Brave Helios	7	1	3	1	3899
Paloma's Prince	4	1	1	0	3249
Cash For Steel	10	2	3	1	4947
Flemensbay	7	1	0	1	2599
Lisheen Hill	3	1	0	1	1949
Powderonthebonnet	12	1	1	1	1949
Muthabir	1	1	0	0	1949
Fire Tower	7	1	1	0	1560
Total winning prize-money					**£42245**
Favourites	**0-7**		**0.0%**		**-7.00**

MISS IMOGEN PICKARD

KINGSLAND, HEREFORDSHIRE

	No. of Hrs	Races Run	1st	2nd	3rd	Unpl	Per cent	£1 Level Stake
NH Flat	*1*	*1*	*0*	*0*	*0*	*1*	*0.0*	*-1.00*
Hurdles	*6*	*19*	*1*	*0*	*2*	*16*	*5.3*	*+7.00*
Chases	*0*	*0*	*0*	*0*	*0*	*0*	*0.0*	*0.00*
Totals	**6**	**20**	**1**	**0**	**2**	**17**	**5.0**	**+6.00**
13-14	*5*	*9*	*0*	*1*	*1*	*7*	*0.0*	*-9.00*

JOCKEYS

	W-R	Per cent	£1 Level Stake
James Banks	1-6	16.7	+20.00

COURSE RECORD

	Total W-R	Non-Hndcps Hurdles	Non-Hndcps Chases	Hndcps Hurdles	Hndcps Chases	NH Flat	Per cent	£1 Level Stake
Ludlow	1-4	1-3	0-0	0-1	0-0	0-0	25.0	+22.00

WINNING HORSES

Horse	Races Run	1st	2nd	3rd	£
Mister Fizz	3	1	0	1	6498
Total winning prize-money					**£6498**
Favourites	**0-0**		**0.0%**		**0.00**

DAVID PIPE

NICHOLASHAYNE, DEVON

	No. of Hrs	Races Run	1st	2nd	3rd	Unpl	Per cent	£1 Level Stake
NH Flat	*31*	*51*	*16*	*4*	*7*	*24*	*31.4*	*+18.92*
Hurdles	*104*	*395*	*68*	*50*	*46*	*231*	*17.2*	*-83.19*
Chases	*37*	*134*	*32*	*17*	*13*	*72*	*23.9*	*+15.80*
Totals	**136**	**580**	**116**	**71**	**66**	**327**	**20.0**	**-48.47**
13-14	*155*	*595*	*91*	*65*	*57*	*382*	*15.3*	*-86.26*
12-13	*159*	*624*	*104*	*72*	*65*	*383*	*16.7*	*-181.32*

BY MONTH

NH Flat	W-R	Per cent	£1 Level Stake	Hurdles	W-R	Per cent	£1 Level Stake
May	4-7	57.1	+5.80	May	6-22	27.3	+19.17
June	2-3	66.7	+5.00	June	0-13	0.0	-13.00
July	0-0	0.0	0.00	July	2-14	14.3	-7.13
August	0-1	0.0	-1.00	August	3-16	18.8	-4.10
September	1-3	33.3	+0.50	September	5-18	27.8	+0.25
October	1-9	11.1	-5.25	October	3-25	12.0	-19.59
November	3-8	37.5	+0.63	November	9-44	20.5	+1.12
December	1-5	20.0	-2.13	December	7-41	17.1	-17.95
January	1-8	12.5	-1.00	January	11-64	17.2	-19.33
February	2-3	66.7	+14.88	February	11-49	22.4	+15.58
March	1-2	50.0	+3.50	March	7-52	13.5	-13.67
April	0-2	0.0	-2.00	April	4-37	10.8	-24.54

Chases	W-R	Per cent	£1 Level Stake	Totals	W-R	Per cent	£1 Level Stake
May	4-9	44.4	+16.30	May	14-38	36.8	+41.27
June	1-3	33.3	+2.00	June	3-19	15.8	-6.00
July	4-9	44.4	+2.75	July	6-23	26.1	-4.38
August	2-6	33.3	-0.30	August	5-23	21.7	-5.40
September	3-6	50.0	+0.01	September	9-27	33.3	+0.76
October	2-11	18.2	-6.75	October	6-45	13.3	-31.59
November	4-23	17.4	-11.32	November	16-75	21.3	-9.57
December	4-16	25.0	+28.00	December	12-62	19.4	+7.92
January	2-13	15.4	-5.83	January	14-85	16.5	-26.16
February	4-12	33.3	+5.90	February	17-64	26.6	+36.36
March	2-12	16.7	-0.95	March	10-66	15.2	-11.12
April	0-14	0.0	-14.00	April	4-53	7.5	-40.54

DISTANCE

Hurdles	W-R	Per cent	£1 Level Stake	Chases	W-R	Per cent	£1 Level Stake
2m-2m3f	33-199	16.6	-74.38	2m-2m3f	5-14	35.7	+3.53
2m4f-2m7f	17-99	17.2	-14.51	2m4f-2m7f	13-42	31.0	+21.22
3m+	8-29	27.6	+26.75	3m+	9-59	15.3	-13.83

TYPE OF RACE

Non-Handicaps	W-R	Per cent	£1 Level Stake	Handicaps	W-R	Per cent	£1 Level Stake
Nov Hrdls	13-74	17.6	-38.08	Nov Hrdls	4-19	21.1	+8.25
Hrdls	13-82	15.9	-44.43	Hrdls	35-215	16.3	-10.75

Nov Chs	13-25	52.0	+3.05
Chases	1-9	11.1	-5.75
Sell/Claim	2-3	66.7	+0.07

Nov Chs	3-16	18.8	+4.38
Chases	15-84	17.9	+14.13
Sell/Claim	1-2	50.0	+1.75

RACE CLASS

	W-R	Per cent	£1 Level Stake
Class 1	3-94	3.2	-76.00
Class 2	17-80	21.3	+33.83
Class 3	23-124	18.5	-7.71
Class 4	51-201	25.4	-5.43
Class 5	9-39	23.1	-7.07
Class 6	13-42	31.0	+14.92

FIRST TIME OUT

	W-R	Per cent	£1 Level Stake
Bumpers	10-31	32.3	+7.38
Hurdles	19-80	23.8	+15.85
Chases	6-25	24.0	-0.82
Totals	35-136	25.7	+22.41

JOCKEYS

	W-R	Per cent	£1 Level Stake
Tom Scudamore	82-325	25.2	+10.97
Kieron Edgar	10-63	15.9	-5.13
Michael Heard	9-48	18.8	+11.05
A P McCoy	6-12	50.0	+9.10
Conor O'Farrell	5-89	5.6	-67.20
Mr J J Codd	1-2	50.0	+8.00
Thomas Viel	1-2	50.0	+15.00
Liam Heard	1-4	25.0	-1.25
Mr D G Noonan	1-10	10.0	-4.00

COURSE RECORD

	Total W-R	Non-Hndcps Hurdles	Non-Hndcps Chases	Hndcps Hurdles	Hndcps Chases	NH Flat	Per cent	£1 Level Stake
Newbury	11-38	1-12	1-2	5-15	4-8	0-1	28.9	+29.03
Chepstow	9-31	1-6	1-2	4-12	1-8	2-3	29.0	+4.42
Taunton	8-51	5-32	0-0	3-15	0-3	0-1	15.7	-8.53
Cheltenham	7-59	0-9	2-9	2-23	1-15	2-3	11.9	-25.38
Ffos Las	6-20	1-1	0-0	2-11	0-2	3-6	30.0	+9.34
Exeter	6-44	5-19	1-2	0-15	0-3	0-5	13.6	-27.09
Perth	5-5	1-1	1-1	0-0	3-3	0-0	100.0	+10.41
Haydock	5-15	0-0	0-1	3-9	2-5	0-0	33.3	+18.50
Plumpton	5-20	0-4	0-1	3-10	1-1	1-4	25.0	+17.88
Worcester	5-24	1-3	0-0	1-11	1-4	2-6	20.8	-6.64
Nton Abbot	5-31	0-6	1-2	4-19	0-3	0-1	16.1	-11.77
Fontwell	4-9	1-4	0-0	2-3	0-1	1-1	44.4	+9.00
Kempton	4-14	2-4	0-1	2-7	0-2	0-0	28.6	+0.63
Fakenham	3-5	2-3	1-2	0-0	0-0	0-0	60.0	-0.56
Leicester	3-5	2-2	0-0	1-2	0-1	0-0	60.0	+1.79
Bangor	3-10	0-2	1-2	2-5	0-1	0-0	30.0	+0.25
Towcester	3-10	0-1	1-1	0-4	0-0	2-4	30.0	+2.80
Ascot	3-11	0-2	1-1	2-6	0-2	0-0	27.3	+3.25
Mrket Rsn	3-16	1-2	2-2	0-6	0-5	0-1	18.8	-7.39
Uttoxeter	3-21	1-4	1-1	0-8	1-3	0-5	14.3	-15.39
Sedgefield	2-4	0-1	0-0	0-1	0-0	2-2	50.0	+2.38
Ludlow	2-13	1-8	0-0	0-2	0-2	1-1	15.4	-7.63
Stratford	2-13	1-6	0-0	0-6	1-1	0-0	15.4	-3.33
Wincanton	2-21	0-6	0-0	1-9	1-6	0-0	9.5	-7.80
Newcastle	1-3	1-1	0-0	0-0	0-1	0-1	33.3	-0.75
Southwell	1-5	0-0	0-1	1-3	0-0	0-1	20.0	-1.00
Warwick	1-8	0-2	0-0	1-4	0-0	0-2	12.5	+5.00
Huntingdon	1-10	0-2	0-0	1-6	0-0	0-2	10.0	-5.00
Wetherby	1-12	0-4	0-1	0-4	1-2	0-1	8.3	-10.20
Sandown	1-16	1-6	0-0	0-8	0-2	0-0	6.3	-14.67
Aintree	1-18	0-3	0-2	0-5	1-8	0-0	5.6	+8.00

WINNING HORSES

Horse	Races Run	1st	2nd	3rd	£
Poole Master	8	1	0	0	43330
The Package	4	1	0	0	35976
Moon Racer	2	2	0	0	38719
Unique De Cotte	5	2	1	0	35764
Shotavodka	8	1	0	1	19494
Monetaire	4	1	1	1	18768
Soll	3	2	0	0	37536
Broadway Buffalo	11	2	2	2	18768
Ainsi Fideles	11	7	2	0	57325
Guess Again	3	2	0	0	22575
Katkeau	5	1	1	0	15377
Kings Palace	4	3	0	0	32937
Bygones Sovereign	8	3	0	0	29927
Virtuel D'Oudon	7	3	1	0	22259
Batavir	4	2	0	1	17751
Unanimite	6	1	1	0	9747
Alternatif	3	1	2	0	9747
His Excellency	3	1	1	0	9495
Tullyesker Hill	2	2	0	0	14152
Saint John Henry	5	3	0	0	14621
Purple 'n Gold	10	2	2	3	10891
Gevrey Chambertin	6	2	0	0	10397
Smiles For Miles	6	3	0	1	14166
Heath Hunter	4	1	0	0	6498
Vazaro Delafayette	3	1	0	1	6498
Rathealy	7	2	2	1	9747
Barton Stacey	6	3	1	0	13348
Famousandfearless	6	2	0	2	10554
*Stars Over The Sea	5	2	0	1	9747
Bidourey	5	4	0	0	13906
Rathlin Rose	5	2	1	1	6636
Vif Argent	8	2	1	0	7148
*Classical Art	8	2	1	0	3899
Azza	6	1	0	2	3833
Street Entertainer	12	3	0	2	7668
Top Wood	6	1	1	1	3769
Sail By The Sea	3	1	0	1	3769
Skylander	8	2	0	4	5216
Obistar	6	1	2	0	3574
Border Breaker	6	2	1	1	6823
Twentytwo's Taken	6	2	1	0	7148
Bathwick Man	6	1	2	1	3509
Hawkhill	4	1	0	0	3509
Franklin Roosevelt	3	1	0	1	3509
*Houston Dynimo	7	1	3	1	3249
The Darling Boy	3	1	0	0	3249
Weather Babe	4	1	1	1	3249
Bladoun	6	1	2	0	3249
*Sir Frank Morgan	4	1	0	0	3249

Makadamia	1	1	0	0	3249
*Perspicace	2	1	0	1	3249
Sinndar's Man	7	2	1	1	6498
*Vayland	4	1	1	0	3249
Taj Badalandabad	7	4	0	0	9552
Herbert Park	5	3	2	0	8209
Molo	5	2	1	1	5263
Bengali	3	2	0	0	4809
Brook	4	1	0	0	3249
Party Girls	4	1	0	1	2738
Sadler's Gold	3	1	0	0	2274
What A Moment	2	1	0	0	1949
Chic Theatre	2	1	0	0	1819
All Force Majeure	5	1	0	0	1560
Cloughernagh Boy	1	1	0	0	1560
Ballywilliam	1	1	0	0	1560
Mount Haven	6	1	1	1	1560
Lady Of Longstone	7	1	1	1	1560
Total winning prize-money					**£760182**
Favourites	**57-128**		**44.5%**		**7.91**

JACKIE DU PLESSIS

TREHAN, CORNWALL

	No. of Hrs	Races Run	1st	2nd	3rd	Unpl	Per cent	£1 Level Stake
NH Flat	*1*	*2*	*0*	*0*	*0*	*2*	*0.0*	*-2.00*
Hurdles	*6*	*24*	*2*	*3*	*6*	*13*	*8.3*	*-7.50*
Chases	*2*	*12*	*2*	*2*	*2*	*6*	*16.7*	*-4.63*
Totals	**8**	**38**	**4**	**5**	**8**	**21**	**10.5**	**-14.13**
13-14	*14*	*37*	*2*	*6*	*5*	*24*	*5.4*	*-19.50*
12-13	*9*	*23*	*2*	*6*	*2*	*13*	*8.7*	*-12.00*

JOCKEYS

	W-R	Per cent	£1 Level Stake
James Best	4-31	12.9	-7.13

COURSE RECORD

	Total W-R	Non-Hndcps Hurdles	Non-Hndcps Chases	Hndcps Hurdles	Hndcps Chases	NH Flat	Per cent	£1 Level Stake
Uttoxeter	2-4	0-0	0-0	0-0	2-4	0-0	50.0	+3.38
Taunton	1-5	0-0	0-0	1-4	0-0	0-1	20.0	+4.00
Exeter	1-7	0-1	0-0	1-5	0-0	0-1	14.3	+0.50

WINNING HORSES

Horse	Races Run	1st	2nd	3rd	£
Ray Diamond	8	2	0	2	6496
Winning Spark	6	1	2	1	3574
Absolutely Bygones	8	1	1	3	3574
Total winning prize-money					**£13644**
Favourites	**0-3**		**0.0%**		**-3.00**

CHARLES POGSON

FARNSFIELD, NOTTS

	No. of Hrs	Races Run	1st	2nd	3rd	Unpl	Per cent	£1 Level Stake
NH Flat	*2*	*2*	*0*	*0*	*0*	*2*	*0.0*	*-2.00*
Hurdles	*13*	*47*	*5*	*7*	*9*	*26*	*10.6*	*-3.00*
Chases	*6*	*33*	*4*	*9*	*6*	*14*	*12.1*	*-17.22*
Totals	**16**	**82**	**9**	**16**	**15**	**42**	**11.0**	**-22.22**
13-14	*11*	*64*	*5*	*11*	*3*	*45*	*7.8*	*-28.00*
12-13	*8*	*40*	*1*	*3*	*4*	*32*	*2.5*	*-35.67*

JOCKEYS

	W-R	Per cent	£1 Level Stake
Adam Pogson	9-82	11.0	-22.22

COURSE RECORD

	Total W-R	Non-Hndcps Hurdles	Non-Hndcps Chases	Hndcps Hurdles	Hndcps Chases	NH Flat	Per cent	£1 Level Stake
Huntingdon	3-6	0-1	0-0	2-3	1-1	0-1	50.0	+8.03
Worcester	2-9	0-3	0-0	1-4	1-2	0-0	22.2	+19.00
Southwell	2-20	0-6	0-1	2-7	0-5	0-1	10.0	-9.50
Bangor	1-2	0-0	0-0	0-0	1-2	0-0	50.0	+2.50
Mrket Rsn	1-15	0-4	0-3	0-5	1-3	0-0	6.7	-12.25

WINNING HORSES

Horse	Races Run	1st	2nd	3rd	£
Minella Forfitness	8	1	2	0	16245
Kayfton Pete	10	2	3	3	7148
Cusheen Bridge	8	3	2	0	8317
Mondo Cane	7	2	1	2	5198
Hopeand	8	1	0	0	2274
Total winning prize-money					**£39182**
Favourites	**4-9**		**44.4%**		**5.03**

MRS SUE POPHAM

TAUNTON, SOMERSET

	No. of Hrs	Races Run	1st	2nd	3rd	Unpl	Per cent	£1 Level Stake
NH Flat	*0*	*0*	*0*	*0*	*0*	*0*	*0.0*	*0.00*
Hurdles	*0*	*0*	*0*	*0*	*0*	*0*	*0.0*	*0.00*
Chases	*2*	*3*	*1*	*0*	*0*	*2*	*33.3*	*-0.25*
Totals	**2**	**3**	**1**	**0**	**0**	**2**	**33.3**	**-0.25**
13-14	*2*	*3*	*0*	*1*	*1*	*1*	*0.0*	*-3.00*
12-13	*2*	*2*	*0*	*0*	*1*	*1*	*0.0*	*-2.00*

JOCKEYS

	W-R	Per cent	£1 Level Stake
Mr M Legg	1-3	33.3	-0.25

COURSE RECORD

	Total W-R	Non-Hndcps Hurdles	Chases	Hndcps Hurdles	Chases	NH Flat	Per cent	£1 Level Stake
Nton Abbot	1-1	0-0	1-1	0-0	0-0	0-0	100.0	+1.75

WINNING HORSES

Horse	Races Run	1st	2nd	3rd	£
Iron Chancellor	2	1	0	0	1317
Total winning prize-money					**£1317**
Favourites	**1-1**		**100.0%**		**1.75**

JONATHAN PORTMAN

UPPER LAMBOURN, BERKS

	No. of Hrs	Races Run	1st	2nd	3rd	Unpl	Per cent	£1 Level Stake
NH Flat	*1*	*2*	*0*	*0*	*0*	*2*	*0.0*	*-2.00*
Hurdles	*3*	*4*	*0*	*0*	*0*	*4*	*0.0*	*-4.00*
Chases	*1*	*2*	*1*	*0*	*0*	*1*	*50.0*	*+3.00*
Totals	**4**	**8**	**1**	**0**	**0**	**7**	**12.5**	**-3.00**
13-14	*8*	*24*	*0*	*3*	*3*	*18*	*0.0*	*-24.00*
12-13	*13*	*36*	*0*	*6*	*7*	*23*	*0.0*	*-36.00*

JOCKEYS

	W-R	Per cent	£1 Level Stake
Gavin Sheehan	1-3	33.3	+2.00

COURSE RECORD

	Total W-R	Non-Hndcps Hurdles	Chases	Hndcps Hurdles	Chases	NH Flat	Per cent	£1 Level Stake
Worcester	1-2	0-0	0-0	0-0	1-2	0-0	50.0	+3.00

WINNING HORSES

Horse	Races Run	1st	2nd	3rd	£
Uncle Pettit	2	1	0	0	2144
Total winning prize-money					**£2144**
Favourites	**0-0**		**0.0%**		**0.00**

JAMIE POULTON

TELSCOMBE, E SUSSEX

	No. of Hrs	Races Run	1st	2nd	3rd	Unpl	Per cent	£1 Level Stake
NH Flat	*2*	*5*	*0*	*1*	*0*	*4*	*0.0*	*-5.00*
Hurdles	*2*	*5*	*0*	*2*	*0*	*3*	*0.0*	*-5.00*
Chases	*2*	*8*	*2*	*0*	*1*	*5*	*25.0*	*+16.00*
Totals	**5**	**18**	**2**	**3**	**1**	**12**	**11.1**	**+6.00**
13-14	*5*	*17*	*2*	*1*	*0*	*14*	*11.8*	*-6.50*
12-13	*6*	*15*	*3*	*0*	*1*	*11*	*20.0*	*+7.75*

JOCKEYS

	W-R	Per cent	£1 Level Stake
Jeremiah McGrath	2-12	16.7	+12.00

COURSE RECORD

	Total W-R	Non-Hndcps Hurdles	Chases	Hndcps Hurdles	Chases	NH Flat	Per cent	£1 Level Stake
Nton Abbot	1-2	0-0	0-0	0-0	1-1	0-1	50.0	+15.00
Uttoxeter	1-3	0-0	0-0	0-1	1-2	0-0	33.3	+4.00

WINNING HORSES

Horse	Races Run	1st	2nd	3rd	£
Farbreaga	6	2	0	1	12140
Total winning prize-money					**£12140**
Favourites	**0-1**		**0.0%**		**-1.00**

BRENDAN POWELL

UPPER LAMBOURN, BERKS

	No. of Hrs	Races Run	1st	2nd	3rd	Unpl	Per cent	£1 Level Stake
NH Flat	*6*	*8*	*2*	*0*	*1*	*5*	*25.0*	*+29.50*
Hurdles	*24*	*55*	*1*	*6*	*4*	*44*	*1.8*	*-51.50*
Chases	*9*	*49*	*5*	*10*	*7*	*27*	*10.2*	*-22.25*
Totals	**34**	**112**	**8**	**16**	**12**	**76**	**7.1**	**-44.25**
13-14	*55*	*239*	*18*	*33*	*33*	*155*	*7.5*	*-93.15*
12-13	*71*	*284*	*26*	*33*	*36*	*189*	*9.2*	*-74.35*

JOCKEYS

	W-R	Per cent	£1 Level Stake
Brendan Powell	7-69	10.1	-4.75
James Banks	1-7	14.3	-3.50

COURSE RECORD

	Total W-R	Non-Hndcps Hurdles	Chases	Hndcps Hurdles	Chases	NH Flat	Per cent	£1 Level Stake
Towcester	3-9	1-2	0-0	0-1	1-3	1-3	33.3	+3.00
Worcester	3-12	0-1	1-3	0-4	1-3	1-1	25.0	+30.75
Sedgefield	1-1	0-0	0-0	0-0	1-1	0-0	100.0	+6.50
Kempton	1-2	0-0	0-0	0-1	1-1	0-0	50.0	+3.50

WINNING HORSES

Horse	Races Run	1st	2nd	3rd	£
Violets Boy	9	1	5	0	6498
Fairyinthewind	6	2	1	2	8084
Morestead	15	1	1	1	3769
Keychain	7	1	0	2	2599
Quinlandio	5	1	2	1	1949
Lettheriverrundry	2	1	0	0	1949
Always Lion	1	1	0	0	1625

Total winning prize-money			**£26473**
Favourites	**0-5**	**0.0%**	**-5.00**

SIR MARK PRESCOTT BT

NEWMARKET, SUFFOLK

	No. of Hrs	Races Run	1st	2nd	3rd	Unpl	Per cent	£1 Level Stake
NH Flat	*1*	*4*	*1*	*1*	*2*	*0*	*25.0*	*-1.00*
Hurdles	*0*	*0*	*0*	*0*	*0*	*0*	*0.0*	*0.00*
Chases	*0*	*0*	*0*	*0*	*0*	*0*	*0.0*	*0.00*
Totals	**1**	**4**	**1**	**1**	**2**	**0**	**25.0**	**-1.00**

JOCKEYS

	W-R	Per cent	£1 Level Stake
Micheal Nolan	1-4	25.0	-1.00

COURSE RECORD

	Total W-R	Non-Hndcps Hurdles	Non-Hndcps Chases	Hndcps Hurdles	Hndcps Chases	NH Flat	Per cent	£1 Level Stake
Southwell	1-1	0-0	0-0	0-0	0-0	1-1	100.0	+2.00

WINNING HORSES

Horse	Races Run	1st	2nd	3rd	£
Sea Pride	4	1	1	2	2053
Total winning prize-money					**£2053**
Favourites	**1-2**		**50.0%**		**1.00**

RICHARD PRICE

ULLINGSWICK, H'FORDS

	No. of Hrs	Races Run	1st	2nd	3rd	Unpl	Per cent	£1 Level Stake
NH Flat	*2*	*3*	*0*	*0*	*0*	*3*	*0.0*	*-3.00*
Hurdles	*5*	*19*	*3*	*2*	*2*	*12*	*15.8*	*+4.50*
Chases	*2*	*8*	*0*	*1*	*2*	*5*	*0.0*	*-8.00*
Totals	**7**	**30**	**3**	**3**	**4**	**20**	**10.0**	**-6.50**
13-14	*8*	*29*	*2*	*1*	*2*	*24*	*6.9*	*-3.00*
12-13	*11*	*24*	*2*	*0*	*4*	*18*	*8.3*	*-5.50*

JOCKEYS

	W-R	Per cent	£1 Level Stake
Richard Johnson	2-9	22.2	+4.50
Nick Scholfield	1-4	25.0	+6.00

COURSE RECORD

	Total W-R	Non-Hndcps Hurdles	Non-Hndcps Chases	Hndcps Hurdles	Hndcps Chases	NH Flat	Per cent	£1 Level Stake
Stratford	1-3	0-0	0-0	1-1	0-2	0-0	33.3	+5.00
Ffos Las	1-3	0-0	0-0	1-1	0-2	0-0	33.3	+2.50
Worcester	1-7	0-0	0-0	1-6	0-1	0-0	14.3	+3.00

WINNING HORSES

Horse	Races Run	1st	2nd	3rd	£
Iguacu	9	2	1	1	6011
Gracchus	11	1	2	3	3119
Total winning prize-money					**£9130**
Favourites	**0-1**		**0.0%**		**-1.00**

PETER PRITCHARD

WHATCOTE, WARWICKS

	No. of Hrs	Races Run	1st	2nd	3rd	Unpl	Per cent	£1 Level Stake
NH Flat	*2*	*4*	*0*	*0*	*0*	*4*	*0.0*	*-4.00*
Hurdles	*4*	*17*	*1*	*2*	*0*	*14*	*5.9*	*+9.00*
Chases	*1*	*3*	*0*	*0*	*0*	*3*	*0.0*	*-3.00*
Totals	**7**	**24**	**1**	**2**	**0**	**21**	**4.2**	**+2.00**
13-14	*6*	*33*	*1*	*1*	*6*	*25*	*3.0*	*-26.50*
12-13	*8*	*36*	*5*	*2*	*0*	*29*	*13.9*	*+44.50*

JOCKEYS

	W-R	Per cent	£1 Level Stake
Tom Bellamy	1-15	6.7	+11.00

COURSE RECORD

	Total W-R	Non-Hndcps Hurdles	Non-Hndcps Chases	Hndcps Hurdles	Hndcps Chases	NH Flat	Per cent	£1 Level Stake
Southwell	1-2	0-0	0-0	1-2	0-0	0-0	50.0	+24.00

WINNING HORSES

Horse	Races Run	1st	2nd	3rd	£
Tisfreetdream	8	1	1	0	3249
Total winning prize-money					**£3249**
Favourites	**0-0**		**0.0%**		**0.00**

R C PUDD

TAUNTON, SOMERSET

	No. of Hrs	Races Run	1st	2nd	3rd	Unpl	Per cent	£1 Level Stake
NH Flat	*0*	*0*	*0*	*0*	*0*	*0*	*0.0*	*0.00*
Hurdles	*0*	*0*	*0*	*0*	*0*	*0*	*0.0*	*0.00*
Chases	*1*	*1*	*1*	*0*	*0*	*0*	*100.0*	*+10.00*
Totals	**1**	**1**	**1**	**0**	**0**	**0**	**100.0**	**+10.00**

JOCKEYS

	W-R	Per cent	£1 Level Stake
Mr Sean Houlihan	1-1	100.0	+10.00

COURSE RECORD

	Total W-R	Non-Hndcps Hurdles	Non-Hndcps Chases	Hndcps Hurdles	Hndcps Chases	NH Flat	Per cent	£1 Level Stake
Nton Abbot	1-1	0-0	1-1	0-0	0-0	0-0	100.0	+10.00

WINNING HORSES

Horse	Races Run	1st	2nd	3rd	£
*Dancing Olga	1	1	0	0	1317
Total winning prize-money					**£1317**
Favourites	**0-0**		**0.0%**		**0.00**

NOEL QUINLAN

NEWMARKET, SUFFOLK

	No. of Hrs	Races Run	1st	2nd	3rd	Unpl	Per cent	£1 Level Stake
NH Flat	*1*	*1*	*0*	*0*	*0*	*1*	*0.0*	*-1.00*
Hurdles	*5*	*14*	*2*	*1*	*3*	*8*	*14.3*	*-4.50*
Chases	*0*	*0*	*0*	*0*	*0*	*0*	*0.0*	*0.00*
Totals	**6**	**15**	**2**	**1**	**3**	**9**	**13.3**	**-5.50**
13-14	*14*	*38*	*3*	*4*	*7*	*24*	*7.9*	*-9.00*
12-13	*15*	*41*	*2*	*4*	*2*	*33*	*4.9*	*-28.00*

JOCKEYS

	W-R	Per cent	£1 Level Stake
Jack Quinlan	2-15	13.3	-5.50

COURSE RECORD

	Total W-R	Non-Hndcps Hurdles	Non-Hndcps Chases	Hndcps Hurdles	Hndcps Chases	NH Flat	Per cent	£1 Level Stake
Bangor	1-1	0-0	0-0	1-1	0-0	0-0	100.0	+3.50
Catterick	1-2	1-2	0-0	0-0	0-0	0-0	50.0	+3.00

WINNING HORSES

Horse	Races Run	1st	2nd	3rd	£
Notnowsam	4	1	0	0	3769
Moyne Nineoseven	4	1	1	2	2274
Total winning prize-money					**£6043**
Favourites	**0-1**		**0.0%**		**-1.00**

JOHN QUINN

SETTRINGTON, N YORKS

	No. of Hrs	Races Run	1st	2nd	3rd	Unpl	Per cent	£1 Level Stake
NH Flat	*3*	*5*	*2*	*2*	*0*	*1*	*40.0*	*+4.00*
Hurdles	*28*	*94*	*17*	*23*	*11*	*43*	*18.1*	*-35.98*
Chases	*5*	*13*	*1*	*5*	*2*	*5*	*7.7*	*-9.75*
Totals	**34**	**112**	**20**	**30**	**13**	**49**	**17.9**	**-41.73**
13-14	*30*	*86*	*18*	*12*	*15*	*41*	*20.9*	*+1.90*
12-13	*26*	*68*	*20*	*8*	*9*	*31*	*29.4*	*+28.27*

BY MONTH

NH Flat	W-R	Per cent	£1 Level Stake	**Hurdles**	W-R	Per cent	£1 Level Stake
May	1-1	100.0	+4.50	May	1-3	33.3	-1.17
June	0-0	0.0	0.00	June	0-1	0.0	-1.00
July	0-0	0.0	0.00	July	2-4	50.0	+7.50
August	0-1	0.0	-1.00	August	1-8	12.5	-5.75
September	0-1	0.0	-1.00	September	0-2	0.0	-2.00
October	1-1	100.0	+2.50	October	2-8	25.0	-5.13
November	0-0	0.0	0.00	November	6-17	35.3	+4.54
December	0-0	0.0	0.00	December	2-13	15.4	-7.97
January	0-1	0.0	-1.00	January	2-11	18.2	+0.50
February	0-0	0.0	0.00	February	1-12	8.3	-10.50
March	0-0	0.0	0.00	March	0-11	0.0	-11.00
April	0-0	0.0	0.00	April	0-4	0.0	-4.00

Chases	W-R	Per cent	£1 Level Stake	**Totals**	W-R	Per cent	£1 Level Stake
May	0-0	0.0	0.00	May	2-4	50.0	+3.33
June	0-3	0.0	-3.00	June	0-4	0.0	-4.00
July	0-0	0.0	0.00	July	2-4	50.0	+7.50
August	0-0	0.0	0.00	August	1-9	11.1	-6.75
September	0-0	0.0	0.00	September	0-3	0.0	-3.00
October	0-1	0.0	-1.00	October	3-10	30.0	-3.63
November	1-3	33.3	+0.25	November	7-20	35.0	+4.79
December	0-1	0.0	-1.00	December	2-14	14.3	-8.97
January	0-4	0.0	-4.00	January	2-16	12.5	-4.50
February	0-1	0.0	-1.00	February	1-13	7.7	-11.50
March	0-0	0.0	0.00	March	0-11	0.0	-11.00
April	0-0	0.0	0.00	April	0-4	0.0	-4.00

DISTANCE

Hurdles	W-R	Per cent	£1 Level Stake	**Chases**	W-R	Per cent	£1 Level Stake
2m-2m3f	14-63	22.2	-19.28	2m-2m3f	1-8	12.5	-4.75
2m4f-2m7f	0-10	0.0	-10.00	2m4f-2m7f	0-2	0.0	-2.00
3m+	0-1	0.0	-1.00	3m+	0-0	0.0	0.00

TYPE OF RACE

Non-Handicaps	W-R	Per cent	£1 Level Stake	**Handicaps**	W-R	Per cent	£1 Level Stake
Nov Hrdls	3-19	15.8	-6.63	Nov Hrdls	0-3	0.0	-3.00
Hrdls	10-34	29.4	-8.84	Hrdls	4-37	10.8	-16.50
Nov Chs	0-4	0.0	-4.00	Nov Chs	1-4	25.0	-0.75
Chases	0-0	0.0	0.00	Chases	0-5	0.0	-5.00
Sell/Claim	0-0	0.0	0.00	Sell/Claim	0-0	0.0	0.00

RACE CLASS

	W-R	Per cent	£1 Level Stake
Class 1	2-12	16.7	-7.59
Class 2	1-10	10.0	-6.50
Class 3	2-18	11.1	-4.50
Class 4	11-57	19.3	-22.97

FIRST TIME OUT

	W-R	Per cent	£1 Level Stake
Bumpers	1-3	33.3	+2.50
Hurdles	10-28	35.7	+16.33
Chases	0-3	0.0	-3.00

Class 5	3-11	27.3	+0.33	Totals	11-34	32.4	+15.83
Class 6	1-4	25.0	-0.50				

JOCKEYS

	W-R	Per cent	£1 Level Stake
Dougie Costello	8-45	17.8	-11.12
James Reveley	5-25	20.0	-13.38
A P McCoy	3-4	75.0	+1.94
Dean Pratt	2-17	11.8	-11.67
Nick Scholfield	1-1	100.0	+2.50
Brian Harding	1-2	50.0	+8.00

COURSE RECORD

	Total W-R	Non-Hndcps Hurdles	Non-Hndcps Chases	Hndcps Hurdles	Hndcps Chases	NH Flat	Per cent	£1 Level Stake
Musselbgh	3-7	3-4	0-0	0-2	0-1	0-0	42.9	+6.30
Sedgefield	3-13	2-6	0-0	0-4	1-2	0-1	23.1	-6.72
Hexham	2-6	1-2	0-1	0-1	0-1	1-1	33.3	-0.67
Wetherby	2-16	1-11	0-0	1-4	0-0	0-1	12.5	-10.59
Towcester	1-1	1-1	0-0	0-0	0-0	0-0	100.0	+0.83
Worcester	1-1	1-1	0-0	0-0	0-0	0-0	100.0	+7.00
Ayr	1-2	0-0	0-0	1-2	0-0	0-0	50.0	+8.00
Stratford	1-3	1-2	0-0	0-1	0-0	0-0	33.3	-0.75
Cartmel	1-4	0-2	0-0	1-2	0-0	0-0	25.0	-0.50
Kelso	1-4	1-3	0-0	0-0	0-0	0-1	25.0	-2.67
Doncaster	1-5	0-2	0-0	1-2	0-1	0-0	20.0	-1.50
Sandown	1-5	1-1	0-0	0-4	0-0	0-0	20.0	-2.50
Aintree	1-6	0-0	0-0	0-3	0-2	1-1	16.7	-0.50
Catterick	1-12	1-9	0-1	0-1	0-1	0-0	8.3	-10.47

WINNING HORSES

Horse	Races Run	1st	2nd	3rd	£
Aurore D'Estruval	3	2	1	0	23919
Kashmir Peak	5	1	2	1	12346
Fisher	4	1	1	0	6498
Forced Family Fun	4	1	0	0	6498
Distime	5	1	1	0	6279
Echo Springs	1	1	0	0	4379
Mr Gallivanter	4	2	0	0	7148
Chieftain's Choice	6	2	1	0	7668
L'Aigle Royal	7	1	1	2	3895
El Beau	5	2	3	0	6888
Poetic Verse	5	1	1	1	3249
*Kashstaree	3	1	0	1	3249
Arthurs Secret	4	1	2	0	2599
Spieta	4	1	1	1	1949
Chebsey Beau	2	1	0	0	1949
Luccombe Down	3	1	2	0	1643
Total winning prize-money					**£100156**
Favourites	**15-29**		**51.7%**		**5.27**

DENIS QUINN

NEWMARKET, SUFFOLK

	No. of Hrs	Races Run	1st	2nd	3rd	Unpl	Per cent	£1 Level Stake
NH Flat	*1*	*1*	*0*	*1*	*0*	*0*	*0.0*	*-1.00*
Hurdles	*6*	*31*	*2*	*1*	*2*	*26*	*6.5*	*-17.50*
Chases	*0*	*0*	*0*	*0*	*0*	*0*	*0.0*	*0.00*
Totals	**7**	**32**	**2**	**2**	**2**	**26**	**6.3**	**-18.50**
13-14	*2*	*3*	*0*	*0*	*0*	*3*	*0.0*	*-3.00*
12-13	*3*	*4*	*0*	*0*	*0*	*4*	*0.0*	*-4.00*

JOCKEYS

	W-R	Per cent	£1 Level Stake
Trevor Whelan	1-5	20.0	-0.50
Jack Quinlan	1-15	6.7	-6.00

COURSE RECORD

	Total W-R	Non-Hndcps Hurdles	Non-Hndcps Chases	Hndcps Hurdles	Hndcps Chases	NH Flat	Per cent	£1 Level Stake
Leicester	1-6	1-3	0-0	0-3	0-0	0-0	16.7	+3.00
Huntingdon	1-10	0-3	0-0	1-7	0-0	0-0	10.0	-5.50

WINNING HORSES

Horse	Races Run	1st	2nd	3rd	£
*Craftybird	6	1	0	1	2599
Helamis	13	1	1	1	2274
Total winning prize-money					**£4873**
Favourites	**0-0**		**0.0%**		**0.00**

ALASTAIR RALPH

LUDLOW, SHROPSHIRE

	No. of Hrs	Races Run	1st	2nd	3rd	Unpl	Per cent	£1 Level Stake
NH Flat	*0*	*0*	*0*	*0*	*0*	*0*	*0.0*	*0.00*
Hurdles	*0*	*0*	*0*	*0*	*0*	*0*	*0.0*	*0.00*
Chases	*3*	*6*	*1*	*2*	*1*	*2*	*16.7*	*-3.38*
Totals	**3**	**6**	**1**	**2**	**1**	**2**	**16.7**	**-3.38**
13-14	*2*	*5*	*0*	*0*	*2*	*3*	*0.0*	*-5.00*
12-13	*1*	*3*	*0*	*0*	*0*	*3*	*0.0*	*-3.00*

JOCKEYS

	W-R	Per cent	£1 Level Stake
Mr T Weston	1-2	50.0	+0.63

COURSE RECORD

	Total W-R	Non-Hndcps Hurdles	Non-Hndcps Chases	Hndcps Hurdles	Hndcps Chases	NH Flat	Per cent	£1 Level Stake
Leicester	1-1	0-0	1-1	0-0	0-0	0-0	100.0	+1.63

WINNING HORSES

Horse	Races Run	1st	2nd	3rd	£
Following Dreams	3	1	1	1	1560
Total winning prize-money					**£1560**
Favourites	**1-1**		**100.0%**		**1.63**

DAVID REES

CLARBESTON, PEMBROKES

	No. of Hrs	Races Run	1st	2nd	3rd	Unpl	Per cent	£1 Level Stake
NH Flat	*1*	*1*	*0*	*0*	*0*	*1*	*0.0*	*-1.00*
Hurdles	*22*	*53*	*2*	*3*	*6*	*42*	*3.8*	*-32.00*
Chases	*7*	*16*	*2*	*1*	*2*	*11*	*12.5*	*+17.00*
Totals	**24**	**70**	**4**	**4**	**8**	**54**	**5.7**	**-16.00**
13-14	*24*	*78*	*7*	*7*	*7*	*57*	*9.0*	*-2.75*
12-13	*25*	*79*	*10*	*6*	*13*	*50*	*12.7*	*+18.50*

JOCKEYS

	W-R	Per cent	£1 Level Stake
Paul Moloney	3-38	7.9	+9.00
Denis O'Regan	1-1	100.0	+6.00

COURSE RECORD

	Total W-R	Non-Hndcps Hurdles	Non-Hndcps Chases	Hndcps Hurdles	Hndcps Chases	NH Flat	Per cent	£1 Level Stake
Ffos Las	2-30	0-6	0-0	1-13	1-11	0-0	6.7	+8.00
Ludlow	1-5	0-2	0-0	0-1	1-2	0-0	20.0	+2.00
Worcester	1-15	1-6	0-0	0-7	0-2	0-0	6.7	-6.00

WINNING HORSES

Horse	Races Run	1st	2nd	3rd	£
Lydstep Point	1	1	0	0	6498
Fishing Bridge	8	1	0	0	6173
*Limpopo Tom	2	1	0	0	5848
Macarthur	7	1	3	0	1949
Total winning prize-money					**£20468**
Favourites	**0-4**		**0.0%**		**-4.00**

ANDREW REID

MILL HILL, LONDON NW7

	No. of Hrs	Races Run	1st	2nd	3rd	Unpl	Per cent	£1 Level Stake
NH Flat	*0*	*0*	*0*	*0*	*0*	*0*	*0.0*	*0.00*
Hurdles	*1*	*4*	*1*	*1*	*0*	*2*	*25.0*	*-1.38*
Chases	*0*	*0*	*0*	*0*	*0*	*0*	*0.0*	*0.00*
Totals	**1**	**4**	**1**	**1**	**0**	**2**	**25.0**	**-1.38**

JOCKEYS

	W-R	Per cent	£1 Level Stake
Brendan Powell	1-1	100.0	+1.63

COURSE RECORD

	Total W-R	Non-Hndcps Hurdles	Non-Hndcps Chases	Hndcps Hurdles	Hndcps Chases	NH Flat	Per cent	£1 Level Stake
Taunton	1-1	1-1	0-0	0-0	0-0	0-0	100.0	+1.63

WINNING HORSES

Horse	Races Run	1st	2nd	3rd	£
Ascendant	4	1	1	0	2053
Total winning prize-money					**£2053**
Favourites	**47-47**		**100.0%**		**76.38**

KEITH REVELEY

LINGDALE, REDCAR & CLEVELAND

	No. of Hrs	Races Run	1st	2nd	3rd	Unpl	Per cent	£1 Level Stake
NH Flat	*8*	*10*	*0*	*0*	*0*	*10*	*0.0*	*-10.00*
Hurdles	*21*	*72*	*14*	*8*	*8*	*42*	*19.4*	*-5.25*
Chases	*10*	*38*	*6*	*7*	*12*	*13*	*15.8*	*-6.83*
Totals	**29**	**120**	**20**	**15**	**20**	**65**	**16.7**	**-22.08**
13-14	*32*	*134*	*19*	*18*	*34*	*63*	*14.2*	*-29.33*
12-13	*39*	*153*	*34*	*21*	*17*	*81*	*22.2*	*+31.25*

BY MONTH

NH Flat	W-R	Per cent	£1 Level Stake	Hurdles	W-R	Per cent	£1 Level Stake
May	0-0	0.0	0.00	May	0-4	0.0	-4.00
June	0-0	0.0	0.00	June	0-1	0.0	-1.00
July	0-0	0.0	0.00	July	0-0	0.0	0.00
August	0-1	0.0	-1.00	August	0-1	0.0	-1.00
September	0-0	0.0	0.00	September	0-1	0.0	-1.00
October	0-0	0.0	0.00	October	2-5	40.0	+2.13
November	0-2	0.0	-2.00	November	1-7	14.3	-4.75
December	0-3	0.0	-3.00	December	2-7	28.6	+11.00
January	0-1	0.0	-1.00	January	0-12	0.0	-12.00
February	0-2	0.0	-2.00	February	3-13	23.1	-0.25
March	0-0	0.0	0.00	March	5-14	35.7	+5.63
April	0-1	0.0	-1.00	April	1-7	14.3	0.00

Chases	W-R	Per cent	£1 Level Stake	Totals	W-R	Per cent	£1 Level Stake
May	2-6	33.3	+0.17	May	2-10	20.0	-3.83
June	0-3	0.0	-3.00	June	0-4	0.0	-4.00
July	0-1	0.0	-1.00	July	0-1	0.0	-1.00
August	0-0	0.0	0.00	August	0-2	0.0	-2.00
September	0-0	0.0	0.00	September	0-1	0.0	-1.00
October	0-2	0.0	-2.00	October	2-7	28.6	+0.13
November	3-5	60.0	+15.50	November	4-14	28.6	+8.75
December	1-3	33.3	+1.50	December	3-13	23.1	+9.50
January	0-6	0.0	-6.00	January	0-19	0.0	-19.00

February	0-8	0.0	-8.00	February	3-23	13.0	-10.25
March	0-1	0.0	-1.00	March	5-15	33.3	+4.63
April	0-3	0.0	-3.00	April	1-11	9.1	-4.00

DISTANCE

Hurdles	W-R	Per cent	£1 Level Stake	Chases	W-R	Per cent	£1 Level Stake
2m-2m3f	10-41	24.4	+6.75	2m-2m3f	3-13	23.1	-2.33
2m4f-2m7f	2-18	11.1	-8.50	2m4f-2m7f	2-6	33.3	+9.00
3m+	1-8	12.5	-3.00	3m+	0-11	0.0	-11.00

TYPE OF RACE

Non-Handicaps	W-R	Per cent	£1 Level Stake	Handicaps	W-R	Per cent	£1 Level Stake
Nov Hrdls	5-19	26.3	-2.00	Nov Hrdls	1-3	33.3	+3.50
Hrdls	1-12	8.3	-9.38	Hrdls	7-38	18.4	+2.63
Nov Chs	0-3	0.0	-3.00	Nov Chs	1-3	33.3	+2.50
Chases	0-0	0.0	0.00	Chases	5-32	15.6	-6.33
Sell/Claim	0-0	0.0	0.00	Sell/Claim	0-0	0.0	0.00

RACE CLASS

	W-R	Per cent	£1 Level Stake
Class 1	1-5	20.0	0.00
Class 2	0-8	0.0	-8.00
Class 3	5-26	19.2	+11.88
Class 4	11-50	22.0	-8.96
Class 5	3-22	13.6	-8.00
Class 6	0-9	0.0	-9.00

FIRST TIME OUT

	W-R	Per cent	£1 Level Stake
Bumpers	0-8	0.0	-8.00
Hurdles	1-13	7.7	-6.00
Chases	2-8	25.0	-0.83
Totals	3-29	10.3	-14.83

JOCKEYS

	W-R	Per cent	£1 Level Stake
James Reveley	19-107	17.8	-12.08
Colm McCormack	1-9	11.1	-6.00

COURSE RECORD

	Total W-R	Non-Hndcps Hurdles	Non-Hndcps Chases	Hndcps Hurdles	Hndcps Chases	NH Flat	Per cent	£1 Level Stake
Sedgefield	5-10	1-1	0-0	2-5	2-4	0-0	50.0	+6.67
Newcastle	4-26	1-8	0-0	2-11	1-4	0-3	15.4	-11.63
Catterick	3-9	2-3	0-0	1-3	0-2	0-1	33.3	+1.75
Doncaster	3-28	1-5	0-2	0-9	2-10	0-2	10.7	-8.50
Musselbgh	2-10	0-2	0-1	1-4	1-3	0-0	20.0	+10.50
Carlisle	1-1	0-0	0-0	1-1	0-0	0-0	100.0	+6.00
Wetherby	1-1	0-0	0-0	1-1	0-0	0-0	100.0	+5.50
Kelso	1-2	1-1	0-0	0-1	0-0	0-0	50.0	+0.63

WINNING HORSES

Horse	Races Run	1st	2nd	3rd	£
Balmusette	6	2	2	0	15445
Robbie	7	2	1	1	13646
Waltz Darling	7	2	1	1	13054
Brave Spartacus	7	3	0	2	11566
Categorical	7	1	1	4	4689
Shadrack	8	2	2	3	7953
Donna's Pride	6	1	1	1	3899
Spiculas	3	2	1	0	7148
*Tekthelot	2	1	1	0	3574
Ivan Boru	6	1	0	1	3379
Midnight Monty	4	1	0	0	3249
Madrasa	6	1	0	0	2599
Whichwaytobougie	7	1	1	2	2274

Total winning prize-money **£92475**

Favourites **6-16** **37.5%** **0.92**

LYDIA RICHARDS

FUNTINGTON, W SUSSEX

	No. of Hrs	Races Run	1st	2nd	3rd	Unpl	Per cent	£1 Level Stake
NH Flat	*2*	*4*	*0*	*0*	*0*	*4*	*0.0*	*-4.00*
Hurdles	*4*	*9*	*1*	*0*	*1*	*7*	*11.1*	*+25.00*
Chases	*4*	*19*	*3*	*1*	*3*	*12*	*15.8*	*-4.75*
Totals	**9**	**32**	**4**	**1**	**4**	**23**	**12.5**	**+16.25**
13-14	*9*	*22*	*1*	*4*	*3*	*14*	*4.5*	*-16.00*
12-13	*5*	*22*	*4*	*5*	*4*	*9*	*18.2*	*-4.50*

JOCKEYS

	W-R	Per cent	£1 Level Stake
Marc Goldstein	3-25	12.0	+17.75
Paddy Brennan	1-2	50.0	+3.50

COURSE RECORD

	Total W-R	Non-Hndcps Hurdles	Non-Hndcps Chases	Hndcps Hurdles	Hndcps Chases	NH Flat	Per cent	£1 Level Stake
Fontwell	3-15	0-2	0-0	1-2	2-10	0-1	20.0	+27.75
Plumpton	1-4	0-0	0-0	0-1	1-3	0-0	25.0	+1.50

WINNING HORSES

Horse	Races Run	1st	2nd	3rd	£
Venetian Lad	10	2	1	3	9422
Aaly	5	1	0	0	3119
*Volio Vincente	4	1	0	0	2274

Total winning prize-money **£14815**

Favourites **0-1** **0.0%** **-1.00**

NICKY RICHARDS

GREYSTOKE, CUMBRIA

	No. of Hrs	Races Run	1st	2nd	3rd	Unpl	Per cent	£1 Level Stake
NH Flat	*5*	*11*	*5*	*2*	*2*	*2*	*45.5*	*+1.05*
Hurdles	*27*	*117*	*33*	*10*	*14*	*59*	*28.2*	*+51.66*
Chases	*15*	*61*	*10*	*8*	*6*	*37*	*16.4*	*-15.13*
Totals	**42**	**189**	**48**	**20**	**22**	**98**	**25.4**	**+37.58**
13-14	*47*	*166*	*25*	*25*	*18*	*98*	*15.1*	*-18.47*
12-13	*45*	*155*	*25*	*19*	*18*	*93*	*16.1*	*-7.87*

BY MONTH

NH Flat	W-R	Per cent	£1 Level Stake
May	0-0	0.0	0.00
June	0-0	0.0	0.00
July	0-0	0.0	0.00
August	0-0	0.0	0.00
September	0-0	0.0	0.00
October	0-0	0.0	0.00
November	3-5	60.0	+3.38
December	1-1	100.0	+0.57
January	1-2	50.0	+0.10
February	0-1	0.0	-1.00
March	0-1	0.0	-1.00
April	0-1	0.0	-1.00

Hurdles	W-R	Per cent	£1 Level Stake
May	3-12	25.0	+11.67
June	0-4	0.0	-4.00
July	3-9	33.3	+6.38
August	2-7	28.6	+0.25
September	1-3	33.3	0.00
October	3-11	27.3	+5.20
November	6-21	28.6	+14.25
December	0-7	0.0	-7.00
January	5-10	50.0	+13.36
February	4-9	44.4	+10.80
March	4-12	33.3	+2.75
April	2-12	16.7	-2.00

Chases	W-R	Per cent	£1 Level Stake
May	1-6	16.7	-2.00
June	1-3	33.3	+3.00
July	1-4	25.0	+2.50
August	1-2	50.0	+2.00
September	1-2	50.0	+2.00
October	2-6	33.3	+0.88
November	0-12	0.0	-12.00
December	1-5	20.0	-0.50
January	0-5	0.0	-5.00
February	0-5	0.0	-5.00
March	0-5	0.0	-5.00
April	2-6	33.3	+4.00

Totals	W-R	Per cent	£1 Level Stake
May	4-18	22.2	+9.67
June	1-7	14.3	-1.00
July	4-13	30.8	+8.88
August	3-9	33.3	+2.25
September	2-5	40.0	+2.00
October	5-17	29.4	+6.08
November	9-38	23.7	+5.63
December	2-13	15.4	-6.93
January	6-17	35.3	+8.46
February	4-15	26.7	+4.80
March	4-18	22.2	-3.25
April	4-19	21.1	+1.00

DISTANCE

Hurdles	W-R	Per cent	£1 Level Stake
2m-2m3f	10-39	25.6	+16.59
2m4f-2m7f	14-40	35.0	+38.22
3m+	8-24	33.3	+7.10

Chases	W-R	Per cent	£1 Level Stake
2m-2m3f	3-5	60.0	+6.38
2m4f-2m7f	2-19	10.5	-11.00
3m+	3-22	13.6	-4.00

TYPE OF RACE

Non-Handicaps

	W-R	Per cent	£1 Level Stake
Nov Hrdls	4-24	16.7	+4.75
Hrdls	5-14	35.7	+16.52
Nov Chs	1-4	25.0	0.00
Chases	0-6	0.0	-6.00
Sell/Claim	1-2	50.0	+1.75

Handicaps

	W-R	Per cent	£1 Level Stake
Nov Hrdls	3-12	25.0	-1.17
Hrdls	20-62	32.3	+32.81
Nov Chs	0-7	0.0	-7.00
Chases	9-44	20.5	-2.13
Sell/Claim	1-3	33.3	+1.00

RACE CLASS

	W-R	Per cent	£1 Level Stake
Class 1	2-15	13.3	-7.00
Class 2	4-17	23.5	-4.70
Class 3	5-37	13.5	-10.17
Class 4	20-70	28.6	+35.43
Class 5	12-41	29.3	+20.97
Class 6	5-9	55.6	+3.05

FIRST TIME OUT

	W-R	Per cent	£1 Level Stake
Bumpers	3-5	60.0	+3.38
Hurdles	5-22	22.7	+19.68
Chases	3-15	20.0	-4.13
Totals	11-42	26.2	+18.93

JOCKEYS

	W-R	Per cent	£1 Level Stake
Brian Harding	36-144	25.0	+28.73
A P McCoy	3-6	50.0	+3.60
Wilson Renwick	2-4	50.0	+7.50
Noel Fehily	2-6	33.3	+1.75
Harry Challoner	2-15	13.3	-6.00
David Mullins	1-1	100.0	+4.50
Davy Russell	1-2	50.0	+3.00
Miss J R Richards	1-7	14.3	-1.50

COURSE RECORD

	Total W-R	Non-Hndcps Hurdles	Non-Hndcps Chases	Hndcps Hurdles	Hndcps Chases	NH Flat	Per cent	£1 Level Stake
Ayr	12-32	3-9	0-1	5-12	1-7	3-3	37.5	+14.94
Kelso	7-23	2-8	0-0	3-6	2-8	0-1	30.4	+5.51
Carlisle	5-21	0-4	1-3	3-6	1-8	0-0	23.8	+10.75
Doncaster	4-13	2-4	0-0	1-4	1-3	0-2	30.8	+17.25
Newcastle	4-14	1-3	0-0	1-3	0-6	2-2	28.6	-1.93
Huntingdon	3-7	1-1	0-1	2-5	0-0	0-0	42.9	+1.85
Perth	3-20	1-2	0-0	2-13	0-5	0-0	15.0	+5.50
Cartmel	2-4	0-0	0-0	1-2	1-2	0-0	50.0	+8.50
Musselbgh	2-6	0-1	0-0	2-4	0-1	0-0	33.3	0.00
Sedgefield	2-6	0-2	0-0	1-2	1-2	0-0	33.3	+1.50
Mrket Rsn	2-9	0-0	0-0	2-8	0-1	0-0	22.2	-2.29
Hexham	1-4	0-2	0-0	0-0	1-2	0-0	25.0	+2.00
Bangor	1-5	0-1	0-0	0-3	1-1	0-0	20.0	-1.00

WINNING HORSES

Horse	Races Run	1st	2nd	3rd	£
Duke Of Navan	5	2	2	0	24703
Glingerburn	5	4	0	0	41701
Simply Ned	4	1	1	0	14115
One For Harry	7	1	1	0	12512
Gold Futures	8	4	0	1	26512
Wicked Spice	7	3	1	0	13646
Cultram Abbey	7	2	0	0	9747
Warriors Tale	5	2	1	0	8967
Top Billing	5	3	0	1	4224
Peachey Moment	7	2	0	3	6758
*Scarlet Fire	3	1	0	2	3899
Bernardelli	3	1	0	0	3899
Sir Vinski	5	2	0	1	3899
Teddy Tee	6	1	1	0	3899
Looking Well	4	2	0	1	7148
Crinkle Crags	6	1	0	0	3379
Winter Alchemy	8	1	1	1	3249
One For Hocky	11	3	2	3	9097
Un Noble	5	1	0	0	3249
Benmadigan	4	1	0	1	3165
St Gregory	7	2	0	0	5068
Early Applause	4	1	1	2	2599
Chidswell	5	1	2	1	2053

Parc Des Princes	5	1	0	1	1949
Another Bill	2	2	0	0	3422
Imada	2	1	0	1	1643
Western Rules	3	2	0	0	3119
Total winning prize-money					**£227621**
Favourites	**17-43**		**39.5%**		**5.44**

DAVID RICHARDS

LLANTILIO CROSSENNY,MONMOUTHS

	No. of Hrs	Races Run	1st	2nd	3rd	Unpl	Per cent	£1 Level Stake
NH Flat	*0*	*0*	*0*	*0*	*0*	*0*	*0.0*	*0.00*
Hurdles	*0*	*0*	*0*	*0*	*0*	*0*	*0.0*	*0.00*
Chases	*1*	*5*	*1*	*0*	*2*	*2*	*20.0*	*+12.00*
Totals	**1**	**5**	**1**	**0**	**2**	**2**	**20.0**	**+12.00**
13-14	*1*	*4*	*0*	*2*	*0*	*2*	*0.0*	*-4.00*
12-13	*2*	*11*	*1*	*0*	*2*	*8*	*9.1*	*-6.67*

JOCKEYS

	W-R	Per cent	£1 Level Stake
Robert Dunne	1-3	33.3	+14.00

COURSE RECORD

	Total W-R	Non-Hndcps Hurdles	Non-Hndcps Chases	Hndcps Hurdles	Hndcps Chases	NH Flat	Per cent	£1 Level Stake
Worcester	1-2	0-0	0-1	0-0	1-1	0-0	50.0	+15.00

WINNING HORSES

Horse	Races Run	1st	2nd	3rd	£
Another Kate	5	1	0	2	4094
Total winning prize-money					**£4094**
Favourites	**0-0**		**0.0%**		**0.00**

JOHN DAVID RICHES

PILLING, LANCASHIRE

	No. of Hrs	Races Run	1st	2nd	3rd	Unpl	Per cent	£1 Level Stake
NH Flat	*1*	*2*	*0*	*0*	*0*	*2*	*0.0*	*-2.00*
Hurdles	*3*	*14*	*1*	*1*	*0*	*12*	*7.1*	*-9.50*
Chases	*0*	*0*	*0*	*0*	*0*	*0*	*0.0*	*0.00*
Totals	**4**	**16**	**1**	**1**	**0**	**14**	**6.3**	**-11.50**

JOCKEYS

	W-R	Per cent	£1 Level Stake
Conor Shoemark	1-5	20.0	-0.50

COURSE RECORD

	Total W-R	Non-Hndcps Hurdles	Non-Hndcps Chases	Hndcps Hurdles	Hndcps Chases	NH Flat	Per cent	£1 Level Stake
Uttoxeter	1-3	0-0	0-0	1-3	0-0	0-0	33.3	+1.50

WINNING HORSES

Horse	Races Run	1st	2nd	3rd	£
*Mubrook	9	1	1	0	2209
Total winning prize-money					**£2209**
Favourites	**0-1**		**0.0%**		**-1.00**

RENEE ROBESON

TYRINGHAM, BUCKS

	No. of Hrs	Races Run	1st	2nd	3rd	Unpl	Per cent	£1 Level Stake
NH Flat	*2*	*3*	*0*	*0*	*2*	*1*	*0.0*	*-3.00*
Hurdles	*11*	*32*	*7*	*5*	*7*	*13*	*21.9*	*+31.25*
Chases	*2*	*5*	*1*	*0*	*0*	*4*	*20.0*	*+4.00*
Totals	**14**	**40**	**8**	**5**	**9**	**18**	**20.0**	**+32.25**
13-14	*23*	*76*	*11*	*7*	*10*	*48*	*14.5*	*-19.25*
12-13	*17*	*69*	*7*	*8*	*11*	*43*	*10.1*	*-19.75*

JOCKEYS

	W-R	Per cent	£1 Level Stake
Joshua Moore	5-16	31.3	+28.25
Jamie Moore	1-1	100.0	+8.00
Paddy Brennan	1-1	100.0	+10.00
Brendan Powell	1-11	9.1	-3.00

COURSE RECORD

	Total W-R	Non-Hndcps Hurdles	Non-Hndcps Chases	Hndcps Hurdles	Hndcps Chases	NH Flat	Per cent	£1 Level Stake
Chepstow	1-1	0-0	0-0	0-0	1-1	0-0	100.0	+8.00
Stratford	1-1	1-1	0-0	0-0	0-0	0-0	100.0	+7.00
Kempton	1-2	0-0	0-0	1-1	0-1	0-0	50.0	+9.00
Aintree	1-3	0-0	0-0	1-2	0-1	0-0	33.3	+4.50
Mrket Rsn	1-3	0-0	0-0	1-3	0-0	0-0	33.3	+5.00
Towcester	1-4	0-1	0-0	1-2	0-0	0-1	25.0	+8.00
Uttoxeter	1-5	0-2	0-0	1-3	0-0	0-0	20.0	+8.00
Huntingdon	1-7	0-2	0-0	1-3	0-1	0-1	14.3	-3.25

WINNING HORSES

Horse	Races Run	1st	2nd	3rd	£
Cloonacool	5	3	1	1	19689
Dawn Commander	2	1	0	1	6256
San Telm	2	1	0	0	5393
Smart Exit	3	1	0	0	3769
Mr Maynard	7	1	1	1	2339
Ereyna	3	1	0	1	2053
Total winning prize-money					**£39499**
Favourites	**0-1**		**0.0%**		**-1.00**

PAULINE ROBSON

KIRKHARLE, NORTHUMBERLAND

	No. of Hrs	Races Run	1st	2nd	3rd	Unpl	Per cent	£1 Level Stake
NH Flat	*0*	*0*	*0*	*0*	*0*	*0*	*0.0*	*0.00*
Hurdles	*11*	*31*	*5*	*4*	*4*	*18*	*16.1*	*-4.75*
Chases	*9*	*29*	*4*	*4*	*4*	*17*	*13.8*	*+0.25*
Totals	**14**	**60**	**9**	**8**	**8**	**35**	**15.0**	**-4.50**
13-14	*11*	*34*	*0*	*5*	*9*	*20*	*0.0*	*-34.00*
12-13	*11*	*35*	*10*	*7*	*2*	*16*	*28.6*	*+9.23*

JOCKEYS

	W-R	Per cent	£1 Level Stake
James Reveley	3-9	33.3	+3.25
Brian Hughes	2-8	25.0	+10.00
Brian Harding	2-18	11.1	-5.50
Graham Watters	1-2	50.0	+1.25
Mr T Hamilton	1-6	16.7	+3.50

COURSE RECORD

	Total W-R	Non-Hndcps Hurdles	Non-Hndcps Chases	Hndcps Hurdles	Hndcps Chases	NH Flat	Per cent	£1 Level Stake
Newcastle	2-5	0-0	0-0	0-2	2-3	0-0	40.0	+11.50
Ayr	2-8	0-0	0-0	2-6	0-2	0-0	25.0	-0.25
Sedgefield	1-1	0-0	0-0	0-0	1-1	0-0	100.0	+9.00
Wetherby	1-2	0-0	0-0	0-1	1-1	0-0	50.0	+0.75
Perth	1-6	0-1	0-0	1-2	0-3	0-0	16.7	-0.50
Musselbgh	1-8	0-0	0-0	1-6	0-2	0-0	12.5	-3.00
Kelso	1-12	0-2	0-1	1-3	0-6	0-0	8.3	-4.00

WINNING HORSES

Horse	Races Run	1st	2nd	3rd	£
Upsilon Bleu	5	1	3	1	12996
Habbie Simpson	5	1	0	1	9747
Sharp Rise	5	1	0	1	6256
Scimon Templar	8	3	0	1	9682
Teo Vivo	5	2	2	0	6671
Full Jack	6	1	1	2	3249
Total winning prize-money					**£48601**
Favourites	**2-13**		**15.4%**		**-7.00**

RICHARD ROWE

SULLINGTON, W SUSSEX

	No. of Hrs	Races Run	1st	2nd	3rd	Unpl	Per cent	£1 Level Stake
NH Flat	*3*	*6*	*0*	*0*	*0*	*6*	*0.0*	*-6.00*
Hurdles	*7*	*18*	*1*	*1*	*3*	*13*	*5.6*	*-7.00*
Chases	*4*	*11*	*1*	*0*	*0*	*10*	*9.1*	*-3.00*
Totals	**11**	**35**	**2**	**1**	**3**	**29**	**5.7**	**-16.00**
13-14	*15*	*50*	*3*	*2*	*5*	*40*	*6.0*	*-26.00*
12-13	*18*	*50*	*1*	*7*	*2*	*40*	*2.0*	*-46.25*

JOCKEYS

	W-R	Per cent	£1 Level Stake
Leighton Aspell	2-22	9.1	-3.00

COURSE RECORD

	Total W-R	Non-Hndcps Hurdles	Non-Hndcps Chases	Hndcps Hurdles	Hndcps Chases	NH Flat	Per cent	£1 Level Stake
Lingfield	1-6	0-1	0-0	0-2	1-3	0-0	16.7	+2.00
Plumpton	1-7	1-2	0-0	0-2	0-0	0-3	14.3	+4.00

WINNING HORSES

Horse	Races Run	1st	2nd	3rd	£
Strange Bird	7	1	0	1	3769
Like Sully	8	1	0	0	3379
Total winning prize-money					**£7148**
Favourites	**0-1**		**0.0%**		**-1.00**

PHILIP ROWLEY

BRIDGNORTH, SHORPSHIRE

	No. of Hrs	Races Run	1st	2nd	3rd	Unpl	Per cent	£1 Level Stake
NH Flat	*0*	*0*	*0*	*0*	*0*	*0*	*0.0*	*0.00*
Hurdles	*0*	*0*	*0*	*0*	*0*	*0*	*0.0*	*0.00*
Chases	*4*	*9*	*1*	*2*	*0*	*6*	*11.1*	*+8.00*
Totals	**4**	**9**	**1**	**2**	**0**	**6**	**11.1**	**+8.00**
13-14	*5*	*13*	*2*	*2*	*2*	*7*	*15.4*	*+19.00*
12-13	*4*	*7*	*3*	*1*	*2*	*1*	*42.9*	*+16.38*

JOCKEYS

	W-R	Per cent	£1 Level Stake
Mr Alex Edwards	1-9	11.1	+8.00

COURSE RECORD

	Total W-R	Non-Hndcps Hurdles	Non-Hndcps Chases	Hndcps Hurdles	Hndcps Chases	NH Flat	Per cent	£1 Level Stake
Bangor	1-2	0-0	1-2	0-0	0-0	0-0	50.0	+15.00

WINNING HORSES

Horse	Races Run	1st	2nd	3rd	£
Temple Grandin	3	1	1	0	1248
Total winning prize-money					**£1248**
Favourites	**0-0**		**0.0%**		**0.00**

LUCINDA RUSSELL

ARLARY, PERTH & KINROSS

	No. of Hrs	Races Run	1st	2nd	3rd	Unpl	Per cent	£1 Level Stake
NH Flat	*20*	*22*	*1*	*2*	*2*	*17*	*4.5*	*-15.00*
Hurdles	*66*	*249*	*13*	*30*	*25*	*181*	*5.2*	*-142.59*

Chases	*59*	*230*	*33*	*32*	*32*	*133*	*14.3*	*-49.81*
Totals	**111**	**501**	**47**	**64**	**59**	**331**	**9.4**	**-207.40**
13-14	*122*	*528*	*67*	*65*	*86*	*309*	*12.7*	*-125.63*
12-13	*103*	*478*	*58*	*68*	*63*	*289*	*12.1*	*-191.07*

BY MONTH

NH Flat	W-R	Per cent	£1 Level Stake
May	0-1	0.0	-1.00
June	0-0	0.0	0.00
July	0-0	0.0	0.00
August	0-0	0.0	0.00
September	0-2	0.0	-2.00
October	0-4	0.0	-4.00
November	0-1	0.0	-1.00
December	0-0	0.0	0.00
January	0-3	0.0	-3.00
February	0-2	0.0	-2.00
March	1-5	20.0	+2.00
April	0-4	0.0	-4.00

Hurdles	W-R	Per cent	£1 Level Stake
May	0-13	0.0	-13.00
June	0-5	0.0	-5.00
July	0-19	0.0	-19.00
August	1-7	14.3	-2.00
September	1-14	7.1	-4.00
October	0-23	0.0	-23.00
November	3-42	7.1	-5.50
December	1-16	6.3	-14.47
January	4-40	10.0	+1.50
February	2-30	6.7	-20.50
March	1-21	4.8	-18.63
April	0-19	0.0	-19.00

Chases	W-R	Per cent	£1 Level Stake
May	2-16	12.5	-8.70
June	2-4	50.0	+6.83
July	1-6	16.7	-1.67
August	3-8	37.5	+8.50
September	1-10	10.0	-6.00
October	5-27	18.5	-5.00
November	3-32	9.4	-22.15
December	1-16	6.3	-9.00
January	7-33	21.2	+10.13
February	8-33	24.2	+22.25
March	0-28	0.0	-28.00
April	0-17	0.0	-17.00

Totals	W-R	Per cent	£1 Level Stake
May	2-30	6.7	-22.70
June	2-9	22.2	+1.83
July	1-25	4.0	-20.67
August	4-15	26.7	+6.50
September	2-26	7.7	-12.00
October	5-54	9.3	-32.00
November	6-75	8.0	-28.65
December	2-32	6.3	-23.47
January	11-76	14.5	+8.63
February	10-65	15.4	-0.25
March	2-54	3.7	-44.63
April	0-40	0.0	-40.00

DISTANCE

Hurdles	W-R	Per cent	£1 Level Stake
2m-2m3f	5-113	4.4	-68.00
2m4f-2m7f	3-77	3.9	-64.47
3m+	3-27	11.1	-14.13

Chases	W-R	Per cent	£1 Level Stake
2m-2m3f	4-38	10.5	-6.50
2m4f-2m7f	13-84	15.5	-18.12
3m+	8-54	14.8	-8.50

TYPE OF RACE

Non-Handicaps

	W-R	Per cent	£1 Level Stake
Nov Hrdls	6-48	12.5	-2.09
Hrdls	2-40	5.0	-10.50
Nov Chs	3-10	30.0	+6.83
Chases	0-2	0.0	-2.00
Sell/Claim	0-1	0.0	-1.00

Handicaps

	W-R	Per cent	£1 Level Stake
Nov Hrdls	1-21	4.8	-15.50
Hrdls	4-137	2.9	-111.50
Nov Chs	8-58	13.8	-17.57
Chases	22-160	13.8	-37.08
Sell/Claim	0-1	0.0	-1.00

RACE CLASS

	W-R	Per cent	£1 Level Stake
Class 1	2-16	12.5	+19.00
Class 2	3-26	11.5	-9.25
Class 3	8-92	8.7	-38.92
Class 4	25-247	10.1	-122.11
Class 5	8-102	7.8	-45.13
Class 6	1-18	5.6	-11.00

FIRST TIME OUT

	W-R	Per cent	£1 Level Stake
Bumpers	0-20	0.0	-20.00
Hurdles	3-53	5.7	-18.50
Chases	8-38	21.1	-6.49
Totals	11-111	9.9	-44.99

JOCKEYS

	W-R	Per cent	£1 Level Stake
Peter Buchanan	20-166	12.0	-21.79
Craig Nichol	12-138	8.7	-72.62
Graham Watters	7-45	15.6	-10.24
Derek Fox	4-66	6.1	-35.00
Brian Hughes	1-1	100.0	+1.75
Ryan Nichol	1-12	8.3	-7.00
Wilson Renwick	1-12	8.3	-8.50
Grant Cockburn	1-32	3.1	-25.00

COURSE RECORD

	Total W-R	Non-Hndcps Hurdles	Non-Hndcps Chases	Hndcps Hurdles	Hndcps Chases	NH Flat	Per cent	£1 Level Stake
Hexham	8-52	1-15	1-1	0-8	6-26	0-2	15.4	-15.74
Musselbgh	8-54	1-8	0-0	2-19	5-26	0-1	14.8	+5.85
Wetherby	5-23	0-3	0-0	0-8	5-11	0-1	21.7	+10.50
Ayr	5-75	1-17	0-2	1-21	3-28	0-7	6.7	-58.13
Perth	5-82	1-14	0-1	1-36	3-28	0-3	6.1	-50.17
Newcastle	4-45	1-7	1-3	1-15	1-17	0-3	8.9	-24.47
Kelso	4-64	1-14	0-1	0-22	2-24	1-3	6.3	-41.63
Haydock	3-17	2-4	0-0	0-4	1-9	0-0	17.6	+22.00
Uttoxeter	2-6	0-0	0-0	0-1	2-5	0-0	33.3	+15.00
Bangor	1-4	0-0	0-0	0-1	1-3	0-0	25.0	+1.50
Cartmel	1-4	0-0	1-1	0-2	0-1	0-0	25.0	0.00
Aintree	1-11	0-1	0-0	0-4	1-6	0-0	9.1	-8.13

WINNING HORSES

Horse	Races Run	1st	2nd	3rd	£
Lie Forrit	5	3	1	0	75970
Reaping The Reward	6	2	1	0	23393
Voyage A New York	7	1	0	1	12143
Thorpe	6	1	2	0	11888
Imjoeking	3	2	1	0	13516
Vengeur De Guye	7	2	0	0	11372
Settledoutofcourt	8	1	2	2	7870
Quito Du Tresor	9	1	1	2	7798
Clondaw Knight	5	2	1	1	12042
Ballyben	6	2	1	0	10397
Back To Bracka	9	1	1	0	6498
Uisge Beatha	8	1	2	3	6498
Ultra Du Chatelet	7	1	1	1	6011
Final Assault	8	1	4	2	5848
Shine A Diamond	11	2	2	1	8686
Ballycool	6	2	0	1	8170
Bescot Springs	12	1	0	2	5523
Rowdy Rocher	6	2	0	3	8997
Lord Of Drums	3	1	0	1	4549
Cobajayisland	6	1	3	0	4549
No Deal	3	1	0	1	4224

Island Heights	6	1	3	0	3994
Present Lodger	7	3	0	1	8837
Kingswell Theatre	6	2	1	1	7018
One For Arthur	6	3	0	2	11372
Itstimeforapint	10	1	2	3	3899
Urban Kode	7	1	1	0	3249
Stylish Chap	7	1	0	1	3249
Morning Time	9	1	2	0	2599
It's High Time	4	1	1	0	2493
Amore Mio	8	1	0	1	2274
Big River	2	1	1	0	1625
Total winning prize-money					**£306551**
Favourites	**12-43**		**27.9%**		**-10.61**

JOHN RYALL

RIMPTON, SOMERSET

	No. of Hrs	Races Run	1st	2nd	3rd	Unpl	Per cent	£1 Level Stake
NH Flat	*2*	*2*	*0*	*0*	*1*	*1*	*0.0*	*-2.00*
Hurdles	*1*	*5*	*0*	*1*	*0*	*4*	*0.0*	*-5.00*
Chases	*1*	*5*	*1*	*0*	*1*	*3*	*20.0*	*+8.00*
Totals	**4**	**12**	**1**	**1**	**2**	**8**	**8.3**	**+1.00**
13-14	*3*	*7*	*0*	*1*	*2*	*4*	*0.0*	*-7.00*
12-13	*5*	*15*	*1*	*3*	*1*	*10*	*6.7*	*-6.50*

JOCKEYS

	W-R	Per cent	£1 Level Stake
Dave Crosse	1-10	10.0	+3.00

COURSE RECORD

	Total W-R	Non-Hndcps Hurdles	Non-Hndcps Chases	Hndcps Hurdles	Hndcps Chases	NH Flat	Per cent	£1 Level Stake
Fontwell	1-4	0-0	0-0	0-2	1-2	0-0	25.0	+9.00

WINNING HORSES

Horse	Races Run	1st	2nd	3rd	£
Cypress Grove	5	1	0	1	2274
Total winning prize-money					**£2274**
Favourites	**0-0**		**0.0%**		**0.00**

AYTACH SADIK

WOLVERLEY, WORCS

	No. of Hrs	Races Run	1st	2nd	3rd	Unpl	Per cent	£1 Level Stake
NH Flat	*1*	*1*	*0*	*0*	*0*	*1*	*0.0*	*-1.00*
Hurdles	*3*	*15*	*0*	*3*	*1*	*11*	*0.0*	*-15.00*
Chases	*3*	*23*	*1*	*1*	*5*	*16*	*4.3*	*-8.00*
Totals	**6**	**39**	**1**	**4**	**6**	**28**	**2.6**	**-24.00**
13-14	*4*	*26*	*1*	*5*	*5*	*15*	*3.8*	*-20.00*
12-13	*5*	*34*	*4*	*1*	*3*	*26*	*11.8*	*+9.88*

JOCKEYS

	W-R	Per cent	£1 Level Stake
Lee Edwards	1-28	3.6	-13.00

COURSE RECORD

	Total W-R	Non-Hndcps Hurdles	Non-Hndcps Chases	Hndcps Hurdles	Hndcps Chases	NH Flat	Per cent	£1 Level Stake
Bangor	1-4	0-0	0-0	0-1	1-3	0-0	25.0	+11.00

WINNING HORSES

Horse	Races Run	1st	2nd	3rd	£
Apache Dawn	11	1	1	0	2395
Total winning prize-money					**£2395**
Favourites	**0-0**		**0.0%**		**0.00**

B SANDERSON

TIVERTON, DEVON

	No. of Hrs	Races Run	1st	2nd	3rd	Unpl	Per cent	£1 Level Stake
NH Flat	*0*	*0*	*0*	*0*	*0*	*0*	*0.0*	*0.00*
Hurdles	*0*	*0*	*0*	*0*	*0*	*0*	*0.0*	*0.00*
Chases	*1*	*2*	*1*	*0*	*1*	*0*	*50.0*	*+0.75*
Totals	**1**	**2**	**1**	**0**	**1**	**0**	**50.0**	**+0.75**

JOCKEYS

	W-R	Per cent	£1 Level Stake
Mr Matthew Hampton	1-2	50.0	+0.75

COURSE RECORD

	Total W-R	Non-Hndcps Hurdles	Non-Hndcps Chases	Hndcps Hurdles	Hndcps Chases	NH Flat	Per cent	£1 Level Stake
Kempton	1-1	0-0	1-1	0-0	0-0	0-0	100.0	+1.75

WINNING HORSES

Horse	Races Run	1st	2nd	3rd	£
Tataniano	2	1	0	1	2496
Total winning prize-money					**£2496**
Favourites	**0-0**		**0.0%**		**0.00**

MARY SANDERSON

TIVERTON, DEVON

	No. of Hrs	Races Run	1st	2nd	3rd	Unpl	Per cent	£1 Level Stake
NH Flat	*1*	*2*	*0*	*1*	*0*	*1*	*0.0*	*-2.00*
Hurdles	*3*	*13*	*2*	*1*	*4*	*6*	*15.4*	*+7.00*
Chases	*2*	*4*	*1*	*0*	*0*	*3*	*25.0*	*+47.00*
Totals	**5**	**19**	**3**	**2**	**4**	**10**	**15.8**	**+52.00**
13-14	*3*	*6*	*0*	*1*	*0*	*5*	*0.0*	*-6.00*
12-13	*2*	*4*	*0*	*0*	*0*	*4*	*0.0*	*-4.00*

JOCKEYS

	W-R	Per cent	£1 Level Stake
Brendan Powell	1-1	100.0	+14.00
Mr Matthew Hampton	1-2	50.0	+49.00
Tom Scudamore	1-6	16.7	-1.00

COURSE RECORD

	Total W-R	Non-Hndcps Hurdles	Non-Hndcps Chases	Hndcps Hurdles	Hndcps Chases	NH Flat	Per cent	£1 Level Stake
Wincanton	1-2	0-1	0-0	1-1	0-0	0-0	50.0	+13.00
Exeter	1-3	0-1	1-2	0-0	0-0	0-0	33.3	+48.00
Nton Abbot	1-13	0-4	0-1	1-6	0-1	0-1	7.7	-8.00

WINNING HORSES

Horse	Races Run	1st	2nd	3rd	£
Applause For Amy	4	2	1	1	4687
Blinding Lights	3	1	0	0	936
Total winning prize-money					**£5623**
Favourites	**1-2**		**50.0%**		**3.00**

JOSE SANTOS

UPPER LAMBOURN, BERKS

	No. of Hrs	Races Run	1st	2nd	3rd	Unpl	Per cent	£1 Level Stake
NH Flat	*1*	*1*	*0*	*0*	*0*	*1*	*0.0*	*-1.00*
Hurdles	*3*	*7*	*1*	*0*	*0*	*6*	*14.3*	*+14.00*
Chases	*1*	*1*	*0*	*0*	*0*	*1*	*0.0*	*-1.00*
Totals	**3**	**9**	**1**	**0**	**0**	**8**	**11.1**	**+12.00**

JOCKEYS

	W-R	Per cent	£1 Level Stake
James Davies	1-7	14.3	+14.00

COURSE RECORD

	Total W-R	Non-Hndcps Hurdles	Non-Hndcps Chases	Hndcps Hurdles	Hndcps Chases	NH Flat	Per cent	£1 Level Stake
Nton Abbot	1-1	0-0	0-0	1-1	0-0	0-0	100.0	+20.00

WINNING HORSES

Horse	Races Run	1st	2nd	3rd	£
Baldadash	3	1	0	0	3422
Total winning prize-money					**£3422**
Favourites	**0-62**		**0.0%**		**-62.00**

DIANNE SAYER

HACKTHORPE, CUMBRIA

	No. of Hrs	Races Run	1st	2nd	3rd	Unpl	Per cent	£1 Level Stake
NH Flat	*6*	*9*	*0*	*0*	*0*	*9*	*0.0*	*-9.00*
Hurdles	*30*	*138*	*18*	*10*	*21*	*89*	*13.0*	*+32.33*
Chases	*18*	*62*	*6*	*10*	*9*	*37*	*9.7*	*-33.17*
Totals	**35**	**209**	**24**	**20**	**30**	**135**	**11.5**	**-9.84**
13-14	*28*	*192*	*28*	*27*	*30*	*107*	*14.6*	*-3.13*
12-13	*28*	*186*	*20*	*16*	*22*	*128*	*10.8*	*-18.98*

BY MONTH

NH Flat	W-R	Per cent	£1 Level Stake	Hurdles	W-R	Per cent	£1 Level Stake
May	0-0	0.0	0.00	May	2-6	33.3	+11.33
June	0-0	0.0	0.00	June	1-5	20.0	+4.00
July	0-0	0.0	0.00	July	1-15	6.7	-9.50
August	0-0	0.0	0.00	August	0-5	0.0	-5.00
September	0-2	0.0	-2.00	September	6-9	66.7	+23.25
October	0-0	0.0	0.00	October	1-14	7.1	-8.50
November	0-3	0.0	-3.00	November	2-17	11.8	-0.50
December	0-0	0.0	0.00	December	2-17	11.8	+58.00
January	0-0	0.0	0.00	January	2-10	20.0	-4.50
February	0-1	0.0	-1.00	February	1-15	6.7	-11.25
March	0-2	0.0	-2.00	March	0-14	0.0	-14.00
April	0-1	0.0	-1.00	April	0-11	0.0	-11.00

Chases	W-R	Per cent	£1 Level Stake	Totals	W-R	Per cent	£1 Level Stake
May	1-7	14.3	-2.50	May	3-13	23.1	+8.83
June	0-5	0.0	-5.00	June	1-10	10.0	-1.00
July	0-5	0.0	-5.00	July	1-20	5.0	-14.50
August	1-4	25.0	+7.00	August	1-9	11.1	+2.00
September	1-4	25.0	-0.75	September	7-15	46.7	+20.50
October	1-6	16.7	-1.67	October	2-20	10.0	-10.17
November	1-6	16.7	-4.00	November	3-26	11.5	-7.50
December	0-4	0.0	-4.00	December	2-21	9.5	+54.00
January	0-5	0.0	-5.00	January	2-15	13.3	-9.50
February	1-4	25.0	-0.25	February	2-20	10.0	-12.50
March	0-7	0.0	-7.00	March	0-23	0.0	-23.00
April	0-5	0.0	-5.00	April	0-17	0.0	-17.00

DISTANCE

Hurdles	W-R	Per cent	£1 Level Stake	Chases	W-R	Per cent	£1 Level Stake
2m-2m3f	13-87	14.9	-7.67	2m-2m3f	1-13	7.7	-9.25
2m4f-2m7f	3-26	11.5	-8.50	2m4f-2m7f	2-22	9.1	-14.25
3m+	0-10	0.0	-10.00	3m+	1-8	12.5	+3.00

TYPE OF RACE

Non-Handicaps	W-R	Per cent	£1 Level Stake	Handicaps	W-R	Per cent	£1 Level Stake
Nov Hrdls	2-18	11.1	-9.17	Nov Hrdls	2-11	18.2	-4.50
Hrdls	1-17	5.9	+50.00	Hrdls	13-92	14.1	-4.00
Nov Chs	0-1	0.0	-1.00	Nov Chs	1-15	6.7	-10.67
Chases	0-1	0.0	-1.00	Chases	5-45	11.1	-20.50
Sell/Claim	1-1	100.0	+3.33	Sell/Claim	0-1	0.0	-1.00

RACE CLASS / FIRST TIME OUT

RACE CLASS	W-R	Per cent	£1 Level Stake	FIRST TIME OUT	W-R	Per cent	£1 Level Stake
Class 1	0-5	0.0	-5.00	Bumpers	0-6	0.0	-6.00
Class 2	0-11	0.0	-11.00	Hurdles	2-20	10.0	-2.67

Class 3	6-36	16.7	-6.67	Chases	1-9	11.1	-4.50
Class 4	10-97	10.3	+14.75				
Class 5	8-53	15.1	+5.08	Totals	3-35	8.6	-13.17
Class 6	0-7	0.0	-7.00				

JOCKEYS

	W-R	Per cent	£1 Level Stake
Brian Hughes	10-43	23.3	+7.83
Henry Brooke	3-23	13.0	+0.25
James Reveley	3-43	7.0	-26.25
Sean Quinlan	2-7	28.6	+3.50
Ryan Mania	2-13	15.4	+1.50
Emma Sayer	2-18	11.1	-6.00
Lucy Alexander	1-5	20.0	-0.67
Colm McCormack	1-27	3.7	+40.00

COURSE RECORD

	Total W-R	Non-Hndcps Hurdles	Non-Hndcps Chases	Hndcps Hurdles	Hndcps Chases	NH Flat	Per cent	£1 Level Stake
Sedgefield	9-24	0-3	0-0	7-16	2-4	0-1	37.5	+24.25
Musselbgh	3-21	0-2	0-0	2-11	1-7	0-1	14.3	-8.75
Cartmel	3-23	1-3	0-0	1-10	1-10	0-0	13.0	-2.17
Perth	3-25	1-1	0-0	2-18	0-6	0-0	12.0	-11.00
Kelso	2-26	0-4	0-1	1-14	1-6	0-1	7.7	-12.50
Doncaster	1-2	0-0	0-0	1-1	0-1	0-0	50.0	+8.00
Aintree	1-6	0-2	0-0	0-2	1-2	0-0	16.7	-1.67
Catterick	1-8	1-4	0-0	0-3	0-1	0-0	12.5	+59.00
Hexham	1-20	0-4	0-0	1-5	0-11	0-0	5.0	-11.00

WINNING HORSES

Horse	Races Run	1st	2nd	3rd	£
Baileys Concerto	10	5	1	1	38170
Cool Baranca	12	1	2	2	6498
Bell Weir	12	1	1	2	5848
Oh Right	5	2	0	1	7798
Gold Chain	12	2	3	3	3899
Cooking Fat	5	1	0	0	3899
Langley House	3	1	0	2	3509
Turtle Cask	11	1	1	0	3509
Sendiym	12	3	1	1	10007
Endeavor	20	2	2	3	5848
Boruma	9	1	0	1	3249
Discoverie	15	2	1	4	4940
Mighty Cliche	9	1	3	0	2599
Tropenfeuer	4	1	0	1	2339
Total winning prize-money					**£102112**
Favourites	**3-17**		**17.6%**		**-8.25**

KATIE SCOTT

GALASHEILS, SCOTTISH BORDERS

	No. of Hrs	Races Run	1st	2nd	3rd	Unpl	Per cent	£1 Level Stake
NH Flat	*3*	*6*	*0*	*0*	*0*	*6*	*0.0*	*-6.00*
Hurdles	*2*	*4*	*0*	*0*	*0*	*4*	*0.0*	*-4.00*
Chases	*3*	*6*	*2*	*1*	*0*	*3*	*33.3*	*+20.00*
Totals	**6**	**16**	**2**	**1**	**0**	**13**	**12.5**	**+10.00**
13-14	*4*	*11*	*0*	*4*	*2*	*5*	*0.0*	*-11.00*
12-13	*1*	*1*	*1*	*0*	*0*	*0*	*100.0*	*+4.50*

JOCKEYS

	W-R	Per cent	£1 Level Stake
Mr T Hamilton	2-4	50.0	+22.00

COURSE RECORD

	Total W-R	Non-Hndcps Hurdles	Non-Hndcps Chases	Hndcps Hurdles	Hndcps Chases	NH Flat	Per cent	£1 Level Stake
Kelso	2-7	0-1	1-3	0-0	1-2	0-1	28.6	+19.00

WINNING HORSES

Horse	Races Run	1st	2nd	3rd	£
*Douglas Julian	4	2	0	0	5771
Total winning prize-money					**£5771**
Favourites	**0-1**		**0.0%**		**-1.00**

JEREMY SCOTT

BROMPTON REGIS, SOMERSET

	No. of Hrs	Races Run	1st	2nd	3rd	Unpl	Per cent	£1 Level Stake
NH Flat	*12*	*23*	*0*	*3*	*2*	*18*	*0.0*	*-23.00*
Hurdles	*31*	*96*	*6*	*7*	*11*	*72*	*6.3*	*-62.42*
Chases	*14*	*62*	*15*	*10*	*10*	*26*	*24.2*	*+29.11*
Totals	**46**	**181**	**21**	**20**	**23**	**116**	**11.6**	**-56.31**
13-14	*47*	*202*	*23*	*19*	*27*	*133*	*11.4*	*-48.72*
12-13	*47*	*209*	*30*	*31*	*33*	*115*	*14.4*	*-43.28*

BY MONTH

NH Flat	W-R	Per cent	£1 Level Stake	Hurdles	W-R	Per cent	£1 Level Stake
May	0-3	0.0	-3.00	May	1-9	11.1	-4.67
June	0-0	0.0	0.00	June	0-2	0.0	-2.00
July	0-0	0.0	0.00	July	1-3	33.3	+5.00
August	0-0	0.0	0.00	August	0-2	0.0	-2.00
September	0-0	0.0	0.00	September	0-2	0.0	-2.00
October	0-3	0.0	-3.00	October	0-6	0.0	-6.00
November	0-3	0.0	-3.00	November	2-15	13.3	-1.25
December	0-3	0.0	-3.00	December	1-12	8.3	-8.00
January	0-3	0.0	-3.00	January	0-12	0.0	-12.00
February	0-2	0.0	-2.00	February	0-12	0.0	-12.00
March	0-2	0.0	-2.00	March	1-11	9.1	-7.50
April	0-4	0.0	-4.00	April	0-10	0.0	-10.00

Chases	W-R	Per cent	£1 Level Stake	Totals	W-R	Per cent	£1 Level Stake
May	1-6	16.7	-1.50	May	2-18	11.1	-9.17
June	1-8	12.5	+2.00	June	1-10	10.0	0.00
July	4-6	66.7	+17.00	July	5-9	55.6	+22.00
August	1-2	50.0	+8.00	August	1-4	25.0	+6.00
September	2-4	50.0	+0.75	September	2-6	33.3	-1.25

October	1-8	12.5	-3.00	October	1-17	5.9	-12.00
November	0-6	0.0	-6.00	November	2-24	8.3	-10.25
December	1-6	16.7	-4.64	December	2-21	9.5	-15.64
January	0-5	0.0	-5.00	January	0-20	0.0	-20.00
February	0-5	0.0	-5.00	February	0-19	0.0	-19.00
March	1-3	33.3	+3.50	March	2-16	12.5	-6.00
April	3-3	100.0	+23.00	April	3-17	17.6	+9.00

DISTANCE

Hurdles	W-R	Per cent	£1 Level Stake	Chases	W-R	Per cent	£1 Level Stake
2m-2m3f	2-22	9.1	-14.50	2m-2m3f	1-6	16.7	-4.64
2m4f-2m7f	3-42	7.1	-23.92	2m4f-2m7f	7-28	25.0	+13.88
3m+	0-4	0.0	-4.00	3m+	4-20	20.0	+13.88

TYPE OF RACE

Non-Handicaps	W-R	Per cent	£1 Level Stake	Handicaps	W-R	Per cent	£1 Level Stake
Nov Hrdls	0-22	0.0	-22.00	Nov Hrdls	1-6	16.7	-2.50
Hrdls	2-11	18.2	+1.33	Hrdls	3-57	5.3	-39.25
Nov Chs	1-3	33.3	-1.64	Nov Chs	3-11	27.3	+8.00
Chases	0-0	0.0	0.00	Chases	11-48	22.9	+22.75
Sell/Claim	0-0	0.0	0.00	Sell/Claim	0-0	0.0	0.00

RACE CLASS / FIRST TIME OUT

RACE CLASS	W-R	Per cent	£1 Level Stake	FIRST TIME OUT	W-R	Per cent	£1 Level Stake
Class 1	1-3	33.3	+7.00	Bumpers	0-12	0.0	-12.00
Class 2	0-10	0.0	-10.00	Hurdles	2-23	8.7	-7.67
Class 3	5-32	15.6	+3.75	Chases	3-11	27.3	+5.88
Class 4	11-87	12.6	-31.89				
Class 5	4-33	12.1	-9.17	Totals	5-46	10.9	-13.79
Class 6	0-16	0.0	-16.00				

JOCKEYS

	W-R	Per cent	£1 Level Stake
Matt Griffiths	11-66	16.7	+2.71
Nick Scholfield	9-76	11.8	-22.76
Tom O'Brien	1-3	33.3	-0.25

COURSE RECORD

	Total W-R	Non-Hndcps Hurdles	Non-Hndcps Chases	Hndcps Hurdles	Hndcps Chases	NH Flat	Per cent	£1 Level Stake
Uttoxeter	3-11	1-2	0-0	0-3	2-4	0-2	27.3	+11.50
Worcester	3-14	1-2	0-0	0-4	2-6	0-2	21.4	+2.33
Bangor	2-3	0-0	1-1	1-1	0-0	0-1	66.7	+1.11
Nton Abbot	2-10	0-1	0-0	0-4	2-5	0-0	20.0	+8.00
Fontwell	2-13	0-0	0-0	0-3	2-9	0-1	15.4	-8.25
Taunton	2-15	0-2	0-0	1-8	1-3	0-2	13.3	-4.50
Chepstow	2-16	0-4	0-0	1-5	1-4	0-3	12.5	-7.50
Perth	1-1	0-0	0-0	0-0	1-1	0-0	100.0	+5.00
Southwell	1-4	0-0	0-0	0-2	1-2	0-0	25.0	-1.00
Warwick	1-7	0-3	0-0	0-2	1-1	0-1	14.3	-2.00
Kempton	1-8	0-1	0-1	0-4	1-1	0-1	12.5	+7.00
Exeter	1-26	0-9	0-1	1-8	0-6	0-2	3.8	-15.00

WINNING HORSES

Horse	Races Run	1st	2nd	3rd	£
Notarfbad	7	1	0	0	22584
Porters War	5	1	2	1	6963
Gunna Be A Devil	6	2	1	2	11512
Kilmurvy	7	1	0	1	6657
Best Boy Barney	9	4	1	1	16794
Daveron	9	1	0	3	5393
Alberobello	7	1	1	2	4549
Moorlands Jack	6	2	0	1	6043
Melodic Rendezvous	4	1	1	2	3899
Decimus	4	1	0	0	3861
*Ladfromhighworth	5	2	1	1	7538
Dream Deal	3	1	0	0	3249
Dashaway	4	1	1	1	3249
Geton Xmoor	4	1	0	0	2599
The Snappy Poet	8	1	1	2	2339
Total winning prize-money					**£107229**
Favourites	**4-14**		**28.6%**		**-5.14**

MRS CAMILLA SCOTT

DULVERTON, SOMERSET

	No. of Hrs	Races Run	1st	2nd	3rd	Unpl	Per cent	£1 Level Stake
NH Flat	*0*	*0*	*0*	*0*	*0*	*0*	*0.0*	*0.00*
Hurdles	*0*	*0*	*0*	*0*	*0*	*0*	*0.0*	*0.00*
Chases	*2*	*2*	*1*	*0*	*0*	*1*	*50.0*	*+24.00*
Totals	**2**	**2**	**1**	**0**	**0**	**1**	**50.0**	**+24.00**
13-14	*1*	*2*	*0*	*0*	*0*	*2*	*0.0*	*-2.00*

JOCKEYS

	W-R	Per cent	£1 Level Stake
Miss V Wade	1-1	100.0	+25.00

COURSE RECORD

	Total W-R	Non-Hndcps Hurdles	Non-Hndcps Chases	Hndcps Hurdles	Hndcps Chases	NH Flat	Per cent	£1 Level Stake
Fontwell	1-1	0-0	1-1	0-0	0-0	0-0	100.0	+25.00

WINNING HORSES

Horse	Races Run	1st	2nd	3rd	£
Ladfromhighworth	1	1	0	0	936
Total winning prize-money					**£936**
Favourites	**0-0**		**0.0%**		**0.00**

MICHAEL SCUDAMORE

BROMSASH, H'FORDS

	No. of Hrs	Races Run	1st	2nd	3rd	Unpl	Per cent	£1 Level Stake
NH Flat	*6*	*10*	*3*	*4*	*1*	*2*	*30.0*	*-2.92*
Hurdles	*12*	*33*	*3*	*3*	*7*	*20*	*9.1*	*-25.15*
Chases	*8*	*35*	*7*	*3*	*4*	*21*	*20.0*	*+5.38*
Totals	**20**	**78**	**13**	**10**	**12**	**43**	**16.7**	**-22.69**
13-14	*22*	*64*	*8*	*8*	*4*	*44*	*12.5*	*+3.25*
12-13	*29*	*105*	*7*	*9*	*9*	*80*	*6.7*	*-29.25*

BY MONTH

NH Flat	W-R	Per cent	£1 Level Stake
May	2-2	100.0	+3.75
June	1-2	50.0	-0.67
July	0-0	0.0	0.00
August	0-0	0.0	0.00
September	0-0	0.0	0.00
October	0-0	0.0	0.00
November	0-1	0.0	-1.00
December	0-1	0.0	-1.00
January	0-0	0.0	0.00
February	0-1	0.0	-1.00
March	0-1	0.0	-1.00
April	0-2	0.0	-2.00

Hurdles	W-R	Per cent	£1 Level Stake
May	1-4	25.0	-2.75
June	0-0	0.0	0.00
July	0-1	0.0	-1.00
August	0-0	0.0	0.00
September	0-2	0.0	-2.00
October	0-3	0.0	-3.00
November	0-3	0.0	-3.00
December	0-5	0.0	-5.00
January	0-5	0.0	-5.00
February	1-4	25.0	+0.50
March	1-1	100.0	+1.10
April	0-5	0.0	-5.00

Chases	W-R	Per cent	£1 Level Stake
May	0-3	0.0	-3.00
June	0-2	0.0	-2.00
July	1-3	33.3	+2.00
August	0-2	0.0	-2.00
September	0-0	0.0	0.00
October	2-3	66.7	+5.75
November	2-6	33.3	-1.38
December	0-3	0.0	-3.00
January	1-5	20.0	0.00
February	0-3	0.0	-3.00
March	1-3	33.3	+14.00
April	0-2	0.0	-2.00

Totals	W-R	Per cent	£1 Level Stake
May	3-9	33.3	-2.00
June	1-4	25.0	-2.67
July	1-4	25.0	+1.00
August	0-2	0.0	-2.00
September	0-2	0.0	-2.00
October	2-6	33.3	+2.75
November	2-10	20.0	-5.38
December	0-9	0.0	-9.00
January	1-10	10.0	-5.00
February	1-8	12.5	-3.50
March	2-5	40.0	+14.10
April	0-9	0.0	-9.00

DISTANCE

Hurdles	W-R	Per cent	£1 Level Stake
2m-2m3f	0-9	0.0	-9.00
2m4f-2m7f	3-17	17.6	-9.15
3m+	0-1	0.0	-1.00

Chases	W-R	Per cent	£1 Level Stake
2m-2m3f	2-7	28.6	+15.00
2m4f-2m7f	2-5	40.0	+3.25
3m+	2-14	14.3	-6.63

TYPE OF RACE

Non-Handicaps	W-R	Per cent	£1 Level Stake
Nov Hrdls	1-9	11.1	-4.50
Hrdls	1-8	12.5	-6.75
Nov Chs	0-1	0.0	-1.00
Chases	0-0	0.0	0.00
Sell/Claim	0-0	0.0	0.00

Handicaps	W-R	Per cent	£1 Level Stake
Nov Hrdls	0-1	0.0	-1.00
Hrdls	1-15	6.7	-12.90
Nov Chs	1-5	20.0	0.00
Chases	6-29	20.7	+6.38
Sell/Claim	0-0	0.0	0.00

RACE CLASS

	W-R	Per cent	£1 Level Stake
Class 1	1-9	11.1	+8.00
Class 2	0-3	0.0	-3.00
Class 3	0-4	0.0	-4.00
Class 4	4-22	18.2	-5.40
Class 5	5-31	16.1	-16.38
Class 6	3-9	33.3	-0.92

FIRST TIME OUT

	W-R	Per cent	£1 Level Stake
Bumpers	2-6	33.3	-0.25
Hurdles	0-8	0.0	-8.00
Chases	0-6	0.0	-6.00
Totals	2-20	10.0	-14.25

JOCKEYS

	W-R	Per cent	£1 Level Stake
Tom Scudamore	7-30	23.3	+4.93
Liam Treadwell	4-23	17.4	-7.38
Mr Robert Hawker	1-1	100.0	+1.75
A P McCoy	1-2	50.0	0.00

COURSE RECORD

	Total W-R	Non-Hndcps Hurdles	Non-Hndcps Chases	Hndcps Hurdles	Hndcps Chases	NH Flat	Per cent	£1 Level Stake
Hexham	4-8	1-1	0-0	0-3	1-2	2-2	50.0	+0.71
Warwick	1-1	0-0	0-0	1-1	0-0	0-0	100.0	+1.10
Wincanton	1-1	1-1	0-0	0-0	0-0	0-0	100.0	+3.50
Stratford	1-2	0-0	0-0	0-1	1-1	0-0	50.0	+3.00
Ayr	1-3	0-1	0-0	0-0	1-2	0-0	33.3	+2.00
Carlisle	1-3	0-0	0-0	0-0	0-0	1-3	33.3	-1.00
Cheltenham	1-4	0-0	0-0	0-1	1-3	0-0	25.0	+13.00
Southwell	1-4	0-0	0-0	0-2	1-2	0-0	25.0	-1.75
Worcester	1-4	0-1	0-0	0-0	1-3	0-0	25.0	+2.00
Ffos Las	1-9	0-2	0-0	0-2	1-4	0-1	11.1	-6.25

WINNING HORSES

Horse	Races Run	1st	2nd	3rd	£
Next Sensation	5	1	0	0	51255
Princesse Fleur	3	1	1	1	4549
No Through Road	10	5	1	0	13622
Streets Of Promise	7	3	1	1	8927
Line D'Aois	5	2	0	1	4038
Grace Tara	1	1	0	0	0
Total winning prize-money					**£82391**
Favourites	**5-15**		**33.3%**		**-5.32**

IAN SEMPLE

HADDINGTON, EAST LOTHIAN

	No. of Hrs	Races Run	1st	2nd	3rd	Unpl	Per cent	£1 Level Stake
NH Flat	*1*	*1*	*0*	*0*	*0*	*1*	*0.0*	*-1.00*
Hurdles	*3*	*8*	*2*	*1*	*0*	*5*	*25.0*	*+14.00*
Chases	*0*	*0*	*0*	*0*	*0*	*0*	*0.0*	*0.00*

Totals	3	9	2	1	0	6	22.2	+13.00
13-14	*3*	*8*	*1*	*2*	*1*	*4*	*12.5*	*+2.00*

JOCKEYS

	W-R	Per cent	£1 Level Stake
Dougie Costello	2-6	33.3	+16.00

COURSE RECORD

	Total W-R	Non-Hndcps Hurdles	Non-Hndcps Chases	Hndcps Hurdles	Hndcps Chases	NH Flat	Per cent	£1 Level Stake
Kelso	1-2	1-1	0-0	0-1	0-0	0-0	50.0	+10.00
Perth	1-3	0-2	0-0	1-1	0-0	0-0	33.3	+7.00

WINNING HORSES

Horse	Races Run	1st	2nd	3rd	£
Bellgrove	4	1	1	0	12512
Calton Entry	3	1	0	0	2599
Total winning prize-money					**£15111**
Favourites	**0-0**		**0.0%**		**0.00**

MATT SHEPPARD

EASTNOR, H'FORDS

	No. of Hrs	Races Run	1st	2nd	3rd	Unpl	Per cent	£1 Level Stake
NH Flat	*0*	*0*	*0*	*0*	*0*	*0*	*0.0*	*0.00*
Hurdles	*9*	*34*	*3*	*3*	*3*	*25*	*8.8*	*-18.50*
Chases	*8*	*43*	*9*	*7*	*6*	*21*	*20.9*	*+52.00*
Totals	**13**	**77**	**12**	**10**	**9**	**46**	**15.6**	**+33.50**
13-14	*14*	*58*	*5*	*7*	*5*	*41*	*8.6*	*-11.00*
12-13	*14*	*65*	*5*	*4*	*7*	*49*	*7.7*	*-43.50*

BY MONTH

NH Flat	W-R	Per cent	£1 Level Stake
May	0-0	0.0	0.00
June	0-0	0.0	0.00
July	0-0	0.0	0.00
August	0-0	0.0	0.00
September	0-0	0.0	0.00
October	0-0	0.0	0.00
November	0-0	0.0	0.00
December	0-0	0.0	0.00
January	0-0	0.0	0.00
February	0-0	0.0	0.00
March	0-0	0.0	0.00
April	0-0	0.0	0.00

Hurdles	W-R	Per cent	£1 Level Stake
May	0-4	0.0	-4.00
June	0-3	0.0	-3.00
July	0-2	0.0	-2.00
August	0-3	0.0	-3.00
September	0-0	0.0	0.00
October	0-4	0.0	-4.00
November	2-5	40.0	+5.00
December	0-4	0.0	-4.00
January	0-1	0.0	-1.00
February	0-1	0.0	-1.00
March	0-2	0.0	-2.00
April	1-5	20.0	+0.50

Chases	W-R	Per cent	£1 Level Stake
May	0-3	0.0	-3.00
June	0-2	0.0	-2.00
July	0-2	0.0	-2.00
August	0-2	0.0	-2.00
September	1-2	50.0	+13.00
October	1-4	25.0	0.00
November	0-6	0.0	-6.00
December	0-4	0.0	-4.00
January	1-6	16.7	+28.00
February	3-4	75.0	+14.50
March	2-6	33.3	+0.50
April	1-2	50.0	+15.00

Totals	W-R	Per cent	£1 Level Stake
May	0-7	0.0	-7.00
June	0-5	0.0	-5.00
July	0-4	0.0	-4.00
August	0-5	0.0	-5.00
September	1-2	50.0	+13.00
October	1-8	12.5	-4.00
November	2-11	18.2	-1.00
December	0-8	0.0	-8.00
January	1-7	14.3	+27.00
February	3-5	60.0	+13.50
March	2-8	25.0	-1.50
April	2-7	28.6	+15.50

DISTANCE

Hurdles	W-R	Per cent	£1 Level Stake
2m-2m3f	3-17	17.6	-1.50
2m4f-2m7f	0-7	0.0	-7.00
3m+	0-1	0.0	-1.00

Chases	W-R	Per cent	£1 Level Stake
2m-2m3f	4-15	26.7	+55.50
2m4f-2m7f	1-12	8.3	-8.00
3m+	0-4	0.0	-4.00

TYPE OF RACE

Non-Handicaps	W-R	Per cent	£1 Level Stake
Nov Hrdls	0-4	0.0	-4.00
Hrdls	0-0	0.0	0.00
Nov Chs	0-1	0.0	-1.00
Chases	0-0	0.0	0.00
Sell/Claim	0-0	0.0	0.00

Handicaps	W-R	Per cent	£1 Level Stake
Nov Hrdls	1-4	25.0	+1.50
Hrdls	2-26	7.7	-16.00
Nov Chs	1-11	9.1	-7.00
Chases	8-31	25.8	+60.00
Sell/Claim	0-0	0.0	0.00

RACE CLASS

	W-R	Per cent	£1 Level Stake
Class 1	0-1	0.0	-1.00
Class 2	1-2	50.0	+15.00
Class 3	1-11	9.1	-7.00
Class 4	9-42	21.4	+42.00
Class 5	1-21	4.8	-15.50
Class 6	0-0	0.0	0.00

FIRST TIME OUT

	W-R	Per cent	£1 Level Stake
Bumpers	0-0	0.0	0.00
Hurdles	0-8	0.0	-8.00
Chases	0-5	0.0	-5.00
Totals	0-13	0.0	-13.00

JOCKEYS

	W-R	Per cent	£1 Level Stake
Charlie Poste	6-41	14.6	+25.50
Trevor Whelan	3-5	60.0	+12.50
Mr Stan Sheppard	2-24	8.3	-1.50
Tom Scudamore	1-1	100.0	+3.00

COURSE RECORD

	Total W-R	Non-Hndcps Hurdles	Non-Hndcps Chases	Hndcps Hurdles	Hndcps Chases	NH Flat	Per cent	£1 Level Stake
Leicester	3-8	0-0	0-0	1-1	2-7	0-0	37.5	+10.50
Taunton	2-5	0-0	0-0	0-1	2-4	0-0	40.0	+33.50
Ludlow	2-8	0-0	0-0	0-2	2-6	0-0	25.0	+1.00
Chepstow	2-10	0-4	0-0	2-5	0-1	0-0	20.0	-1.50
Bangor	1-4	0-0	0-0	0-1	1-3	0-0	25.0	0.00
Nton Abbot	1-4	0-0	0-0	0-2	1-2	0-0	25.0	+13.00
Stratford	1-10	0-0	0-0	0-3	1-7	0-0	10.0	+5.00

WINNING HORSES

Horse	Races Run	1st	2nd	3rd	£
Another Flutter	9	3	2	0	22107
*Diamond Tammy	5	3	1	0	16570
Rock On Rocky	8	2	2	0	9449
Kerryhead Storm	5	3	1	0	15920
Modeligo	5	1	0	0	2599
Total winning prize-money					**£66645**
Favourites	**1-9**		**11.1%**		**-3.50**

OLIVER SHERWOOD

UPPER LAMBOURN, BERKS

	No. of Hrs	Races Run	1st	2nd	3rd	Unpl	Per cent	£1 Level Stake
NH Flat	*16*	*23*	*3*	*4*	*3*	*13*	*13.0*	*-2.75*
Hurdles	*33*	*101*	*8*	*22*	*23*	*48*	*7.9*	*-64.37*
Chases	*19*	*81*	*20*	*17*	*10*	*34*	*24.7*	*+27.78*
Totals	**56**	**205**	**31**	**43**	**36**	**95**	**15.1**	**-39.34**
13-14	*51*	*186*	*34*	*35*	*30*	*87*	*18.3*	*-58.83*
12-13	*46*	*159*	*25*	*29*	*14*	*91*	*15.7*	*-51.57*

BY MONTH

NH Flat	W-R	Per cent	£1 Level Stake	Hurdles	W-R	Per cent	£1 Level Stake
May	0-1	0.0	-1.00	May	0-6	0.0	-6.00
June	0-2	0.0	-2.00	June	0-1	0.0	-1.00
July	0-0	0.0	0.00	July	0-0	0.0	0.00
August	0-0	0.0	0.00	August	0-3	0.0	-3.00
September	0-0	0.0	0.00	September	0-0	0.0	0.00
October	0-2	0.0	-2.00	October	2-7	28.6	+5.00
November	1-5	20.0	-1.75	November	1-15	6.7	-13.60
December	1-1	100.0	+6.00	December	2-12	16.7	-7.02
January	0-1	0.0	-1.00	January	1-17	5.9	-7.00
February	0-3	0.0	-3.00	February	2-15	13.3	-6.75
March	1-6	16.7	+4.00	March	0-15	0.0	-15.00
April	0-2	0.0	-2.00	April	0-10	0.0	-10.00

Chases	W-R	Per cent	£1 Level Stake	Totals	W-R	Per cent	£1 Level Stake
May	0-7	0.0	-7.00	May	0-14	0.0	-14.00
June	1-2	50.0	+1.25	June	1-5	20.0	-1.75
July	2-3	66.7	+7.50	July	2-3	66.7	+7.50
August	0-4	0.0	-4.00	August	0-7	0.0	-7.00
September	0-3	0.0	-3.00	September	0-3	0.0	-3.00
October	1-8	12.5	-4.00	October	3-17	17.6	-1.00
November	5-11	45.5	+13.83	November	7-31	22.6	-1.52
December	0-8	0.0	-8.00	December	3-21	14.3	-9.02
January	1-6	16.7	-1.00	January	2-24	8.3	-9.00
February	3-7	42.9	+5.44	February	5-25	20.0	-4.31
March	3-14	21.4	-1.50	March	4-35	11.4	-12.50
April	4-8	50.0	+28.25	April	4-20	20.0	+16.25

DISTANCE

Hurdles	W-R	Per cent	£1 Level Stake	Chases	W-R	Per cent	£1 Level Stake
2m-2m3f	2-34	5.9	-21.75	2m-2m3f	2-12	16.7	-5.63
2m4f-2m7f	3-31	9.7	-25.62	2m4f-2m7f	8-26	30.8	+5.69
3m+	0-4	0.0	-4.00	3m+	6-29	20.7	+29.50

TYPE OF RACE

Non-Handicaps	W-R	Per cent	£1 Level Stake	Handicaps	W-R	Per cent	£1 Level Stake
Nov Hrdls	5-38	13.2	-26.37	Nov Hrdls	0-7	0.0	-7.00
Hrdls	1-30	3.3	-21.00	Hrdls	2-25	8.0	-9.00
Nov Chs	6-18	33.3	-3.22	Nov Chs	2-9	22.2	+2.50
Chases	2-8	25.0	+0.50	Chases	10-46	21.7	+28.00
Sell/Claim	0-0	0.0	0.00	Sell/Claim	0-0	0.0	0.00

RACE CLASS

	W-R	Per cent	£1 Level Stake
Class 1	4-20	20.0	+23.50
Class 2	2-17	11.8	-2.50
Class 3	7-43	16.3	-13.97
Class 4	13-87	14.9	-45.62
Class 5	2-20	10.0	-3.00
Class 6	3-18	16.7	+2.25

FIRST TIME OUT

	W-R	Per cent	£1 Level Stake
Bumpers	2-16	12.5	-2.75
Hurdles	2-24	8.3	-12.00
Chases	2-16	12.5	-5.50
Totals	6-56	10.7	-20.25

JOCKEYS

	W-R	Per cent	£1 Level Stake
Leighton Aspell	22-147	15.0	-22.07
Thomas Garner	5-31	16.1	-4.75
Ben Ffrench Davis	2-9	22.2	-5.02
Jack Sherwood	1-5	20.0	+3.00
A P McCoy	1-6	16.7	-3.50

COURSE RECORD

	Total W-R	Non-Hndcps Hurdles	Non-Hndcps Chases	Hndcps Hurdles	Hndcps Chases	NH Flat	Per cent	£1 Level Stake
Leicester	2-4	1-1	1-1	0-0	0-2	0-0	50.0	-0.83
Ascot	2-8	0-2	2-4	0-2	0-0	0-0	25.0	-2.25
Taunton	2-8	0-2	0-1	0-1	1-2	1-2	25.0	+9.00
Ludlow	2-9	0-4	0-0	1-2	1-1	0-2	22.2	+4.50
Uttoxeter	2-12	2-6	0-1	0-0	0-4	0-1	16.7	0.00
Fontwell	2-13	1-4	0-2	0-1	0-3	1-3	15.4	-7.50
Towcester	2-13	1-6	0-0	0-1	1-3	0-3	15.4	-8.72
Sandown	2-15	0-2	0-0	1-7	1-5	0-1	13.3	+1.50
Lingfield	1-2	1-1	0-0	0-0	0-1	0-0	50.0	+1.25
Carlisle	1-3	0-0	1-1	0-0	0-2	0-0	33.3	+0.50
Aintree	1-3	0-0	0-1	0-0	1-1	0-1	33.3	+23.00
Stratford	1-3	0-1	0-0	0-0	1-2	0-0	33.3	+5.00
Ayr	1-4	0-0	0-0	0-2	1-2	0-0	25.0	+0.50
Chepstow	1-4	0-2	0-0	0-0	1-2	0-0	25.0	-0.50
Warwick	1-4	0-1	0-1	0-0	1-1	0-1	25.0	-0.25
Cheltenham	1-5	0-2	1-2	0-0	0-1	0-0	20.0	0.00

Nton Abbot	1-5	0-2	1-2	0-0	0-1	0-0	20.0	-2.50
Worcester	1-7	0-1	1-4	0-1	0-0	0-1	14.3	-3.75
Huntingdon	1-9	0-3	0-0	0-1	1-3	0-2	11.1	-5.00
Newbury	1-9	0-2	0-0	0-2	1-4	0-1	11.1	0.00
Plumpton	1-9	0-5	1-1	0-1	0-1	0-1	11.1	-7.17
Exeter	1-10	0-3	0-3	0-1	1-2	0-1	10.0	-7.13
Southwell	1-10	0-5	0-1	0-2	0-1	1-1	10.0	-3.00

WINNING HORSES

Horse	Races Run	1st	2nd	3rd	£
Many Clouds	5	4	0	0	733647
Puffin Billy	7	4	0	1	44344
Rayvin Black	6	1	2	0	15640
Global Power	6	1	2	0	14621
Financial Climate	8	2	0	2	13283
Deputy Dan	7	1	2	2	7798
Milgen Bay	9	3	3	1	14945
Knockalongi	2	1	0	0	6498
Blameitalonmyroots	5	1	2	1	5848
Drum Valley	7	1	3	1	4224
Luci Di Mezzanotte	3	1	1	0	3899
Morning Reggie	7	1	1	1	3899
Come On Laurie	5	2	0	0	6368
Got The Nac	6	1	2	0	3249
Kilgeel Hill	6	2	1	2	6498
Moulin De La Croix	4	1	1	0	2599
*Taniokey	6	1	3	0	2209
Legend Lady	2	1	0	0	2053
Weststreet	5	1	1	2	1643
Robinsson	4	1	0	2	1643
Total winning prize-money					**£894908**
Favourites	**7-37**		**18.9%**		**-21.60**

RAYMOND SHIELS

JEDBURGH, ROXBURGH

	No. of Hrs	Races Run	1st	2nd	3rd	Unpl	Per cent	£1 Level Stake
NH Flat	*0*	*0*	*0*	*0*	*0*	*0*	*0.0*	*0.00*
Hurdles	*2*	*6*	*1*	*0*	*1*	*4*	*16.7*	*+1.00*
Chases	*1*	*2*	*0*	*0*	*1*	*1*	*0.0*	*-2.00*
Totals	**2**	**8**	**1**	**0**	**2**	**5**	**12.5**	**-1.00**
13-14	*2*	*9*	*2*	*1*	*3*	*3*	*22.2*	*+7.50*
12-13	*3*	*10*	*0*	*2*	*2*	*6*	*0.0*	*-10.00*

JOCKEYS

	W-R	Per cent	£1 Level Stake
Daragh Bourke	1-4	25.0	+3.00

COURSE RECORD

	Total W-R	Non-Hndcps Hurdles	Non-Hndcps Chases	Hndcps Hurdles	Hndcps Chases	NH Flat	Per cent	£1 Level Stake
Hexham	1-2	0-1	0-0	1-1	0-0	0-0	50.0	+5.00

WINNING HORSES

Horse	Races Run	1st	2nd	3rd	£
Tikkandemickey	7	1	0	1	3422
Total winning prize-money					**£3422**
Favourites	**0-1**		**0.0%**		**-1.00**

DAN SKELTON

ALCESTER, WARWICKS

	No. of Hrs	Races Run	1st	2nd	3rd	Unpl	Per cent	£1 Level Stake
NH Flat	*38*	*54*	*7*	*6*	*6*	*35*	*13.0*	*-13.92*
Hurdles	*63*	*206*	*44*	*26*	*26*	*110*	*21.4*	*-16.37*
Chases	*32*	*119*	*23*	*15*	*12*	*69*	*19.3*	*-28.90*
Totals	**108**	**379**	**74**	**47**	**44**	**214**	**19.5**	**-59.19**
13-14	*54*	*168*	*26*	*26*	*22*	*94*	*15.5*	*-21.16*

BY MONTH

NH Flat	W-R	Per cent	£1 Level Stake	Hurdles	W-R	Per cent	£1 Level Stake
May	0-1	0.0	-1.00	May	3-6	50.0	+17.00
June	0-2	0.0	-2.00	June	2-7	28.6	-0.88
July	0-0	0.0	0.00	July	1-10	10.0	-5.00
August	0-1	0.0	-1.00	August	0-6	0.0	-6.00
September	0-1	0.0	-1.00	September	1-4	25.0	-1.75
October	0-4	0.0	-4.00	October	6-28	21.4	+8.33
November	0-5	0.0	-5.00	November	1-24	4.2	-20.75
December	2-5	40.0	+11.00	December	6-35	17.1	-3.63
January	0-6	0.0	-6.00	January	3-17	17.6	-4.38
February	0-3	0.0	-3.00	February	5-17	29.4	-3.38
March	5-15	33.3	+9.08	March	7-23	30.4	-0.70
April	0-11	0.0	-11.00	April	9-29	31.0	+4.75

Chases	W-R	Per cent	£1 Level Stake	Totals	W-R	Per cent	£1 Level Stake
May	3-8	37.5	+2.00	May	6-15	40.0	+18.00
June	0-5	0.0	-5.00	June	2-14	14.3	-7.88
July	1-6	16.7	-2.00	July	2-16	12.5	-7.00
August	3-6	50.0	+7.88	August	3-13	23.1	+0.88
September	1-3	33.3	-1.20	September	2-8	25.0	-3.95
October	4-17	23.5	-6.93	October	10-49	20.4	-2.60
November	4-17	23.5	+3.00	November	5-46	10.9	-22.75
December	2-15	13.3	-6.88	December	10-55	18.2	+0.49
January	1-11	9.1	-8.25	January	4-34	11.8	-18.63
February	0-7	0.0	-7.00	February	5-27	18.5	-13.38
March	1-12	8.3	-10.56	March	13-50	26.0	-2.18
April	3-12	25.0	+6.03	April	12-52	23.1	-0.22

DISTANCE

Hurdles	W-R	Per cent	£1 Level Stake	Chases	W-R	Per cent	£1 Level Stake
2m-2m3f	22-88	25.0	+6.26	2m-2m3f	4-31	12.9	-20.43
2m4f-2m7f	11-53	20.8	+0.75	2m4f-2m7f	5-36	13.9	-9.84
3m+	1-3	33.3	+6.00	3m+	10-37	27.0	-8.13

TYPE OF RACE

Non-Handicaps	W-R	Per cent	£1 Level Stake	Handicaps	W-R	Per cent	£1 Level Stake
Nov Hrdls	15-64	23.4	-11.49	Nov Hrdls	1-13	7.7	-10.63
Hrdls	6-47	12.8	-19.25	Hrdls	22-81	27.2	+26.00
Nov Chs	1-11	9.1	-9.43	Nov Chs	6-21	28.6	+6.23
Chases	0-0	0.0	0.00	Chases	16-87	18.4	-25.70
Sell/Claim	0-1	0.0	-1.00	Sell/Claim	0-0	0.0	0.00

RACE CLASS

	W-R	Per cent	£1 Level Stake
Class 1	7-46	15.2	-2.42
Class 2	5-35	14.3	-3.75
Class 3	9-67	13.4	-31.47
Class 4	39-148	26.4	+2.19
Class 5	10-44	22.7	-1.83
Class 6	4-39	10.3	-21.92

FIRST TIME OUT

	W-R	Per cent	£1 Level Stake
Bumpers	3-38	7.9	-24.92
Hurdles	14-48	29.2	+31.96
Chases	7-22	31.8	+0.57
Totals	24-108	22.2	+7.61

JOCKEYS

	W-R	Per cent	£1 Level Stake
Harry Skelton	54-268	20.1	-14.56
Bridget Andrews	12-49	24.5	-13.70
Ryan Mahon	4-32	12.5	-15.50
David England	2-5	40.0	+5.00
Sean Bowen	1-1	100.0	+2.00
Ian Popham	1-5	20.0	-3.43

COURSE RECORD

	Total W-R	Non-Hndcps Hurdles	Non-Hndcps Chases	Hndcps Hurdles	Hndcps Chases	NH Flat	Per cent	£1 Level Stake
Ludlow	6-27	1-8	0-0	3-7	1-7	1-5	22.2	+4.25
Southwell	5-19	2-5	0-0	2-3	1-5	0-6	26.3	+4.25
Fontwell	4-12	1-1	0-0	0-3	3-7	0-1	33.3	+1.50
Chepstow	4-13	2-3	0-1	2-4	0-3	0-2	30.8	+12.50
Wincanton	4-13	3-5	0-0	0-4	1-3	0-1	30.8	-1.25
Stratford	4-19	0-6	0-1	2-3	0-5	2-4	21.1	0.00
Huntingdon	4-21	0-4	0-0	2-8	2-3	0-6	19.0	-3.75
Cheltenham	4-23	1-9	0-0	2-7	1-6	0-1	17.4	+0.25
Sedgefield	3-5	0-0	0-0	1-1	2-3	0-1	60.0	+0.62
Wetherby	3-8	1-1	0-1	0-1	1-3	1-2	37.5	+6.25
Taunton	3-10	2-5	0-0	1-3	0-1	0-1	30.0	-2.20
Bangor	3-11	1-5	0-0	1-1	1-3	0-2	27.3	-2.75
Mrket Rsn	3-12	0-1	0-0	2-4	0-5	1-2	25.0	+1.08
Fakenham	3-17	1-6	0-2	2-4	0-4	0-1	17.6	-6.00
Warwick	3-18	1-7	0-2	0-1	1-2	1-6	16.7	-4.47
Newbury	2-9	2-5	0-0	0-2	0-1	0-1	22.2	+1.38
Uttoxeter	2-14	0-3	0-1	1-3	1-5	0-2	14.3	-3.00
Worcester	2-20	1-5	0-0	1-6	0-6	0-3	10.0	-7.00
Cartmel	1-1	0-0	0-0	0-0	1-1	0-0	100.0	+1.88
Catterick	1-1	0-0	0-0	0-0	1-1	0-0	100.0	+1.75
Lingfield	1-1	0-0	0-0	0-0	1-1	0-0	100.0	+4.50
Newcastle	1-2	1-1	0-0	0-0	0-1	0-0	50.0	+0.38
Towcester	1-4	0-0	0-0	0-1	0-0	1-3	25.0	0.00
Ayr	1-6	0-1	0-0	1-4	0-1	0-0	16.7	-2.00
Exeter	1-6	0-3	1-1	0-1	0-1	0-0	16.7	-4.43
Doncaster	1-11	0-6	0-0	0-0	1-4	0-1	9.1	-9.00
Kempton	1-11	1-5	0-1	0-2	0-1	0-2	9.1	-6.67
Nton Abbot	1-11	0-3	0-0	0-3	1-5	0-0	9.1	-7.75
Sandown	1-12	0-3	0-0	0-6	1-3	0-0	8.3	-5.50
Ascot	1-14	0-2	0-1	0-5	1-5	0-1	7.1	-6.00

WINNING HORSES

Horse	Races Run	1st	2nd	3rd	£
What A Warrior	4	2	0	0	68782
Blue Heron	5	2	0	1	45761
Shelford	5	2	0	0	26679
*Pumped Up Kicks	3	2	0	0	30897
Ballincurrig	5	1	0	0	18768
Bertimont	6	1	2	0	16245
Three Musketeers	3	2	0	1	19195
Rascal	7	4	0	0	26642
Long House Hall	2	2	0	0	22259
Workbench	13	3	1	3	18858
Stephanie Frances	6	3	1	0	21332
Boss Des Mottes	5	1	0	1	9097
What A Good Night	5	2	0	0	10722
Amroth Bay	4	2	0	0	9994
Mister Grez	12	5	3	1	21891
Toby Lerone	7	1	2	1	6564
*Hurricane Hollow	2	1	0	0	6256
Go Odee Go	8	1	2	2	5848
Curragh Hall	6	1	0	1	5198
Hinton Indiana	8	3	2	1	10007
Many Stars	5	1	1	1	4549
Twice Returned	2	1	0	0	4549
Sur La Mer	6	1	2	0	4549
Storm Of Swords	8	3	1	0	11501
Guiding George	6	1	2	1	3994
Dunlough Bay	3	1	0	0	3899
Barrison	2	2	0	0	6498
*Shady Lane	2	1	0	1	3899
Stephen Hero	10	2	2	2	7697
Fascino Rustico	5	2	0	0	7148
Value At Risk	3	1	1	0	3899
Zarib	5	2	0	1	7148
Bon Chic	3	2	0	1	7473
Gaye Memories	5	1	0	0	3509
*Masterful Act	4	1	1	1	3249
Colebrooke	4	1	0	2	3249
*Lochalsh	3	1	1	0	3249
*Rock Of Leon	3	1	1	0	3249
Arthamint	4	1	0	0	3249
Mister Miyagi	3	2	0	1	5198
Popaflora	9	1	3	0	2469
Welsh Shadow	1	1	0	0	1711
Walking In The Air	1	1	0	0	1625
Madame Trigger	5	1	0	2	1560
Two Taffs	1	1	0	0	1560

Total winning prize-money			**£511675**
Favourites	**27-80**	**33.8%**	**-11.10**

EVELYN SLACK

HILTON, CUMBRIA

	No. of Hrs	Races Run	1st	2nd	3rd	Unpl	Per cent	£1 Level Stake
NH Flat	*0*	*0*	*0*	*0*	*0*	*0*	*0.0*	*0.00*
Hurdles	*3*	*10*	*1*	*0*	*2*	*7*	*10.0*	*-2.50*
Chases	*1*	*2*	*0*	*0*	*0*	*2*	*0.0*	*-2.00*
Totals	**4**	**12**	**1**	**0**	**2**	**9**	**8.3**	**-4.50**
13-14	*5*	*21*	*1*	*3*	*2*	*15*	*4.8*	*-8.00*
12-13	*5*	*23*	*2*	*1*	*2*	*18*	*8.7*	*-1.00*

JOCKEYS

	W-R	Per cent	£1 Level Stake
Henry Brooke	1-9	11.1	-1.50

COURSE RECORD

	Total W-R	Non-Hndcps Hurdles	Non-Hndcps Chases	Hndcps Hurdles	Hndcps Chases	NH Flat	Per cent	£1 Level Stake
Ayr	1-1	0-0	0-0	1-1	0-0	0-0	100.0	+6.50

WINNING HORSES

Horse	Races Run	1st	2nd	3rd	£
Omid	6	1	0	1	2599
Total winning prize-money					**£2599**
Favourites	**0-0**		**0.0%**		**0.00**

KENNETH SLACK

HILTON, CUMBRIA

	No. of Hrs	Races Run	1st	2nd	3rd	Unpl	Per cent	£1 Level Stake
NH Flat	*0*	*0*	*0*	*0*	*0*	*0*	*0.0*	*0.00*
Hurdles	*5*	*8*	*1*	*2*	*1*	*4*	*12.5*	*+1.00*
Chases	*1*	*3*	*1*	*1*	*1*	*0*	*33.3*	*0.00*
Totals	**5**	**11**	**2**	**3**	**2**	**4**	**18.2**	**+1.00**

JOCKEYS

	W-R	Per cent	£1 Level Stake
Henry Brooke	2-8	25.0	+4.00

COURSE RECORD

	Total W-R	Non-Hndcps Hurdles	Non-Hndcps Chases	Hndcps Hurdles	Hndcps Chases	NH Flat	Per cent	£1 Level Stake
Catterick	1-1	0-0	0-0	1-1	0-0	0-0	100.0	+8.00
Sedgefield	1-5	0-0	0-0	0-3	1-2	0-0	20.0	-2.00

WINNING HORSES

Horse	Races Run	1st	2nd	3rd	£
Grand Vintage	3	1	0	0	2599
*My Friend George	4	1	2	1	2599
Total winning prize-money					**£5198**
Favourites	**1-3**		**33.3%**		**0.00**

G SLADE-JONES

KINGTON, HEREFORDSHIRE

	No. of Hrs	Races Run	1st	2nd	3rd	Unpl	Per cent	£1 Level Stake
NH Flat	*0*	*0*	*0*	*0*	*0*	*0*	*0.0*	*0.00*
Hurdles	*0*	*0*	*0*	*0*	*0*	*0*	*0.0*	*0.00*
Chases	*2*	*5*	*2*	*1*	*0*	*2*	*40.0*	*+6.75*
Totals	**2**	**5**	**2**	**1**	**0**	**2**	**40.0**	**+6.75**

JOCKEYS

	W-R	Per cent	£1 Level Stake
Mr J Nixon	2-5	40.0	+6.75

COURSE RECORD

	Total W-R	Non-Hndcps Hurdles	Non-Hndcps Chases	Hndcps Hurdles	Hndcps Chases	NH Flat	Per cent	£1 Level Stake
Ludlow	1-1	0-0	1-1	0-0	0-0	0-0	100.0	+8.00
Stratford	1-2	0-0	1-2	0-0	0-0	0-0	50.0	+0.75

WINNING HORSES

Horse	Races Run	1st	2nd	3rd	£
*Tugboat	4	2	1	0	4367
Total winning prize-money					**£4367**
Favourites	**1-1**		**100.0%**		**1.75**

PAM SLY

THORNEY, CAMBS

	No. of Hrs	Races Run	1st	2nd	3rd	Unpl	Per cent	£1 Level Stake
NH Flat	*3*	*5*	*1*	*1*	*1*	*2*	*20.0*	*-0.50*
Hurdles	*11*	*27*	*4*	*0*	*2*	*21*	*14.8*	*-1.50*
Chases	*5*	*14*	*3*	*2*	*2*	*7*	*21.4*	*+5.50*
Totals	**14**	**46**	**8**	**3**	**5**	**30**	**17.4**	**+3.50**
13-14	*16*	*55*	*8*	*7*	*8*	*32*	*14.5*	*+22.83*
12-13	*17*	*60*	*3*	*8*	*9*	*40*	*5.0*	*-37.00*

JOCKEYS

	W-R	Per cent	£1 Level Stake
Kielan Woods	5-30	16.7	+3.50
Gavin Sheehan	1-2	50.0	+2.50
Bridget Andrews	1-2	50.0	+6.00
Harrison Beswick	1-4	25.0	-0.50

COURSE RECORD

	Total W-R	Non-Hndcps Hurdles	Chases	Hndcps Hurdles	Chases	NH Flat	Per cent	£1 Level Stake
Ludlow	2-3	0-0	0-0	0-0	2-3	0-0	66.7	+10.00
Mrket Rsn	2-5	0-2	0-0	1-2	1-1	0-0	40.0	+5.50
Catterick	1-1	0-0	0-0	1-1	0-0	0-0	100.0	+9.00
Towcester	1-4	0-2	0-0	1-2	0-0	0-0	25.0	+4.00
Fakenham	1-6	1-3	0-0	0-2	0-0	0-1	16.7	-2.50
Wetherby	1-6	0-2	0-0	0-0	0-2	1-2	16.7	-1.50

WINNING HORSES

Horse	Races Run	1st	2nd	3rd	£
Arkaim	7	3	1	1	29005
Iconic Rose	6	2	1	0	7018
Bouggietopieces	8	1	0	0	3119
Acertain Circus	6	1	0	1	2738
Grand Turina	1	1	0	0	1643
Total winning prize-money					**£43523**
Favourites	**0-0**		**0.0%**		**0.00**

SUE SMITH

HIGH ELDWICK, W YORKS

	No. of Hrs	Races Run	1st	2nd	3rd	Unpl	Per cent	£1 Level Stake
NH Flat	*6*	*9*	*2*	*2*	*2*	*3*	*22.2*	*+3.00*
Hurdles	*36*	*124*	*9*	*13*	*15*	*87*	*7.3*	*-53.00*
Chases	*41*	*189*	*20*	*29*	*29*	*111*	*10.6*	*-84.58*
Totals	**64**	**322**	**31**	**44**	**46**	**201**	**9.6**	**-134.58**
13-14	*73*	*395*	*61*	*57*	*45*	*232*	*15.4*	*-33.77*
12-13	*58*	*278*	*31*	*30*	*36*	*181*	*11.2*	*-5.70*

BY MONTH

NH Flat	W-R	Per cent	£1 Level Stake	**Hurdles**	W-R	Per cent	£1 Level Stake
May	0-2	0.0	-2.00	May	0-5	0.0	-5.00
June	0-0	0.0	0.00	June	0-3	0.0	-3.00
July	0-0	0.0	0.00	July	0-4	0.0	-4.00
August	0-0	0.0	0.00	August	0-2	0.0	-2.00
September	1-1	100.0	+8.00	September	0-8	0.0	-8.00
October	0-1	0.0	-1.00	October	0-15	0.0	-15.00
November	0-0	0.0	0.00	November	0-24	0.0	-24.00
December	0-2	0.0	-2.00	December	3-16	18.8	+9.00
January	1-1	100.0	+2.00	January	3-10	30.0	+25.50
February	0-2	0.0	-2.00	February	0-9	0.0	-9.00
March	0-0	0.0	0.00	March	3-21	14.3	-10.50
April	0-0	0.0	0.00	April	0-7	0.0	-7.00

Chases	W-R	Per cent	£1 Level Stake	**Totals**	W-R	Per cent	£1 Level Stake
May	2-11	18.2	-3.50	May	2-18	11.1	-10.50
June	0-7	0.0	-7.00	June	0-10	0.0	-10.00
July	0-7	0.0	-7.00	July	0-11	0.0	-11.00
August	0-2	0.0	-2.00	August	0-4	0.0	-4.00
September	0-2	0.0	-2.00	September	1-11	9.1	-2.00
October	1-20	5.0	-15.67	October	1-36	2.8	-31.67
November	3-35	8.6	-23.17	November	3-59	5.1	-47.17
December	7-30	23.3	+3.75	December	10-48	20.8	+10.75
January	4-21	19.0	+3.75	January	8-32	25.0	+31.25
February	2-16	12.5	+3.00	February	2-27	7.4	-8.00
March	1-20	5.0	-16.75	March	4-41	9.8	-27.25
April	0-18	0.0	-18.00	April	0-25	0.0	-25.00

DISTANCE

Hurdles	W-R	Per cent	£1 Level Stake	**Chases**	W-R	Per cent	£1 Level Stake
2m-2m3f	6-56	10.7	+0.50	2m-2m3f	6-42	14.3	-8.00
2m4f-2m7f	3-45	6.7	-30.50	2m4f-2m7f	9-69	13.0	-16.17
3m+	0-9	0.0	-9.00	3m+	3-64	4.7	-52.17

TYPE OF RACE

Non-Handicaps	W-R	Per cent	£1 Level Stake	**Handicaps**	W-R	Per cent	£1 Level Stake
Nov Hrdls	3-25	12.0	+13.25	Nov Hrdls	0-8	0.0	-8.00
Hrdls	0-5	0.0	-5.00	Hrdls	6-77	7.8	-44.25
Nov Chs	5-22	22.7	+11.33	Nov Chs	5-42	11.9	-17.67
Chases	1-5	20.0	+5.00	Chases	9-120	7.5	-83.25
Sell/Claim	0-8	0.0	-8.00	Sell/Claim	0-0	0.0	0.00

RACE CLASS

	W-R	Per cent	£1 Level Stake
Class 1	1-22	4.5	-13.00
Class 2	1-30	3.3	-20.00
Class 3	6-84	7.1	-59.00
Class 4	20-136	14.7	-7.83
Class 5	1-41	2.4	-37.75
Class 6	2-9	22.2	+3.00

FIRST TIME OUT

	W-R	Per cent	£1 Level Stake
Bumpers	1-6	16.7	+3.00
Hurdles	1-32	3.1	-27.00
Chases	0-26	0.0	-26.00
Totals	2-64	3.1	-50.00

JOCKEYS

	W-R	Per cent	£1 Level Stake
Jonathan England	10-95	10.5	-28.75
Danny Cook	7-14	50.0	+24.00
Callum Bewley	5-57	8.8	-36.17
Ryan Mania	4-73	5.5	-56.67
Harry Haynes	3-14	21.4	+19.00
Daragh Bourke	1-6	16.7	+3.00
Dougie Costello	1-18	5.6	-14.00

COURSE RECORD

	Total W-R	Non-Hndcps Hurdles	Chases	Hndcps Hurdles	Chases	NH Flat	Per cent	£1 Level Stake
Catterick	8-19	1-2	2-2	1-6	4-7	0-2	42.1	+44.00
Wetherby	6-47	0-8	0-4	3-16	2-18	1-1	12.8	-16.75
Hexham	3-26	0-9	0-0	1-6	2-10	0-1	11.5	-13.17
Southwell	2-12	0-3	0-0	0-6	1-2	1-1	16.7	+0.75
Uttoxeter	2-21	0-4	1-3	0-5	1-9	0-0	9.5	-13.42
Carlisle	2-24	0-1	0-3	0-6	2-14	0-0	8.3	-10.50
Haydock	2-26	0-0	2-4	0-6	0-16	0-0	7.7	-7.00

Newcastle	2-28	0-1	0-1	0-9	2-16	0-1	7.1	-21.00
Sedgefield	2-38	2-6	0-0	0-11	0-18	0-3	5.3	-25.75
Ayr	1-11	0-0	0-1	1-5	0-5	0-0	9.1	-7.75
Kelso	1-19	0-1	1-3	0-1	0-14	0-0	5.3	-13.00

WINNING HORSES

Horse	Races Run	1st	2nd	3rd	£
Wakanda	9	3	3	1	34342
Mwaleshi	7	1	1	1	12777
Grate Fella	7	2	0	1	12346
Straidnahanna	8	2	1	2	13980
Oorayvic	4	2	1	1	10473
Stagecoach Pearl	7	1	3	0	6498
No Planning	5	1	0	0	6498
Palm Grey	7	1	1	1	6498
De Vous A Moi	5	2	1	0	10279
Smooth Stepper	9	2	0	2	8772
Bennys Well	9	2	0	2	10072
Twice Lucky	3	1	0	0	4449
Clan William	5	1	0	0	4431
Emral Silk	8	1	1	1	4224
Ballymoat	6	1	0	1	3899
*Minella Fiveo	4	1	0	0	3899
Rattlin	7	1	0	0	3798
Groomed	4	1	2	0	3769
Red Danaher	7	1	1	0	3639
Special Wells	8	1	2	0	3249
Hainan	3	1	0	0	3249
Vintage Clouds	4	1	1	1	1643
Herising	1	1	0	0	1560
Total winning prize-money					**£174344**
Favourites	**8-37**		**21.6%**		**-11.50**

SUZY SMITH

LEWES, E SUSSEX

	No. of Hrs	Races Run	1st	2nd	3rd	Unpl	Per cent	£1 Level Stake
NH Flat	*5*	*7*	*0*	*0*	*2*	*5*	*0.0*	*-7.00*
Hurdles	*14*	*56*	*9*	*4*	*11*	*32*	*16.1*	*+12.38*
Chases	*3*	*5*	*0*	*0*	*1*	*4*	*0.0*	*-5.00*
Totals	**17**	**68**	**9**	**4**	**14**	**41**	**13.2**	**+0.38**
13-14	*16*	*49*	*8*	*2*	*4*	*35*	*16.3*	*+38.00*
12-13	*14*	*49*	*9*	*7*	*3*	*30*	*18.4*	*+27.75*

JOCKEYS

	W-R	Per cent	£1 Level Stake
Micheal Nolan	3-8	37.5	+13.00
Mr H A A Bannister	2-9	22.2	-2.63
Tom O'Brien	2-12	16.7	+14.50
Jack Sherwood	1-5	20.0	+2.50
Paddy Brennan	1-18	5.6	-11.00

COURSE RECORD

	Total W-R	Non-Hndcps Hurdles	Non-Hndcps Chases	Hndcps Hurdles	Hndcps Chases	NH Flat	Per cent	£1 Level Stake
Plumpton	4-12	0-1	0-0	4-9	0-0	0-2	33.3	+12.38
Sandown	2-4	0-0	0-0	2-4	0-0	0-0	50.0	+27.00
Fontwell	2-15	0-3	0-0	2-10	0-0	0-2	13.3	-7.50
Fakenham	1-1	0-0	0-0	1-1	0-0	0-0	100.0	+4.50

WINNING HORSES

Horse	Races Run	1st	2nd	3rd	£
Invicta Lake	10	2	0	3	34973
Laughton Park	4	1	1	0	7148
*Little Boy Boru	9	2	1	1	10241
Beau Lake	4	2	0	2	11853
Azabitmour	6	1	1	1	4224
Mariet	5	1	1	0	2599
Total winning prize-money					**£71038**
Favourites	**2-4**		**50.0%**		**1.88**

JULIAN SMITH

TIRLEY, GLOUCS

	No. of Hrs	Races Run	1st	2nd	3rd	Unpl	Per cent	£1 Level Stake
NH Flat	*2*	*3*	*0*	*0*	*0*	*3*	*0.0*	*-3.00*
Hurdles	*6*	*16*	*1*	*1*	*2*	*12*	*6.3*	*-8.00*
Chases	*3*	*9*	*0*	*1*	*3*	*5*	*0.0*	*-9.00*
Totals	**8**	**28**	**1**	**2**	**5**	**20**	**3.6**	**-20.00**
13-14	*10*	*37*	*2*	*6*	*4*	*25*	*5.4*	*-24.63*
12-13	*12*	*35*	*2*	*8*	*4*	*21*	*5.7*	*-2.25*

JOCKEYS

	W-R	Per cent	£1 Level Stake
Mark Grant	1-17	5.9	-9.00

COURSE RECORD

	Total W-R	Non-Hndcps Hurdles	Non-Hndcps Chases	Hndcps Hurdles	Hndcps Chases	NH Flat	Per cent	£1 Level Stake
Bangor	1-5	0-0	0-0	1-3	0-1	0-1	20.0	+3.00

WINNING HORSES

Horse	Races Run	1st	2nd	3rd	£
Pennies And Pounds	4	1	1	0	3422
Total winning prize-money					**£3422**
Favourites	**0-1**		**0.0%**		**-1.00**

R MIKE SMITH

GALSTON, E AYRSHIRE

	No. of Hrs	Races Run	1st	2nd	3rd	Unpl	Per cent	£1 Level Stake
NH Flat	*4*	*5*	*0*	*0*	*1*	*4*	*0.0*	*-5.00*
Hurdles	*5*	*18*	*1*	*3*	*4*	*10*	*5.6*	*-5.00*

Chases	3	11	1	2	0	8	9.1	-4.50
Totals	**9**	**34**	**2**	**5**	**5**	**22**	**5.9**	**-14.50**
13-14	*9*	*27*	*4*	*1*	*1*	*21*	*14.8*	*+11.00*
12-13	*9*	*25*	*1*	*0*	*0*	*24*	*4.0*	*-8.00*

JOCKEYS

	W-R	Per cent	£1 Level Stake
Callum Bewley	2-27	7.4	-7.50

COURSE RECORD

	Total W-R	Non-Hndcps Hurdles	Non-Hndcps Chases	Hndcps Hurdles	Chases	NH Flat	Per cent	£1 Level Stake
Carlisle	1-3	1-1	0-0	0-0	0-0	0-2	33.3	+10.00
Hexham	1-3	0-0	0-1	0-0	1-2	0-0	33.3	+3.50

WINNING HORSES

Horse	Races Run	1st	2nd	3rd	£
U Name It	7	1	2	3	3899
Knight Woodsman	5	1	0	0	2144
Total winning prize-money					**£6043**
Favourites	**0-0**		**0.0%**		**0.00**

MARTIN SMITH

NEWMARKET, SUFFOLK

	No. of Hrs	Races Run	1st	2nd	3rd	Unpl	Per cent	£1 Level Stake
NH Flat	*0*	*0*	*0*	*0*	*0*	*0*	*0.0*	*0.00*
Hurdles	*2*	*11*	*2*	*2*	*2*	*5*	*18.2*	*+10.00*
Chases	*0*	*0*	*0*	*0*	*0*	*0*	*0.0*	*0.00*
Totals	**2**	**11**	**2**	**2**	**2**	**5**	**18.2**	**+10.00**
13-14	*3*	*7*	*1*	*0*	*1*	*5*	*14.3*	*+14.00*

JOCKEYS

	W-R	Per cent	£1 Level Stake
Thomas Cheesman	1-3	33.3	+14.00
Leighton Aspell	1-6	16.7	-2.00

COURSE RECORD

	Total W-R	Non-Hndcps Hurdles	Non-Hndcps Chases	Hndcps Hurdles	Chases	NH Flat	Per cent	£1 Level Stake
Huntingdon	1-1	0-0	0-0	1-1	0-0	0-0	100.0	+3.00
Plumpton	1-1	0-0	0-0	1-1	0-0	0-0	100.0	+16.00

WINNING HORSES

Horse	Races Run	1st	2nd	3rd	£
Ossie's Dancer	6	1	1	1	6498
Amberjam	5	1	1	1	2274
Total winning prize-money					**£8772**
Favourites	**0-0**		**0.0%**		**0.00**

MICHAEL SMITH

KIRKHEATON, NORTHUMBERLAND

	No. of Hrs	Races Run	1st	2nd	3rd	Unpl	Per cent	£1 Level Stake
NH Flat	*7*	*13*	*0*	*2*	*3*	*8*	*0.0*	*-13.00*
Hurdles	*15*	*40*	*3*	*3*	*2*	*32*	*7.5*	*-22.50*
Chases	*8*	*27*	*5*	*3*	*5*	*14*	*18.5*	*-1.00*
Totals	**19**	**80**	**8**	**8**	**10**	**54**	**10.0**	**-36.50**
13-14	*21*	*64*	*9*	*6*	*9*	*40*	*14.1*	*+11.75*
12-13	*11*	*39*	*7*	*3*	*8*	*21*	*17.9*	*+11.16*

JOCKEYS

	W-R	Per cent	£1 Level Stake
Brian Hughes	3-19	15.8	-7.75
Danny Cook	3-28	10.7	-10.50
Adam Nicol	2-17	11.8	-2.25

COURSE RECORD

	Total W-R	Non-Hndcps Hurdles	Non-Hndcps Chases	Hndcps Hurdles	Chases	NH Flat	Per cent	£1 Level Stake
Catterick	2-5	0-0	0-0	0-1	2-4	0-0	40.0	+9.50
Hexham	2-17	2-8	0-0	0-2	0-3	0-4	11.8	-2.50
Ayr	1-2	0-0	0-0	0-1	1-1	0-0	50.0	+2.00
Musselbgh	1-7	0-2	0-0	0-1	1-3	0-1	14.3	-3.25
Wetherby	1-7	0-0	0-0	0-4	1-1	0-2	14.3	-3.25
Kelso	1-12	1-2	0-1	0-6	0-2	0-1	8.3	-9.00

WINNING HORSES

Horse	Races Run	1st	2nd	3rd	£
Bop Along	2	1	1	0	5523
Cango	5	2	2	0	8577
Mister Spingsprong	7	2	1	2	8347
Dream Flyer	4	1	0	0	3994
Benefit In Kind	10	1	1	2	3899
*Brunello	7	1	0	1	3249
Total winning prize-money					**£33589**
Favourites	**3-9**		**33.3%**		**2.25**

GILES SMYLY

WORMINGTON, WORCS

	No. of Hrs	Races Run	1st	2nd	3rd	Unpl	Per cent	£1 Level Stake
NH Flat	*0*	*0*	*0*	*0*	*0*	*0*	*0.0*	*0.00*
Hurdles	*6*	*22*	*3*	*2*	*3*	*14*	*13.6*	*-11.25*
Chases	*4*	*13*	*0*	*2*	*1*	*10*	*0.0*	*-13.00*
Totals	**7**	**35**	**3**	**4**	**4**	**24**	**8.6**	**-24.25**
13-14	*12*	*42*	*3*	*6*	*4*	*29*	*7.1*	*+8.75*
12-13	*10*	*21*	*1*	*2*	*2*	*16*	*4.8*	*+4.00*

JOCKEYS

	W-R	Per cent	£1 Level Stake
Tom Cannon	2-8	25.0	-0.25
Gavin Sheehan	1-6	16.7	-3.00

COURSE RECORD

	Total W-R	Non-Hndcps Hurdles	Non-Hndcps Chases	Hndcps Hurdles	Hndcps Chases	NH Flat	Per cent	£1 Level Stake
Kempton	1-2	0-0	0-0	1-2	0-0	0-0	50.0	+1.25
Warwick	1-2	1-2	0-0	0-0	0-0	0-0	50.0	+1.00
Wincanton	1-6	0-1	0-0	1-5	0-0	0-0	16.7	-1.50

WINNING HORSES

Horse	Races Run	1st	2nd	3rd	£
Letemgo	5	2	0	0	7148
*Maybe Plenty	7	1	1	2	3574

Total winning prize-money £10722

Favourites 1-4 25.0% -1.00

JAMIE SNOWDEN

LAMBOURN, BERKS

	No. of Hrs	Races Run	1st	2nd	3rd	Unpl	Per cent	£1 Level Stake
NH Flat	*12*	*21*	*2*	*3*	*0*	*16*	*9.5*	*-16.70*
Hurdles	*27*	*93*	*10*	*15*	*14*	*53*	*10.8*	*-40.78*
Chases	*13*	*42*	*7*	*6*	*13*	*16*	*16.7*	*-2.40*
Totals	**42**	**156**	**19**	**24**	**27**	**85**	**12.2**	**-59.88**
13-14	*44*	*161*	*21*	*22*	*15*	*103*	*13.0*	*-37.12*
12-13	*36*	*126*	*13*	*14*	*18*	*81*	*10.3*	*-65.56*

BY MONTH

NH Flat	W-R	Per cent	£1 Level Stake
May	0-1	0.0	-1.00
June	0-0	0.0	0.00
July	0-0	0.0	0.00
August	0-0	0.0	0.00
September	0-2	0.0	-2.00
October	0-4	0.0	-4.00
November	0-3	0.0	-3.00
December	0-0	0.0	0.00
January	0-1	0.0	-1.00
February	1-2	50.0	-0.20
March	1-6	16.7	-3.50
April	0-2	0.0	-2.00

Hurdles	W-R	Per cent	£1 Level Stake
May	0-4	0.0	-4.00
June	0-5	0.0	-5.00
July	0-3	0.0	-3.00
August	0-5	0.0	-5.00
September	0-4	0.0	-4.00
October	1-13	7.7	+4.00
November	3-7	42.9	+0.40
December	0-12	0.0	-12.00
January	1-12	8.3	-8.00
February	0-5	0.0	-5.00
March	3-11	27.3	+3.75
April	2-12	16.7	-2.93

Chases	W-R	Per cent	£1 Level Stake
May	0-2	0.0	-2.00
June	0-1	0.0	-1.00
July	0-1	0.0	-1.00
August	1-1	100.0	+14.00
September	0-0	0.0	0.00
October	1-6	16.7	-1.50
November	0-6	0.0	-6.00
December	1-4	25.0	+1.00
January	1-3	33.3	+1.00
February	0-2	0.0	-2.00
March	1-6	16.7	-1.00
April	2-10	20.0	-3.90

Totals	W-R	Per cent	£1 Level Stake
May	0-7	0.0	-7.00
June	0-6	0.0	-6.00
July	0-4	0.0	-4.00
August	1-6	16.7	+9.00
September	0-6	0.0	-6.00
October	2-23	8.7	-1.50
November	3-16	18.8	-8.60
December	1-16	6.3	-11.00
January	2-16	12.5	-8.00
February	1-9	11.1	-7.20
March	5-23	21.7	-0.75
April	4-24	16.7	-8.83

DISTANCE

Hurdles	W-R	Per cent	£1 Level Stake
2m-2m3f	6-47	12.8	-20.33
2m4f-2m7f	2-24	8.3	-17.25
3m+	0-2	0.0	-2.00

Chases	W-R	Per cent	£1 Level Stake
2m-2m3f	4-16	25.0	+13.00
2m4f-2m7f	1-9	11.1	-4.50
3m+	2-12	16.7	-5.90

TYPE OF RACE

Non-Handicaps	W-R	Per cent	£1 Level Stake
Nov Hrdls	5-30	16.7	-13.53
Hrdls	2-26	7.7	-16.50
Nov Chs	0-7	0.0	-7.00
Chases	0-0	0.0	0.00
Sell/Claim	0-3	0.0	-3.00

Handicaps	W-R	Per cent	£1 Level Stake
Nov Hrdls	0-2	0.0	-2.00
Hrdls	3-32	9.4	-5.75
Nov Chs	1-13	7.7	+2.00
Chases	6-22	27.3	+2.60
Sell/Claim	0-1	0.0	-1.00

RACE CLASS

	W-R	Per cent	£1 Level Stake
Class 1	0-7	0.0	-7.00
Class 2	0-4	0.0	-4.00
Class 3	2-18	11.1	-10.75
Class 4	13-88	14.8	-22.43
Class 5	2-22	9.1	-3.00
Class 6	2-17	11.8	-12.70

FIRST TIME OUT

	W-R	Per cent	£1 Level Stake
Bumpers	0-12	0.0	-12.00
Hurdles	0-22	0.0	-22.00
Chases	1-8	12.5	+7.00
Totals	1-42	2.4	-27.00

JOCKEYS

	W-R	Per cent	£1 Level Stake
Brendan Powell	8-77	10.4	-34.10
Micheal Nolan	6-18	33.3	+5.17
Nick Scholfield	1-1	100.0	+2.25
Thomas Garner	1-5	20.0	+12.00
Gavin Sheehan	1-6	16.7	-2.50
Daryl Jacob	1-12	8.3	-7.50
Conor Shoemark	1-13	7.7	-11.20

COURSE RECORD

	Total W-R	Non-Hndcps Hurdles	Non-Hndcps Chases	Hndcps Hurdles	Hndcps Chases	NH Flat	Per cent	£1 Level Stake
Taunton	3-10	3-4	0-0	0-3	0-1	0-2	30.0	+4.57
Fontwell	3-19	0-5	0-0	1-4	1-4	1-6	15.8	-9.45
Southwell	2-8	1-3	0-0	1-3	0-1	0-1	25.0	+12.50
Fakenham	1-3	0-0	0-0	0-0	1-3	0-0	33.3	+1.00
Towcester	1-3	1-3	0-0	0-0	0-0	0-0	33.3	-0.90
Mrket Rsn	1-4	0-3	0-0	0-0	1-1	0-0	25.0	+1.00
Newbury	1-4	0-0	0-0	0-1	1-3	0-0	25.0	+1.00
Chepstow	1-5	0-1	0-0	1-3	0-0	0-1	20.0	+1.00

Exeter	1-5	1-1	0-1	0-2	0-1	0-0	20.0	-1.00
Ffos Las	1-7	0-2	0-0	0-3	0-1	1-1	14.3	-4.50
Nton Abbot	1-8	0-3	0-1	0-1	1-2	0-1	12.5	-4.00
Worcester	1-8	0-3	0-0	0-1	1-3	0-1	12.5	+7.00
Wincanton	1-11	0-4	0-0	0-3	1-4	0-0	9.1	-8.90
Huntingdon	1-12	1-5	0-1	0-2	0-2	0-2	8.3	-10.20

WINNING HORSES

Horse	Races Run	1st	2nd	3rd	£
Alanjou	6	2	0	1	10426
Jean Fleming	3	1	1	1	5824
Tea Caddy	7	1	2	2	4874
Major Milborne	8	1	1	3	4549
*Dino Mite	6	3	0	1	11696
*To The Sky	8	2	2	3	6173
Monbeg Theatre	6	2	2	0	7018
Future Gilded	4	1	0	2	3899
Rhythm Star	6	1	1	2	3661
Kassis	5	1	0	2	3249
Camachoice	7	1	1	1	3119
Souriyan	5	1	2	0	2599
Midnight Silver	4	2	1	0	3574
Total winning prize-money					**£70661**
Favourites	**5-18**		**27.8%**		**-8.63**

MIKE SOWERSBY

GOODMANHAM, E YORKS

	No. of Hrs	Races Run	1st	2nd	3rd	Unpl	Per cent	£1 Level Stake
NH Flat	*2*	*5*	*0*	*0*	*1*	*4*	*0.0*	*-5.00*
Hurdles	*12*	*55*	*4*	*2*	*7*	*42*	*7.3*	*-3.50*
Chases	*1*	*12*	*2*	*1*	*3*	*6*	*16.7*	*-5.38*
Totals	**15**	**72**	**6**	**3**	**11**	**52**	**8.3**	**-13.88**
13-14	*19*	*94*	*5*	*3*	*9*	*77*	*5.3*	*-36.00*
12-13	*15*	*85*	*4*	*1*	*4*	*76*	*4.7*	*-44.00*

JOCKEYS

	W-R	Per cent	£1 Level Stake
Brian Hughes	4-19	21.1	+18.38
Brian Harding	1-3	33.3	+0.75
Adam Nicol	1-30	3.3	-13.00

COURSE RECORD

	Total W-R	Non-Hndcps Hurdles	Non-Hndcps Chases	Hndcps Hurdles	Hndcps Chases	NH Flat	Per cent	£1 Level Stake
Sedgefield	2-6	0-0	0-0	1-5	1-1	0-0	33.3	+6.75
Southwell	2-9	0-1	0-0	2-7	0-1	0-0	22.2	+16.50
Mrket Rsn	1-12	0-0	0-0	0-6	1-3	0-3	8.3	-9.13
Uttoxeter	1-20	0-0	0-0	1-17	0-2	0-1	5.0	-3.00

WINNING HORSES

Horse	Races Run	1st	2nd	3rd	£
Tregaro	12	2	1	3	10990
Moon Melody	5	2	0	2	5653
Feast Of Fire	6	1	0	1	3249
Agent Louise	7	1	0	0	2339
Total winning prize-money					**£22231**
Favourites	**1-1**		**100.0%**		**1.88**

JOHN SPEARING

KINNERSLEY, WORCS

	No. of Hrs	Races Run	1st	2nd	3rd	Unpl	Per cent	£1 Level Stake
NH Flat	*3*	*5*	*0*	*1*	*2*	*2*	*0.0*	*-5.00*
Hurdles	*6*	*21*	*1*	*2*	*5*	*13*	*4.8*	*-18.25*
Chases	*4*	*15*	*4*	*3*	*4*	*4*	*26.7*	*+2.25*
Totals	**10**	**41**	**5**	**6**	**11**	**19**	**12.2**	**-21.00**
13-14	*11*	*46*	*5*	*5*	*7*	*29*	*10.9*	*-7.25*
12-13	*11*	*46*	*5*	*6*	*6*	*29*	*10.9*	*-15.00*

JOCKEYS

	W-R	Per cent	£1 Level Stake
Nico de Boinville	3-20	15.0	-8.75
Jamie Moore	2-14	14.3	-5.25

COURSE RECORD

	Total W-R	Non-Hndcps Hurdles	Non-Hndcps Chases	Hndcps Hurdles	Hndcps Chases	NH Flat	Per cent	£1 Level Stake
Sandown	2-2	0-0	0-0	0-0	2-2	0-0	100.0	+6.75
Southwell	2-2	1-1	0-0	0-0	1-1	0-0	100.0	+3.75
Bangor	1-2	0-0	0-0	0-0	1-2	0-0	50.0	+3.50

WINNING HORSES

Horse	Races Run	1st	2nd	3rd	£
Pearls Legend	6	2	2	1	14296
Barton Gift	5	1	1	1	6498
Over The Air	8	1	2	0	3195
Table Bluff	7	1	0	3	2144
Total winning prize-money					**£26133**
Favourites	**2-4**		**50.0%**		**4.50**

DANIEL STEELE

HENFIELD, W SUSSEX

	No. of Hrs	Races Run	1st	2nd	3rd	Unpl	Per cent	£1 Level Stake
NH Flat	*1*	*1*	*0*	*0*	*0*	*1*	*0.0*	*-1.00*
Hurdles	*7*	*28*	*3*	*1*	*1*	*23*	*10.7*	*+1.50*
Chases	*3*	*10*	*1*	*1*	*0*	*8*	*10.0*	*0.00*
Totals	**7**	**39**	**4**	**2**	**1**	**32**	**10.3**	**+0.50**
13-14	*4*	*22*	*3*	*5*	*0*	*14*	*13.6*	*+5.00*
12-13	*4*	*16*	*0*	*1*	*1*	*14*	*0.0*	*-16.00*

JOCKEYS

	W-R	Per cent	£1 Level Stake
Freddie Mitchell	3-19	15.8	+3.50
Declan Bates	1-1	100.0	+16.00

COURSE RECORD

	Total W-R	Non-Hndcps Hurdles	Non-Hndcps Chases	Hndcps Hurdles	Hndcps Chases	NH Flat	Per cent	£1 Level Stake
Plumpton	3-17	0-3	0-0	2-9	1-5	0-0	17.6	+5.50
Lingfield	1-2	0-0	0-0	1-2	0-0	0-0	50.0	+15.00

WINNING HORSES

Horse	Races Run	1st	2nd	3rd	£
The Sneezer	5	1	1	1	3899
Hold The Bucks	6	2	0	0	5523
According To Them	8	1	0	0	2729
Total winning prize-money					**£12151**
Favourites	**0-1**		**0.0%**		**-1.00**

JACKIE STEPHEN

INVERURIE, ABERDEENS

	No. of Hrs	Races Run	1st	2nd	3rd	Unpl	Per cent	£1 Level Stake
NH Flat	*1*	*2*	*0*	*0*	*0*	*2*	*0.0*	*-2.00*
Hurdles	*3*	*15*	*3*	*3*	*3*	*6*	*20.0*	*+12.50*
Chases	*2*	*3*	*0*	*0*	*1*	*2*	*0.0*	*-3.00*
Totals	**4**	**20**	**3**	**3**	**4**	**10**	**15.0**	**+7.50**
13-14	*3*	*12*	*0*	*2*	*0*	*10*	*0.0*	*-12.00*
12-13	*2*	*3*	*0*	*0*	*0*	*3*	*0.0*	*-3.00*

JOCKEYS

	W-R	Per cent	£1 Level Stake
Tony Kelly	3-15	20.0	+12.50

COURSE RECORD

	Total W-R	Non-Hndcps Hurdles	Non-Hndcps Chases	Hndcps Hurdles	Hndcps Chases	NH Flat	Per cent	£1 Level Stake
Perth	2-11	0-5	0-0	2-4	0-2	0-0	18.2	+10.00
Kelso	1-4	1-1	0-0	0-2	0-1	0-0	25.0	+2.50

WINNING HORSES

Horse	Races Run	1st	2nd	3rd	£
Mo Rouge	7	2	0	4	7697
Amilliontimes	8	1	3	0	3899
Total winning prize-money					**£11596**
Favourites	**0-1**		**0.0%**		**-1.00**

ROBERT STEPHENS

PENHOW, NEWPORT

	No. of Hrs	Races Run	1st	2nd	3rd	Unpl	Per cent	£1 Level Stake
NH Flat	*7*	*11*	*2*	*3*	*1*	*5*	*18.2*	*+19.00*
Hurdles	*12*	*37*	*7*	*6*	*2*	*22*	*18.9*	*+1.88*
Chases	*2*	*5*	*0*	*0*	*0*	*5*	*0.0*	*-5.00*
Totals	**19**	**53**	**9**	**9**	**3**	**32**	**17.0**	**+15.88**
13-14	*11*	*27*	*3*	*3*	*4*	*17*	*11.1*	*+4.00*

JOCKEYS

	W-R	Per cent	£1 Level Stake
Tom O'Brien	8-31	25.8	+32.38
Jack Sherwood	1-1	100.0	+4.50

COURSE RECORD

	Total W-R	Non-Hndcps Hurdles	Non-Hndcps Chases	Hndcps Hurdles	Hndcps Chases	NH Flat	Per cent	£1 Level Stake
Kempton	1-1	1-1	0-0	0-0	0-0	0-0	100.0	+3.00
Southwell (A.W)	1-1	0-0	0-0	0-0	0-0	1-1	100.0	+16.00
Exeter	1-2	1-1	0-0	0-0	0-1	0-0	50.0	+1.00
Ludlow	1-2	1-1	0-0	0-1	0-0	0-0	50.0	+15.00
Mrket Rsn	1-2	1-2	0-0	0-0	0-0	0-0	50.0	+3.50
Uttoxeter	1-3	0-1	0-0	0-1	0-0	1-1	33.3	+10.00
Fontwell	1-4	1-1	0-1	0-1	0-0	0-1	25.0	0.00
Southwell	1-4	0-2	0-0	1-1	0-0	0-1	25.0	-1.13
Stratford	1-4	1-2	0-0	0-1	0-0	0-1	25.0	-1.50

WINNING HORSES

Horse	Races Run	1st	2nd	3rd	£
*Beltor	3	2	0	0	20334
Mile House	6	3	0	0	6910
*Yes Daddy	2	1	0	0	3249
Quebec	3	2	0	0	3249
Bumble Bay	3	1	1	0	1560
Total winning prize-money					**£35302**
Favourites	**3-4**		**75.0%**		**4.38**

MRS S J STILGOE

HUTTON-LE-HOLE, NORTH YORKS

	No. of Hrs	Races Run	1st	2nd	3rd	Unpl	Per cent	£1 Level Stake
NH Flat	*0*	*0*	*0*	*0*	*0*	*0*	*0.0*	*0.00*
Hurdles	*0*	*0*	*0*	*0*	*0*	*0*	*0.0*	*0.00*
Chases	*2*	*9*	*1*	*2*	*2*	*4*	*11.1*	*+3.00*
Totals	**2**	**9**	**1**	**2**	**2**	**4**	**11.1**	**+3.00**
13-14	*1*	*4*	*1*	*1*	*1*	*1*	*25.0*	*+4.00*
12-13	*1*	*1*	*0*	*0*	*0*	*1*	*0.0*	*-1.00*

JOCKEYS

	W-R	Per cent	£1 Level Stake
Mr N Orpwood	1-7	14.3	+5.00

COURSE RECORD

	Total W-R	Non-Hndcps Hurdles	Non-Hndcps Chases	Hndcps Hurdles	Hndcps Chases	NH Flat	Per cent	£1 Level Stake
Kelso	1-2	0-0	1-2	0-0	0-0	0-0	50.0	+10.00

WINNING HORSES

Horse	Races Run	1st	2nd	3rd	£
Nowurhurlin	6	1	2	1	1872
Total winning prize-money					**£1872**
Favourites	**0-0**		**0.0%**		**0.00**

ALI STRONGE

EASTBURY, BERKS

	No. of Hrs	Races Run	1st	2nd	3rd	Unpl	Per cent	£1 Level Stake
NH Flat	*1*	*1*	*0*	*0*	*0*	*1*	*0.0*	*-1.00*
Hurdles	*16*	*45*	*5*	*6*	*5*	*29*	*11.1*	*-9.25*
Chases	*6*	*18*	*2*	*0*	*3*	*13*	*11.1*	*-11.00*
Totals	**18**	**64**	**7**	**6**	**8**	**43**	**10.9**	**-21.25**
13-14	*21*	*70*	*9*	*9*	*6*	*46*	*12.9*	*-1.63*
12-13	*4*	*12*	*0*	*0*	*3*	*9*	*0.0*	*-12.00*

JOCKEYS

	W-R	Per cent	£1 Level Stake
Adam Wedge	2-8	25.0	+8.00
Jack Doyle	2-33	6.1	-17.00
Gavin Sheehan	1-1	100.0	+2.75
Conor Shoemark	1-4	25.0	-1.00
Aidan Coleman	1-6	16.7	-2.00

COURSE RECORD

	Total W-R	Non-Hndcps Hurdles	Non-Hndcps Chases	Hndcps Hurdles	Hndcps Chases	NH Flat	Per cent	£1 Level Stake
Fakenham	2-5	1-2	0-0	0-2	1-1	0-0	40.0	+4.00
Worcester	1-1	0-0	0-0	0-0	1-1	0-0	100.0	+3.00
Nton Abbot	1-3	0-0	0-0	1-2	0-1	0-0	33.3	+0.75
Wincanton	1-4	0-0	0-0	1-3	0-1	0-0	25.0	+9.00
Newbury	1-5	0-1	0-0	1-2	0-2	0-0	20.0	+5.00
Plumpton	1-8	0-1	0-0	1-4	0-3	0-0	12.5	-5.00

WINNING HORSES

Horse	Races Run	1st	2nd	3rd	£
Royal Guardsman	3	1	0	0	12512
Skint	5	1	0	0	6330
Cappielow Park	7	3	2	1	11185
Baku Bay	5	1	2	1	3899
Moneymix	4	1	0	0	3249
Total winning prize-money					**£37175**
Favourites	**2-6**		**33.3%**		**0.00**

ROB SUMMERS

TANWORTH-IN-ARDEN, WARWICKS

	No. of Hrs	Races Run	1st	2nd	3rd	Unpl	Per cent	£1 Level Stake
NH Flat	*1*	*1*	*0*	*0*	*0*	*1*	*0.0*	*-1.00*
Hurdles	*5*	*16*	*1*	*0*	*0*	*15*	*6.3*	*-9.00*
Chases	*5*	*23*	*4*	*1*	*2*	*16*	*17.4*	*+24.50*
Totals	**9**	**40**	**5**	**1**	**2**	**32**	**12.5**	**+14.50**
13-14	*13*	*52*	*0*	*2*	*3*	*47*	*0.0*	*-52.00*
12-13	*10*	*35*	*3*	*3*	*3*	*26*	*8.6*	*-1.00*

JOCKEYS

	W-R	Per cent	£1 Level Stake
Trevor Whelan	2-13	15.4	+4.50
Jake Hodson	2-18	11.1	+12.00
Brendan Powell	1-2	50.0	+5.00

COURSE RECORD

	Total W-R	Non-Hndcps Hurdles	Non-Hndcps Chases	Hndcps Hurdles	Hndcps Chases	NH Flat	Per cent	£1 Level Stake
Stratford	2-7	0-1	0-0	1-4	1-2	0-0	28.6	+9.00
Towcester	2-8	0-1	0-0	0-1	2-6	0-0	25.0	+22.00
Southwell	1-4	0-0	0-0	0-0	1-4	0-0	25.0	+4.50

WINNING HORSES

Horse	Races Run	1st	2nd	3rd	£
Red Whisper	9	2	0	0	5393
Mr Robinson	5	1	0	1	2599
Massachusetts	5	1	0	0	2274
Red Rosso	7	1	1	1	2274
Total winning prize-money					**£12540**
Favourites	**0-0**		**0.0%**		**0.00**

ALAN SWINBANK

MELSONBY, N YORKS

	No. of Hrs	Races Run	1st	2nd	3rd	Unpl	Per cent	£1 Level Stake
NH Flat	*11*	*22*	*4*	*3*	*5*	*10*	*18.2*	*-8.62*
Hurdles	*8*	*32*	*6*	*5*	*6*	*15*	*18.8*	*-1.35*
Chases	*2*	*10*	*3*	*3*	*2*	*2*	*30.0*	*-1.05*
Totals	**20**	**64**	**13**	**11**	**13**	**27**	**20.3**	**-11.02**
13-14	*20*	*58*	*10*	*11*	*4*	*33*	*17.2*	*-6.00*
12-13	*21*	*68*	*10*	*13*	*7*	*38*	*14.7*	*-7.55*

BY MONTH

NH Flat	W-R	Per cent	£1 Level Stake	**Hurdles**	W-R	Per cent	£1 Level Stake
May	0-1	0.0	-1.00	May	0-1	0.0	-1.00

June	0-2	0.0	-2.00	June	0-0	0.0	0.00
July	0-0	0.0	0.00	July	0-0	0.0	0.00
August	0-1	0.0	-1.00	August	0-0	0.0	0.00
September	1-1	100.0	+3.33	September	0-1	0.0	-1.00
October	0-1	0.0	-1.00	October	1-2	50.0	+1.25
November	0-0	0.0	0.00	November	2-11	18.2	-6.10
December	0-2	0.0	-2.00	December	2-3	66.7	+11.50
January	1-3	33.3	-1.20	January	0-5	0.0	-5.00
February	0-2	0.0	-2.00	February	0-3	0.0	-3.00
March	1-6	16.7	-3.25	March	1-3	33.3	+5.00
April	1-3	33.3	+1.50	April	0-3	0.0	-3.00

Chases	W-R	Per cent	£1 Level Stake	Totals	W-R	Per cent	£1 Level Stake
May	0-1	0.0	-1.00	May	0-3	0.0	-3.00
June	0-1	0.0	-1.00	June	0-3	0.0	-3.00
July	0-0	0.0	0.00	July	0-0	0.0	0.00
August	0-0	0.0	0.00	August	0-1	0.0	-1.00
September	0-0	0.0	0.00	September	1-2	50.0	+2.33
October	0-0	0.0	0.00	October	1-3	33.3	+0.25
November	1-3	33.3	+2.00	November	3-14	21.4	-4.10
December	1-1	100.0	+1.38	December	3-6	50.0	+10.88
January	1-2	50.0	-0.43	January	2-10	20.0	-6.63
February	0-1	0.0	-1.00	February	0-6	0.0	-6.00
March	0-1	0.0	-1.00	March	2-10	20.0	+0.75
April	0-0	0.0	0.00	April	1-6	16.7	-1.50

DISTANCE

Hurdles	W-R	Per cent	£1 Level Stake	Chases	W-R	Per cent	£1 Level Stake
2m-2m3f	4-21	19.0	-3.60	2m-2m3f	1-3	33.3	-1.43
2m4f-2m7f	1-5	20.0	-1.75	2m4f-2m7f	2-4	50.0	+3.38
3m+	1-3	33.3	+7.00	3m+	0-1	0.0	-1.00

TYPE OF RACE

Non-Handicaps	W-R	Per cent	£1 Level Stake	Handicaps	W-R	Per cent	£1 Level Stake
Nov Hrdls	2-13	15.4	-2.60	Nov Hrdls	0-2	0.0	-2.00
Hrdls	1-5	20.0	-2.50	Hrdls	3-10	30.0	+7.75
Nov Chs	0-1	0.0	-1.00	Nov Chs	2-3	66.7	+4.38
Chases	0-0	0.0	0.00	Chases	1-6	16.7	-4.43
Sell/Claim	0-1	0.0	-1.00	Sell/Claim	0-0	0.0	0.00

RACE CLASS

	W-R	Per cent	£1 Level Stake
Class 1	0-1	0.0	-1.00
Class 2	1-3	33.3	+7.00
Class 3	4-13	30.8	-0.80
Class 4	3-24	12.5	-9.10
Class 5	2-5	40.0	+2.00
Class 6	3-18	16.7	-9.12

FIRST TIME OUT

	W-R	Per cent	£1 Level Stake
Bumpers	0-11	0.0	-11.00
Hurdles	0-7	0.0	-7.00
Chases	0-2	0.0	-2.00
Totals	0-20	0.0	-20.00

JOCKEYS

	W-R	Per cent	£1 Level Stake
Paul Moloney	10-43	23.3	+3.26
Richard Johnson	1-2	50.0	+0.40
A P McCoy	1-3	33.3	-1.43
Tom O'Brien	1-3	33.3	-0.25

COURSE RECORD

	Total W-R	Non-Hndcps Hurdles	Non-Hndcps Chases	Hndcps Hurdles	Hndcps Chases	NH Flat	Per cent	£1 Level Stake
Carlisle	6-17	2-8	0-0	1-3	2-4	1-2	35.3	+15.27
Hexham	4-6	1-1	0-1	2-2	0-0	1-2	66.7	+7.00
Mrket Rsn	1-2	0-0	0-0	0-0	1-1	0-1	50.0	-0.43
Musselbgh	1-3	0-1	0-0	0-0	0-1	1-1	33.3	-1.20
Kelso	1-3	0-1	0-0	0-1	0-0	1-1	33.3	+1.33

WINNING HORSES

Horse	Races Run	1st	2nd	3rd	£
Phoenix Returns	7	2	2	1	17870
Big Water	9	3	3	1	19653
Deep Resolve	4	2	0	1	6294
Bobs Lord Tara	5	1	1	1	3899
Divine Port	7	2	1	2	4960
Down The Line	3	1	1	1	2599
One More Go	4	1	1	2	1949
Ten Trees	3	1	0	1	1711
Total winning prize-money					**£58935**

Favourites **7-12** **58.3%** **4.65**

TOM SYMONDS

HAREWOOD END, H'FORDS

	No. of Hrs	Races Run	1st	2nd	3rd	Unpl	Per cent	£1 Level Stake
NH Flat	*9*	*13*	*0*	*1*	*1*	*11*	*0.0*	*-13.00*
Hurdles	*25*	*78*	*5*	*10*	*8*	*55*	*6.4*	*-53.42*
Chases	*14*	*68*	*8*	*14*	*13*	*33*	*11.8*	*-28.75*
Totals	**38**	**159**	**13**	**25**	**22**	**99**	**8.2**	**-95.17**
13-14	*39*	*179*	*22*	*17*	*18*	*122*	*12.3*	*-21.17*
12-13	*37*	*132*	*10*	*14*	*17*	*91*	*7.6*	*+0.28*

BY MONTH

NH Flat	W-R	Per cent	£1 Level Stake	Hurdles	W-R	Per cent	£1 Level Stake
May	0-2	0.0	-2.00	May	0-5	0.0	-5.00
June	0-0	0.0	0.00	June	0-2	0.0	-2.00
July	0-0	0.0	0.00	July	0-1	0.0	-1.00
August	0-0	0.0	0.00	August	0-2	0.0	-2.00
September	0-0	0.0	0.00	September	0-3	0.0	-3.00
October	0-0	0.0	0.00	October	1-13	7.7	-10.50
November	0-3	0.0	-3.00	November	2-10	20.0	+4.00
December	0-2	0.0	-2.00	December	1-13	7.7	-9.25
January	0-2	0.0	-2.00	January	1-10	10.0	-5.67
February	0-1	0.0	-1.00	February	0-5	0.0	-5.00
March	0-1	0.0	-1.00	March	0-8	0.0	-8.00
April	0-2	0.0	-2.00	April	0-6	0.0	-6.00

Chases	W-R	Per cent	£1 Level Stake
May	0-2	0.0	-2.00
June	0-5	0.0	-5.00
July	0-4	0.0	-4.00
August	0-2	0.0	-2.00
September	0-0	0.0	0.00
October	0-3	0.0	-3.00
November	1-12	8.3	-6.00
December	0-11	0.0	-11.00
January	4-10	40.0	+7.75
February	2-7	28.6	+4.50
March	1-9	11.1	-5.00
April	0-3	0.0	-3.00

Totals	W-R	Per cent	£1 Level Stake
May	0-9	0.0	-9.00
June	0-7	0.0	-7.00
July	0-5	0.0	-5.00
August	0-4	0.0	-4.00
September	0-3	0.0	-3.00
October	1-16	6.3	-13.50
November	3-25	12.0	-5.00
December	1-26	3.8	-22.25
January	5-22	22.7	+0.08
February	2-13	15.4	-1.50
March	1-18	5.6	-14.00
April	0-11	0.0	-11.00

DISTANCE

Hurdles	W-R	Per cent	£1 Level Stake
2m-2m3f	1-33	3.0	-30.50
2m4f-2m7f	1-20	5.0	-14.00
3m+	0-3	0.0	-3.00

Chases	W-R	Per cent	£1 Level Stake
2m-2m3f	1-16	6.3	-11.50
2m4f-2m7f	2-23	8.7	-13.25
3m+	2-14	14.3	-2.50

TYPE OF RACE

Non-Handicaps	W-R	Per cent	£1 Level Stake
Nov Hrdls	0-13	0.0	-13.00
Hrdls	0-17	0.0	-17.00
Nov Chs	1-4	25.0	-1.25
Chases	0-0	0.0	0.00
Sell/Claim	0-0	0.0	0.00

Handicaps	W-R	Per cent	£1 Level Stake
Nov Hrdls	1-8	12.5	-4.25
Hrdls	4-40	10.0	-19.17
Nov Chs	1-21	4.8	-15.00
Chases	6-43	14.0	-12.50
Sell/Claim	0-0	0.0	0.00

RACE CLASS

	W-R	Per cent	£1 Level Stake
Class 1	0-5	0.0	-5.00
Class 2	2-4	50.0	+11.00
Class 3	1-22	4.5	-19.25
Class 4	4-77	5.2	-55.50
Class 5	6-42	14.3	-17.42
Class 6	0-9	0.0	-9.00

FIRST TIME OUT

	W-R	Per cent	£1 Level Stake
Bumpers	0-9	0.0	-9.00
Hurdles	0-19	0.0	-19.00
Chases	0-10	0.0	-10.00
Totals	0-38	0.0	-38.00

JOCKEYS

	W-R	Per cent	£1 Level Stake
Felix De Giles	7-76	9.2	-40.92
Ben Poste	4-43	9.3	-25.75
Mr J Nixon	2-14	14.3	-2.50

COURSE RECORD

	Total W-R	Non-Hndcps Hurdles	Non-Hndcps Chases	Hndcps Hurdles	Hndcps Chases	NH Flat	Per cent	£1 Level Stake
Uttoxeter	3-15	0-1	0-0	3-8	0-6	0-0	20.0	-4.42
Towcester	2-12	0-3	0-0	0-2	2-4	0-3	16.7	-1.50
Huntingdon	2-14	0-1	0-0	1-4	1-7	0-2	14.3	-4.00
Wetherby	1-3	0-0	0-1	0-1	1-1	0-0	33.3	+4.00
Taunton	1-5	0-0	0-0	0-3	1-2	0-0	20.0	+1.00
Ffos Las	1-6	0-2	0-0	0-2	1-1	0-1	16.7	-2.50
Wincanton	1-7	0-2	0-0	0-2	1-3	0-0	14.3	-1.50
Bangor	1-8	0-0	0-0	1-2	0-5	0-1	12.5	0.00
Ludlow	1-13	0-4	1-1	0-3	0-4	0-1	7.7	-10.25

WINNING HORSES

Horse	Races Run	1st	2nd	3rd	£
Foxcub	5	1	1	0	13646
Midnight Belle	9	2	2	2	19371
Kings Apollo	10	2	4	1	8123
Bertenbar	4	1	0	1	3899
Carhue Princess	10	2	0	4	5848
Alberto's Dream	6	1	1	1	3249
Dixie Bull	7	1	1	3	2885
Eaton Rock	8	1	1	1	2599
Arden Denis	6	1	0	0	2339
Straits Of Messina	2	1	1	0	2209

Total winning prize-money **£64168**

Favourites **5-20** **25.0%** **-1.25**

VICTOR THOMPSON

ALNWICK, NORTHUMBRIA

	No. of Hrs	Races Run	1st	2nd	3rd	Unpl	Per cent	£1 Level Stake
NH Flat	*0*	*0*	*0*	*0*	*0*	*0*	*0.0*	*0.00*
Hurdles	*2*	*8*	*0*	*0*	*3*	*5*	*0.0*	*-8.00*
Chases	*12*	*46*	*1*	*3*	*6*	*36*	*2.2*	*-38.50*
Totals	**14**	**54**	**1**	**3**	**9**	**41**	**1.9**	**-46.50**
13-14	*14*	*25*	*0*	*1*	*2*	*22*	*0.0*	*-25.00*
12-13	*6*	*13*	*3*	*0*	*2*	*8*	*23.1*	*+17.10*

JOCKEYS

	W-R	Per cent	£1 Level Stake
Miss E Todd	1-8	12.5	-0.50

COURSE RECORD

	Total W-R	Non-Hndcps Hurdles	Non-Hndcps Chases	Hndcps Hurdles	Hndcps Chases	NH Flat	Per cent	£1 Level Stake
Southwell	1-5	0-0	0-2	0-1	1-2	0-0	20.0	+2.50

WINNING HORSES

Horse	Races Run	1st	2nd	3rd	£
*Gin Cobbler	11	1	2	1	3899

Total winning prize-money **£3899**

Favourites **0-0** **0.0%** **0.00**

SANDY THOMSON

LAMBDEN, BERWICKS

	No. of Hrs	Races Run	1st	2nd	3rd	Unpl	Per cent	£1 Level Stake
NH Flat	*4*	*5*	*0*	*0*	*2*	*3*	*0.0*	*-5.00*
Hurdles	*15*	*32*	*7*	*2*	*6*	*17*	*21.9*	*+38.40*
Chases	*7*	*35*	*4*	*6*	*5*	*20*	*11.4*	*-15.50*
Totals	**20**	**72**	**11**	**8**	**13**	**40**	**15.3**	**+17.90**
13-14	*15*	*50*	*6*	*5*	*7*	*32*	*12.0*	*+77.75*
12-13	*10*	*31*	*2*	*3*	*0*	*26*	*6.5*	*-11.00*

BY MONTH

NH Flat	W-R	Per cent	£1 Level Stake
May	0-0	0.0	0.00
June	0-0	0.0	0.00
July	0-0	0.0	0.00
August	0-0	0.0	0.00
September	0-0	0.0	0.00
October	0-0	0.0	0.00
November	0-2	0.0	-2.00
December	0-0	0.0	0.00
January	0-0	0.0	0.00
February	0-1	0.0	-1.00
March	0-2	0.0	-2.00
April	0-0	0.0	0.00

Hurdles	W-R	Per cent	£1 Level Stake
May	0-0	0.0	0.00
June	0-0	0.0	0.00
July	0-0	0.0	0.00
August	0-0	0.0	0.00
September	0-0	0.0	0.00
October	1-5	20.0	+1.00
November	2-6	33.3	+25.50
December	1-3	33.3	+6.00
January	1-6	16.7	-2.50
February	0-5	0.0	-5.00
March	1-4	25.0	-0.60
April	1-3	33.3	+14.00

Chases	W-R	Per cent	£1 Level Stake
May	2-6	33.3	+4.00
June	0-1	0.0	-1.00
July	0-0	0.0	0.00
August	0-0	0.0	0.00
September	0-0	0.0	0.00
October	1-3	33.3	+0.50
November	0-3	0.0	-3.00
December	1-5	20.0	+1.00
January	0-5	0.0	-5.00
February	0-4	0.0	-4.00
March	0-4	0.0	-4.00
April	0-4	0.0	-4.00

Totals	W-R	Per cent	£1 Level Stake
May	2-6	33.3	+4.00
June	0-1	0.0	-1.00
July	0-0	0.0	0.00
August	0-0	0.0	0.00
September	0-0	0.0	0.00
October	2-8	25.0	+1.50
November	2-11	18.2	+20.50
December	2-8	25.0	+7.00
January	1-11	9.1	-7.50
February	0-10	0.0	-10.00
March	1-10	10.0	-6.60
April	1-7	14.3	+10.00

DISTANCE

Hurdles	W-R	Per cent	£1 Level Stake
2m-2m3f	3-11	27.3	+26.50
2m4f-2m7f	1-6	16.7	-2.60
3m+	3-14	21.4	+15.50

Chases	W-R	Per cent	£1 Level Stake
2m-2m3f	0-1	0.0	-1.00
2m4f-2m7f	2-11	18.2	-1.00
3m+	2-18	11.1	-8.50

TYPE OF RACE

Non-Handicaps

	W-R	Per cent	£1 Level Stake
Nov Hrdls	1-10	10.0	-4.50
Hrdls	3-9	33.3	+26.40
Nov Chs	0-0	0.0	0.00
Chases	0-0	0.0	0.00
Sell/Claim	0-0	0.0	0.00

Handicaps

	W-R	Per cent	£1 Level Stake
Nov Hrdls	1-1	100.0	+8.00
Hrdls	2-11	18.2	+9.50
Nov Chs	1-5	20.0	+1.50
Chases	3-30	10.0	-17.00
Sell/Claim	0-0	0.0	0.00

RACE CLASS

	W-R	Per cent	£1 Level Stake
Class 1	0-6	0.0	-6.00
Class 2	0-7	0.0	-7.00
Class 3	3-11	27.3	+15.50
Class 4	2-24	8.3	-12.50
Class 5	6-19	31.6	+32.90
Class 6	0-5	0.0	-5.00

FIRST TIME OUT

	W-R	Per cent	£1 Level Stake
Bumpers	0-4	0.0	-4.00
Hurdles	2-11	18.2	+12.00
Chases	1-5	20.0	+1.50
Totals	3-20	15.0	+9.50

JOCKEYS

	W-R	Per cent	£1 Level Stake
Ryan Mania	3-8	37.5	+4.50
Steven Fox	3-21	14.3	+8.40
Brian Hughes	2-8	25.0	+4.50
Danny Cook	1-4	25.0	+22.00
James Reveley	1-6	16.7	-2.50
Derek Fox	1-13	7.7	-7.00

COURSE RECORD

	Total W-R	Non-Hndcps Hurdles	Non-Hndcps Chases	Hndcps Hurdles	Hndcps Chases	NH Flat	Per cent	£1 Level Stake
Kelso	3-21	1-5	0-0	1-4	1-11	0-1	14.3	0.00
Ayr	2-9	1-2	0-0	0-1	1-5	0-1	22.2	-2.10
Musselbgh	2-13	1-3	0-0	1-4	0-5	0-1	15.4	+16.50
Perth	1-2	0-1	0-0	0-0	1-1	0-0	50.0	+1.50
Carlisle	1-5	0-1	0-0	1-1	0-3	0-0	20.0	+12.00
Hexham	1-7	0-1	0-0	0-0	1-5	0-1	14.3	-0.50
Newcastle	1-8	1-4	0-0	0-0	0-3	0-1	12.5	-2.50

WINNING HORSES

Horse	Races Run	1st	2nd	3rd	£
Neptune Equester	6	1	2	1	18838
Any Given Moment	1	1	0	0	6498
Fly Vinnie	5	2	0	1	9097
The Shrimp	7	2	0	1	6693
Seldom Inn	4	2	0	1	6498
Prairie Lad	2	1	0	0	3249
Blue Kascade	7	1	0	2	2599
Mossies Well	5	1	0	2	2599

Total winning prize-money **£56071**

Favourites **2-6** **33.3%** **1.00**

COLIN TIZZARD

MILBORNE PORT, DORSET

	No. of Hrs	Races Run	1st	2nd	3rd	Unpl	Per cent	£1 Level Stake
NH Flat	*18*	*26*	*1*	*3*	*3*	*19*	*3.8*	*-22.00*
Hurdles	*37*	*143*	*23*	*16*	*21*	*83*	*16.1*	*-6.54*

Chases	*30*	*125*	*14*	*15*	*17*	*79*	*11.2*	*-49.67*
Totals	**61**	**294**	**38**	**34**	**41**	**181**	**12.9**	**-78.21**
13-14	*68*	*312*	*26*	*30*	*44*	*212*	*8.3*	*-151.81*
12-13	*64*	*308*	*43*	*29*	*44*	*192*	*14.0*	*-3.94*

BY MONTH

NH Flat	W-R	Per cent	£1 Level Stake
May	0-5	0.0	-5.00
June	0-0	0.0	0.00
July	0-0	0.0	0.00
August	0-0	0.0	0.00
September	0-0	0.0	0.00
October	0-2	0.0	-2.00
November	0-3	0.0	-3.00
December	0-6	0.0	-6.00
January	1-7	14.3	-3.00
February	0-1	0.0	-1.00
March	0-1	0.0	-1.00
April	0-1	0.0	-1.00

Hurdles	W-R	Per cent	£1 Level Stake
May	0-5	0.0	-5.00
June	0-3	0.0	-3.00
July	0-1	0.0	-1.00
August	0-0	0.0	0.00
September	0-0	0.0	0.00
October	1-18	5.6	-9.00
November	4-14	28.6	+9.25
December	2-21	9.5	-3.50
January	5-21	23.8	-6.75
February	4-24	16.7	-0.17
March	1-20	5.0	-16.50
April	6-16	37.5	+29.13

Chases	W-R	Per cent	£1 Level Stake
May	0-6	0.0	-6.00
June	0-2	0.0	-2.00
July	0-4	0.0	-4.00
August	0-0	0.0	0.00
September	0-0	0.0	0.00
October	0-13	0.0	-13.00
November	4-22	18.2	+4.33
December	4-19	21.1	+1.75
January	2-21	9.5	-12.50
February	3-12	25.0	+4.50
March	1-17	5.9	-13.75
April	0-9	0.0	-9.00

Totals	W-R	Per cent	£1 Level Stake
May	0-16	0.0	-16.00
June	0-5	0.0	-5.00
July	0-5	0.0	-5.00
August	0-0	0.0	0.00
September	0-0	0.0	0.00
October	1-33	3.0	-24.00
November	8-39	20.5	+10.58
December	6-46	13.0	-7.75
January	8-49	16.3	-22.25
February	7-37	18.9	+3.33
March	2-38	5.3	-31.25
April	6-26	23.1	+19.13

DISTANCE

Hurdles	W-R	Per cent	£1 Level Stake
2m-2m3f	7-65	10.8	-25.88
2m4f-2m7f	10-45	22.2	+5.25
3m+	2-3	66.7	+25.00

Chases	W-R	Per cent	£1 Level Stake
2m-2m3f	5-31	16.1	-3.17
2m4f-2m7f	6-36	16.7	+0.75
3m+	3-44	6.8	-33.25

TYPE OF RACE

Non-Handicaps	W-R	Per cent	£1 Level Stake
Nov Hrdls	13-68	19.1	+13.83
Hrdls	5-23	21.7	+4.13
Nov Chs	0-12	0.0	-12.00
Chases	4-17	23.5	+2.33
Sell/Claim	0-0	0.0	0.00

Handicaps	W-R	Per cent	£1 Level Stake
Nov Hrdls	1-12	8.3	-1.00
Hrdls	4-39	10.3	-22.50
Nov Chs	4-23	17.4	-5.75
Chases	6-73	8.2	-34.25
Sell/Claim	0-1	0.0	-1.00

RACE CLASS

	W-R	Per cent	£1 Level Stake
Class 1	3-41	7.3	+3.50
Class 2	7-38	18.4	+5.17
Class 3	7-53	13.2	-16.75
Class 4	15-112	13.4	-54.13
Class 5	6-31	19.4	+4.00
Class 6	0-19	0.0	-19.00

FIRST TIME OUT

	W-R	Per cent	£1 Level Stake
Bumpers	1-18	5.6	-14.00
Hurdles	1-20	5.0	-11.50
Chases	3-23	13.0	-8.17
Totals	5-61	8.2	-33.67

JOCKEYS

	W-R	Per cent	£1 Level Stake
Brendan Powell	13-134	9.7	-48.25
Daryl Jacob	9-56	16.1	-5.29
Paul O'Brien	5-38	13.2	-16.63
Aidan Coleman	3-13	23.1	-2.25
Noel Fehily	2-7	28.6	-2.00
Mr M Legg	2-11	18.2	-4.75
Mr Sam Painting	2-11	18.2	-5.38
R Walsh	1-1	100.0	+3.33
Tom Scudamore	1-3	33.3	+23.00

COURSE RECORD

	Total W-R	Non-Hndcps Hurdles	Non-Hndcps Chases	Hndcps Hurdles	Hndcps Chases	NH Flat	Per cent	£1 Level Stake
Exeter	6-38	3-13	1-4	0-9	2-10	0-2	15.8	-3.00
Fontwell	5-20	2-7	0-0	1-6	2-5	0-2	25.0	-0.25
Kempton	4-13	2-5	2-4	0-1	0-3	0-0	30.8	+3.75
Taunton	4-17	1-7	0-0	2-7	1-3	0-0	23.5	+2.25
Wincanton	4-32	1-10	0-0	1-4	2-10	0-8	12.5	-17.75
Newcastle	3-3	2-2	0-0	0-0	1-1	0-0	100.0	+28.00
Ascot	2-12	1-3	0-2	0-1	1-3	0-3	16.7	-4.17
Plumpton	2-14	2-10	0-0	0-0	0-3	0-1	14.3	-2.38
Stratford	1-4	1-2	0-0	0-0	0-2	0-0	25.0	+5.00
Aintree	1-5	1-1	0-1	0-0	0-3	0-0	20.0	+21.00
Ludlow	1-5	0-1	0-0	1-2	0-1	0-1	20.0	-1.50
Haydock	1-6	0-0	1-4	0-0	0-2	0-0	16.7	-1.67
Newbury	1-14	0-3	0-1	0-2	0-7	1-1	7.1	-10.00
Warwick	1-14	1-4	0-2	0-2	0-4	0-2	7.1	-11.00
Chepstow	1-23	1-9	0-0	0-3	0-9	0-2	4.3	-20.00
Cheltenham	1-30	0-5	0-4	0-3	1-17	0-1	3.3	-22.50

WINNING HORSES

Horse	Races Run	1st	2nd	3rd	£
Thistlecrack	6	3	0	0	69720
Hey Big Spender	6	1	0	1	28609
Sew On Target	5	1	1	0	18838
Third Intention	7	2	0	2	29241
Ultragold	4	1	0	0	15640
Masters Hill	5	1	2	0	12512
Native River	7	3	0	1	25250
Kings Lad	7	2	0	1	17976
Theatrical Star	5	1	2	0	7596
Flaming Charmer	5	1	0	0	6498
Dusky Lark	7	2	1	0	9357
Kingscourt Native	5	1	1	2	5848
Murrayana	6	3	1	1	12346
Quite By Chance	9	2	2	1	9680
Wizards Bridge	9	2	1	1	7668
Morello Royale	7	2	2	1	8123

Buckhorn Tom	6	1	1	2	3899
Robinsfirth	3	1	1	0	3574
Kingfisher Creek	8	2	1	1	6693
Buckhorn Timothy	10	2	2	3	5848
Xaarcet	9	1	1	3	2339
Third Act	8	1	0	2	2274
West Approach	2	1	0	0	2053
Theatre Guide	5	1	0	0	0
Total winning prize-money					**£311582**
Favourites	**9-31**		**29.0%**		**-6.88**

MARTIN TODHUNTER

ORTON, CUMBRIA

	No. of Hrs	Races Run	1st	2nd	3rd	Unpl	Per cent	£1 Level Stake
NH Flat	*3*	*4*	*0*	*0*	*0*	*4*	*0.0*	*-4.00*
Hurdles	*14*	*70*	*7*	*4*	*5*	*54*	*10.0*	*-25.71*
Chases	*13*	*46*	*10*	*3*	*7*	*26*	*21.7*	*+17.60*
Totals	**26**	**120**	**17**	**7**	**12**	**84**	**14.2**	**-12.11**
13-14	*35*	*133*	*8*	*8*	*20*	*97*	*6.0*	*-44.60*
12-13	*28*	*82*	*3*	*6*	*5*	*68*	*3.7*	*-57.00*

BY MONTH

NH Flat	W-R	Per cent	£1 Level Stake	Hurdles	W-R	Per cent	£1 Level Stake
May	0-2	0.0	-2.00	May	3-11	27.3	+3.54
June	0-0	0.0	0.00	June	1-5	20.0	+0.50
July	0-0	0.0	0.00	July	0-3	0.0	-3.00
August	0-0	0.0	0.00	August	0-3	0.0	-3.00
September	0-0	0.0	0.00	September	0-4	0.0	-4.00
October	0-1	0.0	-1.00	October	2-7	28.6	+14.00
November	0-0	0.0	0.00	November	1-10	10.0	-6.75
December	0-0	0.0	0.00	December	0-9	0.0	-9.00
January	0-0	0.0	0.00	January	0-7	0.0	-7.00
February	0-0	0.0	0.00	February	0-4	0.0	-4.00
March	0-1	0.0	-1.00	March	0-4	0.0	-4.00
April	0-0	0.0	0.00	April	0-3	0.0	-3.00

Chases	W-R	Per cent	£1 Level Stake	Totals	W-R	Per cent	£1 Level Stake
May	2-7	28.6	+3.50	May	5-20	25.0	+5.04
June	1-5	20.0	+2.00	June	2-10	20.0	+2.50
July	0-1	0.0	-1.00	July	0-4	0.0	-4.00
August	0-3	0.0	-3.00	August	0-6	0.0	-6.00
September	1-1	100.0	+6.00	September	1-5	20.0	+2.00
October	1-7	14.3	-1.00	October	3-15	20.0	+12.00
November	3-5	60.0	+7.10	November	4-15	26.7	+0.35
December	0-6	0.0	-6.00	December	0-15	0.0	-15.00
January	0-2	0.0	-2.00	January	0-9	0.0	-9.00
February	0-1	0.0	-1.00	February	0-5	0.0	-5.00
March	1-2	50.0	+11.00	March	1-7	14.3	+6.00
April	1-6	16.7	+2.00	April	1-9	11.1	-1.00

DISTANCE

Hurdles	W-R	Per cent	£1 Level Stake	Chases	W-R	Per cent	£1 Level Stake
2m-2m3f	6-47	12.8	-8.21	2m-2m3f	1-10	10.0	-3.00
2m4f-2m7f	0-13	0.0	-13.00	2m4f-2m7f	4-18	22.2	+12.00
3m+	0-3	0.0	-3.00	3m+	4-12	33.3	+9.60

TYPE OF RACE

Non-Handicaps	W-R	Per cent	£1 Level Stake	Handicaps	W-R	Per cent	£1 Level Stake
Nov Hrdls	0-10	0.0	-10.00	Nov Hrdls	1-6	16.7	-3.13
Hrdls	0-11	0.0	-11.00	Hrdls	6-42	14.3	-0.58
Nov Chs	0-6	0.0	-6.00	Nov Chs	0-6	0.0	-6.00
Chases	0-0	0.0	0.00	Chases	10-34	29.4	+29.60
Sell/Claim	0-1	0.0	-1.00	Sell/Claim	0-1	0.0	-1.00

RACE CLASS / FIRST TIME OUT

Race Class	W-R	Per cent	£1 Level Stake	First Time Out	W-R	Per cent	£1 Level Stake
Class 1	1-1	100.0	+7.00	Bumpers	0-3	0.0	-3.00
Class 2	0-0	0.0	0.00	Hurdles	2-13	15.4	-0.13
Class 3	3-21	14.3	+4.50	Chases	1-10	10.0	-5.00
Class 4	8-65	12.3	-10.40				
Class 5	5-31	16.1	-11.21	Totals	3-26	11.5	-8.13
Class 6	0-2	0.0	-2.00				

JOCKEYS

	W-R	Per cent	£1 Level Stake
Wilson Renwick	9-41	22.0	+22.10
Graham Watters	5-40	12.5	-19.08
Harry Challoner	2-13	15.4	+8.00
Mr Kit Alexander	1-1	100.0	+1.88

COURSE RECORD

	Total W-R	Non-Hndcps Hurdles	Non-Hndcps Chases	Hndcps Hurdles	Hndcps Chases	NH Flat	Per cent	£1 Level Stake
Ayr	5-14	0-1	0-0	1-5	4-8	0-0	35.7	+18.85
Hexham	3-16	0-3	0-1	1-5	2-7	0-0	18.8	-0.13
Wetherby	2-8	0-1	0-0	1-4	1-3	0-0	25.0	-0.83
Carlisle	2-10	0-2	0-3	2-2	0-3	0-0	20.0	+12.00
Mrket Rsn	1-2	0-0	0-0	0-1	1-1	0-0	50.0	+3.00
Aintree	1-5	0-1	0-0	1-2	0-2	0-0	20.0	+0.50
Newcastle	1-6	0-1	0-1	0-3	1-1	0-0	16.7	-2.50
Perth	1-9	0-2	0-0	0-5	1-2	0-0	11.1	-2.00
Sedgefield	1-17	0-2	0-0	1-10	0-3	0-2	5.9	-8.00

WINNING HORSES

Horse	Races Run	1st	2nd	3rd	£
Presenting Junior	10	7	1	1	53600
Claragh Native	8	1	0	1	6498
Allanard	7	2	1	1	8226
*Playhara	13	3	3	0	8257
Acordingtoscript	5	2	0	0	6888
Indepub	5	1	0	0	3119
De Chissler	11	1	0	2	1949

Total winning prize-money			**£88537**
Favourites	**3-11**	**27.3%**	**-4.36**

EDWIN TUER

BIRKBY, N YORKS

	No. of Hrs	Races Run	1st	2nd	3rd	Unpl	Per cent	£1 Level Stake
NH Flat	*2*	*4*	*0*	*0*	*0*	*4*	*0.0*	*-4.00*
Hurdles	*5*	*11*	*1*	*1*	*0*	*9*	*9.1*	*+6.00*
Chases	*0*	*0*	*0*	*0*	*0*	*0*	*0.0*	*0.00*
Totals	**6**	**15**	**1**	**1**	**0**	**13**	**6.7**	**+2.00**
13-14	*6*	*23*	*1*	*2*	*3*	*17*	*4.3*	*-8.00*
12-13	*4*	*7*	*0*	*2*	*0*	*5*	*0.0*	*-7.00*

JOCKEYS

	W-R	Per cent	£1 Level Stake
Tony Kelly	1-5	20.0	+12.00

COURSE RECORD

	Total W-R	Non-Hndcps Hurdles	Non-Hndcps Chases	Hndcps Hurdles	Hndcps Chases	NH Flat	Per cent	£1 Level Stake
Wetherby	1-2	1-2	0-0	0-0	0-0	0-0	50.0	+15.00

WINNING HORSES

Horse	Races Run	1st	2nd	3rd	£
Bulas Belle	3	1	1	0	3574
Total winning prize-money					**£3574**
Favourites	**0-0**		**0.0%**		**0.00**

JOSEPH TUITE

GREAT SHEFFORD, BERKS

	No. of Hrs	Races Run	1st	2nd	3rd	Unpl	Per cent	£1 Level Stake
NH Flat	*2*	*2*	*1*	*0*	*0*	*1*	*50.0*	*+4.00*
Hurdles	*0*	*0*	*0*	*0*	*0*	*0*	*0.0*	*0.00*
Chases	*0*	*0*	*0*	*0*	*0*	*0*	*0.0*	*0.00*
Totals	**2**	**2**	**1**	**0**	**0**	**1**	**50.0**	**+4.00**

JOCKEYS

	W-R	Per cent	£1 Level Stake
Sam Twiston-Davies	1-1	100.0	+5.00

COURSE RECORD

	Total W-R	Non-Hndcps Hurdles	Non-Hndcps Chases	Hndcps Hurdles	Hndcps Chases	NH Flat	Per cent	£1 Level Stake
Lingfield (A.W)	1-1	0-0	0-0	0-0	0-0	1-1	100.0	+5.00

WINNING HORSES

Horse	Races Run	1st	2nd	3rd	£
Prince Of Poets	1	1	0	0	1560

Total winning prize-money			**£1560**
Favourites	**0-0**	**0.0%**	**0.00**

ANDY TURNELL

BROAD HINTON, WILTS

	No. of Hrs	Races Run	1st	2nd	3rd	Unpl	Per cent	£1 Level Stake
NH Flat	*0*	*0*	*0*	*0*	*0*	*0*	*0.0*	*0.00*
Hurdles	*12*	*29*	*4*	*2*	*0*	*23*	*13.8*	*+23.00*
Chases	*6*	*15*	*2*	*4*	*3*	*6*	*13.3*	*-7.50*
Totals	**16**	**44**	**6**	**6**	**3**	**29**	**13.6**	**+15.50**
13-14	*12*	*40*	*5*	*6*	*2*	*27*	*12.5*	*-7.25*
12-13	*17*	*64*	*5*	*7*	*7*	*45*	*7.8*	*-17.00*

JOCKEYS

	W-R	Per cent	£1 Level Stake
Miss B Hampson	3-6	50.0	+25.00
Mr Sam Painting	1-2	50.0	+19.00
Gerard Tumelty	1-9	11.1	-5.00
James Banks	1-12	8.3	-8.50

COURSE RECORD

	Total W-R	Non-Hndcps Hurdles	Non-Hndcps Chases	Hndcps Hurdles	Hndcps Chases	NH Flat	Per cent	£1 Level Stake
Ffos Las	2-8	1-2	0-0	0-2	1-4	0-0	25.0	+17.00
Chepstow	1-2	0-1	0-0	0-0	1-1	0-0	50.0	+1.50
Fakenham	1-2	1-2	0-0	0-0	0-0	0-0	50.0	+3.50
Huntingdon	1-2	1-1	0-0	0-0	0-1	0-0	50.0	+19.00
Wincanton	1-4	0-1	0-0	1-3	0-0	0-0	25.0	+0.50

WINNING HORSES

Horse	Races Run	1st	2nd	3rd	£
*Candide	8	2	3	0	7576
*Aristocracy	7	1	2	0	3899
*Barneys Honour	2	1	0	0	3422
Waddingtown Hero	6	1	0	1	3249
*Driftashore	1	1	0	0	3249
Total winning prize-money					**£21395**
Favourites	**0-1**		**0.0%**		**-1.00**

BILL TURNER

SIGWELLS, SOMERSET

	No. of Hrs	Races Run	1st	2nd	3rd	Unpl	Per cent	£1 Level Stake
NH Flat	*0*	*0*	*0*	*0*	*0*	*0*	*0.0*	*0.00*
Hurdles	*4*	*17*	*3*	*2*	*3*	*9*	*17.6*	*+5.50*
Chases	*2*	*8*	*0*	*2*	*0*	*6*	*0.0*	*-8.00*
Totals	**5**	**25**	**3**	**4**	**3**	**15**	**12.0**	**-2.50**
13-14	*10*	*30*	*4*	*4*	*3*	*19*	*13.3*	*+29.33*
12-13	*13*	*43*	*3*	*6*	*6*	*28*	*7.0*	*-11.50*

JOCKEYS

	W-R	Per cent	£1 Level Stake
Ryan While	2-8	25.0	+11.50
Chris Davies	1-3	33.3	0.00

COURSE RECORD

	Total W-R	Non-Hndcps Hurdles	Non-Hndcps Chases	Hndcps Hurdles	Hndcps Chases	NH Flat	Per cent	£1 Level Stake
Fakenham	1-2	1-1	0-0	0-0	0-1	0-0	50.0	+1.00
Taunton	1-2	0-0	0-0	1-1	0-1	0-0	50.0	+4.50
Fontwell	1-3	0-0	0-0	1-3	0-0	0-0	33.3	+10.00

WINNING HORSES

Horse	Races Run	1st	2nd	3rd	£
Floral Spinner	9	2	1	3	10262
Edlomond	3	1	1	0	2053
Total winning prize-money					**£12315**
Favourites	**1-1**		**100.0%**		**2.00**

P P C TURNER

HOARWITHY, H'FORDS

	No. of Hrs	Races Run	1st	2nd	3rd	Unpl	Per cent	£1 Level Stake
NH Flat	*0*	*0*	*0*	*0*	*0*	*0*	*0.0*	*0.00*
Hurdles	*0*	*0*	*0*	*0*	*0*	*0*	*0.0*	*0.00*
Chases	*2*	*4*	*1*	*0*	*0*	*3*	*25.0*	*+2.00*
Totals	**2**	**4**	**1**	**0**	**0**	**3**	**25.0**	**+2.00**
12-13	*1*	*2*	*0*	*0*	*0*	*2*	*0.0*	*-2.00*

JOCKEYS

	W-R	Per cent	£1 Level Stake
Miss L M Turner	1-4	25.0	+2.00

COURSE RECORD

	Total W-R	Non-Hndcps Hurdles	Non-Hndcps Chases	Hndcps Hurdles	Hndcps Chases	NH Flat	Per cent	£1 Level Stake
Warwick	1-2	0-0	1-2	0-0	0-0	0-0	50.0	+4.00

WINNING HORSES

Horse	Races Run	1st	2nd	3rd	£
*Pentiffic	3	1	0	0	1248
Total winning prize-money					**£1248**
Favourites	**0-1**		**0.0%**		**-1.00**

NIGEL TWISTON-DAVIES

NAUNTON, GLOUCS

	No. of Hrs	Races Run	1st	2nd	3rd	Unpl	Per cent	£1 Level Stake
NH Flat	*24*	*40*	*3*	*6*	*6*	*25*	*7.5*	*-17.00*
Hurdles	*72*	*247*	*38*	*33*	*26*	*150*	*15.4*	*-80.25*
Chases	*49*	*203*	*32*	*21*	*29*	*121*	*15.8*	*-11.36*
Totals	**119**	**490**	**73**	**60**	**61**	**296**	**14.9**	**-108.61**
13-14	*122*	*563*	*78*	*82*	*72*	*330*	*13.9*	*-103.51*
12-13	*117*	*537*	*73*	*69*	*68*	*327*	*13.6*	*-151.24*

BY MONTH

NH Flat	W-R	Per cent	£1 Level Stake
May	1-5	20.0	+2.00
June	0-4	0.0	-4.00
July	0-1	0.0	-1.00
August	0-3	0.0	-3.00
September	1-2	50.0	+1.00
October	0-1	0.0	-1.00
November	0-4	0.0	-4.00
December	0-4	0.0	-4.00
January	0-2	0.0	-2.00
February	0-2	0.0	-2.00
March	0-6	0.0	-6.00
April	1-6	16.7	+7.00

Hurdles	W-R	Per cent	£1 Level Stake
May	1-21	4.8	-16.00
June	4-14	28.6	+1.83
July	1-4	25.0	-1.13
August	2-5	40.0	+0.04
September	1-13	7.7	-11.56
October	6-21	28.6	+15.38
November	5-33	15.2	-15.08
December	8-31	25.8	+3.69
January	1-25	4.0	-23.83
February	1-25	4.0	-23.17
March	6-28	21.4	+4.58
April	2-27	7.4	-15.00

Chases	W-R	Per cent	£1 Level Stake
May	3-17	17.6	+4.50
June	0-2	0.0	-2.00
July	0-5	0.0	-5.00
August	1-8	12.5	-6.09
September	2-8	25.0	+16.75
October	6-21	28.6	+7.25
November	3-28	10.7	-15.67
December	4-26	15.4	+7.75
January	7-30	23.3	+11.88
February	3-21	14.3	-12.80
March	1-21	4.8	-19.43
April	2-16	12.5	+1.50

Totals	W-R	Per cent	£1 Level Stake
May	5-43	11.6	-9.50
June	4-20	20.0	-4.17
July	1-10	10.0	-7.13
August	3-16	18.8	-9.05
September	4-23	17.4	+6.19
October	12-43	27.9	+21.63
November	8-65	12.3	-34.75
December	12-61	19.7	+7.44
January	8-57	14.0	-13.95
February	4-48	8.3	-37.97
March	7-55	12.7	-20.85
April	5-49	10.2	-6.50

DISTANCE

Hurdles	W-R	Per cent	£1 Level Stake
2m-2m3f	23-80	28.7	+8.86
2m4f-2m7f	5-72	6.9	-55.94
3m+	4-29	13.8	-1.75

Chases	W-R	Per cent	£1 Level Stake
2m-2m3f	7-20	35.0	+11.56
2m4f-2m7f	14-82	17.1	+15.00
3m+	9-73	12.3	-23.67

TYPE OF RACE

Non-Handicaps

	W-R	Per cent	£1 Level Stake
Nov Hrdls	11-62	17.7	-17.61
Hrdls	14-44	31.8	+5.66
Nov Chs	6-17	35.3	+0.68
Chases	1-9	11.1	-6.75
Sell/Claim	2-9	22.2	-3.00

Handicaps

	W-R	Per cent	£1 Level Stake
Nov Hrdls	0-13	0.0	-13.00
Hrdls	10-117	8.5	-56.80
Nov Chs	5-42	11.9	-16.13
Chases	20-135	14.8	+10.83
Sell/Claim	1-3	33.3	+3.50

RACE CLASS

	W-R	Per cent	£1 Level Stake
Class 1	7-62	11.3	-33.33

FIRST TIME OUT

	W-R	Per cent	£1 Level Stake
Bumpers	1-24	4.2	-17.00

Class 2	4-45	8.9	-18.42	Hurdles	10-57	17.5	-3.79
Class 3	15-102	14.7	-22.69	Chases	8-38	21.1	+14.00
Class 4	34-180	18.9	-5.37				
Class 5	10-72	13.9	-12.05	Totals	19-119	16.0	-6.79
Class 6	3-29	10.3	-16.75				

JOCKEYS

	W-R	Per cent	£1 Level Stake
Sam Twiston-Davies	41-232	17.7	-17.05
Ryan Hatch	14-135	10.4	-69.13
Jamie Bargary	9-56	16.1	-4.63
Daryl Jacob	3-9	33.3	+2.33
Tom Bellamy	1-1	100.0	+10.00
James Reveley	1-2	50.0	-0.39
Mark Grant	1-5	20.0	+3.00
Jamie Moore	1-6	16.7	+3.00
Mr S Clements	1-7	14.3	-4.75
David England	1-8	12.5	-2.00

COURSE RECORD

	Total W-R	Non-Hndcps Hurdles	Non-Hndcps Chases	Hndcps Hurdles	Hndcps Chases	NH Flat	Per cent	£1 Level Stake
Ffos Las	9-38	2-9	1-1	0-12	6-12	0-4	23.7	-1.01
Uttoxeter	7-33	2-5	1-2	0-11	4-9	0-6	21.2	+13.32
Leicester	5-19	0-3	0-0	1-3	4-13	0-0	26.3	+10.75
Perth	5-21	1-4	0-1	1-8	1-6	2-2	23.8	+7.44
Cheltenham	5-49	2-12	1-8	1-8	1-20	0-1	10.2	-25.43
Lingfield	4-7	3-5	0-0	0-0	1-2	0-0	57.1	+16.58
Chepstow	4-20	3-4	0-0	0-5	1-8	0-3	20.0	+10.33
Stratford	4-20	2-4	0-0	2-6	0-6	0-4	20.0	-1.13
Mrket Rsn	3-8	3-4	0-0	0-2	0-2	0-0	37.5	+1.33
Kempton	3-10	1-2	0-1	0-1	2-5	0-1	30.0	+1.68
Nton Abbot	3-11	1-4	1-2	0-0	1-4	0-1	27.3	+1.04
Towcester	3-15	0-2	0-0	1-5	1-6	1-2	20.0	+12.00
Haydock	3-17	2-2	0-3	0-3	1-8	0-1	17.6	-2.50
Kelso	2-5	1-2	1-1	0-1	0-1	0-0	40.0	-0.92
Wincanton	2-10	1-4	0-0	0-2	1-4	0-0	20.0	+7.50
Warwick	2-23	0-7	1-2	1-6	0-6	0-2	8.7	-17.05
Sedgefield	1-2	0-0	0-0	1-1	0-1	0-0	50.0	+0.20
Cartmel	1-5	0-1	1-1	0-1	0-2	0-0	20.0	-2.25
Wetherby	1-7	1-2	0-1	0-2	0-2	0-0	14.3	-5.38
Bangor	1-12	0-2	0-0	0-3	1-5	0-2	8.3	-9.63
Southwell	1-13	0-2	0-0	1-6	0-4	0-1	7.7	-7.50
Taunton	1-13	0-1	0-0	1-6	0-5	0-1	7.7	-6.50
Huntingdon	1-14	1-3	0-0	0-4	0-4	0-3	7.1	-11.00
Aintree	1-16	1-4	0-1	0-6	0-5	0-0	6.3	-13.50
Newbury	1-16	0-2	0-1	1-8	0-4	0-1	6.3	-1.00

WINNING HORSES

Horse	Races Run	1st	2nd	3rd	£
The New One	5	4	0	0	192885
Hollow Blue Sky	7	1	0	3	31396
Splash Of Ginge	8	2	0	1	40987
Bristol De Mai	4	1	1	2	19933
Blaklion	8	3	2	1	20204
Bally Braes	8	2	2	0	16884
Sybarite	6	1	0	0	12512
Count Guido Deiro	3	1	0	0	10445
Cogry	6	2	1	0	15882
Five Star Wilsham	11	2	2	0	11618
Ballybolley	7	2	2	1	10756
Mission To Mars	2	1	0	0	6963
Foxbridge	6	3	0	0	16895
Algernon Pazham	5	1	1	1	6498
Brownville	6	1	1	2	6330
Little Jon	7	2	0	1	12586
Goodbye Dancer	4	3	0	0	13478
Pure Science	2	1	0	0	6256
Allthegear No Idea	6	2	1	1	8816
*Valid Point	3	1	0	2	4549
Wood Yer	2	1	0	0	4549
The Musical Guy	6	2	1	0	8317
Fond Memory	8	1	1	2	4549
Buddy Love	7	1	2	1	3899
Big Casino	8	1	0	3	3899
Papradon	9	1	1	1	3798
Listen Boy	3	1	1	0	3798
Winged Crusader	6	1	1	0	3798
Riddleofthesands	2	1	0	0	3769
Frontier Spirit	10	1	1	2	3769
Minella Reception	4	2	1	0	6888
Goldie Horn	13	2	2	1	5278
Bally Beaufort	7	1	1	0	3249
Abigail Lynch	6	2	0	1	5588
I Am Colin	3	1	0	0	3249
Belmount	7	2	1	1	6368
Kilronan High	8	3	1	0	6603
Rally	5	1	0	1	3249
Ballykan	2	1	1	0	3249
A Doll In Milan	5	2	1	0	6368
Millicent Silver	7	1	2	1	3119
Seacon Beg	7	1	1	0	2738
Golden Jubilee	3	1	1	0	2599
Foxtail Hill	4	1	0	1	2599
Dazzling Rita	7	1	2	1	1949
Seranwen	3	1	0	2	1949
Florrie Boy	2	1	0	0	1899
Major Malarkey	5	1	0	0	1872
Lady Fingers	4	1	0	0	1872
Total winning prize-money					**£580703**
Favourites	**27-56**		**48.2%**		**9.23**

MARK USHER

UPPER LAMBOURN, BERKS

	No. of Hrs	Races Run	1st	2nd	3rd	Unpl	Per cent	£1 Level Stake
NH Flat	*1*	*1*	*0*	*0*	*0*	*1*	*0.0*	*-1.00*
Hurdles	*5*	*17*	*2*	*2*	*0*	*13*	*11.8*	*-4.50*
Chases	*0*	*0*	*0*	*0*	*0*	*0*	*0.0*	*0.00*
Totals	**5**	**18**	**2**	**2**	**0**	**14**	**11.1**	**-5.50**
13-14	*4*	*9*	*0*	*3*	*2*	*4*	*0.0*	*-9.00*

12-13	*6*	*14*	*0*	*0*	*1*	*13*	*0.0*	*-14.00*

JOCKEYS

	W-R	Per cent	£1 Level Stake
Dave Crosse	2-16	12.5	-3.50

COURSE RECORD

	Total W-R	Non-Hndcps Hurdles	Non-Hndcps Chases	Hndcps Hurdles	Hndcps Chases	NH Flat	Per cent	£1 Level Stake
Bangor	1-1	0-0	0-0	1-1	0-0	0-0	100.0	+7.50
Fakenham	1-3	1-2	0-0	0-1	0-0	0-0	33.3	+1.00

WINNING HORSES

Horse	Races Run	1st	2nd	3rd	£
Bay Fortuna	4	1	0	0	3422
Haatefina	6	1	0	0	3119
Total winning prize-money					**£6541**
Favourites	**0-0**		**0.0%**		**0.00**

TIM VAUGHAN

ABERTHIN, VALE OF GLAMORGAN

	No. of Hrs	Races Run	1st	2nd	3rd	Unpl	Per cent	£1 Level Stake
NH Flat	*26*	*40*	*3*	*6*	*10*	*21*	*7.5*	*-28.25*
Hurdles	*76*	*215*	*23*	*24*	*22*	*146*	*10.7*	*-102.88*
Chases	*41*	*94*	*12*	*8*	*15*	*59*	*12.8*	*-14.38*
Totals	**116**	**349**	**38**	**38**	**47**	**226**	**10.9**	**-145.51**
13-14	*145*	*498*	*59*	*76*	*54*	*309*	*11.8*	*-146.41*
12-13	*178*	*631*	*83*	*103*	*92*	*353*	*13.2*	*-204.73*

BY MONTH

NH Flat	W-R	Per cent	£1 Level Stake	Hurdles	W-R	Per cent	£1 Level Stake
May	0-2	0.0	-2.00	May	2-13	15.4	-8.08
June	0-0	0.0	0.00	June	1-13	7.7	-5.00
July	0-1	0.0	-1.00	July	3-11	27.3	-3.37
August	0-2	0.0	-2.00	August	2-13	15.4	-6.88
September	0-0	0.0	0.00	September	1-5	20.0	-1.25
October	1-10	10.0	-4.00	October	5-26	19.2	-5.06
November	1-8	12.5	-5.50	November	1-24	4.2	-18.00
December	1-6	16.7	-2.75	December	2-27	7.4	-18.50
January	0-4	0.0	-4.00	January	0-35	0.0	-35.00
February	0-4	0.0	-4.00	February	0-13	0.0	-13.00
March	0-2	0.0	-2.00	March	6-27	22.2	+19.25
April	0-1	0.0	-1.00	April	0-8	0.0	-8.00

Chases	W-R	Per cent	£1 Level Stake	Totals	W-R	Per cent	£1 Level Stake
May	3-22	13.6	-1.00	May	5-37	13.5	-11.08
June	2-9	22.2	+2.00	June	3-22	13.6	-3.00
July	1-9	11.1	-6.13	July	4-21	19.0	-10.50
August	1-3	33.3	+0.50	August	3-18	16.7	-8.38
September	0-1	0.0	-1.00	September	1-6	16.7	-2.25
October	3-7	42.9	+22.00	October	9-43	20.9	+12.94
November	1-11	9.1	-8.75	November	3-43	7.0	-32.25
December	1-12	8.3	-2.00	December	4-45	8.9	-23.25
January	0-8	0.0	-8.00	January	0-47	0.0	-47.00
February	0-4	0.0	-4.00	February	0-21	0.0	-21.00
March	0-3	0.0	-3.00	March	6-32	18.8	+14.25
April	0-5	0.0	-5.00	April	0-14	0.0	-14.00

DISTANCE

Hurdles	W-R	Per cent	£1 Level Stake	Chases	W-R	Per cent	£1 Level Stake
2m-2m3f	13-100	13.0	-35.76	2m-2m3f	2-22	9.1	-12.50
2m4f-2m7f	4-54	7.4	-38.50	2m4f-2m7f	6-37	16.2	+12.13
3m+	2-6	33.3	+3.25	3m+	3-19	15.8	-3.00

TYPE OF RACE

Non-Handicaps	W-R	Per cent	£1 Level Stake	Handicaps	W-R	Per cent	£1 Level Stake
Nov Hrdls	9-65	13.8	-30.74	Nov Hrdls	0-11	0.0	-11.00
Hrdls	3-51	5.9	-36.89	Hrdls	11-81	13.6	-17.25
Nov Chs	1-7	14.3	-1.00	Nov Chs	2-27	7.4	-9.13
Chases	0-3	0.0	-3.00	Chases	9-57	15.8	-1.25
Sell/Claim	0-3	0.0	-3.00	Sell/Claim	0-4	0.0	-4.00

RACE CLASS

	W-R	Per cent	£1 Level Stake
Class 1	0-10	0.0	-10.00
Class 2	1-20	5.0	-14.00
Class 3	5-51	9.8	-26.00
Class 4	16-143	11.2	-39.08
Class 5	13-93	14.0	-36.18
Class 6	3-32	9.4	-20.25

FIRST TIME OUT

	W-R	Per cent	£1 Level Stake
Bumpers	1-26	3.8	-20.00
Hurdles	4-57	7.0	-45.31
Chases	6-33	18.2	+0.88
Totals	11-116	9.5	-64.43

JOCKEYS

	W-R	Per cent	£1 Level Stake
Richard Johnson	18-109	16.5	-14.52
Alan Johns	10-78	12.8	-22.40
Michael Byrne	8-109	7.3	-72.58
Conor Walsh	1-1	100.0	+5.00
Mr B Gibbs	1-5	20.0	+6.00

COURSE RECORD

	Total W-R	Non-Hndcps Hurdles	Non-Hndcps Chases	Hndcps Hurdles	Hndcps Chases	NH Flat	Per cent	£1 Level Stake
Uttoxeter	6-21	2-10	0-0	2-3	1-6	1-2	28.6	+2.16
Southwell	3-15	1-4	0-0	1-5	1-4	0-2	20.0	+12.00
Stratford	3-15	2-8	0-0	0-2	0-2	1-3	20.0	+0.44
Fakenham	3-18	1-6	0-0	1-8	1-4	0-0	16.7	-7.25
Ffos Las	3-45	0-8	0-0	0-13	3-18	0-6	6.7	-30.50
Perth	2-7	1-3	1-2	0-0	0-2	0-0	28.6	+1.10
Fontwell	2-10	1-4	0-0	1-2	0-2	0-2	20.0	+7.00
Worcester	2-13	1-3	0-2	0-2	1-4	0-2	15.4	+3.67
Chepstow	2-26	0-14	0-0	2-5	0-2	0-5	7.7	-19.50
Musselbgh	1-3	0-0	0-0	1-2	0-1	0-0	33.3	+3.00
Lingfield	1-3	0-1	0-0	0-1	1-1	0-0	33.3	-0.75
Aintree	1-3	0-0	0-0	0-0	1-3	0-0	33.3	+2.00

Towcester	1-3	0-0	0-0	0-1	0-1	1-1	33.3	-0.50
Bangor	1-6	1-3	0-1	0-1	0-0	0-1	16.7	-3.63
Haydock	1-6	0-1	0-1	0-2	1-1	0-1	16.7	+4.00
Sedgefield	1-6	0-2	0-0	1-1	0-1	0-2	16.7	-2.75
Warwick	1-6	0-2	0-0	1-1	0-3	0-0	16.7	+9.00
Wincanton	1-6	1-1	0-0	0-2	0-3	0-0	16.7	-2.75
Mrket Rsn	1-9	1-3	0-0	0-4	0-1	0-1	11.1	-5.25
Ludlow	1-11	0-7	0-0	0-0	1-2	0-2	9.1	-2.00
Taunton	1-20	0-9	0-0	1-9	0-1	0-1	5.0	-18.00

WINNING HORSES

Horse	Races Run	1st	2nd	3rd	£
First Fandango	4	2	0	1	23718
Wings Of Smoke	6	1	2	0	9747
Lamool	3	1	0	1	9384
Falcarragh	6	2	2	0	10397
Always Archie	5	1	4	0	5789
Rev It Up	5	1	0	0	5697
Honey Pound	4	2	0	0	7798
*Midnight Diamond	1	1	0	0	4549
*The Omen	11	2	3	2	6043
Be Bop Boru	4	1	0	1	3899
King Rolfe	5	1	0	0	3899
Ashford Wood	5	1	1	1	3798
*Royale Django	4	1	0	0	3329
Alphabetical Order	5	3	0	1	9747
Nathans Pride	7	4	1	0	12782
Tanit River	7	2	0	0	5783
The Wallace Line	5	1	1	1	3119
Kalimantan	6	2	2	1	4687
*Akula	3	1	0	1	2599
Tidestream	4	1	0	0	2496
Spanish Optimist	3	1	0	1	2469
Doc Wells	2	1	0	0	2274
Bens Moor	2	1	0	1	2144
Dalaman	3	1	0	1	1949
Benability	6	1	0	1	1949
Knight's Reward	4	1	0	0	1560
Champagne Chaser	5	1	3	0	1560
Total winning prize-money					**£153165**
Favourites	**14-36**		**38.9%**		**-0.38**

JOHN WADE

MORDON, CO DURHAM

	No. of Hrs	Races Run	1st	2nd	3rd	Unpl	Per cent	£1 Level Stake
NH Flat	*4*	*8*	*0*	*2*	*1*	*5*	*0.0*	*-8.00*
Hurdles	*20*	*64*	*8*	*11*	*5*	*40*	*12.5*	*-30.56*
Chases	*16*	*54*	*7*	*9*	*9*	*29*	*13.0*	*-13.17*
Totals	**37**	**126**	**15**	**22**	**15**	**74**	**11.9**	**-51.73**
13-14	*51*	*180*	*13*	*10*	*27*	*130*	*7.2*	*-78.42*
12-13	*62*	*223*	*23*	*20*	*26*	*154*	*10.3*	*-104.18*

BY MONTH

NH Flat	W-R	Per cent	£1 Level Stake	Hurdles	W-R	Per cent	£1 Level Stake
May	0-3	0.0	-3.00	May	0-10	0.0	-10.00
June	0-0	0.0	0.00	June	0-0	0.0	0.00
July	0-0	0.0	0.00	July	0-0	0.0	0.00
August	0-0	0.0	0.00	August	0-0	0.0	0.00
September	0-0	0.0	0.00	September	0-1	0.0	-1.00
October	0-3	0.0	-3.00	October	0-5	0.0	-5.00
November	0-1	0.0	-1.00	November	4-17	23.5	-0.56
December	0-0	0.0	0.00	December	1-10	10.0	-4.00
January	0-1	0.0	-1.00	January	2-11	18.2	-4.50
February	0-0	0.0	0.00	February	1-4	25.0	+0.50
March	0-0	0.0	0.00	March	0-3	0.0	-3.00
April	0-0	0.0	0.00	April	0-3	0.0	-3.00

Chases	W-R	Per cent	£1 Level Stake	Totals	W-R	Per cent	£1 Level Stake
May	2-14	14.3	-4.50	May	2-27	7.4	-17.50
June	0-1	0.0	-1.00	June	0-1	0.0	-1.00
July	0-0	0.0	0.00	July	0-0	0.0	0.00
August	0-0	0.0	0.00	August	0-0	0.0	0.00
September	0-0	0.0	0.00	September	0-1	0.0	-1.00
October	1-5	20.0	+1.50	October	1-13	7.7	-6.50
November	2-7	28.6	-2.17	November	6-25	24.0	-3.73
December	1-7	14.3	+2.00	December	2-17	11.8	-2.00
January	0-6	0.0	-6.00	January	2-18	11.1	-11.50
February	0-4	0.0	-4.00	February	1-8	12.5	-3.50
March	0-5	0.0	-5.00	March	0-8	0.0	-8.00
April	1-5	20.0	+6.00	April	1-8	12.5	+3.00

DISTANCE

Hurdles	W-R	Per cent	£1 Level Stake	Chases	W-R	Per cent	£1 Level Stake
2m-2m3f	5-29	17.2	-8.06	2m-2m3f	2-14	14.3	-9.18
2m4f-2m7f	1-20	5.0	-14.00	2m4f-2m7f	2-20	10.0	-3.50
3m+	2-14	14.3	-7.50	3m+	3-17	17.6	+2.50

TYPE OF RACE

Non-Handicaps	W-R	Per cent	£1 Level Stake	Handicaps	W-R	Per cent	£1 Level Stake
Nov Hrdls	0-11	0.0	-11.00	Nov Hrdls	2-9	22.2	-3.56
Hrdls	0-1	0.0	-1.00	Hrdls	6-43	14.0	-15.00
Nov Chs	0-2	0.0	-2.00	Nov Chs	1-6	16.7	-3.38
Chases	0-2	0.0	-2.00	Chases	6-44	13.6	-5.80
Sell/Claim	0-0	0.0	0.00	Sell/Claim	0-3	0.0	-3.00

RACE CLASS / FIRST TIME OUT

Race Class	W-R	Per cent	£1 Level Stake	First Time Out	W-R	Per cent	£1 Level Stake
Class 1	0-1	0.0	-1.00	Bumpers	0-4	0.0	-4.00
Class 2	0-5	0.0	-5.00	Hurdles	0-19	0.0	-19.00
Class 3	2-20	10.0	-2.50	Chases	2-14	14.3	-3.50
Class 4	9-60	15.0	-25.93				

Class 5	4-31	12.9	-8.30	Totals	2-37	5.4	-26.50
Class 6	0-9	0.0	-9.00				

JOCKEYS

	W-R	Per cent	£1 Level Stake
Brian Hughes	12-69	17.4	-19.73
Wilson Renwick	2-11	18.2	+3.00
James Reveley	1-7	14.3	+4.00

COURSE RECORD

	Total W-R	Non-Hndcps Hurdles	Non-Hndcps Chases	Hndcps Hurdles	Hndcps Chases	NH Flat	Per cent	£1 Level Stake
Carlisle	4-13	0-0	0-0	3-8	1-4	0-1	30.8	+6.44
Sedgefield	3-27	0-2	0-2	1-10	2-10	0-3	11.1	-14.18
Newcastle	2-10	0-1	0-0	2-4	0-5	0-0	20.0	+0.50
Cartmel	1-2	0-0	0-0	0-1	1-1	0-0	50.0	+3.50
Catterick	1-3	0-0	0-1	1-1	0-1	0-0	33.3	+1.50
Ayr	1-5	0-0	0-0	0-1	1-4	0-0	20.0	+1.50
Musselbgh	1-5	0-0	0-0	1-3	0-1	0-1	20.0	-3.00
Hexham	1-15	0-4	0-0	0-5	1-5	0-1	6.7	-6.00
Kelso	1-17	0-1	0-1	0-3	1-11	0-1	5.9	-13.00

WINNING HORSES

Horse	Races Run	1st	2nd	3rd	£
Always Right	3	1	0	0	7798
Riskier	7	1	3	1	6498
Harris Hawk	2	1	0	0	6498
Runswick Days	7	2	3	1	7221
Walser	7	1	2	1	3899
Allez Cool	5	1	3	0	3899
Jukebox Melody	5	2	0	0	5393
Roseville Cottage	6	1	1	3	3249
Aiaam Al Namoos	4	1	0	0	3249
Spanish Fleet	7	3	1	1	9747
Dingo Bay	7	1	0	1	2469
Total winning prize-money					**£59920**
Favourites	**6-17**		**35.3%**		**-1.23**

LUCY WADHAM

NEWMARKET, SUFFOLK

	No. of Hrs	Races Run	1st	2nd	3rd	Unpl	Per cent	£1 Level Stake
NH Flat	*7*	*15*	*2*	*1*	*3*	*9*	*13.3*	*-2.50*
Hurdles	*19*	*80*	*8*	*13*	*9*	*50*	*10.0*	*-15.38*
Chases	*7*	*37*	*9*	*5*	*7*	*16*	*24.3*	*-0.29*
Totals	**29**	**132**	**19**	**19**	**19**	**75**	**14.4**	**-18.17**
13-14	*24*	*118*	*17*	*22*	*17*	*62*	*14.4*	*-23.00*
12-13	*25*	*114*	*16*	*15*	*15*	*68*	*14.0*	*+3.85*

BY MONTH

NH Flat	W-R	Per cent	£1 Level Stake	**Hurdles**	W-R	Per cent	£1 Level Stake
May	0-1	0.0	-1.00	May	0-7	0.0	-7.00
June	0-0	0.0	0.00	June	0-2	0.0	-2.00
July	0-0	0.0	0.00	July	0-0	0.0	0.00
August	0-0	0.0	0.00	August	0-0	0.0	0.00
September	0-1	0.0	-1.00	September	0-1	0.0	-1.00
October	0-1	0.0	-1.00	October	0-2	0.0	-2.00
November	0-1	0.0	-1.00	November	0-8	0.0	-8.00
December	0-2	0.0	-2.00	December	2-10	20.0	+11.50
January	0-1	0.0	-1.00	January	3-18	16.7	+14.50
February	0-3	0.0	-3.00	February	1-9	11.1	-5.25
March	1-3	33.3	+0.50	March	1-15	6.7	-12.63
April	1-2	50.0	+7.00	April	1-8	12.5	-3.50

Chases	W-R	Per cent	£1 Level Stake	**Totals**	W-R	Per cent	£1 Level Stake
May	0-1	0.0	-1.00	May	0-9	0.0	-9.00
June	0-1	0.0	-1.00	June	0-3	0.0	-3.00
July	1-2	50.0	+5.00	July	1-2	50.0	+5.00
August	0-1	0.0	-1.00	August	0-1	0.0	-1.00
September	0-2	0.0	-2.00	September	0-4	0.0	-4.00
October	2-2	100.0	+5.75	October	2-5	40.0	+2.75
November	1-3	33.3	+5.00	November	1-12	8.3	-4.00
December	0-2	0.0	-2.00	December	2-14	14.3	+7.50
January	1-4	25.0	+2.00	January	4-23	17.4	+15.50
February	2-6	33.3	-1.68	February	3-18	16.7	-9.93
March	2-7	28.6	-3.36	March	4-25	16.0	-15.49
April	0-6	0.0	-6.00	April	2-16	12.5	-2.50

DISTANCE

Hurdles	W-R	Per cent	£1 Level Stake	**Chases**	W-R	Per cent	£1 Level Stake
2m-2m3f	3-18	16.7	-3.50	2m-2m3f	2-8	25.0	-4.36
2m4f-2m7f	3-30	10.0	+14.00	2m4f-2m7f	2-13	15.4	-3.25
3m+	1-12	8.3	-8.25	3m+	4-11	36.4	+10.75

TYPE OF RACE

Non-Handicaps	W-R	Per cent	£1 Level Stake	**Handicaps**	W-R	Per cent	£1 Level Stake
Nov Hrdls	2-14	14.3	-5.75	Nov Hrdls	0-5	0.0	-5.00
Hrdls	2-9	22.2	+14.38	Hrdls	4-52	7.7	-19.00
Nov Chs	1-2	50.0	+5.00	Nov Chs	0-8	0.0	-8.00
Chases	0-1	0.0	-1.00	Chases	8-26	30.8	+3.71
Sell/Claim	0-0	0.0	0.00	Sell/Claim	0-0	0.0	0.00

RACE CLASS

FIRST TIME OUT

	W-R	Per cent	£1 Level Stake		W-R	Per cent	£1 Level Stake
Class 1	0-13	0.0	-13.00	Bumpers	1-7	14.3	-3.50
Class 2	2-15	13.3	-5.25	Hurdles	1-17	5.9	+4.00
Class 3	5-32	15.6	-7.50	Chases	1-5	20.0	+3.00
Class 4	9-45	20.0	+8.35				
Class 5	3-19	15.8	+7.23	Totals	3-29	10.3	+3.50
Class 6	0-8	0.0	-8.00				

JOCKEYS

	W-R	Per cent	£1 Level Stake
Leighton Aspell	10-69	14.5	-20.40

Dougie Costello	3-15	20.0	+18.50
A P McCoy	1-2	50.0	-0.27
Paul Townend	1-2	50.0	+1.50
Daryl Jacob	1-3	33.3	+3.00
Jack Sherwood	1-4	25.0	+5.00
Micheal Nolan	1-7	14.3	-2.50
Jack Quinlan	1-13	7.7	-6.00

COURSE RECORD

	Total W-R	Non-Hndcps Hurdles	Non-Hndcps Chases	Hndcps Hurdles	Chases	NH Flat	Per cent	£1 Level Stake
Fakenham	5-19	0-4	0-0	1-10	3-4	1-1	26.3	+3.73
Huntingdon	3-13	1-5	0-0	1-5	1-2	0-1	23.1	+7.95
Kempton	2-9	0-1	0-0	1-2	1-5	0-1	22.2	-2.59
Sandown	2-10	0-0	0-0	0-5	2-4	0-1	20.0	+4.00
Bangor	1-1	0-0	0-0	0-0	0-0	1-1	100.0	+2.50
Musselbgh	1-2	1-1	0-0	0-1	0-0	0-0	50.0	+1.75
Warwick	1-2	0-0	0-0	0-1	1-1	0-0	50.0	+2.50
Ludlow	1-3	1-1	0-0	0-1	0-0	0-1	33.3	+18.00
Wetherby	1-3	1-1	0-0	0-2	0-0	0-0	33.3	+1.50
Uttoxeter	1-4	0-0	1-1	0-2	0-1	0-0	25.0	+3.00
Leicester	1-5	0-0	0-0	1-4	0-1	0-0	20.0	+0.50

WINNING HORSES

Horse	Races Run	1st	2nd	3rd	£
Le Reve	6	2	1	2	43954
Wiesentraum	6	2	1	0	19126
Shanroe Santos	4	2	0	0	15111
Canuspotit	6	2	1	1	12125
Minstrels Gallery	7	1	1	3	6173
Tealissio	5	1	1	0	5198
Songsmith	6	1	0	0	4549
Watered Silk	4	1	0	1	3961
Artifice Sivola	7	2	1	2	7798
Rendezvous Peak	5	1	0	1	3899
A Boy Named Suzi	6	1	2	0	3422
Mystic Sky	3	1	0	1	3422
Lanceur	4	1	1	0	3249
Sunshine Corner	2	1	0	0	2053
Total winning prize-money					**£134040**
Favourites	**6-17**		**35.3%**		**-3.17**

ROBERT WALEY-COHEN

RATLEY, WARWICKS

	No. of Hrs	Races Run	1st	2nd	3rd	Unpl	Per cent	£1 Level Stake
NH Flat	*2*	*3*	*0*	*0*	*0*	*3*	*0.0*	*-3.00*
Hurdles	*0*	*0*	*0*	*0*	*0*	*0*	*0.0*	*0.00*
Chases	*4*	*11*	*4*	*1*	*0*	*6*	*36.4*	*+23.61*
Totals	**6**	**14**	**4**	**1**	**0**	**9**	**28.6**	**+20.61**
13-14	*2*	*5*	*0*	*0*	*1*	*4*	*0.0*	*-5.00*
12-13	*3*	*8*	*0*	*1*	*1*	*6*	*0.0*	*-8.00*

JOCKEYS

	W-R	Per cent	£1 Level Stake
Mr S Waley-Cohen	4-12	33.3	+22.61

COURSE RECORD

	Total W-R	Non-Hndcps Hurdles	Non-Hndcps Chases	Hndcps Hurdles	Chases	NH Flat	Per cent	£1 Level Stake
Wetherby	2-3	0-0	1-1	0-0	1-1	0-1	66.7	+4.00
Uttoxeter	1-1	0-0	1-1	0-0	0-0	0-0	100.0	+0.61
Aintree	1-2	0-0	0-0	0-0	1-2	0-0	50.0	+24.00

WINNING HORSES

Horse	Races Run	1st	2nd	3rd	£
*Oscar Time	6	3	0	0	80634
*Makadamia	3	1	1	0	4094
Total winning prize-money					**£84728**
Favourites	**2-3**		**66.7%**		**0.11**

MARK WALFORD

SHERRIFF HUTTON, N YORKS

	No. of Hrs	Races Run	1st	2nd	3rd	Unpl	Per cent	£1 Level Stake
NH Flat	*4*	*5*	*0*	*0*	*0*	*5*	*0.0*	*-5.00*
Hurdles	*14*	*33*	*3*	*4*	*2*	*24*	*9.1*	*+4.00*
Chases	*5*	*28*	*7*	*7*	*4*	*10*	*25.0*	*+3.96*
Totals	**17**	**66**	**10**	**11**	**6**	**39**	**15.2**	**+2.96**
13-14	*11*	*26*	*2*	*4*	*5*	*15*	*7.7*	*-5.25*

BY MONTH

NH Flat	W-R	Per cent	£1 Level Stake	Hurdles	W-R	Per cent	£1 Level Stake
May	0-0	0.0	0.00	May	0-5	0.0	-5.00
June	0-0	0.0	0.00	June	1-2	50.0	+6.50
July	0-0	0.0	0.00	July	0-2	0.0	-2.00
August	0-0	0.0	0.00	August	0-0	0.0	0.00
September	0-0	0.0	0.00	September	1-2	50.0	+7.50
October	0-0	0.0	0.00	October	0-3	0.0	-3.00
November	0-1	0.0	-1.00	November	1-4	25.0	+15.00
December	0-2	0.0	-2.00	December	0-3	0.0	-3.00
January	0-0	0.0	0.00	January	0-3	0.0	-3.00
February	0-0	0.0	0.00	February	0-0	0.0	0.00
March	0-2	0.0	-2.00	March	0-5	0.0	-5.00
April	0-0	0.0	0.00	April	0-4	0.0	-4.00

Chases	W-R	Per cent	£1 Level Stake	Totals	W-R	Per cent	£1 Level Stake
May	1-3	33.3	+2.50	May	1-8	12.5	-2.50
June	0-2	0.0	-2.00	June	1-4	25.0	+4.50
July	1-2	50.0	+2.33	July	1-4	25.0	+0.33
August	0-1	0.0	-1.00	August	0-1	0.0	-1.00
September	0-0	0.0	0.00	September	1-2	50.0	+7.50
October	1-3	33.3	+0.75	October	1-6	16.7	-2.25
November	2-5	40.0	+2.38	November	3-10	30.0	+16.38

December	0-3	0.0	-3.00	December	0-8	0.0	-8.00
January	0-1	0.0	-1.00	January	0-4	0.0	-4.00
February	1-2	50.0	+0.50	February	1-2	50.0	+0.50
March	1-4	25.0	+4.50	March	1-11	9.1	-2.50
April	0-2	0.0	-2.00	April	0-6	0.0	-6.00

DISTANCE

Hurdles	W-R	Per cent	£1 Level Stake	Chases	W-R	Per cent	£1 Level Stake
2m-2m3f	1-16	6.3	-7.50	2m-2m3f	1-5	20.0	-0.50
2m4f-2m7f	1-12	8.3	+7.00	2m4f-2m7f	2-7	28.6	+5.25
3m+	0-2	0.0	-2.00	3m+	2-12	16.7	-2.17

TYPE OF RACE

Non-Handicaps	W-R	Per cent	£1 Level Stake	Handicaps	W-R	Per cent	£1 Level Stake
Nov Hrdls	1-7	14.3	+12.00	Nov Hrdls	0-2	0.0	-2.00
Hrdls	0-1	0.0	-1.00	Hrdls	2-23	8.7	-5.00
Nov Chs	0-0	0.0	0.00	Nov Chs	3-10	30.0	+1.13
Chases	0-2	0.0	-2.00	Chases	4-16	25.0	+4.83
Sell/Claim	0-0	0.0	0.00	Sell/Claim	0-0	0.0	0.00

RACE CLASS / FIRST TIME OUT

Race Class	W-R	Per cent	£1 Level Stake	First Time Out	W-R	Per cent	£1 Level Stake
Class 1	0-5	0.0	-5.00	Bumpers	0-4	0.0	-4.00
Class 2	0-3	0.0	-3.00	Hurdles	2-11	18.2	+17.50
Class 3	1-11	9.1	-5.50	Chases	1-2	50.0	+3.50
Class 4	9-29	31.0	+34.46				
Class 5	0-13	0.0	-13.00	Totals	3-17	17.6	+17.00
Class 6	0-5	0.0	-5.00				

JOCKEYS

	W-R	Per cent	£1 Level Stake
Jake Greenall	3-11	27.3	+22.00
Tony Kelly	3-13	23.1	-3.13
Dougie Costello	3-32	9.4	-14.42
Grant Cockburn	1-5	20.0	+3.50

COURSE RECORD

	Total W-R	Non-Hndcps Hurdles	Non-Hndcps Chases	Hndcps Hurdles	Hndcps Chases	NH Flat	Per cent	£1 Level Stake
Uttoxeter	3-8	0-0	0-0	2-3	1-5	0-0	37.5	+14.33
Hexham	2-7	1-1	0-0	0-1	1-5	0-0	28.6	+14.88
Kelso	2-7	0-0	0-1	0-0	2-6	0-0	28.6	+1.25
Catterick	1-2	0-0	0-0	0-0	1-1	0-1	50.0	+0.50
Newcastle	1-6	0-3	0-0	0-1	1-2	0-0	16.7	+2.50
Wetherby	1-14	0-2	0-0	0-7	1-3	0-2	7.1	-8.50

WINNING HORSES

Horse	Races Run	1st	2nd	3rd	£
Uno Valoroso	8	3	2	1	14296
Big Sound	10	2	5	0	10290
Fentara	8	1	1	1	6256
Highlander Ted	5	1	0	1	3769
Oliver's Gold	5	1	1	0	3379
Kodicil	5	1	1	2	3249
Red Tortue	1	1	0	0	3249
Total winning prize-money					**£44488**
Favourites	**4-7**		**57.1%**		**6.46**

ROBERT WALFORD

CHILD OKEFORD, DORSET

	No. of Hrs	Races Run	1st	2nd	3rd	Unpl	Per cent	£1 Level Stake
NH Flat	*2*	*2*	*0*	*0*	*0*	*2*	*0.0*	*-2.00*
Hurdles	*15*	*37*	*4*	*3*	*5*	*25*	*10.8*	*+2.00*
Chases	*8*	*31*	*9*	*7*	*4*	*11*	*29.0*	*+6.03*
Totals	**19**	**70**	**13**	**10**	**9**	**38**	**18.6**	**+6.03**
13-14	*21*	*62*	*12*	*8*	*4*	*38*	*19.4*	*-12.31*
12-13	*12*	*33*	*2*	*4*	*7*	*20*	*6.1*	*-22.00*

BY MONTH

NH Flat	W-R	Per cent	£1 Level Stake	Hurdles	W-R	Per cent	£1 Level Stake
May	0-0	0.0	0.00	May	0-2	0.0	-2.00
June	0-0	0.0	0.00	June	0-1	0.0	-1.00
July	0-0	0.0	0.00	July	0-0	0.0	0.00
August	0-0	0.0	0.00	August	0-0	0.0	0.00
September	0-0	0.0	0.00	September	0-0	0.0	0.00
October	0-1	0.0	-1.00	October	0-1	0.0	-1.00
November	0-0	0.0	0.00	November	1-9	11.1	+3.00
December	0-0	0.0	0.00	December	1-7	14.3	+4.00
January	0-0	0.0	0.00	January	0-7	0.0	-7.00
February	0-0	0.0	0.00	February	0-3	0.0	-3.00
March	0-0	0.0	0.00	March	1-6	16.7	-1.00
April	0-1	0.0	-1.00	April	1-1	100.0	+10.00

Chases	W-R	Per cent	£1 Level Stake	Totals	W-R	Per cent	£1 Level Stake
May	0-0	0.0	0.00	May	0-2	0.0	-2.00
June	0-0	0.0	0.00	June	0-1	0.0	-1.00
July	0-0	0.0	0.00	July	0-0	0.0	0.00
August	0-0	0.0	0.00	August	0-0	0.0	0.00
September	0-0	0.0	0.00	September	0-0	0.0	0.00
October	0-1	0.0	-1.00	October	0-3	0.0	-3.00
November	0-3	0.0	-3.00	November	1-12	8.3	0.00
December	0-5	0.0	-5.00	December	1-12	8.3	-1.00
January	3-4	75.0	+12.50	January	3-11	27.3	+5.50
February	2-7	28.6	+3.00	February	2-10	20.0	0.00
March	1-5	20.0	-1.50	March	2-11	18.2	-2.50
April	3-6	50.0	+1.03	April	4-8	50.0	+10.03

DISTANCE

Hurdles	W-R	Per cent	£1 Level Stake	Chases	W-R	Per cent	£1 Level Stake
2m-2m3f	2-20	10.0	-4.00	2m-2m3f	3-14	21.4	-4.38
2m4f-2m7f	1-11	9.1	0.00	2m4f-2m7f	5-11	45.5	+9.91
3m+	1-1	100.0	+11.00	3m+	1-4	25.0	+2.50

TYPE OF RACE

Non-Handicaps	W-R	Per cent	£1 Level Stake	Handicaps	W-R	Per cent	£1 Level Stake
Nov Hrdls	0-9	0.0	-9.00	Nov Hrdls	0-3	0.0	-3.00
Hrdls	1-7	14.3	+5.00	Hrdls	3-17	17.6	+10.00
Nov Chs	0-1	0.0	-1.00	Nov Chs	2-5	40.0	+4.50
Chases	0-0	0.0	0.00	Chases	7-25	28.0	+2.53
Sell/Claim	0-0	0.0	0.00	Sell/Claim	0-0	0.0	0.00

RACE CLASS / FIRST TIME OUT

	W-R	Per cent	£1 Level Stake		W-R	Per cent	£1 Level Stake
Class 1	1-6	16.7	+6.00	Bumpers	0-2	0.0	-2.00
Class 2	2-4	50.0	+10.50	Hurdles	1-11	9.1	+1.00
Class 3	3-16	18.8	-1.13	Chases	1-6	16.7	-2.50
Class 4	7-35	20.0	-0.34				
Class 5	0-7	0.0	-7.00	Totals	2-19	10.5	-3.50
Class 6	0-2	0.0	-2.00				

JOCKEYS

	W-R	Per cent	£1 Level Stake
Felix De Giles	6-27	22.2	-0.22
Daryl Jacob	3-23	13.0	-1.50
Paul Townend	1-1	100.0	+2.50
David Mullins	1-1	100.0	+10.00
Gavin Sheehan	1-2	50.0	+9.00
Nick Scholfield	1-3	33.3	-0.75

COURSE RECORD

	Total W-R	Non-Hndcps Hurdles	Non-Hndcps Chases	Hndcps Hurdles	Hndcps Chases	NH Flat	Per cent	£1 Level Stake
Taunton	2-6	0-1	0-0	0-1	2-4	0-0	33.3	+3.50
Fontwell	2-8	0-3	0-0	1-2	1-2	0-1	25.0	+4.91
Exeter	2-18	0-5	0-1	0-5	2-7	0-0	11.1	-9.25
Aintree	1-1	0-0	0-0	1-1	0-0	0-0	100.0	+10.00
Stratford	1-2	0-0	0-0	1-1	0-1	0-0	50.0	+3.00
Warwick	1-2	0-1	0-0	0-0	1-1	0-0	50.0	+1.50
Kempton	1-3	1-1	0-0	0-0	0-2	0-0	33.3	+9.00
Nton Abbot	1-3	0-0	0-0	0-1	1-1	0-1	33.3	+0.50
Chepstow	1-6	0-1	0-0	0-1	1-4	0-0	16.7	-3.13
Wincanton	1-7	0-2	0-0	0-1	1-4	0-0	14.3	0.00

WINNING HORSES

Horse	Races Run	1st	2nd	3rd	£
Astre De La Cour	3	2	0	0	31258
Camping Ground	2	1	0	0	18768
Carole's Spirit	3	1	1	0	14305
Saint Raph	5	1	1	1	14128
Brody Bleu	7	3	2	2	14426
Castarnie	4	2	0	1	10397
Sun Wild Life	6	1	2	1	4224
*Tom Neary	3	1	2	0	3899
Rosa Imperialis	4	1	0	1	3249
Total winning prize-money					**£114654**
Favourites	**6-10**		**60.0%**		**6.91**

MARK WALL

CHELTENHAM, GLOUCS

	No. of Hrs	Races Run	1st	2nd	3rd	Unpl	Per cent	£1 Level Stake
NH Flat	*2*	*2*	*0*	*0*	*0*	*2*	*0.0*	*-2.00*
Hurdles	*0*	*0*	*0*	*0*	*0*	*0*	*0.0*	*0.00*
Chases	*1*	*6*	*2*	*1*	*0*	*3*	*33.3*	*-1.63*
Totals	**3**	**8**	**2**	**1**	**0**	**5**	**25.0**	**-3.63**
13-14	*1*	*1*	*0*	*0*	*0*	*1*	*0.0*	*-1.00*
12-13	*1*	*1*	*0*	*0*	*0*	*1*	*0.0*	*-1.00*

JOCKEYS

	W-R	Per cent	£1 Level Stake
Mr M Wall	2-6	33.3	-1.63

COURSE RECORD

	Total W-R	Non-Hndcps Hurdles	Non-Hndcps Chases	Hndcps Hurdles	Hndcps Chases	NH Flat	Per cent	£1 Level Stake
Stratford	1-1	0-0	1-1	0-0	0-0	0-0	100.0	+1.38
Cheltenham	1-2	0-0	1-2	0-0	0-0	0-0	50.0	0.00

WINNING HORSES

Horse	Races Run	1st	2nd	3rd	£
Theatre Queen	6	2	1	0	15735
Total winning prize-money					**£15735**
Favourites	**2-2**		**100.0%**		**2.38**

TREVOR WALL

TWITCHEN, SHROPSHIRE

	No. of Hrs	Races Run	1st	2nd	3rd	Unpl	Per cent	£1 Level Stake
NH Flat	*1*	*1*	*0*	*0*	*0*	*1*	*0.0*	*-1.00*
Hurdles	*5*	*14*	*1*	*2*	*0*	*11*	*7.1*	*+7.00*
Chases	*0*	*0*	*0*	*0*	*0*	*0*	*0.0*	*0.00*
Totals	**6**	**15**	**1**	**2**	**0**	**12**	**6.7**	**+6.00**
13-14	*7*	*25*	*1*	*1*	*3*	*20*	*4.0*	*+1.00*
12-13	*3*	*17*	*0*	*1*	*1*	*15*	*0.0*	*-17.00*

JOCKEYS

	W-R	Per cent	£1 Level Stake
Josh Wall	1-12	8.3	+9.00

COURSE RECORD

	Total W-R	Non-Hndcps Hurdles	Non-Hndcps Chases	Hndcps Hurdles	Hndcps Chases	NH Flat	Per cent	£1 Level Stake
Uttoxeter	1-4	0-1	0-0	1-3	0-0	0-0	25.0	+17.00

WINNING HORSES

Horse	Races Run	1st	2nd	3rd	£
Fairy Alisha	5	1	1	0	2339
Total winning prize-money					**£2339**
Favourites	**0-0**		**0.0%**		**0.00**

JANE WALTON

OTTERBURN, NORTHUMBERLAND

	No. of Hrs	Races Run	1st	2nd	3rd	Unpl	Per cent	£1 Level Stake
NH Flat	*1*	*2*	*0*	*0*	*0*	*2*	*0.0*	*-2.00*
Hurdles	*6*	*22*	*0*	*0*	*1*	*21*	*0.0*	*-22.00*
Chases	*4*	*14*	*3*	*2*	*1*	*8*	*21.4*	*-0.63*
Totals	**8**	**38**	**3**	**2**	**2**	**31**	**7.9**	**-24.63**
13-14	*10*	*37*	*4*	*1*	*4*	*28*	*10.8*	*-16.25*
12-13	*7*	*24*	*0*	*0*	*1*	*23*	*0.0*	*-24.00*

JOCKEYS

	W-R	Per cent	£1 Level Stake
Brian Harding	1-2	50.0	+5.50
James Reveley	1-2	50.0	+1.00
Alistair Findlay	1-28	3.6	-25.13

COURSE RECORD

	Total W-R	Non-Hndcps Hurdles	Non-Hndcps Chases	Hndcps Hurdles	Hndcps Chases	NH Flat	Per cent	£1 Level Stake
Kelso	1-4	0-2	0-0	0-1	1-1	0-0	25.0	+3.50
Newcastle	1-6	0-1	0-0	0-3	1-2	0-0	16.7	-3.00
Hexham	1-10	0-5	0-0	0-2	1-3	0-0	10.0	-7.13

WINNING HORSES

Horse	Races Run	1st	2nd	3rd	£
Have You Had Yours	8	3	2	1	9812
Total winning prize-money					**£9812**
Favourites	**1-3**		**33.3%**		**0.00**

JAMES WALTON

THROPTON, NORTHUMBERLAND

	No. of Hrs	Races Run	1st	2nd	3rd	Unpl	Per cent	£1 Level Stake
NH Flat	*1*	*2*	*0*	*0*	*0*	*2*	*0.0*	*-2.00*
Hurdles	*5*	*26*	*3*	*2*	*3*	*18*	*11.5*	*-2.50*
Chases	*5*	*19*	*0*	*0*	*3*	*16*	*0.0*	*-19.00*
Totals	**10**	**47**	**3**	**2**	**6**	**36**	**6.4**	**-23.50**
13-14	*9*	*26*	*1*	*2*	*1*	*22*	*3.8*	*-11.00*
12-13	*11*	*36*	*5*	*4*	*1*	*26*	*13.9*	*-8.84*

JOCKEYS

	W-R	Per cent	£1 Level Stake
Miss C Walton	2-31	6.5	-15.50
Jamie Hamilton	1-5	20.0	+3.00

COURSE RECORD

	Total W-R	Non-Hndcps Hurdles	Non-Hndcps Chases	Hndcps Hurdles	Hndcps Chases	NH Flat	Per cent	£1 Level Stake
Carlisle	1-1	0-0	0-0	1-1	0-0	0-0	100.0	+10.00
Haydock	1-1	0-0	0-0	1-1	0-0	0-0	100.0	+7.00
Hexham	1-14	0-4	0-2	1-3	0-4	0-1	7.1	-9.50

WINNING HORSES

Horse	Races Run	1st	2nd	3rd	£
Central Flame	7	3	1	2	19494
Total winning prize-money					**£19494**
Favourites	**0-0**		**0.0%**		**0.00**

SHEENA WALTON

HEXHAM, NORTHUMBERLAND

	No. of Hrs	Races Run	1st	2nd	3rd	Unpl	Per cent	£1 Level Stake
NH Flat	*4*	*5*	*0*	*0*	*0*	*5*	*0.0*	*-5.00*
Hurdles	*4*	*10*	*0*	*1*	*0*	*9*	*0.0*	*-10.00*
Chases	*2*	*8*	*1*	*0*	*1*	*6*	*12.5*	*+7.00*
Totals	**8**	**23**	**1**	**1**	**1**	**20**	**4.3**	**-8.00**
13-14	*3*	*17*	*0*	*0*	*0*	*17*	*0.0*	*-17.00*
12-13	*5*	*21*	*0*	*3*	*0*	*18*	*0.0*	*-21.00*

JOCKEYS

	W-R	Per cent	£1 Level Stake
James Reveley	1-2	50.0	+13.00

COURSE RECORD

	Total W-R	Non-Hndcps Hurdles	Non-Hndcps Chases	Hndcps Hurdles	Hndcps Chases	NH Flat	Per cent	£1 Level Stake
Newcastle	1-5	0-0	0-0	0-2	1-2	0-1	20.0	+10.00

WINNING HORSES

Horse	Races Run	1st	2nd	3rd	£
Dystonia's Revenge	6	1	0	1	3769
Total winning prize-money					**£3769**
Favourites	**0-0**		**0.0%**		**0.00**

TRACEY WATKINS

HOLME MARSH, H'FORDS

	No. of Hrs	Races Run	1st	2nd	3rd	Unpl	Per cent	£1 Level Stake
NH Flat	*0*	*0*	*0*	*0*	*0*	*0*	*0.0*	*0.00*
Hurdles	*2*	*6*	*1*	*1*	*1*	*3*	*16.7*	*+20.00*

Chases	*0*	*0*	*0*	*0*	*0*	*0*	*0.0*	*0.00*
Totals	**2**	**6**	**1**	**1**	**1**	**3**	**16.7**	**+20.00**
13-14	*2*	*10*	*0*	*0*	*1*	*9*	*0.0*	*-10.00*
12-13	*3*	*6*	*0*	*0*	*0*	*6*	*0.0*	*-6.00*

JOCKEYS

	W-R	Per cent	£1 Level Stake
Miss B Hampson	1-1	100.0	+25.00

COURSE RECORD

	Total W-R	Non-Hndcps Hurdles	Non-Hndcps Chases	Hndcps Hurdles	Hndcps Chases	NH Flat	Per cent	£1 Level Stake
Ludlow	1-4	0-2	0-0	1-2	0-0	0-0	25.0	+22.00

WINNING HORSES

Horse	Races Run	1st	2nd	3rd	£
One Cool Boy	4	1	1	1	4679

Total winning prize-money **£4679**

Favourites **0-0** **0.0%** **0.00**

SHARON WATT

BROMPTON-ON-SWALE, N YORKS

	No. of Hrs	Races Run	1st	2nd	3rd	Unpl	Per cent	£1 Level Stake
NH Flat	*2*	*2*	*0*	*0*	*0*	*2*	*0.0*	*-2.00*
Hurdles	*3*	*10*	*3*	*0*	*0*	*7*	*30.0*	*+6.63*
Chases	*0*	*0*	*0*	*0*	*0*	*0*	*0.0*	*0.00*
Totals	**4**	**12**	**3**	**0**	**0**	**9**	**25.0**	**+4.63**
13-14	*5*	*11*	*0*	*1*	*1*	*9*	*0.0*	*-11.00*
12-13	*3*	*10*	*1*	*2*	*1*	*6*	*10.0*	*-8.00*

JOCKEYS

	W-R	Per cent	£1 Level Stake
Joseph Palmowski	2-9	22.2	+5.00
Mr H Stock	1-1	100.0	+1.63

COURSE RECORD

	Total W-R	Non-Hndcps Hurdles	Non-Hndcps Chases	Hndcps Hurdles	Hndcps Chases	NH Flat	Per cent	£1 Level Stake
Carlisle	2-2	0-0	0-0	2-2	0-0	0-0	100.0	+10.13
Hexham	1-2	0-1	0-0	1-1	0-0	0-0	50.0	+2.50

WINNING HORSES

Horse	Races Run	1st	2nd	3rd	£
Madam Lilibet	6	3	0	0	9106

Total winning prize-money **£9106**

Favourites **2-2** **100.0%** **5.13**

SIMON WAUGH

MITFORD, NORTHUMBERLAND

	No. of Hrs	Races Run	1st	2nd	3rd	Unpl	Per cent	£1 Level Stake
NH Flat	*3*	*4*	*0*	*0*	*0*	*4*	*0.0*	*-4.00*
Hurdles	*7*	*18*	*1*	*1*	*0*	*16*	*5.6*	*+1.00*
Chases	*4*	*14*	*2*	*3*	*0*	*9*	*14.3*	*-6.88*
Totals	**12**	**36**	**3**	**4**	**0**	**29**	**8.3**	**-9.88**
13-14	*9*	*25*	*2*	*1*	*1*	*21*	*8.0*	*+7.00*
12-13	*5*	*7*	*0*	*0*	*1*	*6*	*0.0*	*-7.00*

JOCKEYS

	W-R	Per cent	£1 Level Stake
Henry Brooke	1-3	33.3	+1.50
Miss A Waugh	1-9	11.1	+10.00
Ryan Mania	1-10	10.0	-7.38

COURSE RECORD

	Total W-R	Non-Hndcps Hurdles	Non-Hndcps Chases	Hndcps Hurdles	Hndcps Chases	NH Flat	Per cent	£1 Level Stake
Newcastle	2-6	0-0	0-0	1-2	1-3	0-1	33.3	+17.50
Mrket Rsn	1-4	0-0	0-0	0-0	1-3	0-1	25.0	-1.38

WINNING HORSES

Horse	Races Run	1st	2nd	3rd	£
Big George	5	1	1	0	2599
Boric	5	1	1	0	2599
*Newyearsresolution	7	1	1	0	2274

Total winning prize-money **£7472**

Favourites **1-3** **33.3%** **-0.38**

PAUL WEBBER

MOLLINGTON, OXON

	No. of Hrs	Races Run	1st	2nd	3rd	Unpl	Per cent	£1 Level Stake
NH Flat	*12*	*16*	*0*	*4*	*4*	*8*	*0.0*	*-16.00*
Hurdles	*36*	*85*	*2*	*7*	*4*	*72*	*2.4*	*-59.00*
Chases	*21*	*69*	*8*	*10*	*10*	*41*	*11.6*	*-6.88*
Totals	**52**	**170**	**10**	**21**	**18**	**121**	**5.9**	**-81.88**
13-14	*60*	*206*	*15*	*31*	*21*	*139*	*7.3*	*-120.13*
12-13	*64*	*192*	*18*	*21*	*17*	*136*	*9.4*	*-78.36*

BY MONTH

NH Flat	W-R	Per cent	£1 Level Stake	Hurdles	W-R	Per cent	£1 Level Stake
May	0-4	0.0	-4.00	May	1-11	9.1	-6.00
June	0-0	0.0	0.00	June	0-0	0.0	0.00
July	0-1	0.0	-1.00	July	0-7	0.0	-7.00
August	0-0	0.0	0.00	August	0-1	0.0	-1.00
September	0-0	0.0	0.00	September	0-1	0.0	-1.00
October	0-0	0.0	0.00	October	0-10	0.0	-10.00

November	0-2	0.0	-2.00	November	1-12	8.3	+9.00
December	0-0	0.0	0.00	December	0-13	0.0	-13.00
January	0-1	0.0	-1.00	January	0-9	0.0	-9.00
February	0-3	0.0	-3.00	February	0-9	0.0	-9.00
March	0-4	0.0	-4.00	March	0-5	0.0	-5.00
April	0-1	0.0	-1.00	April	0-7	0.0	-7.00

Chases	W-R	Per cent	£1 Level Stake	Totals	W-R	Per cent	£1 Level Stake
May	2-7	28.6	+7.00	May	3-22	13.6	-3.00
June	1-9	11.1	+12.00	June	1-9	11.1	+12.00
July	0-3	0.0	-3.00	July	0-11	0.0	-11.00
August	0-1	0.0	-1.00	August	0-2	0.0	-2.00
September	0-0	0.0	0.00	September	0-1	0.0	-1.00
October	0-4	0.0	-4.00	October	0-14	0.0	-14.00
November	0-9	0.0	-9.00	November	1-23	4.3	-2.00
December	3-13	23.1	+4.63	December	3-26	11.5	-8.37
January	0-9	0.0	-9.00	January	0-19	0.0	-19.00
February	0-6	0.0	-6.00	February	0-18	0.0	-18.00
March	1-6	16.7	-2.50	March	1-15	6.7	-11.50
April	1-2	50.0	+4.00	April	1-10	10.0	-4.00

DISTANCE

Hurdles	W-R	Per cent	£1 Level Stake	Chases	W-R	Per cent	£1 Level Stake
2m-2m3f	1-34	2.9	-13.00	2m-2m3f	2-12	16.7	+2.00
2m4f-2m7f	0-25	0.0	-25.00	2m4f-2m7f	4-25	16.0	+15.50
3m+	0-3	0.0	-3.00	3m+	2-18	11.1	-10.38

TYPE OF RACE

Non-Handicaps	W-R	Per cent	£1 Level Stake	Handicaps	W-R	Per cent	£1 Level Stake
Nov Hrdls	2-27	7.4	-1.00	Nov Hrdls	0-5	0.0	-5.00
Hrdls	0-28	0.0	-28.00	Hrdls	0-25	0.0	-25.00
Nov Chs	0-7	0.0	-7.00	Nov Chs	1-17	5.9	-7.00
Chases	0-1	0.0	-1.00	Chases	7-44	15.9	+8.13
Sell/Claim	0-0	0.0	0.00	Sell/Claim	0-0	0.0	0.00

RACE CLASS / FIRST TIME OUT

	W-R	Per cent	£1 Level Stake		W-R	Per cent	£1 Level Stake
Class 1	0-7	0.0	-7.00	Bumpers	0-12	0.0	-12.00
Class 2	1-8	12.5	+3.00	Hurdles	2-28	7.1	-2.00
Class 3	2-21	9.5	-13.38	Chases	2-12	16.7	+2.00
Class 4	7-85	8.2	-15.50				
Class 5	0-38	0.0	-38.00	Totals	4-52	7.7	-12.00
Class 6	0-11	0.0	-11.00				

JOCKEYS

	W-R	Per cent	£1 Level Stake
Liam Treadwell	5-53	9.4	+16.00
Denis O'Regan	2-19	10.5	-11.00
Mr M J P Kendrick	1-4	25.0	+1.00
Tom O'Brien	1-6	16.7	-2.50
Jake Greenall	1-11	9.1	-8.38

COURSE RECORD

	Total W-R	Non-Hndcps Hurdles	Non-Hndcps Chases	Hndcps Hurdles	Hndcps Chases	NH Flat	Per cent	£1 Level Stake
Kempton	2-12	0-3	0-0	0-2	2-7	0-0	16.7	+2.50
Leicester	2-13	1-4	0-0	0-0	1-9	0-0	15.4	+18.00
Sandown	1-4	0-1	0-0	0-2	1-1	0-0	25.0	+1.00
Stratford	1-7	0-2	0-0	0-0	1-4	0-1	14.3	+14.00
Worcester	1-8	0-5	0-0	0-1	1-2	0-0	12.5	-5.00
Doncaster	1-9	0-4	0-0	0-0	1-3	0-2	11.1	-6.38
Southwell	1-11	0-2	0-0	0-3	1-5	0-1	9.1	-5.00
Towcester	1-13	1-4	0-3	0-1	0-4	0-1	7.7	-8.00

WINNING HORSES

Horse	Races Run	1st	2nd	3rd	£
Australia Day	5	1	1	0	15640
Firm Order	5	1	1	1	9126
Sixty Something	6	1	0	1	6657
Rhapando	5	2	0	0	8447
Marley Roca	3	1	0	0	3899
Royalracket	4	1	0	0	3899
Fingers Crossed	5	1	0	0	3899
Lemon's Gent	3	1	1	0	3769
Run On Sterling	5	1	0	1	3119
Total winning prize-money					**£58455**
Favourites	**2-3**		**66.7%**		**2.63**

SIMON WEST

MIDDLEHAM MOOR, N YORKS

	No. of Hrs	Races Run	1st	2nd	3rd	Unpl	Per cent	£1 Level Stake
NH Flat	*5*	*9*	*0*	*0*	*1*	*8*	*0.0*	*-9.00*
Hurdles	*9*	*20*	*3*	*1*	*0*	*16*	*15.0*	*+12.88*
Chases	*0*	*0*	*0*	*0*	*0*	*0*	*0.0*	*0.00*
Totals	**12**	**29**	**3**	**1**	**1**	**24**	**10.3**	**+3.88**
13-14	*8*	*20*	*4*	*0*	*0*	*16*	*20.0*	*+34.50*
12-13	*12*	*41*	*1*	*2*	*2*	*36*	*2.4*	*-28.00*

JOCKEYS

	W-R	Per cent	£1 Level Stake
Joe Colliver	2-18	11.1	-4.13
Dougie Costello	1-3	33.3	+16.00

COURSE RECORD

	Total W-R	Non-Hndcps Hurdles	Non-Hndcps Chases	Hndcps Hurdles	Hndcps Chases	NH Flat	Per cent	£1 Level Stake
Carlisle	2-5	1-2	0-0	1-2	0-0	0-1	40.0	+25.00
Haydock	1-1	1-1	0-0	0-0	0-0	0-0	100.0	+1.88

WINNING HORSES

Horse	Races Run	1st	2nd	3rd	£
Captain Clayton	1	1	0	0	6498
Maximiser	2	2	0	0	9747

Total winning prize-money			**£16245**
Favourites	**0-0**	**0.0%**	**0.00**

SHEENA WEST

FALMER, E SUSSEX

	No. of Hrs	Races Run	1st	2nd	3rd	Unpl	Per cent	£1 Level Stake
NH Flat	*3*	*5*	*0*	*0*	*0*	*5*	*0.0*	*-5.00*
Hurdles	*11*	*45*	*2*	*5*	*9*	*29*	*4.4*	*-19.67*
Chases	*6*	*19*	*2*	*5*	*1*	*11*	*10.5*	*-6.50*
Totals	**16**	**69**	**4**	**10**	**10**	**45**	**5.8**	**-31.17**
13-14	*21*	*92*	*9*	*16*	*12*	*55*	*9.8*	*-10.17*
12-13	*23*	*71*	*10*	*17*	*8*	*36*	*14.1*	*-30.97*

JOCKEYS

	W-R	Per cent	£1 Level Stake
Marc Goldstein	4-59	6.8	-21.17

COURSE RECORD

	Total W-R	Non-Hndcps Hurdles	Non-Hndcps Chases	Hndcps Hurdles	Hndcps Chases	NH Flat	Per cent	£1 Level Stake
Plumpton	3-22	0-2	0-0	1-12	2-8	0-0	13.6	-5.17
Fontwell	1-16	0-1	0-1	1-10	0-2	0-2	6.3	+5.00

WINNING HORSES

Horse	Races Run	1st	2nd	3rd	£
Mr Muddle	5	1	2	0	9747
Hi Note	10	1	2	1	5393
Leg Iron	7	1	2	1	3899
Unidexter	6	1	1	0	2395
Total winning prize-money					**£21434**
Favourites	**0-5**		**0.0%**		**-5.00**

JESS WESTWOOD

MINEHEAD, SOMERSET

	No. of Hrs	Races Run	1st	2nd	3rd	Unpl	Per cent	£1 Level Stake
NH Flat	*3*	*3*	*0*	*1*	*0*	*2*	*0.0*	*-3.00*
Hurdles	*2*	*8*	*0*	*0*	*1*	*7*	*0.0*	*-8.00*
Chases	*1*	*4*	*1*	*1*	*1*	*1*	*25.0*	*+4.00*
Totals	**5**	**15**	**1**	**2**	**2**	**10**	**6.7**	**-7.00**
13-14	*5*	*13*	*0*	*0*	*1*	*12*	*0.0*	*-13.00*
12-13	*2*	*8*	*2*	*1*	*0*	*5*	*25.0*	*-1.00*

JOCKEYS

	W-R	Per cent	£1 Level Stake
Alice Mills	1-4	25.0	+4.00

COURSE RECORD

	Total W-R	Non-Hndcps Hurdles	Non-Hndcps Chases	Hndcps Hurdles	Hndcps Chases	NH Flat	Per cent	£1 Level Stake
Wincanton	1-3	0-0	0-0	0-0	1-2	0-1	33.3	+5.00

WINNING HORSES

Horse	Races Run	1st	2nd	3rd	£
Monkerty Tunkerty	4	1	1	1	12512
Total winning prize-money					**£12512**
Favourites	**0-0**		**0.0%**		**0.00**

JOHN WEYMES

MIDDLEHAM MOOR, N YORKS

	No. of Hrs	Races Run	1st	2nd	3rd	Unpl	Per cent	£1 Level Stake
NH Flat	*3*	*4*	*0*	*2*	*0*	*2*	*0.0*	*-4.00*
Hurdles	*6*	*8*	*1*	*1*	*0*	*6*	*12.5*	*-1.50*
Chases	*0*	*0*	*0*	*0*	*0*	*0*	*0.0*	*0.00*
Totals	**8**	**12**	**1**	**3**	**0**	**8**	**8.3**	**-5.50**
13-14	*6*	*14*	*0*	*1*	*1*	*12*	*0.0*	*-14.00*
12-13	*3*	*9*	*1*	*1*	*1*	*6*	*11.1*	*+42.00*

JOCKEYS

	W-R	Per cent	£1 Level Stake
Nathan Moscrop	1-2	50.0	+4.50

COURSE RECORD

	Total W-R	Non-Hndcps Hurdles	Non-Hndcps Chases	Hndcps Hurdles	Hndcps Chases	NH Flat	Per cent	£1 Level Stake
Stratford	1-4	1-2	0-0	0-1	0-0	0-1	25.0	+2.50

WINNING HORSES

Horse	Races Run	1st	2nd	3rd	£
Elizabeth Coffee	1	1	0	0	1949
Total winning prize-money					**£1949**
Favourites	**0-0**		**0.0%**		**0.00**

DONALD WHILLANS

HAWICK, BORDERS

	No. of Hrs	Races Run	1st	2nd	3rd	Unpl	Per cent	£1 Level Stake
NH Flat	*1*	*1*	*0*	*0*	*0*	*1*	*0.0*	*-1.00*
Hurdles	*9*	*41*	*6*	*8*	*3*	*24*	*14.6*	*-15.63*
Chases	*1*	*3*	*0*	*0*	*0*	*3*	*0.0*	*-3.00*
Totals	**11**	**45**	**6**	**8**	**3**	**28**	**13.3**	**-19.63**
13-14	*17*	*60*	*8*	*7*	*6*	*39*	*13.3*	*+22.25*
12-13	*19*	*78*	*4*	*8*	*8*	*58*	*5.1*	*-58.00*

JOCKEYS

	W-R	Per cent	£1 Level Stake
Callum Whillans	5-35	14.3	-12.00
Peter Buchanan	1-1	100.0	+1.38

COURSE RECORD

	Total W-R	Non-Hndcps Hurdles	Chases	Hndcps Hurdles	Chases	NH Flat	Per cent	£1 Level Stake
Sedgefield	2-3	0-0	0-0	2-3	0-0	0-0	66.7	+7.00
Ayr	1-1	0-0	0-0	1-1	0-0	0-0	100.0	+3.00
Musselbgh	1-4	0-0	0-0	1-4	0-0	0-0	25.0	0.00
Carlisle	1-6	1-1	0-0	0-4	0-1	0-0	16.7	-3.63
Kelso	1-7	1-4	0-0	0-3	0-0	0-0	14.3	-2.00

WINNING HORSES

Horse	Races Run	1st	2nd	3rd	£
Hartforth	6	1	1	0	3899
Snapping Turtle	8	2	2	2	6888
Shades Of Midnight	5	2	0	0	6823
Ellistrin Belle	4	1	0	0	2209
Total winning prize-money					**£19819**
Favourites	**2-2**		**100.0%**		**4.38**

ALISTAIR WHILLANS

NEWMILL-ON-SLITRIG, BORDERS

	No. of Hrs	Races Run	1st	2nd	3rd	Unpl	Per cent	£1 Level Stake
NH Flat	*8*	*16*	*0*	*1*	*1*	*14*	*0.0*	*-16.00*
Hurdles	*16*	*76*	*5*	*6*	*14*	*51*	*6.6*	*-26.67*
Chases	*5*	*20*	*4*	*3*	*1*	*12*	*20.0*	*+20.00*
Totals	**25**	**112**	**9**	**10**	**16**	**77**	**8.0**	**-22.67**
13-14	*33*	*103*	*6*	*12*	*10*	*75*	*5.8*	*-60.75*
12-13	*26*	*106*	*14*	*11*	*6*	*75*	*13.2*	*+13.00*

JOCKEYS

	W-R	Per cent	£1 Level Stake
Ewan Whillans	3-16	18.8	+7.00
Brian Harding	2-16	12.5	+8.00
Ryan Day	1-6	16.7	+2.00
Brian Hughes	1-9	11.1	-4.67
Craig Nichol	1-11	9.1	+6.00
Callum Whillans	1-24	4.2	-11.00

COURSE RECORD

	Total W-R	Non-Hndcps Hurdles	Chases	Hndcps Hurdles	Chases	NH Flat	Per cent	£1 Level Stake
Kelso	3-19	1-6	0-0	1-7	1-4	0-2	15.8	+3.33
Musselbgh	2-11	0-0	0-0	2-10	0-0	0-1	18.2	+10.00
Perth	2-19	0-3	0-0	0-8	2-7	0-1	10.5	-7.00
Haydock	1-2	0-0	0-0	0-0	1-2	0-0	50.0	+15.00
Catterick	1-3	0-0	0-0	1-3	0-0	0-0	33.3	+14.00

WINNING HORSES

Horse	Races Run	1st	2nd	3rd	£
Samstown	6	2	0	0	34323
Gleann Na Ndochais	10	3	2	1	11041
Apachee Prince	8	1	1	2	3899
Funky Munky	10	1	0	1	3249
Claude Carter	15	2	2	2	6498
Total winning prize-money					**£59010**
Favourites	**0-2**		**0.0%**		**-2.00**

ARTHUR WHITEHEAD

ASTON ON CLUN, SHROPSHIRE

	No. of Hrs	Races Run	1st	2nd	3rd	Unpl	Per cent	£1 Level Stake
NH Flat	*0*	*0*	*0*	*0*	*0*	*0*	*0.0*	*0.00*
Hurdles	*3*	*12*	*1*	*3*	*1*	*7*	*8.3*	*-7.67*
Chases	*0*	*0*	*0*	*0*	*0*	*0*	*0.0*	*0.00*
Totals	**3**	**12**	**1**	**3**	**1**	**7**	**8.3**	**-7.67**
13-14	*4*	*23*	*3*	*6*	*3*	*11*	*13.0*	*+11.00*
12-13	*5*	*22*	*1*	*1*	*2*	*18*	*4.5*	*-1.00*

JOCKEYS

W-R	cent	Per Stake	£1 Level
Josh Wall	1-9	11.1	-4.67

COURSE RECORD

	Total W-R	Non-Hndcps Hurdles	Chases	Hndcps Hurdles	Chases	NH Flat	Per cent	£1 Level Stake
Nton Abbot	1-2	0-0	0-0	1-2	0-0	0-0	50.0	+2.33

WINNING HORSES

Horse	Races Run	1st	2nd	3rd	£
Della Sun	4	1	0	1	3509
Total winning prize-money					**£3509**
Favourites	**1-2**		**50.0%**		**2.33**

ARTHUR WHITING

NORTH NIBLEY, GLOUCS

	No. of Hrs	Races Run	1st	2nd	3rd	Unpl	Per cent	£1 Level Stake
NH Flat	*0*	*0*	*0*	*0*	*0*	*0*	*0.0*	*0.00*
Hurdles	*3*	*13*	*1*	*2*	*0*	*10*	*7.7*	*+4.00*
Chases	*1*	*7*	*1*	*1*	*1*	*4*	*14.3*	*-3.00*
Totals	**4**	**20**	**2**	**3**	**1**	**14**	**10.0**	**+1.00**
13-14	*6*	*22*	*3*	*2*	*2*	*15*	*13.6*	*+8.88*
12-13	*6*	*26*	*1*	*0*	*3*	*22*	*3.8*	*-21.50*

JOCKEYS

	W-R	Per cent	£1 Level Stake
Conor Smith	1-2	50.0	+15.00
Nick Scholfield	1-8	12.5	-4.00

COURSE RECORD

	Total W-R	Non-Hndcps Hurdles	Chases	Hndcps Hurdles	Chases	NH Flat	Per cent	£1 Level Stake
Bangor	1-1	0-0	0-0	1-1	0-0	0-0	100.0	+16.00
Taunton	1-4	0-1	0-0	0-2	1-1	0-0	25.0	0.00

WINNING HORSES

Horse	Races Run	1st	2nd	3rd	£
Itsuptoyou	7	1	1	1	4549
The Wee Midget	5	1	0	0	2203
Total winning prize-money					**£6752**
Favourites	**0-1**		**0.0%**		**-1.00**

HARRY WHITTINGTON

SPARSHOLT, OXFORDSHIRE

	No. of Hrs	Races Run	1st	2nd	3rd	Unpl	Per cent	£1 Level Stake
NH Flat	*4*	*4*	*0*	*0*	*1*	*3*	*0.0*	*-4.00*
Hurdles	*7*	*32*	*7*	*4*	*2*	*19*	*21.9*	*+29.44*
Chases	*2*	*6*	*1*	*0*	*4*	*1*	*16.7*	*-3.00*
Totals	**12**	**42**	**8**	**4**	**7**	**23**	**19.0**	**+22.44**
13-14	*10*	*31*	*2*	*3*	*5*	*21*	*6.5*	*-22.75*
12-13	*6*	*14*	*3*	*1*	*1*	*9*	*21.4*	*+44.00*

JOCKEYS

	W-R	Per cent	£1 Level Stake
Paul N O'Brien	3-17	17.6	+4.94
Gavin Sheehan	2-3	66.7	+26.50
Michael Byrne	2-13	15.4	-4.50
Richard Johnson	1-1	100.0	+3.50

COURSE RECORD

	Total W-R	Non-Hndcps Hurdles	Non-Hndcps Chases	Hndcps Hurdles	Hndcps Chases	NH Flat	Per cent	£1 Level Stake
Chepstow	2-4	1-2	0-0	0-0	1-2	0-0	50.0	+0.44
Plumpton	2-4	1-2	0-0	1-2	0-0	0-0	50.0	+3.00
Ludlow	2-5	2-4	0-0	0-1	0-0	0-0	40.0	+26.50
Kempton	1-3	1-2	0-0	0-1	0-0	0-0	33.3	+1.50
Newbury	1-4	1-1	0-0	0-2	0-1	0-0	25.0	+13.00

WINNING HORSES

Horse	Races Run	1st	2nd	3rd	£
*Drifter	5	1	0	0	3899
*Bishop Wulstan	8	2	2	0	3899
Arzal	6	2	1	1	7798
Fourovakind	5	1	0	4	3769
Qasser	4	1	1	0	3444
*Mollasses	3	1	0	1	3249
Total winning prize-money					**£26058**
Favourites	**3-8**		**37.5%**		**-0.06**

IAN WILLIAMS

PORTWAY, WORCS

	No. of Hrs	Races Run	1st	2nd	3rd	Unpl	Per cent	£1 Level Stake
NH Flat	*4*	*8*	*0*	*0*	*1*	*7*	*0.0*	*-8.00*
Hurdles	*42*	*107*	*12*	*10*	*7*	*78*	*11.2*	*-21.75*
Chases	*20*	*76*	*9*	*11*	*9*	*47*	*11.8*	*-21.25*
Totals	**49**	**191**	**21**	**21**	**17**	**132**	**11.0**	**-51.00**
13-14	*47*	*193*	*29*	*28*	*22*	*114*	*15.0*	*-41.93*
12-13	*51*	*111*	*9*	*7*	*15*	*80*	*8.1*	*-44.00*

BY MONTH

NH Flat	W-R	Per cent	£1 Level Stake	Hurdles	W-R	Per cent	£1 Level Stake
May	0-0	0.0	0.00	May	1-14	7.1	-8.50
June	0-0	0.0	0.00	June	1-10	10.0	-7.25
July	0-0	0.0	0.00	July	0-4	0.0	-4.00
August	0-1	0.0	-1.00	August	2-8	25.0	+4.25
September	0-1	0.0	-1.00	September	3-6	50.0	+3.75
October	0-0	0.0	0.00	October	0-11	0.0	-11.00
November	0-0	0.0	0.00	November	1-12	8.3	+1.00
December	0-0	0.0	0.00	December	0-9	0.0	-9.00
January	0-0	0.0	0.00	January	0-8	0.0	-8.00
February	0-0	0.0	0.00	February	0-7	0.0	-7.00
March	0-1	0.0	-1.00	March	3-13	23.1	+14.00
April	0-5	0.0	-5.00	April	1-5	20.0	+10.00

Chases	W-R	Per cent	£1 Level Stake	Totals	W-R	Per cent	£1 Level Stake
May	0-4	0.0	-4.00	May	1-18	5.6	-12.50
June	0-4	0.0	-4.00	June	1-14	7.1	-11.25
July	0-0	0.0	0.00	July	0-4	0.0	-4.00
August	3-8	37.5	+5.00	August	5-17	29.4	+8.25
September	0-4	0.0	-4.00	September	3-11	27.3	-1.25
October	1-8	12.5	-2.00	October	1-19	5.3	-13.00
November	0-10	0.0	-10.00	November	1-22	4.5	-9.00
December	1-6	16.7	0.00	December	1-15	6.7	-9.00
January	0-4	0.0	-4.00	January	0-12	0.0	-12.00
February	2-6	33.3	+2.75	February	2-13	15.4	-4.25
March	2-13	15.4	+8.00	March	5-27	18.5	+21.00
April	0-9	0.0	-9.00	April	1-19	5.3	-4.00

DISTANCE

Hurdles	W-R	Per cent	£1 Level Stake	Chases	W-R	Per cent	£1 Level Stake
2m-2m3f	4-50	8.0	-28.25	2m-2m3f	2-17	11.8	-6.00
2m4f-2m7f	2-24	8.3	-4.75	2m4f-2m7f	6-32	18.8	+5.75
3m+	2-8	25.0	-2.75	3m+	0-16	0.0	-16.00

TYPE OF RACE

Non-Handicaps	W-R	Per cent	£1 Level Stake	Handicaps	W-R	Per cent	£1 Level Stake
Nov Hrdls	1-17	5.9	-14.75	Nov Hrdls	0-5	0.0	-5.00
Hrdls	3-20	15.0	+3.25	Hrdls	8-63	12.7	-3.25
Nov Chs	1-3	33.3	0.00	Nov Chs	2-26	7.7	-5.00
Chases	0-1	0.0	-1.00	Chases	6-46	13.0	-15.25
Sell/Claim	0-2	0.0	-2.00	Sell/Claim	0-0	0.0	0.00

RACE CLASS / FIRST TIME OUT

RACE CLASS	W-R	Per cent	£1 Level Stake	FIRST TIME OUT	W-R	Per cent	£1 Level Stake
Class 1	0-8	0.0	-8.00	Bumpers	0-4	0.0	-4.00
Class 2	1-12	8.3	-8.75	Hurdles	3-36	8.3	-6.50

Class 3	8-52	15.4	-7.00	Chases	0-9	0.0	-9.00
Class 4	8-79	10.1	-21.75				
Class 5	4-36	11.1	-1.50	Totals	3-49	6.1	-19.50
Class 6	0-4	0.0	-4.00				

JOCKEYS

	W-R	Per cent	£1 Level Stake
Will Kennedy	9-74	12.2	-15.75
Richard Johnson	5-16	31.3	+10.75
Rob McCarth	3-57	5.3	-42.00
Tom O'Brien	1-2	50.0	+13.00
Jason Maguire	1-3	33.3	+3.00
Maurice Linehan	1-3	33.3	+10.00
A P McCoy	1-6	16.7	0.00

COURSE RECORD

	Total W-R	Non-Hndcps Hurdles	Non-Hndcps Chases	Hndcps Hurdles	Hndcps Chases	NH Flat	Per cent	£1 Level Stake
Plumpton	3-5	1-1	0-0	2-2	0-2	0-0	60.0	+17.50
Cartmel	2-2	0-0	0-0	1-1	1-1	0-0	100.0	+6.75
Nton Abbot	2-5	1-1	0-0	1-4	0-0	0-0	40.0	+4.25
Worcester	2-8	0-3	0-0	1-3	1-2	0-0	25.0	+5.50
Ludlow	2-10	1-4	0-0	1-5	0-1	0-0	20.0	+8.50
Huntingdon	2-12	0-2	0-0	0-4	2-6	0-0	16.7	0.00
Kempton	1-5	0-1	0-0	1-1	0-2	0-1	20.0	-2.00
Leicester	1-5	0-0	0-0	0-1	1-4	0-0	20.0	-1.25
Fontwell	1-6	0-1	1-1	0-3	0-0	0-1	16.7	-3.00
Warwick	1-6	0-0	0-0	1-2	0-3	0-1	16.7	+11.00
Doncaster	1-7	0-2	0-0	0-2	1-3	0-0	14.3	-2.00
Wetherby	1-10	0-2	0-0	0-4	1-4	0-0	10.0	-4.00
Stratford	1-12	0-4	0-0	0-1	1-7	0-0	8.3	+3.00
Uttoxeter	1-14	1-3	0-0	0-8	0-3	0-0	7.1	-11.25

WINNING HORSES

Horse	Races Run	1st	2nd	3rd	£
Teak	5	2	1	1	21522
*Cool Sky	3	2	0	0	14077
Drumlang	10	2	1	1	11859
Bobcatbilly	8	2	0	0	14296
Fredo	6	1	1	1	7473
A Tail Of Intrigue	16	3	3	1	12505
Etania	8	1	3	0	5198
Mandy's Boy	8	1	1	0	4549
Kapstadt	5	1	0	0	3899
Grand Gigolo	4	1	0	0	3899
Leath Acra Mor	5	1	2	1	3861
Howaboutnow	3	1	0	1	3249
Donapollo	7	1	1	1	3249
Poker School	7	1	2	0	3249
Faithful Mount	1	1	0	0	2599
Total winning prize-money					**£115484**
Favourites	**6-20**		**30.0%**		**-1.25**

NICK WILLIAMS

GEORGE NYMPTON, DEVON

	No. of Hrs	Races Run	1st	2nd	3rd	Unpl	Per cent	£1 Level Stake
NH Flat	*3*	*5*	*1*	*1*	*0*	*3*	*20.0*	*+0.50*
Hurdles	*20*	*65*	*11*	*10*	*9*	*35*	*16.9*	*-0.46*
Chases	*11*	*44*	*1*	*2*	*9*	*32*	*2.3*	*-41.90*
Totals	**30**	**114**	**13**	**13**	**18**	**70**	**11.4**	**-41.86**
13-14	*39*	*128*	*23*	*19*	*10*	*76*	*18.0*	*+44.68*
12-13	*39*	*121*	*20*	*13*	*17*	*71*	*16.5*	*-19.53*

BY MONTH

NH Flat	W-R	Per cent	£1 Level Stake	Hurdles	W-R	Per cent	£1 Level Stake
May	0-0	0.0	0.00	May	0-3	0.0	-3.00
June	0-0	0.0	0.00	June	0-2	0.0	-2.00
July	0-0	0.0	0.00	July	0-2	0.0	-2.00
August	0-0	0.0	0.00	August	0-0	0.0	0.00
September	0-0	0.0	0.00	September	0-0	0.0	0.00
October	0-0	0.0	0.00	October	1-5	20.0	-2.38
November	0-1	0.0	-1.00	November	1-8	12.5	+2.00
December	1-1	100.0	+4.50	December	4-12	33.3	+13.17
January	0-0	0.0	0.00	January	3-12	25.0	+0.75
February	0-1	0.0	-1.00	February	1-11	9.1	-5.00
March	0-2	0.0	-2.00	March	0-7	0.0	-7.00
April	0-0	0.0	0.00	April	1-3	33.3	+5.00

Chases	W-R	Per cent	£1 Level Stake	Totals	W-R	Per cent	£1 Level Stake
May	0-1	0.0	-1.00	May	0-4	0.0	-4.00
June	0-0	0.0	0.00	June	0-2	0.0	-2.00
July	0-0	0.0	0.00	July	0-2	0.0	-2.00
August	0-1	0.0	-1.00	August	0-1	0.0	-1.00
September	0-4	0.0	-4.00	September	0-4	0.0	-4.00
October	0-9	0.0	-9.00	October	1-14	7.1	-11.38
November	0-6	0.0	-6.00	November	1-15	6.7	-5.00
December	1-6	16.7	-3.90	December	6-19	31.6	+13.77
January	0-8	0.0	-8.00	January	3-20	15.0	-7.25
February	0-4	0.0	-4.00	February	1-16	6.3	-10.00
March	0-3	0.0	-3.00	March	0-12	0.0	-12.00
April	0-2	0.0	-2.00	April	1-5	20.0	+3.00

DISTANCE

Hurdles	W-R	Per cent	£1 Level Stake	Chases	W-R	Per cent	£1 Level Stake
2m-2m3f	3-19	15.8	+3.00	2m-2m3f	0-18	0.0	-18.00
2m4f-2m7f	4-15	26.7	+0.38	2m4f-2m7f	1-10	10.0	-7.90
3m+	2-5	40.0	+12.50	3m+	0-9	0.0	-9.00

TYPE OF RACE

Non-Handicaps	W-R	Per cent	£1 Level Stake	Handicaps	W-R	Per cent	£1 Level Stake
Nov Hrdls	4-11	36.4	+6.04	Nov Hrdls	0-3	0.0	-3.00
Hrdls	1-15	6.7	-7.50	Hrdls	5-34	14.7	+1.50

Nov Chs	1-3	33.3	-0.90	Nov Chs	0-6	0.0	-6.00
Chases	0-0	0.0	0.00	Chases	0-35	0.0	-35.00
Sell/Claim	1-1	100.0	+3.50	Sell/Claim	0-1	0.0	-1.00

RACE CLASS

	W-R	Per cent	£1 Level Stake
Class 1	3-28	10.7	-5.00
Class 2	1-17	5.9	-11.00
Class 3	0-26	0.0	-26.00
Class 4	7-34	20.6	-0.86
Class 5	1-7	14.3	-2.50
Class 6	1-2	50.0	+3.50

FIRST TIME OUT

	W-R	Per cent	£1 Level Stake
Bumpers	0-3	0.0	-3.00
Hurdles	3-16	18.8	+4.13
Chases	0-11	0.0	-11.00
Totals	3-30	10.0	-9.87

JOCKEYS

	W-R	Per cent	£1 Level Stake
Lizzie Kelly	8-40	20.0	+2.39
Davy Russell	1-1	100.0	+4.50
Noel Fehily	1-3	33.3	+3.00
A P McCoy	1-7	14.3	-4.25
Richard Johnson	1-15	6.7	-7.00
Daryl Jacob	1-17	5.9	-9.50

COURSE RECORD

	Total W-R	Non-Hndcps Hurdles	Non-Hndcps Chases	Hndcps Hurdles	Hndcps Chases	NH Flat	Per cent	£1 Level Stake
Towcester	2-3	1-1	1-1	0-0	0-0	0-1	66.7	+0.77
Kempton	2-5	1-2	0-0	1-1	0-2	0-0	40.0	+3.13
Taunton	2-10	0-2	0-0	2-5	0-2	0-1	20.0	+2.00
Wincanton	2-11	1-2	0-0	1-4	0-5	0-0	18.2	-0.25
Leicester	1-3	1-1	0-0	0-0	0-2	0-0	33.3	+1.50
Haydock	1-4	0-0	0-0	1-3	0-1	0-0	25.0	+6.00
Ascot	1-5	1-4	0-0	0-1	0-0	0-0	20.0	+2.50
Exeter	1-8	1-3	0-0	0-3	0-2	0-0	12.5	+2.00
Newbury	1-8	0-1	0-1	0-2	0-3	1-1	12.5	-2.50

WINNING HORSES

Horse	Races Run	1st	2nd	3rd	£
Reve De Sivola	3	1	1	0	56270
Aubusson	5	1	1	1	45560
Tea For Two	6	3	1	1	32775
Fox Norton	2	1	0	0	11078
Dolores Delightful	5	1	2	1	3899
Horatio Hornblower	5	1	0	2	3769
After Eight Sivola	6	2	0	1	6823
*Queen Of The Stage	4	1	1	1	3249
Wayward Frolic	4	1	0	0	2599
Amour D'Or	3	1	0	0	1711
Total winning prize-money					**£167733**

Favourites	**3-20**	**15.0%**	**-13.48**

EVAN WILLIAMS

LLANCARFAN, VALE OF GLAMORGAN

	No. of Hrs	Races Run	1st	2nd	3rd	Unpl	Per cent	£1 Level Stake
NH Flat	*24*	*35*	*5*	*4*	*6*	*20*	*14.3*	*+1.91*
Hurdles	*59*	*186*	*32*	*22*	*25*	*107*	*17.2*	*+20.13*
Chases	*47*	*191*	*26*	*32*	*34*	*99*	*13.6*	*-77.34*
Totals	**94**	**412**	**63**	**58**	**65**	**226**	**15.3**	**-55.30**
13-14	*96*	*418*	*55*	*52*	*59*	*252*	*13.2*	*-57.64*
12-13	*120*	*508*	*57*	*63*	*65*	*322*	*11.2*	*-163.33*

BY MONTH

NH Flat	W-R	Per cent	£1 Level Stake
May	0-1	0.0	-1.00
June	0-0	0.0	0.00
July	0-0	0.0	0.00
August	0-1	0.0	-1.00
September	0-1	0.0	-1.00
October	0-2	0.0	-2.00
November	0-4	0.0	-4.00
December	1-6	16.7	+7.00
January	2-6	33.3	+10.50
February	1-2	50.0	-0.09
March	1-8	12.5	-2.50
April	0-4	0.0	-4.00

Hurdles	W-R	Per cent	£1 Level Stake
May	2-15	13.3	+17.00
June	0-11	0.0	-11.00
July	2-9	22.2	+1.10
August	3-9	33.3	+10.00
September	2-7	28.6	-3.77
October	6-17	35.3	+10.70
November	3-22	13.6	-7.75
December	3-21	14.3	+17.00
January	4-23	17.4	+7.00
February	3-20	15.0	-8.86
March	2-17	11.8	-6.20
April	2-15	13.3	-5.09

Chases	W-R	Per cent	£1 Level Stake
May	3-21	14.3	+2.50
June	1-13	7.7	-10.00
July	1-11	9.1	-4.50
August	3-19	15.8	-2.50
September	3-7	42.9	+2.25
October	4-17	23.5	-4.84
November	3-21	14.3	-11.75
December	2-19	10.5	-13.38
January	2-16	12.5	-6.00
February	1-9	11.1	-3.00
March	2-19	10.5	-12.13
April	1-19	5.3	-14.00

Totals	W-R	Per cent	£1 Level Stake
May	5-37	13.5	+18.50
June	1-24	4.2	-21.00
July	3-20	15.0	-3.40
August	6-29	20.7	+6.50
September	5-15	33.3	-2.52
October	10-36	27.8	+3.86
November	6-47	12.8	-23.50
December	6-46	13.0	+10.62
January	8-45	17.8	+11.50
February	5-31	16.1	-11.95
March	5-44	11.4	-20.83
April	3-38	7.9	-23.09

DISTANCE

Hurdles	W-R	Per cent	£1 Level Stake
2m-2m3f	15-83	18.1	+37.83
2m4f-2m7f	10-50	20.0	-6.52
3m+	0-3	0.0	-3.00

Chases	W-R	Per cent	£1 Level Stake
2m-2m3f	14-68	20.6	-6.13
2m4f-2m7f	5-57	8.8	-37.88
3m+	3-33	9.1	-21.09

TYPE OF RACE

Non-Handicaps

	W-R	Per cent	£1 Level Stake
Nov Hrdls	11-47	23.4	-3.57
Hrdls	5-38	13.2	-5.30

Handicaps

	W-R	Per cent	£1 Level Stake
Nov Hrdls	0-4	0.0	-4.00
Hrdls	16-95	16.8	+35.00

Nov Chs	3-15	20.0	-6.50	Nov Chs	4-36	11.1	-20.25
Chases	0-6	0.0	-6.00	Chases	19-134	14.2	-44.59
Sell/Claim	0-0	0.0	0.00	Sell/Claim	0-1	0.0	-1.00

RACE CLASS

	W-R	Per cent	£1 Level Stake
Class 1	1-36	2.8	-10.00
Class 2	2-43	4.7	-32.50
Class 3	18-103	17.5	+17.75
Class 4	33-152	21.7	-6.11
Class 5	6-59	10.2	-31.35
Class 6	3-19	15.8	+6.91

FIRST TIME OUT

	W-R	Per cent	£1 Level Stake
Bumpers	3-24	12.5	+5.50
Hurdles	8-43	18.6	+7.91
Chases	5-27	18.5	-5.00
Totals	16-94	17.0	+8.41

JOCKEYS

	W-R	Per cent	£1 Level Stake
Paul Moloney	40-210	19.0	+6.48
Adam Wedge	13-124	10.5	-32.34
Conor Ring	6-55	10.9	-32.44
Lewis Gordon	3-7	42.9	+14.00
Mr Conor Orr	1-12	8.3	-7.00

COURSE RECORD

	Total W-R	Non-Hndcps Hurdles	Non-Hndcps Chases	Hndcps Hurdles	Hndcps Chases	NH Flat	Per cent	£1 Level Stake
Ffos Las	15-86	4-20	0-1	5-25	3-30	3-10	17.4	+6.80
Ludlow	11-62	3-15	1-1	1-13	4-27	2-6	17.7	-11.43
Nton Abbot	6-31	2-6	1-4	0-5	3-15	0-1	19.4	-15.86
Chepstow	6-32	0-6	0-1	1-13	5-11	0-1	18.8	-3.88
Taunton	4-14	1-2	0-0	2-5	1-6	0-1	28.6	+14.00
Stratford	3-12	1-2	0-0	1-1	1-7	0-2	25.0	+6.00
Huntingdon	2-3	1-1	0-0	0-0	1-1	0-1	66.7	+2.16
Cartmel	2-5	0-0	0-1	0-1	2-3	0-0	40.0	+11.50
Warwick	2-6	1-1	0-1	0-0	1-1	0-3	33.3	-1.45
Mrket Rsn	2-8	0-0	0-1	1-1	1-6	0-0	25.0	+6.50
Uttoxeter	2-9	0-3	0-1	2-3	0-2	0-0	22.2	+5.00
Haydock	2-13	0-2	0-0	2-3	0-7	0-1	15.4	+21.00
Ayr	1-2	0-0	0-0	0-0	1-2	0-0	50.0	+0.75
Fontwell	1-6	1-1	0-0	0-2	0-3	0-0	16.7	-2.00
Bangor	1-10	1-4	0-0	0-1	0-3	0-2	10.0	-7.90
Newbury	1-10	1-2	0-0	0-3	0-2	0-3	10.0	+11.00
Ascot	1-13	0-3	0-0	1-4	0-5	0-1	7.7	-10.00
Cheltenham	1-24	0-3	1-4	0-6	0-11	0-0	4.2	-21.50

WINNING HORSES

Horse	Races Run	1st	2nd	3rd	£
Ballyglasheen	7	1	0	1	34170
On Tour	6	3	1	0	34863
Court Minstrel	6	2	0	0	16457
Zarzal	8	1	1	0	11394
Firebird Flyer	8	2	0	1	15508
Bullet Street	9	2	1	1	12432
Definite Dream	4	2	0	0	11696
Dark Spirit	6	2	2	0	13226
It's A Steal	6	2	2	0	12996
Get It On	8	3	0	0	15270
Makethe Mostofnow	8	1	0	0	6498
Oscar Sunset	5	2	2	0	12021
Going Concern	9	3	0	2	14296
Buck Mulligan	7	1	2	2	6330
Hold Court	9	1	1	1	5848
Tornado In Milan	5	1	1	0	5848
Vinnie Red	4	1	1	1	5848
De Faoithesdream	5	1	1	0	5393
Abbeygrey	12	2	2	1	6879
Sublime Talent	11	1	4	2	4224
Copper Birch	8	1	0	3	4224
Padge	4	1	2	1	4224
Wychwoods Brook	5	1	0	1	4159
Allez Vic	6	1	2	1	4029
Upsanddowns	5	2	1	1	6636
Buywise	5	2	0	0	7798
Islandmagee	7	2	0	3	7630
Timesawastin	7	1	2	1	3769
Traditional Bob	3	1	0	0	3769
Mac Le Couteau	8	2	1	2	5718
Lava Lamp	7	1	0	2	3249
Laser Hawk	3	1	0	1	3249
Bonobo	9	2	0	1	6498
Forgivienne	4	1	1	2	3249
John Constable	2	2	0	0	5848
King's Odyssey	4	1	2	0	3249
Armchair Theatre	3	2	0	0	6498
*Cape Caster	4	1	0	1	3119
Clyne	3	1	0	1	3119
Maxanisi	1	1	0	0	1949
Nansaroy	2	1	0	0	1560
Wabanaki	3	1	1	0	1560

Total winning prize-money **£346300**

Favourites **20-62** **32.3%** **-17.15**

NOEL WILLIAMS

BLEWBURY, OXON

	No. of Hrs	Races Run	1st	2nd	3rd	Unpl	Per cent	£1 Level Stake
NH Flat	*8*	*17*	*1*	*5*	*1*	*10*	*5.9*	*-7.50*
Hurdles	*7*	*32*	*1*	*6*	*3*	*22*	*3.1*	*-23.00*
Chases	*1*	*4*	*1*	*0*	*1*	*2*	*25.0*	*+6.00*
Totals	**11**	**53**	**3**	**11**	**5**	**34**	**5.7**	**-24.50**
13-14	*8*	*14*	*2*	*1*	*1*	*10*	*14.3*	*+7.00*

JOCKEYS

	W-R	Per cent	£1 Level Stake
James Banks	3-33	9.1	-4.50

COURSE RECORD

	Total W-R	Non-Hndcps Hurdles	Non-Hndcps Chases	Hndcps Hurdles	Hndcps Chases	NH Flat	Per cent	£1 Level Stake
Ffos Las	1-1	0-0	0-0	0-0	0-0	1-1	100.0	+8.50

Newbury	1-2	0-0	0-0	1-1	0-0	0-1	50.0	+7.00
Fontwell	1-6	0-1	0-0	0-3	1-2	0-0	16.7	+4.00

WINNING HORSES

Horse	Races Run	1st	2nd	3rd	£
Friendly Society	12	1	2	1	3899
Krackatoa King	6	1	3	1	3899
King Kayf	3	1	1	0	2053
Total winning prize-money					**£9851**
Favourites	**0-3**		**0.0%**		**-3.00**

VENETIA WILLIAMS

KINGS CAPLE, H'FORDS

	No. of Hrs	Races Run	1st	2nd	3rd	Unpl	Per cent	£1 Level Stake
NH Flat	*4*	*6*	*1*	*0*	*1*	*4*	*16.7*	*-1.50*
Hurdles	*55*	*152*	*17*	*11*	*23*	*101*	*11.2*	*-75.33*
Chases	*70*	*290*	*35*	*37*	*37*	*181*	*12.1*	*-80.59*
Totals	**113**	**448**	**53**	**48**	**61**	**286**	**11.8**	**-157.42**
13-14	*120*	*568*	*86*	*73*	*72*	*337*	*15.1*	*-136.64*
12-13	*110*	*537*	*92*	*74*	*65*	*304*	*17.1*	*-28.83*

BY MONTH

NH Flat	W-R	Per cent	£1 Level Stake	Hurdles	W-R	Per cent	£1 Level Stake
May	0-1	0.0	-1.00	May	2-9	22.2	-4.50
June	0-0	0.0	0.00	June	0-0	0.0	0.00
July	0-0	0.0	0.00	July	0-1	0.0	-1.00
August	0-0	0.0	0.00	August	0-0	0.0	0.00
September	0-0	0.0	0.00	September	0-1	0.0	-1.00
October	1-1	100.0	+3.50	October	1-9	11.1	+12.00
November	0-1	0.0	-1.00	November	4-38	10.5	-22.25
December	0-0	0.0	0.00	December	2-19	10.5	-13.43
January	0-2	0.0	-2.00	January	5-19	26.3	-2.15
February	0-1	0.0	-1.00	February	0-24	0.0	-24.00
March	0-0	0.0	0.00	March	3-28	10.7	-15.00
April	0-0	0.0	0.00	April	0-4	0.0	-4.00

Chases	W-R	Per cent	£1 Level Stake	Totals	W-R	Per cent	£1 Level Stake
May	1-11	9.1	0.00	May	3-21	14.3	-5.50
June	1-4	25.0	+11.00	June	1-4	25.0	+11.00
July	1-1	100.0	+0.67	July	1-2	50.0	-0.33
August	0-2	0.0	-2.00	August	0-2	0.0	-2.00
September	0-1	0.0	-1.00	September	0-2	0.0	-2.00
October	1-8	12.5	-1.50	October	3-18	16.7	+14.00
November	13-47	27.7	+41.08	November	17-86	19.8	+17.83
December	7-51	13.7	-9.90	December	9-70	12.9	-23.33
January	4-58	6.9	-39.17	January	9-79	11.4	-43.32
February	2-41	4.9	-33.09	February	2-66	3.0	-58.09
March	3-42	7.1	-29.43	March	6-70	8.6	-44.43
April	2-24	8.3	-17.25	April	2-28	7.1	-21.25

DISTANCE

Hurdles	W-R	Per cent	£1 Level Stake	Chases	W-R	Per cent	£1 Level Stake
2m-2m3f	14-74	18.9	-7.43	2m-2m3f	7-53	13.2	-7.34
2m4f-2m7f	1-33	3.0	-30.13	2m4f-2m7f	7-76	9.2	-37.08
3m+	0-3	0.0	-3.00	3m+	12-114	10.5	-24.33

TYPE OF RACE

Non-Handicaps	W-R	Per cent	£1 Level Stake	Handicaps	W-R	Per cent	£1 Level Stake
Nov Hrdls	8-37	21.6	+2.30	Nov Hrdls	0-9	0.0	-9.00
Hrdls	3-25	12.0	-17.50	Hrdls	5-80	6.3	-53.00
Nov Chs	6-16	37.5	+5.40	Nov Chs	8-60	13.3	+5.25
Chases	0-10	0.0	-10.00	Chases	21-204	10.3	-81.23
Sell/Claim	0-0	0.0	0.00	Sell/Claim	0-0	0.0	0.00

RACE CLASS / FIRST TIME OUT

Race Class	W-R	Per cent	£1 Level Stake	First Time Out	W-R	Per cent	£1 Level Stake
Class 1	4-65	6.2	-29.00	Bumpers	1-4	25.0	+0.50
Class 2	4-69	5.8	-46.00	Hurdles	5-52	9.6	-20.25
Class 3	15-132	11.4	-54.51	Chases	11-57	19.3	+28.50
Class 4	27-155	17.4	-14.28				
Class 5	2-22	9.1	-13.13	Totals	17-113	15.0	+8.75
Class 6	1-5	20.0	-0.50				

JOCKEYS

	W-R	Per cent	£1 Level Stake
Aidan Coleman	31-263	11.8	-75.94
Liam Treadwell	16-120	13.3	-41.85
Callum Whillans	4-28	14.3	-11.38
Mr J S Knox	1-3	33.3	+3.50
Alain Cawley	1-11	9.1	-8.75

COURSE RECORD

	Total W-R	Non-Hndcps Hurdles	Non-Hndcps Chases	Hndcps Hurdles	Hndcps Chases	NH Flat	Per cent	£1 Level Stake
Fontwell	4-10	1-2	0-0	1-1	2-7	0-0	40.0	+22.75
Carlisle	4-11	1-3	1-1	0-2	1-4	1-1	36.4	+13.63
Warwick	4-16	2-3	0-0	0-3	2-10	0-0	25.0	-0.17
Ascot	4-23	0-1	0-0	2-4	2-18	0-0	17.4	+5.25
Ludlow	4-31	0-8	0-1	0-5	4-17	0-0	12.9	-13.15
Mrket Rsn	3-8	0-1	0-0	0-2	3-5	0-0	37.5	+2.25
Kempton	3-14	1-2	1-1	0-3	1-8	0-0	21.4	+5.25
Bangor	3-15	0-2	0-0	0-3	3-10	0-0	20.0	-1.50
Uttoxeter	3-20	1-3	0-0	1-6	1-11	0-0	15.0	-2.13
Chepstow	3-23	1-5	0-0	0-6	2-12	0-0	13.0	-4.13
Huntingdon	2-9	0-1	1-1	0-2	1-5	0-0	22.2	-2.59
Towcester	2-12	0-0	1-2	0-5	1-5	0-0	16.7	-8.60
Taunton	2-13	2-4	0-0	0-4	0-5	0-0	15.4	-8.18
Worcester	1-6	0-1	1-2	0-1	0-2	0-0	16.7	-4.33
Doncaster	1-7	0-0	0-2	0-0	1-5	0-0	14.3	-1.00
Lingfield	1-9	0-1	0-0	0-2	1-6	0-0	11.1	-5.00
Leicester	1-10	0-2	1-1	0-2	0-5	0-0	10.0	-7.00
Nton Abbot	1-10	1-3	0-0	0-2	0-5	0-0	10.0	+11.00
Plumpton	1-11	0-1	0-1	1-4	0-5	0-0	9.1	-6.50

Ffos Las	1-14	0-1	0-0	0-1	1-11	0-1	7.1	-10.50
Wincanton	1-17	1-2	0-0	0-2	0-13	0-0	5.9	-15.27
Haydock	1-18	1-3	0-1	0-4	0-10	0-0	5.6	-15.50
Exeter	1-22	0-3	0-2	0-6	1-10	0-1	4.5	-14.00
Sandown	1-27	0-2	0-4	0-5	1-15	0-1	3.7	-23.00
Cheltenham	1-32	0-2	0-4	0-7	1-19	0-0	3.1	-15.00

WINNING HORSES

Horse	Races Run	1st	2nd	3rd	£
Niceonefrankie	3	2	0	0	72590
Emperor's Choice	4	1	1	0	56950
Baradari	6	1	0	1	28475
Aachen	5	1	0	1	18768
Gardefort	2	1	0	1	16245
Aso	7	3	0	2	23134
Brick Red	6	1	2	0	15640
Howard's Legacy	7	1	1	1	14243
Gorgehous Lliege	5	1	1	0	12660
Ballyoliver	6	1	0	1	12512
Leviathan	7	1	0	0	12512
Richmond	3	1	0	0	9986
Tenor Nivernais	7	1	0	0	9747
Vivaccio	7	2	0	1	17091
Royal Palladium	7	3	0	0	18479
The Clock Leary	2	1	0	0	7535
Union Jack D'Ycy	7	1	1	0	7032
Rocky Bender	5	1	1	0	6657
Abundantly	4	2	1	0	10722
Upepito	6	1	1	2	6498
Tango De Juilley	7	3	2	0	17656
Russborough	5	1	1	1	6498
Arthur's Oak	4	1	0	1	6498
Dubawi Island	5	1	0	0	5697
Otago Trail	4	2	1	1	8772
*Cash And Go	4	2	0	0	9858
Burtons Well	3	1	1	0	5064
Monetary Fund	6	1	1	1	4327
Take The Mick	5	1	1	0	4224
Market Option	4	2	0	0	8362
Huff And Puff	3	1	0	0	3899
John Louis	5	1	1	0	3798
Kingcora	4	1	0	0	3769
Tarraco	5	1	0	1	3769
Cloudy Beach	3	1	0	0	3769
Lochnagar	4	1	0	0	3769
Jupiter Rex	4	1	0	0	3671
Jeanpascal	3	1	0	0	3249
Tuskar Rock	5	1	0	0	2496
*Super Sam	3	1	0	2	1949
Becauseshesaidso	3	1	0	0	1560
Total winning prize-money					**£490130**
Favourites	**22-59**		**37.3%**		**-2.87**

JIM WILSON

HAM, GLOUCS

	No. of Hrs	Races Run	1st	2nd	3rd	Unpl	Per cent	£1 Level Stake
NH Flat	*1*	*2*	*0*	*0*	*0*	*2*	*0.0*	*-2.00*
Hurdles	*2*	*8*	*3*	*0*	*0*	*5*	*37.5*	*+23.50*
Chases	*2*	*3*	*0*	*0*	*0*	*3*	*0.0*	*-3.00*
Totals	**4**	**13**	**3**	**0**	**0**	**10**	**23.1**	**+18.50**
13-14	*3*	*19*	*1*	*1*	*1*	*16*	*5.3*	*-8.00*
12-13	*3*	*7*	*0*	*1*	*0*	*6*	*0.0*	*-7.00*

JOCKEYS

	W-R	Per cent	£1 Level Stake
Liam Treadwell	3-8	37.5	+23.50

COURSE RECORD

	Total W-R	Non-Hndcps Hurdles	Non-Hndcps Chases	Hndcps Hurdles	Hndcps Chases	NH Flat	Per cent	£1 Level Stake
Taunton	1-1	0-0	0-0	1-1	0-0	0-0	100.0	+10.00
Fakenham	1-2	0-0	0-0	1-2	0-0	0-0	50.0	+13.00
Stratford	1-3	0-1	0-0	1-1	0-1	0-0	33.3	+2.50

WINNING HORSES

Horse	Races Run	1st	2nd	3rd	£
Seymour Legend	5	2	0	0	5848
Ruby Valentine	4	1	0	0	2053
Total winning prize-money					**£7901**
Favourites	**0-0**		**0.0%**		**0.00**

NOEL WILSON

MIDDLEHAM, N YORKS

	No. of Hrs	Races Run	1st	2nd	3rd	Unpl	Per cent	£1 Level Stake
NH Flat	*1*	*3*	*1*	*0*	*2*	*0*	*33.3*	*+31.00*
Hurdles	*0*	*0*	*0*	*0*	*0*	*0*	*0.0*	*0.00*
Chases	*0*	*0*	*0*	*0*	*0*	*0*	*0.0*	*0.00*
Totals	**1**	**3**	**1**	**0**	**2**	**0**	**33.3**	**+31.00**
13-14	*3*	*5*	*0*	*0*	*0*	*5*	*0.0*	*-5.00*
12-13	*6*	*13*	*0*	*2*	*1*	*10*	*0.0*	*-13.00*

JOCKEYS

	W-R	Per cent	£1 Level Stake
John Kington	1-3	33.3	+31.00

COURSE RECORD

	Total W-R	Non-Hndcps Hurdles	Non-Hndcps Chases	Hndcps Hurdles	Hndcps Chases	NH Flat	Per cent	£1 Level Stake
Wetherby	1-1	0-0	0-0	0-0	0-0	1-1	100.0	+33.00

WINNING HORSES

Horse	Races Run	1st	2nd	3rd	£
Crockett	3	1	0	2	1711
Total winning prize-money					**£1711**
Favourites	**0-0**		**0.0%**		**0.00**

PETER WINKS

LITTLE HOUGHTON, S YORKS

	No. of Hrs	Races Run	1st	2nd	3rd	Unpl	Per cent	£1 Level Stake
NH Flat	*0*	*0*	*0*	*0*	*0*	*0*	*0.0*	*0.00*
Hurdles	*3*	*20*	*1*	*4*	*5*	*10*	*5.0*	*-16.00*
Chases	*2*	*15*	*1*	*4*	*5*	*5*	*6.7*	*-6.00*
Totals	**5**	**35**	**2**	**8**	**10**	**15**	**5.7**	**-22.00**
13-14	*5*	*34*	*2*	*5*	*5*	*22*	*5.9*	*-4.00*
12-13	*2*	*2*	*0*	*0*	*0*	*2*	*0.0*	*-2.00*

JOCKEYS

	W-R	Per cent	£1 Level Stake
Mr R Winks	2-32	6.3	-19.00

COURSE RECORD

	Total W-R	Non-Hndcps Hurdles	Non-Hndcps Chases	Hndcps Hurdles	Hndcps Chases	NH Flat	Per cent	£1 Level Stake
Bangor	1-3	0-0	0-0	1-2	0-1	0-0	33.3	+1.00
Mrket Rsn	1-4	0-0	0-0	0-1	1-3	0-0	25.0	+5.00

WINNING HORSES

Horse	Races Run	1st	2nd	3rd	£
*Chestnut Ben	8	1	3	3	4549
Ruler Of All	6	1	1	1	3249
Total winning prize-money					**£7798**
Favourites	**0-1**		**0.0%**		**-1.00**

ADRIAN WINTLE

WESTBURY-ON-SEVERN, GLOUCS

	No. of Hrs	Races Run	1st	2nd	3rd	Unpl	Per cent	£1 Level Stake
NH Flat	*3*	*3*	*0*	*0*	*1*	*2*	*0.0*	*-3.00*
Hurdles	*13*	*30*	*1*	*1*	*1*	*27*	*3.3*	*-19.00*
Chases	*3*	*14*	*4*	*2*	*2*	*6*	*28.6*	*+10.50*
Totals	**15**	**47**	**5**	**3**	**4**	**35**	**10.6**	**-11.50**
13-14	*11*	*24*	*1*	*3*	*1*	*19*	*4.2*	*-19.00*
12-13	*5*	*17*	*2*	*1*	*1*	*13*	*11.8*	*+14.00*

JOCKEYS

	W-R	Per cent	£1 Level Stake
Aidan Coleman	4-18	22.2	+6.50
Micheal Nolan	1-6	16.7	+5.00

COURSE RECORD

	Total W-R	Non-Hndcps Hurdles	Non-Hndcps Chases	Hndcps Hurdles	Hndcps Chases	NH Flat	Per cent	£1 Level Stake
Taunton	2-6	0-0	0-0	1-4	1-2	0-0	33.3	+11.00
Southwell	1-1	0-0	1-1	0-0	0-0	0-0	100.0	+3.50
Stratford	1-5	0-2	0-0	0-1	1-2	0-0	20.0	0.00
Worcester	1-13	0-5	1-1	0-3	0-3	0-1	7.7	-4.00

WINNING HORSES

Horse	Races Run	1st	2nd	3rd	£
*Milly Malone	8	2	1	2	8447
Hallings Comet	7	2	1	0	7763
*Billy Congo	5	1	0	0	2924
Total winning prize-money					**£19134**
Favourites	**0-2**		**0.0%**		**-2.00**

RICHARD WOOLLACOTT

SOUTH MOLTON, DEVON

	No. of Hrs	Races Run	1st	2nd	3rd	Unpl	Per cent	£1 Level Stake
NH Flat	*4*	*4*	*1*	*1*	*1*	*1*	*25.0*	*+1.50*
Hurdles	*25*	*81*	*6*	*9*	*10*	*56*	*7.4*	*-28.75*
Chases	*13*	*38*	*4*	*7*	*4*	*23*	*10.5*	*-20.13*
Totals	**38**	**123**	**11**	**17**	**15**	**80**	**8.9**	**-47.38**
13-14	*45*	*162*	*7*	*13*	*13*	*129*	*4.3*	*-114.05*
12-13	*37*	*113*	*16*	*9*	*10*	*78*	*14.2*	*-37.59*

BY MONTH

NH Flat	W-R	Per cent	£1 Level Stake
May	0-0	0.0	0.00
June	1-3	33.3	+2.50
July	0-0	0.0	0.00
August	0-0	0.0	0.00
September	0-0	0.0	0.00
October	0-0	0.0	0.00
November	0-1	0.0	-1.00
December	0-0	0.0	0.00
January	0-0	0.0	0.00
February	0-0	0.0	0.00
March	0-0	0.0	0.00
April	0-0	0.0	0.00

Hurdles	W-R	Per cent	£1 Level Stake
May	1-17	5.9	+9.00
June	0-4	0.0	-4.00
July	0-6	0.0	-6.00
August	0-4	0.0	-4.00
September	0-4	0.0	-4.00
October	0-3	0.0	-3.00
November	2-7	28.6	+4.50
December	1-9	11.1	-5.25
January	1-7	14.3	+2.00
February	1-7	14.3	-5.00
March	0-9	0.0	-9.00
April	0-4	0.0	-4.00

Chases	W-R	Per cent	£1 Level Stake
May	0-4	0.0	-4.00
June	0-3	0.0	-3.00
July	0-4	0.0	-4.00
August	0-2	0.0	-2.00
September	0-1	0.0	-1.00
October	0-0	0.0	0.00
November	0-3	0.0	-3.00
December	0-5	0.0	-5.00
January	2-5	40.0	+5.75

Totals	W-R	Per cent	£1 Level Stake
May	1-21	4.8	+5.00
June	1-10	10.0	-4.50
July	0-10	0.0	-10.00
August	0-6	0.0	-6.00
September	0-5	0.0	-5.00
October	0-3	0.0	-3.00
November	2-11	18.2	+0.50
December	1-14	7.1	-10.25
January	3-12	25.0	+7.75

February	0-4	0.0	-4.00	February	1-11	9.1	-9.00
March	0-3	0.0	-3.00	March	0-12	0.0	-12.00
April	2-4	50.0	+3.13	April	2-8	25.0	-0.87

DISTANCE

Hurdles	W-R	Per cent	£1 Level Stake	Chases	W-R	Per cent	£1 Level Stake
2m-2m3f	3-36	8.3	+4.50	2m-2m3f	0-3	0.0	-3.00
2m4f-2m7f	1-27	3.7	-21.00	2m4f-2m7f	0-13	0.0	-13.00
3m+	0-2	0.0	-2.00	3m+	4-19	21.1	-1.13

TYPE OF RACE

Non-Handicaps	W-R	Per cent	£1 Level Stake	Handicaps	W-R	Per cent	£1 Level Stake
Nov Hrdls	0-14	0.0	-14.00	Nov Hrdls	0-8	0.0	-8.00
Hrdls	1-16	6.3	-14.00	Hrdls	5-41	12.2	+9.25
Nov Chs	0-3	0.0	-3.00	Nov Chs	2-11	18.2	-4.63
Chases	0-0	0.0	0.00	Chases	2-24	8.3	-12.50
Sell/Claim	0-1	0.0	-1.00	Sell/Claim	0-1	0.0	-1.00

RACE CLASS / FIRST TIME OUT

	W-R	Per cent	£1 Level Stake		W-R	Per cent	£1 Level Stake
Class 1	0-1	0.0	-1.00	Bumpers	1-4	25.0	+1.50
Class 2	0-2	0.0	-2.00	Hurdles	1-23	4.3	+3.00
Class 3	0-21	0.0	-21.00	Chases	0-11	0.0	-11.00
Class 4	5-53	9.4	-26.13				
Class 5	5-42	11.9	+1.25	Totals	2-38	5.3	-6.50
Class 6	1-4	25.0	+1.50				

JOCKEYS

	W-R	Per cent	£1 Level Stake
Micheal Nolan	3-23	13.0	-4.50
Daryl Jacob	2-21	9.5	-13.50
Paul John	1-1	100.0	+3.50
A P McCoy	1-2	50.0	+3.50
Paddy Brennan	1-2	50.0	+0.63
Richard Johnson	1-3	33.3	-1.00
Noel Fehily	1-4	25.0	+5.00
Conor O'Farrell	1-39	2.6	-13.00

COURSE RECORD

	Total W-R	Non-Hndcps Hurdles	Non-Hndcps Chases	Hndcps Hurdles	Hndcps Chases	NH Flat	Per cent	£1 Level Stake
Wincanton	3-14	0-2	0-0	1-6	2-6	0-0	21.4	-1.63
Stratford	1-4	0-1	0-0	0-1	0-1	1-1	25.0	+1.50
Taunton	1-9	0-4	0-0	1-4	0-1	0-0	11.1	-5.25
Uttoxeter	1-9	0-1	0-0	1-5	0-1	0-2	11.1	-3.50
Ffos Las	1-9	1-3	0-0	0-3	0-3	0-0	11.1	-7.00
Chepstow	1-11	0-7	0-0	1-3	0-1	0-0	9.1	-2.00
Worcester	1-13	0-2	0-1	1-8	0-1	0-1	7.7	+13.00
Nton Abbot	1-18	0-5	0-1	0-5	1-7	0-0	5.6	-13.50
Exeter	1-20	0-6	0-1	0-8	1-5	0-0	5.0	-13.00

WINNING HORSES

Horse	Races Run	1st	2nd	3rd	£
Silvergrove	8	1	4	1	6498
Bang On Time	8	3	0	0	12776
Cash Injection	9	2	1	2	5523
Positive Vibes	8	1	2	0	2599
Local Show	6	1	2	2	2599
Lady Garvagh	7	1	0	1	2079
Kruseman	7	1	1	0	1949
*Devon General	1	1	0	0	1560

Total winning prize-money **£35583**

Favourites **2-10** **20.0%** **-4.25**

LAURA YOUNG

BROOMFIELD, SOMERSET

	No. of Hrs	Races Run	1st	2nd	3rd	Unpl	Per cent	£1 Level Stake
NH Flat	*3*	*7*	*0*	*0*	*0*	*7*	*0.0*	*-7.00*
Hurdles	*15*	*53*	*4*	*6*	*2*	*41*	*7.5*	*-32.00*
Chases	*4*	*7*	*0*	*0*	*2*	*5*	*0.0*	*-7.00*
Totals	**20**	**67**	**4**	**6**	**4**	**53**	**6.0**	**-46.00**
13-14	*18*	*72*	*4*	*7*	*8*	*53*	*5.6*	*-37.75*
12-13	*16*	*53*	*3*	*6*	*4*	*40*	*5.7*	*-36.50*

JOCKEYS

	W-R	Per cent	£1 Level Stake
Robert Dunne	2-25	8.0	-13.50
A P McCoy	1-1	100.0	+3.50
Sam Twiston-Davies	1-1	100.0	+4.00

COURSE RECORD

	Total W-R	Non-Hndcps Hurdles	Non-Hndcps Chases	Hndcps Hurdles	Hndcps Chases	NH Flat	Per cent	£1 Level Stake
Southwell	2-3	0-0	0-0	2-3	0-0	0-0	66.7	+6.50
Worcester	2-8	0-1	0-0	2-5	0-2	0-0	25.0	+3.50

WINNING HORSES

Horse	Races Run	1st	2nd	3rd	£
Jigsaw Financial	6	2	1	0	4003
Fintan	6	2	2	0	3899

Total winning prize-money **£7902**

Favourites **0-1** **0.0%** **-1.00**

WILLIAM YOUNG JNR

CROSSFORD, S LANARKS

	No. of Hrs	Races Run	1st	2nd	3rd	Unpl	Per cent	£1 Level Stake
NH Flat	*0*	*0*	*0*	*0*	*0*	*0*	*0.0*	*0.00*
Hurdles	*3*	*24*	*1*	*2*	*2*	*19*	*4.2*	*+2.00*
Chases	*1*	*1*	*0*	*0*	*0*	*1*	*0.0*	*-1.00*

Totals	**3**	**25**	**1**	**2**	**2**	**20**	**4.0**	**+1.00**
13-14	*5*	*26*	*0*	*0*	*2*	*24*	*0.0*	*-26.00*
12-13	*2*	*3*	*0*	*0*	*0*	*3*	*0.0*	*-3.00*

JOCKEYS

	W-R	Per cent	£1 Level Stake
Mr J Dixon	1-20	5.0	+6.00

COURSE RECORD

	Total W-R	Non-Hndcps Hurdles	Non-Hndcps Chases	Hndcps Hurdles	Hndcps Chases	NH Flat	Per cent	£1 Level Stake
Cartmel	1-3	0-1	0-0	1-2	0-0	0-0	33.3	+23.00

WINNING HORSES

Horse	Races Run	1st	2nd	3rd	£
Raifteiri	16	1	2	2	2599
Total winning prize-money					**£2599**
Favourites	**0-0**		**0.0%**		**0.00**

LEADING JUMP TRAINERS AT AINTREE (SINCE 2010)

	Total W-R	Nov Hdle	H'cap Hdle	Other Hdle	Nov Chase	H'cap Chase	Other Chase	Hunter Chase	N.H. Flat	Per cent	£1 Level stake
Nicky Henderson	36-203	7-28	7-54	8-37	7-15	4-41	3-16	0-0	1-22	17.7	**2.52**
Paul Nicholls	23-195	2-21	0-28	6-35	5-24	4-68	6-14	0-4	0-7	11.8	-51.49
Peter Bowen	20-130	1-17	2-34	2-7	1-1	7-53	0-1	1-1	6-17	15.4	**35.00**
Philip Hobbs	16-118	2-7	2-43	1-11	2-4	7-40	0-7	0-3	2-8	13.6	-2.00
Nigel Twiston-Davies	14-126	2-14	2-24	3-12	0-5	4-60	0-3	1-3	2-6	11.1	-33.18
Donald McCain	13-175	4-24	2-53	3-26	0-9	3-45	0-2	1-3	0-17	7.4	-102.68
Alan King	12-102	1-14	1-25	6-21	3-6	1-21	0-5	0-0	1-14	11.8	-5.55
Jonjo O'Neill	11-107	1-13	2-33	0-10	2-4	4-32	1-6	0-3	1-9	10.3	-48.83
Rebecca Curtis	9-52	4-11	2-13	0-8	0-5	2-8	0-0	0-2	1-7	17.3	-13.88
Tom George	6-47	0-2	0-6	0-3	1-3	3-21	2-7	0-3	0-3	12.8	-8.88
David Pipe	6-98	0-5	2-29	1-13	1-5	1-44	0-4	0-0	1-3	6.1	-36.25
Gordon Elliott	6-36	0-0	2-6	1-6	1-5	1-15	1-2	0-1	1-2	16.7	**23.00**
Tim Vaughan	5-49	2-8	0-11	0-3	0-2	3-20	0-1	0-3	0-2	10.2	**15.50**
Charlie Longsdon	5-50	0-8	3-23	2-8	0-1	0-9	0-1	0-0	0-5	10.0	-33.17
Lucinda Russell	4-51	1-10	0-13	0-3	0-2	3-17	0-0	0-0	0-6	7.8	-31.38
Colin Tizzard	4-46	1-8	0-5	1-3	0-4	2-23	0-2	0-0	0-1	8.7	**7.00**
Ian Williams	4-42	2-6	1-12	0-9	0-2	1-4	0-0	0-2	0-8	9.5	-18.92
Malcolm Jefferson	3-29	1-4	2-8	1-2	0-1	0-8	0-1	0-0	0-6	10.3	**10.00**
W P Mullins	3-47	1-3	0-1	1-7	0-0	0-24	1-2	0-4	0-6	6.4	-34.75
Howard Johnson	3-35	0-5	0-6	0-4	0-2	3-17	0-0	0-0	0-3	8.6	-3.00
Alistair Whillans	3-16	0-5	2-7	0-1	0-0	1-1	0-0	0-0	0-2	18.8	**4.00**
John Quinn	3-35	0-3	1-12	1-9	0-2	0-7	0-0	0-0	1-2	8.6	-21.13
Dr Richard Newland	3-30	0-0	1-9	0-2	0-0	1-16	0-0	1-4	0-0	10.0	**50.25**
Philip Kirby	3-18	0-1	3-6	0-4	0-0	0-1	0-0	0-0	0-6	16.7	**24.75**
George Moore	2-6	0-1	2-3	0-2	0-0	0-1	0-0	0-0	0-0	33.3	**24.00**
Kevin Bishop	2-3	0-1	1-1	0-0	0-0	1-1	0-0	0-0	0-0	66.7	**10.50**
Henry De Bromhead	2-14	0-2	0-0	0-0	2-3	0-8	0-1	0-0	0-0	14.3	**20.50**
Milton Harris	2-16	0-0	0-4	0-0	0-0	2-8	0-1	0-0	0-3	12.5	**20.00**
Sue Smith	2-43	0-8	0-4	0-2	0-2	2-26	0-0	0-0	0-1	4.7	**28.33**
Charles Egerton	2-5	0-0	0-2	0-0	0-0	0-0	0-0	0-0	2-3	40.0	**17.50**
Kate Walton	2-9	1-1	1-6	0-0	0-0	0-0	0-0	0-0	0-2	22.2	-1.75

LEADING JUMP TRAINERS AT ASCOT (SINCE 2010)

	Total W-R	Nov Hdle	H'cap Hdle	Other Hdle	Nov Chase	H'cap Chase	Other Chase	Hunter Chase	N.H. Flat	Per cent	£1 Level stake
Nicky Henderson	41-174	8-37	4-46	10-44	5-15	2-11	8-21	0-0	5-13	23.6	-59.41
Paul Nicholls	37-150	7-19	4-26	7-28	2-17	6-34	11-24	1-3	0-6	24.7	-7.44
Philip Hobbs	15-104	4-15	2-23	1-12	1-11	3-24	2-11	0-2	2-11	14.4	-35.54
David Pipe	15-90	2-5	5-35	0-12	1-2	4-30	0-5	0-0	3-6	16.7	-1.89
Alan King	15-107	3-21	3-27	7-27	3-10	0-12	1-6	0-0	0-11	14.0	**57.88**
Venetia Williams	9-75	1-6	2-19	0-4	1-10	5-38	0-1	0-0	0-0	12.0	-2.50
Colin Tizzard	7-44	1-4	0-4	1-7	2-5	1-12	1-8	0-0	1-7	15.9	**5.20**
Oliver Sherwood	6-33	1-4	1-9	1-6	1-5	0-5	1-3	0-0	1-2	18.2	-8.68
Gary Moore	6-90	1-14	0-27	1-15	1-9	2-21	1-3	0-1	0-5	6.7	-52.25
Kim Bailey	5-27	0-6	1-6	0-4	3-6	1-4	0-0	0-0	0-1	18.5	**14.13**
Donald McCain	5-33	2-3	2-14	1-7	0-6	0-5	0-0	0-0	0-1	15.2	**0.37**
Harry Fry	5-11	2-3	0-1	3-3	0-0	0-1	0-0	0-0	0-3	45.5	**6.60**
Nigel Twiston-Davies	4-72	1-12	1-12	0-12	0-11	2-22	0-3	0-0	0-1	5.6	-41.17
Jonjo O'Neill	4-50	1-5	0-13	0-11	1-5	0-12	0-4	1-1	1-4	8.0	-24.00
Nick Williams	4-36	0-3	0-3	3-9	1-6	0-9	0-7	0-0	0-0	11.1	-15.25
Evan Williams	4-49	0-3	2-11	0-8	0-5	2-17	0-3	0-1	0-3	8.2	**18.00**
Fergal O'Brien	4-16	0-1	1-2	0-3	0-5	1-2	0-0	1-1	1-2	25.0	**1.66**
Dan Skelton	4-21	1-4	1-5	0-2	1-3	1-5	0-0	0-0	0-2	19.0	**13.50**
Charlie Longsdon	4-53	1-13	0-12	0-7	0-4	1-11	0-2	0-0	2-6	7.5	-9.50
Rebecca Curtis	4-41	2-7	0-4	0-7	1-6	1-7	0-3	0-0	0-8	9.8	-9.00
Henrietta Knight	3-23	0-5	0-1	0-4	1-4	0-1	1-5	1-1	0-2	13.0	**6.50**
Dr Richard Newland	3-21	0-1	2-7	0-3	0-2	1-8	0-2	0-0	0-0	14.3	**22.00**
W P Mullins	2-9	0-1	0-3	2-3	0-0	0-0	0-2	0-0	0-1	22.2	-6.13
John Ferguson	3-11	0-2	1-6	1-1	0-0	0-0	0-0	0-0	2-3	27.3	**4.87**
Richard Rowe	2-12	0-1	0-2	0-0	0-1	2-6	0-1	0-0	0-1	16.7	**20.00**
Lucinda Russell	2-4	0-0	0-1	0-0	1-1	1-2	0-0	0-0	0-0	50.0	**23.50**
Tom George	2-17	0-0	0-3	0-3	1-3	1-8	0-1	0-0	0-0	11.8	-9.50
James Evans	2-8	0-2	0-1	1-1	0-0	1-3	0-0	0-0	0-1	25.0	**5.00**
Victor Dartnall	2-10	0-0	1-2	0-0	0-0	1-6	0-0	0-0	0-2	20.0	**37.00**
Henry Daly	2-18	0-1	0-2	1-3	0-2	1-10	0-0	0-0	0-0	11.1	-10.50
Emma Lavelle	2-51	0-13	1-8	1-10	1-4	0-9	0-5	0-0	0-4	3.9	-45.25

LEADING JUMP TRAINERS AT AYR (SINCE 2010)

	Total W-R	Nov Hdle	H'cap Hdle	Other Hdle	Nov Chase	H'cap Chase	Other Chase	Hunter Chase	N.H. Flat	Per cent	£1 Level stake
Lucinda Russell	37-310	5-34	5-90	4-40	7-24	10-83	3-9	0-0	3-30	11.9	-148.03
Donald McCain	37-141	13-29	2-32	6-18	5-17	5-25	3-7	0-0	3-13	26.2	-12.08
Jim Goldie	30-210	2-27	13-91	2-20	3-7	8-45	0-1	0-0	2-19	14.3	**17.30**
Nicky Richards	28-143	3-30	6-35	5-21	4-11	5-28	2-4	0-0	3-14	19.6	-33.89
James Ewart	12-105	1-12	3-22	1-16	0-6	5-25	1-2	0-0	1-22	11.4	-34.27
S R B Crawford	12-84	2-9	3-24	0-19	1-2	2-13	0-2	0-0	4-15	14.3	-8.50
Nicky Henderson	11-50	1-4	4-20	0-1	1-8	0-9	1-1	0-0	4-7	22.0	-5.72
Paul Nicholls	10-40	1-4	5-14	1-2	0-5	2-13	1-2	0-0	0-0	25.0	**11.68**
J J Lambe	9-50	3-9	4-19	1-7	0-3	1-9	0-1	0-0	0-2	18.0	**17.25**
N W Alexander	9-117	0-12	3-36	0-19	1-5	2-25	0-0	0-1	3-19	7.7	-35.25
Ferdy Murphy	7-60	0-6	1-9	0-5	0-2	5-35	1-2	0-0	0-1	11.7	**6.75**
Maurice Barnes	6-47	0-5	3-17	0-8	0-3	2-8	1-1	0-0	0-5	12.8	**8.41**
Martin Todhunter	6-66	0-4	1-20	0-3	0-5	5-34	0-0	0-0	0-0	9.1	-29.15
Alan Swinbank	6-24	0-5	2-3	0-1	1-3	0-3	0-0	0-0	3-9	25.0	**24.50**
Andrew Parker	5-23	0-2	2-7	0-4	0-1	3-7	0-0	0-0	0-2	21.7	**53.50**
Alistair Whillans	5-74	0-4	1-30	0-9	1-1	2-20	0-0	0-0	1-10	6.8	-40.50
Sue Smith	5-73	1-7	2-21	0-1	1-10	1-31	0-1	0-0	0-2	6.8	-51.88
Donald Whillans	5-32	0-1	4-22	0-1	0-0	1-7	0-0	0-0	0-1	15.6	**0.25**
William Amos	5-43	1-6	0-17	1-6	0-3	2-6	0-0	0-0	1-5	11.6	**11.00**
David Pipe	5-30	1-2	1-10	1-1	1-1	1-14	0-1	0-0	0-1	16.7	-8.95
Chris Grant	5-32	0-1	2-13	0-1	1-2	1-6	0-1	0-0	1-8	15.6	**30.38**
Pauline Robson	5-33	0-2	2-13	0-3	0-1	3-12	0-1	0-0	0-1	15.2	-9.50
Sandy Thomson	4-22	0-0	0-3	2-4	1-2	1-9	0-1	0-0	0-3	18.2	-0.19
Gordon Elliott	5-26	1-5	1-4	1-5	0-3	1-4	0-0	0-0	1-5	19.2	-7.39
Brian Ellison	4-38	0-2	3-14	0-4	0-1	1-15	0-0	0-0	0-2	10.5	**1.50**
Alan King	4-41	1-2	1-14	0-0	0-3	1-16	0-2	0-0	1-4	9.8	-11.75
R T J Wilson	4-18	1-4	2-3	0-2	1-2	0-2	0-1	0-0	0-4	22.2	**7.87**
Malcolm Jefferson	3-42	0-2	0-8	0-2	1-5	1-16	0-0	0-0	1-9	7.1	-22.25
Evelyn Slack	3-9	0-1	3-7	0-0	0-0	0-1	0-0	0-0	0-0	33.3	**9.75**
Howard Johnson	3-32	0-5	0-7	1-3	2-6	0-8	0-2	0-0	0-1	9.4	-19.50
Peter Bowen	3-19	0-0	1-8	0-0	0-0	1-7	0-1	0-0	1-3	15.8	**38.50**

EADING JUMP TRAINERS AT BANGOR-ON-DEE (SINCE 2010)

	Total W-R	Nov Hdle	H'cap Hdle	Other Hdle	Nov Chase	H'cap Chase	Other Chase	Hunter Chase	N.H. Flat	Per cent	£1 Level stake
Donald McCain	78-369	26-103	11-79	12-48	8-40	7-42	5-7	0-1	9-49	21.1	**16.48**
Rebecca Curtis	26-85	11-22	2-11	2-9	4-18	0-5	1-1	1-1	5-18	30.6	**7.91**
Nicky Henderson	19-68	8-17	2-10	2-10	2-8	0-3	0-2	0-0	5-18	27.9	-12.43
Jonjo O'Neill	19-183	3-50	5-42	0-11	3-14	5-47	0-3	0-4	3-12	10.4	-95.01
Charlie Longsdon	18-71	3-12	2-14	2-6	5-8	3-18	0-3	0-0	3-10	25.4	**5.44**
Venetia Williams	15-107	1-22	1-22	3-10	2-9	7-32	1-3	0-0	0-9	14.0	-13.34
Philip Hobbs	13-58	3-10	5-19	0-2	3-6	2-12	0-1	0-0	0-8	22.4	**12.12**
Alan King	13-81	2-20	2-17	3-13	3-9	3-8	0-2	0-0	0-12	16.0	-21.25
Nigel Twiston-Davies	10-73	3-15	2-14	0-9	3-9	2-18	0-0	0-0	0-8	13.7	-15.63
Tim Vaughan	9-72	5-18	0-19	1-14	0-4	3-12	0-0	0-1	0-4	12.5	-13.35
Richard Lee	8-56	0-5	2-7	0-6	0-5	6-29	0-2	0-0	0-2	14.3	-17.50
Evan Williams	8-64	2-17	0-16	3-7	1-11	2-9	0-1	0-0	0-3	12.5	-38.27
Fergal O'Brien	8-34	0-5	3-6	0-3	0-2	3-11	0-1	1-1	1-5	23.5	-6.13
Kim Bailey	7-42	1-10	1-8	2-5	0-2	0-9	1-2	0-0	2-6	16.7	-15.57
Peter Bowen	7-64	1-4	2-23	1-5	0-4	1-18	0-0	0-0	2-10	10.9	-21.35
Brian Ellison	7-35	1-12	2-7	1-7	0-3	2-4	0-0	0-0	1-2	20.0	-13.46
Henry Daly	7-63	1-11	4-11	0-4	0-7	1-14	0-2	0-1	1-13	11.1	-9.75
David Pipe	6-41	0-11	2-16	0-2	2-4	2-6	0-0	0-0	0-2	14.6	-13.75
Jennie Candlish	6-64	1-13	0-21	1-8	1-4	1-6	0-2	0-0	2-10	9.4	-20.40
John O'Shea	5-38	0-7	3-17	0-3	0-0	1-6	0-0	0-0	1-5	13.2	**11.32**
Sue Smith	5-36	0-5	1-10	0-1	1-4	3-11	0-1	0-0	0-4	13.9	-11.47
Paul Webber	5-50	1-12	2-12	0-4	1-4	1-9	0-1	0-0	0-8	10.0	-25.00
Barry Leavy	5-35	0-10	1-12	0-2	1-1	3-9	0-0	0-0	0-1	14.3	**3.50**
Paul Nicholls	4-16	3-6	0-4	0-0	1-3	0-0	0-0	0-1	0-2	25.0	-4.00
Graeme McPherson	5-41	2-12	1-12	0-0	1-1	1-7	0-0	0-0	0-9	12.2	**68.00**
Warren Greatrex	5-24	1-5	1-7	0-1	0-2	0-3	0-0	0-0	3-6	20.8	**14.85**
Tony Carroll	4-30	0-7	1-11	0-3	1-3	2-4	0-0	0-0	0-2	13.3	**6.63**
Brendan Powell	4-20	0-4	0-7	2-2	1-3	1-3	0-0	0-0	0-1	20.0	-1.00
Miss Sally Duckett	4-4	0-0	0-0	0-0	0-0	0-0	0-0	4-4	0-0	100.0	**5.54**
Harry Fry	4-8	0-2	0-0	0-1	2-2	0-0	0-0	0-0	2-3	50.0	**3.10**
Oliver Sherwood	3-33	2-9	0-6	0-5	1-3	0-6	0-0	0-0	0-4	9.1	-13.25

LEADING JUMP TRAINERS AT CARLISLE (SINCE 2010)

	Total W-R	Nov Hdle	H'cap Hdle	Other Hdle	Nov Chase	H'cap Chase	Other Chase	Hunter Chase	N.H. Flat	Per cent	£1 Level stake
Donald McCain	41-208	15-74	4-34	2-9	6-30	1-20	4-11	1-1	8-29	19.7	-63.74
Lucinda Russell	23-217	2-47	1-35	1-3	3-28	13-81	1-5	0-0	2-18	10.6	-74.55
Sue Smith	21-143	5-20	1-23	0-1	0-24	11-52	4-14	0-0	0-9	14.7	-1.90
Nicky Richards	17-76	4-19	6-17	0-1	1-10	4-16	2-4	0-0	0-9	22.4	**26.45**
Alan Swinbank	15-68	5-27	3-11	0-4	3-6	0-1	0-1	0-0	4-18	22.1	**14.95**
Howard Johnson	13-55	3-11	1-9	1-1	7-12	1-9	0-6	0-0	0-7	23.6	-4.73
Jonjo O'Neill	11-53	2-7	6-11	0-0	1-6	0-23	1-5	0-0	1-1	20.8	-15.32
Venetia Williams	9-29	2-7	2-5	0-1	1-3	3-10	0-1	0-0	1-2	31.0	**16.00**
Micky Hammond	8-51	1-10	3-17	0-1	1-6	2-13	0-0	0-0	1-4	15.7	-10.05
John Wade	7-54	2-14	2-13	0-1	0-4	3-17	0-0	0-0	0-5	13.0	**1.44**
Malcolm Jefferson	7-61	0-9	1-8	0-3	1-8	4-15	0-6	0-0	1-12	11.5	-9.04
Maurice Barnes	7-71	2-19	1-22	0-2	0-8	4-8	0-3	0-0	0-9	9.9	-25.75
Dianne Sayer	7-78	2-21	2-24	0-0	1-9	2-20	0-1	0-0	0-3	9.0	-8.75
James Ewart	7-71	0-11	0-9	0-1	3-16	3-19	0-2	0-0	1-13	9.9	-34.98
Charlie Longsdon	7-26	2-5	0-0	0-0	3-6	0-7	1-4	0-0	1-4	26.9	-8.91
Richard Lee	6-21	0-1	0-1	0-0	3-5	3-12	0-2	0-0	0-0	28.6	**8.01**
Nigel Twiston-Davies	6-36	0-6	1-4	0-1	1-3	3-19	1-3	0-0	0-0	16.7	-5.03
James Moffatt	6-43	4-12	1-19	1-1	0-7	0-2	0-1	0-0	0-1	14.0	-11.34
Rose Dobbin	6-61	1-15	2-16	0-2	2-5	0-14	1-1	0-0	0-8	9.8	-30.75
Brian Ellison	5-48	1-14	1-14	0-1	1-4	1-9	0-0	0-0	1-6	10.4	-25.00
George Bewley	5-38	1-6	1-12	1-1	1-4	1-8	0-1	0-0	0-6	13.2	**10.54**
Keith Reveley	5-24	1-5	1-3	0-1	1-2	0-5	0-1	0-0	2-7	20.8	**13.91**
Martin Todhunter	5-65	0-19	2-8	1-2	0-10	2-25	0-0	0-0	0-1	7.7	**2.00**
Jennie Candlish	5-54	0-16	1-12	1-5	0-6	3-9	0-3	0-0	0-3	9.3	-29.74
N W Alexander	5-68	0-9	0-11	0-1	0-10	4-25	0-5	0-0	1-7	7.4	-38.00
Philip Kirby	5-42	2-14	1-10	0-0	1-6	1-5	0-0	0-0	0-7	11.9	**11.08**
Barbara Butterworth	4-28	1-5	2-19	1-1	0-0	0-3	0-0	0-0	0-0	14.3	**41.63**
Peter Bowen	4-13	1-1	0-3	0-0	0-1	3-5	0-0	0-0	0-3	30.8	**25.00**
Alistair Whillans	4-58	2-12	1-21	0-1	0-3	1-12	0-1	0-0	0-8	6.9	-34.50
Ferdy Murphy	4-55	1-10	0-6	0-1	2-11	0-17	1-8	0-0	0-2	7.3	-12.00
William Amos	4-41	0-9	0-3	0-1	1-2	2-19	0-1	0-0	1-6	9.8	-17.75

LEADING JUMP TRAINERS AT CARTMEL (SINCE 2010)

	Total W-R	Nov Hdle	H'cap Hdle	Other Hdle	Nov Chase	H'cap Chase	Other Chase	Hunter Chase	N.H. Flat	Per cent	£1 Level stake
Donald McCain	29-105	9-25	8-28	5-23	3-4	0-14	4-9	0-2	0-0	27.6	-7.83
Dianne Sayer	13-71	4-11	4-31	0-3	0-0	5-26	0-0	0-0	0-0	18.3	**15.08**
Harriet Graham	9-31	0-5	2-9	0-1	0-0	7-16	0-0	0-0	0-0	29.0	**5.24**
Peter Bowen	8-38	0-5	1-10	1-3	0-1	6-16	0-3	0-0	0-0	21.1	**0.12**
Nigel Twiston-Davies	7-35	2-4	3-9	0-2	0-0	1-17	1-3	0-0	0-0	20.0	-9.17
John Quinn	6-16	1-3	3-5	2-8	0-0	0-0	0-0	0-0	0-0	37.5	**7.25**
Jonjo O'Neill	5-15	1-1	3-6	0-0	0-0	1-8	0-0	0-0	0-0	33.3	**6.30**
Brian Ellison	5-25	3-8	0-7	0-4	0-1	2-4	0-1	0-0	0-0	20.0	**11.00**
Sue Smith	5-36	0-5	1-9	0-2	0-0	3-16	1-4	0-0	0-0	13.9	-0.00
Lucinda Russell	5-45	1-8	1-16	1-5	0-1	1-13	1-2	0-0	0-0	11.1	-28.60
Evan Williams	5-28	1-7	1-7	0-2	0-1	2-8	1-2	0-1	0-0	17.9	**0.75**
James Moffatt	5-72	1-10	1-27	3-15	0-1	0-14	0-5	0-0	0-0	6.9	**5.00**
Sophie Leech	5-28	0-3	1-11	0-0	1-1	1-11	2-2	0-0	0-0	17.9	-0.70
John Wade	4-16	1-3	1-2	0-0	0-0	1-8	0-1	1-2	0-0	25.0	**16.83**
Michael Chapman	4-61	1-8	1-16	0-4	0-1	2-31	0-1	0-0	0-0	6.6	-24.25
Richard Ford	4-28	0-6	1-6	0-0	1-1	2-14	0-1	0-0	0-0	14.3	-8.80
Barry Murtagh	4-30	0-2	2-17	0-1	0-1	2-9	0-0	0-0	0-0	13.3	**45.50**
Nicky Richards	4-22	0-6	1-6	1-4	0-0	2-6	0-0	0-0	0-0	18.2	-1.17
George Moore	3-10	1-2	0-5	2-3	0-0	0-0	0-0	0-0	0-0	30.0	**22.50**
Maurice Barnes	3-23	0-4	0-10	1-2	0-0	2-5	0-1	0-1	0-0	13.0	**19.00**
Alistair Whillans	3-26	0-2	3-17	0-1	0-0	0-6	0-0	0-0	0-0	11.5	**4.00**
Tina Jackson	3-11	0-0	3-7	0-3	0-0	0-1	0-0	0-0	0-0	27.3	**3.50**
Tim Vaughan	3-33	1-11	1-8	0-2	0-0	0-9	1-3	0-0	0-0	9.1	-17.64
Gordon Elliott	3-10	1-3	0-2	0-0	0-0	2-4	0-1	0-0	0-0	30.0	-0.87
Mark Michael McNiff	3-7	2-3	0-0	0-1	0-0	1-2	0-1	0-0	0-0	42.9	**16.50**
Ben Haslam	3-17	1-1	1-8	1-5	0-0	0-2	0-0	0-1	0-0	17.6	-4.13
Sue Gardner	2-6	1-2	0-0	0-1	0-0	1-3	0-0	0-0	0-0	33.3	**11.00**
Kate Walton	2-11	1-3	0-5	1-1	0-0	0-2	0-0	0-0	0-0	18.2	-3.00
Martin Todhunter	2-34	0-2	0-14	0-4	0-1	2-13	0-0	0-0	0-0	5.9	-14.50
Tony Carroll	2-9	1-3	1-5	0-0	0-0	0-1	0-0	0-0	0-0	22.2	**0.50**
Joanne Foster	2-18	0-1	0-4	0-1	0-0	1-7	1-4	0-1	0-0	11.1	**5.50**

LEADING JUMP TRAINERS AT CATTERICK (SINCE 2010)

	Total W-R	Nov Hdle	H'cap Hdle	Other Hdle	Nov Chase	H'cap Chase	Other Chase	Hunter Chase	N.H. Flat	Per cent	£1 Level stake
Donald McCain	32-155	11-41	4-32	4-17	3-19	4-12	2-11	0-0	4-23	20.6	-37.66
Keith Reveley	24-100	5-21	5-14	2-7	4-9	5-22	1-4	0-0	2-23	24.0	**73.05**
Sue Smith	19-115	2-16	5-35	0-5	7-12	3-26	2-3	0-0	0-18	16.5	**30.80**
Brian Ellison	13-50	4-15	2-7	3-14	2-4	0-3	1-2	0-0	1-5	26.0	**6.81**
Micky Hammond	10-106	2-15	4-40	0-11	1-9	1-15	1-5	0-0	1-11	9.4	-28.00
John Ferguson	9-16	2-4	0-0	6-7	0-1	0-1	0-1	0-0	1-2	56.3	**10.27**
John Wade	8-62	0-9	1-16	0-2	1-3	6-16	0-4	0-5	0-7	12.9	-9.71
James Ewart	7-38	0-5	1-4	1-3	1-3	1-8	2-5	0-0	1-10	18.4	-2.00
Malcolm Jefferson	6-48	1-13	0-6	0-4	0-2	3-7	1-5	0-0	1-11	12.5	-11.90
Jonjo O'Neill	6-25	3-5	1-4	0-2	0-3	1-6	1-4	0-0	0-1	24.0	-3.84
Michael Easterby	6-41	1-8	1-9	0-4	1-3	1-3	0-2	0-0	2-12	14.6	**4.50**
Howard Johnson	5-43	1-12	1-5	0-2	0-3	1-8	1-7	0-0	1-6	11.6	-12.40
Dianne Sayer	5-46	0-3	4-25	1-6	0-3	0-7	0-0	0-0	0-2	10.9	**66.50**
Chris Grant	5-93	0-17	2-27	0-9	0-6	2-18	1-9	0-0	0-7	5.4	-42.17
Michael Smith	5-12	1-5	0-1	2-2	0-0	2-4	0-0	0-0	0-0	41.7	**20.00**
S R B Crawford	5-20	0-3	0-3	0-0	0-0	0-0	1-3	0-0	4-11	25.0	**8.02**
David O'Meara	5-19	0-4	1-5	1-4	0-0	0-1	1-1	0-0	2-4	26.3	**19.50**
Ferdy Murphy	4-56	0-7	0-10	0-2	1-5	1-21	1-6	0-0	1-5	7.1	-39.05
Andrew Crook	4-35	1-4	1-11	0-6	0-2	2-8	0-0	0-0	0-4	11.4	-1.50
Martin Keighley	4-14	0-3	0-2	0-1	0-1	2-5	1-1	0-0	1-1	28.6	-1.10
Mike Sowersby	3-53	0-4	3-31	0-7	0-1	0-4	0-2	0-0	0-4	5.7	-24.00
George Bewley	3-12	1-1	2-7	0-0	0-0	0-3	0-0	0-0	0-1	25.0	**35.20**
Chris Bealby	3-18	2-6	0-3	0-3	0-1	1-3	0-0	0-0	0-2	16.7	**23.50**
Simon Shirley-Beavan	3-5	0-1	0-0	0-0	2-2	0-0	1-1	0-0	0-1	60.0	**13.08**
John Quinn	3-29	1-6	0-5	2-13	0-1	0-3	0-0	0-0	0-1	10.3	-23.76
Venetia Williams	3-17	0-1	1-1	0-2	0-2	1-9	1-1	0-0	0-1	17.6	-4.92
Joanne Foster	3-30	0-3	1-8	1-3	0-2	1-12	0-2	0-0	0-0	10.0	**46.50**
Tim Easterby	3-43	1-9	0-4	0-8	0-1	2-8	0-2	0-0	0-11	7.0	-26.00
Alan Swinbank	3-33	0-5	0-0	0-6	0-5	0-3	0-2	0-0	3-12	9.1	-13.50
Henry Hogarth	3-31	0-3	1-12	0-2	0-3	2-8	0-1	0-0	0-2	9.7	-2.00
Philip Kirby	3-57	0-11	2-24	0-4	0-2	0-3	0-3	1-2	0-8	5.3	-42.38

LEADING JUMP TRAINERS AT CHELTENHAM (SINCE 2010)

	Total W-R	Nov Hdle	H'cap Hdle	Other Hdle	Nov Chase	H'cap Chase	Other Chase	Hunter Chase	N.H. Flat	Per cent	£1 Level stake
Paul Nicholls	72-499	9-60	13-115	18-94	13-53	12-113	4-62	1-6	2-12	14.4	-58.44
Nicky Henderson	60-452	10-61	11-127	18-82	5-37	7-98	10-44	0-1	3-19	13.3	-103.56
Philip Hobbs	45-329	4-26	9-100	4-30	8-38	13-108	5-20	1-5	3-17	13.7	-36.33
David Pipe	39-339	4-29	11-115	5-43	7-26	11-112	2-24	0-0	3-13	11.5	**15.55**
Nigel Twiston-Davies	30-345	5-41	6-59	3-41	3-49	11-126	1-23	1-2	1-21	8.7	-34.41
W P Mullins	30-240	4-44	7-51	11-45	2-10	0-24	5-45	0-1	2-23	12.5	-37.03
Jonjo O'Neill	24-208	2-18	3-66	3-23	3-20	10-69	3-11	1-7	0-7	11.5	**6.38**
Alan King	16-237	3-28	3-61	1-52	2-15	3-55	3-21	0-0	1-18	6.8	-62.37
Colin Tizzard	12-157	2-25	0-16	0-6	4-28	4-55	1-15	0-0	1-14	7.6	**9.74**
Gordon Elliott	12-106	1-9	4-42	2-14	3-12	0-20	2-8	0-1	0-3	11.3	**9.24**
Fergal O'Brien	9-65	0-4	1-7	1-5	0-4	2-22	0-1	4-11	2-13	13.8	**45.00**
Martin Keighley	9-100	2-19	1-21	1-3	1-11	4-32	0-9	0-1	0-6	9.0	-31.30
Donald McCain	9-126	3-9	2-46	0-24	3-11	1-21	0-12	0-2	0-5	7.1	-22.25
Rebecca Curtis	9-86	2-24	1-18	0-7	2-13	0-4	2-4	0-4	2-12	10.5	-13.12
Neil Mulholland	9-32	0-2	1-6	0-3	1-3	6-12	1-5	0-0	0-1	28.1	**41.25**
Venetia Williams	8-187	1-10	3-62	0-18	0-15	4-76	0-12	0-1	0-2	4.3	-42.00
Tom George	6-89	0-12	2-17	1-17	1-14	2-21	0-6	0-1	0-2	6.7	-38.50
Nick Williams	6-79	1-10	0-11	2-18	1-11	0-18	2-12	0-0	0-1	7.6	-39.13
Evan Williams	6-110	0-12	0-40	2-16	2-11	2-24	0-6	0-0	0-2	5.5	-52.50
A J Martin	5-49	1-6	1-14	0-3	1-3	2-17	0-4	0-0	0-3	10.2	**19.88**
Emma Lavelle	5-77	1-13	1-22	0-12	2-9	1-21	0-4	0-0	0-2	6.5	-38.00
Warren Greatrex	5-52	2-15	1-15	1-9	0-2	0-3	0-1	0-1	1-9	9.6	-18.88
Harry Fry	5-30	1-4	0-8	2-9	0-4	1-5	0-1	0-0	1-2	16.7	-5.25
Robin Dickin	4-35	2-8	2-9	0-5	0-6	0-5	0-1	0-0	0-2	11.4	**1.17**
Henry De Bromhead	4-45	1-6	0-4	0-2	0-8	1-10	2-15	0-0	0-2	8.9	-17.25
Alan Hill	4-12	0-0	0-0	0-0	0-0	0-0	0-0	4-12	0-0	33.3	**1.10**
Peter Bowen	4-50	0-5	2-15	1-3	0-3	1-14	0-1	1-4	0-7	8.0	**2.50**
Mrs Pauline Harkin	4-7	0-0	0-0	0-0	0-0	0-0	0-0	4-7	0-0	57.1	**7.20**
Dan Skelton	4-27	1-6	2-7	0-5	0-0	1-7	0-0	0-0	0-2	14.8	-3.75
John Ferguson	4-51	2-13	1-20	1-7	0-1	0-1	0-1	0-2	0-7	7.8	-25.23
Malcolm Jefferson	3-29	0-1	2-5	1-2	0-5	0-15	1-2	0-0	0-0	10.3	**15.00**

LEADING JUMP TRAINERS AT CHEPSTOW (SINCE 2010)

	Total W-R	Nov Hdle	H'cap Hdle	Other Hdle	Nov Chase	H'cap Chase	Other Chase	Hunter Chase	N.H. Flat	Per cent	£1 Level stake
Philip Hobbs	34-163	4-24	7-39	4-22	5-13	8-40	0-5	0-0	6-21	20.9	-1.62
David Pipe	30-116	6-18	11-38	4-12	1-3	6-32	0-4	0-0	2-9	25.9	**41.04**
Paul Nicholls	28-166	9-27	3-31	7-32	3-18	1-33	4-8	0-0	1-18	16.9	-83.23
Evan Williams	19-156	2-15	6-50	2-25	2-15	7-46	0-2	0-0	0-4	12.2	-9.87
Peter Bowen	16-88	1-10	6-26	0-13	1-4	3-23	0-1	0-0	5-11	18.2	**30.80**
Rebecca Curtis	16-94	2-15	1-12	4-17	3-13	2-12	0-4	0-0	4-21	17.0	-42.42
Nigel Twiston-Davies	14-124	2-14	2-33	3-16	3-6	3-41	1-3	0-0	0-12	11.3	-13.32
Jonjo O'Neill	14-123	4-25	3-32	3-18	0-5	4-36	0-1	0-0	0-6	11.4	-42.95
Victor Dartnall	14-78	0-11	4-19	2-10	1-5	3-21	1-1	0-0	3-11	17.9	**4.88**
Venetia Williams	12-127	2-17	1-27	1-26	0-9	8-45	0-1	0-0	0-3	9.4	-51.88
Colin Tizzard	12-114	3-17	0-14	1-14	3-13	4-39	0-2	0-1	1-14	10.5	-48.47
Tim Vaughan	12-134	1-22	4-35	2-28	0-3	3-27	0-3	1-2	1-14	9.0	-45.15
Richard Lee	10-87	1-13	0-15	1-8	0-6	7-40	1-2	0-0	0-3	11.5	**12.50**
Alan King	10-82	3-18	2-21	2-20	2-5	1-13	0-1	0-0	0-5	12.2	-39.08
Nigel Hawke	9-64	1-9	0-14	0-8	2-3	6-25	0-0	0-0	0-5	14.1	-9.00
Jeremy Scott	8-59	3-11	0-16	2-9	0-0	2-12	0-0	0-0	1-11	13.6	-14.50
Nick Williams	8-40	0-5	2-9	3-8	1-3	0-9	1-1	0-0	1-5	20.0	**40.67**
Martin Keighley	8-67	0-8	5-27	2-10	1-3	0-13	0-0	0-0	0-7	11.9	-11.84
Kim Bailey	7-40	2-8	1-14	0-5	0-1	3-9	0-1	0-0	1-2	17.5	-1.93
Bernard Llewellyn	7-100	3-14	2-55	0-14	0-0	2-9	0-1	0-0	0-7	7.0	-38.00
Emma Lavelle	7-43	2-8	1-11	2-7	1-3	1-9	0-0	0-0	0-5	16.3	-4.25
Donald McCain	7-41	1-6	1-12	2-12	2-3	0-4	0-1	0-0	2-4	17.1	-14.98
Anthony Honeyball	7-44	0-7	2-11	1-8	0-1	1-10	0-0	0-0	3-7	15.9	**31.79**
Sophie Leech	7-57	1-6	4-25	0-3	0-2	2-20	0-0	0-0	0-1	12.3	**1.13**
Neil Mulholland	7-53	2-8	3-16	0-8	0-4	1-12	0-0	0-0	1-5	13.2	-9.75
Tom George	6-72	1-11	0-12	1-12	1-9	3-22	0-1	0-0	0-5	8.3	-49.13
Mark Gillard	6-44	1-6	3-14	0-5	0-3	2-14	0-1	0-0	0-1	13.6	-17.00
Dai Burchell	5-56	1-11	2-21	0-3	0-0	2-18	0-0	0-0	0-3	8.9	-15.75
Matt Sheppard	5-36	0-8	2-11	0-4	0-3	3-6	0-0	0-0	0-4	13.9	-13.00
Henry Daly	5-34	1-5	2-11	1-7	1-1	0-7	0-0	0-0	0-4	14.7	-19.33
Dan Skelton	5-18	2-4	2-5	1-2	0-0	0-4	0-1	0-0	0-2	27.8	**10.75**

LEADING JUMP TRAINERS AT DONCASTER (SINCE 2010)

	Total W-R	Nov Hdle	H'cap Hdle	Other Hdle	Nov Chase	H'cap Chase	Other Chase	Hunter Chase	N.H. Flat	Per cent	£1 Level stake
Nicky Henderson	40-124	13-30	6-21	9-29	6-14	1-15	2-6	0-0	3-9	32.3	**39.57**
Keith Reveley	18-127	2-13	5-28	0-14	3-13	7-42	0-0	0-0	1-17	14.2	-4.83
Paul Nicholls	14-65	1-7	1-7	2-12	8-18	1-18	0-0	0-0	1-3	21.5	-26.06
John Quinn	13-40	5-13	3-8	5-13	0-0	0-4	0-0	0-0	0-2	32.5	**48.75**
Alan King	13-118	5-26	3-25	2-20	1-12	0-20	1-3	0-0	1-12	11.0	-52.48
Emma Lavelle	9-32	0-3	1-7	0-2	0-2	6-14	0-0	0-0	2-4	28.1	**6.83**
Donald McCain	9-90	2-28	1-15	3-21	1-9	1-9	0-3	0-0	1-5	10.0	-27.13
John Ferguson	9-30	3-8	0-1	2-9	1-6	1-1	0-0	0-0	2-5	30.0	**3.89**
James Ewart	8-35	0-3	0-4	0-2	3-5	5-15	0-2	0-0	0-4	22.9	**9.50**
Jonjo O'Neill	7-76	0-12	5-25	0-17	1-4	0-14	0-0	1-2	0-2	9.2	-11.09
Philip Hobbs	6-40	0-5	3-12	0-4	1-8	2-10	0-1	0-0	0-0	15.0	**8.75**
Tony Carroll	6-31	2-10	3-13	1-6	0-1	0-1	0-0	0-0	0-0	19.4	**34.50**
Nicky Richards	6-30	1-8	2-12	1-3	0-0	2-5	0-0	0-0	0-2	20.0	**12.25**
Kim Bailey	5-28	1-4	1-7	1-5	1-3	1-6	0-1	0-0	0-2	17.9	**14.16**
Howard Johnson	5-32	3-9	0-3	0-3	1-3	1-12	0-0	0-0	0-2	15.6	**5.25**
Tom George	5-47	2-10	0-6	1-10	0-4	2-16	0-0	0-0	0-1	10.6	**28.50**
Henry Daly	5-34	0-4	1-6	0-1	1-3	1-13	1-1	0-0	1-6	14.7	**3.83**
Warren Greatrex	5-19	0-3	1-2	1-8	0-2	1-1	0-1	1-1	1-1	26.3	**3.36**
Malcolm Jefferson	4-51	2-12	0-7	0-6	0-5	1-17	0-0	0-0	1-4	7.8	-30.25
Michael Easterby	4-30	0-7	1-4	1-9	1-3	1-3	0-0	0-0	0-4	13.3	**22.00**
Brian Ellison	4-25	0-3	1-9	0-2	1-3	2-4	0-1	0-0	0-3	16.0	-0.38
Neil King	4-41	1-9	1-12	0-9	0-0	0-4	0-0	0-0	2-7	9.8	-5.13
Steve Gollings	4-36	0-10	0-4	1-4	2-7	0-5	0-0	0-0	1-6	11.1	-19.00
David Pipe	4-36	1-5	0-9	0-4	1-1	2-10	0-1	0-0	0-6	11.1	-16.00
Ian Williams	4-43	1-10	0-8	1-11	0-1	1-6	0-0	0-1	1-6	9.3	-27.53
Charlie Longsdon	4-39	1-6	1-8	1-6	0-7	1-11	0-0	0-0	0-1	10.3	-10.65
Harry Fry	4-15	0-2	0-2	1-4	2-4	0-2	1-1	0-0	0-0	26.7	-7.46
Ben Pauling	4-16	1-5	0-1	0-3	3-5	0-1	0-0	0-0	0-1	25.0	**10.00**
John Wade	3-24	1-5	0-4	0-1	0-2	1-9	0-0	0-0	1-3	12.5	**2.00**
John Mackie	3-25	1-7	1-7	0-5	0-0	1-2	0-2	0-0	0-2	12.0	**33.50**
Sue Smith	3-69	0-13	3-10	0-2	0-10	0-30	0-1	0-0	0-3	4.3	-48.50

LEADING JUMP TRAINERS AT EXETER (SINCE 2010)

	Total W-R	Nov Hdle	H'cap Hdle	Other Hdle	Nov Chase	H'cap Chase	Other Chase	Hunter Chase	N.H. Flat	Per cent	£1 Level stake
Philip Hobbs	47-242	14-62	7-52	5-19	3-23	6-46	4-16	1-2	7-22	19.4	-40.01
Paul Nicholls	38-151	14-51	3-15	3-14	8-24	1-15	7-16	0-1	2-15	25.2	-32.64
David Pipe	32-213	7-52	13-77	5-22	0-9	3-35	2-5	0-0	2-13	15.0	-74.63
Victor Dartnall	21-125	1-30	11-39	0-9	2-11	4-18	1-4	1-1	1-13	16.8	**13.77**
Colin Tizzard	20-142	3-32	3-32	2-10	4-15	5-33	3-12	0-0	0-8	14.1	-45.92
Sue Gardner	17-120	5-40	7-47	0-9	0-3	5-13	0-2	0-0	0-6	14.2	**17.83**
Alan King	17-88	2-22	3-20	0-6	6-12	1-8	3-7	0-0	2-13	19.3	-10.14
Jonjo O'Neill	16-114	4-29	3-27	1-10	2-4	4-34	1-5	0-0	1-5	14.0	-19.05
Emma Lavelle	15-98	4-27	1-16	2-11	4-9	3-17	1-10	0-0	0-8	15.3	-44.17
Jeremy Scott	14-128	2-39	7-37	0-13	0-7	4-20	0-5	0-0	1-7	10.9	-38.76
Venetia Williams	12-92	3-20	4-25	1-6	1-10	2-22	1-6	0-0	0-3	13.0	-25.29
Nick Williams	11-58	2-11	0-8	2-8	3-10	1-15	1-4	0-0	2-2	19.0	-1.07
Seamus Mullins	10-86	4-17	1-22	0-12	0-6	5-19	0-4	0-0	0-6	11.6	-9.57
Kim Bailey	9-40	3-12	1-10	1-5	1-1	1-9	2-2	0-0	0-1	22.5	**5.24**
Anthony Honeyball	9-41	0-11	4-15	0-1	1-1	3-9	0-2	0-0	1-2	22.0	**38.75**
Tim Vaughan	8-49	2-14	2-13	0-1	1-5	1-5	0-3	0-0	2-8	16.3	-4.09
Harry Fry	8-26	3-5	1-7	3-7	0-4	1-1	0-1	0-0	0-1	30.8	**13.71**
Oliver Sherwood	7-40	2-12	0-5	1-4	1-3	2-12	0-1	0-0	1-3	17.5	-16.30
Nigel Twiston-Davies	7-76	1-12	1-15	0-1	1-7	4-34	0-5	0-0	0-2	9.2	**15.00**
Chris Down	7-125	0-40	6-45	1-14	0-6	0-6	0-3	0-0	0-11	5.6	-31.50
Tom George	7-52	2-12	1-4	0-4	2-9	2-15	0-4	0-1	0-3	13.5	-1.80
Nicky Henderson	6-27	1-8	1-3	2-4	0-2	0-0	1-3	0-0	1-7	22.2	-13.22
Peter Bowen	6-41	2-9	2-14	0-1	0-2	0-10	1-2	0-0	1-3	14.6	-21.76
Fergal O'Brien	6-40	1-10	1-9	0-3	2-6	1-9	0-1	0-0	1-2	15.0	**5.08**
Charlie Longsdon	6-38	2-11	0-10	0-1	2-4	1-10	1-1	0-0	0-1	15.8	-8.40
Gary Moore	5-25	3-6	1-10	0-0	1-5	0-2	0-2	0-0	0-0	20.0	-3.00
Caroline Keevil	5-80	0-18	1-19	1-8	1-8	2-13	0-5	0-0	0-9	6.3	-40.00
Evan Williams	5-43	3-11	0-14	0-3	1-5	1-5	0-1	0-0	0-4	11.6	-13.50
Martin Hill	4-33	2-10	0-10	2-4	0-1	0-1	0-1	0-0	0-6	12.1	**30.00**
Alex Hales	4-13	0-1	2-3	0-0	1-3	1-5	0-1	0-0	0-0	30.8	**36.50**
Brendan Powell	4-42	0-9	0-13	0-3	0-3	1-6	0-2	0-1	3-5	9.5	-23.27

LEADING JUMP TRAINERS AT FAKENHAM (SINCE 2010)

	Total W-R	Nov Hdle	H'cap Hdle	Other Hdle	Nov Chase	H'cap Chase	Other Chase	Hunter Chase	N.H. Flat	Per cent	£1 Level stake
Nicky Henderson	17-43	7-12	1-6	2-7	0-7	1-1	1-2	1-1	4-7	39.5	-6.00
Lucy Wadham	16-69	1-9	4-22	0-8	2-5	6-14	0-4	2-3	1-4	23.2	**8.04**
Tim Vaughan	15-72	3-17	3-19	2-9	1-4	3-12	3-8	0-0	0-3	20.8	-27.38
Neil King	12-106	2-14	4-33	0-18	0-4	4-26	1-5	0-0	1-6	11.3	-8.40
Evan Williams	11-41	2-9	1-5	0-5	1-4	4-11	3-5	0-0	0-2	26.8	**29.36**
Peter Bowen	10-29	0-3	2-4	2-2	2-3	1-12	2-3	0-0	1-2	34.5	**7.98**
Alex Hales	10-40	2-6	2-15	1-4	2-2	3-10	0-0	0-0	0-3	25.0	**25.61**
Pam Sly	9-45	2-8	1-15	2-6	2-4	0-5	1-2	0-0	1-5	20.0	**29.58**
David Pipe	8-12	4-6	0-0	2-3	2-3	0-0	0-0	0-0	0-0	66.7	**11.00**
Renee Robeson	7-26	0-4	2-6	1-3	2-2	2-5	0-0	0-0	0-6	26.9	**24.88**
John Ferguson	7-32	1-8	0-2	2-9	1-1	0-2	0-1	2-5	1-4	21.9	-0.35
Paul Nicholls	6-20	1-5	0-0	0-1	3-5	0-3	2-6	0-0	0-0	30.0	-7.99
Caroline Bailey	6-38	1-7	1-6	0-6	0-0	4-18	0-1	0-0	0-0	15.8	-11.75
Sarah Humphrey	6-49	0-7	1-12	2-9	0-0	3-17	0-2	0-0	0-2	12.2	-23.20
Michael Gates	6-24	0-4	0-4	0-1	0-1	6-12	0-2	0-0	0-0	25.0	**7.75**
Milton Harris	5-21	1-3	1-4	1-5	0-0	2-6	0-2	0-0	0-1	23.8	**2.17**
Brian Ellison	5-20	0-2	2-8	1-5	0-1	2-4	0-0	0-0	0-0	25.0	**3.83**
Steve Gollings	5-26	1-4	1-5	1-5	0-0	0-5	1-3	0-0	1-4	19.2	-9.56
Jim Best	5-35	1-4	1-16	3-13	0-0	0-1	0-0	0-0	0-1	14.3	-18.13
Ali Stronge	5-10	2-3	2-4	0-1	0-0	1-1	0-0	0-0	0-1	50.0	**32.00**
John Cornwall	4-51	0-0	0-3	0-0	0-12	4-33	0-3	0-0	0-0	7.8	-19.00
Mick Channon	4-8	0-2	0-0	1-3	1-1	0-0	2-2	0-0	0-0	50.0	**8.29**
Lawney Hill	4-30	0-3	0-12	2-4	0-0	2-11	0-0	0-0	0-0	13.3	-17.15
Charlie Mann	4-27	0-1	1-6	2-4	0-3	0-9	1-4	0-0	0-0	14.8	-11.25
Ben Case	4-25	1-2	2-11	1-6	0-1	0-1	0-3	0-0	0-1	16.0	-11.63
Dan Skelton	4-18	0-2	2-4	1-4	0-2	1-4	0-1	0-0	0-1	22.2	-2.50
Dr Richard Newland	4-14	0-0	0-1	3-6	0-0	1-3	0-1	0-2	0-1	28.6	**5.80**
J R Jenkins	3-18	0-2	1-5	1-8	0-0	1-1	0-0	0-0	0-2	16.7	-8.89
Oliver Sherwood	3-17	0-2	0-2	3-5	0-2	0-4	0-1	0-0	0-1	17.6	**7.50**
Chris Bealby	3-32	0-5	1-7	0-4	0-0	2-14	0-0	0-0	0-2	9.4	-11.75
Martin Bosley	3-15	1-1	0-5	0-4	0-1	1-3	0-0	0-0	1-1	20.0	**113.00**

LEADING JUMP TRAINERS AT FFOS LAS (SINCE 2010)

	Total W-R	Nov Hdle	H'cap Hdle	Other Hdle	Nov Chase	H'cap Chase	Other Chase	Hunter Chase	N.H. Flat	Per cent	£1 Level stake
Peter Bowen	59-393	7-57	16-97	6-64	5-21	14-92	1-6	0-2	10-54	15.0	-95.73
Evan Williams	59-448	5-51	14-137	10-50	6-50	18-126	1-5	0-0	5-29	13.2	-48.73
Rebecca Curtis	58-221	15-45	8-46	10-48	6-17	7-20	0-2	0-2	12-41	26.2	**9.82**
Nigel Twiston-Davies	35-192	4-15	6-47	1-17	4-15	17-75	2-5	0-1	1-17	18.2	-20.43
Jonjo O'Neill	35-184	6-14	13-58	1-24	2-12	10-62	1-1	0-2	2-11	19.0	-11.74
Tim Vaughan	35-315	1-48	6-78	6-55	4-23	13-68	0-3	0-1	5-39	11.1	-148.12
Nicky Henderson	26-62	9-16	3-12	3-10	4-8	0-2	0-2	0-0	7-12	41.9	**15.06**
David Pipe	25-149	2-16	7-52	4-19	0-5	4-31	1-1	0-0	7-25	16.8	-14.87
Philip Hobbs	13-94	0-9	3-23	2-16	2-7	2-23	0-2	0-0	4-14	13.8	-36.52
Bernard Llewellyn	12-123	2-21	5-52	3-19	1-7	1-17	0-0	0-0	0-7	9.8	**44.50**
David Rees	12-106	1-9	5-41	2-16	2-9	2-30	0-1	0-0	0-0	11.3	**44.50**
Anthony Honeyball	12-52	1-5	2-12	0-9	1-3	3-7	0-1	0-0	5-15	23.1	**10.96**
Richard Lee	10-51	0-3	2-11	0-4	1-1	6-29	0-1	0-0	1-2	19.6	**47.46**
John Flint	10-77	1-11	6-29	1-7	0-1	1-12	0-1	0-0	1-16	13.0	**67.63**
Keith Goldsworthy	10-126	1-20	2-35	2-19	0-7	2-19	0-1	1-1	2-24	7.9	-35.25
Dr Richard Newland	10-26	0-2	6-14	1-1	0-1	3-8	0-0	0-0	0-0	38.5	**19.35**
Debra Hamer	9-72	1-14	2-15	0-12	2-4	3-17	1-1	0-0	0-9	12.5	-0.04
Paul Nicholls	8-31	2-5	3-6	2-8	1-2	0-5	0-1	0-1	0-3	25.8	-3.57
Sophie Leech	8-36	1-3	3-14	2-2	0-3	2-12	0-0	0-0	0-2	22.2	**2.38**
Kim Bailey	7-38	1-2	2-13	2-6	0-6	0-6	0-0	0-0	2-5	18.4	-7.75
Charlie Mann	7-43	3-6	0-15	1-6	1-6	2-7	0-0	0-0	0-3	16.3	**21.78**
Warren Greatrex	6-29	0-2	1-5	3-8	0-3	1-5	0-1	0-0	1-5	20.7	-12.33
Venetia Williams	7-45	0-4	1-7	0-6	1-4	4-22	1-1	0-0	0-1	15.6	**14.25**
Mark Bradstock	6-12	0-0	3-4	0-0	1-1	2-3	0-0	0-0	0-4	50.0	**20.13**
Henry Daly	6-22	3-4	2-7	0-0	0-5	0-1	1-2	0-0	0-3	27.3	**0.75**
Bob Buckler	5-19	0-4	1-5	0-1	0-0	4-8	0-0	0-0	0-1	26.3	**20.98**
Alan King	5-42	0-5	1-9	0-3	1-5	2-7	0-2	0-0	1-11	11.9	-6.88
Martin Keighley	5-34	0-2	2-10	0-4	1-5	0-8	0-0	0-0	2-5	14.7	-0.25
Paul Henderson	5-19	0-0	2-4	0-1	1-2	1-11	0-0	0-0	1-1	26.3	**6.50**
Neil Mulholland	5-45	0-4	4-14	0-3	0-2	1-16	0-0	0-0	0-6	11.1	-4.50
Jamie Snowden	5-27	1-3	1-10	2-9	0-1	0-2	0-0	0-0	1-2	18.5	**8.50**

LEADING JUMP TRAINERS AT FONTWELL (SINCE 2010)

	Total W-R	Nov Hdle	H'cap Hdle	Other Hdle	Nov Chase	H'cap Chase	Other Chase	Hunter Chase	N.H. Flat	Per cent	£1 Level stake
Chris Gordon	43-309	2-35	24-114	1-35	3-14	11-90	0-0	0-1	2-20	13.9	**37.84**
Gary Moore	40-307	4-29	13-103	6-48	5-20	7-79	4-8	0-0	1-20	13.0	-97.65
Paul Nicholls	28-92	3-10	1-8	2-18	7-19	1-10	10-16	1-1	3-10	30.4	-17.73
Tim Vaughan	22-119	6-18	5-34	2-10	2-10	6-29	0-5	0-0	1-13	18.5	-29.11
Oliver Sherwood	19-70	3-11	4-15	3-9	0-6	3-14	1-2	0-0	5-13	27.1	**58.25**
Alan King	19-78	6-17	1-9	6-24	2-7	1-6	1-7	0-0	2-8	24.4	-6.84
Neil Mulholland	18-113	6-17	8-44	0-11	0-5	3-27	1-3	0-0	0-6	15.9	**0.34**
Nicky Henderson	16-45	3-5	1-6	1-6	3-5	1-2	2-4	1-1	4-16	35.6	-4.65
Seamus Mullins	16-153	0-9	4-29	2-17	2-8	7-64	0-5	0-0	1-21	10.5	**26.00**
David Pipe	16-82	3-14	3-33	3-14	1-3	2-5	1-1	0-0	3-12	19.5	-21.23
Charlie Longsdon	16-93	5-19	0-25	4-13	0-1	4-23	1-2	0-0	2-10	17.2	-29.56
Jonjo O'Neill	15-81	2-9	4-28	0-2	1-4	6-31	0-3	1-1	1-3	18.5	-13.94
Jamie Snowden	15-89	3-14	3-15	1-15	0-7	4-19	0-2	0-0	4-17	16.9	**9.15**
Victor Dartnall	14-47	1-6	5-11	0-6	1-1	5-14	0-2	1-1	1-6	29.8	**28.32**
Venetia Williams	14-74	0-7	5-19	3-8	2-8	2-23	1-3	0-0	1-6	18.9	**0.96**
Brendan Powell	14-170	1-20	8-55	0-11	0-7	4-63	0-1	0-0	1-13	8.2	-78.44
Lawney Hill	13-75	0-7	8-34	1-2	0-5	4-22	0-2	0-0	0-3	17.3	-7.16
Colin Tizzard	13-72	1-8	1-13	3-11	3-6	2-18	0-2	0-0	3-14	18.1	-19.93
Emma Lavelle	13-61	3-11	1-12	3-7	1-3	4-16	1-7	0-0	0-5	21.3	**20.25**
Anthony Honeyball	13-39	0-3	5-8	0-6	1-2	1-4	0-1	0-0	6-15	33.3	**4.75**
Philip Hobbs	12-55	4-11	4-15	2-10	0-1	0-11	0-2	0-0	2-5	21.8	-3.29
Caroline Keevil	11-68	0-11	5-24	1-7	1-2	2-9	1-2	0-0	1-13	16.2	**37.55**
Evan Williams	11-61	2-6	1-16	2-7	1-4	3-20	1-4	0-0	1-4	18.0	-20.70
Lydia Richards	10-66	0-3	1-9	0-8	0-5	9-34	0-0	0-0	0-7	15.2	**8.25**
David Bridgwater	10-49	2-6	0-5	1-6	0-2	7-26	0-3	0-0	0-1	20.4	-9.15
Sheena West	8-75	0-10	3-37	4-16	0-0	0-4	0-2	0-0	1-6	10.7	**3.25**
Neil King	8-69	0-7	0-16	2-12	1-4	5-24	0-0	0-0	0-6	11.6	**13.86**
Charlie Mann	8-66	2-8	1-15	0-13	2-4	2-20	0-2	0-0	1-4	12.1	-15.52
Nick Gifford	8-86	1-17	1-14	0-13	0-5	3-19	1-8	0-0	2-10	9.3	-49.77
Dr Richard Newland	8-20	1-3	2-6	3-4	0-1	2-4	0-0	0-0	0-2	40.0	**0.26**
Richard Rowe	7-108	1-19	0-30	1-7	0-3	5-31	0-2	0-0	0-16	6.5	-62.92

LEADING JUMP TRAINERS AT HAYDOCK (SINCE 2010)

	Total W-R	Nov Hdle	H'cap Hdle	Other Hdle	Nov Chase	H'cap Chase	Other Chase	Hunter Chase	N.H. Flat	Per cent	£1 Level stake
Donald McCain	38-174	13-25	7-54	5-27	3-17	4-28	2-5	0-1	4-18	21.8	-16.45
Paul Nicholls	14-65	1-4	2-18	1-11	3-7	2-12	5-12	0-0	0-2	21.5	-1.50
David Pipe	14-74	0-2	8-41	2-4	0-0	5-25	0-3	0-0	0-0	18.9	**38.70**
Nicky Henderson	12-69	2-11	3-31	4-11	0-5	0-3	2-6	0-0	1-4	17.4	-16.82
Sue Smith	12-125	0-13	0-26	0-7	5-15	6-57	1-5	0-0	0-3	9.6	-8.75
Venetia Williams	12-100	3-7	3-28	2-9	2-10	2-42	0-2	0-1	0-1	12.0	-32.80
Alan King	11-63	2-4	1-20	2-8	1-3	1-16	1-3	0-1	3-8	17.5	-22.71
Lucinda Russell	10-63	3-6	0-15	0-2	1-5	5-32	0-1	0-0	1-2	15.9	**27.50**
Nigel Twiston-Davies	9-90	0-5	2-21	2-9	1-6	1-40	1-2	1-2	1-7	10.0	-45.22
Brian Ellison	8-54	1-2	4-33	0-6	1-2	2-11	0-0	0-0	0-0	14.8	**7.75**
Evan Williams	8-53	0-3	5-20	0-4	1-3	2-21	0-1	0-0	0-1	15.1	**58.50**
Philip Hobbs	7-68	0-4	3-32	0-1	1-6	2-18	0-3	0-0	1-4	10.3	-24.25
Henry Daly	7-34	0-2	2-7	1-3	2-6	0-11	0-0	1-1	1-4	20.6	-2.17
Malcolm Jefferson	6-50	1-6	0-15	1-5	0-0	4-19	0-0	0-0	0-6	12.0	-2.27
Jonjo O'Neill	6-71	0-6	2-32	0-4	2-4	0-19	1-2	0-1	1-3	8.5	-13.44
Tom George	6-34	0-1	1-7	1-1	1-8	3-14	0-2	0-0	0-1	17.6	**2.50**
Colin Tizzard	6-23	0-0	1-2	0-2	1-4	2-10	2-5	0-0	0-0	26.1	**11.16**
Charlie Longsdon	6-44	0-2	3-16	1-1	0-0	1-21	0-0	0-0	1-4	13.6	-15.50
Emma Lavelle	5-18	0-2	2-7	2-5	0-3	0-0	0-0	0-0	1-1	27.8	**12.73**
Nick Williams	5-22	1-3	1-9	1-3	1-2	1-4	0-1	0-0	0-1	22.7	**9.83**
Peter Bowen	4-36	0-4	1-9	1-3	0-2	1-15	0-1	0-0	1-3	11.1	-4.00
Keith Reveley	4-35	0-4	3-14	0-1	0-3	1-11	0-0	0-0	0-2	11.4	-21.43
Jennie Candlish	4-36	0-0	2-22	1-7	0-0	1-4	0-0	0-0	0-4	11.1	-13.50
John Quinn	3-12	0-1	1-5	2-4	0-0	0-1	0-0	0-0	0-1	25.0	**10.25**
Tim Easterby	3-41	0-5	1-16	0-8	0-0	1-8	0-1	0-0	1-3	7.3	-7.50
Caroline Bailey	3-12	0-1	0-1	0-0	0-0	3-10	0-0	0-0	0-0	25.0	**9.75**
Ian Williams	3-21	0-4	1-9	0-0	2-4	0-3	0-0	0-0	0-1	14.3	-10.00
Robin Dickin	2-9	1-1	0-3	1-1	0-1	0-2	0-0	0-0	0-1	22.2	**2.00**
John Wade	2-19	0-0	0-6	0-0	0-0	2-11	0-0	0-1	0-1	10.5	-0.00
Jeremy Scott	2-14	1-1	0-8	1-2	0-0	0-1	0-1	0-0	0-1	14.3	-3.25
Howard Johnson	2-15	1-3	0-5	0-0	0-2	1-4	0-1	0-0	0-0	13.3	**10.00**

LEADING JUMP TRAINERS AT HEXHAM (SINCE 2010)

	Total W-R	Nov Hdle	H'cap Hdle	Other Hdle	Nov Chase	H'cap Chase	Other Chase	Hunter Chase	N.H. Flat	Per cent	£1 Level stake
Lucinda Russell	47-246	3-39	5-49	8-24	8-29	16-87	2-2	0-0	5-16	19.1	-35.25
Sue Smith	24-145	1-24	6-26	2-16	4-12	6-53	2-2	0-0	3-12	16.6	-31.34
Donald McCain	19-116	8-35	2-25	5-21	1-13	0-10	0-2	0-0	3-10	16.4	-65.27
Ferdy Murphy	15-102	3-11	2-11	2-16	3-13	4-39	0-6	0-0	1-6	14.7	**8.63**
Howard Johnson	13-50	3-16	0-7	2-6	2-7	4-7	0-2	0-0	2-5	26.0	**0.38**
Stuart Coltherd	12-45	1-3	1-10	0-4	1-5	9-22	0-1	0-0	0-0	26.7	**76.00**
Malcolm Jefferson	10-47	2-15	2-10	1-2	1-6	3-6	0-0	0-0	1-8	21.3	-4.51
N W Alexander	10-60	1-12	3-16	1-5	0-2	3-14	1-2	1-3	0-6	16.7	**17.20**
Martin Todhunter	9-81	1-8	1-27	1-5	0-7	6-32	0-0	0-0	0-2	11.1	-11.62
James Ewart	9-48	1-4	0-3	0-5	2-6	6-18	0-3	0-0	0-9	18.8	**10.87**
George Moore	8-30	3-11	2-3	1-4	2-6	0-3	0-0	0-0	0-3	26.7	-0.63
Brian Ellison	8-43	2-11	2-8	3-14	1-4	0-3	0-0	0-0	0-3	18.6	-12.83
Micky Hammond	8-56	2-13	5-16	1-2	0-5	0-14	0-0	0-0	0-6	14.3	-23.93
Maurice Barnes	7-103	2-22	2-26	1-18	1-13	1-17	0-0	0-0	0-7	6.8	-10.01
Donald Whillans	7-66	0-6	3-31	0-5	0-2	3-16	0-1	0-0	1-5	10.6	-26.50
John Quinn	7-17	0-4	0-4	5-5	0-1	0-1	0-0	0-0	2-2	41.2	**3.40**
Alan Swinbank	7-25	1-7	2-5	1-3	0-1	0-0	1-1	0-0	2-8	28.0	-0.13
Nicky Richards	7-30	1-5	1-8	1-7	2-3	1-5	1-1	0-0	0-1	23.3	-1.47
Ann Hamilton	6-34	0-4	3-8	0-4	1-2	2-12	0-0	0-1	0-3	17.6	-2.13
Dianne Sayer	6-76	0-11	4-21	0-10	0-8	2-23	0-0	0-0	0-3	7.9	-33.63
S R B Crawford	6-20	1-1	0-5	1-2	2-5	0-4	0-0	0-0	2-3	30.0	-4.99
Karen McLintock	6-25	0-3	0-1	0-3	2-3	0-2	0-0	0-0	4-13	24.0	-0.25
Philip Kirby	6-54	1-18	1-12	1-5	0-1	2-9	0-1	0-3	1-5	11.1	-16.75
John Wade	5-63	0-15	1-9	0-3	1-6	3-22	0-1	0-2	0-5	7.9	-20.13
Michael Scudamore	6-18	0-0	0-4	1-2	0-0	2-7	0-0	0-0	3-5	33.3	**6.58**
Alistair Whillans	5-66	1-10	3-30	0-3	0-2	0-14	1-1	0-0	0-6	7.6	-39.00
Andrew Crook	5-42	0-5	1-12	0-8	0-0	4-15	0-0	0-0	0-2	11.9	**38.00**
Keith Reveley	5-33	2-9	1-4	2-4	0-3	0-10	0-0	0-0	0-3	15.2	-9.44
J J Lambe	5-30	2-6	1-11	1-4	0-3	1-3	0-1	0-0	0-2	16.7	-3.92
Rose Dobbin	5-49	1-10	1-7	0-3	0-3	3-21	0-0	0-0	0-5	10.2	-4.25
Tim Walford	4-26	0-6	4-14	0-4	0-1	0-1	0-0	0-0	0-0	15.4	-7.63

LEADING JUMP TRAINERS AT HUNTINGDON (SINCE 2010)

	Total W-R	Nov Hdle	H'cap Hdle	Other Hdle	Nov Chase	H'cap Chase	Other Chase	Hunter Chase	N.H. Flat	Per cent	£1 Level stake
Nicky Henderson	40-106	12-33	2-10	10-19	6-12	1-4	3-9	0-0	6-19	37.7	**0.47**
Alan King	28-134	7-32	4-31	5-21	5-15	3-11	0-1	0-0	4-23	20.9	**0.10**
Jonjo O'Neill	26-142	1-34	14-49	1-17	2-7	6-23	0-0	0-1	2-11	18.3	-21.22
Charlie Longsdon	19-112	5-23	4-31	1-6	3-15	3-18	1-3	0-0	2-16	17.0	-14.07
John Ferguson	17-49	9-21	0-3	4-14	0-2	0-1	0-0	0-0	4-8	34.7	**24.05**
Gary Moore	15-115	1-23	8-31	3-20	2-15	0-16	0-3	0-1	1-6	13.0	**3.70**
Kim Bailey	13-58	2-15	2-12	2-3	2-5	3-12	0-1	0-0	2-10	22.4	**15.00**
Neil King	13-148	2-25	4-59	4-20	0-5	2-21	0-1	0-0	1-17	8.8	-4.75
Venetia Williams	13-98	3-13	5-28	0-13	2-14	3-23	0-1	0-0	0-6	13.3	**34.66**
Lawney Hill	9-58	0-5	2-25	2-7	0-3	4-13	1-2	0-0	0-3	15.5	**10.60**
Ian Williams	9-51	1-7	4-18	1-7	2-5	1-8	0-1	0-0	0-5	17.6	**5.04**
J R Jenkins	8-54	0-5	6-26	0-8	1-5	0-1	0-1	0-0	1-8	14.8	**36.50**
Lucy Wadham	8-65	2-11	2-23	1-9	1-3	1-8	0-0	0-0	1-11	12.3	-8.31
Ben Case	8-51	0-5	6-25	1-3	0-5	1-4	0-0	0-0	0-9	15.7	**22.25**
Philip Hobbs	7-54	1-15	0-5	1-8	2-9	0-5	1-3	0-1	2-8	13.0	-25.00
Oliver Sherwood	7-47	0-8	0-8	0-7	1-5	3-6	0-1	0-0	3-12	14.9	-9.51
Jeremy Scott	7-22	5-8	0-5	0-1	1-1	0-5	0-0	0-0	1-2	31.8	**3.04**
Paul Nicholls	7-18	4-5	0-3	0-1	0-1	0-2	1-4	1-1	1-1	38.9	**1.43**
Brendan Powell	7-70	1-6	0-21	1-11	0-7	3-20	0-0	1-2	1-3	10.0	-35.25
Dr Richard Newland	7-30	0-1	5-12	1-5	0-3	1-6	0-2	0-1	0-0	23.3	**3.09**
Tim Vaughan	7-42	1-10	1-10	2-6	1-4	2-6	0-0	0-1	0-5	16.7	-7.59
Neil Mulholland	7-32	0-3	2-14	2-2	1-3	2-9	0-0	0-0	0-1	21.9	-5.93
Robin Dickin	6-31	1-13	1-6	0-3	2-3	1-4	0-0	0-0	1-2	19.4	**31.00**
Nigel Twiston-Davies	6-83	1-10	0-19	1-7	2-13	2-24	0-0	0-0	0-10	7.2	-59.64
David Pipe	6-38	0-3	3-19	1-6	2-2	0-3	0-0	0-0	0-5	15.8	-17.84
Caroline Bailey	6-58	1-15	0-15	0-5	0-4	5-16	0-1	0-0	0-2	10.3	-23.00
Henry Daly	6-55	0-15	4-6	0-7	2-11	0-8	0-2	0-0	0-6	10.9	**1.62**
Dan Skelton	6-32	0-5	2-8	1-3	1-2	2-5	0-0	0-0	0-9	18.8	-10.13
Pam Sly	5-56	1-10	1-18	0-5	2-9	1-6	0-0	0-0	0-8	8.9	-28.17
Sheena West	5-35	1-8	1-11	1-7	1-4	0-4	1-1	0-0	0-0	14.3	-18.97
Claire Dyson	5-55	0-7	3-32	0-3	0-2	2-10	0-0	0-0	0-1	9.1	-14.92

LEADING JUMP TRAINERS AT KELSO (SINCE 2010)

	Total W-R	Nov Hdle	H'cap Hdle	Other Hdle	Nov Chase	H'cap Chase	Other Chase	Hunter Chase	N.H. Flat	Per cent	£1 Level stake
Donald McCain	40-164	12-39	4-23	6-31	6-23	9-32	0-7	0-0	3-9	24.4	**28.36**
Lucinda Russell	29-298	7-72	3-62	2-23	7-38	8-83	1-4	0-0	1-16	9.7	-118.91
Nicky Richards	25-130	5-33	5-35	3-15	2-8	4-21	1-3	1-2	4-13	19.2	-6.17
James Ewart	19-119	4-21	5-22	2-12	1-16	5-38	1-2	0-0	1-8	16.0	**7.86**
N W Alexander	15-144	3-34	2-23	1-13	2-8	6-36	0-2	1-16	0-12	10.4	**10.95**
Rose Dobbin	14-128	5-45	1-31	1-13	1-7	3-17	1-2	0-2	2-11	10.9	**5.16**
Chris Grant	13-85	4-29	4-19	0-4	0-6	4-15	0-2	0-0	1-10	15.3	**120.89**
Stuart Coltherd	11-95	0-23	4-15	0-7	2-18	3-22	0-1	2-8	0-1	11.6	**36.12**
John Wade	10-66	0-9	2-13	1-2	0-10	4-23	1-1	2-3	0-5	15.2	**18.50**
Howard Johnson	10-48	3-15	2-7	1-5	2-6	1-9	0-0	0-0	1-6	20.8	**35.63**
Jim Goldie	10-94	3-18	5-39	0-8	1-6	0-16	0-0	0-0	1-7	10.6	-46.40
Ann Hamilton	9-44	0-7	3-7	1-4	0-2	3-18	1-1	1-2	0-3	20.5	**17.83**
Sue Smith	9-73	1-10	1-13	0-2	4-14	3-29	0-3	0-0	0-2	12.3	-8.82
Dianne Sayer	9-112	2-19	3-47	0-8	2-5	2-30	0-1	0-0	0-2	8.0	-39.50
George Charlton	9-87	3-24	2-25	0-5	0-7	3-14	0-1	0-0	1-11	10.3	-30.60
Malcolm Jefferson	8-68	1-13	0-12	1-2	2-8	2-20	0-2	0-0	2-11	11.8	-11.75
Alistair Whillans	8-88	2-20	3-42	0-4	1-1	0-13	0-0	0-0	2-8	9.1	-40.34
Michael Smith	8-44	5-14	0-9	1-6	0-6	0-3	0-0	0-0	2-6	18.2	**38.12**
Maurice Barnes	7-98	2-27	3-26	0-12	2-10	0-14	0-1	0-0	0-8	7.1	-47.90
Keith Reveley	7-36	1-4	0-7	2-3	1-3	3-10	0-0	0-0	0-9	19.4	-1.47
Alan Swinbank	7-40	3-15	0-6	2-6	0-2	0-0	1-1	0-0	1-10	17.5	-12.05
Nicky Henderson	6-10	1-2	0-0	1-2	2-2	0-0	2-2	0-0	0-2	60.0	**2.36**
George Bewley	6-50	1-8	4-21	1-7	0-3	0-7	0-1	0-0	0-3	12.0	**17.50**
Karen McLintock	6-21	1-5	2-4	0-2	0-0	2-3	0-1	0-0	1-6	28.6	**18.50**
George Moore	5-24	0-3	1-8	2-4	1-2	1-3	0-0	0-0	0-4	20.8	**7.50**
Patrick Griffin	5-20	1-6	0-3	2-4	0-1	1-2	1-1	0-0	0-3	25.0	**10.25**
Andrew Parker	5-22	1-4	1-6	0-0	2-3	1-8	0-0	0-0	0-1	22.7	-1.59
Ferdy Murphy	5-64	0-6	0-11	0-4	1-9	3-26	1-6	0-0	0-2	7.8	-32.06
Robert Johnson	4-32	0-12	0-0	1-3	1-4	2-9	0-1	0-0	0-3	12.5	**16.50**
Sandy Thomson	4-53	0-15	1-12	1-6	0-3	1-10	0-0	1-5	0-2	7.5	-27.50
William Amos	4-40	0-6	1-13	1-2	2-6	0-11	0-0	0-0	0-2	10.0	-21.38

LEADING JUMP TRAINERS AT KEMPTON (SINCE 2010)

	Total W-R	Nov Hdle	H'cap Hdle	Other Hdle	Nov Chase	H'cap Chase	Other Chase	Hunter Chase	N.H. Flat	Per cent	£1 Level stake
Nicky Henderson	71-237	14-50	12-58	13-40	9-26	6-25	9-26	0-0	10-19	30.0	**59.90**
Paul Nicholls	36-166	5-27	3-23	7-28	8-25	6-27	8-28	0-1	0-9	21.7	-11.36
Alan King	23-179	8-47	3-41	5-24	3-16	1-24	1-10	0-0	2-20	12.8	-73.66
Philip Hobbs	21-124	6-22	3-35	2-13	2-9	4-25	3-11	0-1	1-12	16.9	-17.15
Jonjo O'Neill	12-92	2-23	1-20	3-12	0-3	5-23	1-4	0-1	0-6	13.0	-32.60
Emma Lavelle	12-76	5-26	4-15	0-4	0-7	2-14	0-3	0-0	1-9	15.8	-7.98
Gary Moore	9-123	2-28	2-36	0-18	1-14	1-19	2-8	0-0	1-2	7.3	-61.72
Tom George	9-58	1-8	1-6	1-4	3-8	3-27	0-3	0-0	0-2	15.5	-10.75
David Pipe	9-66	1-4	2-31	3-12	2-2	1-13	0-7	0-0	0-1	13.6	-38.56
Paul Webber	8-78	0-24	0-10	1-10	0-2	4-18	3-8	0-0	0-6	10.3	-27.20
Colin Tizzard	7-61	2-9	0-8	1-2	0-9	1-16	1-10	0-0	2-7	11.5	-32.52
Nigel Twiston-Davies	6-52	0-8	0-8	2-8	1-6	2-18	0-2	0-0	1-3	11.5	-20.82
Venetia Williams	6-80	1-10	0-25	0-5	0-2	3-34	2-6	0-0	0-0	7.5	-40.75
Charlie Longsdon	6-59	1-12	2-22	0-6	1-6	1-11	0-0	0-0	1-5	10.2	-12.00
Chris Gordon	6-28	0-3	1-7	0-2	0-1	5-12	0-1	0-0	0-2	21.4	**42.43**
Harry Fry	6-14	1-3	1-3	2-3	0-0	2-3	0-0	0-0	0-2	42.9	**13.32**
Lucy Wadham	5-29	1-5	3-12	0-1	0-3	1-6	0-0	0-0	0-2	17.2	-0.09
Nick Williams	5-23	2-4	3-7	1-4	0-5	0-3	0-1	0-0	0-0	21.7	**12.63**
Jim Best	5-15	2-6	1-2	2-6	0-0	0-0	0-0	0-0	0-1	33.3	**12.60**
David Arbuthnot	4-27	1-4	2-13	0-2	0-2	0-4	0-0	0-0	1-3	14.8	-8.05
Kim Bailey	4-45	0-9	1-14	0-2	0-5	2-11	0-1	0-0	1-3	8.9	**16.00**
Jeremy Scott	4-33	2-4	1-16	0-3	0-1	1-7	0-0	0-0	0-3	12.1	**3.00**
Andy Turnell	4-32	1-5	1-8	0-2	1-3	1-8	0-2	0-0	0-4	12.5	**1.33**
Tony Carroll	4-27	1-5	2-14	0-1	0-2	0-2	1-2	0-0	0-1	14.8	**54.75**
Evan Williams	4-26	1-7	2-8	0-4	1-1	0-6	0-0	0-0	0-0	15.4	**1.25**
Tim Vaughan	4-37	3-8	0-14	0-3	0-5	1-5	0-1	0-0	0-2	10.8	-14.93
Warren Greatrex	4-44	0-13	2-12	0-6	1-2	0-7	1-3	0-0	0-3	9.1	-21.25
John Ferguson	4-25	2-12	1-4	0-5	0-2	0-0	0-0	0-0	1-2	16.0	-14.33
Robin Dickin	3-30	1-5	0-2	0-3	1-6	1-7	0-2	0-0	0-5	10.0	-7.50
Henrietta Knight	3-26	0-4	0-3	0-5	1-3	1-5	1-2	0-0	0-4	11.5	-16.58
Mick Channon	3-14	0-3	0-1	2-7	0-2	1-1	0-0	0-0	0-0	21.4	-3.25

LEADING JUMP TRAINERS AT LEICESTER (SINCE 2010)

	Total W-R	Nov Hdle	H'cap Hdle	Other Hdle	Nov Chase	H'cap Chase	Other Chase	Hunter Chase	N.H. Flat	Per cent	£1 Level stake
Nigel Twiston-Davies	16-79	2-11	2-10	1-6	3-15	8-33	0-3	0-1	0-0	20.3	**15.97**
Tom George	13-52	0-0	0-1	0-3	6-20	7-27	0-0	0-1	0-0	25.0	**13.86**
Nicky Henderson	11-30	2-7	0-1	2-4	5-13	1-3	1-2	0-0	0-0	36.7	**14.87**
Venetia Williams	11-53	1-7	0-11	0-5	2-10	5-17	3-3	0-0	0-0	20.8	-14.00
Caroline Bailey	10-62	0-10	1-5	0-3	3-11	6-30	0-3	0-0	0-0	16.1	-3.00
David Pipe	9-26	4-5	2-7	0-4	1-3	2-7	0-0	0-0	0-0	34.6	-2.87
Tony Carroll	8-75	0-6	2-28	3-13	2-11	1-17	0-0	0-0	0-0	10.7	-13.00
Neil King	7-31	1-5	0-5	3-7	1-3	1-10	1-1	0-0	0-0	22.6	**3.25**
Charlie Longsdon	7-29	0-8	0-3	0-2	1-4	4-8	2-4	0-0	0-0	24.1	**8.10**
Jonjo O'Neill	6-58	1-14	2-10	1-2	1-11	1-21	0-0	0-0	0-0	10.3	-31.20
Paul Webber	6-50	1-7	0-4	0-3	1-13	3-20	1-3	0-0	0-0	12.0	**6.05**
Philip Hobbs	5-21	1-3	1-3	0-2	0-5	3-8	0-0	0-0	0-0	23.8	-8.84
Richard Lee	5-17	0-3	1-3	0-0	2-4	2-7	0-0	0-0	0-0	29.4	**13.33**
Oliver Sherwood	5-21	0-2	0-1	2-4	1-5	1-7	1-2	0-0	0-0	23.8	**2.25**
Lucy Wadham	5-29	2-6	1-7	1-3	0-5	0-7	1-1	0-0	0-0	17.2	-7.13
Ian Williams	5-15	0-1	1-3	0-1	1-3	3-7	0-0	0-0	0-0	33.3	**1.88**
Emma Lavelle	5-12	2-3	0-0	0-1	2-4	1-4	0-0	0-0	0-0	41.7	**1.46**
Alan King	5-37	1-12	0-3	1-3	1-9	0-6	2-4	0-0	0-0	13.5	-17.31
John Ferguson	5-8	4-4	0-0	0-2	0-1	0-0	1-1	0-0	0-0	62.5	**2.08**
Robin Dickin	4-27	0-4	0-2	1-4	2-3	1-12	0-2	0-0	0-0	14.8	-0.50
Seamus Mullins	4-11	0-1	0-0	0-0	2-6	2-4	0-0	0-0	0-0	36.4	**13.50**
John Flint	4-6	0-0	3-3	1-2	0-0	0-1	0-0	0-0	0-0	66.7	**9.50**
Michael Appleby	4-11	0-1	1-5	3-5	0-0	0-0	0-0	0-0	0-0	36.4	**13.16**
David Bridgwater	4-20	1-4	0-1	2-4	1-5	0-6	0-0	0-0	0-0	20.0	-0.25
Fergal O'Brien	4-22	0-1	1-3	0-2	1-5	1-10	0-0	1-1	0-0	18.2	**27.00**
Barry Brennan	3-18	0-0	1-6	2-5	0-3	0-2	0-1	0-1	0-0	16.7	**14.00**
Matt Sheppard	3-14	0-0	1-1	0-2	0-2	2-9	0-0	0-0	0-0	21.4	**4.50**
Steve Flook	3-12	0-0	0-0	0-0	0-0	1-1	0-0	2-11	0-0	25.0	**17.00**
Nick Williams	3-7	1-1	0-0	1-1	0-1	1-4	0-0	0-0	0-0	42.9	**13.50**
Evan Williams	3-26	0-5	0-6	1-4	2-5	0-4	0-2	0-0	0-0	11.5	-12.78
Ben Case	3-18	0-4	0-3	0-3	0-2	3-4	0-2	0-0	0-0	16.7	-6.12

LEADING JUMP TRAINERS AT LINGFIELD (SINCE 2010)

	Total W-R	Nov Hdle	H'cap Hdle	Other Hdle	Nov Chase	H'cap Chase	Other Chase	Hunter Chase	N.H. Flat	Per cent	£1 Level stake
Gary Moore	13-88	1-12	2-26	2-14	2-5	6-26	0-5	0-0	0-0	14.8	-14.08
Venetia Williams	7-56	0-9	0-12	1-6	2-7	4-20	0-2	0-0	0-0	12.5	**6.37**
Nigel Twiston-Davies	6-26	4-9	0-3	1-3	0-1	1-9	0-1	0-0	0-0	23.1	**3.37**
Seamus Mullins	6-29	1-5	2-3	0-5	0-4	3-10	0-2	0-0	0-0	20.7	**24.25**
David Pipe	6-20	1-4	2-6	1-4	0-1	2-5	0-0	0-0	0-0	30.0	**5.35**
Philip Hobbs	5-10	1-4	0-1	2-2	1-1	1-2	0-0	0-0	0-0	50.0	**2.55**
Tim Vaughan	5-16	0-3	2-5	1-4	0-2	2-2	0-0	0-0	0-0	31.3	**5.16**
Charlie Longsdon	5-24	1-5	0-4	0-1	2-4	2-10	0-0	0-0	0-0	20.8	-12.34
Nick Gifford	4-15	1-2	0-2	1-3	0-2	1-5	1-1	0-0	0-0	26.7	**13.75**
Laura Mongan	4-22	0-6	3-7	0-2	0-1	1-6	0-0	0-0	0-0	18.2	**21.50**
Warren Greatrex	4-11	3-3	1-2	0-3	0-2	0-1	0-0	0-0	0-0	36.4	**11.98**
Richard Lee	3-4	0-0	0-0	0-0	0-0	3-4	0-0	0-0	0-0	75.0	**12.50**
Oliver Sherwood	3-12	1-4	0-0	1-2	1-1	0-4	0-1	0-0	0-0	25.0	-2.75
Nicky Henderson	3-10	0-2	0-0	3-6	0-1	0-0	0-1	0-0	0-0	30.0	-0.10
Tom George	3-15	0-1	0-1	0-1	1-1	2-10	0-1	0-0	0-0	20.0	-3.25
Alan King	3-21	0-8	1-5	0-2	1-1	1-5	0-0	0-0	0-0	14.3	-6.50
Brendan Powell	3-20	0-2	1-9	1-1	0-3	1-5	0-0	0-0	0-0	15.0	-5.50
Anthony Middleton	3-9	1-1	1-4	0-1	0-0	0-2	1-1	0-0	0-0	33.3	**15.50**
Chris Gordon	3-29	1-5	2-12	0-1	0-3	0-8	0-0	0-0	0-0	10.3	-18.00
Jonjo O'Neill	2-32	0-6	1-5	0-9	0-2	0-9	1-1	0-0	0-0	6.3	-21.25
Jamie Poulton	2-11	0-2	1-3	0-0	0-3	1-3	0-0	0-0	0-0	18.2	**11.00**
Richard Rowe	2-27	0-9	0-4	0-1	1-4	1-9	0-0	0-0	0-0	7.4	-10.50
Charlie Mann	2-15	0-4	0-1	0-3	0-0	2-5	0-2	0-0	0-0	13.3	-3.13
Paul Webber	2-6	1-2	0-0	1-2	0-1	0-0	0-1	0-0	0-0	33.3	**5.00**
Lucy Wadham	2-15	0-4	2-8	0-2	0-0	0-1	0-0	0-0	0-0	13.3	-1.25
Anna Newton-Smith	2-24	0-5	0-2	0-1	1-1	1-15	0-0	0-0	0-0	8.3	-18.00
Emma Lavelle	2-13	1-5	0-1	0-3	1-3	0-1	0-0	0-0	0-0	15.4	-6.67
Dan Skelton	2-3	0-0	0-0	0-1	0-0	2-2	0-0	0-0	0-0	66.7	**4.75**
George Baker	2-5	0-2	1-1	0-1	0-0	1-1	0-0	0-0	0-0	40.0	**0.38**
Neil Mulholland	2-16	0-1	1-5	0-1	0-3	1-6	0-0	0-0	0-0	12.5	-6.00
Kate Buckett	2-5	1-2	1-1	0-0	0-0	0-1	0-1	0-0	0-0	40.0	**36.00**

LEADING JUMP TRAINERS AT LUDLOW (SINCE 2010)

	Total W-R	Nov Hdle	H'cap Hdle	Other Hdle	Nov Chase	H'cap Chase	Other Chase	Hunter Chase	N.H. Flat	Per cent	£1 Level stake
Evan Williams	61-322	5-34	5-57	15-69	9-42	14-82	5-9	0-3	8-26	18.9	-66.63
Nicky Henderson	36-127	6-20	3-18	12-40	0-9	0-8	3-5	0-0	12-27	28.3	-31.51
Philip Hobbs	21-118	5-17	3-12	1-29	3-11	6-33	2-5	1-3	0-8	17.8	-26.59
Nigel Twiston-Davies	18-175	0-16	2-26	5-40	2-17	7-62	0-2	0-2	2-10	10.3	-79.12
Henry Daly	18-143	1-19	1-24	5-23	2-12	4-38	0-2	4-7	1-18	12.6	-58.91
Venetia Williams	17-139	0-13	2-30	0-21	5-21	8-48	1-4	0-1	1-1	12.2	-68.98
Rebecca Curtis	15-56	2-2	3-6	5-20	0-6	0-5	0-0	1-3	4-14	26.8	-4.75
Jonjo O'Neill	11-85	1-7	1-17	1-19	0-5	3-29	1-1	3-6	1-1	12.9	-30.88
Tom George	11-64	0-8	0-2	2-16	3-7	5-23	0-2	0-0	1-6	17.2	-6.81
Kim Bailey	10-66	2-12	2-17	1-12	1-4	2-13	0-4	0-0	2-4	15.2	**13.46**
Ian Williams	10-46	1-4	2-13	3-13	3-8	1-5	0-1	0-0	0-2	21.7	**1.94**
Oliver Sherwood	8-53	2-8	1-7	2-16	0-2	1-5	0-1	0-0	2-14	15.1	-15.75
Tim Vaughan	8-59	1-11	1-13	1-15	1-2	2-7	0-0	1-2	1-9	13.6	**8.00**
Paul Webber	7-68	3-15	0-8	2-20	0-2	0-11	1-3	0-0	1-9	10.3	-25.25
David Pipe	7-48	0-6	2-14	2-19	1-3	0-3	0-0	0-0	2-3	14.6	-26.59
Martin Keighley	7-29	1-2	1-6	2-5	0-1	3-12	0-0	0-0	0-3	24.1	**4.46**
Dan Skelton	7-35	1-6	3-8	0-6	0-3	1-5	0-0	0-0	2-7	20.0	-1.95
Neil Mulholland	7-23	1-1	3-10	2-4	1-2	0-4	0-0	0-0	0-2	30.4	**35.01**
Robin Dickin	6-67	1-14	1-19	2-13	0-2	0-5	0-0	0-0	2-14	9.0	**12.50**
Paul Nicholls	6-40	1-3	0-3	1-10	2-6	1-12	0-0	1-1	0-5	15.0	-22.47
Richard Lee	5-74	0-3	0-10	1-16	2-11	1-30	1-1	0-0	0-3	6.8	-54.20
Peter Bowen	5-66	0-8	2-17	1-9	0-2	0-15	0-3	0-2	2-10	7.6	-13.50
David Evans	5-63	0-6	3-20	1-20	1-3	0-5	0-2	0-0	0-7	7.9	-28.75
Tom Symonds	5-50	0-4	2-8	1-12	0-10	0-7	2-3	0-0	0-6	10.0	-21.25
Steve Flook	5-35	0-2	0-0	0-0	0-0	0-0	0-0	5-32	0-1	14.3	**11.53**
Martin Bosley	5-18	0-2	2-5	0-2	1-3	2-5	0-0	0-0	0-1	27.8	**20.83**
Colin Tizzard	5-27	0-0	2-5	1-4	1-3	0-10	0-1	0-0	1-4	18.5	**19.60**
Keith Goldsworthy	5-28	2-7	1-7	1-5	0-1	0-2	0-1	1-2	0-3	17.9	**101.67**
Dr Richard Newland	5-27	0-2	1-10	2-6	0-0	2-6	0-0	0-3	0-0	18.5	**7.25**
Charlie Longsdon	5-47	2-9	0-7	2-11	0-3	0-11	1-2	0-0	0-4	10.6	-20.60
Brian Ellison	4-28	0-4	2-9	2-10	0-1	0-3	0-1	0-0	0-0	14.3	-10.42

LEADING JUMP TRAINERS AT MARKET RASEN (SINCE 2010)

	Total W-R	Nov Hdle	H'cap Hdle	Other Hdle	Nov Chase	H'cap Chase	Other Chase	Hunter Chase	N.H. Flat	Per cent	£1 Level stake
Jonjo O'Neill	37-241	5-47	9-61	0-14	3-21	18-83	0-7	0-1	2-9	15.4	-59.51
Charlie Longsdon	32-122	8-20	3-24	1-12	2-8	11-40	2-2	0-0	5-18	26.2	-14.04
Nicky Henderson	28-74	9-16	2-18	4-9	3-6	2-9	0-3	0-0	8-17	37.8	**27.58**
Peter Bowen	26-115	2-12	6-31	1-12	2-10	11-42	0-1	0-0	4-15	22.6	**40.54**
Malcolm Jefferson	23-138	7-33	6-34	1-8	2-7	1-22	1-3	0-0	5-31	16.7	**35.65**
Brian Ellison	20-114	6-21	7-48	5-28	1-5	1-16	0-0	0-0	0-2	17.5	**37.93**
Steve Gollings	17-102	4-23	5-25	4-16	1-12	3-13	0-5	0-0	2-13	16.7	-35.87
Tim Vaughan	17-135	7-33	1-43	3-21	3-14	0-20	2-5	1-1	0-5	12.6	-51.27
Donald McCain	14-116	2-24	0-32	5-24	1-12	1-12	2-8	0-0	3-10	12.1	-58.16
Chris Bealby	12-94	1-20	3-16	0-4	1-9	6-31	0-4	0-0	1-10	12.8	-24.88
Philip Kirby	11-80	2-18	6-39	0-6	1-5	1-5	0-0	0-1	1-6	13.8	-6.12
John Ferguson	11-33	3-10	4-9	4-9	0-1	0-0	0-1	0-0	2-7	33.3	**10.66**
Nigel Twiston-Davies	10-56	2-10	0-13	2-6	2-4	3-20	1-1	0-0	0-3	17.9	-4.75
James Evans	10-21	1-1	1-5	1-1	0-0	6-13	0-0	0-0	1-1	47.6	**35.96**
David Pipe	10-65	2-5	2-28	2-13	2-4	1-19	1-2	0-0	0-2	15.4	-22.89
Dr Richard Newland	10-64	0-6	3-21	1-11	2-3	5-27	0-2	0-1	0-0	15.6	-11.77
Sue Smith	9-102	1-12	4-22	1-7	0-9	3-42	0-1	0-0	0-10	8.8	**31.50**
Kim Bailey	8-49	1-7	0-9	0-1	3-6	2-15	2-5	0-0	0-6	16.3	-24.95
Anabel K Murphy	8-35	1-4	5-21	0-1	0-3	1-2	1-1	0-0	0-3	22.9	**52.00**
Nigel Hawke	8-25	0-3	0-1	1-4	0-1	7-16	0-0	0-0	0-0	32.0	**29.04**
Dianne Sayer	8-52	1-8	6-30	0-1	0-4	1-7	0-0	0-0	0-2	15.4	-2.83
Alan Swinbank	8-28	2-2	0-5	1-3	1-2	1-2	0-0	0-0	3-14	28.6	-3.15
Venetia Williams	7-30	1-4	1-8	1-2	2-6	2-10	0-0	0-0	0-0	23.3	-0.25
Ian Williams	7-36	0-0	3-13	1-5	2-7	1-7	0-1	0-0	0-4	19.4	-4.38
Nicky Richards	7-51	2-8	5-22	0-2	0-4	0-11	0-1	0-1	0-2	13.7	-18.75
Evan Williams	7-69	2-9	2-28	1-13	1-5	1-20	0-2	0-0	0-0	10.1	-19.00
Fergal O'Brien	7-30	1-5	3-8	0-1	0-2	3-10	0-1	0-0	0-3	23.3	**18.75**
Alex Hales	7-47	0-10	3-16	0-4	0-1	4-12	0-0	0-0	0-5	14.9	**2.85**
Nick Kent	7-70	2-17	4-26	0-4	0-1	0-10	0-1	1-1	0-10	10.0	-22.75
Pam Sly	6-58	2-16	2-21	0-7	0-3	2-4	0-1	0-0	0-8	10.3	-15.00
Paul Webber	6-46	1-7	2-17	1-8	0-3	0-6	1-6	0-0	2-6	13.0	-7.00

LEADING JUMP TRAINERS AT MUSSELBURGH (SINCE 2010)

	Total W-R	Nov Hdle	H'cap Hdle	Other Hdle	Nov Chase	H'cap Chase	Other Chase	Hunter Chase	N.H. Flat	Per cent	£1 Level stake
Donald McCain	35-138	6-20	2-41	9-24	3-11	6-28	3-4	0-1	6-10	25.4	**16.53**
Lucinda Russell	26-233	1-21	6-69	2-30	5-18	11-74	0-6	0-0	1-15	11.2	-80.92
Brian Ellison	15-114	0-7	7-59	2-25	1-3	3-16	2-2	0-0	0-7	13.2	-51.91
Jim Goldie	12-123	3-13	5-69	2-19	1-3	0-11	0-1	0-0	1-7	9.8	-16.25
James Ewart	11-91	0-13	2-16	6-15	0-4	1-19	1-5	0-0	1-19	12.1	-47.39
John Ferguson	11-35	2-4	3-12	5-14	0-1	1-2	0-0	0-2	1-2	31.4	**3.79**
Howard Johnson	9-45	2-10	2-14	1-5	0-3	1-5	1-3	0-1	2-4	20.0	-0.41
Nicky Richards	9-55	1-9	6-25	1-6	0-0	0-6	0-1	0-0	1-9	16.4	**11.70**
Dianne Sayer	8-70	1-4	4-35	0-8	0-4	3-17	0-0	0-0	0-2	11.4	**8.75**
Chris Grant	8-81	0-7	1-22	1-13	0-6	5-26	0-1	0-0	1-6	9.9	-26.00
N W Alexander	8-66	0-4	3-24	1-6	0-1	4-20	0-0	0-2	0-9	12.1	-14.00
Sandy Thomson	7-34	1-3	5-18	1-3	0-0	0-7	0-0	0-0	0-3	20.6	**39.25**
Keith Reveley	7-45	1-5	2-11	2-8	2-5	0-8	0-1	0-0	0-7	15.6	**10.00**
Peter Niven	7-33	0-3	3-10	0-7	0-0	0-3	0-0	0-0	4-10	21.2	**32.50**
John Quinn	6-33	1-2	1-16	4-9	0-1	0-3	0-0	0-0	0-2	18.2	-6.40
Rose Dobbin	6-56	0-7	1-20	0-8	0-3	3-10	0-0	0-0	2-8	10.7	**19.50**
Nicky Henderson	5-21	1-4	2-8	1-3	1-5	0-1	0-0	0-0	0-1	23.8	-5.29
Michael Smith	5-29	1-2	1-6	1-14	0-0	1-3	0-0	0-0	1-4	17.2	-7.09
Philip Kirby	5-36	0-3	4-21	0-4	0-1	1-5	0-1	0-0	0-1	13.9	**1.00**
John Wade	4-45	0-4	2-12	0-1	1-2	1-17	0-1	0-1	0-7	8.9	-22.10
Malcolm Jefferson	4-22	1-1	1-8	0-2	0-1	0-3	0-0	0-0	2-7	18.2	-2.75
Bruce Mactaggart	4-16	0-0	0-2	0-1	2-2	2-11	0-0	0-0	0-0	25.0	**1.75**
David Pipe	4-7	0-0	3-3	0-1	0-0	0-2	0-0	0-0	1-1	57.1	**5.75**
Donald Whillans	4-16	0-0	3-10	0-2	0-2	0-0	0-0	0-0	1-2	25.0	**100.50**
Kate Walton	4-18	0-0	3-15	0-1	0-1	1-1	0-0	0-0	0-0	22.2	**8.00**
Venetia Williams	4-14	0-0	3-7	0-0	0-0	1-5	0-1	0-1	0-0	28.6	**1.75**
Alan Swinbank	4-19	1-2	1-4	0-3	0-0	0-1	0-0	0-0	2-9	21.1	-7.22
S R B Crawford	4-23	0-2	3-10	0-3	0-1	0-1	0-0	0-0	1-6	17.4	**1.88**
Tim Vaughan	4-26	0-3	2-9	1-5	0-2	0-2	0-1	0-1	1-3	15.4	-6.50
Gordon Elliott	4-11	2-5	0-2	1-2	0-0	1-1	0-0	0-0	0-1	36.4	**0.80**
Martin Todhunter	3-25	0-3	0-8	2-6	0-0	1-7	0-0	0-0	0-1	12.0	**32.00**

LEADING JUMP TRAINERS AT NEWBURY (SINCE 2010)

	Total W-R	Nov Hdle	H'cap Hdle	Other Hdle	Nov Chase	H'cap Chase	Other Chase	Hunter Chase	N.H. Flat	Per cent	£1 Level stake
Nicky Henderson	55-270	15-64	6-57	16-47	5-34	3-35	5-11	0-0	7-28	20.4	-48.49
Paul Nicholls	53-240	3-29	8-50	12-34	13-41	9-52	6-23	0-1	3-16	22.1	**0.84**
Alan King	28-222	4-43	2-49	7-32	7-28	2-34	0-8	0-0	7-33	12.6	-50.42
Philip Hobbs	23-160	5-18	2-44	2-18	3-17	10-53	1-3	0-0	0-8	14.4	**59.33**
David Pipe	22-145	2-20	8-44	2-19	4-11	4-41	0-3	0-0	2-7	15.2	**29.42**
Jonjo O'Neill	14-117	5-23	2-25	1-23	4-20	0-16	0-2	1-3	1-6	12.0	-43.52
Venetia Williams	14-113	0-9	2-20	1-12	3-23	8-47	0-2	0-0	0-1	12.4	-44.03
Nigel Twiston-Davies	12-125	1-24	5-26	0-5	2-19	4-39	0-6	0-1	0-5	9.6	-9.92
Tom George	12-91	0-13	1-15	1-10	4-20	3-28	2-4	0-0	1-3	13.2	-28.50
Gary Moore	10-118	1-27	4-32	1-18	1-15	1-15	0-3	0-0	2-10	8.5	**35.00**
Colin Tizzard	9-104	2-15	2-15	1-9	2-17	1-29	0-3	0-0	1-17	8.7	-32.25
Harry Fry	9-24	1-2	1-3	1-4	1-2	1-5	1-2	0-0	3-6	37.5	**8.92**
Nick Williams	8-53	1-5	1-5	1-7	2-10	1-16	1-3	0-0	1-7	15.1	-15.83
Charlie Longsdon	7-58	1-10	0-10	0-5	1-4	4-22	0-1	0-0	1-7	12.1	-15.63
Warren Greatrex	7-53	1-15	1-9	0-13	1-3	2-9	0-0	1-1	1-3	13.2	**0.87**
Oliver Sherwood	6-42	0-8	0-7	3-6	0-1	3-16	0-0	0-0	0-5	14.3	**13.25**
Kim Bailey	6-56	0-19	0-9	0-6	2-7	3-12	1-2	0-0	0-1	10.7	-21.00
Emma Lavelle	6-65	2-16	1-14	1-7	2-5	1-13	0-1	0-0	0-10	9.2	-28.80
Richard Lee	5-26	1-3	2-7	0-1	1-3	1-12	0-0	0-0	0-0	19.2	**1.50**
Donald McCain	5-48	2-10	0-10	2-11	0-7	1-6	0-5	0-0	0-1	10.4	-11.92
Mark Bradstock	4-16	0-4	0-1	0-0	1-1	2-8	1-1	0-0	0-1	25.0	**9.88**
Paul Webber	4-36	0-4	0-3	0-5	1-10	1-8	1-1	0-0	1-6	11.1	-10.97
Fergal O'Brien	4-25	0-6	0-2	1-3	0-4	2-7	0-0	0-0	1-3	16.0	**28.00**
Rebecca Curtis	4-53	1-11	2-13	1-9	0-8	0-6	0-1	0-0	0-7	7.5	-27.25
Peter Bowen	3-25	1-3	1-9	0-0	0-1	1-9	0-0	0-1	0-2	12.0	**1.50**
Tony Carroll	3-33	1-8	2-11	0-6	0-1	0-3	0-2	0-0	0-2	9.1	-9.00
Evan Williams	3-33	2-8	0-5	1-2	0-4	0-8	0-1	0-1	0-4	9.1	**2.63**
Tim Vaughan	3-47	1-4	0-15	1-11	0-4	1-10	0-0	0-0	0-4	6.4	-26.33
Neil Mulholland	3-13	0-2	3-5	0-2	0-2	0-2	0-0	0-0	0-0	23.1	**11.50**
Robin Dickin	2-13	0-3	0-1	0-3	0-0	1-2	1-1	0-0	0-3	15.4	-4.75
R Barber	2-2	0-0	0-0	0-0	0-0	0-0	0-0	2-2	0-0	100.0	**3.57**

LEADING JUMP TRAINERS AT NEWCASTLE (SINCE 2010)

	Total W-R	Nov Hdle	H'cap Hdle	Other Hdle	Nov Chase	H'cap Chase	Other Chase	Hunter Chase	N.H. Flat	Per cent	£1 Level stake
Lucinda Russell	30-205	6-27	6-52	1-15	2-17	12-78	1-4	0-0	2-12	14.6	-26.63
Donald McCain	25-123	8-42	4-19	5-15	3-13	2-19	2-3	0-0	1-12	20.3	**3.69**
Keith Reveley	23-116	3-22	3-28	3-11	2-4	10-35	0-0	0-0	2-16	19.8	-19.38
Chris Grant	16-141	2-38	7-33	0-7	0-7	5-34	0-2	0-0	2-20	11.3	-60.55
Sue Smith	14-132	2-17	2-35	1-6	3-17	6-48	0-0	0-0	0-9	10.6	-49.22
Nicky Richards	13-74	4-20	3-18	0-6	0-5	1-14	0-2	0-0	5-9	17.6	-12.96
Malcolm Jefferson	12-59	3-16	2-14	0-6	0-2	3-10	1-2	0-0	3-9	20.3	**45.25**
N W Alexander	12-98	1-20	5-27	2-11	1-5	3-28	0-1	0-0	0-6	12.2	-12.88
James Ewart	10-92	2-23	1-11	1-12	0-6	3-25	3-4	0-0	0-11	10.9	-45.75
John Wade	9-82	0-20	2-14	0-3	2-7	5-34	0-0	0-0	0-4	11.0	-49.85
Ann Hamilton	8-34	1-4	0-2	0-0	5-8	2-19	0-0	0-0	0-1	23.5	**3.88**
Howard Johnson	8-48	2-17	0-11	0-1	2-3	2-8	1-4	0-0	1-4	16.7	-3.81
Martin Todhunter	8-53	1-4	2-17	0-3	2-5	3-22	0-1	0-0	0-1	15.1	**4.50**
Alistair Whillans	6-56	2-11	2-20	0-4	0-1	1-11	0-0	0-0	1-9	10.7	-27.75
John Quinn	6-19	2-4	3-9	1-4	0-2	0-0	0-0	0-0	0-0	31.6	**12.23**
Stuart Coltherd	6-50	0-5	1-16	0-5	1-4	4-20	0-0	0-0	0-0	12.0	**2.50**
Micky Hammond	5-41	1-11	3-12	0-1	0-3	1-11	0-0	0-0	0-3	12.2	**1.50**
Donald Whillans	5-52	1-13	3-26	0-3	0-0	1-6	0-0	0-0	0-4	9.6	-2.37
Tim Easterby	5-42	3-14	1-5	0-4	0-3	0-7	1-2	0-0	0-7	11.9	-26.59
David Pipe	5-18	1-2	0-2	2-2	0-1	1-8	0-0	0-0	1-3	27.8	-1.82
Colin Tizzard	5-6	1-2	0-0	1-1	0-0	3-3	0-0	0-0	0-0	83.3	**34.50**
Philip Kirby	5-51	3-12	1-25	0-1	0-1	0-5	0-0	0-0	1-7	9.8	-3.25
David O'Meara	5-21	2-7	1-4	0-1	0-2	1-4	0-0	0-0	1-3	23.8	**0.62**
Keith Dalgleish	5-12	0-2	2-4	0-1	0-0	3-3	0-0	0-0	0-2	41.7	**9.38**
Brian Ellison	4-54	0-10	2-15	0-7	1-5	1-12	0-0	0-0	0-5	7.4	-39.09
Sandy Thomson	4-24	1-6	0-2	0-1	0-2	2-9	0-0	0-0	1-4	16.7	**57.50**
Ferdy Murphy	4-44	1-10	0-5	0-1	1-5	1-20	1-3	0-0	0-0	9.1	-23.97
Kate Walton	4-24	1-7	0-8	0-0	0-0	2-6	0-0	0-0	1-3	16.7	**12.00**
Jennie Candlish	4-16	0-2	2-6	0-2	0-0	1-4	0-0	0-0	1-2	25.0	**6.20**
George Moore	3-26	1-9	1-5	1-3	0-0	0-2	0-2	0-0	0-5	11.5	-11.38
Nicky Henderson	3-4	0-0	0-0	3-4	0-0	0-0	0-0	0-0	0-0	75.0	**1.02**

LEADING JUMP TRAINERS AT NEWTON ABBOT (SINCE 2010)

	Total W-R	Nov Hdle	H'cap Hdle	Other Hdle	Nov Chase	H'cap Chase	Other Chase	Hunter Chase	N.H. Flat	Per cent	£1 Level stake
Paul Nicholls	46-151	9-24	2-19	8-25	11-30	6-32	5-13	0-2	5-6	30.5	**26.71**
Evan Williams	29-148	5-26	5-30	5-19	7-20	7-50	0-1	0-0	0-2	19.6	-27.68
Jonjo O'Neill	27-144	5-21	11-48	3-17	2-9	4-41	0-3	0-0	2-5	18.8	**6.46**
Philip Hobbs	25-155	3-21	3-32	4-25	3-12	12-59	0-2	0-0	0-4	16.1	-12.42
David Pipe	24-191	4-15	11-96	4-33	1-4	2-33	1-5	0-0	1-5	12.6	-81.24
Colin Tizzard	18-160	2-22	2-37	1-14	5-17	8-62	0-2	0-0	0-6	11.3	-43.75
Tim Vaughan	17-130	4-22	3-39	3-26	0-6	3-25	0-2	0-0	4-10	13.1	-58.19
Nigel Twiston-Davies	16-69	2-12	5-20	2-7	1-4	6-21	0-1	0-1	0-3	23.2	**26.67**
Nicky Henderson	15-34	7-9	2-12	2-6	1-1	1-3	0-0	0-0	2-3	44.1	**12.38**
Martin Hill	14-85	3-15	8-41	0-7	1-3	1-13	0-0	0-0	1-6	16.5	**54.63**
Peter Bowen	13-106	2-16	4-35	2-8	1-6	4-30	0-2	0-0	0-9	12.3	-27.89
Jimmy Frost	11-130	2-31	4-43	1-20	0-7	4-23	0-2	0-1	0-3	8.5	-42.38
Paul Henderson	11-92	0-15	3-26	1-4	2-12	5-33	0-1	0-0	0-1	12.0	**1.75**
Mark Gillard	10-87	1-16	3-27	1-17	0-7	5-19	0-1	0-0	0-0	11.5	-13.67
Sophie Leech	10-82	2-11	6-38	0-11	0-5	1-13	1-2	0-1	0-1	12.2	-6.87
Jim Best	9-34	2-5	2-10	2-10	0-1	2-4	1-2	0-0	0-2	26.5	-14.61
Jeremy Scott	8-43	1-6	2-16	1-8	1-2	3-8	0-1	0-0	0-2	18.6	**12.86**
Dr Richard Newland	8-27	0-4	4-9	0-2	2-3	2-9	0-0	0-0	0-0	29.6	**8.11**
Bernard Llewellyn	7-75	1-11	3-51	3-9	0-1	0-3	0-0	0-0	0-0	9.3	-0.12
Sue Gardner	7-93	1-18	6-50	0-16	0-2	0-1	0-0	0-0	0-6	7.5	-35.50
David Bridgwater	7-31	2-8	0-3	0-1	0-3	5-15	0-1	0-0	0-0	22.6	**14.00**
Alison Thorpe	7-35	1-5	2-14	3-9	0-0	1-4	0-0	0-0	0-3	20.0	**12.19**
Brendan Powell	7-42	1-8	0-11	3-8	1-4	0-6	1-1	0-0	1-4	16.7	**2.25**
Alan Jones	7-50	1-9	2-15	0-4	1-4	1-7	0-2	0-0	2-9	14.0	**10.00**
Martin Keighley	7-43	0-1	1-14	1-2	0-5	3-17	1-1	0-0	1-3	16.3	-6.59
Neil Mulholland	7-95	2-29	1-21	1-9	0-4	3-27	0-0	0-0	0-5	7.4	-50.93
Chris Down	6-69	1-11	3-29	1-15	0-1	1-8	0-0	0-0	0-5	8.7	-27.63
Seamus Mullins	6-74	0-16	2-17	1-11	0-5	2-16	0-1	0-0	1-8	8.1	-28.00
Charlie Longsdon	6-26	1-4	0-6	1-3	1-1	3-9	0-0	0-0	0-3	23.1	**14.08**
Warren Greatrex	6-20	0-0	3-10	0-3	0-1	0-2	0-0	0-0	3-4	30.0	-2.36
John Ferguson	6-21	2-6	2-9	1-2	0-0	0-2	0-0	0-0	1-2	28.6	**0.41**

LEADING JUMP TRAINERS AT PERTH (SINCE 2010)

	Total W-R	Nov Hdle	H'cap Hdle	Other Hdle	Nov Chase	H'cap Chase	Other Chase	Hunter Chase	N.H. Flat	Per cent	£1 Level stake
Gordon Elliott	81-271	20-42	23-79	18-49	10-35	7-50	0-4	0-0	3-12	29.9	**31.59**
Lucinda Russell	42-418	9-74	14-122	4-41	5-46	9-107	1-3	0-1	0-24	10.0	-141.18
Nigel Twiston-Davies	32-125	5-18	4-36	5-11	7-18	7-33	0-1	0-0	4-8	25.6	**27.47**
Donald McCain	22-121	8-26	2-26	6-27	4-16	1-14	0-0	0-0	1-12	18.2	-39.84
Tim Vaughan	20-61	3-13	6-16	3-6	5-12	2-12	0-0	0-0	1-2	32.8	**18.81**
Peter Bowen	17-44	2-5	4-8	0-1	2-4	6-20	0-0	0-0	3-6	38.6	**26.63**
Jim Goldie	17-120	1-16	11-63	3-15	0-10	1-13	0-1	0-0	1-2	14.2	-3.50
Lisa Harrison	13-87	1-15	5-31	1-11	1-3	5-19	0-0	0-0	0-8	14.9	**12.08**
Nicky Richards	11-89	2-14	4-32	1-12	1-4	2-25	0-0	0-1	1-1	12.4	-4.54
N W Alexander	11-119	1-18	2-31	1-20	1-5	4-22	0-2	1-9	1-12	9.2	**11.50**
S R B Crawford	11-122	1-15	3-36	3-27	2-12	0-16	0-0	0-0	2-16	9.0	-71.93
Alistair Whillans	9-90	0-14	2-41	0-8	2-7	5-15	0-0	0-0	0-5	10.0	-11.50
A J Martin	9-38	1-10	3-10	1-4	1-5	1-6	0-0	0-1	2-2	23.7	**14.40**
Tom George	9-54	1-5	1-9	1-3	2-11	3-22	0-0	0-1	1-3	16.7	-4.33
David Pipe	9-23	0-0	2-7	1-1	2-3	4-11	0-0	0-0	0-1	39.1	**9.35**
Dianne Sayer	9-96	2-14	4-58	0-0	0-1	3-22	0-0	0-0	0-1	9.4	-43.40
Lucy Normile	8-125	0-17	3-51	0-25	2-8	3-17	0-0	0-1	0-6	6.4	-64.25
Malcolm Jefferson	7-36	0-4	0-6	0-3	3-4	3-13	1-1	0-0	0-5	19.4	**36.25**
Fergal O'Brien	7-31	0-4	2-7	0-1	1-5	3-10	0-0	1-1	0-3	22.6	**10.63**
Maurice Barnes	6-84	2-14	1-24	0-16	1-8	2-17	0-0	0-0	0-5	7.1	-3.50
R Mike Smith	6-35	0-3	0-2	0-5	0-2	5-16	0-1	1-3	0-3	17.1	**3.50**
Victor Dartnall	5-19	2-4	1-5	0-2	2-4	0-4	0-0	0-0	0-0	26.3	-0.62
C A McBratney	5-64	3-19	1-16	1-11	0-2	0-13	0-1	0-0	0-2	7.8	-43.77
Philip Hobbs	4-25	0-1	0-4	2-5	1-4	1-11	0-0	0-0	0-0	16.0	-11.77
George Bewley	4-32	0-4	2-16	0-3	0-1	0-2	0-0	0-0	2-6	12.5	-11.25
Pauline Robson	4-20	2-4	1-5	0-6	0-3	0-1	0-0	0-0	1-1	20.0	-2.00
John Joseph Hanlon	4-17	0-2	0-1	2-5	0-1	0-4	0-0	0-0	2-4	23.5	-4.46
Robert Alan Hennessy	4-15	1-1	1-4	0-1	1-3	1-6	0-0	0-0	0-0	26.7	**7.00**
Rose Dobbin	4-54	1-9	0-21	0-7	1-6	2-7	0-0	0-0	0-4	7.4	-39.63
P Monteith	3-23	1-3	0-5	0-4	0-3	2-6	0-0	0-0	0-2	13.0	-0.17
Kim Bailey	3-5	2-2	0-1	0-0	0-1	1-1	0-0	0-0	0-0	60.0	**5.08**

LEADING JUMP TRAINERS AT PLUMPTON (SINCE 2010)

	Total W-R	Nov Hdle	H'cap Hdle	Other Hdle	Nov Chase	H'cap Chase	Other Chase	Hunter Chase	N.H. Flat	Per cent	£1 Level stake
Gary Moore	47-244	10-39	11-87	10-44	7-29	8-39	0-2	0-0	1-4	19.3	-15.67
Alan King	28-71	9-17	3-17	5-13	8-14	2-4	1-3	0-0	0-3	39.4	**25.25**
Seamus Mullins	21-170	0-17	6-43	0-16	4-19	11-63	0-1	0-0	0-11	12.4	-61.54
Venetia Williams	21-85	4-15	2-19	5-17	2-9	7-20	0-1	0-0	1-4	24.7	-14.09
David Pipe	19-68	1-11	5-24	4-12	2-5	2-7	0-0	0-0	5-9	27.9	**11.54**
Suzy Smith	17-70	1-10	15-42	1-7	0-0	0-5	0-0	0-0	0-6	24.3	**75.63**
Chris Gordon	16-151	2-18	4-73	2-10	3-12	5-31	0-0	0-0	0-7	10.6	-10.50
David Bridgwater	13-51	0-11	0-8	2-7	4-9	7-14	0-0	0-0	0-2	25.5	**6.29**
Charlie Longsdon	13-66	2-14	1-14	2-11	0-6	7-17	0-0	0-0	1-4	19.7	-15.07
Neil King	11-78	2-6	1-26	2-8	1-2	5-33	0-1	0-0	0-2	14.1	-17.38
Anna Newton-Smith	11-128	0-12	6-56	0-8	0-7	5-41	0-0	0-0	0-4	8.6	-22.67
Colin Tizzard	11-65	3-14	3-9	1-8	1-5	2-23	1-1	0-0	0-5	16.9	-22.18
Nick Gifford	11-81	0-17	1-19	1-10	3-9	2-18	1-2	0-0	3-6	13.6	-27.25
Sheena West	10-79	1-12	5-38	1-13	0-1	3-12	0-0	0-0	0-3	12.7	-24.68
Jim Best	10-81	3-18	3-33	2-19	0-0	0-3	0-1	0-0	2-7	12.3	-29.00
Tim Vaughan	10-85	0-13	3-24	4-22	1-6	2-13	0-0	0-0	0-7	11.8	-38.13
Paul Henderson	10-54	0-2	2-16	0-3	0-4	8-29	0-0	0-0	0-0	18.5	**11.38**
Zoe Davison	9-114	0-10	7-71	0-10	0-5	2-13	0-0	0-0	0-5	7.9	-12.25
Linda Jewell	8-89	0-16	2-23	0-8	0-7	6-30	0-1	0-0	0-4	9.0	-25.75
Emma Lavelle	8-44	2-10	1-11	1-5	2-3	2-10	0-1	0-0	0-4	18.2	-12.25
Evan Williams	8-37	1-5	3-16	1-7	1-2	2-7	0-0	0-0	0-0	21.6	**1.36**
Anthony Honeyball	8-27	1-6	4-10	0-2	0-0	0-2	0-1	0-0	3-6	29.6	**9.09**
Warren Greatrex	8-44	3-12	2-12	1-13	1-2	0-1	0-0	0-0	1-4	18.2	-15.23
Oliver Sherwood	7-34	1-6	2-5	0-5	1-3	2-11	0-0	0-0	1-4	20.6	**5.96**
Michael Madgwick	7-46	0-8	3-10	2-4	0-4	2-17	0-1	0-0	0-2	15.2	-3.25
Charlie Mann	7-36	1-5	0-7	1-4	4-7	0-12	1-1	0-0	0-0	19.4	**5.86**
Caroline Keevil	7-35	0-5	3-11	0-0	2-4	2-10	0-0	0-0	0-5	20.0	**53.38**
Nicky Henderson	6-30	2-7	0-2	2-13	1-7	0-0	1-1	0-0	0-0	20.0	-13.70
Peter Bowen	6-26	0-0	3-11	0-0	1-1	2-13	0-0	0-0	0-1	23.1	**6.25**
Richard Rowe	6-85	2-10	2-25	1-10	1-7	0-27	0-0	0-0	0-6	7.1	-53.75

LEADING JUMP TRAINERS AT SANDOWN (SINCE 2010)

	Total W-R	Nov Hdle	H'cap Hdle	Other Hdle	Nov Chase	H'cap Chase	Other Chase	Hunter Chase	N.H. Flat	Per cent	£1 Level stake
Paul Nicholls	42-172	3-12	7-42	2-16	9-20	8-51	9-30	3-3	1-6	24.4	**12.26**
Nicky Henderson	40-175	16-42	8-56	8-30	4-13	3-19	3-17	0-0	0-9	22.9	**14.96**
Gary Moore	15-123	0-21	4-42	3-25	1-6	2-26	4-7	0-0	1-4	12.2	**5.22**
Philip Hobbs	14-95	3-12	4-28	3-9	0-7	3-33	1-6	0-0	1-5	14.7	-17.85
Alan King	13-93	0-9	4-35	2-15	1-7	5-19	0-5	0-0	1-8	14.0	-1.17
Venetia Williams	12-101	0-8	2-29	1-11	3-8	6-44	0-4	0-0	0-3	11.9	-42.93
David Pipe	11-87	2-7	3-46	2-15	2-2	0-16	1-6	0-0	1-3	12.6	-32.73
Charlie Longsdon	10-49	1-5	3-15	2-4	1-4	3-16	1-3	0-0	0-4	20.4	**32.50**
Jonjo O'Neill	7-79	4-20	0-25	1-6	1-7	1-17	0-0	0-1	0-6	8.9	-32.88
Charlie Mann	7-44	0-3	2-13	0-8	0-1	3-12	2-10	0-0	0-0	15.9	**39.75**
Nick Williams	6-46	0-6	1-15	0-5	1-3	3-12	0-4	0-0	1-2	13.0	-0.00
Victor Dartnall	5-32	0-4	2-8	0-1	0-1	3-15	0-0	0-1	0-3	15.6	**16.33**
Lucy Wadham	5-30	0-2	3-21	1-3	0-0	2-3	0-1	0-0	0-3	16.7	**13.50**
Neil King	4-17	0-0	1-9	1-6	0-0	2-3	0-1	0-0	0-0	23.5	**13.50**
Nick Gifford	4-38	0-4	1-10	0-5	1-4	2-16	0-0	0-1	0-1	10.5	-6.50
Donald McCain	4-40	0-5	2-15	0-5	0-3	1-10	1-3	0-0	0-0	10.0	-10.83
Oliver Sherwood	3-45	0-4	1-19	0-4	0-1	2-12	0-0	0-0	0-6	6.7	-7.50
David Arbuthnot	3-22	2-6	0-8	0-3	0-2	0-3	0-0	0-0	1-1	13.6	-1.14
W P Mullins	3-6	1-2	0-1	0-0	1-1	0-1	0-0	0-0	1-1	50.0	**9.50**
Sheena West	3-11	0-1	0-5	2-4	0-0	0-1	1-1	0-0	0-0	27.3	**15.00**
Seamus Mullins	3-22	0-2	3-12	0-2	0-1	0-1	0-3	0-0	0-1	13.6	**12.50**
Ian Williams	3-27	1-7	0-9	0-3	0-0	1-5	0-3	1-1	0-0	11.1	-18.10
Tom George	2-29	0-4	0-5	0-1	0-1	2-14	0-5	0-0	0-0	6.9	-17.50
Emma Lavelle	3-36	2-8	1-12	0-4	0-1	0-9	0-1	0-0	0-3	8.3	-19.50
Dr Richard Newland	3-29	0-5	1-9	0-5	0-1	2-12	0-0	0-0	0-0	10.3	**21.00**
John Spearing	2-2	0-0	0-0	0-0	0-0	2-2	0-0	0-0	0-0	100.0	**6.75**
Jeremy Scott	2-16	1-2	0-8	0-0	0-0	1-3	0-0	0-0	0-3	12.5	-8.00
John Quinn	2-7	0-0	1-6	1-2	0-0	0-0	0-0	0-0	0-0	28.6	-1.00
Paul Webber	2-35	1-11	0-5	0-2	0-1	1-12	0-3	0-0	0-1	5.7	-15.00
Colin Tizzard	2-30	0-1	0-7	0-1	0-4	2-13	0-5	0-0	0-0	6.7	-20.75
Henry Daly	2-26	0-1	1-9	0-2	0-1	1-10	0-1	0-0	0-2	7.7	**4.00**

LEADING JUMP TRAINERS AT SEDGEFIELD (SINCE 2010)

	Total W-R	Nov Hdle	H'cap Hdle	Other Hdle	Nov Chase	H'cap Chase	Other Chase	Hunter Chase	N.H. Flat	Per cent	£1 Level stake
Donald McCain	60-220	19-63	6-38	15-34	2-17	4-23	3-11	0-0	11-34	27.3	-42.84
Sue Smith	30-217	3-28	7-49	1-11	2-22	15-79	1-9	0-0	1-19	13.8	-47.24
Malcolm Jefferson	22-101	4-18	3-20	0-6	2-7	11-34	0-3	0-0	2-13	21.8	**22.04**
Brian Ellison	21-108	7-31	7-31	4-18	1-7	1-11	0-1	0-0	1-9	19.4	-23.61
Ferdy Murphy	20-137	1-23	1-23	4-8	3-11	7-52	4-12	0-0	0-8	14.6	-19.65
Dianne Sayer	19-111	3-15	10-52	0-6	1-11	5-25	0-0	0-0	0-2	17.1	**29.00**
Micky Hammond	16-98	0-12	5-39	1-8	2-6	4-19	0-2	0-0	4-12	16.3	**19.00**
Chris Grant	16-124	3-26	7-35	1-9	1-3	3-30	1-6	0-1	0-14	12.9	-39.83
Keith Reveley	15-66	4-13	3-19	1-6	3-6	3-18	0-2	0-0	1-2	22.7	**21.38**
Howard Johnson	13-52	4-15	2-13	0-2	2-3	1-5	4-7	0-0	0-7	25.0	-10.04
Alan Swinbank	12-64	1-17	1-9	0-4	1-2	2-6	1-4	0-0	6-22	18.8	-16.27
Rose Dobbin	12-83	1-8	4-36	0-5	1-6	4-22	0-1	0-1	2-4	14.5	**12.00**
John Wade	11-192	0-44	2-31	0-7	2-14	6-62	0-7	0-5	1-22	5.7	-118.18
Tim Vaughan	11-68	0-16	6-19	1-5	1-3	3-15	0-2	0-0	0-8	16.2	-33.49
Barry Murtagh	10-69	2-5	7-42	0-2	1-3	0-11	0-1	0-0	0-5	14.5	**25.83**
Martin Todhunter	10-113	2-16	3-41	1-6	2-9	2-33	0-2	0-0	0-6	8.8	-46.00
Philip Kirby	10-97	2-16	3-44	1-9	0-2	2-10	0-0	1-2	1-14	10.3	-31.05
Andrew Crook	9-91	0-9	1-30	0-4	0-8	7-33	0-0	0-0	1-7	9.9	-13.90
Joanne Foster	9-65	0-5	2-13	0-2	1-9	6-31	0-2	0-1	0-2	13.8	**7.00**
Nicky Richards	9-42	3-13	2-12	1-3	1-5	2-6	0-2	0-0	0-1	21.4	**1.45**
S R B Crawford	9-38	1-7	0-7	1-6	1-1	1-1	0-0	0-0	5-16	23.7	**5.02**
George Moore	8-70	1-15	2-19	1-9	0-5	2-9	1-3	0-0	1-10	11.4	-25.30
Maurice Barnes	8-87	1-17	4-31	1-9	0-7	2-12	0-3	0-0	0-8	9.2	**12.00**
Tim Easterby	8-82	5-25	0-14	1-20	0-1	0-6	1-4	0-0	1-12	9.8	-45.94
William Amos	7-52	0-4	2-13	0-0	0-6	4-26	1-2	0-0	0-1	13.5	-23.42
John Quinn	7-25	1-8	1-5	4-6	1-1	0-1	0-1	0-0	0-3	28.0	-10.07
James Ewart	7-41	1-7	0-11	0-1	0-1	6-19	0-0	0-0	0-2	17.1	-6.63
Mike Sowersby	6-35	0-5	1-17	0-0	0-1	5-9	0-1	0-0	0-2	17.1	**54.75**
Jennie Candlish	6-46	2-8	4-19	0-3	0-3	0-8	0-0	0-0	0-5	13.0	-19.33
James Moffatt	6-43	2-7	2-30	1-1	0-0	0-1	1-1	0-0	0-3	14.0	**8.50**
Ben Haslam	6-36	0-5	4-18	0-6	2-4	0-1	0-1	0-0	0-1	16.7	**9.88**

LEADING JUMP TRAINERS AT SOUTHWELL (SINCE 2010)

	Total W-R	Nov Hdle	H'cap Hdle	Other Hdle	Nov Chase	H'cap Chase	Other Chase	Hunter Chase	N.H. Flat	Per cent	£1 Level stake
Jonjo O'Neill	28-156	2-17	10-61	6-29	2-8	6-27	0-1	1-3	1-10	17.9	-34.63
Charlie Longsdon	18-72	6-17	2-15	1-11	2-5	4-10	0-1	0-1	3-12	25.0	**1.01**
Nicky Henderson	16-61	3-16	0-9	5-13	2-6	0-1	0-2	0-0	6-14	26.2	-22.61
Keith Reveley	16-64	4-8	4-19	1-10	0-1	5-19	0-0	0-0	2-7	25.0	**17.46**
Tim Vaughan	16-81	3-13	3-23	4-19	2-8	2-10	0-3	0-1	2-4	19.8	-2.79
Peter Bowen	13-63	0-8	4-20	1-5	2-7	5-17	0-0	0-0	1-6	20.6	**19.25**
Tom George	13-55	2-8	1-7	2-9	0-1	4-21	1-1	0-0	3-8	23.6	**13.34**
Caroline Bailey	13-70	1-16	5-15	0-10	2-8	4-17	1-3	0-0	0-1	18.6	**30.71**
Nigel Twiston-Davies	12-86	3-16	2-19	0-11	1-5	2-24	1-3	0-0	3-8	14.0	-30.08
Kim Bailey	12-38	2-7	2-12	3-8	2-2	3-6	0-1	0-0	0-2	31.6	**29.48**
Sue Smith	11-84	0-12	4-23	0-4	1-7	5-27	0-0	0-0	1-11	13.1	**7.25**
Venetia Williams	10-44	0-3	3-11	1-5	0-7	4-14	1-2	0-0	1-2	22.7	**0.34**
Alan King	10-67	4-14	0-16	3-11	0-5	1-8	1-3	0-0	1-10	14.9	-28.60
Dan Skelton	9-27	2-7	2-5	2-3	0-1	2-6	0-0	0-0	1-5	33.3	**21.75**
Charlie Mann	8-36	1-3	1-9	2-6	2-3	1-12	1-1	0-0	0-2	22.2	**18.50**
David Bridgwater	8-18	1-3	0-1	0-2	4-5	3-7	0-0	0-0	0-0	44.4	**5.27**
Evan Williams	8-73	1-11	3-21	2-16	0-6	1-13	1-3	0-1	0-2	11.0	-13.06
Donald McCain	8-54	2-11	1-11	2-15	2-6	1-7	0-1	0-0	0-3	14.8	-33.78
Mike Sowersby	7-67	0-5	5-28	0-10	0-3	2-17	0-0	0-0	0-4	10.4	**30.50**
Neil Mulholland	7-38	0-3	3-16	0-3	0-1	3-11	0-0	0-0	1-4	18.4	**29.88**
John Cornwall	6-87	0-1	0-11	0-1	1-16	5-58	0-0	0-0	0-0	6.9	-43.75
Lucy Wadham	6-30	0-6	1-8	1-5	0-0	3-6	0-0	0-0	1-5	20.0	-7.80
Charles Pogson	6-75	2-20	2-15	1-16	0-6	1-15	0-0	0-0	0-3	8.0	-30.50
Chris Bealby	6-68	1-11	0-15	0-10	1-4	3-17	0-2	1-1	0-8	8.8	-38.13
Seamus Mullins	6-40	0-5	1-9	0-4	0-0	3-15	0-0	0-0	2-7	15.0	**1.13**
Martin Keighley	6-43	1-5	3-18	0-6	0-0	1-10	0-0	0-0	1-4	14.0	**4.40**
Dr Richard Newland	6-19	0-0	0-6	5-10	0-0	1-3	0-0	0-0	0-0	31.6	-1.52
Philip Kirby	6-44	0-5	3-20	0-5	0-5	0-3	1-1	0-0	2-5	13.6	-6.59
Michael Scudamore	6-37	0-1	0-6	0-6	0-2	5-18	1-1	0-0	0-3	16.2	-16.25
John Ferguson	6-24	2-4	2-7	1-6	0-2	1-1	0-0	0-0	0-4	25.0	**0.75**
Robin Dickin	5-69	0-18	2-12	0-8	1-5	1-17	0-0	0-0	1-9	7.2	-32.50

LEADING JUMP TRAINERS AT STRATFORD (SINCE 2010)

	Total W-R	Nov Hdle	H'cap Hdle	Other Hdle	Nov Chase	H'cap Chase	Other Chase	Hunter Chase	N.H. Flat	Per cent	£1 Level stake
Jonjo O'Neill	23-136	5-20	5-32	2-12	1-15	9-46	0-2	0-3	1-6	16.9	**18.27**
Tim Vaughan	22-124	5-28	3-26	9-28	1-10	2-23	1-1	0-1	1-7	17.7	**6.64**
Nigel Twiston-Davies	17-118	0-14	3-24	5-13	4-13	3-37	0-5	0-1	2-11	14.4	**39.38**
Peter Bowen	16-96	4-15	5-17	0-5	0-6	4-26	0-2	0-1	3-24	16.7	-19.59
Nicky Henderson	15-61	4-14	7-21	2-6	0-2	0-10	1-2	0-0	1-6	24.6	-12.37
Evan Williams	15-111	2-21	2-18	2-22	5-11	3-32	0-1	0-0	1-6	13.5	-37.23
Charlie Longsdon	15-75	1-8	5-18	2-12	0-4	5-18	0-3	0-0	2-12	20.0	**7.55**
Warren Greatrex	14-38	5-11	0-6	3-7	1-1	3-6	0-1	2-2	0-4	36.8	**15.37**
Philip Hobbs	12-87	1-9	0-17	2-11	1-6	7-34	1-2	0-3	0-5	13.8	-29.49
Ian Williams	12-64	6-16	2-16	1-8	2-4	0-8	0-3	0-2	1-7	18.8	**26.43**
Rebecca Curtis	12-50	4-10	1-10	3-5	2-3	1-9	1-2	0-2	0-9	24.0	**6.62**
Alan King	11-46	2-4	3-13	2-9	1-4	3-10	0-1	0-0	0-5	23.9	**9.45**
Paul Nicholls	10-45	1-7	0-3	0-6	4-8	1-12	0-0	1-3	3-6	22.2	-10.20
Paul Webber	10-62	2-9	3-12	0-10	2-5	3-20	0-2	0-0	0-4	16.1	**22.50**
David Pipe	10-65	4-14	1-23	2-11	1-2	1-11	0-0	0-0	1-4	15.4	-1.18
Henry Daly	9-53	0-4	3-12	0-6	2-10	3-15	1-1	0-2	0-3	17.0	**23.13**
David Bridgwater	9-71	1-19	0-3	1-16	1-10	5-18	0-1	0-0	1-4	12.7	**49.33**
Dan Skelton	9-34	0-5	2-6	1-4	2-5	2-7	0-0	0-1	2-6	26.5	**6.42**
Dr Richard Newland	9-35	1-2	3-9	3-8	0-3	2-12	0-0	0-1	0-0	25.7	**0.27**
Phil Middleton	9-40	0-5	6-17	1-6	0-5	2-5	0-0	0-0	0-2	22.5	**25.66**
John Ferguson	8-28	3-6	1-7	3-9	0-0	0-2	0-0	0-1	1-3	28.6	-1.04
Neil King	7-69	1-6	4-28	0-11	0-5	1-16	0-1	0-0	1-2	10.1	-14.00
David Evans	6-33	1-6	1-7	2-11	0-1	2-5	0-0	0-0	0-3	18.2	**9.74**
Tom George	6-35	1-4	0-1	0-3	0-4	4-20	1-1	0-1	0-1	17.1	-6.02
Shaun Lycett	6-33	0-7	3-16	0-3	0-1	2-3	0-0	0-0	1-3	18.2	**47.50**
Anthony Honeyball	6-16	2-4	1-2	0-1	1-2	0-2	1-1	0-0	1-4	37.5	**10.91**
Milton Harris	5-40	1-7	0-9	1-7	2-4	1-9	0-2	0-0	0-2	12.5	-4.00
Lawney Hill	5-41	2-5	0-7	0-3	1-2	2-22	0-1	0-0	0-1	12.2	-18.84
Sheena West	5-35	0-7	1-13	4-13	0-0	0-0	0-1	0-0	0-1	14.3	-16.72
Gary Moore	5-32	0-3	2-10	2-10	1-3	0-4	0-0	0-0	0-2	15.6	-2.70
John Quinn	5-15	0-1	1-7	3-6	0-0	0-0	0-0	0-0	1-1	33.3	**1.08**

LEADING JUMP TRAINERS AT TAUNTON (SINCE 2010)

	Total W-R	Nov Hdle	H'cap Hdle	Other Hdle	Nov Chase	H'cap Chase	Other Chase	Hunter Chase	N.H. Flat	Per cent	£1 Level stake
Paul Nicholls	64-204	23-61	11-49	11-25	10-23	3-20	1-4	1-3	4-19	31.4	-11.84
David Pipe	28-222	6-80	12-77	4-33	0-5	5-13	0-2	0-0	1-12	12.6	-89.67
Philip Hobbs	25-149	10-42	3-46	1-15	5-13	4-13	0-1	0-1	2-18	16.8	-52.72
Evan Williams	20-117	4-21	6-42	3-11	4-14	2-22	0-4	0-0	1-3	17.1	**38.51**
Venetia Williams	16-91	3-21	8-33	0-6	1-10	3-14	1-4	0-0	0-3	17.6	-13.59
Colin Tizzard	14-122	3-24	4-32	0-6	1-14	3-27	2-5	0-0	1-14	11.5	-56.26
Alan King	12-106	5-29	2-37	2-11	2-11	0-6	0-1	0-0	1-11	11.3	-47.62
Emma Lavelle	10-41	1-10	3-10	1-2	1-4	2-9	1-1	0-0	1-5	24.4	**26.90**
Tim Vaughan	10-76	3-18	4-31	1-9	0-3	1-7	0-1	0-0	1-7	13.2	**1.62**
Nicky Henderson	9-52	3-16	1-17	2-8	2-6	0-0	0-0	0-0	1-5	17.3	-20.67
Anthony Honeyball	9-55	1-18	7-15	0-4	0-4	0-5	0-1	0-0	1-8	16.4	**20.96**
Jeremy Scott	8-57	1-16	3-22	0-3	0-4	2-3	0-1	0-0	2-8	14.0	-2.38
Bob Buckler	8-56	0-11	2-15	1-5	0-4	4-15	0-0	0-1	1-5	14.3	-16.13
Chris Down	8-103	0-19	7-65	0-6	0-1	1-2	0-0	0-0	0-10	7.8	-9.50
Victor Dartnall	8-60	4-15	3-25	0-2	0-4	0-9	0-0	1-1	0-4	13.3	-2.04
Harry Fry	8-33	4-14	0-5	1-5	0-0	1-1	0-0	0-0	2-8	24.2	-3.64
Nick Williams	7-32	2-7	3-10	0-2	1-4	1-5	0-1	0-0	0-3	21.9	**0.50**
Neil Mulholland	7-85	0-20	4-33	0-3	1-6	1-16	1-2	0-0	0-5	8.2	-28.88
Charlie Mann	6-30	0-8	3-8	0-2	1-7	1-3	1-2	0-0	0-0	20.0	**7.45**
Caroline Keevil	6-80	0-21	3-24	0-8	0-8	3-11	0-0	0-0	0-8	7.5	-49.00
Jamie Snowden	6-31	2-8	1-8	1-4	0-0	1-6	0-1	0-0	1-4	19.4	**12.07**
Alexandra Dunn	6-39	0-6	5-20	1-6	0-0	0-5	0-0	0-0	0-2	15.4	**7.25**
Oliver Sherwood	4-22	1-4	0-7	0-3	1-2	0-1	1-1	0-1	1-3	18.2	**4.75**
Patrick Rodford	4-15	0-0	0-0	0-2	1-3	2-8	0-0	0-0	1-2	26.7	**6.35**
Kevin Bishop	4-44	0-1	4-36	0-2	0-0	0-2	0-0	0-0	0-3	9.1	-12.25
Arthur Whiting	4-20	0-3	0-5	0-1	1-4	2-4	0-0	0-0	1-3	20.0	**76.88**
Lawney Hill	4-14	0-2	3-7	0-1	0-1	0-1	0-0	0-0	1-2	28.6	**0.62**
Michael Blake	4-23	0-0	0-15	3-4	0-1	1-2	0-0	0-0	0-1	17.4	-5.33
Brendan Powell	4-45	0-8	2-23	1-4	1-6	0-2	0-0	0-0	0-2	8.9	-6.00
Dan Skelton	4-16	2-4	1-4	0-1	1-4	0-1	0-0	0-0	0-2	25.0	**2.80**
John Ferguson	4-8	1-1	1-3	0-0	0-2	0-0	0-0	0-0	2-2	50.0	**10.01**

LEADING JUMP TRAINERS AT TOWCESTER (SINCE 2010)

	Total W-R	Nov Hdle	H'cap Hdle	Other Hdle	Nov Chase	H'cap Chase	Other Chase	Hunter Chase	N.H. Flat	Per cent	£1 Level stake
Nicky Henderson	19-64	9-15	1-4	2-12	2-3	0-0	0-3	0-0	5-27	29.7	-2.87
Kim Bailey	19-80	2-13	5-25	4-12	1-4	5-19	1-2	0-0	1-5	23.8	**23.74**
Venetia Williams	18-105	4-19	2-23	1-12	6-15	3-23	0-4	0-0	2-9	17.1	-47.20
Jonjo O'Neill	17-122	4-28	4-29	0-20	1-5	8-33	0-1	0-2	0-4	13.9	-45.97
Tim Vaughan	17-68	5-13	4-20	1-7	0-5	2-10	2-3	0-1	3-9	25.0	-7.56
Nigel Twiston-Davies	15-130	3-24	1-24	1-14	1-8	5-39	1-6	0-1	3-14	11.5	-50.20
David Pipe	15-57	2-9	2-13	3-8	2-3	2-7	0-2	0-0	4-15	26.3	**4.18**
Alan King	15-55	4-16	1-9	4-8	0-4	0-3	0-1	0-0	6-14	27.3	**1.81**
Robin Dickin	14-120	1-19	2-23	4-17	3-13	4-32	0-2	0-0	0-14	11.7	-49.56
Fergal O'Brien	14-68	2-14	1-10	6-13	2-5	1-14	0-1	0-0	2-11	20.6	**2.55**
Oliver Sherwood	13-69	3-18	1-9	1-10	1-8	4-11	2-4	0-0	1-9	18.8	-6.65
Martin Keighley	12-76	1-19	2-18	0-6	1-5	5-17	0-0	0-0	3-11	15.8	-17.00
Jim Old	11-44	0-3	5-12	2-7	0-6	2-13	2-2	0-0	0-1	25.0	**37.50**
Tony Carroll	11-84	1-7	3-30	2-14	0-4	5-23	0-1	0-0	0-5	13.1	-0.75
Charlie Longsdon	10-73	2-14	2-16	0-10	1-3	2-15	1-5	0-0	2-10	13.7	**2.88**
Henry Daly	9-63	3-14	2-9	1-15	1-3	1-10	0-3	1-1	0-8	14.3	-2.65
Brendan Powell	9-64	1-7	1-16	1-11	0-3	2-8	0-4	1-2	3-13	14.1	-8.00
Donald McCain	9-78	0-23	0-10	2-15	0-6	1-8	4-8	0-0	2-8	11.5	-48.18
Ben Pauling	9-23	0-4	4-8	0-1	0-0	5-8	0-0	0-0	0-2	39.1	**19.13**
Seamus Mullins	8-85	0-9	2-24	1-12	0-7	1-17	1-1	0-0	3-15	9.4	-14.00
Ian Williams	8-40	0-4	1-8	2-14	1-3	1-4	3-3	0-0	0-4	20.0	-2.40
Richard Lee	7-38	0-2	0-6	3-7	0-5	2-14	1-1	0-0	1-3	18.4	**33.50**
Lucy Wadham	7-39	2-5	3-17	1-7	0-0	0-1	1-3	0-0	0-6	17.9	-10.80
Jamie Snowden	7-40	2-9	2-10	2-15	0-1	0-2	0-0	0-0	1-3	17.5	-4.67
Philip Hobbs	6-21	1-4	2-3	2-7	1-3	0-1	0-2	0-0	0-1	28.6	**1.92**
David Bridgwater	6-32	0-5	0-2	1-8	0-3	3-10	1-2	0-0	1-2	18.8	**0.25**
Ben Case	6-43	2-10	1-9	0-11	1-5	1-5	0-0	0-0	1-3	14.0	**1.75**
Alex Hales	6-47	2-8	1-8	0-5	0-2	2-17	0-0	0-0	1-7	12.8	**4.25**
Anthony Middleton	6-38	1-2	2-19	0-4	0-0	3-11	0-0	0-0	0-2	15.8	**3.50**
David Arbuthnot	5-12	3-5	0-2	0-0	0-0	0-1	0-0	0-0	2-4	41.7	**0.90**
Lawney Hill	5-46	0-2	4-20	0-4	0-2	0-9	0-1	0-0	1-8	10.9	-7.50

LEADING JUMP TRAINERS AT UTTOXETER (SINCE 2010)

	Total W-R	Nov Hdle	H'cap Hdle	Other Hdle	Nov Chase	H'cap Chase	Other Chase	Hunter Chase	N.H. Flat	Per cent	£1 Level stake
Jonjo O'Neill	40-298	5-36	16-104	6-42	2-21	9-73	1-8	1-1	0-13	13.4	-80.59
Donald McCain	39-271	9-51	4-52	13-81	0-13	1-22	6-18	0-0	6-34	14.4	-91.73
Nigel Twiston-Davies	31-151	5-18	4-35	8-24	5-14	7-40	0-3	0-0	2-17	20.5	**15.25**
Tim Vaughan	29-166	7-29	5-36	12-51	2-10	0-20	1-11	0-0	2-9	17.5	**8.80**
David Pipe	26-142	3-14	5-51	6-28	1-7	7-25	2-3	0-0	2-14	18.3	**7.15**
Kim Bailey	19-139	2-29	6-34	4-30	0-5	3-21	1-7	0-0	3-13	13.7	-19.97
Dr Richard Newland	19-60	3-10	7-23	5-12	2-2	1-9	1-3	0-0	0-1	31.7	**17.58**
Charlie Longsdon	19-94	5-15	4-28	5-20	1-5	1-12	2-3	0-0	1-11	20.2	-18.35
Peter Bowen	18-126	1-14	6-40	4-20	1-5	4-28	0-2	0-0	2-17	14.3	-38.48
Neil King	17-93	1-18	5-27	3-18	2-4	4-17	0-0	0-0	2-9	18.3	**13.57**
Nicky Henderson	16-56	3-10	2-15	6-15	0-2	0-1	2-4	0-0	3-9	28.6	-2.12
Alan King	16-93	1-19	3-15	5-20	3-8	0-8	1-5	0-0	3-18	17.2	-31.36
Philip Hobbs	15-85	1-8	3-19	5-19	1-8	2-19	0-3	0-0	3-9	17.6	-4.68
Sue Smith	14-94	1-12	3-22	1-12	1-9	5-27	2-4	0-0	1-8	14.9	**22.45**
Jennie Candlish	13-112	1-21	6-43	0-15	3-10	3-13	0-5	0-0	0-5	11.6	-8.29
Evan Williams	12-108	1-13	4-23	1-28	1-6	5-29	0-5	0-0	0-4	11.1	-22.63
Venetia Williams	11-104	2-15	3-25	2-13	2-12	2-29	0-2	0-0	0-8	10.6	-57.07
Jim Best	11-50	1-7	4-23	5-17	0-1	0-0	0-1	0-0	1-1	22.0	-8.53
Rebecca Curtis	11-40	1-7	1-7	4-9	1-2	1-2	1-3	0-0	2-10	27.5	-2.37
Fergal O'Brien	10-86	3-18	1-20	0-17	2-6	2-15	0-2	0-0	2-8	11.6	-29.38
Tony Carroll	9-96	2-20	5-50	1-10	0-7	1-5	0-0	0-0	0-4	9.4	-20.09
Emma Lavelle	9-55	2-9	0-9	1-4	1-3	2-9	2-9	0-0	1-12	16.4	**4.42**
Henry Daly	8-45	0-6	2-13	1-7	2-2	1-8	0-2	0-0	2-7	17.8	**2.88**
Charlie Mann	8-32	3-7	2-11	1-4	0-2	2-6	0-2	0-0	0-0	25.0	**6.08**
Phil Middleton	8-21	1-2	6-14	0-0	0-2	1-3	0-0	0-0	0-0	38.1	**41.75**
Jeremy Scott	7-34	0-3	1-9	1-4	1-4	1-6	1-3	0-0	2-5	20.6	**11.38**
Nigel Hawke	7-35	1-3	0-8	0-2	2-3	3-15	1-1	0-0	0-3	20.0	**16.88**
Colin Tizzard	7-31	0-2	1-6	0-1	1-4	3-13	2-4	0-0	0-1	22.6	**3.25**
Ian Williams	7-85	2-17	1-32	3-21	0-5	1-7	0-0	0-0	0-3	8.2	-44.88
Anthony Honeyball	7-34	0-5	4-16	1-5	0-1	0-3	1-1	0-0	1-3	20.6	-0.87
Tom Symonds	7-51	3-13	3-18	0-7	0-3	0-4	1-1	0-0	0-5	13.7	**30.96**

LEADING JUMP TRAINERS AT WARWICK (SINCE 2010)

	Total W-R	Nov Hdle	H'cap Hdle	Other Hdle	Nov Chase	H'cap Chase	Other Chase	Hunter Chase	N.H. Flat	Per cent	£1 Level stake
Alan King	26-122	5-23	2-19	7-26	6-16	4-16	0-0	0-0	2-22	21.3	-37.59
Nigel Twiston-Davies	21-138	4-24	4-28	0-11	1-10	5-46	1-1	1-1	5-17	15.2	**2.72**
Philip Hobbs	17-90	3-16	1-15	3-11	3-7	3-23	0-1	1-2	3-15	18.9	-19.75
Venetia Williams	17-98	5-19	1-20	1-12	2-7	7-34	0-1	1-1	0-4	17.3	**2.32**
Nicky Henderson	14-41	3-8	2-5	2-8	4-8	1-2	0-2	0-0	2-8	34.1	-2.15
Jonjo O'Neill	13-117	1-22	7-38	1-16	1-4	1-23	0-2	1-3	1-9	11.1	-31.27
Paul Nicholls	11-37	1-7	0-0	1-4	6-15	1-4	1-3	0-0	1-4	29.7	**3.51**
David Pipe	11-56	1-5	3-20	2-6	0-2	4-15	0-0	0-0	1-8	19.6	-6.97
Charlie Longsdon	10-71	0-10	2-17	2-12	1-4	0-12	1-3	0-0	4-13	14.1	**13.20**
Henry Daly	8-69	2-16	1-13	0-9	1-5	2-17	0-1	0-0	2-8	11.6	-7.25
Charlie Mann	7-34	2-7	1-6	1-5	1-6	2-9	0-0	0-0	0-1	20.6	**0.92**
Richard Lee	6-32	1-6	1-6	1-2	1-2	1-13	0-0	0-0	1-3	18.8	**37.00**
Tom George	6-31	0-4	0-4	0-2	2-6	3-7	0-2	0-1	1-5	19.4	**8.75**
Colin Tizzard	6-47	2-10	0-5	0-2	0-8	3-12	0-0	0-0	1-10	12.8	**12.50**
Ian Williams	6-48	1-7	3-10	1-12	0-3	0-6	0-0	0-0	1-10	12.5	**3.00**
Robin Dickin	5-62	2-19	2-17	0-4	0-3	1-10	0-0	0-0	0-9	8.1	**52.08**
Neil King	5-37	0-1	2-10	1-6	1-1	0-13	0-0	0-0	1-6	13.5	-20.45
Richard Phillips	5-41	1-9	2-17	0-4	2-3	0-4	0-0	0-0	0-4	12.2	**12.50**
Nick Williams	5-20	0-0	0-2	0-3	1-3	1-8	2-3	0-0	1-1	25.0	**11.88**
Evan Williams	5-31	1-5	1-9	1-4	1-2	1-7	0-0	0-1	0-3	16.1	-8.29
Brendan Powell	5-22	0-2	1-5	1-5	0-1	2-5	1-1	0-0	0-3	22.7	**18.25**
W P Mullins	4-6	1-2	0-0	3-3	0-0	0-1	0-0	0-0	0-0	66.7	**2.47**
Tim Vaughan	5-21	0-4	2-2	2-8	0-1	0-4	0-0	1-1	0-1	23.8	**25.08**
Ben Case	4-22	1-4	0-6	0-3	2-2	0-2	0-0	0-0	1-5	18.2	**47.00**
Dr Richard Newland	4-15	0-3	2-4	0-2	0-0	2-6	0-0	0-0	0-0	26.7	**21.75**
Jeremy Scott	3-20	0-4	2-7	0-2	0-0	1-3	0-0	0-0	0-4	15.0	**8.00**
Peter Bowen	3-19	0-2	2-5	0-1	0-3	0-5	0-0	0-0	1-3	15.8	**20.50**
Anabel K Murphy	3-20	0-1	3-15	0-1	0-0	0-0	0-0	0-1	0-2	15.0	**14.00**
Sheena West	3-12	0-1	0-3	1-2	0-0	1-5	0-0	0-0	1-1	25.0	**16.13**
Seamus Mullins	3-26	0-4	0-2	1-6	0-2	2-5	0-1	0-0	0-6	11.5	-10.50
Paul Webber	3-42	0-8	1-8	2-9	0-5	0-4	0-0	0-0	0-8	7.1	-10.00

LEADING JUMP TRAINERS AT WETHERBY (SINCE 2010)

	Total W-R	Nov Hdle	H'cap Hdle	Other Hdle	Nov Chase	H'cap Chase	Other Chase	Hunter Chase	N.H. Flat	Per cent	£1 Level stake
Sue Smith	29-238	3-36	9-59	1-21	3-26	12-85	0-2	0-0	1-9	12.2	-92.35
Donald McCain	28-162	8-32	3-37	5-32	2-21	3-24	4-7	0-0	3-9	17.3	-47.13
Jonjo O'Neill	22-87	4-11	7-23	3-9	2-5	3-26	2-4	0-4	1-5	25.3	-1.76
Brian Ellison	22-120	2-13	4-44	9-32	4-9	3-17	0-1	0-0	0-4	18.3	-1.99
Malcolm Jefferson	15-97	2-12	2-16	1-16	2-8	7-32	1-3	0-0	0-10	15.5	**13.51**
Lucinda Russell	12-112	0-13	4-25	0-13	2-13	6-38	0-3	0-0	0-7	10.7	-22.00
Tim Easterby	12-112	4-20	1-17	0-26	0-7	6-26	1-2	0-0	0-14	10.7	-27.52
Michael Easterby	11-66	0-11	6-21	1-11	2-3	1-11	0-0	0-0	1-9	16.7	**19.70**
Howard Johnson	11-59	1-12	2-13	3-13	1-6	1-7	0-2	0-1	3-5	18.6	**41.81**
Chris Grant	11-115	2-23	5-26	1-25	2-11	1-21	0-2	0-0	0-7	9.6	-31.40
Charlie Longsdon	11-46	0-6	1-7	2-10	1-1	5-15	0-1	0-0	2-6	23.9	-0.54
Warren Greatrex	11-25	2-8	2-8	2-3	2-2	1-1	0-0	0-0	2-3	44.0	**21.48**
Micky Hammond	10-172	3-32	4-72	0-13	0-4	2-36	0-2	0-0	1-13	5.8	-98.09
John Quinn	10-49	2-12	3-11	4-20	0-0	0-1	0-0	0-0	1-5	20.4	**2.92**
Alan King	10-57	2-12	2-12	2-16	1-4	1-7	1-2	0-0	1-4	17.5	-18.13
Philip Kirby	9-78	2-22	2-28	0-9	0-2	2-6	0-0	0-1	3-10	11.5	-26.76
John Wade	8-118	0-20	1-26	0-4	2-12	5-46	0-3	0-2	0-5	6.8	-82.88
Kim Bailey	7-24	0-2	1-5	2-6	1-3	1-2	2-4	0-0	0-2	29.2	**13.13**
Maurice Barnes	7-78	2-16	1-32	1-9	0-4	3-11	0-2	0-0	0-4	9.0	-30.90
Paul Nicholls	7-19	0-3	0-0	3-6	2-3	1-2	1-5	0-0	0-0	36.8	**1.76**
Steve Gollings	7-22	3-7	1-7	2-3	0-1	0-2	0-1	0-0	1-1	31.8	**14.17**
Martin Todhunter	7-63	0-6	2-16	0-9	0-6	5-23	0-3	0-0	0-0	11.1	-27.00
David Pipe	7-45	2-7	0-10	0-6	2-3	2-11	1-3	0-0	0-5	15.6	-28.69
Caroline Bailey	7-28	1-1	0-3	0-1	1-2	5-20	0-0	0-0	0-1	25.0	**34.13**
Ian Williams	7-33	0-3	4-15	0-2	2-5	1-6	0-1	0-0	0-1	21.2	**3.58**
Tim Vaughan	7-50	1-10	1-17	1-9	2-7	1-4	0-1	0-0	1-2	14.0	-28.12
Nigel Twiston-Davies	6-38	2-5	0-4	1-4	1-2	1-17	0-2	1-1	0-3	15.8	-11.75
David O'Meara	6-41	1-9	2-13	0-8	2-5	1-2	0-0	0-0	0-4	14.6	-8.17
George Moore	5-72	1-22	3-15	0-14	1-6	0-4	0-3	0-0	0-8	6.9	-43.17
Nicky Henderson	5-24	1-1	0-6	3-8	1-4	0-2	0-3	0-0	0-0	20.8	-8.37
Ferdy Murphy	5-75	0-10	1-16	1-4	0-4	3-39	0-1	0-0	0-1	6.7	-42.50

LEADING JUMP TRAINERS AT WINCANTON (SINCE 2010)

	Total W-R	Nov Hdle	H'cap Hdle	Other Hdle	Nov Chase	H'cap Chase	Other Chase	Hunter Chase	N.H. Flat	Per cent	£1 Level stake
Paul Nicholls	70-272	26-73	13-54	7-29	9-30	10-55	1-3	0-2	4-26	25.7	-42.37
David Pipe	36-203	7-36	11-83	3-21	2-8	12-45	0-0	0-0	1-10	17.7	-30.73
Colin Tizzard	31-217	2-42	5-43	5-19	3-20	11-63	0-2	0-1	5-27	14.3	-37.17
Philip Hobbs	30-196	3-38	11-45	2-18	7-20	3-53	1-1	0-1	3-20	15.3	-39.27
Alan King	17-116	1-28	5-34	4-13	2-13	3-14	0-2	0-1	2-11	14.7	-32.50
Harry Fry	15-54	2-9	3-12	3-11	1-4	2-5	0-0	0-0	4-13	27.8	**17.50**
Tom George	13-64	0-7	0-4	0-2	3-9	9-38	0-1	1-1	0-2	20.3	-16.46
Venetia Williams	13-115	3-14	2-25	0-9	4-15	4-48	0-2	0-0	0-2	11.3	-59.60
Emma Lavelle	13-71	3-13	1-16	1-6	0-6	3-17	1-2	0-0	4-11	18.3	**9.08**
Nicky Henderson	11-57	3-13	2-17	5-11	1-6	0-2	0-0	0-0	0-8	19.3	-28.49
Jeremy Scott	11-105	3-24	4-29	2-7	1-9	1-21	0-3	0-0	0-12	10.5	-47.88
Tim Vaughan	11-49	4-9	3-22	0-1	1-7	1-5	0-0	1-2	1-3	22.4	**18.64**
Chris Down	10-79	2-18	6-39	0-7	0-2	2-6	0-0	0-0	0-7	12.7	**60.50**
Andy Turnell	9-45	3-15	4-15	0-5	1-3	0-5	0-0	0-0	1-2	20.0	-4.40
Seamus Mullins	9-100	3-26	2-33	1-7	2-9	1-17	0-0	0-0	0-8	9.0	-39.92
Brendan Powell	9-59	1-14	4-23	0-5	1-3	2-11	0-0	0-0	1-3	15.3	**48.08**
Neil Mulholland	9-101	3-28	0-25	0-11	1-6	5-20	0-0	0-0	0-11	8.9	-54.67
Kim Bailey	8-54	1-17	4-21	1-5	0-2	1-7	1-1	0-0	0-1	14.8	-9.07
Victor Dartnall	8-77	0-10	3-29	0-4	1-5	4-22	0-0	0-2	0-5	10.4	-12.50
Nick Williams	7-45	1-6	1-9	2-6	1-3	1-17	0-0	0-0	1-4	15.6	-0.83
Nigel Twiston-Davies	6-43	1-7	1-8	0-3	0-4	4-19	0-0	0-0	0-2	14.0	**9.98**
Sue Gardner	6-43	0-6	3-21	0-5	0-1	3-6	0-0	0-0	0-4	14.0	**15.00**
Gary Moore	6-48	1-5	1-24	2-5	2-5	0-6	0-0	0-0	0-3	12.5	-6.45
Paul Henderson	6-115	2-17	1-36	0-5	0-10	3-39	0-0	0-0	0-8	5.2	-56.00
Ben De Haan	5-23	2-8	0-2	1-5	2-5	0-2	0-0	0-0	0-1	21.7	**21.93**
Charlie Mann	5-43	1-11	1-9	0-3	0-2	2-16	1-1	0-1	0-0	11.6	-28.88
Dan Skelton	5-16	1-4	0-3	2-3	1-1	0-3	0-0	0-0	1-2	31.3	-0.25
Rebecca Curtis	5-18	1-3	1-7	1-3	1-1	0-2	0-0	0-0	1-2	27.8	**5.30**
Jamie Snowden	5-47	0-8	1-10	0-8	1-8	3-11	0-0	0-0	0-2	10.6	-12.52
Ron Hodges	4-40	1-4	0-18	0-0	2-4	1-12	0-0	0-0	0-2	10.0	-19.82
David Arbuthnot	4-17	0-1	2-5	0-2	0-1	1-6	0-1	0-0	1-1	23.5	**6.50**

LEADING JUMP TRAINERS AT WORCESTER (SINCE 2010)

	Total W-R	Nov Hdle	H'cap Hdle	Other Hdle	Nov Chase	H'cap Chase	Other Chase	Hunter Chase	N.H. Flat	Per cent	£1 Level stake
Jonjo O'Neill	51-271	7-30	16-82	3-37	3-22	13-68	3-9	1-2	5-21	18.8	-38.76
Paul Nicholls	23-69	5-8	2-10	6-11	4-11	3-11	2-12	0-0	1-6	33.3	**7.55**
Tim Vaughan	20-140	4-22	5-42	5-23	3-11	2-30	1-4	0-0	0-8	14.3	-33.52
David Pipe	19-142	1-10	4-59	5-13	1-10	3-27	1-4	0-0	4-19	13.4	-72.31
Donald McCain	18-96	2-14	6-17	5-27	1-8	4-15	0-2	0-0	0-13	18.8	**5.31**
Rebecca Curtis	18-63	1-8	3-13	3-12	5-9	1-4	1-2	0-0	4-15	28.6	-10.57
Philip Hobbs	17-93	1-7	3-20	4-18	1-10	4-23	3-5	0-0	1-10	18.3	-10.70
Nicky Henderson	16-60	6-10	0-16	2-10	1-2	2-4	1-2	0-0	4-16	26.7	-2.31
Peter Bowen	16-107	0-18	2-22	1-12	1-10	5-28	0-3	0-0	7-14	15.0	-14.25
Charlie Longsdon	16-79	0-9	2-14	1-11	2-9	4-18	1-1	0-0	6-17	20.3	**0.49**
Nigel Twiston-Davies	14-113	3-13	1-31	3-13	4-11	3-35	0-1	0-0	0-9	12.4	-30.75
Dr Richard Newland	13-62	4-9	2-26	2-9	1-6	3-6	1-6	0-0	0-0	21.0	-22.05
Lawney Hill	12-56	3-15	1-10	2-4	1-6	5-15	0-0	0-0	0-6	21.4	**72.00**
Evan Williams	12-116	2-15	2-21	3-26	1-13	4-39	0-2	0-0	0-0	10.3	-41.97
Kim Bailey	10-54	2-5	1-16	3-8	2-6	2-10	0-4	0-0	0-5	18.5	-5.12
Brendan Powell	10-81	1-16	1-27	1-11	2-5	3-16	0-2	0-0	2-4	12.3	**5.85**
Neil Mulholland	10-76	1-4	6-28	0-12	0-4	2-20	1-2	0-0	0-6	13.2	-10.95
Jeremy Scott	9-40	1-5	3-13	1-2	2-6	2-8	0-1	0-0	0-5	22.5	**0.46**
Jim Best	9-38	1-7	4-15	3-9	0-0	1-3	0-1	0-0	0-3	23.7	**2.53**
Anthony Honeyball	9-36	0-5	5-11	0-6	1-2	0-1	1-1	0-0	2-10	25.0	**29.25**
Ian Williams	8-44	2-5	2-17	0-12	0-4	3-3	1-2	0-0	0-1	18.2	**4.41**
Shaun Lycett	8-80	1-9	4-39	2-18	0-2	0-2	0-0	0-0	1-10	10.0	-20.55
Seamus Mullins	7-50	1-5	1-8	0-8	1-5	1-7	1-3	0-0	2-14	14.0	**4.25**
Paul Webber	7-63	0-5	0-6	0-14	0-9	4-16	0-3	0-0	3-10	11.1	-27.63
Martin Keighley	7-94	2-10	2-31	0-16	1-7	1-18	0-3	0-0	1-9	7.4	-7.50
John Ferguson	7-20	3-4	2-5	0-6	0-0	0-1	0-0	0-0	2-4	35.0	-1.71
Richard Lee	6-64	0-3	1-14	1-7	0-2	4-33	0-1	0-0	0-4	9.4	-20.75
Richard Phillips	6-62	1-11	3-25	2-8	0-0	0-8	0-0	0-0	0-10	9.7	-17.00
David Rees	6-50	1-9	2-21	2-9	1-2	0-7	0-0	0-0	0-2	12.0	-16.00
David Bridgwater	6-63	1-8	0-5	3-16	1-13	1-15	0-0	0-0	0-6	9.5	-23.40
Michael Gates	6-48	0-5	0-10	0-8	0-2	6-20	0-0	0-0	0-3	12.5	**11.50**

LEADING TRAINERS BY MONTH 2010-2014

JANUARY

	Total W-R	Nov Hdle	H'cap Hdle	Other Hdle	Nov Chase	H'cap Chase	Other Chase	Hunter Chase	N.H. Flat	Per cent	£1 Level stake
Nicky Henderson	102-357	30-92	6-49	25-86	24-52	2-34	7-21	0-0	9-27	28.6	-26.46
Donald McCain	76-405	25-91	6-80	10-72	13-47	10-63	6-24	0-0	6-29	18.8	-105.53
David Pipe	72-393	16-72	17-111	16-68	5-19	12-82	2-20	0-0	4-25	18.3	-50.11
Paul Nicholls	67-326	12-57	8-57	15-62	9-42	9-69	14-29	0-0	1-12	20.6	-53.75
Venetia Williams	66-421	13-57	18-103	4-43	4-48	24-153	2-10	0-0	1-8	15.7	**12.87**
Philip Hobbs	59-330	9-72	9-70	9-49	10-36	14-77	1-10	1-1	6-19	17.9	-53.95
Alan King	46-304	14-73	7-64	10-49	9-40	4-39	2-13	0-0	0-28	15.1	-44.11
Evan Williams	37-244	4-31	9-73	5-44	7-29	8-46	1-6	0-2	3-13	15.2	**42.88**
Jonjo O'Neill	36-368	6-82	12-92	3-55	2-28	8-88	4-11	0-2	1-10	9.8	-194.28
Nigel Twiston-Davies	33-313	5-49	5-61	2-30	4-37	14-108	0-12	0-0	3-17	10.5	-18.28
Lucinda Russell	31-284	4-33	7-76	6-34	1-17	11-99	1-8	0-0	1-17	10.9	-104.35
Sue Smith	27-181	2-30	13-48	0-9	3-15	7-67	1-4	0-0	1-8	14.9	**7.71**
Tom George	25-179	2-30	2-19	1-22	7-30	11-64	0-6	0-0	2-8	14.0	-54.44
Gary Moore	24-215	3-38	4-54	4-33	4-32	7-49	1-5	0-0	1-6	11.2	**13.84**
Colin Tizzard	23-225	4-34	5-41	2-15	4-24	4-65	1-15	0-0	3-31	10.2	-86.38
Keith Reveley	22-118	3-17	5-22	1-15	4-10	5-32	0-1	0-0	4-21	18.6	-12.23
John Ferguson	22-71	6-22	1-8	12-28	1-6	0-1	0-1	0-0	2-5	31.0	**13.23**
Charlie Longsdon	21-166	5-41	4-39	2-17	2-14	3-41	1-3	0-0	4-14	12.7	-43.77
Howard Johnson	20-103	6-24	0-19	2-9	4-7	2-23	3-13	0-0	3-8	19.4	-0.33
Rebecca Curtis	20-91	3-16	2-20	7-20	3-11	2-10	0-3	0-0	3-11	22.0	**30.89**
Malcolm Jefferson	19-105	4-21	3-21	0-6	0-6	7-29	1-5	0-0	4-17	18.1	**42.38**
Henry Daly	19-120	1-22	4-19	4-22	3-18	4-29	2-2	1-1	0-7	15.8	-31.90
Brian Ellison	19-118	4-19	5-49	3-17	2-6	2-16	2-3	0-0	1-8	16.1	-42.91
Nicky Richards	19-98	3-26	4-25	4-15	2-8	3-15	1-3	0-0	2-6	19.4	-9.00
Seamus Mullins	18-128	3-21	3-28	1-15	2-15	7-27	0-6	0-0	2-17	14.1	**33.70**
Neil Mulholland	18-118	1-26	8-38	2-11	2-13	4-22	1-3	0-0	0-6	15.3	**19.00**
Nick Williams	16-98	2-8	4-18	5-19	2-18	3-29	1-6	0-0	0-1	16.3	-5.14
Victor Dartnall	15-99	2-23	4-22	0-7	4-11	3-27	1-2	0-2	1-5	15.2	**4.65**
Jim Goldie	14-116	2-15	6-52	2-14	1-3	2-19	0-3	0-0	1-10	12.1	-1.00
James Ewart	14-108	0-13	2-18	1-13	0-6	6-29	3-6	0-0	2-23	13.0	-30.86
Micky Hammond	13-88	3-16	5-37	0-5	1-5	2-17	0-2	0-0	2-6	14.8	**44.25**
Tony Carroll	13-95	3-15	5-28	1-15	1-7	3-23	0-4	0-0	0-3	13.7	**37.00**
Lucy Wadham	13-99	0-15	5-42	3-13	1-6	1-8	2-7	0-0	1-8	13.1	-9.20
Harry Fry	13-33	2-7	2-7	3-7	1-2	1-4	2-3	0-0	2-3	39.4	**22.18**
Neil King	12-123	1-27	2-31	2-24	1-5	4-24	1-3	0-0	1-10	9.8	-60.51
Emma Lavelle	12-138	3-34	3-28	0-21	2-16	2-17	0-5	0-0	2-19	8.7	-68.63
Alex Hales	12-78	2-14	2-24	0-9	3-7	5-21	0-2	0-0	0-1	15.4	-0.17
Martin Keighley	12-112	1-20	4-29	0-12	1-8	4-29	0-5	0-0	2-9	10.7	-32.92
Dr Richard Newland	12-61	0-7	4-15	2-7	1-3	5-28	0-0	0-0	0-1	19.7	**10.50**
Tom Symonds	12-62	0-6	3-16	0-12	1-8	5-13	2-3	0-0	1-6	19.4	**2.79**
Peter Bowen	11-109	1-10	3-31	3-21	1-5	1-30	0-1	0-0	2-11	10.1	-32.53
Charlie Mann	11-115	1-23	2-22	2-17	4-13	1-34	1-3	0-0	0-4	9.6	-45.97
David Bridgwater	11-48	2-13	0-7	2-3	2-3	4-17	1-3	0-0	0-2	22.9	**10.66**
Richard Lee	10-83	3-12	1-18	0-6	2-10	3-32	0-3	0-0	1-2	12.0	-25.92
Oliver Sherwood	10-109	2-26	2-16	3-29	1-9	1-18	1-3	0-1	0-7	9.2	**37.50**
John Quinn	10-56	4-16	2-11	4-17	0-2	0-6	0-1	0-0	0-3	17.9	**12.30**
Nick Gifford	10-83	0-14	0-13	1-8	4-14	3-27	1-4	0-0	1-3	12.0	-26.70
Tim Vaughan	10-198	1-38	3-53	1-35	1-14	1-29	2-10	0-0	1-20	5.1	-141.61
Robin Dickin	9-78	3-25	1-10	1-10	0-2	4-21	0-3	0-0	0-7	11.5	-26.25
Kim Bailey	9-112	1-24	2-28	3-21	0-8	1-17	0-4	0-0	2-10	8.0	-31.03
Steve Gollings	9-46	2-13	2-9	2-6	0-4	1-7	1-3	0-0	1-4	19.6	-17.88

FEBRUARY

	Total W-R	Nov Hdle	H'cap Hdle	Other Hdle	Nov Chase	H'cap Chase	Other Chase	Hunter Chase	N.H. Flat	Per cent	£1 Level stake
Nicky Henderson	114-397	37-104	5-66	26-81	15-46	4-28	13-33	2-2	12-38	28.7	-94.83
Paul Nicholls	85-370	21-74	12-64	15-60	14-46	5-51	10-41	4-8	4-26	23.0	-85.75
David Pipe	77-355	11-68	21-110	11-48	7-20	16-69	0-5	0-0	11-35	21.7	**6.04**
Donald McCain	76-424	22-107	12-97	13-58	11-56	5-50	5-19	0-2	8-36	17.9	-74.34
Venetia Williams	66-435	5-52	13-93	10-57	10-49	21-153	5-14	0-2	2-15	15.2	-127.33
Alan King	61-405	11-96	8-84	6-58	17-36	6-43	5-28	0-2	8-58	15.1	-79.41
Jonjo O'Neill	58-374	15-89	18-96	6-65	5-20	7-65	1-5	4-15	2-19	15.5	-81.96
Philip Hobbs	42-303	7-51	10-67	3-33	4-27	8-70	3-17	0-4	7-34	13.9	-94.44
Nigel Twiston-Davies	38-365	7-53	9-76	2-41	4-30	8-110	1-16	4-9	3-30	10.4	-52.78
Lucinda Russell	34-262	5-32	4-67	0-21	8-28	14-92	2-4	0-0	1-18	13.0	-55.98
Colin Tizzard	33-206	5-35	5-45	3-19	2-20	8-53	4-8	0-1	6-25	16.0	-51.55
Evan Williams	32-261	5-31	8-76	6-57	2-22	7-61	1-5	1-2	2-7	12.3	**61.58**
Gary Moore	28-215	4-40	7-67	5-40	3-15	8-36	1-8	0-0	0-9	13.0	-73.60
Sue Smith	26-212	0-24	7-62	0-4	7-28	12-73	0-5	0-0	0-16	12.3	-41.36
Tom George	25-184	3-15	0-18	2-26	6-24	10-77	2-13	1-2	1-9	13.6	-8.35
Charlie Longsdon	23-166	6-33	3-38	5-17	1-15	6-37	0-3	0-0	2-23	13.9	**2.82**
Tim Vaughan	22-203	4-37	7-65	3-30	2-19	1-23	2-2	1-4	2-23	10.8	-58.81
Nicky Richards	20-95	3-17	5-29	3-10	2-4	3-18	1-5	0-0	3-13	21.1	**9.41**
Rebecca Curtis	20-119	2-19	1-22	6-25	2-14	0-7	0-2	3-8	6-22	16.8	-33.51
John Ferguson	20-75	6-20	4-14	6-24	0-3	1-2	0-0	0-3	4-11	26.7	-15.16
Kim Bailey	18-86	4-18	2-25	3-10	1-4	3-17	3-5	0-0	2-7	20.9	**52.97**
Richard Lee	17-119	1-12	4-23	2-17	4-13	4-50	1-1	0-0	1-3	14.3	-25.96
Brian Ellison	16-158	3-32	8-69	1-24	2-7	1-18	1-1	0-0	0-12	10.1	-84.89
Keith Reveley	16-133	4-23	6-31	0-9	2-9	2-32	0-1	0-0	2-28	12.0	-56.17
Anthony Honeyball	16-68	1-15	7-17	0-4	0-2	2-10	1-3	0-0	5-17	23.5	**30.06**
Chris Grant	15-116	1-25	3-28	1-7	0-9	6-27	1-5	0-0	3-15	12.9	**2.96**
Ian Williams	15-98	2-21	3-25	3-15	3-9	2-15	1-3	0-2	1-8	15.3	-29.70
Warren Greatrex	15-96	3-23	4-28	4-19	0-4	1-9	0-0	1-1	2-12	15.6	**22.93**
Oliver Sherwood	14-117	1-21	1-22	3-18	1-8	6-33	0-2	0-0	2-13	12.0	-38.82
Nick Williams	14-87	4-14	1-20	1-10	3-7	4-24	0-5	0-0	1-7	16.1	-6.90
Jim Goldie	13-81	1-7	8-41	1-6	0-1	3-17	0-0	0-0	0-9	16.0	**17.30**
Charlie Mann	13-116	2-13	1-21	1-20	1-16	4-28	3-11	0-0	1-7	11.2	**17.65**
Victor Dartnall	13-104	3-25	3-22	0-4	1-7	3-26	0-0	1-4	2-16	12.5	-12.38
Lucy Wadham	13-99	4-15	3-42	0-7	0-8	4-15	1-3	0-1	1-9	13.1	-27.81
Emma Lavelle	13-124	5-33	1-23	2-15	2-8	0-19	1-5	0-0	2-21	10.5	-52.77
Henry Daly	12-113	2-20	2-18	0-19	2-9	0-26	1-4	2-2	3-15	10.6	-55.90
Martin Keighley	12-64	1-8	4-24	2-5	0-1	3-15	1-2	0-1	1-8	18.8	-6.96
Harry Fry	12-39	1-6	0-7	3-8	2-4	4-5	1-2	0-0	1-7	30.8	**12.24**
Howard Johnson	11-112	3-31	4-28	1-8	0-11	1-18	1-5	0-2	1-9	9.8	**5.38**
Alan Swinbank	11-59	1-12	2-7	0-2	2-5	1-6	0-2	0-0	5-25	18.6	**20.50**
Nick Gifford	11-71	0-9	2-13	1-8	1-2	3-25	2-5	0-1	2-8	15.5	**17.83**
James Ewart	11-103	2-16	0-22	4-13	1-6	3-26	1-4	0-0	0-16	10.7	-45.83
Philip Kirby	11-87	1-11	7-44	0-5	1-4	1-11	0-1	0-1	1-10	12.6	**5.91**
Malcolm Jefferson	10-111	3-23	2-25	0-8	1-8	3-26	0-4	0-0	1-17	9.0	-22.77
Micky Hammond	10-80	3-14	3-27	1-10	1-7	1-10	0-0	0-0	1-12	12.5	-4.62
Stuart Coltherd	10-55	0-7	1-12	0-4	2-5	6-22	0-0	1-3	0-2	18.2	**49.50**
Tim Easterby	10-73	2-17	2-14	1-9	1-4	3-15	0-1	0-0	1-13	13.7	-33.44
N W Alexander	10-92	1-10	2-25	1-8	1-4	3-26	0-3	0-5	2-11	10.9	**55.50**
David Arbuthnot	9-42	3-7	1-5	0-5	2-5	1-13	0-0	0-0	2-7	21.4	**10.19**
John Quinn	9-64	2-16	2-26	4-15	0-0	0-5	0-0	0-0	1-2	14.1	-22.34
Tony Carroll	9-91	1-13	4-44	1-6	2-4	1-18	0-3	0-0	0-3	9.9	-9.70

MARCH

	Total W-R	Nov Hdle	H'cap Hdle	Other Hdle	Nov Chase	H'cap Chase	Other Chase	Hunter Chase	N.H. Flat	Per cent	£1 Level stake
Nicky Henderson	100-534	26-107	22-139	21-94	5-41	2-59	10-46	0-1	15-62	18.7	-27.02
Paul Nicholls	82-439	20-69	15-96	12-68	14-51	10-70	4-59	3-11	4-27	18.7	-60.18
Donald McCain	75-496	30-132	9-119	13-62	3-44	6-60	3-28	0-1	11-53	15.1	-180.79
Philip Hobbs	62-453	15-66	9-136	6-51	11-37	14-107	2-17	1-6	6-47	13.7	-82.19
Venetia Williams	60-462	9-63	12-117	3-50	12-49	20-156	2-16	1-1	1-18	13.0	-194.33
Alan King	60-464	11-86	5-128	13-69	7-29	8-74	5-23	0-0	12-66	12.9	-157.13
David Pipe	54-419	9-63	21-165	6-51	2-20	13-99	3-19	0-0	2-22	12.9	-24.31
Evan Williams	50-354	10-55	13-93	7-44	8-32	7-93	2-9	0-2	3-30	14.1	-81.64
Nigel Twiston-Davies	48-406	5-43	10-97	5-43	4-29	16-142	2-15	1-5	5-41	11.8	-88.71
Jonjo O'Neill	47-381	5-56	7-110	8-69	4-22	17-97	3-13	2-10	2-15	12.3	-43.79
Charlie Longsdon	38-269	9-42	5-75	3-23	2-17	11-65	1-7	0-1	8-43	14.1	-46.87
Lucinda Russell	37-307	5-63	8-73	0-13	5-27	15-101	1-5	0-0	3-25	12.1	-98.86
Tim Vaughan	36-299	6-49	12-85	3-40	0-21	7-61	1-11	3-6	4-28	12.0	-135.86
Sue Smith	33-301	5-37	11-82	1-13	2-25	10-111	2-14	0-0	2-20	11.0	-27.62
Gary Moore	31-282	5-42	9-102	7-43	6-35	2-53	1-4	0-0	1-8	11.0	-53.44
Keith Reveley	31-174	5-26	6-46	4-21	5-9	9-44	0-2	0-0	2-28	17.8	-17.26
Tom George	29-205	3-27	0-24	3-23	7-31	14-79	0-8	0-2	2-12	14.1	-46.94
Rebecca Curtis	29-128	7-30	6-26	4-22	4-10	2-11	3-6	0-4	3-19	22.7	**3.92**
Colin Tizzard	27-217	3-33	6-51	3-16	5-20	7-66	1-7	0-2	2-25	12.4	**54.25**
Malcolm Jefferson	22-158	4-35	5-33	1-13	1-10	8-37	0-5	0-0	4-26	13.9	**3.00**
Brian Ellison	22-149	4-28	9-66	3-29	1-3	4-23	0-0	0-0	1-4	14.8	-37.06
Howard Johnson	21-149	7-42	0-32	1-7	6-14	2-22	3-15	0-0	2-19	14.1	-59.10
Warren Greatrex	21-138	5-39	5-44	2-21	1-3	5-16	0-2	1-2	2-14	15.2	**7.62**
Charlie Mann	20-149	3-23	7-44	2-17	2-7	4-40	2-10	0-4	0-6	13.4	-11.13
Tony Carroll	20-141	4-23	11-77	1-14	1-9	3-14	0-1	0-0	0-5	14.2	**68.62**
Dan Skelton	20-79	1-10	5-16	4-11	2-10	2-12	0-0	0-1	6-19	25.3	**5.57**
Victor Dartnall	19-134	2-18	6-40	1-8	0-15	4-33	2-2	2-4	2-15	14.2	-34.41
Ian Williams	19-123	0-12	9-52	3-9	2-5	4-29	0-6	1-3	0-9	15.4	-9.55
Nicky Richards	19-123	5-31	6-37	0-3	3-9	0-18	2-5	0-0	3-20	15.4	-36.68
Jennie Candlish	19-109	4-16	6-41	2-18	2-5	4-18	0-0	0-0	1-14	17.4	**14.22**
Anthony Honeyball	18-91	1-10	9-29	0-16	3-6	2-12	1-4	0-0	2-16	19.8	-0.42
Neil Mulholland	18-129	2-15	7-42	1-15	1-9	3-33	1-5	0-0	3-11	14.0	-33.04
Kim Bailey	17-185	1-35	2-50	2-22	3-15	5-41	1-5	0-0	3-18	9.2	-76.23
Caroline Bailey	17-78	0-11	1-10	0-5	2-6	13-38	1-4	0-0	0-4	21.8	**41.13**
James Ewart	17-125	2-19	2-25	3-9	2-13	4-36	2-4	0-0	2-20	13.6	-45.19
Oliver Sherwood	16-160	0-27	1-28	3-18	1-9	4-40	2-6	0-0	5-32	10.0	-60.92
Chris Grant	16-137	1-32	9-35	1-8	0-9	2-34	3-5	0-0	0-14	11.7	-25.88
Jeremy Scott	15-98	1-14	8-45	1-9	0-4	4-20	0-0	0-0	1-10	15.3	-6.55
Neil King	15-132	2-11	5-52	1-21	1-4	5-38	0-0	0-0	1-9	11.4	-52.00
Dianne Sayer	15-118	3-14	9-58	0-6	0-8	3-28	0-1	0-0	0-3	12.7	-16.50
Alan Swinbank	15-87	2-18	3-9	0-6	1-8	2-7	1-5	0-0	6-34	17.2	-16.49
Henry Daly	15-165	0-24	4-33	1-14	3-15	5-47	0-4	1-4	1-25	9.1	-48.12
Seamus Mullins	14-158	2-35	2-42	0-18	0-9	10-41	0-4	0-0	0-10	8.9	-70.30
Jim Goldie	14-87	3-16	3-36	0-7	2-3	4-18	0-0	0-0	2-7	16.1	-10.27
John Quinn	14-68	3-14	5-28	5-17	0-0	0-5	0-0	0-0	1-4	20.6	**15.28**
Lucy Wadham	14-110	1-10	4-44	4-24	1-3	3-22	1-3	0-1	1-6	12.7	-27.73
Nigel Hawke	14-72	2-11	2-15	0-3	1-6	8-31	0-2	0-0	1-4	19.4	-2.40
Emma Lavelle	14-144	4-25	2-35	1-20	2-7	4-34	0-5	0-0	1-24	9.7	-84.31
Fergal O'Brien	14-114	3-21	0-25	1-16	1-7	5-29	1-2	1-3	2-11	12.3	**19.33**
Brendan Powell	14-154	1-19	5-56	1-17	5-12	0-28	0-0	1-4	1-19	9.1	-42.17
Richard Lee	13-100	4-11	2-17	0-9	2-11	5-49	0-1	0-0	0-2	13.0	-32.50

APRIL

	Total W-R	Nov Hdle	H'cap Hdle	Other Hdle	Nov Chase	H'cap Chase	Other Chase	Hunter Chase	N.H. Flat	Per cent	£1 Level stake
Nicky Henderson	105-499	24-75	18-137	19-86	8-36	7-56	7-37	0-0	27-94	21.0	-12.86
Paul Nicholls	98-496	23-77	11-98	15-58	19-66	14-122	7-29	1-10	8-44	19.8	-120.20
Donald McCain	73-444	17-91	11-129	11-57	12-51	8-71	3-6	2-4	9-41	16.4	-101.49
Philip Hobbs	69-384	12-47	15-105	6-33	10-29	17-111	2-14	1-5	6-45	18.0	-2.70
David Pipe	53-340	10-47	20-123	7-44	5-12	8-96	1-9	0-0	2-14	15.6	-85.15
Alan King	52-387	15-65	9-92	10-64	9-31	3-62	0-9	0-0	7-74	13.4	-72.84
Jonjo O'Neill	44-326	9-43	8-97	6-35	3-16	9-81	3-14	3-13	3-32	13.5	-35.63
Nigel Twiston-Davies	39-372	2-44	8-80	9-38	5-18	9-147	0-7	1-4	6-39	10.5	-126.40
Tim Vaughan	35-252	5-43	5-72	3-21	3-16	11-63	1-5	1-9	6-26	13.9	-0.97
Gary Moore	32-205	6-27	9-76	3-20	5-24	5-42	2-6	0-1	2-10	15.6	**5.48**
Kim Bailey	31-172	4-31	9-56	1-12	3-8	6-34	2-4	0-0	6-30	18.0	**38.32**
Peter Bowen	30-165	0-16	11-48	2-13	1-7	9-52	0-2	0-1	8-28	18.2	**102.89**
Evan Williams	27-274	6-45	5-67	5-40	5-32	6-70	0-5	0-4	0-13	9.9	-107.89
Rebecca Curtis	27-124	7-20	0-27	7-24	2-12	4-14	0-0	0-2	7-27	21.8	-7.19
Colin Tizzard	25-178	4-28	2-28	3-12	6-22	6-58	0-5	0-0	4-25	14.0	-17.39
Lucinda Russell	24-270	1-33	5-69	2-21	2-30	11-89	1-4	0-0	2-24	8.9	-98.95
Tom George	24-159	1-20	1-18	5-20	5-21	11-60	1-9	0-5	0-10	15.1	-12.38
Charlie Longsdon	23-212	4-41	4-64	1-22	4-9	7-53	0-1	0-0	3-27	10.8	-89.72
Oliver Sherwood	21-134	3-28	2-28	2-9	5-15	7-23	1-3	0-3	1-27	15.7	-16.75
Jeremy Scott	21-105	6-16	7-31	0-11	1-7	5-19	0-1	0-1	2-20	20.0	**94.01**
Howard Johnson	21-117	2-23	3-27	0-9	7-15	6-30	1-2	0-0	2-13	17.9	**33.00**
Henry Daly	21-155	3-26	7-38	1-13	2-12	5-41	0-0	2-5	1-24	13.5	-10.18
Warren Greatrex	21-110	3-20	2-34	2-13	2-3	2-12	0-1	1-1	9-26	19.1	-41.74
Malcolm Jefferson	20-150	5-24	4-41	1-5	5-14	2-35	1-2	0-0	3-30	13.3	-23.39
Sue Smith	20-205	2-25	2-45	0-5	3-27	13-90	0-0	0-0	0-13	9.8	-1.92
Venetia Williams	20-275	6-30	4-62	1-28	4-31	5-108	0-8	0-3	0-9	7.3	-170.14
Brian Ellison	19-125	2-17	10-62	4-12	0-5	3-28	0-0	0-0	0-2	15.2	-3.74
Fergal O'Brien	19-100	1-17	3-22	2-10	1-5	7-28	0-1	3-3	3-17	19.0	**26.48**
Emma Lavelle	17-123	3-21	1-22	1-10	2-14	7-38	0-2	0-0	3-17	13.8	-25.09
Seamus Mullins	16-144	1-20	6-36	2-16	2-16	3-37	0-0	0-0	2-21	11.1	**4.55**
Neil King	16-119	2-12	3-39	3-12	1-1	6-39	0-1	0-0	1-17	13.4	**18.36**
Victor Dartnall	16-105	3-13	8-32	0-3	4-13	0-28	0-0	0-1	1-15	15.2	-7.93
Dan Skelton	15-80	2-15	6-19	1-7	4-7	2-16	0-0	0-0	0-16	18.8	-16.18
Dr Richard Newland	15-76	0-1	8-26	1-6	1-1	4-38	0-0	1-5	0-0	19.7	**67.28**
Philip Kirby	15-95	4-14	6-43	0-1	0-5	4-14	0-1	0-4	1-13	15.8	**11.70**
Andy Turnell	13-78	3-10	0-17	2-7	1-8	6-31	0-0	0-1	1-6	16.7	**5.03**
Keith Reveley	13-89	2-10	2-25	1-5	2-7	5-30	0-0	0-0	1-13	14.6	-13.50
Nicky Richards	13-117	3-25	4-48	0-8	0-3	4-19	1-4	0-1	1-11	11.1	-20.52
James Ewart	13-108	0-16	5-23	1-8	2-12	4-31	0-3	0-1	1-14	12.0	-23.93
Chris Gordon	13-118	1-15	6-40	0-9	3-7	3-37	0-0	0-3	0-7	11.0	-12.25
Lucy Wadham	12-89	5-22	2-22	2-11	0-6	1-17	0-0	1-2	1-11	13.5	-18.92
Dianne Sayer	12-98	1-12	8-56	0-1	0-2	3-24	0-0	0-0	0-3	12.2	-17.33
Nick Williams	12-80	0-13	2-10	3-15	1-3	1-18	2-15	0-0	3-6	15.0	**27.65**
John Wade	11-122	0-21	4-27	0-2	1-10	4-45	0-0	1-7	1-10	9.0	-6.67
Ian Williams	11-101	1-23	3-30	2-6	3-8	1-22	0-0	1-3	0-10	10.9	-31.50
David Arbuthnot	11-36	2-6	3-9	1-1	2-2	1-9	0-0	0-0	2-9	30.6	**37.58**
N W Alexander	11-112	3-14	2-30	1-15	0-7	2-21	0-0	2-14	1-11	9.8	-24.00
Sue Gardner	10-58	3-18	4-25	0-2	0-1	2-6	0-0	0-0	1-6	17.2	**67.50**
Alan Swinbank	10-46	2-8	0-6	1-5	1-2	0-1	0-0	0-0	6-25	21.7	-7.00
Caroline Bailey	10-65	0-4	1-10	0-5	1-6	7-35	1-1	0-0	0-4	15.4	-16.79
Brendan Powell	10-133	2-20	3-53	0-17	0-4	4-30	0-0	0-2	1-9	7.5	-60.68

MAY

	Total W-R	Nov Hdle	H'cap Hdle	Other Hdle	Nov Chase	H'cap Chase	Other Chase	Hunter Chase	N.H. Flat	Per cent	£1 Level stake
Donald McCain	68-315	20-59	7-75	18-66	8-26	5-46	3-11	0-3	7-29	21.6	-92.48
Jonjo O'Neill	53-294	9-42	14-94	3-28	4-16	17-73	2-8	3-15	1-18	18.0	-67.16
Nicky Henderson	52-222	11-32	7-48	6-27	3-9	5-24	4-17	0-0	16-65	23.4	**2.09**
Peter Bowen	50-209	4-26	10-61	8-20	5-11	11-53	1-5	2-5	9-28	23.9	**99.42**
Tim Vaughan	44-221	7-38	6-58	11-35	5-16	12-51	1-6	1-4	1-13	19.9	**39.40**
David Pipe	41-212	4-21	12-87	5-28	4-10	5-32	3-12	0-0	8-22	19.3	-11.52
Paul Nicholls	39-143	11-24	5-27	3-17	6-17	4-27	3-13	2-4	5-14	27.3	**4.16**
Evan Williams	37-229	6-33	7-60	6-33	2-22	14-69	2-9	0-0	0-3	16.2	**7.22**
Philip Hobbs	29-187	2-11	9-71	4-16	4-11	6-44	3-10	1-8	0-16	15.5	-45.26
Kim Bailey	22-127	1-21	4-34	9-21	2-9	2-19	1-12	0-0	3-11	17.3	**24.63**
Lucinda Russell	21-156	6-27	2-36	1-13	1-19	9-51	1-2	0-1	1-7	13.5	-44.93
Alan King	20-171	6-34	1-42	4-21	3-11	1-25	0-9	0-0	5-29	11.7	-83.89
Nigel Twiston-Davies	19-200	2-25	3-59	2-17	1-10	8-69	1-3	0-1	2-16	9.5	-94.74
Venetia Williams	19-105	3-13	2-30	5-8	3-13	3-36	1-1	0-0	2-4	18.1	-34.32
Rebecca Curtis	18-71	5-13	6-20	1-8	3-4	0-5	0-4	0-2	3-15	25.4	-7.06
Sue Smith	17-106	2-14	3-14	1-11	1-13	7-40	2-4	0-0	1-10	16.0	-8.81
Gary Moore	17-146	2-11	8-68	3-18	1-7	1-29	1-4	0-2	1-7	11.6	-46.70
Fergal O'Brien	17-85	3-17	3-18	2-11	0-1	1-15	1-2	4-13	3-8	20.0	**43.13**
Seamus Mullins	15-146	1-15	4-38	1-19	1-10	5-41	2-4	0-0	1-19	10.3	-42.82
Paul Webber	14-99	2-13	3-18	0-11	0-6	6-28	1-6	0-0	2-17	14.1	-22.38
Martin Keighley	14-100	1-11	1-32	2-9	2-7	6-29	1-2	0-0	1-10	14.0	-35.29
Dr Richard Newland	14-53	0-2	4-25	2-3	1-1	7-15	0-1	0-6	0-0	26.4	-2.58
Charlie Longsdon	14-104	0-10	0-28	2-6	4-13	2-28	2-4	0-1	4-14	13.5	-29.45
Dianne Sayer	13-79	3-15	6-30	0-2	1-9	3-23	0-0	0-0	0-0	16.5	**8.33**
Oliver Sherwood	12-83	2-9	1-20	2-12	1-8	3-14	0-3	0-1	3-16	14.5	-11.00
Charlie Mann	12-73	3-13	5-20	0-11	1-5	1-17	1-5	0-0	1-2	16.4	**21.41**
Philip Kirby	12-84	1-15	7-38	1-7	0-5	1-7	1-1	1-3	0-8	14.3	-7.27
Neil Mulholland	12-105	5-21	5-33	1-12	1-8	0-22	0-1	0-0	0-8	11.4	**6.72**
Warren Greatrex	12-33	3-3	1-6	0-6	1-3	1-4	1-1	1-1	4-9	36.4	**7.76**
Malcolm Jefferson	11-69	0-10	1-13	2-8	0-6	5-19	0-0	0-0	3-13	15.9	-10.38
Chris Gordon	11-90	0-4	6-41	1-9	1-6	2-23	0-0	1-4	0-3	12.2	**8.50**
John Ferguson	11-41	6-10	2-11	2-10	0-3	0-3	0-0	0-2	1-2	26.8	**6.14**
Milton Harris	10-50	1-3	4-24	1-8	1-2	3-9	0-3	0-0	0-1	20.0	**23.50**
Brian Ellison	10-55	2-12	2-20	2-12	1-5	3-5	0-1	0-0	0-0	18.2	-12.10
Tom George	10-92	0-13	1-8	0-13	2-10	2-30	3-10	0-4	2-4	10.9	-16.87
Keith Reveley	10-55	3-8	0-9	1-9	1-3	4-21	1-2	0-0	0-3	18.2	-15.06
Martin Todhunter	10-87	1-15	5-28	0-6	1-4	3-28	0-0	0-0	0-6	11.5	-18.63
Tony Carroll	10-84	1-14	4-35	1-13	1-1	2-11	1-3	0-0	0-7	11.9	-24.09
Ian Williams	10-67	3-13	2-20	1-10	1-3	1-8	2-3	0-3	0-7	14.9	-18.75
Brendan Powell	10-102	1-20	1-30	1-7	0-6	4-22	1-5	1-2	1-10	9.8	-47.75
George Moore	9-30	1-6	2-9	2-2	3-6	0-4	1-1	0-0	0-2	30.0	-0.60
Alistair Whillans	9-53	2-10	4-26	0-1	2-5	1-7	0-0	0-0	0-4	17.0	**9.08**
Neil King	9-93	1-12	3-32	0-8	0-4	5-32	0-1	0-0	0-4	9.7	-30.00
Chris Grant	9-87	2-12	4-30	1-11	1-7	1-20	0-0	0-1	0-6	10.3	-19.53
Nicky Richards	9-78	2-16	2-24	1-10	1-6	2-16	0-1	1-3	0-2	11.5	-20.11
Ben Case	9-41	2-5	4-15	1-6	1-5	0-0	0-3	0-0	1-7	22.0	**28.29**
Michael Scudamore	9-60	0-5	3-20	1-5	0-1	2-18	1-1	1-4	1-6	15.0	**33.25**
Rose Dobbin	9-65	3-20	0-16	0-3	2-9	2-11	0-0	0-1	2-5	13.8	-19.00
John Wade	8-106	1-21	1-17	0-4	1-13	5-32	0-3	0-4	0-12	7.5	-49.50
Howard Johnson	8-42	2-6	0-11	2-7	2-6	2-9	0-1	0-0	0-2	19.0	-5.25
Maurice Barnes	8-107	1-15	2-42	2-18	1-7	2-17	0-0	0-1	0-7	7.5	-40.01

JUNE

	Total W-R	Nov Hdle	H'cap Hdle	Other Hdle	Nov Chase	H'cap Chase	Other Chase	Hunter Chase	N.H. Flat	Per cent	£1 Level stake
Peter Bowen	51-200	5-28	10-46	3-13	4-20	20-64	1-2	0-1	8-26	25.5	-1.56
Jonjo O'Neill	48-249	5-18	16-82	5-25	4-22	13-84	2-7	0-0	3-11	19.3	**1.58**
Tim Vaughan	35-202	8-37	7-62	7-31	5-20	3-38	2-3	0-1	3-10	17.3	-60.54
Nicky Henderson	27-91	7-13	3-29	6-15	2-3	2-10	0-0	0-0	7-21	29.7	**0.49**
Evan Williams	27-177	2-27	8-49	3-21	6-22	5-52	3-5	0-1	0-0	15.3	-34.97
Donald McCain	27-172	7-32	8-41	6-44	1-13	3-23	0-0	0-1	2-18	15.7	-60.13
Nigel Twiston-Davies	23-137	4-19	6-40	4-13	2-4	6-49	0-1	0-0	1-11	16.8	-6.92
Dr Richard Newland	19-65	1-5	7-23	5-14	4-6	2-10	0-6	0-0	0-1	29.2	**16.55**
Paul Nicholls	18-76	3-8	2-14	2-15	7-13	3-16	1-7	0-1	0-2	23.7	-13.24
Lucinda Russell	18-104	4-20	3-25	2-8	3-11	5-33	0-1	0-0	1-6	17.3	-3.71
David Pipe	16-153	1-13	4-71	3-18	1-8	4-30	0-1	0-0	3-12	10.5	-88.09
Jim Best	13-53	3-9	5-18	3-19	0-1	2-2	0-1	0-0	0-3	24.5	-16.76
Philip Hobbs	12-82	1-10	1-19	1-10	0-5	6-29	1-3	0-1	2-5	14.6	-21.05
Kim Bailey	12-50	4-8	0-12	0-5	3-7	4-12	1-4	0-0	0-2	24.0	-9.30
Tony Carroll	12-81	2-11	6-38	1-13	1-7	2-7	0-0	0-0	0-5	14.8	-13.41
Rebecca Curtis	12-36	3-6	2-10	0-2	2-5	4-7	0-1	0-1	1-4	33.3	**4.31**
Seamus Mullins	11-65	0-5	5-13	1-7	1-6	3-23	0-3	0-0	1-8	16.9	**7.12**
Charlie Longsdon	11-47	1-6	2-9	1-4	2-7	5-18	0-0	0-0	0-3	23.4	**13.83**
Neil Mulholland	11-77	2-12	5-27	0-6	0-4	2-22	0-0	0-0	2-6	14.3	**10.91**
Paul Webber	9-59	1-7	2-13	0-5	0-10	2-15	1-4	0-0	3-5	15.3	**3.78**
Charlie Mann	8-40	2-5	2-14	1-4	2-4	1-12	0-1	0-0	0-0	20.0	**6.77**
David Bridgwater	8-48	1-6	0-4	1-10	0-6	6-21	0-0	0-0	0-1	16.7	-4.25
Alan King	8-40	1-6	1-16	6-8	0-2	0-7	0-0	0-0	0-1	20.0	-8.92
Keith Goldsworthy	8-40	0-5	1-11	0-4	0-1	3-5	0-0	0-1	4-13	20.0	**21.32**
Malcolm Jefferson	7-38	2-7	0-6	0-1	1-4	3-12	0-0	0-0	1-8	18.4	**16.50**
Brian Ellison	7-44	1-7	1-10	2-14	2-3	1-5	0-0	0-0	0-5	15.9	-14.78
Gary Moore	7-56	0-13	3-12	1-7	0-7	2-14	1-3	0-0	0-0	12.5	-14.75
Richard Phillips	7-53	0-7	4-22	2-6	0-0	1-10	0-0	0-0	0-8	13.2	**3.50**
Dianne Sayer	7-53	3-10	4-26	0-0	0-1	0-14	0-0	0-0	0-2	13.2	-2.62
Ian Williams	7-68	3-12	1-26	1-15	1-3	1-7	0-0	0-0	0-5	10.3	-26.51
Michael Blake	7-44	2-4	2-22	2-7	0-1	1-8	0-1	0-0	0-1	15.9	-7.29
Paul Henderson	7-40	0-5	2-8	0-1	1-5	4-17	0-0	0-0	0-4	17.5	**5.75**
Anthony Honeyball	7-26	1-3	2-6	0-3	0-2	2-7	0-0	0-0	2-5	26.9	**3.32**
John Ferguson	7-39	1-3	4-15	1-11	0-0	0-4	0-1	0-1	1-4	17.9	-8.46
Milton Harris	6-40	0-3	1-14	2-9	1-3	2-7	0-3	0-0	0-1	15.0	**6.00**
Sue Smith	6-71	0-10	3-9	1-11	0-3	1-29	0-0	0-0	1-9	8.5	-42.75
Lawney Hill	6-49	0-4	3-20	3-7	0-4	0-14	0-0	0-0	0-0	12.2	**22.54**
Debra Hamer	6-32	2-7	3-13	0-2	1-2	0-8	0-0	0-0	0-0	18.8	**9.50**
Tom George	6-38	0-4	1-3	1-4	3-6	0-15	1-1	0-1	0-4	15.8	-19.71
Martin Todhunter	6-49	0-4	1-17	1-7	0-3	4-16	0-0	0-0	0-2	12.2	-7.00
John Flint	6-43	1-9	2-18	2-6	0-1	1-6	0-0	0-0	0-3	14.0	-3.87
Fergal O'Brien	6-62	2-7	0-17	1-5	1-9	2-15	0-1	0-0	0-8	9.7	-33.63
Chris Gordon	6-46	0-3	4-19	0-2	0-4	2-16	0-0	0-0	0-2	13.0	-15.20
Jamie Snowden	6-41	0-4	1-12	1-6	0-4	3-11	1-2	0-0	0-2	14.6	**16.37**
Warren Greatrex	6-16	0-1	3-6	0-1	0-1	2-5	0-0	0-0	1-2	37.5	**14.58**
George Moore	5-20	2-5	1-5	0-0	1-2	1-6	0-0	0-0	0-2	25.0	**0.92**
Micky Hammond	5-30	1-9	3-5	1-5	0-2	0-6	0-0	0-0	0-3	16.7	-3.13
Sue Gardner	5-36	1-4	2-19	0-5	1-1	1-3	0-0	0-1	0-3	13.9	-4.25
Neil King	5-62	1-9	0-14	1-21	0-2	3-10	0-0	0-0	0-6	8.1	**14.75**
Venetia Williams	5-30	0-3	0-6	1-1	2-3	2-17	0-0	0-0	0-0	16.7	**4.75**
Nigel Hawke	5-26	2-7	2-8	0-5	1-2	0-4	0-0	0-0	0-0	19.2	**26.41**

JULY

	Total W-R	Nov Hdle	H'cap Hdle	Other Hdle	Nov Chase	H'cap Chase	Other Chase	Hunter Chase	N.H. Flat	Per cent	£1 Level stake
Peter Bowen	47-198	4-18	13-53	4-19	4-14	13-66	0-8	0-0	9-26	23.7	**48.17**
Jonjo O'Neill	41-238	6-22	17-95	4-15	4-22	9-70	0-8	0-0	1-7	17.2	-31.81
Tim Vaughan	41-209	11-41	7-54	11-46	5-20	4-37	1-6	0-0	2-7	19.6	**3.38**
Donald McCain	37-170	12-33	5-42	9-43	3-15	3-18	3-8	0-0	2-13	21.8	**7.33**
Evan Williams	18-165	4-31	2-41	3-31	3-10	6-49	0-5	0-0	0-2	10.9	-55.10
Lawney Hill	17-72	2-11	4-25	1-4	6-9	4-22	0-0	0-0	0-1	23.6	**19.06**
David Pipe	17-135	2-10	7-68	1-24	1-4	3-23	3-6	0-0	0-7	12.6	-53.81
Dr Richard Newland	17-72	4-7	6-28	2-15	1-2	3-14	1-7	0-0	0-1	23.6	**0.73**
Nigel Twiston-Davies	16-86	3-14	3-27	4-8	3-11	3-23	0-2	0-0	0-2	18.6	**0.95**
Lucinda Russell	11-104	1-19	3-44	2-7	2-9	3-22	0-0	0-0	0-3	10.6	-34.17
Jim Best	10-51	1-8	2-21	5-13	0-1	0-2	1-2	0-0	1-4	19.6	-6.80
John Ferguson	10-35	2-5	5-15	4-12	0-1	0-1	0-0	0-0	1-3	28.6	**4.60**
Philip Hobbs	9-70	1-3	2-20	2-18	1-3	3-26	0-2	0-0	0-1	12.9	-16.74
Nicky Henderson	9-52	6-14	0-19	0-3	1-4	0-5	1-3	0-0	1-4	17.3	-30.01
Paul Nicholls	9-49	1-2	1-5	1-7	0-4	1-15	5-16	0-0	0-0	18.4	**19.38**
Martin Keighley	9-65	2-5	4-26	1-11	0-3	2-16	0-0	0-0	0-4	13.8	**41.50**
Jeremy Scott	8-31	1-5	2-9	1-3	1-2	3-10	0-2	0-0	0-0	25.8	**11.75**
Neil King	8-44	0-5	2-13	2-13	2-3	1-8	0-1	0-0	1-2	18.2	**26.41**
Dianne Sayer	8-72	1-8	4-42	0-1	0-1	3-19	0-0	0-0	0-1	11.1	-16.50
Nicky Richards	8-46	0-4	6-27	0-2	0-0	2-12	0-0	0-0	0-1	17.4	**9.71**
David Bridgwater	8-65	2-17	1-4	3-10	0-10	2-16	0-3	0-0	0-5	12.3	-22.40
Sophie Leech	8-70	1-7	5-22	0-9	1-7	1-19	0-4	0-0	0-2	11.4	-5.50
Paul Webber	7-48	0-5	3-16	1-11	0-2	2-11	0-3	0-0	2-5	14.6	**10.75**
Brendan Powell	7-59	1-6	1-16	3-12	0-6	1-12	1-3	0-0	0-4	11.9	-3.13
Charlie Longsdon	7-47	0-1	2-16	1-3	2-3	0-17	2-4	0-0	0-4	14.9	-19.77
Rebecca Curtis	7-27	1-3	0-4	2-7	3-6	0-1	1-4	0-0	0-2	25.9	-9.55
Mike Sowersby	6-43	0-5	5-23	0-1	0-2	1-8	0-0	0-0	0-4	14.0	**43.00**
Sue Smith	6-54	0-5	0-8	0-6	0-4	4-25	1-3	0-0	1-4	11.1	-14.27
Tony Carroll	6-67	1-10	2-29	0-9	2-8	1-7	0-0	0-0	0-4	9.0	-16.50
Martin Hill	6-22	1-2	3-10	0-3	1-1	0-6	0-0	0-0	1-1	27.3	**50.38**
David Rees	6-38	0-3	3-18	1-7	1-1	1-8	0-1	0-0	0-0	15.8	**16.75**
Lucy Normile	6-36	0-2	2-17	0-4	1-5	3-8	0-0	0-0	0-0	16.7	**16.50**
Jimmy Frost	6-31	2-5	1-6	0-8	0-0	3-9	0-2	0-0	0-1	19.4	**39.00**
Anthony Honeyball	6-23	0-4	4-11	0-1	0-1	0-2	2-2	0-0	0-2	26.1	**8.50**
Philip Kirby	6-48	2-9	4-26	0-7	0-3	0-2	0-0	0-0	0-1	12.5	**9.55**
Warren Greatrex	6-18	2-4	1-4	1-4	0-1	1-3	0-0	0-0	1-2	33.3	**2.22**
Kim Bailey	5-36	1-6	2-12	1-3	0-0	1-11	0-2	0-0	0-2	13.9	**8.25**
David Evans	5-29	0-2	1-8	2-8	1-2	1-8	0-0	0-0	0-1	17.2	**1.33**
Maurice Barnes	5-47	1-9	0-13	1-7	0-5	3-11	0-0	0-0	0-2	10.6	**9.00**
Brian Ellison	5-48	2-10	1-13	1-15	0-4	1-7	0-1	0-0	0-0	10.4	**7.00**
Seamus Mullins	5-40	0-5	0-6	0-8	0-3	2-12	0-0	0-0	3-6	12.5	**13.00**
Ian Williams	5-32	2-4	1-12	0-7	0-2	1-3	1-3	0-0	0-1	15.6	-13.96
Alan King	5-33	1-7	4-11	0-9	0-3	0-4	0-1	0-0	0-0	15.2	-4.43
Alison Thorpe	5-31	1-2	2-16	2-10	0-0	0-3	0-0	0-0	0-0	16.1	**12.17**
Michael Blake	5-37	2-3	2-20	0-3	0-1	1-10	0-0	0-0	0-0	13.5	-15.00
Sarah Humphrey	5-22	1-2	0-6	1-4	0-2	2-4	0-2	0-0	1-2	22.7	**1.88**
Simon West	5-17	0-1	2-8	1-4	0-0	2-4	0-0	0-0	0-1	29.4	**27.50**
Richard Woollacott	5-29	0-8	0-2	1-5	0-0	4-10	0-3	0-0	0-1	17.2	-9.05
Malcolm Jefferson	4-27	0-2	1-6	0-1	1-3	0-9	2-2	0-0	0-4	14.8	**4.13**
Michael Easterby	4-33	1-7	0-5	0-1	0-1	1-14	0-0	0-0	2-5	12.1	-10.59
Bob Buckler	4-18	0-5	0-0	0-1	0-0	4-12	0-0	0-0	0-0	22.2	-4.67

AUGUST

	Total W-R	Nov Hdle	H'cap Hdle	Other Hdle	Nov Chase	H'cap Chase	Other Chase	Hunter Chase	N.H. Flat	Per cent	£1 Level stake
Tim Vaughan	51-260	16-59	10-67	11-48	3-20	10-49	1-6	0-0	0-11	19.6	-38.62
Jonjo O'Neill	46-210	7-24	17-68	0-12	1-12	19-86	0-0	0-0	2-8	21.9	-14.74
Donald McCain	30-145	11-38	8-36	5-34	2-8	1-15	1-3	0-0	2-11	20.7	-20.47
Evan Williams	25-187	2-19	5-42	6-29	4-17	8-73	0-4	0-0	0-3	13.4	-64.70
Nigel Twiston-Davies	24-114	0-9	7-27	2-10	3-10	9-47	3-4	0-0	0-7	21.1	**27.34**
Peter Bowen	23-165	4-33	7-44	0-9	0-9	8-53	1-2	0-0	3-15	13.9	-60.84
David Pipe	19-132	3-12	7-67	3-12	3-10	3-27	0-0	0-0	0-4	14.4	-41.36
Brian Ellison	14-51	8-17	3-17	2-10	0-1	1-4	0-1	0-0	0-1	27.5	**7.12**
Lawney Hill	13-68	2-11	2-17	0-6	2-9	6-22	1-1	0-0	0-2	19.1	**11.25**
Philip Hobbs	12-64	0-6	2-14	2-6	3-9	5-27	0-0	0-0	0-2	18.8	**21.49**
Paul Nicholls	12-43	5-9	0-5	0-2	4-10	2-15	0-1	0-0	1-1	27.9	-8.32
Lucinda Russell	12-80	3-16	2-24	0-6	2-7	4-22	1-2	0-0	0-3	15.0	-27.13
Neil Mulholland	12-58	0-4	6-22	0-2	1-5	5-25	0-0	0-0	0-0	20.7	**3.88**
Colin Tizzard	11-50	0-1	1-9	0-2	2-7	8-30	0-0	0-0	0-1	22.0	**20.25**
Brendan Powell	11-71	1-9	2-19	2-13	3-11	1-16	1-1	0-0	1-2	15.5	-21.01
Jim Best	10-40	1-7	4-17	3-7	0-0	2-5	0-0	0-0	0-4	25.0	-10.52
Rebecca Curtis	10-30	3-7	0-2	1-4	3-5	1-6	0-0	0-0	2-6	33.3	-8.40
John Ferguson	10-28	3-9	3-8	3-8	0-0	0-1	0-0	0-0	1-2	35.7	**1.90**
Kim Bailey	9-27	2-4	1-10	4-5	0-1	2-6	0-1	0-0	0-0	33.3	**7.34**
Paul Webber	9-28	2-6	0-2	1-4	1-3	3-8	1-2	0-0	1-3	32.1	**7.92**
Ian Williams	9-41	2-4	3-14	0-8	0-3	2-7	1-3	0-0	1-2	22.0	**10.63**
Nicky Richards	9-38	3-8	3-22	1-3	0-0	2-4	0-0	0-0	0-1	23.7	**13.00**
Gary Moore	8-34	0-4	3-13	4-8	0-1	0-6	0-1	0-0	1-1	23.5	**14.15**
Dianne Sayer	8-48	0-6	2-24	0-2	0-2	6-14	0-0	0-0	0-0	16.7	**7.85**
Alan King	8-25	2-4	0-6	1-6	0-1	5-8	0-0	0-0	0-0	32.0	**18.72**
Sophie Leech	8-64	2-10	2-26	0-6	1-4	1-15	2-2	0-0	0-1	12.5	-21.83
Nicky Henderson	7-24	4-8	3-10	0-1	0-1	0-2	0-0	0-0	0-2	29.2	-2.42
Martin Keighley	7-60	0-2	2-22	1-6	0-5	3-20	0-0	0-0	1-5	11.7	-8.09
Anthony Honeyball	7-24	0-3	2-6	0-3	4-5	0-0	1-3	0-0	0-4	29.2	**6.25**
Philip Kirby	7-37	3-11	2-18	1-3	0-1	0-2	0-0	0-0	1-2	18.9	-7.41
Don Cantillon	6-15	2-5	2-3	0-3	1-1	0-0	1-1	0-0	0-2	40.0	-1.88
Harriet Graham	6-12	0-2	2-5	0-0	0-0	4-5	0-0	0-0	0-0	50.0	**6.24**
John Quinn	6-20	0-3	2-7	4-9	0-0	0-0	0-0	0-0	0-1	30.0	**0.63**
John Flint	6-34	2-4	3-15	1-7	0-1	0-6	0-0	0-0	0-1	17.6	-5.95
Alan Swinbank	6-17	2-4	0-1	1-2	0-1	0-1	1-1	0-0	2-7	35.3	-1.00
Alan Jones	6-19	1-4	1-8	0-0	0-2	2-3	0-0	0-0	2-2	31.6	**20.50**
Chris Gordon	6-46	0-6	5-23	0-3	0-3	1-10	0-0	0-0	0-1	13.0	**8.50**
Sue Smith	5-47	0-6	2-13	0-2	0-4	3-18	0-1	0-0	0-3	10.6	**14.50**
Bernard Llewellyn	5-33	0-3	2-21	3-5	0-2	0-1	0-0	0-0	0-1	15.2	**10.38**
David Bridgwater	5-48	2-8	0-6	2-8	1-7	0-13	0-2	0-0	0-4	10.4	-10.00
Alison Thorpe	5-27	1-1	1-10	2-9	0-0	1-6	0-0	0-0	0-1	18.5	**0.94**
Keith Goldsworthy	5-29	2-9	1-6	1-5	0-1	0-1	0-0	0-0	1-7	17.2	**3.58**
Sarah Humphrey	5-21	0-5	1-4	1-3	0-2	3-6	0-0	0-0	0-1	23.8	**10.54**
Dr Richard Newland	5-48	2-9	1-9	1-11	0-4	1-12	0-3	0-0	0-0	10.4	-35.22
Warren Greatrex	5-20	0-2	1-8	1-2	1-3	0-2	0-0	0-0	2-3	25.0	-5.86
Tim Walford	4-10	0-1	3-6	0-1	0-1	1-1	0-0	0-0	0-0	40.0	**25.00**
John O'Shea	4-30	0-4	2-15	0-1	0-2	1-6	0-0	0-0	1-2	13.3	-11.43
Alistair Whillans	4-23	0-2	4-17	0-1	0-0	0-2	0-0	0-0	0-1	17.4	**3.75**
Micky Hammond	4-25	0-2	1-6	1-4	1-2	1-11	0-0	0-0	0-0	16.0	**18.63**
Jim Goldie	4-17	0-3	2-8	1-2	0-1	0-2	0-0	0-0	1-1	23.5	**0.75**
Charlie Mann	4-27	1-3	1-11	0-3	1-2	1-8	0-0	0-0	0-0	14.8	-6.00

SEPTEMBER

	Total W-R	Nov Hdle	H'cap Hdle	Other Hdle	Nov Chase	H'cap Chase	Other Chase	Hunter Chase	N.H. Flat	Per cent	£1 Level stake
Nigel Twiston-Davies	31-119	7-25	1-25	2-12	7-12	10-34	0-2	0-0	4-9	26.1	20.92
Jonjo O'Neill	25-149	2-17	9-48	1-12	2-12	9-56	0-0	0-0	2-5	16.8	-15.25
Charlie Longsdon	23-64	4-8	2-12	3-9	1-2	7-15	1-5	0-0	5-14	35.9	45.91
Tim Vaughan	19-145	4-30	4-41	5-32	2-9	2-27	1-6	0-0	1-5	13.1	-80.49
David Pipe	18-116	1-11	5-52	3-15	3-9	4-23	0-2	0-0	2-5	15.5	-32.70
Evan Williams	18-123	3-18	2-30	3-21	4-16	5-37	1-3	0-0	0-2	14.6	-48.16
Peter Bowen	16-149	2-19	2-45	0-16	1-6	6-43	0-2	0-0	5-20	10.7	-60.20
Philip Hobbs	15-86	3-9	0-15	1-10	2-10	4-31	4-7	0-0	1-4	17.4	-18.73
Brian Ellison	13-58	3-9	3-15	3-22	1-4	3-12	0-0	0-0	0-0	22.4	11.64
Dr Richard Newland	13-42	1-4	3-18	6-12	0-2	3-10	1-1	0-0	0-0	31.0	8.29
Donald McCain	12-90	4-20	1-18	5-35	1-8	0-7	1-3	0-0	0-3	13.3	-54.70
Dianne Sayer	10-47	3-8	5-22	0-2	0-1	2-11	0-0	0-0	0-3	21.3	16.00
Nicky Henderson	9-27	2-3	3-16	2-7	0-1	0-0	1-1	0-0	1-3	33.3	6.47
Fergal O'Brien	9-40	1-10	2-6	0-2	2-6	4-14	0-1	0-0	0-1	22.5	21.63
Sheena West	8-35	0-4	5-19	3-9	0-1	0-1	0-0	0-0	0-1	22.9	26.66
Brendan Powell	8-50	1-5	2-13	2-12	1-1	1-14	0-1	0-0	1-4	16.0	31.75
Chris Gordon	8-43	1-7	6-20	0-1	0-0	1-12	0-1	0-0	0-2	18.6	36.00
Kim Bailey	7-24	4-7	0-7	0-1	2-2	0-5	1-1	0-0	0-1	29.2	3.54
Bernard Llewellyn	7-45	1-5	5-31	1-5	0-1	0-2	0-0	0-0	0-1	15.6	31.13
Gary Moore	7-40	2-8	2-13	2-11	0-1	0-6	1-1	0-0	0-0	17.5	8.75
Sophie Leech	7-42	2-9	2-14	1-2	1-4	1-13	0-0	0-0	0-0	16.7	23.60
Neil Mulholland	7-52	1-12	4-14	0-4	0-3	1-16	1-1	0-0	0-2	13.5	13.62
John Ferguson	7-20	3-6	1-4	1-7	0-0	0-0	0-0	0-0	2-5	35.0	-5.06
Paul Nicholls	6-24	2-4	0-1	0-1	3-8	1-8	0-1	0-0	0-1	25.0	-9.17
Lawney Hill	6-47	0-2	1-17	0-3	0-5	5-17	0-0	0-0	0-3	12.8	-15.63
Lucinda Russell	6-104	2-23	3-25	0-8	0-10	1-29	0-1	0-0	0-8	5.8	-63.50
Emma Lavelle	6-29	0-2	2-7	1-2	0-6	3-10	0-2	0-0	0-0	20.7	36.25
Martin Keighley	6-59	0-9	2-19	0-8	1-4	2-12	1-2	0-0	0-6	10.2	-15.25
Paul Henderson	6-37	0-8	1-9	0-0	0-2	4-16	0-0	0-0	1-2	16.2	1.25
Rebecca Curtis	6-26	1-4	0-5	2-6	1-1	0-2	1-1	0-0	1-7	23.1	-13.54
Malcolm Jefferson	5-45	1-6	0-10	0-2	2-4	2-11	0-2	0-0	0-10	11.1	2.50
Jeremy Scott	5-16	1-1	0-5	0-1	2-2	2-6	0-0	0-0	0-1	31.3	-3.78
Mike Sowersby	5-30	0-10	1-12	0-2	0-0	4-6	0-0	0-0	0-0	16.7	21.75
John O'Shea	5-25	0-7	2-9	1-4	1-1	0-1	0-0	0-0	1-3	20.0	23.00
Chris Grant	5-30	1-5	2-9	1-6	0-0	1-8	0-1	0-0	0-2	16.7	-12.92
Ian Williams	5-37	1-2	2-16	1-8	0-3	1-5	0-1	0-0	0-3	13.5	-1.75
Alan King	5-24	1-6	1-5	1-8	1-1	1-4	0-0	0-0	0-0	20.8	-1.50
Jim Best	5-37	1-7	4-18	0-8	0-0	0-2	0-0	0-0	0-2	13.5	-19.53
David Evans	4-29	0-3	0-6	1-10	1-1	1-4	0-0	0-0	1-5	13.8	-6.50
Maurice Barnes	4-36	1-9	2-12	0-6	0-2	1-5	0-0	0-0	0-2	11.1	18.00
Sue Smith	4-43	1-5	1-14	0-3	1-4	0-12	0-0	0-0	1-5	9.3	-18.90
Jim Goldie	4-30	1-5	3-13	0-7	0-2	0-2	0-0	0-0	0-1	13.3	25.00
Richard Phillips	4-20	0-6	1-5	1-1	0-0	0-2	0-0	0-0	2-6	20.0	3.50
Martin Todhunter	4-26	1-5	0-13	0-1	0-0	3-6	0-1	0-0	0-0	15.4	-0.25
Colin Tizzard	4-30	2-3	0-8	0-0	1-2	1-17	0-0	0-0	0-0	13.3	-8.00
Nicky Richards	4-18	0-4	2-5	0-0	1-1	1-8	0-0	0-0	0-0	22.2	0.50
David Bridgwater	4-29	0-8	0-1	1-6	2-3	0-8	0-2	0-0	1-1	13.8	20.25
Rose Dobbin	4-21	0-4	1-6	0-0	2-2	1-8	0-0	0-0	0-1	19.0	-0.75
Ben Haslam	4-17	1-2	1-6	0-5	1-2	1-2	0-0	0-0	0-0	23.5	-8.66
Neil King	3-35	0-3	0-11	1-10	0-0	2-10	0-0	0-0	0-1	8.6	30.50
Tom George	3-9	1-2	0-0	1-1	0-1	1-3	0-1	0-0	0-1	33.3	11.77

OCTOBER

	Total W-R	Nov Hdle	H'cap Hdle	Other Hdle	Nov Chase	H'cap Chase	Other Chase	Hunter Chase	N.H. Flat	Per cent	£1 Level stake
Paul Nicholls	67-263	16-56	7-36	16-44	13-38	5-52	8-20	0-0	3-19	25.5	-32.50
Charlie Longsdon	63-257	10-48	16-56	9-39	5-19	11-53	5-13	0-0	7-29	24.5	-54.77
Philip Hobbs	59-302	13-52	11-71	8-39	6-27	11-75	2-14	0-0	8-28	19.5	-17.20
Nigel Twiston-Davies	57-303	10-40	9-48	10-38	10-47	15-102	2-11	0-0	1-18	18.8	**73.85**
Jonjo O'Neill	54-388	8-66	21-111	4-41	6-30	11-109	0-10	0-0	4-22	13.9	-132.67
Donald McCain	41-316	9-63	6-60	12-63	3-37	6-48	1-12	0-0	5-35	13.0	-112.17
Evan Williams	40-241	6-36	7-63	5-34	7-30	6-51	5-15	0-0	4-14	16.6	-59.31
Tim Vaughan	40-272	11-53	8-69	9-53	3-20	7-43	0-7	0-0	2-28	14.7	-51.90
David Pipe	35-207	5-29	4-80	10-33	5-11	7-33	2-5	0-0	2-16	16.9	-88.06
Alan King	34-148	4-30	8-36	11-37	7-17	2-22	1-4	0-0	1-6	23.0	-3.49
Nicky Henderson	28-127	7-27	7-36	2-20	3-15	2-12	2-7	0-0	5-11	22.0	-18.12
Lucinda Russell	24-230	0-34	2-43	4-21	4-25	12-82	0-5	0-0	2-20	10.4	-107.13
Emma Lavelle	24-129	6-21	5-34	4-11	3-9	6-37	1-10	0-0	0-8	18.6	**17.41**
Rebecca Curtis	22-134	2-22	4-23	4-28	3-18	2-8	0-5	0-0	7-30	16.4	-33.58
Kim Bailey	20-139	5-32	5-34	3-23	1-10	4-29	1-4	0-0	1-7	14.4	-37.33
Neil Mulholland	20-139	5-21	5-40	4-22	0-9	6-29	0-4	0-0	0-14	14.4	-9.29
Peter Bowen	19-202	4-24	2-50	2-29	1-15	8-61	1-2	0-0	1-21	9.4	-47.55
Colin Tizzard	18-170	2-38	2-17	4-15	4-18	5-58	1-9	0-0	0-16	10.6	-73.66
Sue Smith	17-169	2-27	3-37	2-14	2-18	7-54	1-8	0-0	0-11	10.1	-50.47
Tom George	17-119	2-10	0-13	2-13	1-13	6-45	3-12	0-0	3-13	14.3	-34.21
Martin Keighley	16-114	1-16	4-32	3-12	4-11	2-27	0-4	0-0	2-13	14.0	-34.94
Anthony Honeyball	16-56	1-10	3-10	2-9	0-1	2-8	0-0	0-0	8-18	28.6	**43.34**
Gary Moore	14-147	3-20	2-40	4-37	2-16	1-22	2-9	0-0	0-5	9.5	-72.49
John Ferguson	16-68	8-27	0-7	4-14	0-1	0-3	1-2	0-0	3-14	23.5	**5.55**
Nicky Richards	14-93	3-15	3-26	3-19	1-10	3-13	1-5	0-0	0-5	15.1	-16.04
Dr Richard Newland	14-58	2-7	5-26	1-4	0-2	6-18	0-0	0-0	0-1	24.1	-11.96
Jeremy Scott	13-88	2-20	1-23	0-12	2-7	4-15	2-2	0-0	2-9	14.8	-9.39
Brian Ellison	13-87	0-9	3-25	5-19	2-10	2-17	0-1	0-0	1-6	14.9	**5.88**
Oliver Sherwood	12-81	2-15	2-13	3-14	0-10	1-16	2-5	0-0	2-8	14.8	**0.82**
David Bridgwater	12-63	0-8	0-6	1-16	2-5	7-24	1-3	0-0	1-1	19.0	-12.02
Maurice Barnes	11-99	3-20	5-35	0-12	1-9	2-14	0-2	0-0	0-7	11.1	**42.50**
Sheena West	11-37	1-3	3-18	5-15	0-0	0-0	2-2	0-0	0-1	29.7	**23.90**
Paul Webber	11-101	3-23	1-15	2-19	1-12	3-23	1-7	0-0	0-2	10.9	-31.54
Ian Williams	11-86	1-7	5-27	2-23	3-10	0-7	0-5	0-0	0-7	12.8	-13.74
Brendan Powell	11-110	2-15	4-35	2-17	0-7	1-29	0-1	0-0	2-6	10.0	-28.08
Dan Skelton	11-62	3-11	3-18	0-7	0-4	4-15	1-3	0-0	0-4	17.7	-7.60
Robin Dickin	10-78	1-22	2-15	2-9	2-8	1-16	0-0	0-0	2-9	12.8	**51.75**
John Quinn	10-40	1-6	0-11	8-18	0-2	0-2	0-0	0-0	1-1	25.0	-4.98
Nick Williams	10-84	2-16	1-10	1-12	1-7	2-23	3-14	0-0	0-2	11.9	-14.66
Chris Gordon	10-89	0-10	3-28	1-12	2-6	4-24	0-1	0-0	0-8	11.2	-1.17
Jamie Snowden	10-75	1-13	3-14	2-21	1-9	2-11	0-0	0-0	1-7	13.3	-12.60
Rose Dobbin	10-78	2-15	2-20	1-12	1-3	1-14	1-2	0-0	2-12	12.8	**50.16**
Warren Greatrex	10-63	0-11	2-16	3-10	0-4	0-5	1-3	0-0	4-14	15.9	-14.33
Richard Lee	9-64	0-4	1-12	1-6	0-4	7-34	0-1	0-0	0-3	14.1	**17.00**
Malcolm Jefferson	9-82	1-13	1-15	0-6	4-10	2-19	0-4	0-0	1-15	11.0	-32.93
Venetia Williams	9-106	1-14	2-30	0-16	1-6	3-32	1-4	0-0	1-6	8.5	-30.63
N W Alexander	9-67	0-18	2-12	1-10	0-3	6-16	0-1	0-0	0-7	13.4	-5.25
Howard Johnson	8-45	1-8	0-8	3-14	2-5	2-7	0-2	0-0	0-1	17.8	-15.18
James Ewart	8-40	1-4	1-5	1-9	0-7	4-8	0-1	0-0	1-6	20.0	-0.30
Graeme McPherson	8-62	0-4	6-26	0-6	1-6	1-10	0-0	0-0	0-10	12.9	**9.00**
Seamus Mullins	7-82	2-13	0-10	1-12	1-5	2-26	0-4	0-0	1-12	8.5	-29.00

NOVEMBER

	Total W-R	Nov Hdle	H'cap Hdle	Other Hdle	Nov Chase	H'cap Chase	Other Chase	Hunter Chase	N.H. Flat	Per cent	£1 Level stake
Paul Nicholls	124-480	16-70	16-84	23-90	26-74	14-97	24-55	0-0	6-26	25.8	**3.93**
Nicky Henderson	99-384	19-63	11-79	35-99	7-32	7-48	13-39	0-0	10-36	25.8	-79.32
Donald McCain	78-369	21-82	6-64	18-71	3-32	7-50	12-28	0-0	11-46	21.1	-44.56
Alan King	71-410	12-72	6-92	19-82	14-50	10-67	6-19	0-0	5-37	17.3	-68.27
Philip Hobbs	64-374	10-63	14-81	11-61	6-35	14-97	9-26	0-0	1-19	17.1	-8.51
David Pipe	59-367	7-47	18-122	9-55	7-20	13-93	0-10	0-0	8-32	16.1	-42.59
Jonjo O'Neill	54-454	7-79	19-125	4-64	4-28	11-117	5-21	0-0	4-27	11.9	-174.74
Venetia Williams	52-347	4-47	8-90	4-36	9-33	23-114	3-21	0-0	1-12	15.0	**23.34**
Emma Lavelle	42-169	13-47	6-29	7-22	4-18	4-31	5-12	0-0	4-13	24.9	**47.61**
Evan Williams	41-252	6-35	6-60	8-37	4-32	12-65	3-12	0-0	2-12	16.3	-38.89
Nigel Twiston-Davies	40-380	12-71	2-61	5-43	6-47	12-132	2-16	0-0	1-16	10.5	-189.85
Lucinda Russell	40-311	5-43	5-63	4-39	11-38	10-105	2-9	0-0	3-14	12.9	-69.16
Sue Smith	33-244	5-39	1-34	1-22	7-32	14-92	5-16	0-0	0-10	13.5	-56.88
Colin Tizzard	32-216	7-34	2-27	4-26	4-33	8-60	6-20	0-0	1-19	14.8	-39.42
Charlie Longsdon	32-244	6-41	1-54	4-39	3-20	10-59	1-8	0-0	7-27	13.1	-81.69
Oliver Sherwood	29-139	4-31	3-21	4-23	3-10	6-26	4-9	0-0	5-21	20.9	-1.20
Tim Vaughan	29-257	6-55	5-58	8-56	2-16	3-42	1-9	0-0	4-22	11.3	-96.25
Kim Bailey	27-163	2-40	5-35	2-16	5-16	9-34	2-13	0-0	2-10	16.6	**20.56**
Tom George	27-205	5-30	5-25	1-27	3-24	10-68	2-14	0-0	1-19	13.2	-56.74
Neil Mulholland	27-135	2-26	10-39	3-17	3-12	8-28	1-3	0-0	0-10	20.0	**28.23**
Rebecca Curtis	26-153	12-32	0-15	4-31	3-27	2-16	2-5	0-0	3-30	17.0	-43.88
Warren Greatrex	25-124	5-27	4-17	8-28	2-12	1-11	0-6	0-0	5-23	20.2	-32.83
Fergal O'Brien	23-122	4-29	4-21	3-20	2-10	5-25	0-2	0-0	5-15	18.9	**45.76**
James Ewart	23-110	2-17	3-15	2-11	5-16	10-37	1-3	0-0	0-12	20.9	**20.56**
Gary Moore	21-236	1-38	6-67	4-45	4-24	4-53	0-5	0-0	2-9	8.9	-100.09
Harry Fry	21-67	8-17	2-14	3-10	2-4	0-6	0-2	0-0	6-14	31.3	-1.21
Richard Lee	19-114	0-10	3-18	3-14	1-9	12-52	0-6	0-0	0-5	16.7	**20.88**
Brian Ellison	19-162	2-21	3-52	5-37	4-14	4-28	0-1	0-0	1-10	11.7	-48.37
Nicky Richards	19-121	4-31	7-30	1-9	0-10	3-26	0-4	0-0	4-11	15.7	-35.28
Neil King	18-115	4-26	3-31	5-17	1-5	3-26	0-1	0-0	2-9	15.7	-43.27
Keith Reveley	18-114	2-16	3-26	4-14	3-10	5-30	0-3	0-0	1-15	15.8	-10.75
Nick Williams	18-113	0-10	2-15	3-23	2-16	5-29	6-20	0-0	0-3	15.9	**51.42**
John Quinn	17-69	3-16	4-18	9-26	1-3	0-2	0-1	0-0	0-4	24.6	-5.12
Henry Daly	17-128	2-20	5-23	1-20	3-15	3-30	1-8	0-0	2-13	13.3	-31.75
John Ferguson	17-69	9-21	2-18	2-14	0-4	0-0	1-1	0-0	4-12	24.6	**11.30**
Malcolm Jefferson	16-120	3-16	3-25	1-17	1-9	5-31	1-5	0-0	2-18	13.3	-25.17
Martin Keighley	16-132	2-19	5-30	0-15	1-15	6-38	0-9	0-0	2-8	12.1	-40.00
Peter Bowen	15-165	3-28	6-46	0-14	1-12	4-42	0-7	0-0	1-18	9.1	-66.20
Dr Richard Newland	15-66	3-10	5-27	2-12	2-4	3-15	0-2	0-0	0-0	22.7	-12.19
Victor Dartnall	14-84	0-13	5-22	0-8	2-5	7-30	0-0	0-0	0-6	16.7	**8.25**
Ian Williams	14-137	2-24	5-40	4-37	1-10	1-17	0-4	0-0	1-7	10.2	-49.67
Dan Skelton	14-82	2-15	2-16	0-11	1-7	8-21	0-1	0-0	1-11	17.1	-6.88
Tom Symonds	14-90	1-19	8-20	2-20	1-11	1-7	0-0	0-0	1-13	15.6	**20.12**
John Wade	13-102	2-17	3-25	0-5	3-9	5-41	0-1	0-0	0-4	12.7	-18.24
Lucy Wadham	13-80	2-14	6-34	1-15	1-2	2-12	1-4	0-0	0-3	16.3	-9.57
Steve Gollings	13-62	2-10	2-12	1-8	2-6	3-7	0-6	0-0	3-13	21.0	**6.58**
Robin Dickin	12-90	0-19	3-25	3-8	2-8	2-15	1-4	0-0	1-11	13.3	**36.38**
Jeremy Scott	12-119	2-23	6-41	0-11	0-7	2-21	0-5	0-0	2-12	10.1	-52.58
Charlie Mann	12-115	0-18	1-22	1-19	2-17	7-33	1-6	0-0	0-1	10.4	-40.80
Paul Webber	12-147	2-25	1-22	2-29	3-21	2-29	2-12	0-0	0-10	8.2	-55.75
Jamie Snowden	12-81	4-19	2-7	2-18	2-8	2-15	0-4	0-0	0-10	14.8	-42.50

DECEMBER

	Total W-R	Nov Hdle	H'cap Hdle	Other Hdle	Nov Chase	H'cap Chase	Other Chase	Hunter Chase	N.H. Flat	Per cent	£1 Level stake
Nicky Henderson	103-376	22-71	12-76	35-92	15-56	5-39	10-36	0-0	6-18	27.4	-9.93
Paul Nicholls	87-377	9-50	7-51	14-69	24-63	12-83	19-53	0-0	2-15	23.1	-11.46
Donald McCain	78-371	18-73	7-69	13-68	9-45	12-51	8-27	0-0	11-39	21.0	**4.16**
David Pipe	58-355	10-50	14-106	9-56	5-14	11-85	0-18	0-0	9-31	16.3	-42.07
Philip Hobbs	54-309	11-49	8-57	8-41	7-45	9-76	5-22	0-0	6-20	17.5	-75.17
Nigel Twiston-Davies	47-346	7-44	9-55	7-49	5-43	17-128	0-11	0-0	2-17	13.6	-81.09
Alan King	45-298	10-61	10-60	11-58	3-39	5-36	2-16	0-0	5-30	15.1	-58.67
Jonjo O'Neill	40-371	10-72	7-83	4-65	5-40	8-86	2-14	0-0	4-12	10.8	-130.38
Venetia Williams	40-343	4-43	8-72	2-44	5-41	21-125	0-11	0-0	0-10	11.7	-104.77
Charlie Longsdon	37-199	9-38	4-42	2-28	7-18	11-54	2-10	0-0	2-10	18.6	**26.25**
Tim Vaughan	28-229	2-36	9-75	4-43	4-21	6-35	0-4	0-0	3-18	12.2	-79.22
Nick Williams	27-105	3-9	2-11	10-28	5-13	1-31	4-11	0-0	2-4	25.7	**62.23**
Sue Smith	25-207	1-29	4-39	1-9	7-35	11-76	1-5	0-0	0-14	12.1	-58.88
Lucinda Russell	24-194	5-35	2-48	2-16	4-19	6-62	3-7	0-0	2-7	12.4	-65.54
Tom George	21-171	1-17	0-18	3-28	6-30	8-59	1-13	0-0	2-7	12.3	-44.01
Evan Williams	21-190	1-18	1-56	4-22	2-23	10-52	0-3	0-0	3-16	11.1	-17.88
John Ferguson	21-84	6-18	1-14	9-30	2-14	1-2	0-1	0-0	2-7	25.0	-17.38
Richard Lee	20-84	2-7	1-12	2-4	3-5	9-51	2-2	0-0	1-3	23.8	**90.06**
Kim Bailey	20-136	3-20	5-28	2-25	2-11	5-41	2-5	0-0	1-7	14.7	-45.66
Keith Reveley	20-98	2-16	6-18	1-9	1-7	7-32	1-2	0-0	2-14	20.4	**99.00**
Colin Tizzard	20-181	4-36	2-17	1-14	3-31	9-50	0-15	0-0	1-18	11.0	-45.56
Henry Daly	19-116	3-23	6-25	5-17	2-10	2-26	0-4	0-0	1-11	16.4	**26.36**
Emma Lavelle	19-123	1-28	5-22	2-17	6-16	4-21	0-6	0-0	1-13	15.4	-35.91
Gary Moore	18-163	4-29	2-41	1-36	2-16	6-32	3-5	0-0	0-8	11.0	-50.17
Oliver Sherwood	16-104	4-20	1-18	4-22	1-12	4-24	0-3	0-0	2-6	15.4	-15.56
Malcolm Jefferson	16-91	3-15	1-14	2-10	0-6	6-31	2-3	0-0	2-12	17.6	**30.00**
Brian Ellison	16-131	2-21	7-52	5-32	1-8	1-10	0-3	0-0	0-8	12.2	-54.18
Neil King	16-99	2-13	6-34	3-16	0-3	2-21	1-1	0-0	2-11	16.2	**27.62**
Dan Skelton	16-87	3-14	4-16	2-23	1-7	3-17	0-0	0-0	3-10	18.4	**6.67**
Dr Richard Newland	16-72	2-17	6-22	2-12	2-9	4-14	0-0	0-0	0-1	22.2	**12.27**
Rebecca Curtis	16-118	3-26	4-17	1-20	1-14	1-18	0-2	0-0	6-22	13.6	-61.05
Jeremy Scott	14-99	3-21	5-29	2-9	1-12	2-16	0-4	0-0	1-8	14.1	-22.98
Martin Keighley	14-104	1-5	4-34	0-10	2-7	7-36	0-6	0-0	0-6	13.5	**7.87**
John Wade	13-102	1-17	2-17	1-4	2-12	7-39	0-4	0-0	0-9	12.7	-35.38
Peter Bowen	12-125	0-19	6-36	0-8	1-7	2-45	0-2	0-0	3-8	9.6	-29.62
Steve Gollings	12-45	1-9	3-11	3-10	1-4	1-7	2-3	0-0	1-4	26.7	**0.41**
Paul Webber	12-118	1-24	1-23	1-15	3-15	4-29	2-6	0-0	0-6	10.2	-42.99
Nicky Richards	12-80	2-15	4-22	1-9	2-8	2-16	0-6	0-0	1-4	15.0	-4.83
Brendan Powell	12-111	0-19	2-38	3-16	0-10	3-16	1-3	0-0	3-10	10.8	-37.80
Warren Greatrex	12-110	5-29	5-27	0-20	1-10	1-9	0-5	0-0	0-11	10.9	-33.77
Harry Fry	12-48	3-11	1-8	2-9	3-5	0-5	2-4	0-0	1-6	25.0	**7.14**
John Quinn	11-51	2-7	3-11	6-28	0-2	0-1	0-0	0-0	0-3	21.6	**6.59**
Ian Williams	11-95	2-21	3-19	1-25	2-12	2-10	1-2	0-0	0-6	11.6	-58.69
Seamus Mullins	10-111	1-23	4-32	0-6	1-10	3-26	0-2	0-0	1-12	9.0	-22.50
Charlie Mann	10-102	1-16	2-17	0-15	2-18	5-31	0-4	0-0	0-2	9.8	-25.00
Victor Dartnall	10-82	0-10	6-22	1-12	0-5	2-29	0-0	0-0	1-4	12.2	-32.17
Michael Smith	9-23	2-5	0-3	2-4	1-2	3-6	0-0	0-0	1-3	39.1	**39.66**
Jennie Candlish	9-100	2-18	3-40	1-17	1-7	2-15	0-1	0-0	0-3	9.0	-61.69
Philip Kirby	9-63	3-17	3-22	0-6	0-3	1-5	0-1	0-0	2-9	14.3	**21.88**
Sheena West	8-35	0-2	0-9	2-9	0-1	3-9	1-2	0-0	2-3	22.9	**82.13**
Stuart Coltherd	8-48	1-10	2-9	0-3	1-8	4-15	0-1	0-0	0-2	16.7	**25.50**

LEADING JUMPS TRAINERS 2014/15

TRAINER	WINS-RUNS		2NDS	3RDS	4THS	WIN PRIZE	TOTAL PRIZE	£1 STAKE
Paul Nicholls	124-518	24%	89	80	46	£2,383,883	£3,246,894	+58.40
Nicky Henderson	129-500	26%	90	61	49	£1,130,446	£1,905,755	-59.50
Philip Hobbs	102-552	18%	93	77	52	£1,020,176	£1,509,917	-81.06
W P Mullins	16-91	18%	8	13	8	£889,987	£1,385,931	-12.58
David Pipe	116-580	20%	71	66	62	£781,676	£1,260,650	-51.21
Alan King	75-448	17%	78	43	51	£768,235	£1,140,598	-136.18
Oliver Sherwood	31-204	15%	43	36	24	£894,907	£1,041,945	-38.35
Jonjo O'Neill	104-634	16%	87	70	61	£513,442	£978,167	-185.21
Nigel Twiston-Davies	73-488	15%	60	61	66	£597,785	£889,206	-106.61
Venetia Williams	53-441	12%	47	61	58	£490,128	£859,211	-150.41
Tom George	36-262	14%	40	38	37	£259,962	£717,772	-48.05
Dan Skelton	73-377	19%	47	44	52	£492,905	£714,164	-63.69
Donald McCain	98-687	14%	96	104	71	£392,870	£643,730	-285.31
John Ferguson	56-214	26%	49	18	18	£364,772	£614,729	-8.83
Evan Williams	63-410	15%	58	65	57	£346,299	£608,228	-53.30
Gordon Elliott	35-120	29%	21	15	11	£463,168	£588,076	+43.43
Colin Tizzard	38-294	13%	34	41	44	£319,993	£560,935	-79.46
Warren Greatrex	51-272	19%	31	34	34	£395,347	£546,881	-79.92
Harry Fry	36-157	23%	21	27	18	£298,417	£528,346	-29.51
Lucinda Russell	47-501	9%	64	59	60	£306,548	£496,581	-207.40
Charlie Longsdon	50-338	15%	50	43	36	£285,689	£447,716	-126.35
Kim Bailey	61-268	23%	32	31	31	£336,774	£439,192	+24.08
Mark Bradstock	8-24	33%	1	3	0	£429,341	£436,704	+20.46
Gary Moore	39-313	12%	38	33	45	£271,622	£426,199	-98.89
Neil Mulholland	51-262	19%	38	26	27	£316,649	£406,957	+8.69
Rebecca Curtis	45-221	20%	34	39	25	£287,295	£400,719	+23.42
Peter Bowen	57-373	15%	58	66	41	£245,907	£399,395	-90.07
Sue Smith	31-322	10%	44	46	52	£174,342	£348,320	-134.58
Nicky Richards	48-189	25%	21	22	12	£235,418	£345,554	+37.58
Brian Ellison	35-289	12%	55	41	25	£162,771	£314,239	-173.33
Nick Williams	13-113	12%	13	18	9	£167,733	£296,162	-40.86
Dr Richard Newland	35-149	23%	23	17	16	£207,557	£285,745	-14.92
Fergal O'Brien	27-247	11%	32	29	30	£152,221	£270,618	-29.13
Emma Lavelle	21-190	11%	19	22	17	£142,727	£269,005	-56.14
Henry De Bromhead	3-15	20%	2	2	0	£179,181	£268,596	+0.50
Lucy Wadham	19-132	14%	19	19	13	£134,039	£249,797	-18.17
David Bridgwater	33-184	18%	26	26	19	£165,883	£247,232	-17.17
Neil King	29-201	14%	28	45	32	£155,301	£244,477	+11.58
Tim Vaughan	38-351	11%	38	48	34	£153,164	£244,389	-147.51
Richard Lee	19-108	18%	16	14	7	£151,337	£232,000	+18.13
Michael Scudamore	13-78	17%	10	12	11	£83,400	£230,569	-23.19
Malcolm Jefferson	25-161	16%	20	17	19	£159,538	£220,350	-49.09
Mick Channon	8-54	15%	11	1	11	£47,496	£218,043	-32.67
Charlie Mann	23-152	15%	20	12	30	£122,834	£198,458	-2.24
Chris Gordon	30-198	15%	31	24	18	£135,151	£197,949	+7.02
Henry Daly	21-181	12%	42	18	15	£85,338	£181,958	-3.58
David Dennis	32-208	15%	12	37	28	£130,881	£181,307	-1.90
Martin Keighley	17-210	8%	29	27	23	£117,613	£180,743	-56.75
John Quinn	20-112	18%	30	13	8	£100,157	£178,222	-41.73
Ian Williams	21-191	11%	21	17	31	£115,483	£174,386	-51.00